**MOTOROLA**

MC68030

ENHANCED 32-BIT
MICROPROCESSOR USER'S MANUAL

Third Edition

PRENTICE HALL, Englewood Cliffs, N.J. 07632

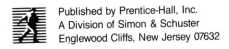

Published by Prentice-Hall, Inc.
A Division of Simon & Schuster
Englewood Cliffs, New Jersey 07632

The publisher offers discounts on this book when ordered
in bulk quantities. For more information, write:

Special Sales/College Marketing
Prentice-Hall, Inc.
College Technical and Reference Division
Englewood Cliffs, New Jersey 07632

Printed in the United States of America

10 9 8 7 6 5 4 3 2

ISBN   0-13-566423-3

Prentice-Hall International (UK) Limited, *London*
Prentice-Hall of Australia Pty. Limited, *Sydney*
Prentice-Hall Canada Inc., *Toronto*
Prentice-Hall Hispanoamericana, S.A., *Mexico*
Prentice-Hall of India Private Limited, *New Delhi*
Prentice-Hall of Japan, Inc., *Tokyo*
Simon & Schuster Asia Pte. Ltd., *Singapore*
Editora Prentice-Hall do Brasil, Ltda., *Rio de Janeiro*

TABLE OF CONTENTS

TABLE OF CONTENTS (Continued)

Section 3
Instruction Set Summary

TABLE OF CONTENTS (Continued)

Section 4
Processing States

Section 5
Signal Description

TABLE OF CONTENTS (Continued)

Section 6
On-Chip Cache Memories

TABLE OF CONTENTS (Continued)

TABLE OF CONTENTS (Continued)

Section 8
Exception Processing

TABLE OF CONTENTS (Continued)

Section 9
Memory Management Unit

TABLE OF CONTENTS (Continued)

TABLE OF CONTENTS (Continued)

TABLE OF CONTENTS (Continued)

TABLE OF CONTENTS (Continued)

Section 11
Instruction Execution Timing

TABLE OF CONTENTS (Continued)

Section 12
Applications Information

TABLE OF CONTENTS (Concluded)

LIST OF ILLUSTRATIONS

LIST OF ILLUSTRATIONS (Continued)

LIST OF ILLUSTRATIONS (Continued)

LIST OF ILLUSTRATIONS (Continued)

LIST OF ILLUSTRATIONS (Continued)

LIST OF ILLUSTRATIONS (Continued)

LIST OF ILLUSTRATIONS (Continued)

LIST OF ILLUSTRATIONS (Concluded)

LIST OF TABLES

LIST OF TABLES (Continued)

PREFACE

The *MC68030 User's Manual* describes the capabilities, operation, and programming of the MC68030 32-bit second-generation enhanced microprocessor. The manual consists of the following sections and appendix. For detailed information on the MC68030 instruction set refer to M68000PM/AD, *M68000 Family Programmer's Reference Manual.*

NOTE

In this manual, assertion and negation are used to specify forcing a signal to a particular state. In particular, assertion and assert refer to a signal that is active or true; negation and negate indicate a signal that is inactive or false. These terms are used independently of the voltage level (high or low) that they represent.

The audience of this manual includes systems designers, systems programmers, and applications programmers. Systems designers need some knowledge of all sections, with particular emphasis on Sections 1, 5, 6, 7, 13, 14, and Appendix A. Designers who implement a coprocessor for their system also need a thorough knowledge of Section 10. Systems programmers should become familiar with Sections 1, 2, 3, 4, 6, 8, 9, 11, and Appendix A. Applications programmers can find most of the information they need in Sections 1, 2, 3, 4, 9, 11, 12, and Appendix A.

From a different viewpoint, the audience for this book consists of users of other M68000 Family members and those who are not familiar with these microprocessors. Users of the other family members can find references to similarities to and differences from the other Motorola microprocessors throughout the manual. However, Section 1 and Appendix A specifically identify the MC68030 within the rest of the family and contrast its differences.

SECTION 1

INTRODUCTION

The MC68030 is a second-generation full 32-bit enhanced microprocessor from Motorola. The MC68030 is a member of the M68000 Family of devices that combines a central processing unit (CPU) core, a data cache, an instruction cache, an enhanced bus controller, and a memory management unit (MMU) in a single VLSI device. The processor is designed to operate at clock speeds beyond 20 MHz. The MC68030 is implemented with 32-bit registers and data paths, 32-bit addresses, a rich instruction set, and versatile addressing modes.

The MC68030 is upward object code compatible with the earlier members of the M68000 Family and has the added features of an on-chip MMU, a data cache, and an improved bus interface. It retains the flexible coprocessor interface pioneered in the MC68020 and provides full IEEE floating-point support through this interface with the MC68881 or MC68882 floating-point coprocessor. Also, the internal functional blocks of this microprocessor are designed to operate in parallel, allowing instruction execution to be overlapped. In addition to instruction execution, the internal caches, the on-chip MMU, and the external bus controller all operate in parallel.

The MC68030 fully supports the nonmultiplexed bus structure of the MC68020, with 32 bits of address and 32 bits of data. The MC68030 bus has an enhanced controller that supports both asynchronous and synchronous bus cycles and burst data transfers. It also supports the MC68020 dynamic bus sizing mechanism that automatically determines device port sizes on a cycle-by-cycle basis as the processor transfers operands to or from external devices.

A block diagram of the MC68030 is shown in Figure 1-1. The instructions and data required by the processor are supplied from the internal caches whenever possible. The MMU translates the logical address generated by the processor into a physical address utilizing its address translation cache (ATC). The bus controller manages the transfer of data between the CPU and memory or devices at the physical address.

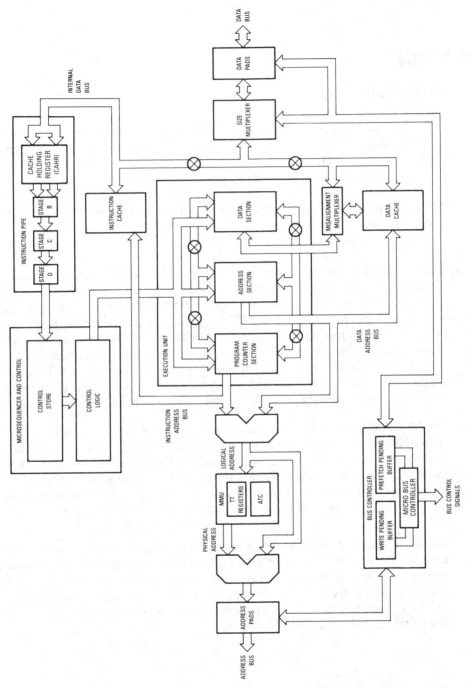

Figure 1-1. Block Diagram

MC68030 USER'S MANUAL MOTOROLA

1.1 FEATURES

The features of the MC68030 microprocessor are:

- Object Code Compatible with the MC68020 and Earlier M68000 Micro-processors

- Complete 32-Bit Nonmultiplexed Address and Data Buses

- 16 32-Bit General-Purpose Data and Address Registers

- Two 32-Bit Supervisor Stack Pointers and 10 Special-Purpose Control Registers

- 256-Byte Instruction Cache and 256-Byte Data Cache Can Be Accessed Simultaneously

- Paged MMU that Translates Addresses in Parallel with Instruction Execution and Internal Cache Accesses

- Two Transparent Segments Allow Untranslated Access to Physical Memory To Be Defined for Systems That Transfer Large Blocks of Data between Predefined Physical Addresses — e.g., Graphics Applications

- Pipelined Architecture with Increased Parallelism Allows Accesses to Internal Caches To Occur in Parallel with Bus Transfers and Instruction Execution To Be Overlapped

- Enhanced Bus Controller Supports Asynchronous Bus Cycles (three clocks minimum), Synchronous Bus Cycles (two clocks minimum), and Burst Data Transfers (one clock minimum) all to the Physical Address Space

- Dynamic Bus Sizing Supports 8-, 16-, 32-Bit Memories and Peripherals

- Support for Coprocessors with the M68000 Coprocessor Interface — e.g., Full IEEE Floating-Point Support Provided by the MC68881/MC68882 Floating-Point Coprocessors

- 4-Gbyte Logical and Physical Addressing Range

- Implemented in Motorola's HCMOS Technology That Allows CMOS and HMOS (High-Density NMOS) Gates to be Combined for Maximum Speed, Low Power, and Optimum Die Size

- Processor Speeds Beyond 20 MHz

Both improved performance and increased functionality result from the on-chip implementation of the MMU and the data and instruction caches. The enhanced bus controller and the internal parallelism also provide increased system performance. Finally, the improved bus interface, the reduction in physical size, and the lower power consumption combine to reduce system costs and satisfy cost/performance goals of the system designer.

1.2 MC68030 EXTENSIONS TO THE M68000 FAMILY

In addition to the on-chip instruction cache present in the MC68020, the MC68030 has an internal data cache. Data that is accessed during read cycles may be stored in the on-chip cache, where it is available for subsequent accesses. The data cache reduces the number of external bus cycles when the data operand required by an instruction is already in the data cache.

Performance is enhanced further because the on-chip caches can be internally accessed in a single clock cycle. In addition, the bus controller provides a two-clock cycle synchronous mode and burst mode accesses that can transfer data in as little as one clock per long word.

The MC68030 enhanced microprocessor contains an on-chip MMU that allows address translation to operate in parallel with the CPU core, the internal caches, and the bus controller.

Additional signals support emulation and system analysis. External debug equipment can disable the on-chip caches and the MMU to freeze the MC68030 internal state during breakpoint processing. In addition, the MC68030 indicates:

1. The start of a refill of the instruction pipe
2. Instruction boundaries
3. Pending trace or interrupt processing
4. Exception processing
5. Halt conditions

This status and control information allows external debugging equipment to trace the MC68030 activity and interact nonintrusively with the MC68030 to effectively reduce system debug effort.

1.3 PROGRAMMING MODEL

The programming model of the MC68030 consists of two groups of registers: the user model and the supervisor model. This corresponds to the user and supervisor privilege levels. User programs executing at the user privilege level use the registers of the user model. System software executing at the supervisor level uses the control registers of the supervisor level to perform supervisor functions.

Figure 1-2 shows the user programming model, consisting of 16 32-bit general-purpose registers and two control registers:

- General-Purpose 32-Bit Registers (D0–D7, A0–A7)
- 32-Bit Program Counter (PC)
- 8-Bit Condition Code Register (CCR)

The supervisor programming model consists of the registers available to the user plus 14 control registers:

- Two 32-Bit Supervisor Stack Pointers (ISP and MSP)
- 16-Bit Status Register (SR)
- 32-Bit Vector Base Register (VBR)
- 32-Bit Alternate Function Code Registers (SFC and DFC)
- 32-Bit Cache Control Register (CACR)
- 32-Bit Cache Address Register (CAAR)
- 64-Bit CPU Root Pointer (CRP)
- 64-Bit Supervisor Root Pointer (SRP)
- 32-Bit Translation Control Register (TC)
- 32-Bit Transparent Translation Registers (TT0 and TT1)
- 16-Bit MMU Status Register (MMUSR)

The user programming model remains unchanged from previous M68000 Family microprocessors. The supervisor programming model supplements the user programming model and is used exclusively by the MC68030 system programmers who utilize the supervisor privilege level to implement sensitive operating system functions, I/O control, and memory management subsystems. The supervisor programming model contains all the controls to access and enable the special features of the MC68030. This segregation was carefully planned so that all application software is written to run at the nonprivileged user level and migrates to the MC68030 from any M68000 platform without modification. Since system software is usually modified by system programmers when ported to a new design, the control features are properly placed in the supervisor programming model. For example, the transparent translation feature of the MC68030 is new to the family supervisor programming model for the MC68030 and the two translation registers are new additions to the family supervisor programming model for the MC68030. Only supervisor code uses this feature, and user application programs remain unaffected.

Registers D0–D7 are used as data registers for bit and bit field (1 to 32 bits), byte (8 bit), word (16 bit), long-word (32 bit), and quad-word (64 bit) operations. Registers A0–A6 and the user, interrupt, and master stack pointers are address registers that may be used as software stack pointers or base address registers. Register A7 (shown as A7' and A7'' in Figure 1-3) is a register designation that applies to the user stack pointer in the user privilege level and to either the interrupt or master stack pointer in the supervisor privilege level. In the supervisor privilege level, the active stack pointer (interrupt or master) is called the supervisor stack pointer (SSP). In addition,

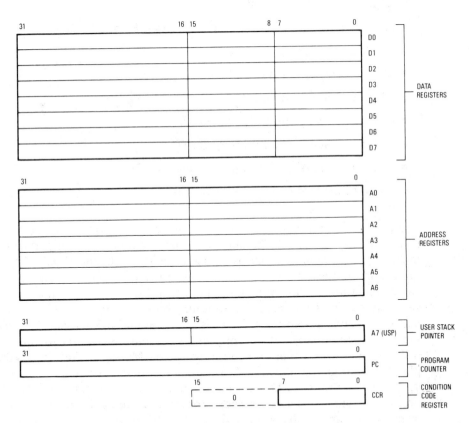

Figure 1-2. User Programming Model

the address registers may be used for word and long-word operations. All of the 16 general-purpose registers (D0–D7, A0–A7) may be used as index registers.

The program counter (PC) contains the address of the next instruction to be executed by the MC68030. During instruction execution and exception processing, the processor automatically increments the contents of the PC or places a new value in the PC, as appropriate.

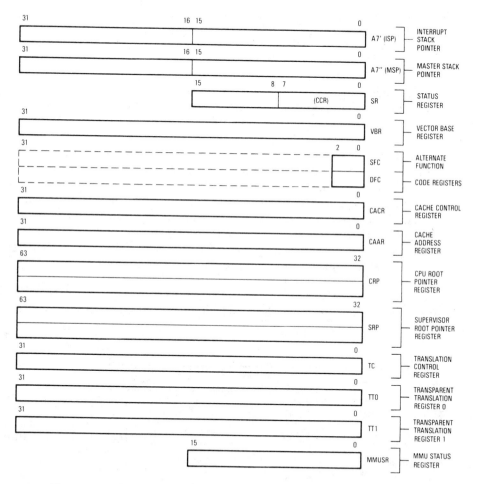

Figure 1-3. Supervisor Programming Model Supplement

The status register, SR, (see Figure 1-4) stores the processor status. It contains the condition codes that reflect the results of a previous operation and can be used for conditional instruction execution in a program. The condition codes are extend (X), negative (N), zero (Z), overflow (V), and carry (C). The user byte containing the condition codes is the only portion of the status register information available in the user privilege level, and it is referenced as the CCR in user programs. In the supervisor privilege level, software can access the full status register, including the interrupt priority mask (three bits) as well as additional control bits. These bits indicate whether the processor is in:

1. One of two trace modes (T1, T0)
2. Supervisor or user privilege level (S)
3. Master or interrupt mode (M)

The vector base register (VBR) contains the base address of the exception vector table in memory. The displacement of an exception vector is added to the value in this register to access the vector table.

Alternate function code registers, SFC and DFC, contain 3-bit function codes. Function codes can be considered extensions of the 32-bit linear address that optionally provide as many as eight 4-Gbyte address spaces. Function codes are automatically generated by the processor to select address spaces for data and program at the user and supervisor privilege levels and a CPU address space for processor functions (e.g., coprocessor communications). Registers SFC and DFC are used by certain instructions to explicitly specify the function codes for operations.

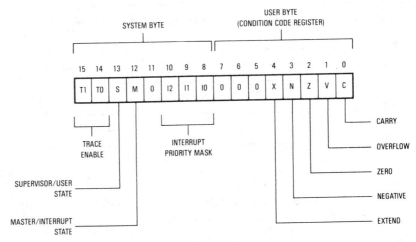

Figure 1-4. Status Register

The cache control register (CACR) controls the on-chip instruction and data caches of the MC68030. The cache address register (CAAR) stores an address for cache control functions.

The CPU root pointer (CRP) contains a pointer to the root of the translation tree for the currently executing task of the MC68030. This tree contains the mapping information for the task's address space. When the MC68030 is configured to provide a separate address space for supervisor routines, the supervisor root pointer (SRP) contains a pointer to the root of the translation tree describing the supervisor's address space.

The translation control register (TC) consists of several fields that control address translation. These fields enable and disable address translation, enable and disable the use of SRP for the supervisor address space, and select or ignore the function codes in translating addresses. Other fields define the size of memory pages, the number of address bits used in translation, and the translation table structure.

The transparent translation registers, TT0 and TT1, can each specify separate blocks of memory as directly accessible without address translation. Logical addresses in these areas become the physical addresses for memory access. Function codes and the eight most significant bits of the address can be used to define the area of memory and type of access; either read, write, or both types of memory access can be directly mapped. The transparent translation feature allows rapid movement of large blocks of data in memory or I/O space without disturbing the context of the on-chip address translation cache or incurring delays associated with translation table lookups. This feature is useful to graphics, controller, and real-time applications.

The MMU status register (MMUSR) contains memory management status information resulting from a search of the address translation cache or the translation tree for a particular logical address.

1.4 DATA TYPES AND ADDRESSING MODES

Seven basic data types are supported:
1. Bits
2. Bit Fields (Fields of consecutive bits, 1–32 bits long)
3. BCD Digits (Packed: 2 digits/byte, Unpacked: 1 digit/byte)
4. Byte Integers (8 bits)
5. Word Integers (16 bits)
6. Long-Word Integers (32 bits)
7. Quad-Word Integers (64 bits)

In addition, the instruction set supports operations on other data types such as memory addresses. The coprocessor mechanism allows direct support of floating-point operations with the MC68881 and MC68882 floating-point co-processors as well as specialized user-defined data types and functions.

The 18 addressing modes, shown in Table 1-1, include nine basic types:
1. Register Direct
2. Register Indirect
3. Register Indirect with Index
4. Memory Indirect
5. Program Counter Indirect with Displacement
6. Program Counter Indirect with Index
7. Program Counter Memory Indirect
8. Absolute
9. Immediate

The register indirect addressing modes can also postincrement, predecrement, offset, and index addresses. The program counter relative mode also has index and offset capabilities. As in the MC68020, both modes are extended to provide indirect reference through memory. In addition to these addressing modes, many instructions implicitly specify the use of the condition code register, stack pointer, and/or program counter.

1.5 INSTRUCTION SET OVERVIEW

The instructions in the MC68030 instruction set are listed in Table 1-2. The instruction set has been tailored to support structured high-level languages and sophisticated operating systems. Many instructions operate on bytes, words, or long words, and most instructions can use any of the 18 addressing modes.

MC68030 USER'S MANUAL MOTOROLA

Table 1-1. Addressing Modes

Addressing Modes	Syntax
Register Direct	
Data Register Direct	Dn
Address Register Direct	An
Register Indirect	
Address Register Indirect	(An)
Address Register Indirect with Postincrement	(An)+
Address Register Indirect with Predecrement	−(An)
Address Register Indirect with Displacement	(d_{16},An)
Register Indirect with Index	
Address Register Indirect with Index (8-Bit Displacement)	(d_8,An,Xn)
Address Register Indirect with Index (Base Displacement)	(bd,An,Xn)
Memory Indirect	
Memory Indirect Postindexed	([bd,An],Xn,od)
Memory Indirect Preindexed	([bd,An,Xn],od)
Program Counter Indirect with Displacement	(d_{16},PC)
Program Counter Indirect with Index	
PC Indirect with Index (8-Bit Displacement)	(d_8,PC,Xn)
PC Indirect with Index (Base Displacement)	(bd,PC,Xn)
Program Counter Memory Indirect	
PC Memory Indirect Postindexed	([bd,PC],Xn,od)
PC Memory Indirect Preindexed	([bd,PC,Xn],od)
Absolute	
Absolute Short	(xxx).W
Absolute Long	(xxx).L
Immediate	#⟨data⟩

NOTES:

Dn = Data Register, D0–D7

An = Address Register, A0–A7

d_8, d_{16} = A twos-complement or sign-extended displacement; added as part of the effective address calculation; size is 8 (d_8) or 16 (d_{16}) bits; when omitted, assemblers use a value of zero.

Xn = Address or data register used as an index register; form is Xn.SIZE*SCALE, where SIZE is .W or .L (indicates index register size) and SCALE is 1, 2, 4, or 8 (index register is multiplied by SCALE); use of SIZE and/or SCALE is optional.

bd = A twos-complement base displacement; when present, size can be 16 or 32 bits.

od = Outer displacement, added as part of effective address calculation after any memory indirection; use is optional with a size of 16 or 32 bits.

PC = Program Counter

⟨data⟩ = Immediate value of 8, 16, or 32 bits

( ) = Effective Address

[ ] = Use as indirect access to long-word address.

1.6 VIRTUAL MEMORY AND VIRTUAL MACHINE CONCEPTS

The full addressing range of the MC68030 is 4 Gbytes (4,294,967,296 bytes) in each of eight address spaces. Even though most systems implement a smaller physical memory, the system can be made to appear to have a full 4 Gbytes of memory available to each user program by using virtual memory techniques.

In a virtual memory system, a user program can be written as if it has a large amount of memory available, when the physical memory actually present is much smaller. Similarly, a system can be designed to allow user programs to access devices that are not physically present in the system, such as tape drives, disk drives, printers, terminals, and so forth. With proper software emulation, a physical system can appear to be any other M68000 computer system to a user program, and the program can be given full access to all of the resources of that emulated system. Such an emulated system is called a virtual machine.

1.6.1 Virtual Memory

A system that supports virtual memory has a limited amount of high-speed physical memory that can be accessed directly by the processor and maintains an image of a much larger virtual memory on a secondary storage device such as a large-capacity disk drive. When the processor attempts to access a location in the virtual memory map that is not resident in physical memory, a page fault occurs. The access to that location is temporarily suspended while the necessary data is fetched from secondary storage and placed in physical memory. The suspended access is then either restarted or continued.

The MC68030 uses instruction continuation to support virtual memory. When a bus cycle is terminated with a bus error, the microprocessor suspends the current instruction and executes the virtual memory bus error handler. When the bus error handler has completed execution, it returns control to the program that was executing when the error was detected, reruns the faulted bus cycle (when required), and continues the suspended instruction.

Table 1-2. Instruction Set

Mnemonic	Description
ABCD	Add Decimal with Extend
ADD	Add
ADDA	Add Address
ADDI	Add Immediate
ADDQ	Add Quick
ADDX	Add with Extend
AND	Logical AND
ANDI	Logical AND Immediate
ASL, ASR	Arithmetic Shift Left and Right
Bcc	Branch Conditionally
BCHG	Test Bit and Change
BCLR	Test Bit and Clear
BFCHG	Test Bit Field and Change
BFCLR	Test Bit Field and Clear
BFEXTS	Signed Bit Field Extract
BFEXTU	Unsigned Bit Field Extract
BFFFO	Bit Field Find First One
BFINS	Bit Field Insert
BFSET	Test Bit Field and Set
BFTST	Test Bit Field
BKPT	Breakpoint
BRA	Branch
BSET	Test Bit and Set
BSR	Branch to Subroutine
BTST	Test Bit
CAS	Compare and Swap Operands
CAS2	Compare and Swap Dual Operands
CHK	Check Register Against Bound
CHK2	Check Register Against Upper and Lower Bounds
CLR	Clear
CMP	Compare
CMPA	Compare Address
CMPI	Compare Immediate
CMPM	Compare Memory to Memory
CMP2	Compare Register Against Upper and Lower Bounds
DBcc	Test Condition, Decrement and Branch
DIVS, DIVSL	Signed Divide
DIVU, DIVUL	Unsigned Divide
EOR	Logical Exclusive OR
EORI	Logical Exclusive OR Immediate
EXG	Exchange Registers
EXT, EXTB	Sign Extend
ILLEGAL	Take Illegal Instruction Trap
JMP	Jump
JSR	Jump to Subroutine
LEA	Load Effective Address
LINK	Link and Allocate
LSL, LSR	Logical Shift Left and Right
MOVE	Move
MOVEA	Move Address
MOVE CCR	Move Condition Code Register
MOVE SR	Move Status Register

Mnemonic	Description
MOVE USP	Move User Stack Pointer
MOVEC	Move Control Register
MOVEM	Move Multiple Registers
MOVEP	Move Peripheral
MOVEQ	Move Quick
MOVES	Move Alternate Address Space
MULS	Signed Multiply
MULU	Unsigned Multiply
NBCD	Negate Decimal with Extend
NEG	Negate
NEGX	Negate with Extend
NOP	No Operation
NOT	Logical Complement
OR	Logical Inclusive OR
ORI	Logical Inclusive OR Immediate
ORI CCR	Logical Inclusive OR Immediate to Condition Codes
ORI SR	Logical Inclusive OR Immediate to Status Register
PACK	Pack BCD
PEA	Push Effective Address
PFLUSH	Flush Entry(ies) in the ATC
PFLUSHA	Flush All Entries in the ATC
PLOADR, PLOADW	Load Entry into the ATC
PMOVE	Move to/from MMU Registers
PMOVEFD	Move to/from MMU Registers with Flush Disable
PTESTR, PTESTW	Test a Logical Address
RESET	Reset External Devices
ROL, ROR	Rotate Left and Right
ROXL, ROXR	Rotate with Extend Left and Right
RTD	Return and Deallocate
RTE	Return from Exception
RTR	Return and Restore Codes
RTS	Return from Subroutine
SBCD	Subtract Decimal with Extend
Scc	Set Conditionally
STOP	Stop
SUB	Subtract
SUBA	Subtract Address
SUBI	Subtract Immediate
SUBQ	Subtract Quick
SUBX	Subtract with Extend
SWAP	Swap Register Words
TAS	Test Operand and Set
TRAP	Trap
TRAPcc	Trap Conditionally
TRAPV	Trap on Overflow
TST	Test Operand
UNLK	Unlink
UNPK	Unpack BCD

Coprocessor Instructions

Mnemonic	Description
cpBcc	Branch Conditionally
cpDBcc	Test Coprocessor Condition, Decrement and Branch
cpGEN	Coprocessor General Instruction

Mnemonic	Description
cpRESTORE	Restore Internal State of Coprocessor
cpSAVE	Save Internal State of Coprocessor
cpScc	Set Conditionally
cpTRAPcc	Trap Conditionally

1.6.2 Virtual Machine

A typical use for a virtual machine system is the development of software, such as an operating system, for a new machine also under development and not yet available for programming use. In a virtual machine system, a governing operating system emulates the hardware of the new machine and allows the new software to be executed and debugged as though it were running on the new hardware. Since the new software is controlled by the governing operating system, it is executed at a lower privilege level than the governing operating system. Thus, any attempts by the new software to use virtual resources that are not physically present (and should be emulated) are trapped to the governing operating system and performed by its software.

In the MC68030 implementation of a virtual machine, the virtual application runs at the user privilege level. The governing operating system executes at the supervisor privilege level and any attempt by the new operating system to access supervisor resources or execute privileged instructions causes a trap to the governing operating system.

Instruction continuation is used to support virtual I/O devices in memory-mapped input/output systems. Control and data registers for the virtual device are simulated in the memory map. An access to a virtual register causes a fault and the function of the register is emulated by software.

1.7 THE MEMORY MANAGEMENT UNIT

The MMU supports virtual memory systems by translating logical addresses to physical addresses using translation tables stored in memory. The MMU stores address mappings in an address translation cache (ATC) that contains the most recently used translations. When the ATC contains the address for a bus cycle requested by the CPU, a translation table search is not performed. Features of the MMU include:

- Multiple Level Translation Tables with Short- and Long-Format Descriptors for Efficient Table Space Usage

- Table Searches Automatically Performed in Microcode

- 22-Entry Fully Associative ATC

- Address Translations and Internal Instruction and Data Cache Accesses Performed in Parallel

- Eight Page Sizes Available Ranging from 256 to 32K Bytes

- Two Optional Transparent Blocks

- User and Supervisor Root Pointer Registers

- Write Protection and Supervisor Protection Attributes

- Translations Enabled/Disabled by Software

- Translations Can Be Disabled with External $\overline{\text{MMUDIS}}$ Signal

- Used and Modified Bits Automatically Maintained in Tables and ATC

- Cache Inhibit Output ($\overline{\text{CIOUT}}$) Signal Can Be Asserted on a Page-by-Page Basis

- 32-Bit Internal Logical Address with Capability To Ignore as many as 15 Upper Address Bits

- 3-Bit Function Code Supports Separate Address Spaces

- 32-Bit Physical Address

The memory management function performed by the MMU is called demand paged memory management. Since a task specifies the areas of memory it requires as it executes, memory allocation is supported on a demand basis. If a requested access to memory is not currently mapped by the system, then the access causes a demand for the operating system to load or allocate the required memory image. The technique used by the MC68030 is paged memory management because physical memory is managed in blocks of a specified number of bytes, called page frames. The logical address space is divided into fixed-size pages that contain the same number of bytes as the page frames. Memory management assigns a physical base address to a logical page. The system software then transfers data between secondary storage and memory one or more pages at a time.

1.8 PIPELINED ARCHITECTURE

The MC68030 uses a three-stage pipelined internal architecture to provide for optimum instruction throughput. The pipeline allows as many as three words of a single instruction or three consecutive instructions to be decoded concurrently.

1.9 THE CACHE MEMORIES

Due to locality of reference, instructions and data that are used in a program have a high probability of being reused within a short time. Additionally, instructions and data operands that reside in proximity to the instructions and data currently in use also have a high probability of being utilized within a short period. To exploit these locality characteristics, the MC68030 contains two on-chip logical caches, a data cache, and an instruction cache.

Each of the caches stores 256 bytes of information, organized as 16 entries, each containing a block of four long words (16 bytes). The processor fills the cache entries either one long word at a time or, during burst mode accesses, four long words consecutively. The burst mode of operation not only fills the cache efficiently but also captures adjacent instruction or data items that are likely to be required in the near future due to locality characteristics of the executing task.

The caches improve the overall performance of the system by reducing the number of bus cycles required by the processor to fetch information from memory and by increasing the bus bandwidth available for other bus masters in the system. Addition of the data cache in the MC68030 extends the benefits of cache techniques to all memory accesses. During a write cycle, the data cache circuitry writes data to a cached data item as well as to the item in memory, maintaining consistency between data in the cache and that in memory. However, writing data that is not in the cache may or may not cause the data item to be stored in the cache, depending on the write allocation policy selected in the cache control register (CACR).

MC68030 USER'S MANUAL   MOTOROLA

SECTION 2
DATA ORGANIZATION AND ADDRESSING CAPABILITIES

Most external references to memory by a microprocessor are either program references or data references; they either access instruction words or operands (data items) for an instruction. Program references are references to the program space, the section of memory that contains the program instructions and any immediate data operands that reside in the instruction stream. Refer to M68000PM/AD, *M68000 Programmer's Reference Manual*, for descriptions of the instructions in the program space. Data references refer to the data space, the section of memory that contains the program data. Data items in the instruction stream can be accessed with the program counter relative addressing modes, and these accesses are classified as program references. A third type of external reference used for coprocessor communications, interrupt acknowledge cycles, and breakpoint acknowledge cycles is classified as a CPU space reference. The MC68030 automatically sets the function codes to access the program space, the data space, or the CPU space for special functions as required. The function codes can be used by the memory management unit to organize separate program (read only) and data (read-write) memory areas.

This section describes the data organization and addressing capabilities of the MC68030. It lists the types of operands used by instructions and describes the registers and their use as operands. Next, the section describes the organization of data in memory and the addressing modes available to access data in memory. Last, the section describes the system stack and user program stacks and queues.

2.1 INSTRUCTION OPERANDS

The MC68030 supports a general-purpose set of operands to serve the requirements of a large range of applications. Operands of MC68030 instructions may reside in registers, in memory, or within the instructions themselves. An instruction operand might also reside in a coprocessor. An operand may be a single bit, a bit field of from 1 to 32 bits in length, a byte (8 bits), a word (16 bits), a long word (32 bits), or a quad word (64 bits). The operand size for each instruction is either explicitly encoded in the instruction or implicitly defined by the instruction operation. Coprocessors are designed to support special computation models that require very specific but widely varying data operand types and sizes. Hence, coprocessor instructions can specify operands of any size.

2.2 ORGANIZATION OF DATA IN REGISTERS

The eight data registers can store data operands of 1, 8, 16, 32, and 64 bits, addresses of 16 or 32 bits, or bit fields of 1 to 32 bits. The seven address registers and the three stack pointers are used for address operands of 16 or 32 bits. The control registers (SR, VBR, SFC, DFC, CACR, CAAR, CRP, SRP, TC, TT0, TT1, and MMUSR) vary in size according to function. Coprocessors may define unique operand sizes and support them with on-chip registers accordingly.

2.2.1 Data Registers

Each data register is 32 bits wide. Byte operands occupy the low-order 8 bits, word operands the low-order 16 bits, and long-word operands the entire 32 bits. When a data register is used as either a source or destination operand, only the appropriate low-order byte or word (in byte or word operations, respectively) is used or changed; the remaining high-order portion is neither used nor changed. The least significant bit of a long-word integer is addressed as bit zero, and the most significant bit is addressed as bit 31. For bit fields, the most significant bit is addressed as bit zero, and the least significant bit is addressed as the width of the field minus one. If the width of the field plus the offset is greater than 32, the bit field wraps around within the register. The following illustration shows the organization of various types of data in the data registers.

Quad-word data consists of two long words: for example, the product of 32-bit multiply or the quotient of 32-bit divide operations (signed and unsigned). Quad words may be organized in any two data registers without restrictions on order or pairing. There are no explicit instructions for the management of this data type, although the MOVEM instruction can be used to move a quad word into or out of the registers.

Binary-coded decimal (BCD) data represents decimal numbers in binary form. Although many BCD codes have been devised, the BCD instructions of the M68000 Family support formats in which the four least significant bits consist of a binary number having the numeric value of the corresponding decimal number. Two BCD formats are used. In the unpacked BCD format, a byte

Bit (0≤Modulo (Offset)<31, Offset of 0 = MSB)

31	30	29		1	0
MSB			•••		LSB

Byte

31	24	23	16	15	8	7	0
High-Order Byte		Middle-High Byte		Middle-Low Byte		Low-Order Byte	

16-Bit Word

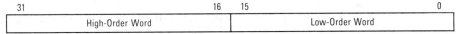

31	16	15	0
High-Order Word		Low-Order Word	

Long Word

31	0
Long Word	

Quad Word

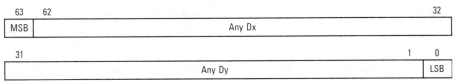

63	62	32
MSB	Any Dx	

31	1	0
Any Dy		LSB

Bit Field (0≤Offset<32, 0<Width≤32)

31	Width		0
Offset	MSB ••• LSB		

Note: If width + offset<32, bit field wraps around within the register.

Unpacked BCD (a = MSB)

31	8	7	6	5	4	3	2	1	0
		x	x	x	x	a	b	c	d

Packed BCD (a = MSB First Digit, e = MSB Second Digit)

31	8	7	6	5	4	3	2	1	0
		a	b	c	d	e	f	g	h

Data Organization in Data Registers

contains one digit; the four least significant bits contain the binary value and the four most significant bits are undefined. Each byte of the packed BCD format contains two digits; the least significant four bits contain the least significant digit.

2.2.2 Address Registers

Each address register and stack pointer is 32 bits wide and holds a 32-bit address. Address registers cannot be used for byte-sized operands. Therefore, when an address register is used as a source operand, either the low-order word or the entire long-word operand is used, depending upon the operation size. When an address register is used as the destination operand, the entire register is affected, regardless of the operation size. If the source operand is a word size, it is first sign-extended to 32 bits and then used in the operation to an address register destination. Address registers are used primarily for addresses and to support address computation. The instruction set includes instructions that add to, subtract from, compare, and move the contents of address registers. The following example shows the organization of addresses in address registers.

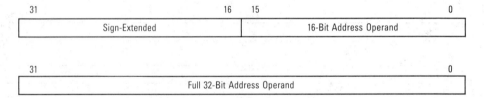

Address Organization in Address Registers

2.2.3 Control Registers

The control registers described in this section contain control information for supervisor functions and vary in size. With the exception of the user portion of the status register (CCR), they are accessed only by instructions at the supervisor privilege level.

The status register (SR), shown in Figure 1-4, is 16 bits wide. Only 12 bits of the status register are defined; all undefined values are reserved by Motorola for future definition. The undefined bits are read as zeros and should be written as zeros for future compatibility. The lower byte of the status register is the CCR. Operations to the CCR can be performed at the supervisor or user privilege level. All operations to the status register and CCR are word-sized operations, but for all CCR operations, the upper byte is read as all zeros and is ignored when written, regardless of privilege level.

The supervisor programming model (see Figure 1-3) shows the control registers. The cache control register (CACR) provides control and status information for the on-chip instruction and data caches. The cache address register (CAAR) contains the address for cache control functions. The vector base register (VBR) provides the base address of the exception vector table. All operations involving the CACR, CAAR, and VBR are long-word operations, whether these registers are used as the source or the destination operand.

The alternate function code registers (SFC and DFC) are 32-bit registers with only bits 2:0 implemented that contain the address space values (FC0–FC2) for the read or write operands of MOVES, PLOAD, PFLUSH, and PTEST instructions. The MOVEC instruction is used to transfer values to and from the alternate function code registers. These are long-word transfers; the upper 29 bits are read as zeros and are ignored when written.

The remaining control registers in the supervisor programming model are used by the memory management unit (MMU). The CPU root pointer (CRP) and supervisor root pointer (SRP) contain pointers to the user and supervisor address translation trees. Transfers of data to and from these 64-bit registers are quad-word transfers. The translation control register (TC) contains control information for the MMU. The MC68030 always uses long-word transfers to access this 32-bit register. The transparent translation registers (TT0 and TT1) also contain 32 bits each; they identify memory areas for direct addressing without address translation. Data transfers to and from these registers are long-word transfers. The MMU status register (MMUSR) stores the status of the MMU after execution of a PTEST instruction. It is a 16-bit register, and transfers to and from the MMUSR are word transfers. Refer to **SECTION 9 MEMORY MANAGEMENT UNIT** for more detail.

2.3 ORGANIZATION OF DATA IN MEMORY

Memory is organized on a byte-addressable basis where lower addresses correspond to higher order bytes. The address, N, of a long-word data item corresponds to the address of the most significant byte of the highest order word. The lower order word is located at address N + 2, leaving the least significant byte at address N + 3 (refer to Figure 2-1). Notice that the MC68030 does not require data to be aligned on word boundaries (refer to Figure 2-2), but the most efficient data transfers occur when data is aligned on the same byte boundary as its operand size. However, instruction words must be aligned on word boundaries.

The data types supported in memory by the MC68030 are bit and bit field data; integer data of 8, 16, or 32 bits; 32-bit addresses; and BCD data (packed and unpacked). These data types are organized in memory as shown in Figure 2-2. Note that all of these data types can be accessed at any byte address.

Coprocessors can implement any data types and lengths up to 255 bytes. For example, the MC68881/MC68882 floating-point coprocessors support memory accesses for quad-word-sized items (double-precision floating-point values).

A bit operand is specified by a base address that selects one byte in memory (the base byte) and a bit number that selects the one bit in this byte. The most significant bit of the byte is bit 7.

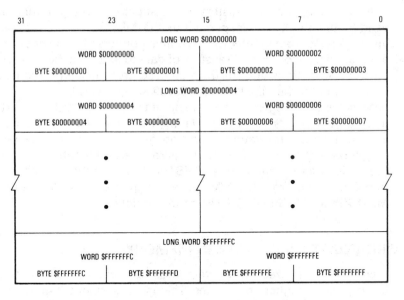

Figure 2-1. Memory Operand Address

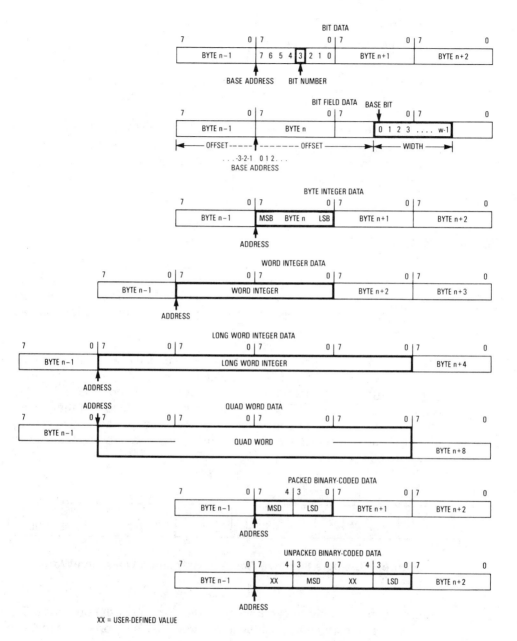

Figure 2-2. Memory Data Organization

A bit field operand is specified by:

1. A base address that selects one byte in memory,

2. A bit field offset that indicates the leftmost (base) bit of the bit field in relation to the most significant bit of the base byte, and

3. A bit field width that determines how many bits to the right of the base bit are in the bit field.

The most significant bit of the base byte is bit field offset 0, the least significant bit of the base byte is bit field offset 7, and the least significant bit of the previous byte in memory is bit offset -1. Bit field offsets may have values in the range of -2^{31} to $2^{31}-1$, and bit field widths may range between 1 and 32 bits.

2.4 ADDRESSING MODES

The addressing mode of an instruction can specify the value of an operand (with an immediate operand), a register that contains the operand (with the register direct addressing mode), or how the effective address of an operand in memory is derived. An assembler syntax has been defined for each addressing mode.

Figure 2-3 shows the general format of the single effective address instruction operation word. The effective address field specifies the addressing mode for an operand that can use one of the numerous defined modes. The ⟨ea⟩ designation is composed of two 3-bit fields: the mode field and the register field. The value in the mode field selects one or a set of addressing modes. The register field specifies a register for the mode or a submode for modes that do not use registers.

15	14	13	12	11	10	9	8	7	6	5					0
										EFFECTIVE ADDRESS					
X	X	X	X	X	X	X	X	X	X	MODE			REGISTER		

Figure 2-3. Single Effective Address Instruction Operation Word

Many instructions imply the addressing mode for one of the operands. The formats of these instructions include appropriate fields for operands that use only one addressing mode.

The effective address field may require additional information to fully specify the operand address. This additional information, called the effective address extension, is contained in an additional word or words and is considered part of the instruction. Refer to **2.5 EFFECTIVE ADDRESS ENCODING SUMMARY** for a description of the extension word formats.

The notational conventions used in the addressing mode descriptions in this section are:

> EA—Effective address
> An—Address register n
> > Example: A3 is address register 3
> Dn—Data register n
> > Example: D5 is data register 5
> Xn.SIZE*SCALE—Denotes index register n (data or address), the index size (W for word, L for long word), and a scale factor (1, 2, 4, or 8, for no, word, long-word or 8 for quad-word scaling, respectively).
> PC—The program counter
> d_n—Displacement value, n bits wide
> bd—Base displacement
> od—Outer displacement
> L—Long-word size
> W—Word size
> ( )—Identify an indirect address in a register
> [ ]—Identify an indirect address in memory

When the addressing mode uses a register, the register field of the operation word specifies the register to be used. Other fields within the instruction specify whether the register selected is an address or data register and how the register is to be used.

2.4.1 Data Register Direct Mode

In the data register direct mode, the operand is in the data register specified by the effective address register field.

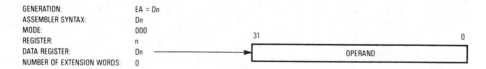

```
GENERATION:                  EA = Dn
ASSEMBLER SYNTAX:            Dn
MODE:                        000
REGISTER:                    n
DATA REGISTER:               Dn
NUMBER OF EXTENSION WORDS:   0
```

2.4.2 Address Register Direct Mode

In the address register direct mode, the operand is in the address register specified by the effective address register field.

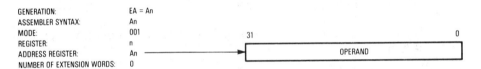

```
GENERATION:              EA = An
ASSEMBLER SYNTAX:        An
MODE:                    001
REGISTER:                n
ADDRESS REGISTER:        An
NUMBER OF EXTENSION WORDS:  0
```

2.4.3 Address Register Indirect Mode

In the address register indirect mode, the operand is in memory, and the address of the operand is in the address register specified by the register field.

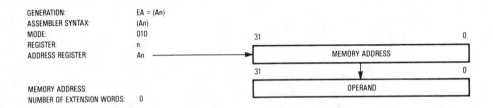

```
GENERATION:              EA = (An)
ASSEMBLER SYNTAX:        (An)
MODE:                    010
REGISTER:                n
ADDRESS REGISTER:        An

MEMORY ADDRESS:
NUMBER OF EXTENSION WORDS:  0
```

2.4.4 Address Register Indirect with Postincrement Mode

In the address register indirect with postincrement mode, the operand is in memory, and the address of the operand is in the address register specified by the register field. After the operand address is used, it is incremented by one, two, or four depending on the size of the operand: byte, word, or long word. Coprocessors may support incrementing for any size of operand up to 255 bytes. If the address register is the stack pointer and the operand size is byte, the address is incremented by two rather than one to keep the stack pointer aligned to a word boundary.

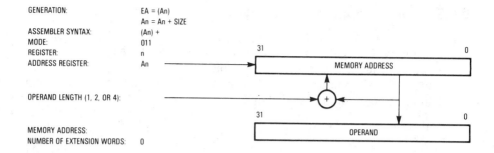

GENERATION:	EA = (An)
	An = An + SIZE
ASSEMBLER SYNTAX:	(An) +
MODE:	011
REGISTER:	n
ADDRESS REGISTER:	An
OPERAND LENGTH (1, 2, OR 4):	
MEMORY ADDRESS:	
NUMBER OF EXTENSION WORDS:	0

2.4.5 Address Register Indirect with Predecrement Mode

In the address register indirect with predecrement mode, the operand is in memory, and the address of the operand is in the address register specified by the register field. Before the operand address is used, it is decremented by one, two, or four depending on the operand size: byte, word, or long word. Coprocessors may support decrementing for any operand size up to 255 bytes. If the address register is the stack pointer and the operand size is byte, the address is decremented by two rather than one to keep the stack pointer aligned to a word boundary.

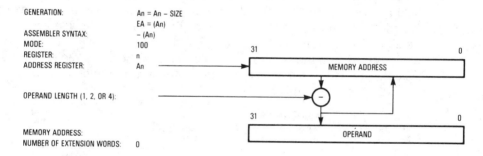

GENERATION:	An = An – SIZE
	EA = (An)
ASSEMBLER SYNTAX:	– (An)
MODE:	100
REGISTER:	n
ADDRESS REGISTER:	An
OPERAND LENGTH (1, 2, OR 4):	
MEMORY ADDRESS:	
NUMBER OF EXTENSION WORDS:	0

2.4.6 Address Register Indirect with Displacement Mode

In the address register indirect with displacement mode, the operand is in memory. The address of the operand is the sum of the address in the address register plus the sign-extended 16-bit displacement integer in the extension word. Displacements are always sign-extended to 32 bits prior to being used in effective address calculations.

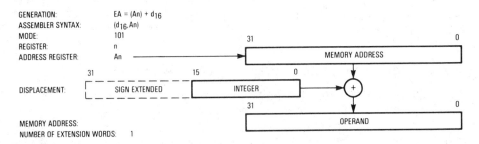

2.4.7 Address Register Indirect with Index (8-Bit Displacement) Mode

This addressing mode requires one extension word that contains the index register indicator and an 8-bit displacement. The index register indicator includes size and scale information. In this mode, the operand is in memory. The address of the operand is the sum of the contents of the address register, the sign-extended displacement value in the low-order eight bits of the extension word, and the sign-extended contents of the index register (possibly scaled). The user must specify the displacement, the address register, and the index register in this mode.

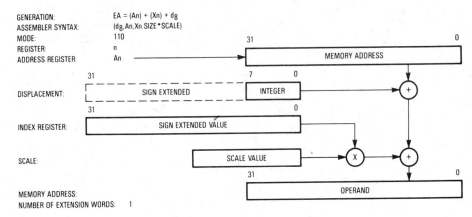

2.4.8 Address Register Indirect with Index (Base Displacement) Mode

This addressing mode requires an index register indicator and an optional 16- or 32-bit sign-extended base displacement. The index register indicator includes size and scaling information. The operand is in memory. The address of the operand is the sum of the contents of the address register, the scaled contents of the sign-extended index register, and the base displacement.

In this mode, the address register, the index register, and the displacement are all optional. If none is specified, the effective address is zero. This mode provides a data register indirect address when no address register is specified and the index register is a data register (Dn).

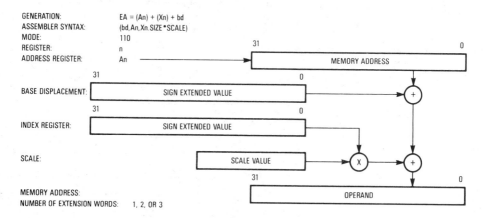

GENERATION: EA = (An) + (Xn) + bd
ASSEMBLER SYNTAX: (bd,An,Xn.SIZE*SCALE)
MODE: 110
REGISTER: n
ADDRESS REGISTER: An

MEMORY ADDRESS

BASE DISPLACEMENT: SIGN EXTENDED VALUE

INDEX REGISTER: SIGN EXTENDED VALUE

SCALE: SCALE VALUE

MEMORY ADDRESS: OPERAND
NUMBER OF EXTENSION WORDS: 1, 2, OR 3

2.4.9 Memory Indirect Postindexed Mode

In this mode, the operand and its address are in memory. The processor calculates an intermediate indirect memory address using the base register (An) and base displacement (bd). The processor accesses a long word at this address and adds the index operand (Xn.SIZE*SCALE) and the outer displacement to yield the effective address. Both displacements and the index register contents are sign-extended to 32 bits.

In the syntax for this mode, brackets enclose the values used to calculate the intermediate memory address. All four user-specified values are optional. Both the base and outer displacements may be null, word, or long word. When a displacement is omitted or an element is suppressed, its value is taken as zero in the effective address calculation.

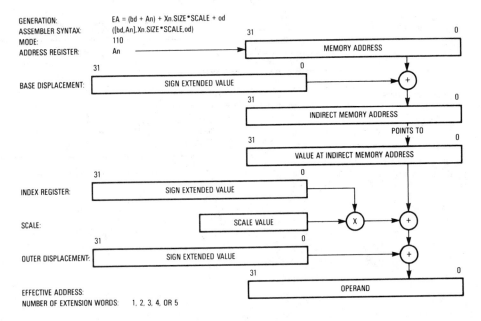

GENERATION: EA = (bd + An) + Xn.SIZE*SCALE + od
ASSEMBLER SYNTAX: ([bd,An],Xn.SIZE*SCALE,od)
MODE: 110
ADDRESS REGISTER: An

BASE DISPLACEMENT:
INDEX REGISTER:
SCALE:
OUTER DISPLACEMENT:
EFFECTIVE ADDRESS:
NUMBER OF EXTENSION WORDS: 1, 2, 3, 4, OR 5

2.4.10 Memory Indirect Preindexed Mode

In this mode, the operand and its address are in memory. The processor calculates an intermediate indirect memory address using the base register (An), a base displacement (bd), and the index operand (Xn.SIZE * SCALE). The processor accesses a long word at this address and adds the outer displacement to yield the effective address. Both displacements and the index register contents are sign-extended to 32 bits.

In the syntax for this mode, brackets enclose the values used to calculate the intermediate memory address. All four user-specified values are optional. Both the base and outer displacements may be null, word, or long word. When a displacement is omitted or an element is suppressed, its value is taken as zero in the effective address calculation.

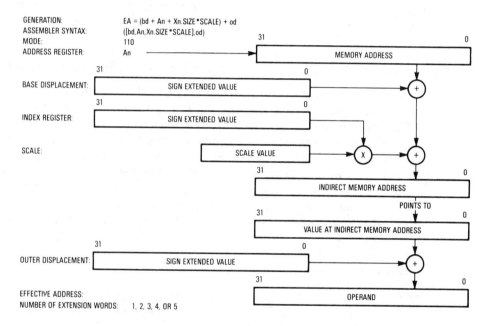

2.4.11 Program Counter Indirect with Displacement Mode

In this mode, the operand is in memory. The address of the operand is the sum of the address in the PC and the sign-extended 16-bit displacement integer in the extension word. The value in the PC is the address of the extension word. The reference is a program space reference and is only allowed for reads (refer to **4.2 ADDRESS SPACE TYPES**).

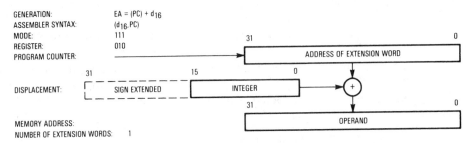

```
GENERATION:              EA = (PC) + d16
ASSEMBLER SYNTAX:        (d16,PC)
MODE:                    111
REGISTER:                010
PROGRAM COUNTER:
```

2.4.12 Program Counter Indirect with Index (8-Bit Displacement) Mode

This mode is similar to the address register indirect with index (8-bit displacement) mode described in **2.4.7 Address Register Indirect with Index (8-Bit Displacement) Mode**, but the PC is used as the base register. The operand is in memory. The address of the operand is the sum of the address in the PC, the sign-extended displacement integer in the lower eight bits of the extension word, and the sized, scaled, and sign-extended index operand. The value in the PC is the address of the extension word. This reference is a program space reference and is only allowed for reads. The user must include the displacement, the PC, and the index register when specifying this addressing mode.

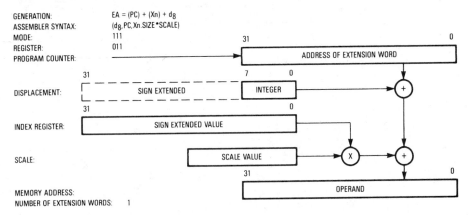

```
GENERATION:              EA = (PC) + (Xn) + d8
ASSEMBLER SYNTAX:        (d8,PC,Xn.SIZE*SCALE)
MODE:                    111
REGISTER:                011
PROGRAM COUNTER:
```

2.4.13 Program Counter Indirect with Index (Base Displacement) Mode

This mode is similar to the address register indirect with index (base displacement) mode described in **2.4.8 Address Register Indirect with Index (Base Displacement) Mode**, but the PC is used as the base register. It requires an index register indicator and an optional 16- or 32-bit sign-extended base displacement. The operand is in memory. The address of the operand is the sum of the contents of the PC, the scaled contents of the sign-extended index register, and the base displacement. The value of the PC is the address of the first extension word. The reference is a program space reference and is only allowed for reads (refer to **4.2 ADDRESS SPACE TYPES**).

In this mode, the PC, the index register, and the displacement are all optional. However, the user must supply the assembler notation "ZPC" (zero value is taken for the PC) to indicate that the PC is not used. This allows the user to access the program space without using the PC in calculating the effective address. The user can access the program space with a data register indirect access by placing ZPC in the instruction and specifying a data register (Dn) as the index register.

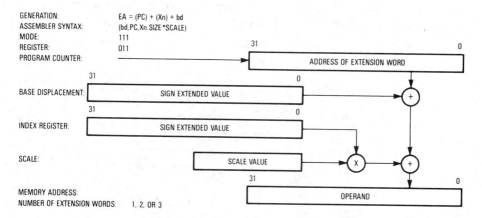

```
GENERATION:              EA = (PC) + (Xn) + bd
ASSEMBLER SYNTAX:        (bd,PC,Xn.SIZE *SCALE)
MODE:                    111
REGISTER:                011
```

2.4.14 Program Counter Memory Indirect Postindexed Mode

This mode is similar to the memory indirect postindexed mode described in **2.4.9 Memory Indirect Postindexed Mode**, but the PC is used as the base register. Both the operand and operand address are in memory. The processor calculates an intermediate indirect memory address by adding a base displacement (bd) to the PC contents. The processor accesses a long word at that address and adds the scaled contents of the index register and the optional outer displacement (od) to yield the effective address. The value of the PC used in the calculation is the address of the first extension word. The reference is a program space reference and is only allowed for reads (refer to **4.2 ADDRESS SPACE TYPES**).

In the syntax for this mode, brackets enclose the values used to calculate the intermediate memory address. All four user-specified values are optional. However, the user must supply the assembler notation ZPC (zero value is taken for the PC) to indicate that the PC is not used. This allows the user to access the program space without using the PC in calculating the effective address. Both the base and outer displacements may be null, word, or long word. When a displacement is omitted or an element is suppressed, its value is taken as zero in the effective address calculation.

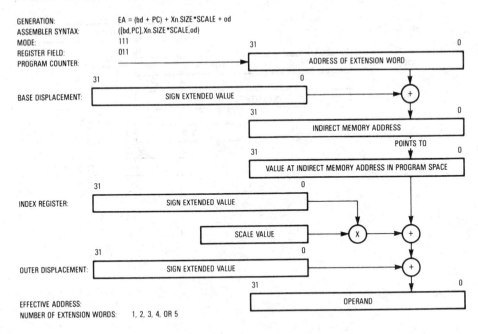

GENERATION: EA = (bd + PC) + Xn.SIZE *SCALE + od
ASSEMBLER SYNTAX: ([bd,PC],Xn.SIZE *SCALE,od)
MODE: 111
REGISTER FIELD: 011
PROGRAM COUNTER: ADDRESS OF EXTENSION WORD
BASE DISPLACEMENT: SIGN EXTENDED VALUE
INDIRECT MEMORY ADDRESS
POINTS TO
VALUE AT INDIRECT MEMORY ADDRESS IN PROGRAM SPACE
INDEX REGISTER: SIGN EXTENDED VALUE
SCALE VALUE
OUTER DISPLACEMENT: SIGN EXTENDED VALUE
EFFECTIVE ADDRESS: OPERAND
NUMBER OF EXTENSION WORDS: 1, 2, 3, 4, OR 5

2.4.15 Program Counter Memory Indirect Preindexed Mode

This mode is similar to the memory indirect preindexed mode described in **2.4.10 Memory Indirect Preindexed Mode**, but the PC is used as the base register. Both the operand and operand address are in memory. The processor calculates an intermediate indirect memory address by adding the PC contents, a base displacement (bd), and the scaled contents of an index register. The processor accesses a long word at that address and adds the optional outer displacement (od) to yield the effective address. The value of the PC is the address of the first extension word. The reference is a program space reference and is only allowed for reads (refer to **4.2 ADDRESS SPACE TYPES**).

In the syntax for this mode, brackets enclose the values used to calculate the intermediate memory address. All four user-specified values are optional. However, the user must supply the assembler notation ZPC (zero value is taken for the PC) to indicate that the PC is not used. This allows the user to access the program space without using the PC in calculating the effective address. Both the base and outer displacements may be null, word, or long word. When a displacement is omitted or an element is suppressed, its value is taken as zero in the effective address calculation.

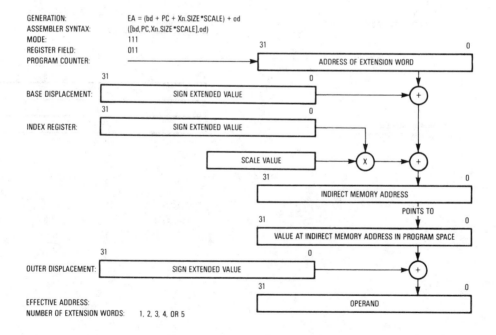

GENERATION: EA = (bd + PC + Xn.SIZE*SCALE) + od
ASSEMBLER SYNTAX: ([bd,PC,Xn.SIZE*SCALE],od)
MODE: 111
REGISTER FIELD: 011

2.4.16 Absolute Short Addressing Mode

In this addressing mode, the operand is in memory, and the address of the operand is in the extension word. The 16-bit address is sign-extended to 32 bits before it is used.

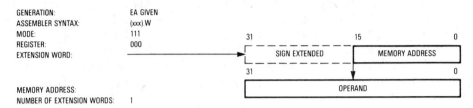

```
GENERATION:                  EA GIVEN
ASSEMBLER SYNTAX:            (xxx).W
MODE:                        111
REGISTER:                    000
EXTENSION WORD:

MEMORY ADDRESS:
NUMBER OF EXTENSION WORDS:   1
```

2.4.17 Absolute Long Addressing Mode

In this mode, the operand is in memory, and the address of the operand occupies the two extension words following the instruction word in memory. The first extension word contains the high-order part of the address; the low-order part of the address is the second extension word.

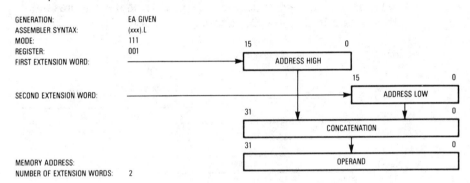

```
GENERATION:                  EA GIVEN
ASSEMBLER SYNTAX:            (xxx).L
MODE:                        111
REGISTER:                    001
FIRST EXTENSION WORD:

SECOND EXTENSION WORD:

MEMORY ADDRESS:
NUMBER OF EXTENSION WORDS:   2
```

2.4.18 Immediate Data

In this addressing mode, the operand is in one or two extension words:

Byte Operation
> Operand is in the low-order byte of the extension word

Word Operation
> Operand is in the extension word

Long-Word Operation
> The high-order 16 bits of the operand are in the first extension word; the low-order 16 bits are in the second extension word.

Coprocessor instructions can support immediate data of any size. The instruction word is followed by as many extension words as are required.

Generation:	Operand given
Assembler Syntax:	#xxx
Mode Field:	111
Register Field:	100
Number of Extension Words:	1 or 2, except for coprocessor instructions

2.5 EFFECTIVE ADDRESS ENCODING SUMMARY

Most of the addressing modes use one of the three formats shown in Figure 2-4. The single effective address instruction is in the format of the instruction word. The encoding of the mode field of this word selects the addressing mode. The register field contains the general register number or a value that selects the addressing mode when the mode field contains "111". Table 2-2 shows the encoding of these fields. Some indexed or indirect modes use the instruction word followed by the brief format extension word. Other indexed or indirect modes consist of the instruction word and the full format of extension words. The longest instruction for the MC68030 contains 10 extension words. It is a MOVE instruction with full format extension words for both the source and destination effective addresses and with 32-bit base displacements and 32-bit outer displacements for both addresses. However, coprocessor instructions can have any number of extension words. Refer to the coprocessor instruction formats in **SECTION 10 COPROCESSOR INTERFACE DESCRIPTION**.

For effective addresses that use the full format, the index suppress (IS) bit and the index/indirect selection (I/IS) field determine the type of indexing and indirection. Table 2-1 lists the indexing and indirection operations corresponding to all combinations of IS and I/IS values.

Table 2-1. IS-I/IS Memory Indirection Encodings

IS	Index/Indirect	Operation
0	000	No Memory Indirection
0	001	Indirect Preindexed with Null Outer Displacement
0	010	Indirect Preindexed with Word Outer Displacement
0	011	Indirect Preindexed with Long Outer Displacement
0	100	Reserved
0	101	Indirect Postindexed with Null Outer Displacement
0	110	Indirect Postindexed with Word Outer Displacement
0	111	Indirect Postindexed with Long Outer Displacement
1	000	No Memory Indirection
1	001	Memory Indirect with Null Outer Displacement
1	010	Memory Indirect with Word Outer Displacement
1	011	Memory Indirect with Long Outer Displacement
1	100–111	Reserved

Single Effective Address Instruction Format

15	14	13	12	11	10	9	8	7	6	5		0
X	X	X	X	X	X	X	X	X	X	EFFECTIVE ADDRESS		
										MODE		REGISTER

Brief Format Extension Word

15	14		12	11	10	9	8	7			0
D/A	REGISTER			W/L	SCALE		0	DISPLACEMENT			

Full Format Extension Word(s)

15	14		12	11	10	9	8	7	6	5	4	3	2		0
D/A	REGISTER			W/L	SCALE		1	BS	IS	BD SIZE		0	I/IS		
BASE DISPLACEMENT (0, 1, OR 2 WORDS)															
OUTER DISPLACEMENT (0, 1, OR 2 WORDS)															

Field	Definition
Instruction:	
Register	General Register Number
Extensions:	
Register	Index Register Number
D/A	Index Register Type
	0 = Dn
	1 = An
W/L	Word/Long-Word Index Size
	0 = Sign-Extended Word
	1 = Long Word
Scale	Scale Factor
	00 = 1
	01 = 2
	10 = 4
	11 = 8

Field	Definition
BS	Base Register Suppress:
	0 = Base Register Added
	1 = Base Register Suppressed
IS	Index Suppress:
	0 = Evaluate and Add Index Operand
	1 = Suppress Index Operand
BD SIZE	Base Displacement Size:
	00 = Reserved
	01 = Null Displacement
	10 = Word Displacement
	11 = Long Displacement
I/IS	Index/Indirect Selection: Indirect and Indexing Operand Determined in Conjunction with Bit 6, Index Suppress

Figure 2-4. Effective Address Specification Formats

Effective address modes are grouped according to the use of the mode. They can be classified as follows:

Data   A data addressing effective address mode is one that refers to data operands.

Memory   A memory addressing effective address mode is one that refers to memory operands.

Alterable An alterable addressing effective address mode is one that refers to alterable (writable) operands.

Control   A control addressing effective address mode is one that refers to memory operands without an associated size.

Table 2-2 shows the categories to which each of the effective addressing modes belong.

Table 2-2. Effective Addressing Mode Categories

Address Modes	Mode	Register	Data	Memory	Control	Alterable	Assembler Syntax
Data Register Direct	000	reg. no.	X	—	—	X	Dn
Address Register Direct	001	reg. no.	—	—	—	X	An
Address Register Indirect	010	reg. no.	X	X	X	X	(An)
Address Register Indirect with Postincrement	011	reg. no.	X	X	—	X	(An) +
Address Register Indirect with Predecrement	100	reg. no.	X	X	—	X	– (An)
Address Register Indirect with Displacement	101	reg. no.	X	X	X	X	(d_{16},An)
Address Register Indirect with Index (8-Bit Displacement)	110	reg. no.	X	X	X	X	(d_8,An,Xn)
Address Register Indirect with Index (Base Displacement)	110	reg. no.	X	X	X	X	(bd,An,Xn)
Memory Indirect Postindexed	110	reg. no.	X	X	X	X	([bd,An],Xn,od)
Memory Indirect Preindexed	110	reg. no.	X	X	X	X	([bd,An,Xn],od)
Absolute Short	111	000	X	X	X	X	(xxx).W
Absolute Long	111	001	X	X	X	X	(xxx).L
Program Counter Indirect with Displacement	111	010	X	X	X	—	(d_{16},PC)
Program Counter Indirect with Index (8-Bit) Displacement	111	011	X	X	X	—	(d_8,PC,Xn)
Program Counter Indirect with Index (Base Displacement)	111	011	X	X	X	—	(bd,PC,Xn)
PC Memory Indirect Postindexed	111	011	X	X	X	—	([bd,PC],Xn,od
PC Memory Indirect Preindexed	111	011	X	X	X	—	([bd,PC,Xn],od)
Immediate	111	100	X	X	—	—	#(data)

These categories are sometimes combined, forming new categories that are more restrictive. Two combined classifications are alterable memory or data alterable. The former refers to those addressing modes that are both alterable and memory addresses, and the latter refers to addressing modes that are both data and alterable.

2.6 PROGRAMMER'S VIEW OF ADDRESSING MODES

Extensions to the indexed addressing modes, indirection, and full 32-bit displacements provide additional programming capabilities for both the MC68020 and the MC68030. This section describes addressing techniques that exploit these capabilities and summarizes the addressing modes from a programming point of view.

Several of the addressing techniques described in this section use data registers and address registers interchangeably. While the MC68030 provides this capability, its performance has been optimized for addressing with address registers. The performance of a program that uses address registers in address calculations is superior to that of a program that similarly uses data registers. The specification of addresses with data registers should be used sparingly (if at all), particularly in programs that require maximum performance.

2.6.1 Addressing Capabilities

In both the MC68020 and the MC68030, setting the base register suppress (BS) bit in the full format extension word (see Figure 2-4) suppresses use of the base address register in calculating the effective address. This allows any index register to be used in place of the base register. Since any of the data registers can be index registers, this provides a data register indirect form (Dn). The mode could be called register indirect (Rn) since either a data register or an address register can be used. This addressing mode is an extension to the M68000 Family because the MC68030 and MC68020 can use both the data registers and the address registers to address memory. The capability of specifying the size and scale of an index register (Xn.SIZE*SCALE) in these modes provides additional addressing flexibility. Using the SIZE parameter, either the entire contents of the index register can be used, or the least significant word can be sign-extended to provide a 32-bit index value (refer to Figure 2-5).

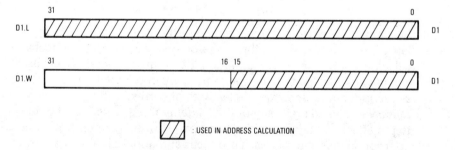

Figure 2-5. Using SIZE in the Index Selection

For both the MC68020 and the MC68030, the register indirect modes can be extended further. Since displacements can be 32 bits wide, they can represent absolute addresses or the results of expressions that contain absolute addresses. This allows the general register indirect form to be (bd,Rn) or (bd,An,Rn) when the base register is not suppressed. Thus, an absolute address can be directly indexed by one or two registers (refer to Figure 2-6).

SYNTAX: (bd,An,Rn)

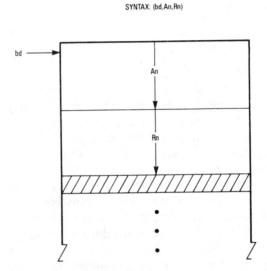

Figure 2-6. Using Absolute Address with Indexes

Scaling provides an optional shifting of the value in an index register to the left by zero, one, two, or three bits before using it in the effective address calculation (the actual value in the index register remains unchanged). This is equivalent to multiplying the register by one, two, four, or eight for direct subscripting into an array of elements of corresponding size using an arithmetic value residing in any of the 16 general registers. Scaling does not add to the effective address calculation time. However, when combined with the appropriate derived modes, it produces additional capabilities. Arrayed structures can be addressed absolutely and then subscripted, (bd,Rn*scale), for example. Optionally, an address register that contains a dynamic displacement can be included in the address calculation (bd,An,Rn*scale). Another variation that can be derived is (An,Rn*scale). In the first case, the array address is the sum of the contents of a register and a displacement, as shown in Figure 2-7. In the second example, An contains the address of an array and Rn contains a subscript.

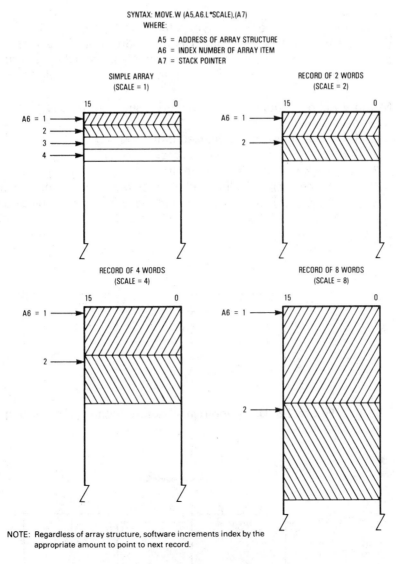

SYNTAX: MOVE.W (A5,A6.L*SCALE),(A7)
WHERE:

A5 = ADDRESS OF ARRAY STRUCTURE
A6 = INDEX NUMBER OF ARRAY ITEM
A7 = STACK POINTER

SIMPLE ARRAY
(SCALE = 1)

RECORD OF 2 WORDS
(SCALE = 2)

RECORD OF 4 WORDS
(SCALE = 4)

RECORD OF 8 WORDS
(SCALE = 8)

NOTE: Regardless of array structure, software increments index by the appropriate amount to point to next record.

Figure 2-7. Addressing Array Items

The memory indirect addressing modes use a long-word pointer in memory to access an operand. Any of the modes previously described can be used to address the memory pointer. Because the base and index registers can both be suppressed, the displacement acts as an absolute address, providing indirect absolute memory addressing (refer to Figure 2-8).

The outer displacement (od) available in the memory indirect modes is added to the pointer in memory. The syntax for these modes is ([bd,An],Xn,od) and ([bd,An,Xn],od). When the pointer is the address of a structure in memory and the outer displacement is the offset of an item in the structure, the memory indirect modes can access the item efficiently (refer to Figure 2-9).

Memory indirect addressing modes are used with a base displacement in five basic forms:
1. [bd,An] — Indirect, suppressed index register
2. ([bd,An,Xn]) — Preindexed indirect
3. ([bd,An],Xn) — Postindexed indirect
4. ([bd,An,Xn],od) — Preindexed indirect with outer displacement
5. ([bd,An],Xn,od) — Postindexed indirect with outer displacement

SYNTAX: ([bd])

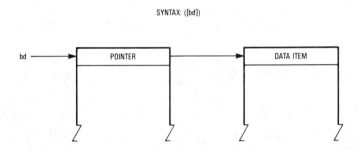

Figure 2-8. Using Indirect Absolute Memory Addressing

SYNTAX: ([An],od)

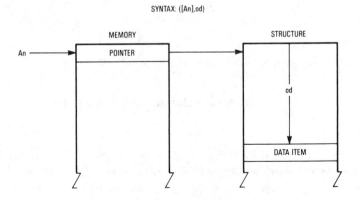

Figure 2-9. Accessing an Item in a Structure Using Pointer

The indirect, suppressed index register mode (see Figure 2-10) uses the contents of register An as an index to the pointer located at the address specified by the displacement. The actual data item is at the address in the selected pointer.

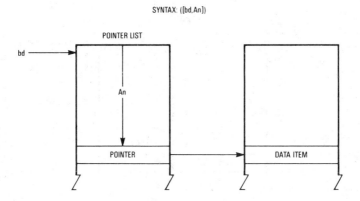

Figure 2-10. Indirect Addressing, Suppressed Index Register

The preindexed indirect mode (see Figure 2-11) uses the contents of An as an index to the pointer list structure at the displacement. Register Xn is the index to the pointer, which contains the address of the data item.

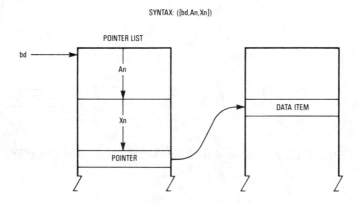

Figure 2-11. Preindexed Indirect Addressing

The postindexed indirect mode (see Figure 2-12) uses the contents of An as an index to the pointer list at the displacement. Register Xn is used as an index to the structure of data items located at the address specified by the pointer. Figure 2-13 shows the preindexed indirect addressing with outer displacement mode.

SYNTAX: ([bd,An],Xn)

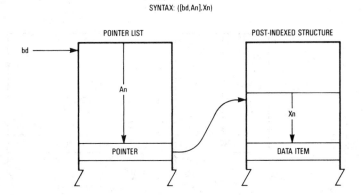

Figure 2-12. Postindexed Indirect Addressing

SYNTAX: ([bd,An,Xn],od)

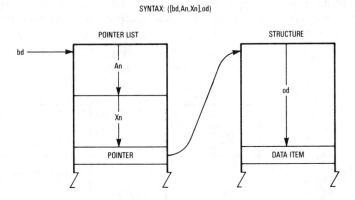

Figure 2-13. Preindexed Indirect Addressing with Outer Displacement

The postindexed indirect mode with outer displacement (see Figure 2-14) uses the contents of An as an index to the pointer list at the displacement. Register Xn is used as an index to the structure of data structures at the address in the pointer. The outer displacement (od) is the displacement of the data item within the selected data structure.

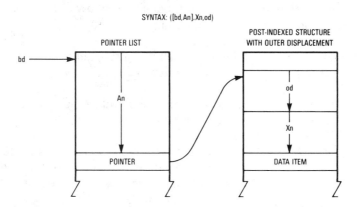

Figure 2-14. Postindexed Indirect Addressing with Outer Displacement

2.6.2 General Addressing Mode Summary

The addressing modes described in the previous section are derived from specific combinations of options in the indexing mode or a selection of two alternate addressing modes. For example, the addressing mode called register indirect (Rn) assembles as the address register indirect if the register is an address register. If Rn is a data register, the assembler uses the address register indirect with index mode using the data register as the indirect register and suppresses the address register by setting the base suppress bit in the effective address specification. Assigning an address register as Rn provides higher performance than using a data register as Rn. Another case is (bd,An), which selects an addressing mode depending on the size of the displacement. If the displacement is 16 bits or less, the address register indirect with displacement mode (d_{16},An) is used. When a 32-bit displacement is required, the address register indirect with index (bd,An,Xn) is used with the index register suppressed.

It is useful to examine the derived addressing modes available to a programmer (without regard to the MC68030 effective addressing mode actually encoded) because the programmer need not be concerned about these decisions. The assembler can choose the more efficient addressing mode to encode.

In the list of derived addressing modes that follows, common programming terms are used. The following definitions apply:

pointer — Long-word value in a register or in memory which represents an address.

base — A pointer combined with a displacement to represent an address.

index — A constant or variable value added into an effective address calculation. A constant index is a displacement. A variable index is always represented by a register containing the value.

disp — Displacement, a constant index.

subscript — The use of any of the data or address registers as a variable index subscript into arrays of items 1, 2, 4, or 8 bytes in size.

relative — An address calculated from the program counter contents. The address is position independent and is in program space. All other addresses but psaddr are in data space.

addr — An absolute address.

psaddr — An absolute address in program space. All other addresses but PC relative are in data space.

preindexed — All modes from absolute address through program counter relative.

postindexed — Any of the following modes:

    addr — Absolute address in data space

    psaddr,ZPC — Absolute address in program space

    An — Register pointer

    disp,An — Register pointer with constant displacement

    addr,An — Absolute address with single variable name

    disp,PC — Simple PC relative

The addressing modes defined in programming terms, which are derivations of the addressing modes provided by the MC68030 architecture, are as follows:

Immediate Data — #data:
The data is a constant located in the instruction stream.

Register Direct — Rn:
The contents of a register contain the operand.

Scanning Modes:
(An)+
Address register pointer automatically incremented after use.

−(An)
Address register pointer automatically decremented before use.

Absolute Address:
(addr)
Absolute address in data space.

(psaddr,ZPC)
Absolute address in program space. Symbol ZPC suppresses the PC, but retains PC relative mode to directly access the program space.

Register Pointer:
(Rn)
Register as a pointer.

(disp,Rn)
Register as a pointer with constant index (or base address).

Indexing:
(An,Rn)
Register pointer An with variable index Rn.

(disp,An,Rn)
Register pointer with constant and variable index (or a base address with a variable index).

(addr,Rn)
Absolute address with variable index.

(addr,An,Rn)
Absolute address with two variable indexes.

Subscripting:
(An,Rn*scale)
Address register pointer subscript.

(disp,An,Rn*scale)
Address register pointer subscript with constant displacement (or base address with subscript).

(addr, Rn*scale)
Absolute address with subscript.

(addr,An,Rn*scale)
Absolute address subscript with variable index.

Program Relative:
(disp,PC)
Simple PC relative.

(disp,PC,Rn)
PC relative with variable index.

(disp,PC,Rn*scale)
PC relative with subscript.

Memory Pointer:
  ([preindexed])
    Memory pointer directly to data operand.

  ([preindexed],disp)
    Memory pointer as base with displacement to data operand.

  ([postindexed],Rn)
    Memory pointer with variable index.

  ([postindexed],disp,Rn)
    Memory pointer with constant and variable index.

  ([postindexed],Rn*scale)
    Memory pointer subscripted.

  ([postindexed], disp, Rn*scale)
    Memory pointer subscripted with constant index.

2.7 M68000 FAMILY ADDRESSING COMPATIBILITY

Programs can be easily transported from one member of the M68000 Family to another in an upward compatible fashion. The user object code of each early member of the family is upward compatible with newer members and can be executed on the newer microprocessor without change. The address extension word(s) are encoded with the information that allows the MC68020/MC68030 to distinguish the new address extensions to the basic M68000 Family architecture. The address extension words for the early MC68000/MC68008/MC68010 microprocessors and for the newer 32-bit MC68020/MC68030 microprocessors are shown in Figure 2-15. Notice the encoding for SCALE used by the MC68020/MC68030 is a compatible extension of the M68000 architecture. A value of zero for SCALE is the same encoding for both extension words; hence, software that uses this encoding is both upward and downward compatible across all processors in the product line. However, the other values of SCALE are not found in both extension formats; thus, while software can be easily migrated in an upward compatible direction, only nonscaled addressing is supported in a downward fashion. If the MC68000 were to execute an instruction that encoded a scaling factor, the scaling factor would be ignored and not access the desired memory address. The earlier microprocessors have no knowledge of the extension word formats implemented by newer processors; while they do detect illegal instructions, they do not decode invalid encodings of the extension words as exceptions.

2.8 OTHER DATA STRUCTURES

Stacks and queues are widely used data structures. The MC68030 implements a system stack and also provides instructions that support the use of user stacks and queues.

2.8.1 System Stack

Address register seven (A7) is used as the system stack pointer (SP). Any of the three system stack registers is active at any one time. The M and S bits of the status register determine which stack pointer is used. When $S = 0$ indicating user mode (user privilege level), the user stack pointer (USP) is the active system stack pointer, and the master and interrupt stack pointers cannot be referenced. When $S = 1$ indicating supervisor mode (at supervisor privilege level) and $M = 1$, the master stack pointer (MSP) is the active system stack pointer. When $S = 1$ and $M = 0$, the interrupt stack pointer (ISP) is the active system stack pointer. This mode is the MC68030 default mode after reset and corresponds to the MC68000, MC68008, and MC68010 supervisor

**MC68000/MC68008/MC68010 Address
Extension Word**

15	14	12	11	10	9	8	7	0
D/A	REGISTER		W/L	0	0	0	DISPLACEMENT INTEGER	

D/A: 0 = Data Register Select
           1 = Address Register Select
W/L: 0 = Word-Sized Operation
           1 = Long-Word-Sized Operation

**MC68020/MC68030 Address
Extension Word**

15	14	12	11	10	9	8	7	0
D/A	REGISTER		W/L	SCALE		0	DISPLACEMENT INTEGER	

D/A: 0 = Data Register Select
            1 = Address Register Select
W/L: 0 = Word-Sized Operation
            1 = Long-Word-Sized Operation
SCALE: 00 = Scale Factor 1 (Compatible with MC68000)
          01 = Scale Factor 2 (Extension to MC68000)
          10 = Scale Factor 4 (Extension to MC68000)
          11 = Scale Factor 8 (Extension to MC68000)

Figure 2-15. M68000 Family Address Extension Words

mode. The term supervisor stack pointer (SSP) refers to the master or interrupt stack pointers, depending on the state of the M bit. When M = 1, the term SSP (or A7) refers to the MSP address register. When M = 0, the term SSP (or A7) refers to the ISP address register. The active system stack pointer is implicitly referenced by all instructions that use the system stack. Each system stack fills from high to low memory.

A subroutine call saves the program counter on the active system stack, and the return restores it from the active system stack. During the processing of traps and interrupts, both the program counter and the status register are saved on the supervisor stack (either master or interrupt). Thus, the execution of supervisor code is independent of user code and the condition of the user stack; conversely, user programs use the user stack pointer independently of supervisor stack requirements.

To keep data on the system stack aligned for maximum efficiency, the active stack pointer is automatically decremented or incremented by two for all byte-sized operands moved to or from the stack. In long-word-organized memory, aligning the stack pointer on a long-word address significantly increases the efficiency of stacking exception frames, subroutine calls and returns, and other stacking operations.

2.8.2 User Program Stacks

The user can implement stacks with the address register indirect with post-increment and predecrement addressing modes. With address register An (n = 0–6), the user can implement a stack that is filled either from high to low memory or from low to high memory. Important considerations are:

- Use the predecrement mode to decrement the register before its contents are used as the pointer to the stack.

- Use the postincrement mode to increment the register after its contents are used as the pointer to the stack.

- Maintain the stack pointer correctly when byte, word, and long-word items are mixed in these stacks.

To implement stack growth from high to low memory, use:

−(An) to push data on the stack,

(An)+ to pull data from the stack.

For this type of stack, after either a push or a pull operation, register An points to the top item on the stack. This is illustrated as:

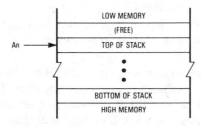

To implement stack growth from low to high memory, use:

(An)+ to push data on the stack,

−(An) to pull data from the stack.

In this case, after either a push or pull operation, register An points to the next available space on the stack. This is illustrated as:

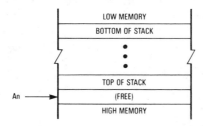

2.8.3 Queues

The user can implement queues with the address register indirect with post-increment or predecrement addressing modes. Using a pair of address registers (two of A0–A6), the user can implement a queue which is filled either from high to low memory or from low to high memory. Two registers are used because queues are pushed from one end and pulled from the other. One register, An, contains the "put" pointer; the other, Am, the "get" pointer.

To implement growth of the queue from low to high memory, use:

  (An)+ to put data into the queue,

  (Am)+ to get data from the queue.

After a "put" operation, the "put" address register points to the next available space in the queue, and the unchanged "get" address register points to the next item to be removed from the queue. After a "get" operation, the "get" address register points to the next item to be removed from the queue, and the unchanged "put" address register points to the next available space in the queue. This is illustrated as:

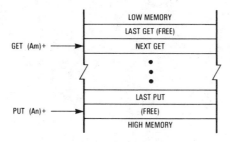

To implement the queue as a circular buffer, the relevant address register should be checked and adjusted, if necessary, before performing the "put" or "get" operation. The address register is adjusted by subtracting the buffer length (in bytes) from the register.

To implement growth of the queue from high to low memory, use:

- $-(An)$ to put data into the queue,

- $-(Am)$ to get data from the queue.

After a "put" operation, the "put" address register points to the last item placed in the queue, and the unchanged "get" address register points to the last item removed from the queue. After a "get" operation, the "get" address register points to the last item removed from the queue, and the unchanged "put" address register points to the last item placed in the queue. This is illustrated as:

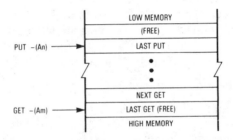

To implement the queue as a circular buffer, the "get" or "put" operation should be performed first, and then the relevant address register should be checked and adjusted, if necessary. The address register is adjusted by adding the buffer length (in bytes) to the register contents.

SECTION 3
INSTRUCTION SET SUMMARY

This section briefly describes the MC68030 instruction set. Refer to the MC68000PM/AD, *MC68000 Programmer's Reference Manual*, for complete details on the MC68030 instruction set.

The following paragraphs include descriptions of the instruction format and the operands used by instructions, followed by a summary of the instruction set. The integer condition codes and floating-point details are discussed. Programming examples for selected instructions are also presented.

3.1 INSTRUCTION FORMAT

All MC68030 instructions consist of at least one word; some have as many as 11 words (see Figure 3-1). The first word of the instruction, called the operation word, specifies the length of the instruction and the operation to be performed. The remaining words, called extension words, further specify the instruction and operands. These words may be floating-point command words, conditional predicates, immediate operands, extensions to the effective address mode specified in the operation word, branch displacements, bit number or bit field specifications, special register specifications, trap operands, pack/unpack constants, or argument counts.

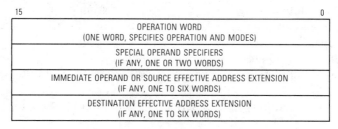

Figure 3-1. Instruction Word General Format

Besides the operation code, which specifies the function to be performed, an instruction defines the location of every operand for the function. Instructions specify an operand location in one of three ways:

1. Register Specification — A register field of the instruction contains the number of the register.

2. Effective Address — An effective address field of the instruction contains address mode information.

3. Implicit Reference — The definition of an instruction implies the use of specific registers.

The register field within an instruction specifies the register to be used. Other fields within the instruction specify whether the register selected is an address or data register and how the register is to be used. **SECTION 1 INTRODUCTION** contains register information.

Effective address information includes the registers, displacements, and absolute addresses for the effective address mode. **SECTION 2 DATA ORGANIZATION AND ADDRESSING CAPABILITIES** describes the effective address modes in detail.

Certain instructions operate on specific registers. These instructions imply the required registers.

3.2 INSTRUCTION SUMMARY

The instructions form a set of tools to perform the following operations:

Data Movement	Bit Field Manipulation
Integer Arithmetic	Binary-Coded Decimal Arithmetic
Logical	Program Control
Shift and Rotate	System Control
Bit Manipulation	Multiprocessor Communications

Each instruction type is described in detail in the following paragraphs.

The following notations are used in this section. In the operand syntax statements of the instruction definitions, the operand on the right is the destination operand.

An = any address register, A7–A0
Dn = any data register, D7–D0
Rn = any address or data register
CCR = condition code register (lower byte of status register)
cc = condition codes from CCR
SR = status register
SP = active stack pointer
USP = user stack pointer
ISP = supervisor/interrupt stack pointer
MSP = supervisor/master stack pointer
SSP = supervisor (master or interrupt) stack pointer
DFC = destination function code register
SFC = source function code register
Rc = control register (VBR, SFC, DFC, CACR)
MRc = MMU control register (SRP, URP, TC, DTT0, DTT1, ITT0, ITT1, MMUSR)
MMUSR = MMU status register
B, W, L = specifies a signed integer data type (twos complement) of byte, word, or long word
S = single-precision real data format (32 bits)
D = double-precision real data format (64 bits)
X = extended-precision real data format (96 bits, 16 bits unused)
P = packed BCD real data format (96 bits, 12 bytes)
FPm, FPn = any floating-point data register, FP7–FP0
PFcr = floating-point system control register (FPCR, FPSR, or FPIAR)
k = a twos-complement signed integer (-64 to $+17$) that specifies the format of a number to be stored in the packed BCD format
d = displacement; d_{16} is a 16-bit displacement
<ea> = effective address
list = list of registers, for example D3–D0
#<data> = immediate data; a literal integer
{offset:width} = bit field selection
label = assemble program label
[m] = bit m of an operand
[m:n] = bits m through n of operand

X = extend (X) bit in CCR
N = negative (N) bit in CCR
Z = Zero (Z) bit in CCR
V = overflow (V) bit in CCR
C = carry (C) bit in CCR
+ = arithmetic addition or postincrement indicator
− = arithmetic subtraction or predecrement indicator
× = arithmetic multiplication
÷ = arithmetic division or conjunction symbol
~ = invert; operand is logically complemented
Λ = logical AND
V = logical OR
⊕ = logical exclusive OR
Dc = data register, D7–D0 used during compare
Du = data register, D7–D0 used during update
Dr, Dq = data registers, remainder or quotient of divide
Dh, Dl = data registers, high- or low-order 32 bits of product
MSW = most significant word
LSW = least significant word
MSB = most significant bit
FC = function code
{R/W} = read or write indicator
[An] = address extensions

3.2.1 Data Movement Instructions

The MOVE instructions with their associated addressing modes are the basic means of transferring and storing addresses and data. MOVE instructions transfer byte, word, and long-word operands from memory to memory, memory to register, register to memory, and register to register. Address movement instructions (MOVE or MOVEA) transfer word and long-word operands and ensure that only valid address manipulations are executed. In addition to the general MOVE instructions, there are several special data movement instructions: move multiple registers (MOVEM), move peripheral data (MOVEP), move quick (MOVEQ), exchange registers (EXG), load effective address (LEA), push effective address (PEA), link stack (LINK), and unlink stack (UNLK).

Table 3-1 is a summary of the integer and floating-point data movement operations.

Table 3-1. Data Movement Operations

Instruction	Operand Syntax	Operand Size	Operation
EXG	Rn, Rn	32	Rn ⟷ Rn
LEA	<ea>,An	32	<ea> ◆ An
LINK	An,#<d>	16,32	Sp − 4 ◆ SP; An ◆ (SP); SP ◆ An, SP + D ◆ SP
MOVE MOVEA	<ea>,<ea> <ea>,An	8,16,32 16,32 ◆ 32	source ◆ destination
MOVEM	list,<ea> <ea>,list	16,32 16,32 ◆ 32	listed registers ◆ destination source ◆ listed registers
MOVEP	Dn, (d$_{16}$,An) (d$_{16}$,An),Dn	16,32	Dn[31:24] ◆ (An + d); Dn[23:16] ◆ An + d + 2); Dn[15:8] ◆ (An + d + 4); Dn[7:0] ◆ (An + d + 6) (An + d) ◆ Dn[31:24]; (An + d + 2) ◆ Dn[23:16]; (An + d + 4) ◆ Dn[15:8]; (An + d + 6) ◆ Dn[7:0]
MOVEQ	#<data>,Dn	8 ◆ 32	immediate data ◆ destination
PEA	<ea>	32	SP − 4 ◆ SP; <ea> ◆ (SP)
UNLK	An	32	An ◆ SP; (SP) ◆ An; SP + 4 ◆ SP

3.2.2 Integer Arithmetic Instructions

The integer arithmetic operations include the four basic operations of add (ADD), subtract (SUB), multiply (MUL), and divide (DIV) as well as arithmetic compare (CMP, CMPM, CMP2), clear (CLR), and negate (NEG). The instruction set includes ADD, CMP, and SUB instructions for both address and data operations with all operand sizes valid for data operations. Address operands consist of 16 or 32 bits. The clear and negate instructions apply to all sizes of data operands.

Signed and unsigned MUL and DIV instructions include:
- Word multiply to produce a long-word product
- Long-word multiply to produce and long-word or quad-word product
- Division of a long word divided by a word divisor (word quotient and word remainder)
- Division of a long word or quad word dividend by a long-word divisor (long-word quotient and long-word remainder)

A set of extended instructions provides multiprecision and mixed-size arithmetic. These instructions are add extended (ADDX), subtract extended (SUBX), sign extended (EXT), and negate binary with extend (NEGX). Refer to Table 3-2 for a summary of the integer arithmetic operations.

Table 3-2. Integer Arithmetic Operations

Instruction	Operand Syntax	Operand Size	Operation
ADD	Dn,⟨ea⟩	8, 16, 32	source + destination ⬧ destination
	⟨ea⟩,Dn	8, 16, 32	
ADDA	⟨ea⟩,An	16, 32	
ADDI	#⟨data⟩,⟨ea⟩	8, 16, 32	immediate data + destination ⬧ destination
ADDQ	#⟨data⟩,⟨ea⟩	8, 16, 32	
ADDX	Dn,Dn	8, 16, 32	source + destination + X ⬧ destination
	−(An),−(An)	8, 16, 32	
CLR	⟨ea⟩	8, 16, 32	0 ⬧ destination
CMP	⟨ea⟩,Dn	8, 16, 32	destination − source
CMPA	⟨ea⟩,An	16, 32	
CMPI	#⟨data⟩,⟨ea⟩	8, 16, 32	destination − immediate data
CMPM	(An)+,(An)+	8, 16, 32	destination − source
CMP2	⟨ea⟩,Rn	8, 16, 32	lower bound ⟨ = Rn ⟨ = upper bound
DIVS/DIVU	⟨ea⟩,Dn	32/16 ⬧ 16:16	destination/source ⬧ destination (signed or unsigned)
	⟨ea⟩,Dr:Dq	64/32 ⬧ 32:32	
	⟨ea⟩,Dq	32/32 ⬧ 32	
DIVSL/DIVUL	⟨ea⟩,Dr:Dq	32/32 ⬧ 32:32	
EXT	Dn	8 ⬧ 16	sign extended destination ⬧ destination
	Dn	16 ⬧ 32	
EXTB	Dn	8 ⬧ 32	
MULS/MULU	⟨ea⟩,Dn	16 × 16 ⬧ 32	source × destination ⬧ destination (signed or unsigned)
	⟨ea⟩,Dl	32 × 32 ⬧ 32	
	⟨ea⟩,Dh:Dl	32 × 32 ⬧ 64	
NEG	⟨ea⟩	8, 16, 32	0 − destination ⬧ destination
NEGX	⟨ea⟩	8, 16, 32	0 − destination − X ⬧ destination
SUB	⟨ea⟩,Dn	8, 16, 32	destination = source ⬧ destination
	Dn,⟨ea⟩	8, 16, 32	
SUBA	⟨ea⟩,An	16, 32	
SUBI	#⟨data⟩,⟨ea⟩	8, 16, 32	destination − immediate data ⬧ destination
SUBQ	#⟨data⟩,⟨ea⟩	8, 16, 32	
SUBX	Dn,Dn	8, 16, 32	destination − source − X ⬧ destination
	−(An),−(An)	8, 16, 32	

3.2.3 Logical Instructions

The logical operation instructions (AND, OR, EOR, and NOT) perform logical operations with all sizes of integer data operands. A similar set of immediate instructions (ANDI, ORI, and EORI) provide these logical operations with all sizes of immediate data. The TST instruction compares the operand with zero arithmetically, placing the result in the condition code register. Table 3-3 summarizes the logical operations.

MC68030 USER'S MANUAL

Table 3-3. Logical Operations

Instruction	Operand Syntax	Operand Size	Operation
AND	(ea),Dn Dn,(ea)	8, 16, 32 8, 16, 32	source $\land$ destination $\rightarrow$ destination
ANDI	#<data>,<ea>	8, 16,32	immediate data $\land$ destination $\rightarrow$ destination
EOR	Dn,<data>,<ea>	8, 16, 32	source $\oplus$ destination $\rightarrow$ destination
EORI	#(data),(ea)	8, 16, 32	immediate data $\oplus$ destination $\rightarrow$ destination
NOT	(ea)	8, 16, 32	$\sim$ destination $\rightarrow$ destination
OR	(ea),Dn Dn,(ea)	8, 16, 32 8, 16, 32	source $\lor$ destination $\rightarrow$ destination
ORI	#(data),(ea)	8, 16, 32	immediate data $\lor$ destination $\rightarrow$ destination
TST	(ea)	8, 16, 32	source — 0 to set condition codes

3.2.4 Shift and Rotate Instructions

The arithmetic shift instructions (ASR and ASL) and logical shift instructions (LSR and LSL) provide shift operations in both directions. The ROR, ROL, ROXR, and ROXL instructions perform rotate (circular shift) operations, with and without the extend bit. All shift and rotate operations can be performed on either registers or memory.

Register shift and rotate operations shift all operand sizes. The shift count may be specified in the instruction operation word (to shift from 1–8 places) or in a register (modulo 64 shift count).

Memory shift and rotate operations shift word-length operands one bit position only. The SWAP instruction exchanges the 16-bit halves of a register. Performance of shift/rotate instructions is enhanced so that use of the ROR and ROL instructions with a shift count of eight allows fast byte swapping. Table 3-4 is a summary of the shift and rotate operations.

Table 3-4. Shift and Rotate Operations

Instruction	Operand Syntax	Operand Size	Operation
ASL	Dn,Dn #⟨data⟩,Dn ⟨ea⟩	8, 16, 32 8, 16, 32 16	X/C ← ← ← 0
ASR	Dn,Dn #⟨data⟩,Dn ⟨ea⟩	8, 16, 32 8, 16, 32 16	→ → X/C
LSL	Dn,Dn #⟨data⟩,Dn ⟨ea⟩	8, 16, 32 8, 16, 32 16	X/C ← ← ← 0
LSR	Dn,Dn #⟨data⟩,Dn ⟨ea⟩	8, 16, 32 8, 16, 32 16	0 → → → X/C
ROL	Dn,Dn #⟨data⟩,Dn ⟨ea⟩	8, 16, 32 8, 16, 32 16	C ← ← ←
ROR	Dn,Dn #⟨data⟩,Dn ⟨ea⟩	8, 16, 32 8, 16, 32 16	→ → C
ROXL	Dn,Dn #⟨data⟩,Dn ⟨ea⟩	8, 16, 32 8, 16, 32 16	C ← ← ← X
ROXR	Dn,Dn #⟨data⟩,Dn ⟨ea⟩	8, 16, 32 8, 16, 32 16	X → → → C
SWAP	Dn	32	MSW | LSW

3.2.5 Bit Manipulation Instructions

Bit manipulation operations are accomplished using the following instructions: bit test (BTST), bit test and set (BSET), bit test and clear (BCLR), and bit test and change (BCHG). All bit manipulation operations can be performed on either registers or memory. The bit number is specified as immediate data or in a data register. Register operands are 32 bits long, and memory operands are 8 bits long. In Table 3-5, the summary of the bit manipulation operations, Z refers to bit 2, the zero bit of the status register.

MC68030 USER'S MANUAL MOTOROLA

Table 3-5. Bit Manipulation Operations

Instruction	Operand Syntax	Operand Size	Operation
BCHG	Dn,⟨ea⟩ #⟨data⟩,⟨ea⟩	8, 32 8, 32	~ (⟨bit number⟩ of destination) ♦ Z ♦ bit of destination
BCLR	Dn,⟨ea⟩ #⟨data⟩,⟨ea⟩	8, 32 8, 32	~ (⟨bit number⟩ of destination) ♦ Z; 0 ♦ bit of destination
BSET	Dn,⟨ea⟩ #⟨data⟩,⟨ea⟩	8, 32 8, 32	~ (⟨bit number⟩ of destination) ♦ Z; 1 ♦ bit of destination
BTST	Dn,⟨ea⟩ #⟨data⟩,⟨ea⟩	8, 32 8, 32	~ (⟨bit number⟩ of destination) ♦ Z

3

3.2.6 Bit Field Instructions

The MC68030 supports variable-length bit field operations on fields of up to 32 bits. The bit field insert (BFINS) instruction inserts a value into a bit field. Bit field extract unsigned (BFEXTU) and bit field extract signed (BFEXTS) extract a value from the field. Bit field find first one (BFFFO) finds the first bit that is set in a bit field. Also included are instructions that are analogous to the bit manipulation operations; bit field test (BFTST), bit field test and set (BFSET), bit field test and clear (BFCLR), and bit field test and change (BFCHG). Table 3-6 is a summary of the bit field operations.

Table 3-6. Bit Field Operations

Instruction	Operand Syntax	Operand Size	Operation
BFCHG	⟨ea⟩ {offset:width}	1–32	~ Field ♦ Field
BFCLR	⟨ea⟩ {offset:width}	1–32	0's ♦ Field
BFEXTS	⟨ea⟩ {offset:width},Dn	1–32	Field ♦ Dn; Sign Extended
BFEXTU	⟨ea⟩ {offset:width},Dn	1–32	Field ♦ Dn; Zero Extended
BFFFO	⟨ea⟩ {offset:width},Dn	1–32	Scan for first bit set in field; offset ♦ Dn
BFINS	Dn,⟨ea⟩ {offset:width}	1–32	Dn ♦ Field
BFSET	⟨ea⟩ {offset:width}	1–32	1's ♦ Field
BFTST	⟨ea⟩ {offset:width}	1–32	Field MSB ♦ N; ~ (OR of all bits in field) ♦ Z

NOTE: All bit field instructions set the N and Z bits as shown for BFTST before performing the specified operation.

3.2.7 Binary-Coded Decimal Instructions

Five instructions support operations on binary-coded decimal (BCD) numbers. The arithmetic operations on packed BCD numbers are add decimal with extend (ABCD), subtract decimal with extend (SBCD), and negate decimal with extend (NBCD). PACK and UNPACK instructions aid in the conversion of byte encoded numeric data, such as ASCII or EBCDIC strings, to BCD data and vice versa. Table 3-7 is a summary of the BCD operations.

Table 3-7. BCD Operations

Instruction	Operand Syntax	Operand Size	Operation
ABCD	Dn,Dn − (An), − (An)	8 8	source$_{10}$ + destination$_{10}$ + X $\blacklozenge$ destination
NBCD	⟨ea⟩	8	0 − destination$_{10}$ − X $\blacklozenge$ destination
PACK	− (An), − (An) #⟨data⟩ Dn,Dn,#⟨data⟩	16 $\blacklozenge$ 8 16 $\blacklozenge$ 8	unpackaged source + immediate data $\blacklozenge$ packed destination
SBCD	Dn,Dn − (An), − (An)	8 8	destination$_{10}$ − source$_{10}$ − X $\blacklozenge$ destination
UNPK	− (An), − (An) #⟨data⟩ Dn,Dn,#⟨data⟩	8 $\blacklozenge$ 16 8 $\blacklozenge$ 16	packed source $\blacklozenge$ unpacked source unpacked source + immediate data $\blacklozenge$ unpacked destination

3.2.8 Program Control Instructions

A set of subroutine call and return instructions and conditional and unconditional branch instructions perform program control operations. The no operation instruction (NOP) may be used to force synchronization of the internal pipelines. Table 3-8 summarizes these instructions.

Table 3-8. Program Control Operations

Instruction	Operand Syntax	Operand Size	Operation
Integer and Floating-Point Conditional			
Bcc	\<label\>	8,16,32	if condition true, then PC + d → PC
DBcc	Dn,\<label\>	16	if condition false, then Dn − 1 → Dn if Dn ≠ − 1, then PC + d → PC
Scc	\<ea\>	8	if condition true, then 1's → destination; else 0's → destination
Unconditional			
BRA	\<label\>	8,16,32	PC + d → PC
BSR	\<label\>	8,16,32	SP − 4 → SP; PC → (SP); PC + d → PC
JMP	\<ea\>	none	destination → PC
JSR	\<ea\>	none	SP − 4 → SP; PC → (SP); destination → PC
NOP	none	none	PC + 2 → PC
Returns			
RTD	#\<d\>	16	(SP) → PC; SP + 4 + d → SP
RTR	none	none	(SP) → CCR; SP + 2 → SP; (SP) → PC; SP + 4 → SP
RTS	none	none	(SP) → PC; SP + 4 → SP

Letters cc in the integer instruction mnemonics Bcc, DBcc, and Scc specify testing one of the following conditions:

CC — Carry clear
LS — Lower or same
CS — Carry set
LT — Less than
EQ — Equal
MI — Minus
F — Never true*
NE — Not equal

GE — Greater or equal
PL — Plus
GT — Greater than
T — Always true*
HI — Higher
VC — Overflow clear
LE — Less or equal
VS — Overflow set

*Not applicable to the Bcc or cpBcc instructions.

3.2.9 System Control Instructions

Privileged instructions, trapping instructions, and instructions that use or modify the condition code register (CCR) provide system control operations. Table 3-9 summarizes these instructions. The TRAPcc instruction uses the same conditional tests as the corresponding program control instructions. All of these instructions cause the processor to flush the instruction pipe.

Table 3-9. System Control Operations

Instruction	Operand Syntax	Operand Size	Operation
Privileged			
ANDI	#<data>,SR	16	immediate data Λ SR → SR
EORI	#<data>,SR	16	immediate data $\oplus$ SR → SR
MOVE	<ea>,SR SR,<ea>	16 16	source → SR SR → destination
MOVE	USP,An An,USP	32 32	USP → An An → USP
MOVEC	Rc,Rn Rn,Rc	32 32	Rc → Rn Rn → Rc
MOVES	Rn,<ea> <ea>,Rn	8,16,32	Rn → destination using DFC source using SFC → Rn
ORI	#<data>,SR	16	immediate data V SR → SR
RESET	none	none	assert $\overline{\text{RESET}}$ line
RTE	none	none	(SP) → SR; SP+2 → SP; (SP) → PC; SP+4 → SP; Restore stack according to format
STOP	#<data>	16	immediate data → SR; STOP
Trap Generating			
BKPT	#<data>	none	run breakpoint cycle, then trap as illegal instruction
CHK	<ea>,Dn	16,32	if Dn<0 or Dn>(ea), then CHK exception
CHK2	<ea>,Rn	8,16,32	if Rn<lower bound or Rn>upper bound, the CHK exception
ILLEGAL	none	none	SSP −2 → SSP; Vector Offset → (SSP); SSP −4 → SSP; PC → (SSP); SSP −2 → SSP; SR → (SSP); Illegal Instruction Vector Address → PC
TRAP	#<data>	none	SSP −2 → SSP; Format and Vector Offset → (SSP) SSP −4 → SSP; PC → (SSP); SSP −2 → SSP; SR → (SSP); Vector Address → PC
TRAPcc	none #<data>	none 16,32	if cc true, then TRAP exception
TRAPV	none	none	if V then take overflow TRAP exception
Condition Code Register			
ANDI	#<data>,CCR	8	immediate data Λ CCR → CCR
EORI	#<data>,CCR	8	immediate data $\oplus$ CCR → CCR
MOVE	<ea>,CCR CCR,<ea>	16 16	source → CCR CCR → destination
ORI	#<data>,CCR	8	immediate data V CCR → CCR

3.2.10 Memory Management Unit Instructions

The PFLUSH instructions flush the address translation caches (ATCs) and can optionally select only nonglobal entries for flushing. PTEST performs a search of the address translation tables, storing results in the MMU status register and loading the entry into the ATC. Table 3-10 summarizes these instructions.

Table 3-10. MMU Instructions

Instruction	Operand Syntax	Operand Size	Operation
PFLUSHA	none	none	Invalidate all ATC entries
PFLUSHA.N	none	none	Invalidate all nonglobal ATC entries
PFLUSH	(An)	none	Invalidate ATC entries at effective address
PFLUSH.N	(An)	none	Invalidate nonglobal ATC entries at effective address
PTEST	(An)	none	Information about logical address ♦ MMU status register

3.2.11 Multiprocessor Instructions

The TAS, CAS, and CAS2 instructions coordinate the operations of processors in multiprocessing systems. These instructions use read-modify-write bus cycles to ensure uninterrupted updating of memory. Coprocessor instructions control the coprocessor operations. Table 3-11 lists these instructions.

Table 3-11. Multiprocessor Operations (Read-Modify-Write)

Instruction	Operand Syntax	Operand Size	Operation
		Read-Modify-Write	
CAS	Dc,Du,<ea>	8,16,32	destination — Dc ♦ CC; if Z then Du ♦ destination else destination ♦ Dc
CAS2	Dc1:Dc2, Du1:Du2, (Rn):(Rn)	8,16,32	dual operand CAS
TAS	<ea>	8	destination — 0; set condition codes; 1 ♦ destination [7]
		Coprocessor	
cpBcc	⟨label⟩	16, 32	if cpcc true then pc + d ♦ PC
cpDBcc	⟨label⟩,Dn	16	if cpcc false then Dn − 1 ♦ Dn if Dn ≠ − 1, then PC + d ♦ PC
cpGEN	User Defined	User Defined	operand ♦ coprocessor
cp RESTORE	⟨ea⟩	none	restore coprocessor state from ⟨ea⟩
cpSAVE	⟨ea⟩	none	save coprocessor state at ⟨ea⟩
cpScc	⟨ea⟩	8	if cpcc true, then 1's ♦ destination; else 0's ♦ destination
cpTRAPcc	none #⟨data⟩	none 16, 32	if cpcc true then TRAPcc exception

3.3 INTEGER CONDITION CODES

The CCR portion of the SR contains five bits which indicate the results of many integer instructions. Program and system control instructions use certain combinations of these bits to control program and system flow.

The first four bits represent a condition resulting from a processor operation. The X bit is an operand for multiprecision computations; when it is used, it is set to the value of the C bit. The carry bit and the multiprecision extend bit are separate in the M68000 Family to simplify programming techniques that use them (refer to Table 3-8 as an example).

The condition codes were developed to meet two criteria:
- Consistency — across instructions, uses, and instances
- Meaningful Results — no change unless it provides useful information

Consistency across instructions means that all instructions that are special cases of more general instructions affect the condition codes in the same way. Consistency across instances means that all instances of an instruction affect the condition codes in the same way. Consistency across uses means that conditional instructions test the condition codes similarly and provide the same results, regardless of whether the condition codes are set by a compare, test, or move instruction.

In the instruction set definitions, the CCR is shown as follows:

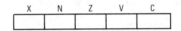

where:
X (extend)
Set to the value of the C bit for arithmetic operations. Otherwise not affected or set to a specified result.

N (negative)
Set if the most significant bit of the result is set. Cleared otherwise.

Z (zero)
Set if the result equals zero. Cleared otherwise.

V (overflow)
Set if arithmetic overflow occurs. This implies that the result cannot be represented in the operand size. Cleared otherwise.

C (carry)
Set if a carry out of the most significant bit of the operand occurs for an addition. Also set if a borrow occurs in a subtraction. Cleared otherwise.

MC68030 USER'S MANUAL   MOTOROLA

3

3.3.1 Condition Code Computation

Most operations take a source operand and a destination operand, compute, and store the result in the destination location. Single-operand operations take a destination operand, compute, and store the result in the destination location. Table 3-12 lists each instruction and how it affects the condition code bits.

Table 3-12. Condition Code Computations (Sheet 1 of 2)

Operations	X	N	Z	V	C	Special Definition
ABCD	*	U	?	U	?	C = Decimal Carry $Z = Z \wedge \overline{Rm} \wedge \ldots \wedge \overline{R0}$
ADD, ADDI, ADDQ	*	*	*	?	?	$V = Sm \wedge Dm \wedge \overline{Rm} \vee \overline{Sm} \wedge \overline{Dm} \wedge Rm$ $C = Sm \wedge Dm \vee \overline{Rm} \wedge Dm \vee Sm \wedge \overline{Rm}$
ADDX	*	*	?	?	?	$V = Sm \wedge Dm \wedge \overline{Rm} \vee \overline{Sm} \wedge \overline{Dm} \wedge Rm$ $C = Sm \wedge Dm \vee \overline{Rm} \wedge Dm \vee Sm \wedge \overline{Rm}$ $Z = Z \wedge \overline{Rm} \wedge \ldots \wedge \overline{R0}$
AND, ANDI, EOR, EORI, MOVEQ, MOVE, OR, ORI, CLR, EXT, NOT, TAS, TST	—	*	*	0	0	
CHK	—	*	U	U	U	
CHK2, CMP2	—	U	?	U	?	$Z = (R = LB) \vee (R = UB)$ $C = (LB <\, = UB) \wedge (IR < LB) \vee (R > UB))$ $\vee (UB < LB) \wedge (R > UB) \wedge (R < LB)$
SUB, SUBI, SUBQ	*	*	*	?	?	$V = \overline{Sm} \wedge Dm \wedge \overline{Rm} \vee Sm \wedge \overline{Dm} \wedge Rm$ $C = Sm \wedge \overline{Dm} \vee Rm \wedge \overline{Dm} \vee Sm \wedge Rm$
SUBX	*	*	?	?	?	$V = \overline{Sm} \wedge Dm \wedge \overline{Rm} \vee Sm \wedge \overline{Dm} \wedge Rm$ $C = Sm \wedge \overline{Dm} \vee Rm \wedge \overline{Dm} \vee Sm \wedge Rm$ $Z = Z \wedge \overline{Rm} \wedge \ldots \wedge \overline{R0}$
CAS, CAS2, CMP, CMPI, CMPM	—	*	*	?	?	$V = \overline{Sm} \wedge Dm \wedge \overline{Rm} \vee Sm \wedge \overline{Dm} \wedge Rm$ $C = Sm \wedge \overline{Dm} \vee Rm \wedge \overline{Dm} \vee Sm \wedge Rm$
DIVS, DUVI	—	*	*	?	0	V = Division Overflow
MULS, MULU	—	*	*	?	0	V = Multiplication Overflow
SBCD, NBCD	*	U	?	U	?	C = Decimal Borrow $Z = Z \wedge \overline{Rm} \wedge \ldots \wedge \overline{R0}$
NEG	*	*	*	?	?	$V = Dm \wedge Rm$ $C = Dm \vee Rm$
NEGX	*	*	?	?	?	$V = Dm \wedge Rm$ $C = Dm \vee Rm$ $Z = Z \wedge \overline{Rm} \wedge \ldots \wedge \overline{R0}$

Table 3-12. Condition Code Computations (Sheet 2 of 2)

Operations	X	N	Z	V	C	Special Definition
BTST, BCHG, BSET, BCLR	—	—	?	—	—	$Z = \overline{Dn}$
BFTST, BFCHG, BFSET, BFCLR	—	?	?	0	0	$N = Dm$ $Z = \overline{Dm} \setminus \overline{DM-1} \setminus \ldots \setminus \overline{D0}$
BFEXTS, BFEXTU, BFFFO	—	?	?	0	0	$N = Sm$ $Z = \overline{Sm} \setminus \overline{Sm-1} \setminus \ldots \setminus \overline{S0}$
BFINS	—	?	?	0	0	$N = Dm$ $Z = \overline{Dm} \setminus \overline{DM-1} \setminus \ldots \setminus \overline{D0}$
ASL	*	*	*	?	?	$V = Dm \setminus (\overline{Dm-1} V \ldots V \overline{Dm-r}) V \overline{Dm} \setminus (DM-1 V \ldots + Dm-r)$ $C = \overline{Dm-r+1}$
ASL (R = 0)	—	*	*	0	0	
LSL, ROXL	*	*	*	0	?	$C = Dm - r + 1$
LSR (r = 0)	—	*	*	0	0	
ROXL (r = 0)	—	*	*	0	?	$C = X$
ROL	—	*	*	0	?	$C = Dm - r + 1$
ROL (r = 0)	—	*	*	0	0	
ASR, LSR, ROXR	*	*	*	0	?	$C = Dr - 1$
ASR, LSR (r = 0)	—	*	*	0	0	
ROXR (r = 0)	—	*	*	0	?	$C = X$
ROR	—	*	*	0	?	$C = Dr - 1$
ROR (r = 0)	—	*	*	0	0	

— = Not Affected
U = Undefined, Result Meaningless
? = Other — See Special Definition
* = General Case
    X = C
    N = $\overline{Rm}$
    Z = $\overline{Rm} \setminus \ldots \setminus \overline{R0}$
Sm = Source Operand — Most Significant Bit
Dm = Destination Operand — Most Significant Bit

Rm = Result Operand — Most Significant Bit
R = Register Tested
n = Bit Number
r = Shift Count
LB = Lower Bound
UB = Upper Bound
$\setminus$ = Boolean AND
V = Boolean OR
$\overline{Rm}$ = NOT Rm

3.3.2 Conditional Tests

Table 3-13 lists the condition names, encodings, and tests for the conditional branch and set instructions. The test associated with each condition is a logical formula using the current states of the condition codes. If this formula evaluates to one, the condition is true. If the formula evaluates to zero, the condition is false. For example, the T condition is always true, and the EQ condition is true only if the Z bit condition code is currently true.

Table 3-13. Conditional Tests

Mnemonic	Condition	Encoding	Test
T*	True	0000	1
F*	False	0001	0
HI	High	0010	$\overline{C} \cdot \overline{Z}$
LS	Low or Same	0011	$C + Z$
CC(HS)	Carry Clear	0100	$\overline{C}$
CS(LO)	Carry Set	0101	C
NE	Not Equal	0110	$\overline{Z}$
EQ	Equal	0111	Z
VC	Overflow Clear	1000	$\overline{V}$
VS	Overflow Set	1001	V
PL	Plus	1010	$\overline{N}$
MI	Minus	1011	N
GE	Greater or Equal	1100	$N \cdot V + \overline{N} \cdot \overline{V}$
LT	Less Than	1101	$N \cdot \overline{V} + \overline{N} \cdot V$
GT	Greater Than	1110	$N \cdot V \cdot \overline{Z} + \overline{N} \cdot \overline{V} \cdot \overline{Z}$
LE	Less or Equal	1111	$Z + N \cdot \overline{V} + \overline{N} \cdot V$

$\cdot$ = Boolean AND
$+$ = Boolean OR
$\overline{N}$ = Boolean NOT N

*Not available for the Bcc instruction.

3.4 INSTRUCTION SET SUMMARY

Table 3-14 provides a alphabetized listing of the MC68030 instruction set listed by opcode, operation, and syntax.

Table 3-14 use notational conventions for the operands, the subfields and qualifiers, and the operations performed by the instructions. In the syntax descriptions, the left operand is the source operand, and the right operand is the destination operand. The following list contains the notations used in Table 3-14.

Notation for operands:

PC—Program counter
SR—Status register
V—Overflow condition code
Immediate Data—Immediate data from the instruction
Source—Source contents
Destination—Destination contents
Vector—Location of exception vector
+inf—Positive infinity
–inf—Negative infinity
<fmt>—Operand data format: byte (B), word (W), long (L), single (S), double (D), extended (X), or packed (P).
FPm—One of eight floating-point data registers (always specifies the source register)
FPn—One of eight floating-point data registers (always specifies the detination register)

Notation for subfields and qualifiers:

<bit> of <operand>—Selects a single bit of the operand
<ea>{offset:width}—Selects a bit field
(<operand>)—The contents of the referenced location
<operand>10—The operand is binary coded decimal, operations are performed in decimal
(<address register>)—The register indirect operator
–(<address register>)—Indicates that the operand register points to the memory
(<address register>)+—Location of the instruction operand — the optional mode qualifiers are –, +, (d), and (d,ix)
#xxx or #<data>—Immediate data that follows the instruction word(s)

Notations for operations that have two operands, written <operand> <op> <operand>, where <op> is one of the following:

     ➤—The source operand is moved to the destination operand

     ⧏—The two operands are exchanged

     +—The operands are added

     −—The destination operand is subtracted from the source operand

     ×—The operands are multiplied

     ÷—The source operand is divided by the destination operand

     <—Relational test, true if source operand is less than destination operand

     >—Relational test, true if source operand is greater than destination operand

     V—Logical OR

     ⊕—Logical exclusive OR

     Λ—Logical AND

shifted by, rotated by—The source operand is shifted or rotated by the number of positions specified by the second operand

Notation for single-operand operations:

     ~<operand>—The operand is logically complemented

<operand>sign-extended—The operand is sign extended; all bits of the upper portion are made equal to the high-order bit of the lower portion

<operand>tested—The operand is compared to zero, and the condition codes are set appropriately

Notation for other operations:

     TRAP—Equivalent to Format/Offset Word ➤ (SSP); SSP − 2 ➤ SSP; PC ➤ (SSP); SSP − 4 ➤ SSP; SR ➤ (SSP); SSP − 2 ➤ SSP; (vector) ➤ PC

     STOP—Enter the stopped state, waiting for interrupts

If <condition> then—The condition is tested. If true, the operations <operations> else after "then" are performed. If the condition is <operations> false and the optional "else" clause is present, the operations after "else" are performed. If the condition is false and else is omitted, the instruction performs no operation. Refer to the Bcc instruction description as an example.

Table 3-14. Instruction Set Summary (Sheet 1 of 5)

Opcode	Operation	Syntax
ABCD	Source$_{10}$ + Destination$_{10}$ + X ♦ Destination	ABCD Dy,Dx ABCD −(Ay), −(Ax)
ADD	Source + Destination ♦ Destination	ADD ⟨ea⟩,Dn ADD Dn,⟨ea⟩
ADDA	Source + Destination ♦ Destination	ADDA ⟨ea⟩,An
ADDI	Immediate Data + Destination ♦ Destination	ADDI #⟨data⟩,⟨ea⟩
ADDQ	Immediate Data + Destination ♦ Destination	ADDQ #⟨data⟩,⟨ea⟩
ADDX	Source + Destination + X ♦ Destination	ADDX Dy,Dx ADDX −(Ay), −(Ax)
AND	Source \ Destination ♦ Destination	AND ⟨ea⟩,Dn AND Dn,⟨ea⟩
ANDI	Immediate Data \ Destination ♦ Destination	ANDI #⟨data⟩,⟨ea⟩
ANDI to CCR	Source \ CCR ♦CCR	ANDI #⟨data⟩,CCR
ANDI to SR	If supervisor state the Source \ SR ♦ SR else TRAP	ANDI #⟨data⟩,SR
ASL,ASR	Destination Shifted by ⟨count⟩ ♦ Destination	ASd Dx,Dy ASd #⟨data⟩,Dy ASd ⟨ea⟩
Bcc	If (condition true) then PC + d ♦ PC	Bcc ⟨label⟩
BCHG	~(⟨number⟩ of Destination) ♦ Z; ~(⟨number⟩ of Destination) ♦ ⟨bit number⟩ of Destination	BCHG Dn,⟨ea⟩ BCHG #⟨data⟩,⟨ea⟩
BCLR	~(⟨bit number⟩ of Destination) ♦ Z; 0 ♦ ⟨bit number⟩ of Destination	BCLR Dn,⟨ea⟩ BCLR #⟨data⟩,⟨ea⟩
BFCHG	~(⟨bit field⟩ of Destination) ♦ ⟨bit field⟩ of Destination	BFCHG ⟨ea⟩{offset:width}
BFCLR	0 ♦ ⟨bit field⟩ of Destination	BFCLR ⟨ea⟩{offset:width}
BFEXTS	⟨bit field⟩ of Source ♦ Dn	BFEXTS ⟨ea⟩{offset:width},Dn
BFEXTU	⟨bit offset⟩ of Source ♦ Dn	BFEXTU ⟨ea⟩{offset:width},Dn
BFFFO	⟨bit offset⟩ of Source Bit Scan ♦ Dn	BFFFO ⟨ea⟩{offset:width},Dn
BFINS	Dn ♦ ⟨bit field⟩ of Destination	BFINS Dn,⟨ea⟩{offset:width}
BFSET	1s ♦ ⟨bit field⟩ of Destination	BFSET ⟨ea⟩{offset:width}
BFTST	⟨bit field⟩ of Destination	BFTST ⟨ea⟩{offset:width}
BKPT	Run breakpoint acknowledge cycle; TRAP as illegal instruction	BKPT #⟨data⟩
BRA	PC + d ♦ PC	BRA ⟨label⟩
BSET	~(⟨bit number⟩ of Destination) ♦ Z; 1 ♦ ⟨bit number⟩ of Destination	BSET Dn,⟨ea⟩ BSET #⟨data⟩,⟨ea⟩
BSR	SP − 4 ♦ SP; PC ♦ (SP); PC + d ♦ PC	BSR ⟨label⟩
BTST	−(⟨bit number⟩ of Destination) ♦ Z;	BTST Dn,⟨ea⟩ BTST #⟨data⟩,⟨ea⟩

Table 3-14. Instruction Set Summary (Sheet 2 of 5)

Opcode	Operation	Syntax
CAS CAS2	CAS Destination — Compare Operand ♦ cc; if Z, Update Operand ♦ Destination else Destination ♦ Compare Operand CAS2 Destination 1 — Compare 1 ♦ cc; if Z, Destination 2 — Compare 2 ♦ cc; if Z, Update 1 ♦ Destination 1; Update 2 ♦ Destination 2 else Destination 1 ♦ Compare 1; Destination 2 ♦ Compare 2	CAS Dc,Du,⟨ea⟩ CAS2 Dc1:Dc2,Du1:Du2,(Rn1):(Rn2)
CHK	If Dn < 0 or Dn > Source then TRAP	CHK ⟨ea⟩,Dn
CHK2	If Rn < lower bound or Rn > upper bound then TRAP	CHK2 ⟨ea⟩,Rn
CLR	0 ♦ Destination	CLR ⟨ea⟩
CMP	Destination — Source ♦ cc	CMP ⟨ea⟩,Dn
CMPA	Destination — Source	CMPA ⟨ea⟩,An
CMPI	Destination — Immediate Data	CMPI #⟨data⟩,⟨ea⟩
CMPM	Destination — Source ♦ cc	CMPM (Ay)+,(Ax)+
CMP2	Compare Rn < lower-bound or Rn > upper-bound and Set Condition Codes	CMP2 ⟨ea⟩,Rn
cpBcc	If cpcc true then scanPC+d ♦ PC	cpBcc ⟨label⟩
cpDBcc	If cpcc false then (Dn − 1 ♦ Dn; If Dn ≠ − 1 then scanPC+d ♦ PC)	cpDBcc Dn,⟨label⟩
cpGEN	Pass Command Word to Coprocessor	cpGEN ⟨parameters as defined by co-processor⟩
cpRESTORE	If supervisor state then Restore Internal State of Coprocessor else TRAP	cpRESTORE ⟨ea⟩
cpSAVE	If supervisor state then Save Internal State of Coprocessor else TRAP	cpSAVE ⟨ea⟩
cpScc	If cpcc true then 1s ♦ Destination else 0s ♦ Destination	cpScc ⟨ea⟩
cpTRAPcc	If cpcc true then TRAP	cpTRAPcc cpTRAPcc #⟨data⟩
DBcc	If condition false then (Dn−1 ♦ Dn; If Dn ≠ −1 then PC+d ♦ PC)	DBcc Dn,⟨label⟩
DIVS DIVSL	Destination/Source ♦ Destination	DIVS.W ⟨ea⟩,Dn 32/16 ♦ 16r:16q DIVS.L ⟨ea⟩,Dq 32/32 ♦ 32q DIVS.L ⟨ea⟩,Dr:Dq 64/32 ♦ 32r:32q DIVSL.L ⟨ea⟩,Dr:Dq 32/32 ♦ 32r:32q
DIVU DIVUL	Destination/Source ♦ Destination	DIVU.W ⟨ea⟩,Dn 32/16 ♦ 16r:16q DIVU.L ⟨ea⟩,Dq 32/32 ♦ 32q DIVU.L ⟨ea⟩,Dr:Dq 64/32 ♦ 32r:32q DIVUL.L ⟨ea⟩,Dr:Dq 32/32 ♦ 32r:32q
EOR	Source ⊕ Destination ♦ Destination	EOR Dn,⟨ea⟩
EORI	Immediate Data ⊕ Destination ♦ Destination	EORI #⟨data⟩,⟨ea⟩

3

Table 3-14. Instruction Set Summary (Sheet 3 of 5)

Opcode	Operation	Syntax
EORI to CCR	Source $\oplus$ CCR $\blacklozenge$ CCR	EORI #⟨data⟩,CCR
EORI to SR	If supervisor state the Source $\oplus$ SR $\blacklozenge$ SR else TRAP	EORI #⟨data⟩,SR
EXG	Rx $\blacklozenge\blacklozenge$ Ry	EXG Dx,Dy EXG Ax,Ay EXG Dx,Ay EXG Ay,Dx
EXT EXTB	Destination Sign-Extended $\blacklozenge$ Destination	EXT.W Dn extend byte to word EXT.L L Dn extend word to long word EXTB.L Dn extend byte to long word
ILLEGAL	SSP − 2 $\blacklozenge$ SSP; Vector Offset $\blacklozenge$ (SSP); SSP − 4 $\blacklozenge$ SSP; PC $\blacklozenge$ (SSP); SSp − 2 $\blacklozenge$ SSP; SR $\blacklozenge$ (SSP); Illegal Instruction Vector Address $\blacklozenge$ PC	ILLEGAL
JMP	Destination Address $\blacklozenge$ PC	JMP ⟨ea⟩
JSR	SP − 4 $\blacklozenge$ SP; PC $\blacklozenge$ (SP) Destination Address $\blacklozenge$ PC	JSR ⟨ea⟩
LEA	⟨ea⟩ $\blacklozenge$ An	LEA ⟨ea⟩,An
LINK	SP − 4 $\blacklozenge$ SP; An $\blacklozenge$ (SP) SP $\blacklozenge$ An, SP + d $\blacklozenge$ SP	LINK An,#⟨displacement⟩
LSL,LSR	Destination Shifted by ⟨count⟩ $\blacklozenge$ Destination	LSd^5 Dx,Dy LSd^5 #⟨data⟩,Dy LSd^5 ⟨ea⟩
MOVE	Source $\blacklozenge$ Destination	MOVE ⟨ea⟩,⟨ea⟩
MOVEA	Source $\blacklozenge$ Destination	MOVEA ⟨ea⟩,An
MOVE from CCR	CCR $\blacklozenge$ Destination	MOVE CCR,⟨ea⟩
MOVE to CCR	Source $\blacklozenge$ CCR	MOVE ⟨ea⟩,CCR
MOVE from SR	If supervisor state then SR $\blacklozenge$ Destination else TRAP	MOVE SR,⟨ea⟩
MOVE to SR	If supervisor state then Source $\blacklozenge$ SR else TRAP	MOVE ⟨ea⟩,SR
MOVE USP	If supervisor state then USP $\blacklozenge$ An or An $\blacklozenge$ USP else TRAP	MOVE USP,An MOVE An,USP
MOVEC	If supervisor state then Rc $\blacklozenge$ Rn or Rn $\blacklozenge$ Rc else TRAP	MOVEC Rc,Rn MOVEC Rn,Rc
MOVEM	Registers $\blacklozenge$ Destination Source $\blacklozenge$ Registers	MOVEM register list,(ea) MOVEM ⟨ea⟩,register list
MOVEP	Source $\blacklozenge$ Destination	MOVEP Dx,(d,Ay) MOVEP (d,Ay),Dx
MOVEQ	Immediate Data $\blacklozenge$ Destination	MOVEQ #⟨data⟩,Dn

Table 3-14. Instruction Set Summary (Sheet 4 of 5)

Opcode	Operation	Syntax
MOVES	If supervisor state then Rn ♦ Destination [DFC] or Source [SFC] ♦ Rn else TRAP	MOVES Rn,⟨ea⟩ MOVES ⟨ea⟩,Rn
MULS	Source × Destination ♦ Destination	MULS.W ⟨ea⟩,Dn 16 × 16 ♦ 32 MULS.L ⟨ea⟩,Dl 32 × 32 ♦ 32 MULS.L ⟨ea⟩,Dh:Dl 32 × 32 ♦ 64
MULU	Source × Destination ♦ Destination	MULU.W ⟨ea⟩,Dn 16 × 16 ♦ 32 MULU.L ⟨ea⟩,Dl 32 × 32 ♦ 32 MULU.L ⟨ea⟩,Dh:Dl 32 × 32 ♦ 64
NBCD	$0 - (\text{Destination}_{10}) - X$ ♦ Destination	NBCD ⟨ea⟩
NEG	0 − (Destination) ♦ Destination	NEG ⟨ea⟩
NEGX	0 − (Destination) − X ♦ Destination	NEGX ⟨ea⟩
NOP	None	NOP
NOT	~Destination ♦ Destination	NOT ⟨ea⟩
OR	Source V Destination ♦ Destination	OR ⟨ea⟩,Dn OR Dn,⟨ea⟩
ORI	Immediate Data V Destination ♦ Destination	ORI #⟨data⟩,⟨ea⟩
ORI to CCR	Source V CCR ♦ CCR	ORI #⟨data⟩,CCR
ORI to SR	If supervisor state then Source V SR ♦ SR else TRAP	ORI #⟨data⟩,SR
PACK	Source (Unpacked BCD) + adjustment ♦ Destintion (Packed BCD)	PACK − (Ax), − (Ay),#⟨adjustment⟩ PACK Dx,Dy,#⟨adjustment⟩
PEA	Sp − 4 ♦ SP; ⟨ea⟩ ♦ (SP)	PEA ⟨ea⟩
PFLUSH	If supervisor state then invalidate instruction and data ATC entries for destination address else TRAP	PFLUSH (An) PFLUSHN (An) PFLUSHA PFLUSHAN
PLOAD	If supervisor state then entry ♦ ATC else TRAP	PLOADR ⟨function code⟩,⟨ea⟩ PLOADW ⟨function code⟩,⟨ea⟩
PMOVE	If supervisor state then (Source) ♦ MRn or MRn ♦ (Destination)	PMOVE MRn,⟨ea⟩ PMOVE ⟨ea⟩,MRn PMOVEFD ⟨ea⟩,MRn
PTEST	If supervisor state then logical address status ♦ MMUSR; entry ♦ ATC else TRAP	PTESTR (An) PTESTW (An)
RESET	If supervisor state then Assert RSTO Line else TRAP	RESET
ROL,ROR	Destination Rotated by ⟨count⟩ ♦ Destination	ROd[5] Rx,Dy ROd[5] #⟨data⟩,Dy ROd[5] ⟨ea⟩
ROXL,ROXR	Destination Rotated with X by ⟨count⟩ ♦ Destination	ROXd[5] Dx,Dy ROXd[5] #⟨data⟩,Dy ROXd[5] ⟨ea⟩

3

Table 3-14. Instruction Set Summary (Sheet 5 of 5)

Opcode	Operation	Syntax
RTD	(SP) → PC; SP + 4 + d → SP	RTD #⟨displacement⟩

RTE	If supervisor state
	  the (SP) → SR; SP + 2 → SP; (SP) → PC;
	  SP + 4 → SP;
	  restore state and deallocate stack according to (SP)
	else TRAP
		RTE

RTR	(SP) → CCR; SP + 2 → SP; (SP) → PC; SP + 4 → SP	RTR
RTS	(SP) → PC; SP + 4 → SP	RTS
SBCD	$\text{Destination}_{10} - \text{Source}_{10} - X \rightarrow \text{Destination}$	SBCD Dx,Dy SBCD − (Ax), − (Ay)
Scc	If Condition True then 1s → Destination else 0s → Destination	Scc ⟨ea⟩
STOP	If supervisor state then Immediate Data → SR; STOP else TRAP	STOP #⟨data⟩
SUB	Destination − Source → Destination	SUB ⟨ea⟩,Dn SUB Dn,⟨ea⟩
SUBA	Destination − Source → Destination	SUBA ⟨ea⟩,An
SUBI	Destination − Immediate Data → Destination	SUBI #⟨data⟩,⟨ea⟩
SUBQ	Destination − Immediate Data → Destination	SUBQ #⟨data⟩,⟨ea⟩
SUBX	Destination − Source − X → Destination	SUBX Dx,Dy SUBX − (Ax), − (Ay)
SWAP	Register [31:16] ↔ Register [15:0]	SWAP Dn
TAS	Destination Tested → Condition Codes; 1 → bit 7 of Destination	TAS ⟨ea⟩
TRAP	SSP − 2 → SSP; Format/Offset → (SSP); SSP − 4 → SSP; PC → (SSP); SSP − 2 → SSP; SR → (SSP); Vector Address → PC	TRAP #⟨vector⟩
TRAPcc	If cc then TRAP	TRAPcc TRAPcc.W #⟨data⟩ TRAPcc.L #⟨data⟩
TRAPV	If V then TRAP	TRAPV
TST	Destination Tested → Condition Codes	TST ⟨ea⟩
UNLK	An → SP; (SP) → An; SP + 4 → SP	UNLK An
UNPK	Source (Packed BCD) + adjustment → Destination (Unpacked BCD)	UNPACK − (Ax), − (Ay),#⟨adjustment⟩ UNPACK Dx,Dy,#⟨adjustment⟩

NOTES:
1. Specifies either the instruction (IC), data (DC), or IC/DC caches.
2. Where r is rounding precision, S or D.
3. A list of any combination of the eight floating-point data registers, with individual register names separated by a slash (/); and/or contiguous blocks of registers specified by the first and last register names separated by a dash (−).
4. A list of any combination of the three floating-point system control registers (FPCR, FPSR, and FPIAR) with individual register names separated by a slash (/).
5. where d is direction, L or R.

3.5 INSTRUCTION EXAMPLES

The following paragraphs provide examples of how to use selected instructions.

3.5.1 Using the CAS and CAS2 Instructions

The CAS instruction compares the value in a memory location with the value in a data register, and copies a second data register into the memory location if the compared values are equal. This provides a means of updating system counters, history information, and globally shared pointers. The instruction uses an indivisible read-modify-write cycle; after CAS reads the memory location, no other instruction can change that location before CAS has written the new value. This provides security in single-processor systems, in multitasking environments, and in multiprocessor environments. In a single-processor system, the operation is protected from instructions of an interrupt routine. In a multitasking environment, no other task can interfere with writing the new value of a system variable. In a multiprocessor environment, the other processors must wait until the CAS instruction completes before accessing a global pointer.

The following code fragment shows a routine to maintain a count, in location SYS_CNTR, of the executions of an operation that may be performed by any process or processor in a system. The routine obtains the current value of the count in register D0 and stores the new count value in register D1. The CAS instruction copies the new count into SYS_CNTR if it is valid. However, if another user has incremented the counter between the time the count was stored and the read-modify-write cycle of the CAS instruction, the write portion of the cycle copies the new count in SYS_CNTR into D0, and the routine branches to repeat the test. The following code sequence guarantees that SYS_CNTR is correctly incremented.

```
          MOVE.W   SYS_CNTR,D0      get the old value of the counter
INC_LOOP  MOVE.W   D0,D1            make a copy of it
          ADDQ.W   #1,D1            and increment it
          CAS.W    D0,D1,SYS_CNTR   if counter value is still the same, update it
          BNE      INC_LOOP         if not, try again
```

The CAS and CAS2 instructions together allow safe operations in the manipulation of system linked lists. Controlling a single location, HEAD in the example, manages a last-in-first-out linked list (see Figure 3-2). If the list is empty, HEAD contains the NULL pointer (0); otherwise, HEAD contains the address of the element most recently added to the list. The code fragment shown in Figure 3-2 illustrates the code for inserting an element. The MOVE instructions load the address in location HEAD into D0 and into the NEXT pointer in the element being inserted, and the address of the new element into D1. The CAS instruction stores the address of the inserted element into location HEAD if the address in HEAD remains unaltered. If HEAD contains a new address, the instruction loads the new address into D0 and branches to the second MOVE instruction to try again.

The CAS2 instruction is similar to the CAS instruction except that it performs two comparisons and updates two variables when the results of the comparisons are equal. If the results of both comparisons are equal, CAS2 copies new values into the destination addresses. If the result of either comparison is not equal, the instruction copies the values in the destination addresses into the compare operands.

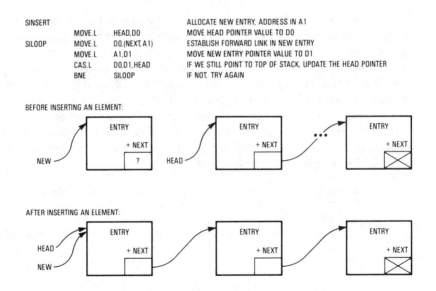

Figure 3-2. Linked List Insertion

The next code (see Figure 3-3) fragment shows the use of a CAS2 instruction to delete an element from a linked list. The first LEA instruction loads the effective address of HEAD into A0. The MOVE instruction loads the address in pointer HEAD into D0. The TST instruction checks for an empty list, and the BEQ instruction branches to a routine at label SDEMPTY if the list is empty. Otherwise, a second LEA instruction loads the address of the NEXT pointer in the newest element on the list into A1, and the following MOVE instruction loads the pointer contents into D1. The CAS2 instruction compares the address of the newest structure to the value in HEAD and the address in D1 to the pointer in the address in A1. If no element has been inserted or deleted by another routine while this routine has been executing, the results of these comparisons are equal, and the CAS2 instruction stores the new value into location HEAD. If an element has been inserted or deleted, the CAS2 instruction loads the new address in location HEAD into D0, and the BNE instruction branches to the TST instruction to try again.

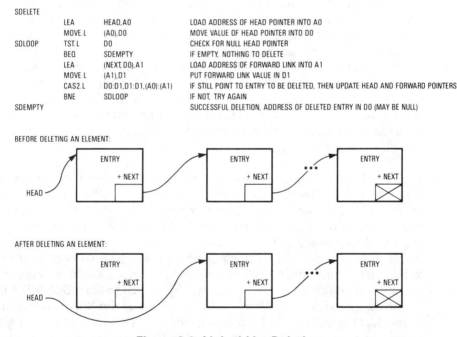

```
SDELETE
            LEA       HEAD,A0               LOAD ADDRESS OF HEAD POINTER INTO A0
            MOVE.L    (A0),D0               MOVE VALUE OF HEAD POINTER INTO D0
SDLOOP      TST.L     D0                    CHECK FOR NULL HEAD POINTER
            BEQ       SDEMPTY               IF EMPTY, NOTHING TO DELETE
            LEA       (NEXT,D0),A1          LOAD ADDRESS OF FORWARD LINK INTO A1
            MOVE.L    (A1),D1               PUT FORWARD LINK VALUE IN D1
            CAS2.L    D0:D1,D1:D1,(A0):(A1) IF STILL POINT TO ENTRY TO BE DELETED, THEN UPDATE HEAD AND FORWARD POINTERS
            BNE       SDLOOP                IF NOT, TRY AGAIN
SDEMPTY                                     SUCCESSFUL DELETION, ADDRESS OF DELETED ENTRY IN D0 (MAY BE NULL)
```

BEFORE DELETING AN ELEMENT:

AFTER DELETING AN ELEMENT:

Figure 3-3. Linked List Deletion

The CAS2 instruction can also be used to correctly maintain a first-in-first-out doubly linked list. A doubly linked list needs two controlled locations, LIST_PUT and LIST_GET, which contain pointers to the last element inserted in the list and the next to be removed, respectively. If the list is empty, both pointers are NULL (0).

The code fragment shown in Figure 3-4 illustrates the insertion of an element in a doubly linked list. The first two instructions load the effective addresses of LIST_PUT and LIST_GET into registers A0 and A1, respectively. The next instruction moves the address of the new element into register D2. Another MOVE instruction moves the address in LIST_PUT into register D0. At label DILOOP, a TST instruction tests the value in D0, and the BEQ instruction branches to the MOVE instruction when D0 is equal to zero. Assuming the list is empty, this MOVE instruction is executed next; it moves the zero in D0 into the NEXT and LAST pointers of the new element. Then the CAS2 instruction moves the address of the new element into both LIST_PUT and LIST_GET, assuming that both of these pointers still contain zero. If not, the BNE instruction branches to the TST instruction at label DILOOP to try again. This time, the BEQ instruction does not branch, and the following MOVE instruction moves the address in D0 to the NEXT pointer of the new element. The CLR instruction clears register D1 to zero, and the MOVE instruction moves the zero into the LAST pointer of the new element. The LEA instruction loads the address of the LAST pointer of the most recently inserted element into register A1. Assuming the LIST_PUT pointer and the pointer in A1 have not been changed, the CAS2 instruction stores the address of the new element into these pointers.

The code fragment to delete an element from a doubly linked list is similar (see Figure 3-5). The first two instructions load the effective addresses of pointers LIST_PUT and LIST_GET into registers A0 and A1, respectively. The MOVE instruction at label DDLOOP moves the LIST_GET pointer into register D1. The BEQ instruction that follows branches out of the routine when the pointer is zero. The MOVE instruction moves the LAST pointer of the element to be deleted into register D2. Assuming this is not the last element in the list, the Z condition code is not set, and the branch to label DDEMPTY does not occur. The LEA instruction loads the address of the NEXT pointer of the element at the address in D2 into register A2. The next instruction, a CLR instruction, clears register D0 to zero. The CAS2 instruction compares the address in D1 to the LIST_GET pointer and to the address in register A2. If the pointers have not been updated, the CAS2 instruction loads the address in D2 into the LIST_GET pointer and zero into the address in register A2.

```
DINSERT                                      (ALLOCATE NEW LIST ENTRY, LOAD ADDRESS INTO A2)
            LEA      LIST_PUT, A0            LOAD ADDRESS OF HEAD POINTER INTO A0
            LEA      LIST_GET, A1            LOAD ADDRESS OF TAIL POINTER INTO A1
            MOVE.L   A2,D2                   LOAD NEW ENTRY POINTER INTO D2
            MOVE.L   (A0),D0                 LOAD POINTER TO HEAD ENTRY INTO D0
DILOOP      TST.L    D0                      IS HEAD POINTER NULL (0 ENTRIES IN LIST)?
            BEQ      DIEMPTY                 IF SO, WE NEED ONLY TO ESTABLISH POINTERS
            MOVE.L   D0,(NEXT, A2)          PUT HEAD POINTER INTO FORWARD POINTER OF NEW ENTRY
            CLR.L    D1                      PUT NULL POINTER VALUE IN D1
            MOVE.L   D1,(LAST, A2)          PUT NULL POINTER IN BACKWARD POINTER OF NEW ENTRY
            LEA      (LAST, D0),A1          LOAD BACKWARD POINTER OF OLD HEAD ENTRY INTO A1
            CAS2.L   D0:D1,D2:D2,(A0):(A1)  IF WE STILL POINT TO OLD HEAD ENTRY, UPDATE POINTERS
            BNE      DILOOP                  IF NOT, TRY AGAIN
            BRA      DIDONE
DIEMPTY     MOVE.L   D0,(NEXT, A2)          PUT NULL POINTER IN FORWARD POINTER OF NEW ENTRY
            MOVE.L   D0,(LAST, A2)          PUT NULL POINTER IN BACKWARD POINTER OF NEW ENTRY
            CAS2.L   D0:D0,D2:D2,(A0):(A1)  IF WE STILL HAVE NO ENTRIES, SET BOTH POINTERS TO THIS ENTRY
            BNE      DILOOP                  IF NOT, TRY AGAIN
DIDONE                                       SUCCESSFUL LIST ENTRY INSERTION
```

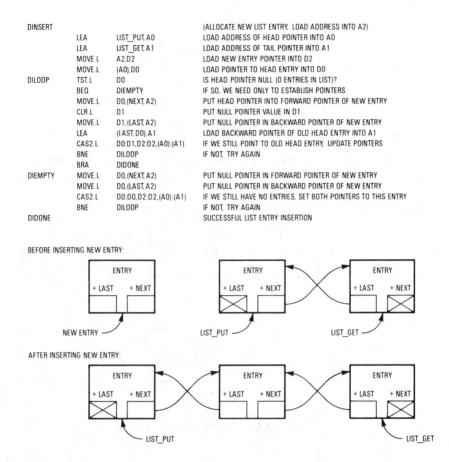

Figure 3-4. Doubly Linked List Insertion

When the list contains only one element, the routine branches to the CAS2 instruction at label DDEMPTY after moving a zero pointer value into D2. This instruction checks the addresses in LIST–PUT and LIST–GET to verify that no other routine has inserted another element or deleted the last element. Then the instruction moves zero into both pointers, and the list is empty.

```
DDELETE
          LEA       LIST_PUT,A0      GET ADDRESS OF HEAD POINTER IN A0
          LEA       LIST_GET,A1      GET ADDRESS OF TAIL POINTER IN A1
DDLOOP    MOVE.L    (A1),D1          MOVE TAIL POINTER INTO D1
          BEQ       DDDONE           IF NO LIST, QUIT
          MOVE.L    (LAST,D1),D2     PUT BACKWARD POINTER IN D2
          BEQ       DDEMPTY          IF ONLY ONE ELEMENT, UPDATE POINTERS
          LEA       (NEXT,D2),A2     PUT ADDRESS OF FORWARD POINTER IN A2
          CLR.L     D0               PUT NULL POINTER VALUE IN D0
          CAS2.L    D1:D1,D2:D0,(A1):(A2)   IF BOTH POINTERS STILL POINT TO THIS ENTRY, UPDATE THEM
          BNE       DDLOOP           IF NOT, TRY AGAIN
          BRA       DDDONE
DDEMPTY   CAS2.L    D1:D1,D2:D2,(A1):(A0)   IF STILL FIRST ENTRY, SET HEAD AND TAIL POINTERS TO NULL
          BNE       DDLOOP           IF NOT, TRY AGAIN
DDDONE                               SUCCESSFUL ENTRY DELETION, ADDRESS OF DELETED ENTRY IN D1 (MAY BE NULL)
```

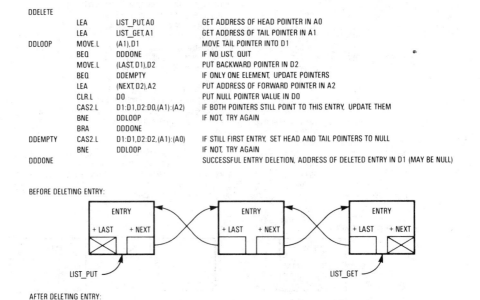

Figure 3-5. Doubly Linked List Deletion

3.5.2 Nested Subroutine Calls

The LINK instruction pushes an address onto the stack, saves the stack address at which the address is stored, and reserves an area of the stack. Using this instruction in a series of subroutine calls results in a linked list of stack frames.

The UNLK instruction removes a stack frame from the end of the list by loading an address into the stack pointer and pulling the value at that address from the stack. When the operand of the instruction is the address of the link address at the bottom of a stack frame, the effect is to remove the stack frame from the stack and from the linked list.

3.5.3 Bit Field Operations

One data type provided by the MC68030 is the bit field, consisting of as many as 32 consecutive bits. A bit field is defined by an offset from an effective address and a width value. The offset is a value in the range of -2^{31} through $2^{31}-1$ from the most significant bit (bit 7) at the effective address. The width is a positive number, 1–32. The most significant bit of a bit field is bit 0; the bits number in a direction opposite to the bits of an integer.

The instruction set includes eight instructions that have bit field operands. The insert bit field (BFINS) instruction inserts a bit field stored in a register into a bit field. The extract bit field signed (BFEXTS) instruction loads a bit field into the least significant bits of a register and extends the sign to the left, filling the register. The extract bit field unsigned (BFEXTU) also loads a bit field, but zero fills the unused portion of the destination register.

The set bit field (BFSET) instruction sets all the bits of a field to ones. The clear bit field (BFCLR) instruction clears a field. The change bit field (BFCHG) instruction complements all the bits in a bit field. These three instructions all test the previous value of the bit field, setting the condition codes accordingly. The test bit field (BFTST) instruction tests the value in the field, setting the condition codes appropriately without altering the bit field. The find first one in bit field (BFFFO) instruction scans a bit field from bit 0 to the right until it finds a bit set to one and loads the bit offset of the first set bit into the specified data register. If no bits in the field are set, the field offset and the field width is loaded into the register.

An important application of bit field instructions is the manipulation of the exponent field in a floating-point number. In the IEEE standard format, the most significant bit is the sign bit of the mantissa. The exponent value begins at the next most significant bit position; the exponent field does not begin on a byte boundary. The extract bit field (BFEXTU) instruction and the BFTST instruction are the most useful for this application, but other bit field instructions can also be used.

Programming of input and output operations to peripherals requires testing, setting, and inserting of bit fields in the control registers of the peripherals, which is another application for bit field instructions. However, control register locations are not memory locations; therefore, it is not always possible to insert or extract bit fields of a register without affecting other fields within the register.

Another widely used application for bit field instructions is bit-mapped graphics. Because byte boundaries are ignored in these areas of memory, the field definitions used with bit field instructions are very helpful.

3.5.4 Pipeline Synchronization with the NOP Instruction

Although the no operation (NOP) instruction performs no visible operation, it serves an important purpose. It forces synchronization of the integer unit pipeline by waiting for all pending bus cycles to complete. All previous integer instructions and floating-point external operand accesses complete execution before the NOP begins. The NOP instruction does not synchronize the FPU pipeline; floating-point instructions with floating-point register operand destinations can be executing when the NOP begins.

SECTION 4
PROCESSING STATES

This section describes the processing states of the MC68030. It describes the functions of the bits in the supervisor portion of the status register and the actions taken by the processor in response to exception conditions.

Unless the processor has halted, it is always in either the normal or the exception processing state. Whenever the processor is executing instructions or fetching instructions or operands, it is in the normal processing state. The processor is also in the normal processing state while it is storing instruction results or communicating with a coprocessor.

NOTE

Exception processing refers specifically to the transition from normal processing of a program to normal processing of system routines, interrupt routines, and other exception handlers. Exception processing includes all stacking operations, the fetch of the exception vector, and filling of the instruction pipe caused by an exception. It has completed when execution of the first instruction of the exception handler routine begins.

The processor enters the exception processing state when an interrupt is acknowledged, when an instruction is traced or results in a trap, or when some other exceptional condition arises. Execution of certain instructions or unusual conditions occurring during the execution of any instructions can cause exceptions. External conditions, such as interrupts, bus errors, and some coprocessor responses, also cause exceptions. Exception processing provides an efficient transfer of control to handlers and routines that process the exceptions.

A catastrophic system failure occurs whenever the processor receives a bus error or generates an address error while in the exception processing state. This type of failure halts the processor. For example, if during the exception processing of one bus error another bus error occurs, the MC68030 has not completed the transition to normal processing and has not completed saving the internal state of the machine, so the processor assumes that the system is not operational and halts. Only an external reset can restart a halted processor. (When the processor executes a STOP instruction, it is in a special type of normal processing state, one without bus cycles. It is stopped, not halted.)

4.1 PRIVILEGE LEVELS

The processor operates at one of two levels of privilege: the user level or the supervisor level. The supervisor level has higher privileges than the user level. Not all processor or coprocessor instructions are permitted to execute in the lower privileged user level, but all are available at the supervisor level. This allows a separation of supervisor and user so the supervisor can protect system resources from uncontrolled access. The processor uses the privilege level indicated by the S bit in the status register to select either the user or supervisor privilege level and either the user stack pointer or a supervisor stack pointer for stack operations. The processor identifies a bus access (supervisor or user mode) via the function codes so that differentiation between supervisor and user can be maintained. The memory management unit uses the indication of privilege level to control and translate memory accesses to protect supervisor code, data, and resources from access by user programs.

In many systems, the majority of programs execute at the user level. User programs can access only their own code and data areas and can be restricted from accessing other information. The operating system typically executes at the supervisor privilege level. It has access to all resources, performs the overhead tasks for the user level programs, and coordinates their activities.

4.1.1 Supervisor Privilege Level

The supervisor level is the higher privilege level. The privilege level is determined by the S bit of the status register; if the S bit is set, the supervisor privilege level applies, and all instructions are executable. The bus cycles for instructions executed at the supervisor level are normally classified as supervisor references, and the values of the function codes on FC0–FC2 refer to supervisor address spaces.

In a multitasking operating system, it is more efficient to have a supervisor stack space associated with each user task and a separate stack space for interrupt associated tasks. The MC68030 provides two supervisor stacks, master and interrupt; the M bit of the status register selects which of the two is active. When the M bit is set to one, supervisor stack pointer references (either implicit or by specifying address register A7) access the master stack pointer (MSP). The operating system sets the MSP for each task to point to a task-related area of supervisor data space. This separates task-related supervisor activity from asynchronous, I/O-related supervisor tasks that may be only coincidental to the currently executing task. The master stack (MSP) can separately maintain task control information for each currently executing user task, and the software updates the MSP when a task switch is performed, providing an efficient means for transferring task-related stack items. The other supervisor stack (ISP) can be used for interrupt control information and workspace area as interrupt handling routines require.

When the M bit is clear, the MC68030 is in the interrupt mode of the supervisor privilege level, and operation is the same as in the MC68000, MC68008, and MC68010 supervisor mode. (The processor is in this mode after a reset operation.) All supervisor stack pointer references access the interrupt stack pointer (ISP) in this mode.

The value of the M bit in the status register does not affect execution of privileged instructions; both master and interrupt modes are at the supervisor privilege level. Instructions that affect the M bit are MOVE to SR, ANDI to SR, EORI to SR, ORI to SR, and RTE. Also, the processor automatically saves the M-bit value and clears it in the SR as part of the exception processing for interrupts.

All exception processing is performed at the supervisor privilege level. All bus cycles generated during exception processing are supervisor references, and all stack accesses use the active supervisor stack pointer.

4.1.2 User Privilege Level

The user level is the lower privilege level. The privilege level is determined by the S bit of the status register; if the S bit is clear, the processor executes instructions at the user privilege level.

Most instructions execute at either privilege level, but some instructions that have important system effects are privileged and can only be executed at the supervisor level. For instance, user programs are not allowed to execute the STOP instruction or the RESET instruction. To prevent a user program from entering the supervisor privilege level, except in a controlled manner, instructions that can alter the S bit in the status register are privileged. The TRAP #n instruction provides controlled access to operating system services for user programs.

The bus cycles for an instruction executed at the user privilege level are classified as user references, and the values of the function codes on FC0–FC2 specify user address spaces. The memory management unit of the processor, when it is enabled, uses the value of the function codes to distinguish between user and supervisor activity and to control access to protected portions of the address space. While the processor is at the user level, references to the system stack pointer implicitly, or to address register seven (A7) explicitly, refer to the user stack pointer (USP).

4.1.3 Changing Privilege Level

To change from the user to the supervisor privilege level, one of the conditions that causes the processor to perform exception processing must occur. This causes a change from the user level to the supervisor level and can cause a change from the master mode to the interrupt mode. Exception processing saves the current values of the S and M bits of the status register (along with the rest of the status register) on the active supervisor stack, and then sets the S bit, forcing the processor into the supervisor privilege level. When the exception being processed is an interrupt and the M bit is set, the M bit is cleared, putting the processor into the interrupt mode. Execution of instructions continues at the supervisor level to process the exception condition.

To return to the user privilege level, a system routine must execute one of the following instructions: MOVE to SR, ANDI to SR, EORI to SR, ORI to SR, or RTE. The MOVE, ANDI, EORI, and ORI to SR and RTE instructions execute at the supervisor privilege level and can modify the S bit of the status register. After these instructions execute, the instruction pipeline is flushed and is refilled from the appropriate address space. This is indicated externally by the assertion of the REFILL signal.

The RTE instruction returns to the program that was executing when the exception occurred. It restores the exception stack frame saved on the supervisor stack. If the frame on top of the stack was generated by an interrupt, trap, or instruction exception, the RTE instruction restores the status register and program counter to the values saved on the supervisor stack. The processor then continues execution at the restored program counter address and at the privilege level determined by the S bit of the restored status register. If the frame on top of the stack was generated by a bus fault (bus error or address error exception), the RTE instruction restores the entire saved processor state from the stack.

4.2 ADDRESS SPACE TYPES

The processor specifies a target address space for every bus cycle with the function code signals according to the type of access required. In addition to distinguishing between supervisor/user and program/data, the processor can identify special processor cycles, such as the interrupt acknowledge cycle, and the memory management unit can control accesses and translate addresses appropriately. Table 4-1 lists the types of accesses defined for the MC68030 and the corresponding values of function codes FC0–FC2.

Table 4-1. Address Space Encodings

FC2	FC1	FC0	Address Space
0	0	0	(Undefined, Reserved)*
0	0	1	User Data Space
0	1	0	User Program Space
0	1	1	(Undefined, Reserved)*
1	0	0	(Undefined, Reserved)*
1	0	1	Supervisor Data Space
1	1	0	Supervisor Program Space
1	1	1	CPU Space

*Address space 3 is reserved for user definition, while 0 and 4 are reserved for future use by Motorola.

The memory locations of user program and data accesses are not predefined. Neither are the locations of supervisor data space. During reset, the first two long words beginning at memory location zero in the supervisor program space are used for processor initialization. No other memory locations are explicitly defined by the MC68030.

A function code of $7 ([FC2:FC0] = 111) selects the CPU address space. This is a special address space that does not contain instructions or operands but is reserved for special processor functions. The processor uses accesses in this space to communicate with external devices for special purposes. For example, all M68000 processors use the CPU space for interrupt acknowledge cycles. The MC68020 and MC68030 also generate CPU space accesses for breakpoint acknowledge and coprocessor operations.

Supervisor programs can use the MOVES instruction to access all address spaces, including the user spaces and the CPU address space. Although the MOVES instruction can be used to generate CPU space cycles, this may interfere with proper system operation. Thus, the use of MOVES to access the CPU space should be done with caution.

4.3 EXCEPTION PROCESSING

An exception is defined as a special condition that pre-empts normal processing. Both internal and external conditions cause exceptions. External conditions that cause exceptions are interrupts from external devices, bus errors, coprocessor detected errors, and reset. Instructions, address errors, tracing, and breakpoints are internal conditions that cause exceptions. The TRAP, TRAPcc, TRAPV, cpTRAPcc, CHK, CHK2, RTE, and DIV instructions can all generate exceptions as part of their normal execution. In addition, illegal instructions, privilege violations, and coprocessor protocol violations cause exceptions.

Exception processing, which is the transition from the normal processing of a program to the processing required for the exception condition, involves the exception vector table and an exception stack frame. The following paragraphs describe the vector table and a generalized exception stack frame. Exception processing is discussed in detail in **SECTION 8 EXCEPTION PROCESSING**. Coprocessor detected exceptions are discussed in detail in **SECTION 10 COPROCESSOR INTERFACE DESCRIPTION**.

4.3.1 Exception Vectors

The vector base register (VBR) contains the base address of the 1024-byte exception vector table, which consists of 256 exception vectors. Exception vectors contain the memory addresses of routines that begin execution at the completion of exception processing. These routines perform a series of operations appropriate for the corresponding exceptions. Because the exception vectors contain memory addresses, each consists of one long word, except for the reset vector. The reset vector consists of two long words: the address used to initialize the interrupt stack pointer and the address used to initialize the program counter.

The address of an exception vector is derived from an 8-bit vector number and the VBR. The vector numbers for some exceptions are obtained from an external device; others are supplied automatically by the processor. The processor multiplies the vector number by four to calculate the vector offset, which it adds to the VBR. The sum is the memory address of the vector. All exception vectors are located in supervisor data space, except the reset vector, which is located in supervisor program space. Only the initial reset vector is fixed in the processor's memory map; once initialization is complete, there are no fixed assignments. Since the VBR provides the base address of the vector table, the vector table can be located anywhere in memory; it can even be dynamically relocated for each task that is executed by an operating system. Details of exception processing are provided in **SECTION 8 EXCEPTION PROCESSING**, and Table 8-1 lists the exception vector assignments.

4.3.2 Exception Stack Frame

Exception processing saves the most volatile portion of the current processor context on the top of the supervisor stack. This context is organized in a format called the exception stack frame. This information always includes a copy of the status register, the program counter, the vector offset of the vector, and the frame format field. The frame format field identifies the type of stack frame. The RTE instruction uses the value in the format field to properly restore the information stored in the stack frame and to deallocate the stack space. The general form of the exception stack frame is illustrated in Figure 4-1. Refer to **SECTION 8 EXCEPTION PROCESSING** for a complete list of exception stack frames.

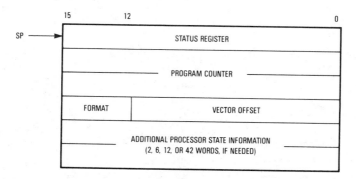

Figure 4-1. General Exception Stack Frame

4

SECTION 5
SIGNAL DESCRIPTION

This section contains brief descriptions of the input and output signals in their functional groups, as shown in Figure 5-1. Each signal is explained in a brief paragraph with reference to other sections that contain more detail about the signal and the related operations.

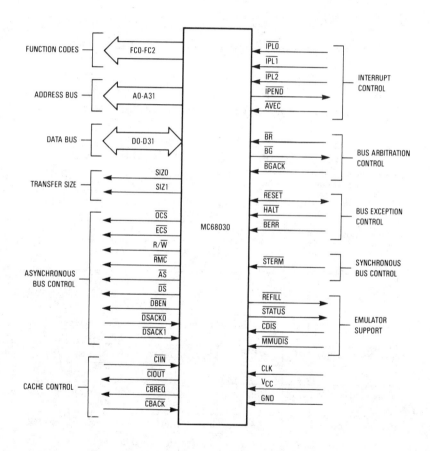

Figure 5-1. Functional Signal Groups

NOTE

In this section and in the remainder of the manual, **assertion** and **negation** are used to specify forcing a signal to a particular state. In particular, assertion and assert refer to a signal that is active or true; negation and negate indicate a signal that is inactive or false. These terms are used independently of the voltage level (high or low) that they represent.

5.1 SIGNAL INDEX

The input and output signals for the MC68030 are listed in Table 5-1. Both the names and mnemonics are shown along with brief signal descriptions. For more detail on each signal, refer to the paragraph in this section named for the signal and the reference in that paragraph to a description of the related operations.

Guaranteed timing specifications for the signals listed in Table 5-1 can be found in M68030EC/D, *MC68030 Electrical Specifications.*.

Table 5-1. Signal Index (Sheet 1 of 2)

Signal Name	Mnemonic	Function
Function Codes	FC0–FC2	3-bit function code used to identify the address space of each bus cycle.
Address Bus	A0–A31	32-bit address bus.
Data Bus	D0–D31	32-bit data bus used to transfer 8, 16, 24, or 32 bits of data per bus cycle.
Size	SIZ0/SIZ1	Indicates the number of bytes remaining to be transferred for this cycle. These signals, together with A0 and A1, define the active sections of the data bus.
Operand Cycle Start	$\overline{OCS}$	Identical operation to that of $\overline{ECS}$ except that $\overline{OCS}$ is asserted only during the first bus cycle of an operand transfer.
External Cycle Start	$\overline{ECS}$	Provides an indication that a bus cycle is beginning.
Read/Write	$R/\overline{W}$	Defines the bus transfer as a processor read or write.
Read-Modify-Write Cycle	$\overline{RMC}$	Provides an indicator that the current bus cycle is part of an indivisible read-modify-write operation.
Address Strobe	$\overline{AS}$	Indicates that a valid address is on the bus.
Data Strobe	$\overline{DS}$	Indicates that valid data is to be placed on the data bus by an external device or has been placed on the data bus by the MC68030.
Data Buffer Enable	$\overline{DBEN}$	Provides an enable signal for external data buffers.

Table 5-1. Signal Index (Sheet 2 of 2)

Signal Name	Mnemonic	Function
Data Transfer and Size Acknowledge	DSACK0/ DSACK1	Bus response signals that indicate the requested data transfer operation is completed. In addition, these two lines indicate the size of the external bus port on a cycle-by-cycle basis and are used for asynchronous transfers.
Synchronous Termination	STERM	Bus response signal that indicates a port size of 32 bits and that data may be latched on the next falling clock edge.
Cache Inhibit In	CIIN	Prevents data from being loaded into the MC68030 instruction and data caches.
Cache Inhibit Out	CIOUT	Reflects the CI bit in ATC entries or TTx register; indicates that external caches should ignore these accesses.
Cache Burst Request	CBREQ	Indicates a burst request for the instruction or data cache.
Cache Burst Acknowledge	CBACK	Indicates that the accessed device can operate in burst mode.
Interrupt Priority Level	IPL0–IPL2	Provides an encoded interrupt level to the processor.
Interrupt Pending	IPEND	Indicates that an interrupt is pending.
Autovector	AVEC	Requests an autovector during an interrupt acknowledge cycle.
Bus Request	BR	Indicates that an external device requires bus mastership.
Bus Grant	BG	Indicates that an external device may assume bus mastership.
Bus Grant Acknowledge	BGACK	Indicates that an external device has assumed bus mastership.
Reset	RESET	System reset.
Halt	HALT	Indicates that the processor should suspend bus activity.
Bus Error	BERR	Indicates that an erroneous bus operation is being attempted.
Cache Disable	CDIS	Dynamically disables the on-chip cache to assist emulator support.
MMU Disable	MMUDIS	Dynamically disables the translation mechanism of the MMU.
Pipe Refill	REFILL	Indicates when the MC68030 is beginning to fill pipeline.
Microsequencer Status	STATUS	Indicates the state of the microsequencer.
Clock	CLK	Clock input to the processor.
Power Supply	V_{CC}	Power supply.
Ground	GND	Ground connection.

5

5.2 FUNCTION CODE SIGNALS (FC0–FC2)

These three-state outputs identify the address space of the current bus cycle. Table 4-1 shows the relationship of the function code signals to the privilege levels and the address spaces. Refer to **4.2 ADDRESS SPACE TYPES** for more information.

5.3 ADDRESS BUS (A0–A31)

These three-state outputs provide the address for the current bus cycle, except in the CPU address space. Refer to **4.2 ADDRESS SPACE TYPES** for more information on the CPU address space. A31 is the most significant address signal. Refer to **7.1.2 Address Bus** for information on the address bus and its relationship to bus operation.

5.4 DATA BUS (D0–D31)

These three-state bidirectional signals provide the general-purpose data path between the MC68030 and all other devices. The data bus can transfer 8, 16, 24, or 32 bits of data per bus cycle. D31 is the most significant bit of the data bus. Refer to **7.1.4 Data Bus** for more information on the data bus and its relationship to bus operation.

5.5 TRANSFER SIZE SIGNALS (SIZ0, SIZ1)

These three-state outputs indicate the number of bytes remaining to be transferred for the current bus cycle. With A0, A1, $\overline{\text{DSACK0}}$, $\overline{\text{DSACK1}}$, and $\overline{\text{STERM}}$, SIZ0 and SIZ1 define the number of bits transferred on the data bus. Refer to **7.2.1 Dynamic Bus Sizing** for more information on the size signals and their use in dynamic bus sizing.

5.6 BUS CONTROL SIGNALS

The following signals control synchronous bus transfer operations for the MC68030.

5.6.1 Operand Cycle Start ($\overline{\text{OCS}}$)

This output signal indicates the beginning of the first external bus cycle for an instruction prefetch or a data operand transfer. $\overline{\text{OCS}}$ is not asserted for subsequent cycles that are performed due to dynamic bus sizing or operand misalignment. Refer to **7.1.1 Bus Control Signals** for information about the relationship of $\overline{\text{OCS}}$ to bus operation.

5.6.2 External Cycle Start ($\overline{\text{ECS}}$)

This output signal indicates the beginning of a bus cycle of any type. Refer to **7.1.1 Bus Control Signals** for information about the relationship of $\overline{\text{ECS}}$ to bus operation.

5.6.3 Read/Write (R/$\overline{\text{W}}$)

This three-state output signal defines the type of bus cycle. A high level indicates a read cycle; a low level indicates a write cycle. Refer to **7.1.1 Bus Control Signals** for information about the relationship of R/$\overline{\text{W}}$ to bus operation.

5.6.4 Read-Modify-Write Cycle ($\overline{\text{RMC}}$)

This three-state output signal identifies the current bus cycle as part of an indivisible read-modify-write operation; it remains asserted during all bus cycles of the read-modify-write operation. Refer to **7.1.1 Bus Control Signals** for information about the relationship of $\overline{\text{RMC}}$ to bus operation.

5.6.5 Address Strobe ($\overline{\text{AS}}$)

This three-state output indicates that a valid address is on the address bus. The function code, size, and read/write signals are also valid when $\overline{\text{AS}}$ is asserted. Refer to **7.1.3 Address Strobe** for information about the relationship of $\overline{\text{AS}}$ to bus operation.

5.6.6 Data Strobe (DS)

During a read cycle, this three-state output indicates that an external device should place valid data on the data bus. During a write cycle, the data strobe indicates that the MC68030 has placed valid data on the bus. During two-clock synchronous write cycles, the MC68030 does not assert DS. Refer to **7.1.5 Data Strobe** for more information about the relationship of DS to bus operation.

5.6.7 Data Buffer Enable (DBEN)

This output is an enable signal for external data buffers. This signal may not be required in all systems. The timing of this signal may preclude its use in a system that supports two-clock synchronous bus cycles. Refer to **7.1.6 Data Buffer Enable** for more information about the relationship of DBEN to bus operation.

5.6.8 Data Transfer and Size Acknowledge (DSACK0, DSACK1)

These inputs indicate the completion of a requested data transfer operation. In addition, they indicate the size of the external bus port at the completion of each cycle. These signals apply only to asynchronous bus cycles. Refer to **7.1.7 Bus Cycle Termination Signals** for more information on these signals and their relationship to dynamic bus sizing.

5.6.9 Synchronous Termination (STERM)

This input is a bus handshake signal indicating that the addressed port size is 32 bits and that data is to be latched on the next falling clock edge for a read cycle. This signal applies only to synchronous operation. Refer to **7.1.7 Bus Cycle Termination Signals** for more information about the relationship of STERM to bus operation.

5.7 CACHE CONTROL SIGNALS

The following signals relate to the on-chip caches.

5.7.1 Cache Inhibit Input ($\overline{\text{CIIN}}$)

This input signal prevents data from being loaded into the MC68030 instruction and data caches. It is a synchronous input signal and is interpreted on a bus-cycle-by-bus-cycle basis. $\overline{\text{CIIN}}$ is ignored during all write cycles. Refer to **6.1 ON-CHIP CACHE ORGANIZATION AND OPERATION** for information on the relationship of $\overline{\text{CIIN}}$ to the on-chip caches.

5.7.2 Cache Inhibit Output ($\overline{\text{CIOUT}}$)

This three-state output signal reflects the state of the CI bit in the address translation cache entry for the referenced logical address, indicating that an external cache should ignore the bus transfer. When the referenced logical address is within an area specified for transparent translation, the CI bit of the appropriate transparent translation register controls the state of $\overline{\text{CIOUT}}$. Refer to **SECTION 9 MEMORY MANAGEMENT UNIT** for more information about the address translation cache and transparent translation. Also, refer to **SECTION 6 ON-CHIP CACHE MEMORIES** for the effect of $\overline{\text{CIOUT}}$ on the internal caches.

5.7.3 Cache Burst Request ($\overline{\text{CBREQ}}$)

This three-state output signal requests a burst mode operation to fill a line in the instruction or data cache. Refer to **6.1.3 Cache Filling** for filling information and **7.3.7 Burst Operation Cycles** for bus cycle information pertaining to burst mode operations.

5.7.4 Cache Burst Acknowledge ($\overline{\text{CBACK}}$)

This input signal indicates that the accessed device can operate in the burst mode and can supply at least one more long word for the instruction or data cache. Refer to **7.3.7 Burst Operation Cycles** for information about burst mode operation.

5.8 INTERRUPT CONTROL SIGNALS

The following signals are the interrupt control signals for the MC68030.

5.8.1 Interrupt Priority Level Signals

These input signals provide an indication of an interrupt condition and the encoding of the interrupt level from a peripheral or external prioritizing circuitry. $\overline{IPL2}$ is the most significant bit of the level number. For example, since the $\overline{IPLn}$ signals are active low, $\overline{IPL0}$–$\overline{IPL2}$ equal to $5 corresponds to an interrupt request at interrupt level 2. Refer to **8.1.9 Interrupt Exceptions** for information on MC68030 interrupts.

5.8.2 Interrupt Pending ($\overline{IPEND}$)

This output signal indicates that an interrupt request has been recognized internally and exceeds the current interrupt priority mask in the status register (SR). This output is for use by external devices (coprocessors and other bus masters, for example) to predict processor operation on the following instruction boundaries. Refer to **8.1.9 Interrupt Exceptions** for interrupt information. Also, refer to **7.4.1 Interrupt Acknowledge Bus Cycles** for bus information related to interrupts.

5.8.3 Autovector ($\overline{AVEC}$)

This input signal indicates that the MC68030 should generate an automatic vector during an interrupt acknowledge cycle. Refer to **7.4.1.2 AUTOVECTOR INTERRUPT ACKNOWLEDGE CYCLE** for more information about automatic vectors.

5.9 BUS ARBITRATION CONTROL SIGNALS

The following signals are the three bus arbitration control signals used to determine which device in a system is the bus master.

5.9.1 Bus Request ($\overline{BR}$)

This input signal indicates that an external device needs to become the bus master. This is typically a "wire-ORed" input (but does not need to be constructed from open-collector devices). Refer to **7.7 BUS ARBITRATION** for more information.

5.9.2 Bus Grant ($\overline{\text{BG}}$)

This output indicates that the MC68030 will release ownership of the bus master when the current processor bus cycle completes. Refer to **7.7.2 Bus Grant** for more information.

5.9.3 Bus Grant Acknowledge ($\overline{\text{BGACK}}$)

This input indicates that an external device has become the bus master. Refer to **7.7.3 Bus Grant Acknowledge** for more information.

5.10 BUS EXCEPTION CONTROL SIGNALS

The following signals are the bus exception control signals for the MC68030.

5.10.1 Reset ($\overline{\text{RESET}}$)

This bidirectional open-drain signal is used to initiate a system reset. An external reset signal resets the MC68030 as well as all external devices. A reset signal from the processor (asserted as part of the RESET instruction) resets external devices only; the internal state of the processor is not altered. Refer to **7.8 RESET OPERATION** for a description of reset bus operation and **8.1.1 Reset Exception** for information about the reset exception.

5.10.2 Halt ($\overline{\text{HALT}}$)

The halt signal indicates that the processor should suspend bus activity or, when used with $\overline{\text{BERR}}$, that the processor should retry the current cycle. Refer to **7.5 BUS EXCEPTION CONTROL CYCLES** for a description of the effects of $\overline{\text{HALT}}$ on bus operations.

5.10.3 Bus Error ($\overline{\text{BERR}}$)

The bus error signal indicates that an invalid bus operation is being attempted or, when used with $\overline{\text{HALT}}$, that the processor should retry the current cycle. Refer to **7.5 BUS EXCEPTION CONTROL CYCLES** for a description of the effects of $\overline{\text{BERR}}$ on bus operations.

5.11 EMULATOR SUPPORT SIGNALS

The following signals support emulation by providing a means for an emulator to disable the on-chip caches and memory management unit and by supplying internal status information to an emulator. Refer to **SECTION 12 APPLICATIONS INFORMATION** for more detailed information on emulation support.

5.11.1 Cache Disable (CDIS)

The cache disable signal dynamically disables the on-chip caches to assist emulator support. Refer to **6.1 ON-CHIP CACHE ORGANIZATION AND OPERATION** for information about the caches; refer to **SECTION 12 APPLICATIONS INFORMATION** for a description of the use of this signal by an emulator. CDIS does not flush the data and instruction caches; entries remain unaltered and become available again when CDIS is negated.

5.11.2 MMU Disable (MMUDIS)

The MMU disable signal dynamically disables the translation of addresses by the MMU. Refer to **9.4 ADDRESS TRANSLATION CACHE** for a description of address translation; refer to **SECTION 12 APPLICATIONS INFORMATION** for a description of the use of this signal by an emulator. The assertion of MMUDIS does not flush the address translation cache (ATC); ATC entries become available again when MMUDIS is negated.

5.11.3 Pipeline Refill (REFILL)

The pipeline refill signal indicates that the MC68030 is beginning to refill the internal instruction pipeline. Refer to **SECTION 12 APPLICATIONS INFORMATION** for a description of the use of this signal by an emulator.

5.11.4 Internal Microsequencer Status (STATUS)

The microsequencer status signal indicates the state of the internal microsequencer. The varying number of clocks for which this signal is asserted indicates instruction boundaries, pending exceptions, and the halted condition. Refer to **SECTION 12 APPLICATIONS INFORMATION** for a description of the use of this signal by an emulator.

5.12 CLOCK (CLK)

The clock signal is the clock input to the MC68030. It is a TTL-compatible signal. Refer to **SECTION 12 APPLICATIONS INFORMATION** for suggestions on clock generation.

5.13 POWER SUPPLY CONNECTIONS

The MC68030 requires connection to a V_{CC} power supply, positive with respect to ground. The V_{CC} connections are grouped to supply adequate current for the various sections of the processor. The ground connections are similarly grouped. **SECTION 14 ORDERING INFORMATION AND ME-CHANICAL DATA** describes the groupings of V_{CC} and ground connections, and **SECTION 12 APPLICATIONS INFORMATION** describes a typical power supply interface.

5.14 SIGNAL SUMMARY

Table 5-2 provides a summary of the electrical characteristics of the signals discussed in this section.

Table 5-2. Signal Summary

Signal Function	Signal Name	Input/Output	Active State	Three-State
Function Codes	FC0–FC2	Output	High	Yes
Address Bus	A0–A31	Output	High	Yes
Data Bus	D0–D31	Input/Output	High	Yes
Transfer Size	SIZ0/SIZ1	Output	High	Yes
Operand Cycle Start	$\overline{OCS}$	Output	Low	No
External Cycle Start	$\overline{ECS}$	Output	Low	No
Read/Write	R/$\overline{W}$	Output	High/Low	Yes
Read-Modify-Write Cycle	$\overline{RMC}$	Output	Low	Yes
Address Strobe	$\overline{AS}$	Output	Low	Yes
Data Strobe	$\overline{DS}$	Output	Low	Yes
Data Buffer Enable	$\overline{DBEN}$	Output	Low	Yes
Data Transfer and Size Acknowledge	$\overline{DSACK0}$/$\overline{DSACK1}$	Input	Low	—
Synchronous Termination	$\overline{STERM}$	Input	Low	—
Cache Inhibit In	$\overline{CIIN}$	Input	Low	—
Cache Inhibit Out	$\overline{CIOUT}$	Output	Low	Yes
Cache Burst Request	$\overline{CBREQ}$	Output	Low	Yes
Cache Burst Acknowledge	$\overline{CBACK}$	Input	Low	—
Interrupt Priority Level	$\overline{IPL0}$–$\overline{IPL2}$	Input	Low	—
Interrupt Pending	$\overline{IPEND}$	Output	Low	No
Autovector	$\overline{AVEC}$	Input	Low	—
Bus Request	$\overline{BR}$	Input	Low	—
Bus Grant	$\overline{BG}$	Output	Low	No
Bus Grant Acknowledge	$\overline{BGACK}$	Input	Low	—
Reset	$\overline{RESET}$	Input/Output	Low	No
Halt	$\overline{HALT}$	Input	Low	—
Bus Error	$\overline{BERR}$	Input	Low	—
Cache Disable	$\overline{CDIS}$	Input	Low	—
MMU Disable	$\overline{MMUDIS}$	Input	Low	—
Pipeline Refill	$\overline{REFILL}$	Output	Low	No
Microsequencer Status	$\overline{STATUS}$	Output	Low	No
Clock	CLK	Input	—	—
Power Supply	V_{CC}	Input	—	—
Ground	GND	Input	—	—

SECTION 6
ON-CHIP CACHE MEMORIES

The MC68030 microprocessor includes a 256-byte on-chip instruction cache and a 256-byte on-chip data cache that are accessed by logical (virtual) addresses. These caches improve performance by reducing external bus activity and increasing instruction throughput.

Reduced external bus activity increases overall performance by increasing the availability of the bus for use by external devices (in systems with more than one bus master, such as a processor and a DMA device) without degrading the performance of the MC68030. An increase in instruction throughput results when instruction words and data required by a program are available in the on-chip caches and the time required to access them on the external bus is eliminated. Additionally, instruction throughput increases when instruction words and data can be accessed simultaneously.

As shown in Figure 6-1, the instruction cache and the data cache are connected to separate on-chip address and data buses. The address buses are combined to provide the logical address to the memory management unit (MMU). The MC68030 initiates an access to the appropriate cache for the requested instruction or data operand at the same time that it initiates an access for the translation of the logical address in the address translation cache of the MMU. When a hit occurs in the instruction or data cache and the MMU validates the access on a write, the information is transferred from the cache (on a read) or to the cache and the bus controller (on a write). When a hit does not occur, the MMU translation of the address is used for an external bus cycle to obtain the instruction or operand. Regardless of whether or not the required operand is located in one of the on-chip caches, the address translation cache of the MMU performs logical-to-physical address translation in parallel with the cache lookup in case an external cycle is required.

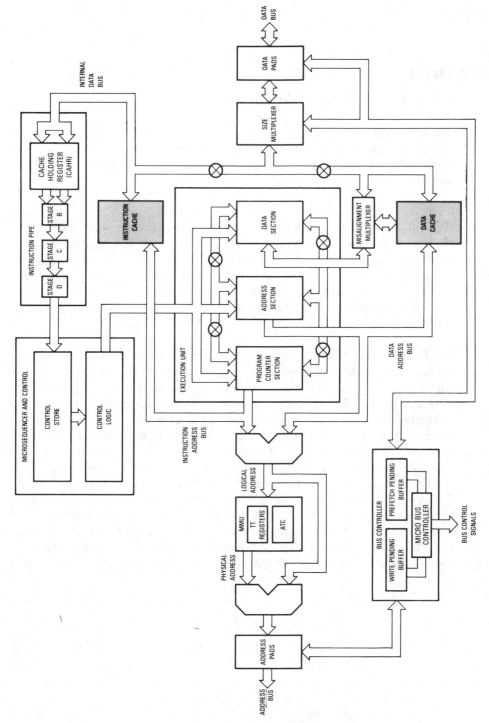

Figure 6-1. Internal Caches and the MC68030

6.1 ON-CHIP CACHE ORGANIZATION AND OPERATION

Both on-chip caches are 256-byte direct-mapped caches, each organized as 16 lines. Each line consists of four entries, and each entry contains four bytes. The tag field for each line contains a valid bit for each entry in the line; each entry is independently replaceable. When appropriate, the bus controller requests a burst mode operation to replace an entire cache line. The cache control register (CACR) is accessible by supervisor programs to control the operation of both caches.

System hardware can assert the cache disable ($\overline{\text{CDIS}}$) signal to disable both caches. The assertion of $\overline{\text{CDIS}}$ disables the caches, regardless of the state of the enable bits in CACR. $\overline{\text{CDIS}}$ is primarily intended for use by in-circuit emulators.

Another input signal, cache inhibit in ($\overline{\text{CIIN}}$), inhibits caching of data reads or instruction prefetches on a bus-cycle by bus-cycle basis. Examples of data that should not be cached are data for I/O devices and data from memory devices that cannot supply a full port width of data, regardless of the size of the required operand.

Subsequent paragraphs describe how $\overline{\text{CIIN}}$ is used during the filling of the caches.

An output signal, cache inhibit out ($\overline{\text{CIOUT}}$), reflects the state of the cache inhibit (CI) bit from the MMU of either the address translation cache entry that corresponds to a specified logical address or the transparent translation register that corresponds to that address. Whenever the appropriate CI bit is set for either a read or a write access and an external bus cycle is required, $\overline{\text{CIOUT}}$ is asserted and the instruction and data caches are ignored for the access. This signal can also be used by external hardware to inhibit caching in external caches.

Whenever a read access occurs and the required instruction word or data operand is resident in the appropriate on-chip cache (no external bus cycle is required), the MMU is completely ignored, unless an invalid translation resides in the MMU at that time (see next two paragraphs). Therefore, the state of the corresponding CI bits in the MMU are also ignored. The MMU is used to validate all accesses that require external bus cycles; an address translation must be available and valid, protections are checked, and the $\overline{\text{CIOUT}}$ signal is asserted appropriately.

6

An external access is defined as "cachable" for either the instruction or data cache when all the following conditions apply:

- The cache is enabled with the appropriate bit in the CACR set.
- The $\overline{\text{CDIS}}$ signal is negated.
- The $\overline{\text{CIIN}}$ signal is negated for the access.
- The $\overline{\text{CIOUT}}$ signal is negated for the access.
- The MMU validates the access.

Because both the data and instruction caches are referenced by logical addresses, they should be flushed during a task switch or at any time the logical-to-physical address mapping changes, including when the MMU is first enabled. In addition, if a page descriptor is currently marked as valid and is later changed to the invalid type (due to a context switch *or* a page replacement operation) *entries in the on-chip instruction or data cache corresponding to the physical page must be first cleared (invalidated).* Otherwise, if on-chip cache entries are valid for pages with descriptors in memory marked invalid, processor operation is unpredictable.

Data read and write accesses to the same address should also have consistent cachability status to ensure that the data in the cache remains consistent with external memory. For example, if $\overline{\text{CIOUT}}$ is negated for read accesses within a page and the MMU configuration is changed so that $\overline{\text{CIOUT}}$ is subsequently asserted for write accesses within the same page, those write accesses do not update data in the cache, and stale data may result. Similarly, when the MMU maps multiple logical addresses to the same physical address, all accesses to those logical addresses should have the same cachability status.

6.1.1 Instruction Cache

The instruction cache is organized with a line size of four long words, as shown in Figure 6-2. Each of these long words is considered a separate cache entry as each has a separate valid bit. All four entries in a line have the same tag address. Burst filling all four long words can be advantageous when the time spent in filling the line is not long relative to the equivalent bus-cycle time for four nonburst long-word accesses, because of the probability that the contents of memory adjacent to or close to a referenced operand or instruction is also required by subsequent accesses. Dynamic RAMs supporting fast access modes (page, nibble, or static column) are easily employed to support the MC68030 burst mode.

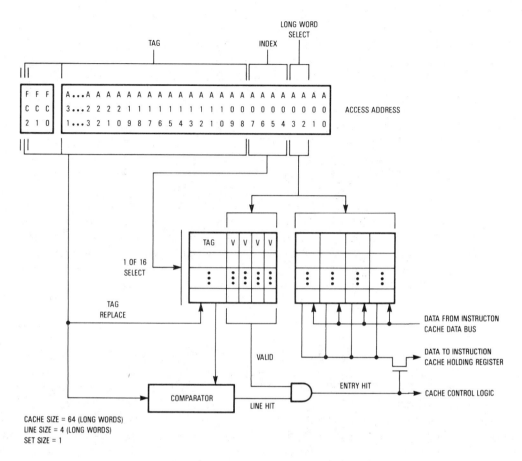

Figure 6-2. On-Chip Instruction Cache Organization

When enabled, the instruction cache is used to store instruction prefetches (instruction words and extension words) as they are requested by the CPU. Instruction prefetches are normally requested from sequential memory addresses except when a change of program flow occurs (e.g., a branch taken) or when an instruction is executed that can modify the status register, in which cases the instruction pipe is automatically flushed and refilled. The output signal REFILL indicates this condition. For more information on the operation of this signal, refer to **SECTION 12 APPLICATIONS INFORMATION**.

In the instruction cache, each of the 16 lines has a tag consisting of the 24 most significant logical address bits, the FC2 function code bit (used to distinguish between user and supervisor accesses), and the four valid bits (one corresponding to each long word). Refer to Figure 6-2 for the instruction cache organization. Address bits A7–A4 select one of 16 lines and its associated tag. The comparator compares the address and function code bits in the selected tag with address bits A31–A8 and FC2 from the internal prefetch request to determine if the requested word is in the cache. A cache hit occurs when there is a tag match and the corresponding valid bit (selected by A3–A2) is set. On a cache hit, the word selected by address bit A1 is supplied to the instruction pipe.

When the address and function code bits do not match or the requested entry is not valid, a miss occurs. The bus controller initiates a long-word prefetch operation for the required instruction word and loads the cache entry, provided the entry is cachable. A burst mode operation may be requested to fill an entire cache line. If the function code and address bits match and the corresponding long word is not valid (but one or more of the other three valid bits for that line are set) a single entry fill operation replaces the required long word only, using a normal prefetch bus cycle or cycles (no burst).

6.1.2 Data Cache

The data cache stores data references to any address space except CPU space (FC = $7), including those references made with PC relative addressing modes and accesses made with the MOVES instruction. Operation of the data cache is similar to that of the instruction cache, except for the address comparison and cache filling operations. The tag of each line in the data cache contains function code bits FC0, FC1, and FC2 in addition to address bits A31–A8. The cache control circuitry selects the tag using bits A7–A4 and compares it to the corresponding bits of the access address to determine if a tag match has occurred. Address bits A3–A2 select the valid bit for the appropriate long word in the cache to determine if an entry hit has occurred. Misaligned data transfers may span two data cache entries. In this case, the processor checks for a hit one entry at a time. Therefore, it is possible that a portion of the access results in a hit and a portion results in a miss. The hit and miss are treated independently. Figure 6-3 illustrates the organization of the data cache.

The operation of the data cache differs for read and write cycles. A data read cycle operates exactly like an instruction cache read cycle; when a miss occurs, an external cycle is initiated to obtain the operand from memory, and the data is loaded into the cache if the access is cachable. In the case of a misaligned operand that spans two cache entries, two long words are required from memory. Burst mode operation may also be initiated to fill an entire line of the data cache. Read accesses from the CPU address space and address translation table search accesses are not stored in the data cache.

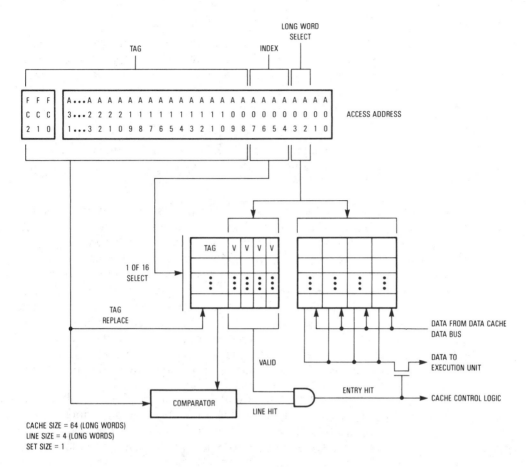

Figure 6-3. On-Chip Data Cache Organization

The data cache on the MC68030 is a writethrough cache. When a hit occurs on a write cycle, the data is written both to the cache and to external memory (provided the MMU validates the access), regardless of the operand size and even if the cache is frozen. If the MMU determines that the access is invalid, the write is aborted, the corresponding entry is invalidated, and a bus error exception is taken. Since the write to the cache completes before the write to external memory, the cache contains the new value even if the external write terminates in a bus error. The value in the data cache might be used by another instruction before the external write cycle has completed, although this should not have any adverse consequences. Refer to **7.6 BUS SYNCHRONIZATION** for the details of bus synchronization.

6.1.2.1 WRITE ALLOCATION. The supervisor program can configure the data cache for either of two types of allocation for data cache entries that miss on write cycles. The state of the write allocation (WA) bit in the cache control register specifies either no write allocation or write allocation with partial validation of the data entries in the cache on writes.

When no write allocation is selected (WA = 0), write cycles that miss do not alter the data cache contents. In this mode, the processor does not replace entries in the cache during write operations. The cache is updated only during a write hit.

When write allocation is selected (WA = 1), the processor always updates the data cache on cachable write cycles, but only validates an updated entry that hits or an entry that is updated with long-word data that is long-word aligned. When a tag miss occurs on a write of long-word data that is long-word aligned, the corresponding tag is replaced, and only the long word being written is marked as valid. The other three entries in the cache line are invalidated when a tag miss occurs on a misaligned long-word write or on a byte or word write, the data is not written in the cache, the tag is unaltered, and the valid bit(s) are cleared. Thus, an aligned long-word data write may replace a previously valid entry; whereas, a misaligned data write or a write of data that is not long word may invalidate a previously valid entry or entries.

Write allocation eliminates stale data that may reside in the cache because of either of two unique situations: multiple mapping of two or more logical addresses to one physical address within the same task or allowing the same physical location to be accessed by both supervisor and user mode cycles. Stale data conditions can arise when operating in the no-write-allocation mode and all the following conditions are satisfied:

- Multiple mapping (object aliasing) is allowed by the operating system.
- A read cycle loads a value for an "aliased" physical address into the data cache.
- A write cycle occurs, referencing the same aliased physical object as above but using a different logical address, causing a cache miss and no update to the cache (has the same page offset).
- The physical object is then read using the first alias, which provides stale data from the cache.

In this case, the data in the cache no longer matches that in physical memory and is stale. Since the write-allocation mode updates the cache during write cycles, the data in the cache remains consistent with physical memory. Note that when CIOUT is asserted, the data cache is completely ignored, even on write cycles operating in the write-allocation mode. Also note that since the CIIN signal is ignored on write cycles, cache entries may be created for noncachable data (when CIIN is asserted on a write) when operating in the write-allocation mode. Figure 6-4 shows the manner in which each mode operates in five different situations.

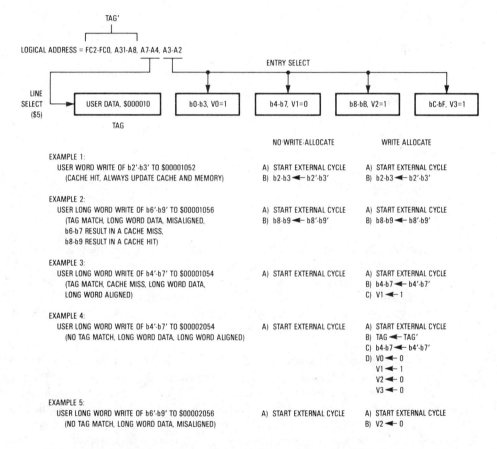

Figure 6-4. No-Write-Allocation and Write-Allocation Mode Examples

6.1.2.2 READ-MODIFY-WRITE ACCESSES. The read portion of a read-modify-write cycle is always forced to miss in the data cache. However, if the system allows internal caching of read-modify-write cycle operands ($\overline{\text{CIOUT}}$ and $\overline{\text{CIIN}}$ both negated), the processor either uses the data read from memory to update a matching entry in the data cache or creates a new entry with the read data in the case of no matching entry. The write portion of a read-modify-write operation also updates a matching entry in the data cache. In the case of a cache miss on the write, the allocation of a new cache entry for the data being written is controlled by the WA bit. Table search accesses, however, are completely ignored by the data cache; it is never updated for a table search access.

6.1.3 Cache Filling

The bus controller can load either cache in either of two ways:

- Single entry mode
- Burst fill mode

In the single entry mode, the bus controller loads a single long-word entry of a cache line. In the burst fill mode, an entire line (four long words) can be filled. Refer to **SECTION 7 BUS OPERATION** for detailed information about the bus cycles required for both modes.

6.1.3.1 SINGLE ENTRY MODE. When a cachable access is initiated and a burst mode operation is not requested by the MC68030 or is not supported by external hardware, the bus controller transfers a single long word for the corresponding cache entry. An entire long word is required. If the port size of the responding device is smaller than 32 bits, the MC68030 executes all bus cycles necessary to fill the long word.

When a device cannot supply its entire port width of data, regardless of the size of the transfer, the responding device must consistently assert the cache inhibit input ($\overline{\text{CIIN}}$) signal. For example, a 32-bit port must always supply 32 bits, even for 8- and 16-bit transfers; a 16-bit port must supply 16 bits, even for 8-bit transfers. The MC68030 assumes that a 32-bit termination signal for the bus cycle indicates availability of 32 valid data bits, even if only 16 or 8 bits are requested. Similarly, the processor assumes that a 16-bit termination signal indicates that all 16 bits are valid. If the device cannot supply its full port width of data, it must assert $\overline{\text{CIIN}}$ for all bus cycles corresponding to a cache entry.

When a cachable read cycle provides data with both $\overline{\text{CIIN}}$ and $\overline{\text{BERR}}$ negated, the MC68030 attempts to fill the cache entry. Figure 6-5 shows the organization of a line of data in the caches. The notation b0, b1, b2, and so forth identifies the bytes within the line. For each entry in the line, a valid bit in the associated tag corresponds to a long-word entry to be loaded. Since a single valid bit applies to an entire long word, a single entry mode operation must provide a full 32 bits of data. Ports less than 32 bits wide require several read cycles for each entry.

Figure 6-5 shows an example of a byte data operand read cycle starting at byte address $03 from an 8-bit port. Provided the data item is cachable, this operation results in four bus cycles. The first cycle requested by the MC68030 reads a byte from address $03. The 8-bit $\overline{\text{DSACKx}}$ response causes the MC68030 to fetch the remainder of the long word starting at address $00. The bytes are latched in the following order: b3, b0, b1, and b2. Note that during cache loading operations, devices must indicate the same port size consistently throughout all cycles for that long-word entry in the cache.

Figure 6-6 shows the access of a byte data operand from a 16-bit port. This operation requires two read cycles. The first cycle requests the byte at address $03. If the device responds with a 16-bit $\overline{\text{DSACKx}}$ encoding, the word at address $02 (including the requested byte) is accepted by the MC68030. The second cycle requests the word at address $00. Since the device again responds with a 16-bit $\overline{\text{DSACKx}}$ encoding, the remaining two bytes of the long word are latched, and the cache entry is filled.

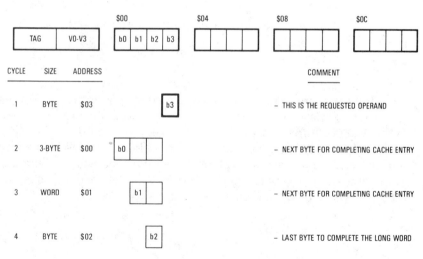

Figure 6-5. Single Entry Mode Operation — 8-Bit Port

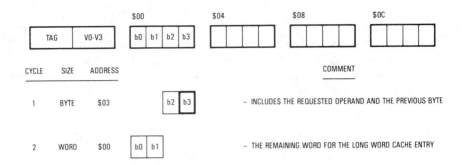

Figure 6-6. Single Entry Mode Operation — 16-Bit Port

With a 32-bit port, the same operation is shown in Figure 6-7. Only one read cycle is required. All four bytes (including the requested byte) are latched during the cycle.

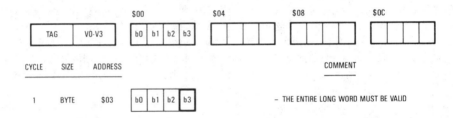

Figure 6-7. Single Entry Mode Operation — 32-Bit Port

If a requested access is misaligned and spans two cache entries, the bus controller attempts to fill both associated long-word cache entries. An example of this is an operand request for a long word on an odd-word boundary. The MC68030 first fetches the initial byte(s) of the operand (residing in the first long word) and then requests the remaining bytes to fill that cache entry (if the port size is less than 32 bits) before it requests the remainder of the operand and corresponding long word to fill the second cache entry. If the port size is 32 bits, the processor performs two accesses, one for each cache entry.

Figure 6-8 shows a misaligned access of a long word at address $06 from an 8-bit port requiring eight bus cycles to complete. Reading this long-word operand requires eight read cycles, since accesses to all eight addresses return 8-bit port-size encodings. These cycles fetch the two cache entries that the requested long-word spans. The first cycle requests a long word at address $06 and accepts the first requested byte (b6). The subsequent transfers of the first long word are performed in the following order: b7, b4, b5. The remaining four read cycles transfer the four bytes of the second cache entry. The sequence of access for the entire operation is b6, b7, b4, b5, b8, b9, bA, and bB.

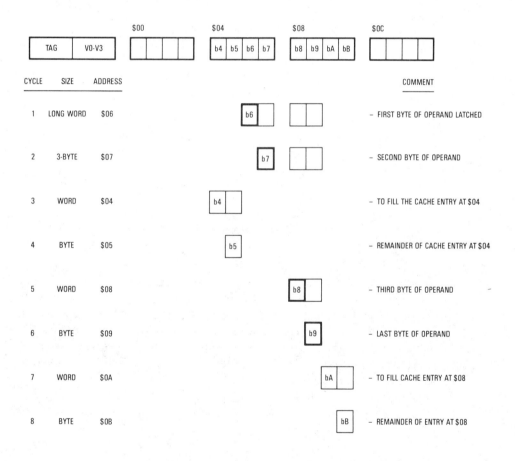

Figure 6-8. Single Entry Mode Operation —
Misaligned Long Word and 8-Bit Port

The next example, shown in Figure 6-9, is a read of a misaligned long-word operand from devices that return 16-bit $\overline{\text{DSACKx}}$ encodings. The processor accepts the first portion of the operand, the word from address $06, and requests a word from address $04 to fill the cache entry. Next, the processor reads the word at address $08, the second portion of the operand, and stores it in the cache also. Finally, the processor accesses the word at $0A to fill the second long-word cache entry.

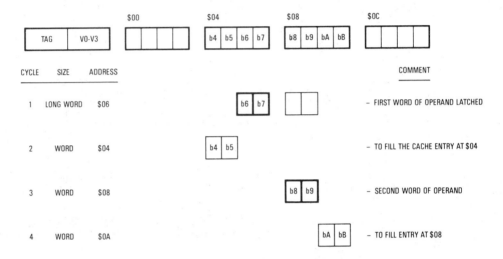

**Figure 6-9. Single Entry Mode Operation —
Misaligned Long Word and 16-Bit Port**

Two read cycles are required for a misaligned long-word operand transfer from devices that return 32-bit $\overline{\text{DSACKx}}$ encodings. As shown in Figure 6-10, the first read cycle requests the long word at address $06 and latches the long word at address $04. The second read cycle requests and latches the long word corresponding to the second cache entry at address $08. Two read cycles are also required if $\overline{\text{STERM}}$ is used to indicate a 32-bit port instead of the 32-bit $\overline{\text{DSACKx}}$ encoding.

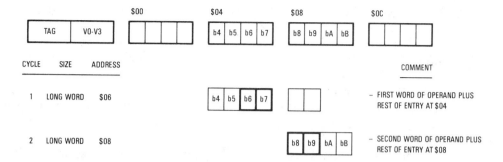

**Figure 6-10. Single Entry Mode Operation —
Misaligned Long Word and 32-Bit $\overline{\text{DSACKx}}$ Port**

If all bytes of a long word are cachable, $\overline{\text{CIIN}}$ must be negated for all bus cycles required to fill the entry. If any byte is not cachable, $\overline{\text{CIIN}}$ must be asserted for all corresponding bus cycles. The assertion of the $\overline{\text{CIIN}}$ signal prevents the caches from being updated during read cycles. Write cycles (including the write portion of a read-modify-write cycle) ignore the assertion of the $\overline{\text{CIIN}}$ signal and may cause the data cache to be altered, depending on the state of the cache (whether or not the write cycle hits), the state of the WA bit in the CACR, and the conditions indicated by the MMU.

The occurrence of a bus error while attempting to load a cache entry aborts the entry fill operation but does not necessarily cause a bus error exception. If the bus error occurs on a read cycle for a portion of the required operand (not the remaining bytes of the cache entry) to be loaded into the data cache, the processor immediately takes a bus error exception. If the read cycle in error is made only to fill the data cache (the data is not part of the target operand), no exception occurs, but the corresponding entry is marked invalid. For the instruction cache, the processor marks the entry as invalid, but only takes an exception if the execution unit attempts to use the instruction word(s).

6.1.3.2 BURST MODE FILLING. Burst mode filling is enabled by bits in the cache control register. The data burst enable bit must be set to enable burst filling of the data cache. Similarly, the instruction burst enable bit must be set to enable burst filling of the instruction cache. When burst filling is enabled and the corresponding cache is enabled, the bus controller requests a burst mode fill operation in either of these cases:

- A read cycle for either the instruction or data cache misses due to the indexed tag not matching.

- A read cycle tag matches, but all long words in the line are invalid.

The bus controller requests a burst mode fill operation by asserting the cache burst request signal ($\overline{\text{CBREQ}}$). The responding device may sequentially supply one to four long words of cachable data, or it may assert the cache inhibit input signal ($\overline{\text{CIIN}}$) when the data in a long word is not cachable. If the responding device does not support the burst mode and it terminates cycles with $\overline{\text{STERM}}$, it should not acknowledge the request with the assertion of the cache burst acknowledge ($\overline{\text{CBACK}}$) signal. The MC68030 ignores the assertion of $\overline{\text{CBACK}}$ during cycles terminated with $\overline{\text{DSACKx}}$.

The cache burst request signal ($\overline{\text{CBREQ}}$) requests burst mode operation from the referenced external device. To operate in the burst mode, the device or external hardware must be able to increment the low-order address bits if required, and the current cycle must be a 32-bit synchronous transfer ($\overline{\text{STERM}}$ must be asserted) as described in **SECTION 7 BUS OPERATION**. The device must also assert $\overline{\text{CBACK}}$ (at the same time as $\overline{\text{STERM}}$) at the end of the cycle in which the MC68030 asserts $\overline{\text{CBREQ}}$. $\overline{\text{CBACK}}$ causes the processor to continue driving the address and bus control signals and to latch a new data value for the next cache entry at the completion of each subsequent cycle (as defined by $\overline{\text{STERM}}$), for a total of up to four cycles (until four long words have been read).

When a cache burst is initiated, the first cycle attempts to load the cache entry corresponding to the instruction word or data item explicitly requested by the execution unit. The subsequent cycles are for the subsequent entries in the cache line. In the case of a misaligned transfer when the operand spans two cache entries within a cache line, the first cycle corresponds to the cache entry containing the portion of the operand at the lower address.

Figure 6-11 illustrates the four cycles of a burst operation and shows that the second, third, and fourth cycles are run in burst mode. A distinction is made between the first cycle of a burst operation and the subsequent cycles because the first cycle is requested by the microsequencer and the burst fill cycles are requested by the bus controller. Therefore, when data from the first cycle is returned, it is immediately available for the execution unit (EU). However, data from the burst fill cycles is not available to the EU until the burst operation is complete. Since the microsequencer makes two separate requests for misaligned data operands, only the first portion of the misaligned operand returned during a burst operation is available to the EU after the first cycle is complete. The microsequencer must wait for the burst operation to complete before requesting the second portion of the operand. Normally, the request for the second portion results in a data cache hit unless the second cycle of the burst operation terminates abnormally.

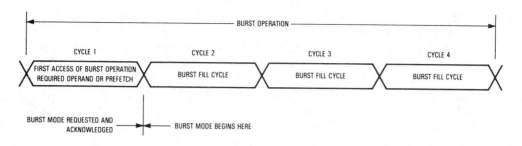

Figure 6-11. Burst Operation Cycles and Burst Mode

The bursting mechanism allows addresses to wrap around so that the entire four long words in the cache line can be filled in a single burst operation, regardless of the initial address and operand alignment. Depending on the structure of the external memory system, address bits A2 and A3 may have to be incremented externally to select the long words in the proper order for loading into the cache. The MC68030 holds the entire address bus constant for the duration of the burst cycle. Figure 6-12 shows an example of this address wraparound. The initial cycle is a long-word access from address $6. Because the responding device returns $\overline{CBACK}$ and $\overline{STERM}$ (signaling a 32-bit port), the entire long word at base address $04 is transferred. Since the initial address is $06 when $\overline{CBREQ}$ is asserted, the next entry to be burst filled into the cache should correspond to address $08, then $0C, and last, $00. This addressing is compatible with existing nibble-mode dynamic RAMs, and can be supported by page and static column modes with an external modulo 4 counter for A2 and A3.

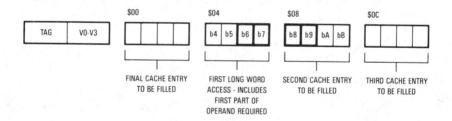

Figure 6-12. Burst Filling Wraparound Example

The MC68030 does not assert $\overline{\text{CBREQ}}$ during the first portion of a misaligned access if the remainder of the access does not correspond to the same cache line. Figure 6-13 shows an example in which the first portion of a misaligned access is at address $0F. With a 32-bit port, the first access corresponds to the cache entry at address $0C, which is filled using a single-entry load operation. The second access, at address $10 corresponding to the second cache line, requests a burst fill and the processor asserts $\overline{\text{CBREQ}}$. During this burst operation, long words $10, $14, $18, and $1C are all filled in that order.

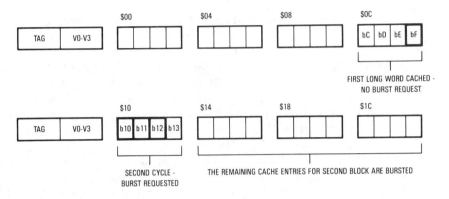

Figure 6-13. Deferred Burst Filling Example

The processor does not assert $\overline{\text{CBREQ}}$ if any of the following conditions exist:

- The appropriate cache is not enabled
- Burst filling for the cache is not enabled
- The cache freeze bit for the appropriate cache is set
- The current operation is the read portion of a read-modify-write operation
- The MMU has inhibited caching for the current page
- The cycle is for the first access of an operand that spans two cache lines (crosses a modulo 16 boundary)

Additionally, the assertion of $\overline{\text{CIIN}}$ and $\overline{\text{BERR}}$ and the premature negation of $\overline{\text{CBACK}}$ affect burst operation as described in the following paragraphs.

The assertion of $\overline{\text{CIIN}}$ during the first cycle of a burst operation causes the data to be latched by the processor, and if the requested operand is aligned (the entire operand is latched in the first cycle), the data is passed on to the instruction pipe or execution unit. However, the data is not loaded into its corresponding cache. In addition, the MC68030 negates $\overline{\text{CBREQ}}$, and the burst operation is aborted. If a portion of the requested operand remains to be read (due to misalignment), a second read cycle is initiated at the appropriate address with $\overline{\text{CBREQ}}$ negated.

The assertion of $\overline{\text{CIIN}}$ during the second, third, or fourth cycle of a burst operation prevents the data during that cycle from being loaded into the appropriate cache and causes $\overline{\text{CBREQ}}$ to negate, aborting the burst operation. However, if the data for the cycle contains part of the requested operand, the execution unit uses that data.

The premature negation of the $\overline{\text{CBACK}}$ signal during the burst operation causes the current cycle to complete normally, loading the data successfully transferred into the appropriate cache. However, the burst operation aborts and $\overline{\text{CBREQ}}$ negates.

A bus error occurring during a burst operation also causes the burst operation to abort. If the bus error occurs during the first cycle of a burst (i.e., before burst mode is entered), the data read from the bus is ignored, and the entire associated cache line is marked "invalid". If the access is a data cycle, exception processing proceeds immediately. If the cycle is for an instruction fetch, a bus error exception is made pending. This bus error is processed only if the execution unit attempts to use either instruction word. Refer to **11.2.2 Instruction Pipe** for more information about pipeline operation.

For either cache, when a bus error occurs after the burst mode has been entered (that is, on the second cycle or later), the cache entry corresponding to that cycle is marked invalid, but the processor does not take an exception (the microsequencer has not yet requested the data). In the case of an instruction cache burst, the data from the aborted cycle is completely ignored. Pending instruction prefetches are still pending and are subsequently run by the processor. If the second cycle is for a portion of a misaligned data operand fetch and a bus error occurs, the processor terminates the burst operation and negates $\overline{\text{CBREQ}}$. Once the burst terminates, the microsequencer requests a read cycle for the second portion. Since the burst terminated abnormally for the second cycle of the burst, the data cache results in a miss, and a second external cycle is required. If $\overline{\text{BERR}}$ is again asserted, the MC68030 then takes an exception.

On the initial access of a burst operation, a "retry" (indicated by the assertion of $\overline{BERR}$ and $\overline{HALT}$) causes the processor to retry the bus cycle and assert $\overline{CBREQ}$ again. However, signaling a retry with simultaneous $\overline{BERR}$ and $\overline{HALT}$ during the second, third, or fourth cycle of a burst operation does not cause a retry operation, even if the requested operand is misaligned. Assertion of $\overline{BERR}$ and $\overline{HALT}$ during burst fill cycles of a burst operation causes independent bus error and halt operations. The processor remains halted until $\overline{HALT}$ is negated, and then handles the bus error as described in the previous paragraphs.

6.2 CACHE RESET

When a hardware reset of the processor occurs, all valid bits of both caches are cleared. The cache enable bits, burst enable bits, and the freeze bits in the cache control register (CACR) for both caches (refer to Figure 6-14) are also cleared, effectively disabling both caches. The WA bit in the CACR is also cleared.

6.3 CACHE CONTROL

Only the MC68030 cache control circuitry can directly access the cache arrays, but the supervisor program can set bits in the CACR to exercise control over cache operations. The supervisor also has access to the cache address register (CAAR), which contains the address for a cache entry to be cleared.

6.3.1 Cache Control Register

The CACR, shown in Figure 6-14, is a 32-bit register that can be written or read by the MOVEC instruction or indirectly modified by a reset. Five of the bits (4–0) control the instruction cache; six other bits (13–8) control the data cache. Each cache is controlled independently of the other, although a similar operation can be performed for both caches by a single MOVEC instruction. For example, loading a long word in which bits 3 and 11 are set into the CACR clears both caches. Bits 31–14 and 7–5 are reserved for Motorola definition. They are currently read as zeros and are ignored when written. For future compatibility, writes should not set these bits.

31		14	13	12	11	10	9	8	7	6	5	4	3	2	1	0
0 0 0 0 0 0 0 0 0 0 0 0 0 0 0 0 0 0			WA	DBE	CD	CED	FD	ED	0	0	0	IBE	CI	CEI	FI	EI

WA = Write Allocate
DBE = Data Burst Enable
CD = Clear Data Cache
CED = Clear Entry in Data Cache
FD = Freeze Data Cache
ED = Enable Data Cache
IBE = Instruction Burst Enable
CI = Clear Instruction Cache
CEI = Clear Entry in Instruction Cache
FI = Freeze Instruction Cache
EI = Enable Instruction Cache

Figure 6-14. Cache Control Register

6.3.1.1 WRITE ALLOCATE. Bit 13, the WA bit, is set to select the write-allocation mode (refer to **6.1.2.1 WRITE ALLOCATION**) for write cycles. Clearing this bit selects the no-write-allocation mode. A reset operation clears this bit. The supervisor should set this bit when it shares data with the user task or when any task maps multiple logical addresses to one physical address. If the data cache is disabled or frozen, the WA bit is ignored.

6.3.1.2 DATA BURST ENABLE. Bit 12, the DBE bit, is set to enable burst filling of the data cache. Operating systems and other software set this bit when burst filling of the data cache is desired. A reset operation clears the DBE bit.

6.3.1.3 CLEAR DATA CACHE. Bit 11, the CD bit, is set to clear all entries in the data cache. Operating systems and other software set this bit to clear data from the cache prior to a context switch. The processor clears all valid bits in the data cache at the time a MOVEC instruction loads a one into the CD bit of the CACR. The CD bit is always read as a zero.

6.3.1.4 CLEAR ENTRY IN DATA CACHE. Bit 10, the CED bit, is set to clear an entry in the data cache. The index field of the CAAR (see Figure 6-15) corresponding to the index and long-word select portion of an address specifies the entry to be cleared. The processor clears only the specified long word by clearing the valid bit for the entry at the time a MOVEC instruction loads a one into the CED bit of the CACR, regardless of the states of the ED and FD bits. The CED bit is always read as a zero.

6.3.1.5 FREEZE DATA CACHE. Bit 9, the FD bit, is set to freeze the data cache. When the FD bit is set and a miss occurs during a read or write of the data cache, the indexed entry is not replaced. However, write cycles that hit in the data cache cause the entry to be updated even when the cache is frozen. When the FD bit is clear, a miss in the data cache during a read cycle causes the entry (or line) to be filled, and the filling of entries on writes that miss are then controlled by the WA bit. A reset operation clears the FD bit.

6.3.1.6 ENABLE DATA CACHE. Bit 8, the ED bit, is set to enable the data cache. When it is cleared, the data cache is disabled. A reset operation clears the ED bit. The supervisor normally enables the data cache, but it can clear ED for system debugging or emulation, as required. Disabling the data cache does not flush the entries. If it is enabled again, the previously valid entries remain valid and can be used.

6.3.1.7 INSTRUCTION BURST ENABLE. Bit 4, the IBE bit, is set to enable burst filling of the instruction cache. Operating systems and other software set this bit when burst filling of the instruction cache is desired. A reset operation clears the IBE bit.

6.3.1.8 CLEAR INSTRUCTION CACHE. Bit 3, the CI bit, is set to clear all entries in the instruction cache. Operating systems and other software set this bit to clear instructions from the cache prior to a context switch. The processor clears all valid bits in the instruction cache at the time a MOVEC instruction loads a one into the CI bit of the CACR. The CI bit is always read as a zero.

6.3.1.9 CLEAR ENTRY IN INSTRUCTION CACHE. Bit 2, the CEI bit, is set to clear an entry in the instruction cache. The index field of the CAAR (see Figure 6-15) corresponding to the index and long-word select portion of an address specifies the entry to be cleared. The processor clears only the specified long word by clearing the valid bit for the entry at the time a MOVEC instruction loads a one into the CEI bit of the CACR, regardless of the states of the EI and FI bits. The CEI bit is always read as a zero.

6.3.1.10 FREEZE INSTRUCTION CACHE. Bit 1, the FI bit, is set to freeze the instruction cache. When the FI bit is set and a miss occurs in the instruction cache, the entry (or line) is not replaced. When the FI bit is cleared to zero, a miss in the instruction cache causes the entry (or line) to be filled. A reset operation clears the FI bit.

6.3.1.11 ENABLE INSTRUCTION CACHE. Bit 0, the EI bit, is set to enable the instruction cache. When it is cleared, the instruction cache is disabled. A reset operation clears the EI bit. The supervisor normally enables the instruction cache, but it can clear EI for system debugging or emulation, as required. Disabling the instruction cache does not flush the entries. If it is enabled again, the previously valid entries remain valid and may be used.

6.3.2 Cache Address Register

The CAAR is a 32-bit register shown in Figure 6-15. The index field (bits 7–2) contains the address for the "clear cache entry" operations. The bits of this field correspond to bits 7–2 of addresses; they specify the index and a long word of a cache line. Although only the index field is used currently, all 32 bits of the register are implemented and are reserved for use by Motorola.

Figure 6-15. Cache Address Register

SECTION 7
BUS OPERATION

This section provides a functional description of the bus, the signals that control it, and the bus cycles provided for data transfer operations. It also describes the error and halt conditions, bus arbitration, and the reset operation. Operation of the bus is the same whether the processor or an external device is the bus master; the names and descriptions of bus cycles are from the point of view of the bus master. For exact timing specifications, refer to **SECTION 13 ELECTRICAL CHARACTERISTICS**.

The MC68030 architecture supports byte, word, and long-word operands, allowing access to 8-, 16-, and 32-bit data ports through the use of asynchronous cycles controlled by the data transfer and size acknowledge inputs ($\overline{\text{DSACK0}}$ and $\overline{\text{DSACK1}}$).

Synchronous bus cycles controlled by the synchronous termination signal ($\overline{\text{STERM}}$) can only be used to transfer data to and from 32-bit ports.

The MC68030 allows byte, word, and long-word operands to be located in memory on any byte boundary. For a misaligned transfer, more than one bus cycle may be required to complete the transfer, regardless of port size. For a port less than 32 bits wide, multiple bus cycles may be required for an operand transfer due to either misalignment or a port width smaller than the operand size. Instruction words and their associated extension words must be aligned on word boundaries. The user should be aware that misalignment of word or long-word operands can cause the MC68030 to perform multiple bus cycles for the operand transfer; therefore, processor performance is optimized if word and long-word memory operands are aligned on word or long-word boundaries, respectively.

7.1 BUS TRANSFER SIGNALS

The bus transfers information between the MC68030 and an external memory, coprocessor, or peripheral device. External devices can accept or provide 8 bits, 16 bits, or 32 bits in parallel and must follow the handshake protocol described in this section. The maximum number of bits accepted or provided during a bus transfer is defined as the port width. The MC68030 contains an address bus that specifies the address for the transfer and a data bus that transfers the data. Control signals indicate the beginning of the cycle, the address space and the size of the transfer, and the type of cycle. The selected device then controls the length of the cycle with the signal(s) used to terminate the cycle. Strobe signals, one for the address bus and another for the data bus, indicate the validity of the address and provide timing information for the data.

The bus can operate in an asynchronous mode identical to the MC68020 bus for any port width. The bus and control input signals used for asynchronous operation are internally synchronized to the MC68030 clock, introducing a delay. This delay is the time period required for the MC68030 to sample an asynchronous input signal, synchronize the input to the internal clocks of the processor, and determine whether it is high or low. Figure 7-1 shows the relationship between the clock signal and the associated internal signal of a typical asynchronous input.

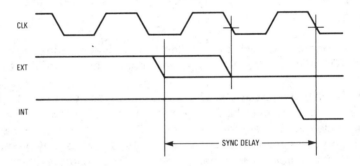

Figure 7-1. Relationship between External and Internal Signals

Furthermore, for all asynchronous inputs, the processor latches the level of the input during a sample window around the falling edge of the clock signal. This window is illustrated in Figure 7-2. To ensure that an input signal is recognized on a specific falling edge of the clock, that input must be stable during the sample window. If an input makes a transition during the window time period, the level recognized by the processor is not predictable; however, the processor always resolves the latched level to either a logic high or low before using it. In addition to meeting input setup and hold times for deterministic operation, all input signals must obey the protocols described in this section.

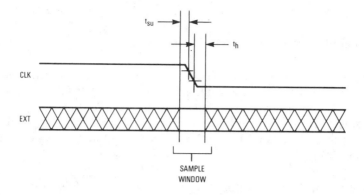

Figure 7-2. Asynchronous Input Sample Window

A device with a 32-bit port size can also provide a synchronous mode transfer. In synchronous operation, input signals are externally synchronized to the processor clock, and the synchronizing delay is not incurred.

Synchronous inputs ($\overline{\text{STERM}}$, $\overline{\text{CBACK}}$, and $\overline{\text{CIIN}}$) must remain stable during a sample window for all rising edges of the clock during a bus cycle (i.e., while address strobe ($\overline{\text{AS}}$) is asserted), regardless of when the signals are asserted or negated, to ensure proper operation. This sample window is defined by the synchronous input setup and hold times (see MC68030EC/D, *MC68030 Electrical Specifications*).

7.1.1 Bus Control Signals

The external cycle start ($\overline{\text{ECS}}$) signal is the earliest indication that the processor is initiating a bus cycle. The MC68030 initiates a bus cycle by driving the address, size, function code, read/write, and cache inhibit-out outputs and by asserting $\overline{\text{ECS}}$. However, if the processor finds the required program or data item in an on-chip cache, if a miss occurs in the address translation cache (ATC) of the memory management unit (MMU), or if the MMU finds a fault with the access, the processor aborts the cycle before asserting $\overline{\text{AS}}$. $\overline{\text{ECS}}$ can be used to initiate various timing sequences that are eventually qualified with $\overline{\text{AS}}$. Qualification with $\overline{\text{AS}}$ may be required since, in the case of an internal cache hit, an ATC miss, or an MMU fault, a bus cycle may be aborted after $\overline{\text{ECS}}$ has been asserted. The assertion of $\overline{\text{AS}}$ ensures that the cycle has not been aborted by these internal conditions.

During the first external bus cycle of an operand transfer, the operand cycle start ($\overline{\text{OCS}}$) signal is asserted with $\overline{\text{ECS}}$. When several bus cycles are required to transfer the entire operand, $\overline{OCS}$ is asserted only at the beginning of the first external bus cycle. With respect to $\overline{OCS}$, an "operand" is any entity required by the execution unit, whether a program or data item.

The function code signals (FC0–FC2) are also driven at the beginning of a bus cycle. These three signals select one of eight address spaces (refer to Table 4-1) to which the address applies. Five address spaces are presently defined. Of the remaining three, one is reserved for user definition and two are reserved by Motorola for future use. The function code signals are valid while $\overline{AS}$ is asserted.

At the beginning of a bus cycle, the size signals (SIZ0 and SIZ1) are driven along with $\overline{ECS}$ and the FC0–FC2. SIZ0 and SIZ1 indicate the number of bytes remaining to be transferred during an operand cycle (consisting of one or more bus cycles) or during a cache fill operation from a device with a port size that is less than 32 bits. Table 7-2 shows the encoding of SIZ0 and SIZ1. These signals are valid while $\overline{AS}$ is asserted.

The read/write (R/$\overline{W}$) signal determines the direction of the transfer during a bus cycle. This signal changes state, when required, at the beginning of a bus cycle and is valid while $\overline{AS}$ is asserted. R/$\overline{W}$ only transitions when a write cycle is preceded by a read cycle or vice versa. The signal may remain low for two consecutive write cycles.

The read-modify-write cycle signal ($\overline{RMC}$) is asserted at the beginning of the first bus cycle of a read-modify-write operation and remains asserted until completion of the final bus cycle of the operation. The $\overline{RMC}$ signal is guaranteed to be negated before the end of state 0 for a bus cycle following a read-modify-write operation.

7.1.2 Address Bus

The address bus signals (A0–A31) define the address of the byte (or the most significant byte) to be transferred during a bus cycle. The processor places the address on the bus at the beginning of a bus cycle. The address is valid while $\overline{AS}$ is asserted.

7.1.3 Address Strobe

$\overline{AS}$ is a timing signal that indicates the validity of an address on the address bus and of many control signals. It is asserted one-half clock after the beginning of a bus cycle.

7.1.4 Data Bus

The data bus signals (D0–D31) comprise a bidirectional, nonmultiplexed parallel bus that contains the data being transferred to or from the processor. A read or write operation may transfer 8, 16, 24, or 32 bits of data (one, two, three, or four bytes) in one bus cycle. During a read cycle, the data is latched by the processor on the last falling edge of the clock for that bus cycle. For a write cycle, all 32 bits of the data bus are driven, regardless of the port width or operand size. The processor places the data on the data bus one-half clock cycle after $\overline{AS}$ is asserted in a write cycle.

7.1.5 Data Strobe

The data strobe ($\overline{DS}$) is a timing signal that applies to the data bus. For a read cycle, the processor asserts $\overline{DS}$ to signal the external device to place data on the bus. It is asserted at the same time as $\overline{AS}$ during a read cycle. For a write cycle, $\overline{DS}$ signals to the external device that the data to be written is valid on the bus. The processor asserts $\overline{DS}$ one full clock cycle after the assertion of $\overline{AS}$ during a write cycle.

7.1.6 Data Buffer Enable

The data buffer enable signal ($\overline{DBEN}$) can be used to enable external data buffers while data is present on the data bus. During a read operation, $\overline{DBEN}$ is asserted one clock cycle after the beginning of the bus cycle and is negated as $\overline{DS}$ is negated. In a write operation, $\overline{DBEN}$ is asserted at the time $\overline{AS}$ is asserted and is held active for the duration of the cycle. In a synchronous system supporting two-clock bus cycles, $\overline{DBEN}$ timing may prevent its use.

7.1.7 Bus Cycle Termination Signals

During asynchronous bus cycles, external devices assert the data transfer and size acknowledge signals ($\overline{DSACK0}$ and/or $\overline{DSACK1}$) as part of the bus protocol. During a read cycle, the assertion of $\overline{DSACKx}$ signals the processor to terminate the bus cycle and to latch the data. During a write cycle, the assertion of $\overline{DSACKx}$ indicates that the external device has successfully stored the data and that the cycle may terminate. These signals also indicate to the processor the size of the port for the bus cycle just completed, as shown in Table 7-1. Refer to **7.3.1 Asynchronous Read Cycle** for timing relationships of $\overline{DSACK0}$ and $\overline{DSACK1}$.

For synchronous bus cycles, external devices assert the synchronous termination signal ($\overline{\text{STERM}}$) as part of the bus protocol. During a read cycle, the assertion of $\overline{\text{STERM}}$ causes the processor to latch the data. During a write cycle, it indicates that the external device has successfully stored the data. In either case, it terminates the cycle and indicates that the transfer was made to a 32-bit port. Refer to **7.3.2 Asynchronous Write Cycle** for timing relationships of $\overline{\text{STERM}}$.

The bus error ($\overline{\text{BERR}}$) signal is also a bus cycle termination indicator and can be used in the absence of $\overline{\text{DSACKx}}$ or $\overline{\text{STERM}}$ to indicate a bus error condition. It can also be asserted in conjunction with $\overline{\text{DSACKx}}$ or $\overline{\text{STERM}}$ to indicate a bus error condition, provided it meets the appropriate timing described in this section and in MC68030EC/D, *MC68030 Electrical Specifications*. Additionally, the $\overline{\text{BERR}}$ and $\overline{\text{HALT}}$ signals can be asserted together to indicate a retry termination. Again, the $\overline{\text{BERR}}$ and $\overline{\text{HALT}}$ signals can be asserted simultaneously in lieu of or in conjunction with the $\overline{\text{DSACKx}}$ or $\overline{\text{STERM}}$ signals.

Finally, the autovector ($\overline{\text{AVEC}}$) signal can be used to terminate interrupt acknowledge cycles, indicating that the MC68030 should internally generate a vector number to locate an interrupt handler routine. $\overline{\text{AVEC}}$ is ignored during all other bus cycles.

7.2 DATA TRANSFER MECHANISM

The MC68030 architecture supports byte, word, and long-word operands allowing access to 8-, 16-, and 32-bit data ports through the use of asynchronous cycles controlled by $\overline{\text{DSACK0}}$ and $\overline{\text{DSACK1}}$. It also supports synchronous bus cycles to and from 32-bit ports, terminated by $\overline{\text{STERM}}$. Byte, word, and long-word operands can be located on any byte boundary, but misaligned transfers may require additional bus cycles, regardless of port size.

When the processor requests a burst mode fill operation, it asserts the cache burst request ($\overline{\text{CBREQ}}$) signal to attempt to fill four entries within a line in one of the on-chip caches. This mode is compatible with nibble, static column, or page mode dynamic RAMs. The burst fill operation uses synchronous bus cycles, each terminated by $\overline{\text{STERM}}$, to fetch as many as four long words.

7.2.1 Dynamic Bus Sizing

The MC68030 dynamically interprets the port size of the addressed device during each bus cycle, allowing operand transfers to or from 8-, 16-, and 32-bit ports. During an asynchronous operand transfer cycle, the slave device signals its port size (byte, word, or long word) and indicates completion of the bus cycle to the processor through the use of the $\overline{\text{DSACKx}}$ inputs. Refer to Table 7-1 for $\overline{\text{DSACKx}}$ encodings and assertion results.

Table 7-1. $\overline{\text{DSACK}}$ Codes and Results

$\overline{\text{DSACK1}}$	$\overline{\text{DSACK0}}$	Result
H	H	Insert Wait States in Current Bus Cycle
H	L	Complete Cycle — Data Bus Port Size is 8 Bits
L	H	Complete Cycle — Data Bus Port Size is 16 Bits
L	L	Complete Cycle — Data Bus Port Size is 32 Bits

For example, if the processor is executing an instruction that reads a long-word operand from a long-word aligned address, it attempts to read 32 bits during the first bus cycle. (Refer to **7.2.2 Misaligned Operands** for the case of a word or byte address.) If the port responds that it is 32 bits wide, the MC68030 latches all 32 bits of data and continues with the next operation. If the port responds that it is 16 bits wide, the MC68030 latches the 16 bits of valid data and runs another bus cycle to obtain the other 16 bits. The operation for an 8-bit port is similar, but requires four read cycles. The addressed device uses the $\overline{\text{DSACKx}}$ signals to indicate the port width. For instance, a 32-bit device *always* returns $\overline{\text{DSACKx}}$ for a 32-bit port (regardless of whether the bus cycle is a byte, word, or long-word operation).

Dynamic bus sizing requires that the portion of the data bus used for a transfer to or from a particular port size be fixed. A 32-bit port must reside on data bus bits 0–31, a 16-bit port must reside on data bus bits 16–32, and an 8-bit port must reside on data bus bits 24–31. This requirement minimizes the number of bus cycles needed to transfer data to 8- and 16-bit ports and ensures that the MC68030 correctly transfers valid data. The MC68030 always attempts to transfer the maximum amount of data on all bus cycles; for a long-word operation, it always assumes that the port is 32 bit wide when beginning the bus cycle.

The bytes of operands are designated as shown in Figure 7-3. The most significant byte of a long-word operand is OP0, and OP3 is the least significant byte. The two bytes of a word-length operand are OP2 (most significant) and OP3. The single byte of a byte-length operand is OP3. These designations are used in the figures and descriptions that follow.

7

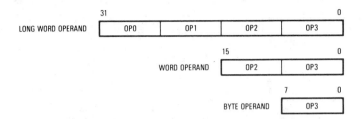

Figure 7-3. Internal Operand Representation

Figure 7-4 shows the required organization of data ports on the MC68030 bus for 8-, 16-, and 32-bit devices. The four bytes shown in Figure 7-4 are connected through the internal data bus and data multiplexer to the external data bus. This path is the means through which the MC68030 supports dynamic bus sizing and operand misalignment. Refer to **7.2.2 Misaligned Operands** for the definition of misaligned operand. The data multiplexer establishes the necessary connections for different combinations of address and data sizes.

The multiplexer takes the four bytes of the 32-bit bus and routes them to their required positions. For example, OP0 can be routed to D24–D31, as would be the normal case, or it can be routed to any other byte position to support a misaligned transfer. The same is true for any of the operand bytes. The positioning of bytes is determined by the size (SIZ0 and SIZ1) and address (A0 and A1) outputs.

The SIZ0 and SIZ1 outputs indicate the remaining number of bytes to be transferred during the current bus cycle, as shown in Table 7-2.

The number of bytes transferred during a write or noncachable read bus cycle is equal to or less than the size indicated by the SIZ0 and SIZ1 outputs, depending on port width and operand alignment. For example, during the first bus cycle of a long-word transfer to a word port, the size outputs indicate that four bytes are to be transferred, although only two bytes are moved on that bus cycle. Cachable read cycles must always transfer the number of bytes indicated by the port size.

A0 and A1 also affect operation of the data multiplexer. During an operand transfer, A2–A31 indicate the long-word base address of that portion of the operand to be accessed; A0 and A1 indicate the byte offset from the base. Table 7-3 shows the encodings of A0 and A1 and the corresponding byte offsets from the long-word base.

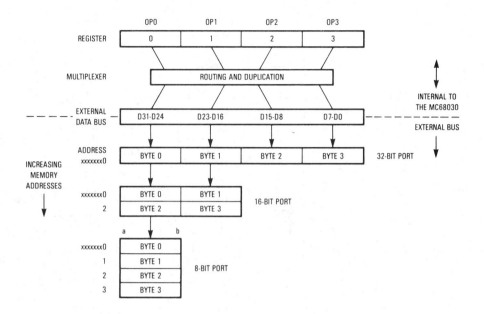

Figure 7-4. MC68030 Interface to Various Port Sizes

Table 7-4 lists the bytes required on the data bus for read cycles that are cachable. The entries shown as OPn are portions of the requested operand that are read or written during that bus cycle and are defined by SIZ0, SIZ1, A0, and A1 for the bus cycle. The PRn and the Nn bytes correspond to the previous and next bytes in memory, respectively, that must be valid on the data bus for the specified port size (long word or word) so that the internal caches operate correctly. (For cachable accesses, the MC68030 assumes that all portions of the data bus for a given port size are valid.) This same table applies to noncachable read cycles except that the bytes labeled PRn and Nn are not required and can be replaced by "don't cares".

Table 7-2. Size Signal Encoding

SIZ1	SIZ0	Size
0	1	Byte
1	0	Word
1	1	3 Bytes
0	0	Long Word

Table 7-3. Address Offset Encodings

A1	A0	Offset
0	0	+0 Bytes
0	1	+1 Byte
1	0	+2 Bytes
1	1	+3 Bytes

Table 7-4. Data Bus Requirements for Read Cycles

Transfer Size	Size		Address		Long-Word Port External Data Bytes Required				Word Port External Data Bytes Required		Byte Port External Data Bytes Required
	SIZ1	SIZ0	A1	A0	D31:D24	D23:D16	D15:D8	D7:D0	D31:D24	D23:D16	D31:D24
Byte	0	1	0	0	OP3	N	N1	N2	OP3	N	OP3
	0	1	0	1	PR	OP3	N	N1	PR	OP3	OP3
	0	1	1	0	PR1	PR	OP3	N	OP3	N	OP3
	0	1	1	1	PR2	PR1	PR	OP3	PR	OP3	OP3
Word	1	0	0	0	OP2	OP3	N	N1	OP2	OP3	OP2
	1	0	0	1	PR	OP2	OP3	N	PR	OP2	OP2
	1	0	1	0	PR1	PR	OP2	OP3	OP2	OP3	OP2
	1	0	1	1	PR2	PR1	PR	OP2	PR	OP2	OP2
3 Byte	1	1	0	0	OP1	OP2	OP3	N	OP1	OP2	OP1
	1	1	0	1	PR	OP1	OP2	OP3	PR	OP1	OP1
	1	1	1	0	PR1	PR	OP1	OP2	OP1	OP2	OP1
	1	1	1	1	PR2	PR1	PR	OP1	PR	OP1	OP1
Long Word	0	0	0	0	OP0	OP1	OP2	OP3	OP0	OP1	OP0
	0	0	0	1	PR	OP0	OP1	OP2	PR	OP0	OP0
	0	0	1	0	PR1	PR	OP0	OP1	OP0	OP1	OP0
	0	0	1	1	PR2	PR1	PR	OP0	PR	OP0	OP0

NOTE: The bytes labeled as Nn (Next n) and PRn (Previous n) are only required to be valid for cachable read cycles. They can be interpreted as don't cares for noncachable read cycles.

Table 7-5 lists the combinations of SIZ0, SIZ1, A0, and A1 and the corresponding pattern of the data transfer for write cycles from the internal multiplexer of the MC68030 to the external data bus.

Figure 7-5 shows the transfer of a long-word operand to a word port. In the first bus cycle, the MC68030 places the four operand bytes on the external bus. Since the address is long-word aligned in this example, the multiplexer follows the pattern in the entry of Table 7-5 corresponding to SIZ0_SIZ1_A0_A1 = 0000. The port latches the data on bits D16–D31 of the data bus, asserts $\overline{DSACK1}$ ($\overline{DSACK0}$ remains negated), and the processor

MC68030 USER'S MANUAL

Table 7-5. MC68030 Internal to External Data Bus Multiplexer — Write Cycles

Transfer Size	Size		Address		External Data Bus Connection			
	SIZ1	SIZ0	A1	A0	D31:D24	D23:D16	D15:D8	D7:D0
Byte	0	1	x	x	OP3	OP3	OP3	OP3
Word	1	0	x	0	OP2	OP3	OP2	OP3
	1	0	x	1	OP2	OP2	OP3	OP2
3 Byte	1	1	0	0	OP1	OP2	OP3	OP0*
	1	1	0	1	OP1	OP1	OP2	OP3
	1	1	1	0	OP1	OP2	OP1	OP2
	1	1	1	1	OP1	OP1	OP2*	OP1
Long Word	0	0	0	0	OP0	OP1	OP2	OP3
	0	0	0	1	OP0	OP0	OP1	OP2
	0	0	1	0	OP0	OP1	OP0	OP1
	0	0	1	1	OP0	OP0	OP1*	OP0

*Due to the current implementation, this byte is output but never used.
x = don't care
NOTE: The OP tables on the external data bus refer to a particular byte of the operand that is written on that section of the data bus.

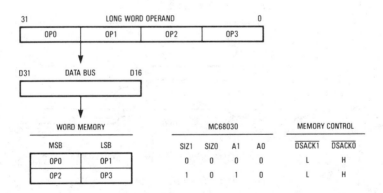

Figure 7-5. Example of Long-Word Transfer to Word Port

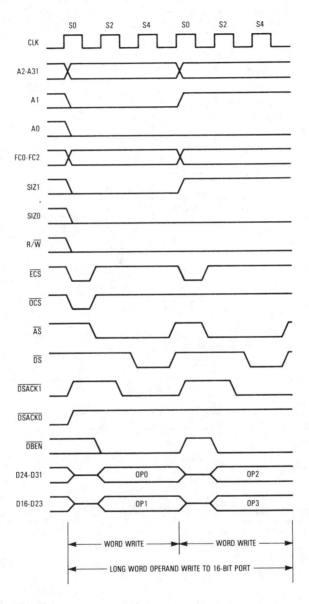

Figure 7-6. Long-Word Operand Write Timing (16-Bit Data Port)

terminates the bus cycle. It then starts a new bus cycle with SIZ0_SIZ1_A0_A1 = 1010 to transfer the remaining 16 bits. SIZ0 and SIZ1 indicate that a word remains to be transferred; A0 and A1 indicate that the word corresponds to an offset of two from the base address. The multiplexer follows the pattern corresponding to this configuration of the size and address signals and places the two least significant bytes of the long word on the word portion of the bus (D16–D31). The bus cycle transfers the remaining bytes to the word-size port. Figure 7-6 shows the timing of the bus transfer signals for this operation.

Figure 7-7 shows a word transfer to an 8-bit bus port. Like the preceding example, this example requires two bus cycles. Each bus cycle transfers a single byte. The size signals for the first cycle specify two bytes; for the second cycle, one byte. Figure 7-8 shows the associated bus transfer signal timing.

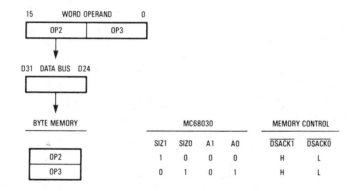

Figure 7-7. Example of Word Transfer to Byte Port

7.2.2 Misaligned Operands

Since operands may reside at any byte boundaries, they may be misaligned. A byte operand is properly aligned at any address; a word operand is misaligned at an odd address; a long word is misaligned at an address that is not evenly divisible by four. The MC68000, MC68008, and MC68010 implementations allow long-word transfers on odd-word boundaries but force exceptions if word or long-word operand transfers are attempted at odd-byte addresses. Although the MC68030 does not enforce any alignment restrictions for data operands (including PC relative data addresses), some performance degradation occurs when additional bus cycles are required for

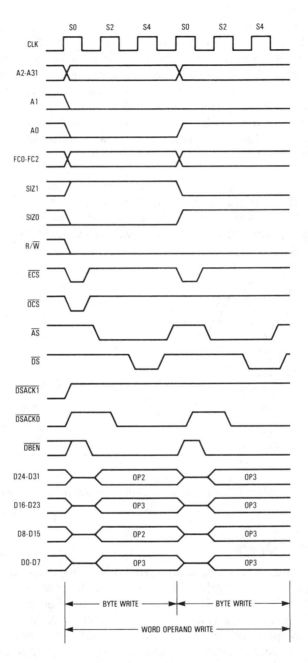

Figure 7-8. Word Operand Write Timing (8-Bit Data Port)

long-word or word operands that are misaligned. For maximum performance, data items should be aligned on their natural boundaries. All instruction words and extension words must reside on word boundaries. Attempting to prefetch an instruction word at an odd address causes an address error exception.

Figure 7-9 shows the transfer of a long-word operand to an odd address in word-organized memory, which requires three bus cycles. For the first cycle, the size signals specify a long-word transfer, and the address offset (A2:A0) is 001. Since the port width is 16 bits, only the first byte of the long word is transferred. The slave device latches the byte and acknowledges the data transfer, indicating that the port is 16 bits wide. When the processor starts the second cycle, the size signals specify that three bytes remain to be transferred with an address offset (A2:A0) of 010. The next two bytes are transferred during this cycle. The processor then initiates the third cycle, with the size signals indicating one byte remaining to be transferred. The address offset (A2:A0) is now 100; the port latches the final byte; and the operation is complete. Figure 7-10 shows the associated bus transfer signal timing.

Figure 7-11 shows the equivalent operation for a cachable data read cycle.

Figures 7-12 and 7-13 show a word transfer to an odd address in word-organized memory. This example is similar to the one shown in Figures 7-9 and 7-10 except that the operand is word sized and the transfer requires only two bus cycles.

Figure 7-14 shows the equivalent operation for a cachable data read cycle.

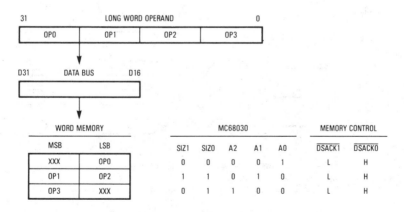

Figure 7-9. Misaligned Long-Word Transfer to Word Port Example

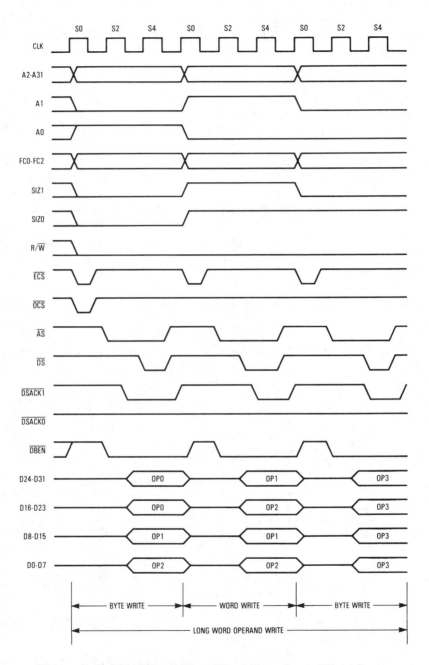

Figure 7-10. Misaligned Long-Word Transfer to Word Port

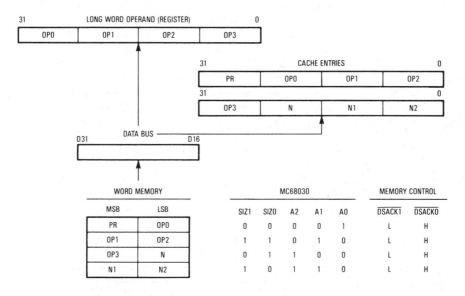

Figure 7-11. Misaligned Cachable Long-Word Transfer from Word Port Example

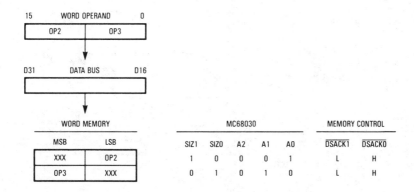

Figure 7-12. Misaligned Word Transfer to Word Port Example

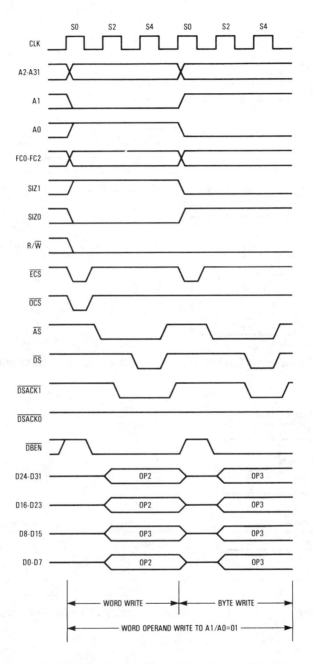

Figure 7-13. Misaligned Word Transfer to Word Port

Figures 7-15 and 7-16 show an example of a long-word transfer to an odd address in long-word-organized memory. In this example, a long-word access is attempted beginning at the least significant byte of a long-word-organized memory. Only one byte can be transferred in the first bus cycle. The second bus cycle then consists of a three-byte access to a long-word boundary. Since the memory is long-word organized, no further bus cycles are necessary.

Figure 7-17 shows the equivalent operation for a cachable data read cycle.

7.2.3 Effects of Dynamic Bus Sizing and Operand Misalignment

The combination of operand size, operand alignment, and port size determines the number of bus cycles required to perform a particular memory access. Table 7-6 shows the number of bus cycles required for different operand sizes to different port sizes with all possible alignment conditions for write cycles and noncachable read cycles.

Table 7-6. Memory Alignment and Port Size Influence on Write Bus Cycles

A1/A0	Number of Bus Cycles			
	00	01	10	11
Instruction*	1:2:4	N/A	N/A	N/A
Byte Operand	1:1:1	1:1:1	1:1:1	1:1:1
Word Operand	1:1:2	1:2:2	1:1:2	2:2:2
Long-Word Operand	1:2:4	2:3:4	2:2:4	2:3:4

Data Port Size — 32 Bits:16 Bits:8 Bits
*Instruction prefetches are always two words from a long-word boundary.

This table shows that bus cycle throughput is significantly affected by port size and alignment. The MC68030 system designer and programmer should be aware of and account for these effects, particularly in time-critical applications.

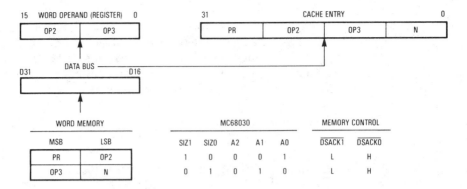

Figure 7-14. Example of Misaligned Cachable Word Transfer from Word Bus

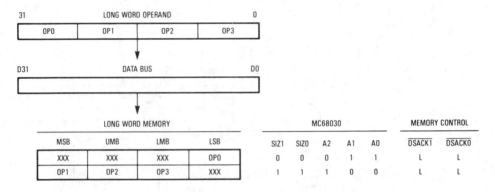

Figure 7-15. Misaligned Long-Word Transfer to Long-Word Port

Table 7-6 shows that the processor always prefetches instructions by reading a long word from a long-word address (A1:A0 = 00), regardless of port size or alignment. When the required instruction begins at an odd-word boundary, the processor attempts to fetch the entire 32 bits and loads both words into the instruction cache, if possible, although the second one is the required word. Even if the instruction access is not cached, the entire 32 bits are latched into an internal cache holding register from which the two instructions words can subsequently be referenced. Refer to **SECTION 11 INSTRUCTION EXE-CUTION TIMING** for a complete description of the cache holding register and pipeline operation.

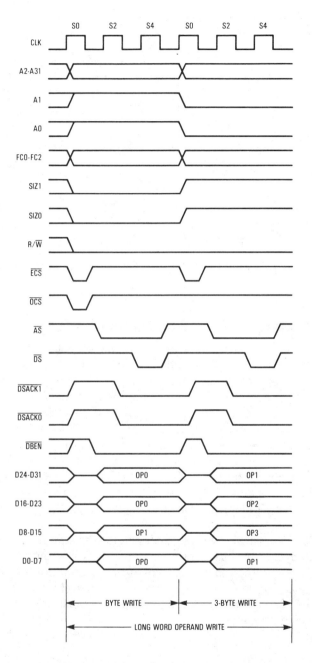

Figure 7-16. Misaligned Write Cycles to Long-Word Port

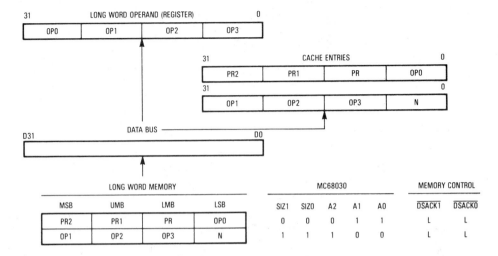

Figure 7-17. Misaligned Cachable Long-Word Transfer from Long-Word Bus

7.2.4 Address, Size, and Data Bus Relationships

The data transfer examples show how the MC68030 drives data onto or receives data from the correct byte sections of the data bus. Table 7-7 shows the combinations of the size signals and address signals that are used to generate byte enable signals for each of the four sections of the data bus for noncachable read cycles and all write cycles if the addressed device requires them. The port size also affects the generation of these enable signals as shown in the table. The four columns on the right correspond to the four byte enable signals. Letters B, W, and L refer to port sizes: B for 8-bit ports, W for 16-bit ports, and L for 32-bit ports. The letters B, W, and L imply that the byte enable signal should be true for that port size. A dash (—) implies that the byte enable signal does not apply.

The MC68030 always drives all sections of the data bus because, at the start of a write cycle, the bus controller does not know the port size. The byte enable signals in the table apply only to read operations that are not to be internally cached and to write operations. For cachable read cycles, during which the data is cached, the addressed port must drive all sections of the bus on which it resides.

Table 7-7. Data Bus Write Enable Signals for Byte, Word, and Long-Word Ports

Transfer Size	SIZ1	SIZ0	A1	A0	Data Bus Active Sections Byte (B) – Word (W) – Long-Word (L) Ports			
					D31:D24	D23:D16	D15:D8	D7:D0
Byte	0	1	0	0	B W L	—	—	—
	0	1	0	1	B	W L	—	—
	0	1	1	0	B W	—	L	—
	0	1	1	1	B	W	—	L
Word	1	0	0	0	B W L	W L	—	—
	1	0	0	1	B	W L	L	—
	1	0	1	0	B W	W	L	L
	1	0	1	1	B	W	—	L
3 Byte	1	1	0	0	B W L	W L	L	—
	1	1	0	1	B	W L	L	L
	1	1	1	0	B W	W	L	L
	1	1	1	1	B	W	—	L
Long Word	0	0	0	0	B W L	W L	L	L
	0	0	0	1	B	W L	L	L
	0	0	1	0	B W	W	L	L
	0	0	1	1	B	W	—	L

The table shows that the MC68030 transfers the number of bytes specified by the size signals to or from the specified address unless the operand is misaligned or the number of bytes is greater than the port width. In these cases, the device transfers the greatest number of bytes possible for the port. For example, if the size is four bytes and the address offset (A1:A0) is 01, a 32-bit slave can only receive three bytes in the current bus cycle. A 16- or 8-bit slave can only receive one byte. The table defines the byte enables for all port sizes. Byte data strobes can be obtained by combining the enable signals with the data strobe signal. Devices residing on 8-bit ports can use the data strobe by itself since there is only one valid byte for every transfer. These enable or strobe signals select only the bytes required for write cycles or for noncachable read cycles. The other bytes are not selected, which prevents incorrect accesses in sensitive areas such as I/O.

Figure 7-18 shows a logic diagram for one method for generating byte data enable signals for 16- and 32-bit ports from the size and address encodings and the read/write signal.

7.2.5 MC68030 versus MC68020 Dynamic Bus Sizing

The MC68030 supports the dynamic bus sizing mechanism of the MC68020 for asynchronous bus cycles (terminated with $\overline{DSACKx}$) with two restrictions. First, for a cachable access within the boundaries of an aligned long word, the port size must be consistent throughout the transfer of each long word. For example, when a byte port resides at address $00, addresses $01, $02, and $03 must also correspond to byte ports. Second, the port must supply as much data as it signals as port size, regardless of the transfer size indicated with the size signals and the address offset indicated by A0 and A1 for cachable accesses. Otherwise, dynamic bus sizing is identical in the two processors.

7.2.6 Cache Filling

The on-chip data and instruction caches, described in **SECTION 6 ON-CHIP CACHE MEMORIES**, are each organized as 16 lines of four long-word entries each. For each line, a tag contains the most significant bits of the logical address, FC2 (instruction cache) or FC0–FC2 (data cache), and a valid bit for each entry in the line. An entry fill operation loads an entire long word accessed from memory into a cache entry. This type of fill operation is performed when one entry of a line is not valid and an access is cachable. A burst fill operation is requested when a tag miss occurs for the current cycle or when all four entires in the cache line are invalid (provided the cache is enabled and burst filling for the cache is enabled). The burst fill operation attempts to fill all four entries in the line. To support burst filling, the slave device must have a 32-bit port and must have a burst mode capability; that is, it must acknowledge a burst request with the cache burst acknowledge ($\overline{CBACK}$) signal. It must also terminate the burst accesses with $\overline{STERM}$ and place a long word on the data bus for each transfer. The device may continue to supply successive long words, asserting $\overline{STERM}$ with each one, until the cache line is full. For further information about filling the cache, both entry fills and burst mode fills, refer to **6.1.3 Cache Filling**, **7.3.4 Synchronous Read Cycle**, **7.3.5 Synchronous Write Cycle**, and **7.3.7 Burst Operation Cycles**, which discuss in detail the required bus cycles.

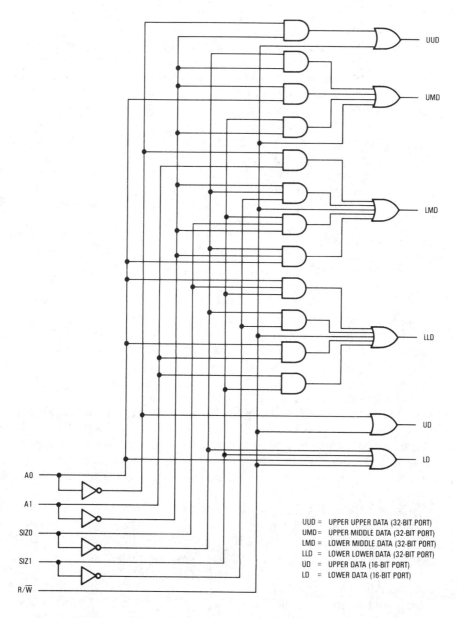

UUD = UPPER UPPER DATA (32-BIT PORT)
UMD = UPPER MIDDLE DATA (32-BIT PORT)
LMD = LOWER MIDDLE DATA (32-BIT PORT)
LLD = LOWER LOWER DATA (32-BIT PORT)
UD = UPPER DATA (16-BIT PORT)
LD = LOWER DATA (16-BIT PORT)

NOTE: These select lines can be combined with the address decode circuitry, or all
can be generated within the same programmed array logic unit.

Figure 7-18. Byte Data Select Generation for 16- and 32-Bit Ports

7.2.7 Cache Interactions

The organization and requirements of the on-chip instruction and data caches affect the interpretation of the $\overline{\text{DSACKx}}$ and $\overline{\text{STERM}}$ signals. Since the MC68030 attempts to load all data operands and instructions that are cachable into the on-chip caches, the bus may operate differently when caching is enabled. Specifically, on cachable read cycles that terminate normally, the low-order address signals (A0 and A1) and the size signals do not apply.

The slave device must supply as much aligned data on the data bus as its port size allows, regardless of the requested operand size. This means that an 8-bit port must supply a byte, a 16-bit port must supply a word, and a 32-bit port must supply an entire long word. This data is loaded into the cache. For a 32-bit port, the slave device ignores A0 and A1 and supplies the long word beginning at the long-word boundary on the data bus. For a 16-bit port, the device ignores A0 and supplies the entire word beginning at the lower word boundary on D16–D31 of the data bus. For a byte port, the device supplies the addressed byte on D24–D31.

If the addressed device cannot supply port-sized data or if the data should not be cached, the device must assert cache inhibit in ($\overline{\text{CIIN}}$) as it terminates the read cycle. If the bus cycle terminates abnormally, the MC68030 does not cache the data. For details of interactions of port sizes, misalignments, and cache filling, refer to **6.1.3 Cache Filling**.

The caches can also affect the assertion of $\overline{\text{AS}}$ and the operation of a read cycle. The search of the appropriate cache by the processor begins when the microsequencer requires an instruction or a data item. At this time, the bus controller may also initiate an external bus cycle in case the requested item is not resident in the instruction or data cache. If the bus is not occupied with another read or write cycle, the bus controller asserts the $\overline{\text{ECS}}$ signal (and the $\overline{\text{OCS}}$ signal, if appropriate). If an internal cache hit occurs, the external cycle aborts, and $\overline{\text{AS}}$ is not asserted. This makes it possible to have $\overline{\text{ECS}}$ asserted on multiple consecutive clock cycles. Notice that there is a minimum time specified from the negation of ECS to the next assertion of $\overline{\text{ECS}}$ (refer to MC68030EC/D, *MC68030 Electrical Specifications*.

Instruction prefetches can occur every other clock so that if, after an aborted cycle due to an instruction cache hit, the bus controller asserts $\overline{\text{ECS}}$ on the next clock, this second cycle is for a data fetch. However, data accesses that hit in the data cache can also cause the assertion of $\overline{\text{ECS}}$ and an aborted cycle. Therefore, since instruction and data accesses are mixed, it is possible to see multiple successive $\overline{\text{ECS}}$ assertions on the external bus if the processor is hitting in both caches and if the bus controller is free. Note that, if the bus controller is executing other cycles, these aborted cycles due to cache hits may not be seen externally. Also, $\overline{OCS}$ is asserted for the first *external* cycle of an operand transfer. Therefore, in the case of a misaligned data transfer where the first portion of the operand results in a cache hit (but the bus controller did not begin an external cycle and then abort it) and the second portion in a cache miss, $\overline{OCS}$ is asserted for the second portion of the operand.

7.2.8 Asynchronous Operation

The MC68030 bus may be used in an asynchonous manner. In that case, the external devices connected to the bus can operate at clock frequencies different from the clock for the MC68030. Asynchronous operation requires using only the handshake line ($\overline{AS}$, $\overline{DS}$, $\overline{DSACK1}$, $\overline{DSACK0}$, $\overline{BERR}$, and $\overline{HALT}$) to control data transfers. Using this method, $\overline{AS}$ signals the start of a bus cycle, and $\overline{DS}$ is used as a condition for valid data on a write cycle. Decoding the size outputs and lower address lines (A0 and A1) provides strobes that select the active portion of the data bus. The slave device (memory or peripheral) then responds by placing the requested data on the correct portion of the data bus for a read cycle or latching the data on a write cycle, and asserting the $\overline{DSACK1}/\overline{DSACK0}$ combination that corresponds to the port size to terminate the cycle. If no slave responds or the access is invalid, external control logic asserts the $\overline{BERR}$ or $\overline{BERR}$ and $\overline{HALT}$ signal(s) to abort or retry the bus cycle, respectively.

The $\overline{DSACKx}$ signals can be asserted before the data from a slave device is valid on a read cycle. The length of time that $\overline{DSACKx}$ may precede data is given by parameter #31, and it must be met in any asynchronous system to insure that valid data is latched into the processor. (Refer to MC68030EC/D, *MC68030 Electrical Specifications* for timing parameters.) Notice that no maximum time is specified from the assertion of $\overline{AS}$ to the assertion of $\overline{DSACKx}$. Although the processor can transfer data in a minimum of three clock cycles when the cycle is terminated with $\overline{DSACKx}$, the processor inserts wait cycles in clock period increments until $\overline{DSACKx}$ is recognized.

The $\overline{BERR}$ and/or $\overline{HALT}$ signals can be asserted after the $\overline{DSACKx}$ signal(s) is asserted. $\overline{BERR}$ and/or $\overline{HALT}$ must be asserted within the time given as parameter #48, after $\overline{DSACKx}$ is asserted in any asynchronous system. If this maximum delay time is violated, the processor may exhibit erratic behavior.

For asynchronous read cycles, the value of $\overline{\text{CIIN}}$ is internally latched on the rising edge of bus cycle state 4. Refer to **7.3.1 Asynchronous Read Cycle** for more details on the states for asynchonous read cycles.

During any bus cycle terminated by $\overline{\text{DSACKx}}$ or $\overline{\text{BERR}}$, the assertion of $\overline{\text{CBACK}}$ is completely ignored.

7.2.9 Synchronous Operation with $\overline{\text{DSACKx}}$

Although cycles terminated with the $\overline{\text{DSACKx}}$ signals are classified as asynchronous and cycles terminated with $\overline{\text{STERM}}$ are classified as synchronous, cycles terminated with $\overline{\text{DSACKx}}$ can also operate synchronously in that signals are interpreted relative to clock edges.

The devices that use these cycles must synchronize the responses to the MC68030 clock to be synchronous. Since they terminate bus cycles with the $\overline{\text{DSACKx}}$ signals, the dynamic bus sizing capabilities of the MC68030 are available. In addition, the minimum cycle time for these cycles is also three clocks.

To support those systems that use the system clock to generate $\overline{\text{DSACKx}}$ and other asynchronous inputs, the asynchronous input setup time (parameter #47A) and the asynchronous input hold time (parameter #47B) are given. If the setup and hold times are met for the assertion or negation of a signal, such as $\overline{\text{DSACKx}}$, the processor can be guaranteed to recognize that signal level on that specific falling edge of the system clock. If the assertion of $\overline{\text{DSACKx}}$ is recognized on a particular falling edge of the clock, valid data is latched into the processor (for a read cycle) on the next falling clock edge provided the data meets the data setup time (parameter #27). In this case, parameter #31 for asynchronous operation can be ignored. The timing parameters referred to are described in MC68030EC/D, *MC68030 Electrical Specifications*. If a system asserts $\overline{\text{DSACKx}}$ for the required window around the falling edge of S2 and obeys the proper bus protocol by maintaining $\overline{\text{DSACKx}}$ (and/or $\overline{\text{BERR/HALT}}$) until and throughout the clock edge that negates $\overline{\text{AS}}$ (with the appropriate asynchronous input hold time specified by parameter #47B), no wait states are inserted. The bus cycle runs at its maximum speed (three clocks per cycle) for bus cycles terminated with $\overline{\text{DSACKx}}$.

To assure proper operation in a synchronous system when $\overline{\text{BERR}}$ or $\overline{\text{BERR}}$ and $\overline{\text{HALT}}$ is asserted after $\overline{\text{DSACKx}}$, $\overline{\text{BERR}}$ (and $\overline{\text{HALT}}$) must meet the appropriate setup time (parameter #27A) prior to the falling clock edge one clock cycle after $\overline{\text{DSACKx}}$ is recognized. This setup time is critical, and the MC68030 may exhibit erratic behavior if it is violated.

When operating synchronously, the data-in setup and hold times for synchronous cycles may be used instead of the timing requirements for data relative to the $\overline{\text{DS}}$ signal.

The value of $\overline{\text{CIIN}}$ is latched on the rising edge of bus cycle state 4 for all cycles terminated with $\overline{\text{DSACKx}}$.

7.2.10 Synchronous Operation with $\overline{\text{STERM}}$

The MC68030 supports synchronous bus cycles terminated with $\overline{\text{STERM}}$. These cycles, for 32-bit ports only, are similar to cycles terminated with $\overline{\text{DSACKx}}$. The main difference is that $\overline{\text{STERM}}$ can be asserted (and data can be transferred) earlier than for a cycle terminated with $\overline{\text{DSACKx}}$, causing the processor to perform a minimum access time transfer in two clock periods. However, wait cycles can be inserted by delaying the assertion of $\overline{\text{STERM}}$ appropriately.

Using $\overline{\text{STERM}}$ instead of $\overline{\text{DSACKx}}$ in any bus cycle makes the cycle synchronous. Any bus cycle is synchronous if:

1. Neither $\overline{\text{DSACKx}}$ nor $\overline{\text{AVEC}}$ is recognized during the cycle.

2. The port size is 32 bits.

3. Synchronous input setup and hold time requirements (specifications #60 and #61) for $\overline{\text{STERM}}$ are met.

Burst mode operation requires the use of $\overline{\text{STERM}}$ to terminate each of its cycles. The first cycle of any burst transfer must be a synchronous cycle as described in the preceding paragraph. The exact timing of this cycle is controlled by the assertion of $\overline{\text{STERM}}$, and wait cycles can be inserted as necessary. However, the minimum cycle time is two clocks. If a burst operation is initiated and allowed to terminate normally, the second, third, and fourth cycles latch data on successive falling edges of the clock at a minimum. Again, the exact timing for these subsequent cycles is controlled by the timing of $\overline{\text{STERM}}$ for each of these cycles, and wait cycles can be inserted as necessary.

Although the synchronous input signals ($\overline{\text{STERM}}$, $\overline{\text{CIIN}}$, and $\overline{\text{CBACK}}$) must be stable for the appropriate setup and hold times relative to every rising edge of the clock during which $\overline{\text{AS}}$ is asserted, the assertion or negation of $\overline{\text{CBACK}}$ and $\overline{\text{CIIN}}$ is internally latched on the rising edge of the clock for which $\overline{\text{STERM}}$ is asserted in a synchronous cycle.

The $\overline{\text{STERM}}$ signal can be generated from the address bus and function code value and does not need to be qualified with the $\overline{\text{AS}}$ signal. If $\overline{\text{STERM}}$ is asserted and no cycle is in progress (even if the cycle has begun, $\overline{\text{ECS}}$ is asserted and then the cycle is aborted), $\overline{\text{STERM}}$ is ignored by the MC68030.

Similarly, $\overline{\text{CBACK}}$ can be asserted independently of the assertion of $\overline{\text{CBREQ}}$. If a cache burst is not requested, the assertion of $\overline{\text{CBACK}}$ is ignored.

The assertion of $\overline{\text{CIIN}}$ is ignored when the appropriate cache is not enabled or when cache inhibit out ($\overline{\text{CIOUT}}$) is asserted. It is also ignored during write cycles or translation table searches.

NOTE

$\overline{\text{STERM}}$ and $\overline{\text{DSACKx}}$ should *never* be asserted during the same bus cycle.

7.3 DATA TRANSFER CYCLES

The transfer of data between the processor and other devices involves the following signals:

- Address Bus A0–A31
- Data Bus D0–D31
- Control Signals

The address and data buses are both parallel nonmultiplexed buses. The bus master moves data on the bus by issuing control signals, and the asynchronous/synchronous bus uses a handshake protocol to insure correct movement of the data. In all bus cycles, the bus master is responsible for de-skewing all signals it issues at both the start and the end of the cycle. In addition, the bus master is responsible for de-skewing the acknowledge and data signals from the slave devices. The following paragraphs define read, write, and read-modify-write cycle operations. An additional paragraph describes burst mode transfers.

MC68030 USER'S MANUAL

MOTOROLA

Each of the bus cycles is defined as a succession of states. These states apply to the bus operation and are different from the processor states described in **SECTION 4 PROCESSING STATES**. The clock cycles used in the descriptions and timing diagrams of data transfer cycles are independent of the clock frequency. Bus operations are described in terms of external bus states.

7.3.1 Asynchronous Read Cycle

During a read cycle, the processor receives data from a memory, coprocessor, or peripheral device. If the instruction specifies a long-word operation, the MC68030 attempts to read four bytes at once. For a word operation, it attempts to read two bytes at once, and for a byte operation, one byte. For some operations, the processor requests a three-byte transfer. The processor properly positions each byte internally. The section of the data bus from which each byte is read depends on the operand size, address signals (A0–A1), CIIN and CIOUT, whether the internal caches are enabled, and the port size. Refer to **7.2.1 Dynamic Bus Sizing**, **7.2.2 Misaligned Operands**, and **7.2.6 Cache Filling** for more information on dynamic bus sizing, misaligned operands, and cache interactions.

Figure 7-19 is a flowchart of an asynchronous long-word read cycle. Figure 7-20 is a flowchart of a byte read cycle. The following figures show functional read cycle timing diagrams specified in terms of clock periods. Figure 7-21 corresponds to byte and word read cycles from a 32-bit port. Figure 7-22 corresponds to a long-word read cycle from an 8-bit port. Figure 7-23 also applies to a long-word read cycle, but from a 16-bit port.

State 0

The read cycle starts in state 0 (S0). The processor drives ECS low, indicating the beginning of an external cycle. When the cycle is the first external cycle of a read operand operation, operand cycle start (OCS) is driven low at the same time. During S0, the processor places a valid address on A0–A31 and valid function codes on FC0–FC2. The function codes select the address space for the cycle. The processor drives R/W high for a read cycle and drives DBEN inactive to disable the data buffers. SIZ0–SIZ1 become valid, indicating the number of bytes requested to be transferred. CIOUT also becomes valid, indicating the state of the MMU CI bit in the address translation descriptor or in the appropriate TTx register.

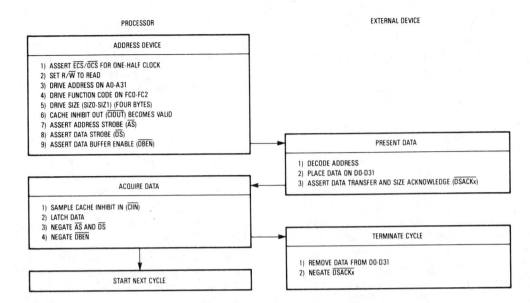

Figure 7-19. Asynchronous Long-Word Read Cycle Flowchart

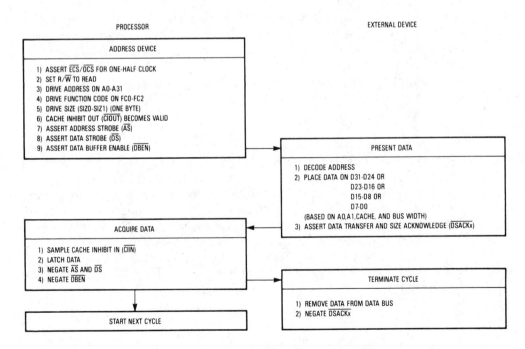

Figure 7-20. Asynchronous Byte Read Cycle Flowchart

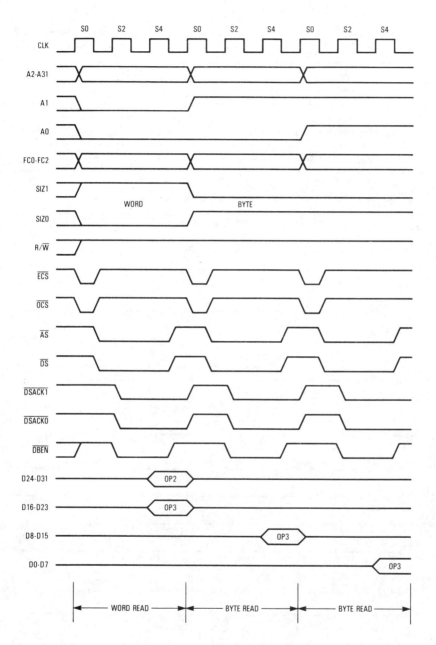

Figure 7-21. Asynchronous Byte and Word Read Cycles — 32-Bit Port

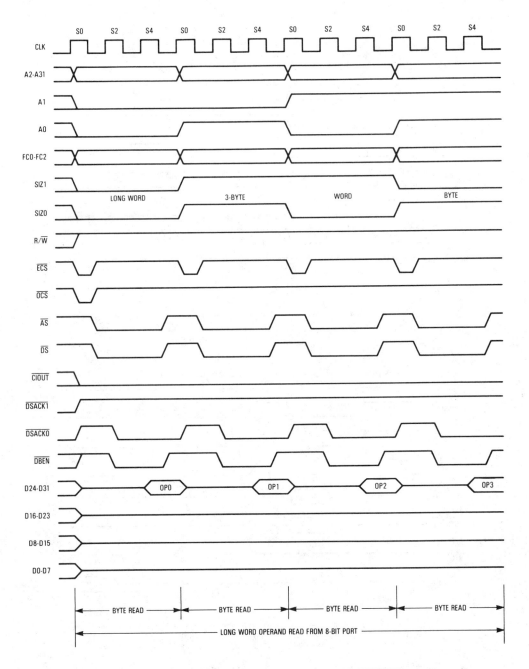

Figure 7-22. Long-Word Read — 8-Bit Port with CIOUT Asserted

MC68030 USER'S MANUAL

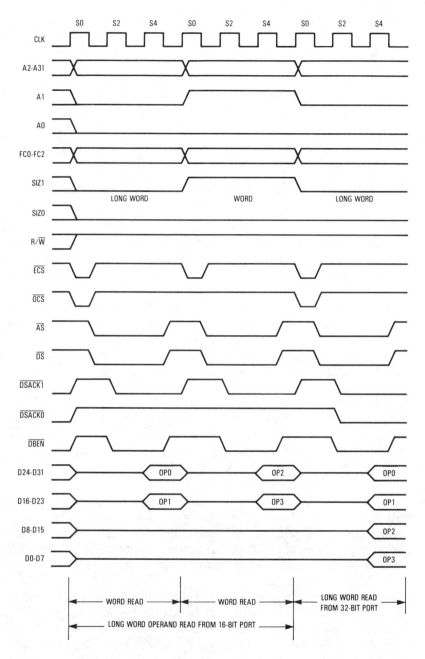

Figure 7-23. Long-Word Read — 16-Bit and 32-Bit Port

State 1

One-half clock later in state 1 (S1), the processor asserts $\overline{\text{AS}}$ indicating that the address on the address bus is valid. The processor also asserts $\overline{\text{DS}}$ also during S1. In addition, the $\overline{\text{ECS}}$ (and $\overline{\text{OCS}}$, if asserted) signal is negated during S1.

State 2

During state 2 (S2), the processor asserts $\overline{\text{DBEN}}$ to enable external data buffers. The selected device uses R/$\overline{\text{W}}$, SIZ0–SIZ1, A0–A1, $\overline{\text{CIOUT}}$, and $\overline{\text{DS}}$ to place its information on the data bus, and drives $\overline{\text{CIIN}}$ if appropriate. Any or all of the bytes (D24–D31, D16–D23, D8–D15, and D0–D7) are selected by SIZ0–SIZ1 and A0–A1. Concurrently, the selected device asserts $\overline{\text{DSACKx}}$.

State 3

As long as at least one of the $\overline{\text{DSACKx}}$ signals is recognized by the end of S2 (meeting the asynchronous input setup time requirement), data is latched on the next falling edge of the clock, and the cycle terminates. If $\overline{\text{DSACKx}}$ is not recognized by the start of state 3 (S3), the processor inserts wait states instead of proceeding to states 4 and 5. To ensure that wait states are inserted, both $\overline{\text{DSACK0}}$ and $\overline{\text{DSACK1}}$ must remain negated throughout the asynchronous input setup and hold times around the end of S2. If wait states are added, the processor continues to sample the $\overline{\text{DSACKx}}$ signals on the falling edges of the clock until one is recognized.

State 4

The processor samples $\overline{\text{CIIN}}$ at the beginning of state 4 (S4). Since $\overline{\text{CIIN}}$ is defined as a synchronous input, whether asserted or negated, it must meet the appropriate synchronous input setup and hold times on every rising edge of the clock while $\overline{\text{AS}}$ is asserted. At the end of S4, the processor latches the incoming data.

State 5

The processor negates $\overline{\text{AS}}$, $\overline{\text{DS}}$, and $\overline{\text{DBEN}}$ during state 5 (S5). It holds the address valid during S5 to provide address hold time for memory systems. R/$\overline{\text{W}}$, SIZ0–SIZ1, and FC0–FC2 also remain valid throughout S5.

The external device keeps its data and $\overline{\text{DSACKx}}$ signals asserted until it detects the negation of $\overline{\text{AS}}$ or $\overline{\text{DS}}$ (whichever it detects first). The device must remove its data and negate $\overline{\text{DSACKx}}$ within approximately one clock period after sensing the negation of $\overline{\text{AS}}$ or $\overline{\text{DS}}$. $\overline{\text{DSACKx}}$ signals that remain asserted beyond this limit may be prematurely detected for the next bus cycle.

7.3.2 Asynchronous Write Cycle

During a write cycle, the processor transfers data to memory or a peripheral device.

Figure 7-24 is a flowchart of a write cycle operation for a long-word transfer. The following figures show the functional write cycle timing diagrams specified in terms of clock periods. Figure 7-25 shows two write cycles (between two read cycles with no idle time) for a 32-bit port. Figure 7-26 shows byte and word write cycles to a 32-bit port. Figure 7-27 shows a long-word write cycle to an 8-bit port. Figure 7-28 shows a long-word write cycle to a 16-bit port.

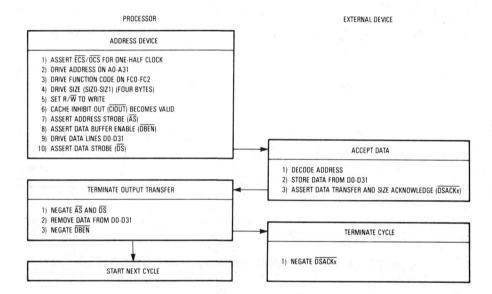

PROCESSOR

EXTERNAL DEVICE

ADDRESS DEVICE

1) ASSERT $\overline{ECS}/\overline{OCS}$ FOR ONE-HALF CLOCK
2) DRIVE ADDRESS ON A0-A31
3) DRIVE FUNCTION CODE ON FC0-FC2
4) DRIVE SIZE (SIZ0-SIZ1) (FOUR BYTES)
5) SET R/$\overline{W}$ TO WRITE
6) CACHE INHIBIT OUT ($\overline{CIOUT}$) BECOMES VALID
7) ASSERT ADDRESS STROBE ($\overline{AS}$)
8) ASSERT DATA BUFFER ENABLE ($\overline{DBEN}$)
9) DRIVE DATA LINES D0-D31
10) ASSERT DATA STROBE ($\overline{DS}$)

ACCEPT DATA

1) DECODE ADDRESS
2) STORE DATA FROM D0-D31
3) ASSERT DATA TRANSFER AND SIZE ACKNOWLEDGE ($\overline{DSACKx}$)

TERMINATE OUTPUT TRANSFER

1) NEGATE $\overline{AS}$ AND $\overline{DS}$
2) REMOVE DATA FROM D0-D31
3) NEGATE $\overline{DBEN}$

TERMINATE CYCLE

1) NEGATE $\overline{DSACKx}$

START NEXT CYCLE

Figure 7-24. Asynchronous Write Cycle Flowchart

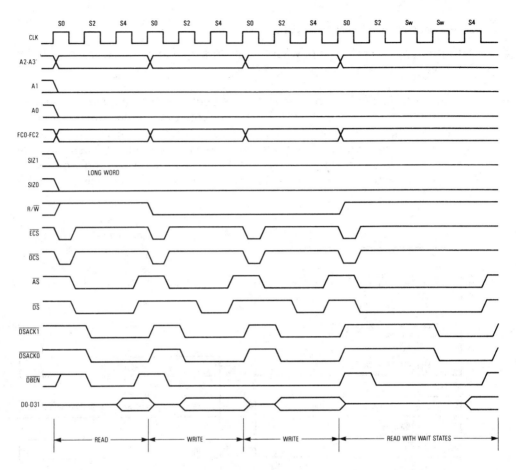

Figure 7-25. Asynchronous Read-Write-Read Cycles — 32-Bit Port

State 0

The write cycle starts in S0. The processor drives $\overline{\text{ECS}}$ low, indicating the beginning of an external cycle. When the cycle is the first external cycle of a write operation, $\overline{\text{OCS}}$ is driven low at the same time. During S0, the processor places a valid address on A0–A31 and valid function codes on FC0–FC2. The function codes select the address space for the cycle. The processor drives R/$\overline{\text{W}}$ low for a write cycle. SIZ0–SIZ1 become valid, indicating the number of bytes to be transferred. $\overline{\text{CIOUT}}$ also becomes valid, indicating the state of the MMU CI bit in the address translation descriptor or in the appropriate TTx register.

MC68030 USER'S MANUAL   MOTOROLA

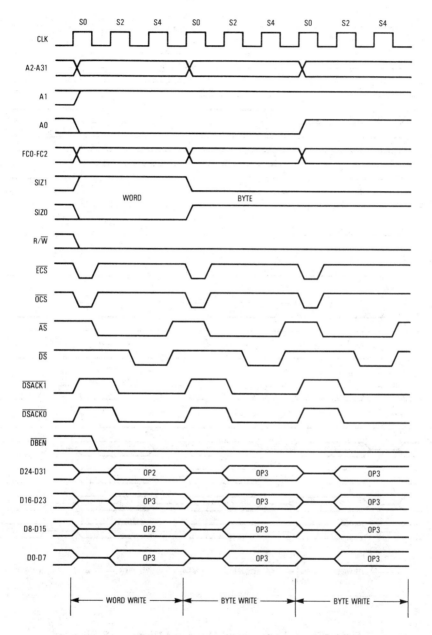

Figure 7-26. Asynchronous Byte and Word Write Cycles — 32-Bit Port

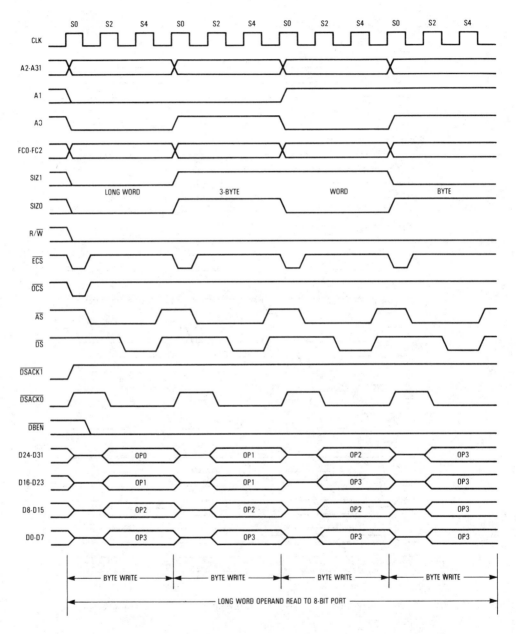

Figure 7-27. Long-Word Operand Write — 8-Bit Port

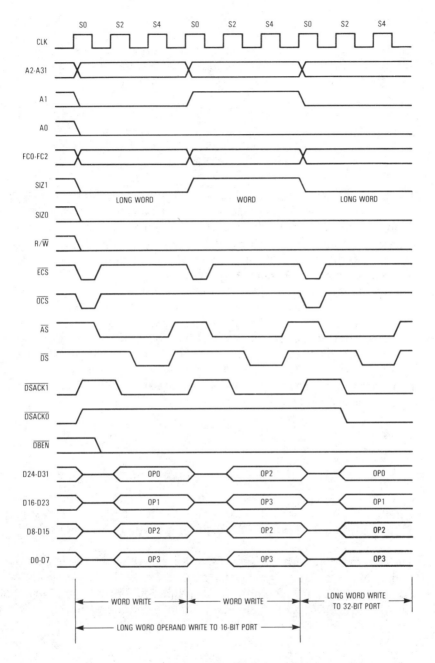

Figure 7-28. Long-Word Operand Write — 16-Bit Port

State 1

One-half clock later in S1, the processor asserts $\overline{AS}$, indicating that the address on the address bus is valid. The processor also asserts $\overline{DBEN}$ during S1, which can enable external data buffers. In addition, the $\overline{ECS}$ (and $\overline{OCS}$, if asserted) signal is negated during S1.

State 2

During S2, the processor places the data to be written onto the D0–D31, and samples $\overline{DSACKx}$ at the end of S2.

State 3

The processor asserts $\overline{DS}$ during S3, indicating that the data is stable on the data bus. As long as at least one of the $\overline{DSACKx}$ signals is recognized by the end of S2 (meeting the asynchronous input setup time requirement), the cycle terminates one clock later. If $\overline{DSACKx}$ is not recognized by the start of S3, the processor inserts wait states instead of proceeding to S4 and S5. To ensure that wait states are inserted, both $\overline{DSACK0}$ and $\overline{DSACK1}$ must remain negated throughout the asynchronous input setup and hold times around the end of S2. If wait states are added, the processor continues to sample the $\overline{DSACKx}$ signals on the falling edges of the clock until one is recognized. The selected device uses R/$\overline{W}$, $\overline{DS}$, SIZ0–SIZ1, and A0–A1 to latch data from the appropriate byte(s) of the data bus (D24–D31, D16–D23, D8–D15, and D0–D7). SIZ0–SIZ1 and A0–A1 select the bytes of the data bus. If it has not already done so, the device asserts $\overline{DSACKx}$ to signal that it has successfully stored the data.

State 4

The processor issues no new control signals during S4.

State 5

The processor negates $\overline{AS}$ and $\overline{DS}$ during S5. It holds the address and data valid during S5 to provide address hold time for memory systems. R/$\overline{W}$, SIZ0–SIZ1, FC0–FC2, and $\overline{DBEN}$ also remain valid throughout S5.

The external device must keep $\overline{DSACKx}$ asserted until it detects the negation of $\overline{AS}$ or $\overline{DS}$ (whichever it detects first). The device must negate $\overline{DSACKx}$ within approximately one clock period after sensing the negation of $\overline{AS}$ or $\overline{DS}$. $\overline{DSACKx}$ signals that remain asserted beyond this limit may be prematurely detected for the next bus cycle.

7.3.3 Asynchronous Read-Modify-Write Cycle

The read-modify-write cycle performs a read, conditionally modifies the data in the arithmetic logic unit, and may write the data out to memory. In the MC68030 processor, this operation is indivisible, providing semaphore capabilities for multiprocessor systems. During the entire read-modify-write sequence, the MC68030 asserts the $\overline{RMC}$ signal to indicate that an indivisible operation is occurring. The MC68030 does not issue a bus grant ($\overline{BG}$) signal in response to a bus request ($\overline{BR}$) signal during this operation. The read portion of a read-modify-write operation is forced to miss in the data cache because the data in the cache would not be valid if another processor had altered the value being read. However, read-modify-write cycles may alter the contents of the data cache as described in **6.1.2. Data Cache**.

No burst filling of the data cache occurs during a read-modify-write operation.

The test and set (TAS) and compare and swap (CAS and CAS2) instructions are the only MC68030 instructions that utilize read-modify-write operations. Depending on the compare results of the CAS and CAS2 instructions, the write cycle(s) may not occur. Table search accesses required for the MMU are always read-modify-write cycles to the supervisor data space. During these cycles, a write does not occur unless a descriptor is updated. No data is internally cached for table search accesses since the MMU uses physical addresses to access the tables. Refer to **SECTION 9 MEMORY MANAGEMENT UNIT** for information about the MMU.

Figure 7-29 is a flowchart of the asynchronous read-modify-write cycle operation. Figure 7-30 is an example of a functional timing diagram of a TAS instruction specified in terms of clock periods.

State 0

The processor asserts $\overline{ECS}$ and $\overline{OCS}$ in S0 to indicate the beginning of an external operand cycle. The processor also asserts $\overline{RMC}$ in S0 to identify a read-modify-write cycle. The processor places a valid address on A0–A31 and valid function codes on FC0–FC2. The function codes select the address space for the operation. SIZ0–SIZ1 become valid in S0 to indicate the operand size. The processor drives R/$\overline{W}$ high for the read cycle and sets $\overline{CIOUT}$ according to the value of the MMU CI bit in the address translation descriptor or in the appropriate TTx register.

State 1

One-half clock later in S1, the processor asserts $\overline{AS}$, indicating that the address on the address bus is valid. The processor asserts $\overline{DS}$ during S1. In addition, the $\overline{ECS}$ (and $\overline{OCS}$, if asserted) signal is negated during S1.

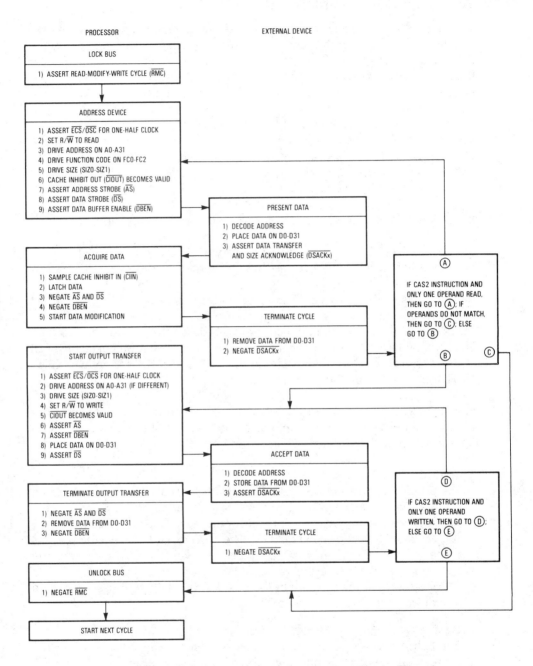

Figure 7-29. Asynchronous Read-Modify-Write Cycle Flowchart

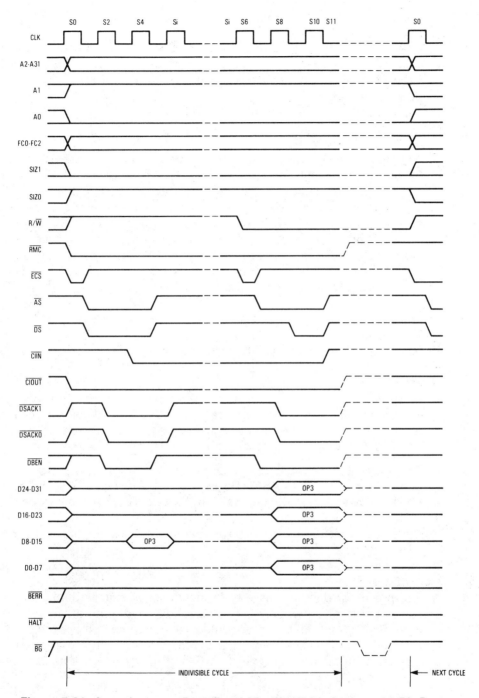

**Figure 7-30. Asynchronous Byte Read-Modify-Write Cycle — 32-Bit Port
(TAS Instruction with CIOUT or CIIN Asserted)**

State 2

During state 2 (S2), the processor drives $\overline{\text{DBEN}}$ active to enable external data buffers. The selected device uses R/$\overline{\text{W}}$, SIZ0–SIZ1, A0–A1, and $\overline{\text{DS}}$ to place information on the data bus. Any or all of the bytes (D24–D31, D16–D23, D8–D15, and D0–D7) are selected by SIZ0–SIZ1 and A0–A1. Concurrently, the selected device may assert the $\overline{\text{DSACKx}}$ signals.

State 3

As long as at least one of the $\overline{\text{DSACKx}}$ signals is recognized by the end of S2 (meeting the asynchronous input setup time requirement), data is latched on the next falling edge of the clock, and the cycle terminates. If $\overline{\text{DSACKx}}$ is not recognized by the start of S3, the processor inserts wait states instead of proceeding to S4 and S5. To ensure that wait states are inserted, both $\overline{\text{DSACK0}}$ and $\overline{\text{DSACK1}}$ must remain negated throughout the asynchronous input setup and hold times around the end of S2. If wait states are added, the processor continues to sample the $\overline{\text{DSACKx}}$ signals on the falling edges of the clock until one is recognized.

State 4

The processor samples the level of $\overline{\text{CIIN}}$ at the beginning of S4. At the end of S4, the processor latches the incoming data.

State 5

The processor negates $\overline{\text{AS}}$, $\overline{\text{DS}}$, and $\overline{\text{DBEN}}$ during S5. If more than one read cycle is required to read in the operand(s), S0–S5 are repeated for each read cycle. When finished reading, the processor holds the address, R/$\overline{\text{W}}$, and FC0–FC2 valid in preparation for the write portion of the cycle.

The external device keeps its data and $\overline{\text{DSACKx}}$ signals asserted until it detects the negation of $\overline{\text{AS}}$ or $\overline{\text{DS}}$ (whichever it detects first). The device must remove the data and negate $\overline{\text{DSACKx}}$ within approximately one clock period after sensing the negation of $\overline{\text{AS}}$ or $\overline{\text{DS}}$. $\overline{\text{DSACKx}}$ signals that remain asserted beyond this limit may be prematurely detected for the next portion of the operation.

Idle States

The processor does not assert any new control signals during the idle states, but it may internally begin the modify portion of the cycle at this time. S6–S11 are omitted if no write cycle is required. If a write cycle is required, the R/$\overline{\text{W}}$ signal remains in the read mode until S6 to prevent bus conflicts with the preceding read portion of the cycle; the data bus is not driven until S8.

MC68030 USER'S MANUAL

MOTOROLA

State 6

The processor asserts $\overline{\text{ECS}}$ and $\overline{\text{OCS}}$ in S6 to indicate that another external cycle is beginning. The processor drives R/$\overline{\text{W}}$ low for a write cycle. $\overline{\text{CIOUT}}$ also becomes valid, indicating the state of the MMU CI bit in the address translation descriptor or in a relevant TTx register. Depending on the write operation to be performed, the address lines may change during S6.

State 7

In S7, the processor asserts $\overline{\text{AS}}$, indicating that the address on the address bus is valid. The processor also asserts $\overline{\text{DBEN}}$, which can be used to enable data buffers during S7. In addition, the $\overline{\text{ECS}}$ (and $\overline{\text{OCS}}$, if asserted) signal is negated during S7.

State 8

During S8, the processor places the data to be written onto D0–D31.

State 9

The processor asserts $\overline{\text{DS}}$ during S9 indicating that the data is stable on the data bus. As long as at least one of the $\overline{\text{DSACKx}}$ signals is recognized by the end of S8 (meeting the asynchronous input setup time requirement), the cycle terminates one clock later. If $\overline{\text{DSACKx}}$ is not recognized by the start of S9, the processor inserts wait states instead of proceeding to S10 and S11. To ensure that wait states are inserted, both $\overline{\text{DSACK0}}$ and $\overline{\text{DSACK1}}$ must remain negated throughout the asynchronous input setup and hold times around the end of S8. If wait states are added, the processor continues to sample $\overline{\text{DSACKx}}$ signals on the falling edges of the clock until one is recognized.

The selected device uses R/$\overline{\text{W}}$, $\overline{\text{DS}}$, SIZ0–SIZ1, and A0–A1 to latch data from the appropriate section(s) of the data bus (D24–D31, D16–D23, D8–D15, and D0–D7). SIZ0–SIZ1 and A0–A1 select the data bus sections. If it has not already done so, the device asserts $\overline{\text{DSACKx}}$ when it has successfully stored the data.

State 10

The processor issues no new control signals during S10.

State 11

The processor negates $\overline{AS}$ and $\overline{DS}$ during S11. It holds the address and data valid during S11 to provide address hold time for memory systems. R/$\overline{W}$ and FC0–FC2 also remain valid throughout S11.

If more than one write cycle is required, S6–S11 are repeated for each write cycle.

The external device keeps $\overline{DSACKx}$ asserted until it detects the negation of $\overline{AS}$ or $\overline{DS}$ (whichever it detects first). The device must remove its data and negate $\overline{DSACKx}$ within approximately one clock period after sensing the negation of $\overline{AS}$ or $\overline{DS}$.

7.3.4 Synchronous Read Cycle

A synchronous read cycle is terminated differently from an asynchronous read cycle; otherwise, the cycles assert and respond to the same signals, in the same sequence. $\overline{STERM}$ rather than $\overline{DSACKx}$ is asserted by the addressed external device to terminate a synchronous read cycle. Since $\overline{STERM}$ must meet the synchronous setup and hold times with respect to all rising edges of the clock while $\overline{AS}$ is asserted, it does not need to be synchronized by the processor. Only devices with 32-bit ports may assert $\overline{STERM}$. $\overline{STERM}$ is also used with the $\overline{CBREQ}$ and $\overline{CBACK}$ signals during burst mode operation. It provides a two-clock (minimum) bus cycle for 32-bit ports and single-clock (minimum) burst accesses, although wait states can be inserted for these cycles as well. Therefore, a synchronous cycle terminated with $\overline{STERM}$ with one wait cycle is a three-clock bus cycle. However, note that $\overline{STERM}$ is asserted one-half clock later than $\overline{DSACKx}$ would be for a similar asynchronous cycle with zero wait cycles (also three clocks). Thus, if dynamic bus sizing is not needed, $\overline{STERM}$ can be used to provide more decision time in an external cache design than is available with $\overline{DSACKx}$ for three-clock accesses.

Figure 7-31 is a flowchart of a synchronous long-word read cycle. Byte and word operations are similar. Figure 7-32 is a functional timing diagram of a synchronous long-word read cycle.

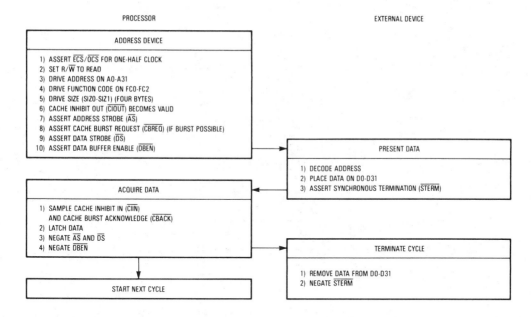

ADDRESS DEVICE

1) ASSERT ECS/OCS FOR ONE-HALF CLOCK
2) SET R/W TO READ
3) DRIVE ADDRESS ON A0-A31
4) DRIVE FUNCTION CODE ON FC0-FC2
5) DRIVE SIZE (SIZ0-SIZ1) (FOUR BYTES)
6) CACHE INHIBIT OUT (CIOUT) BECOMES VALID
7) ASSERT ADDRESS STROBE (AS)
8) ASSERT CACHE BURST REQUEST (CBREQ) (IF BURST POSSIBLE)
9) ASSERT DATA STROBE (DS)
10) ASSERT DATA BUFFER ENABLE (DBEN)

PRESENT DATA

1) DECODE ADDRESS
2) PLACE DATA ON D0-D31
3) ASSERT SYNCHRONOUS TERMINATION (STERM)

ACQUIRE DATA

1) SAMPLE CACHE INHIBIT IN (CIIN)
   AND CACHE BURST ACKNOWLEDGE (CBACK)
2) LATCH DATA
3) NEGATE AS AND DS
4) NEGATE DBEN

TERMINATE CYCLE

1) REMOVE DATA FROM D0-D31
2) NEGATE STERM

START NEXT CYCLE

Figure 7-31. Synchronous Long-Word Read Cycle Flowchart — No Burst Allowed

State 0

The read cycle starts with S0. The processor drives ECS low, indicating the beginning of an external cycle. When the cycle is the first cycle of a read operand operation, OCS is driven low at the same time. During S0, the processor places a valid address on A0–A31 and valid function codes on FC0–FC2. The function codes select the address space for the cycle. The processor drives R/W high for a read cycle and drives DBEN inactive to disable the data buffers. SIZ1–SIZ0 become valid, indicating the number of bytes to be transferred. CIOUT also becomes valid, indicating the state of the MMU CI bit in the address translation descriptor or in the appropriate TTx register.

State 1

One-half clock later in S1, the processor asserts AS, indicating that the address on the address bus is valid. The processor also asserts DS during S1. If the burst mode is enabled for the appropriate on-chip cache and all four long words of the cache entry are invalid, (i.e., four long words can be read in), CBREQ is asserted. In addition, the ECS (and OCS, if asserted) signal is negated during S1.

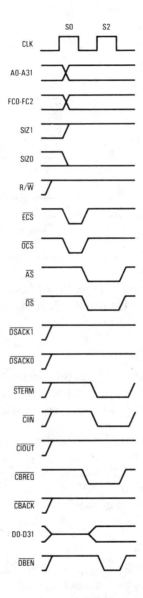

Figure 7-32. Synchronous Read with $\overline{\text{CIIN}}$ Asserted and $\overline{\text{CBACK}}$ Negated

MC68030 USER'S MANUAL   MOTOROLA

State 2

The selected device uses R/$\overline{\text{W}}$, SIZ0–SIZ1, A0–A1, and $\overline{\text{CIOUT}}$ to place its information on the data bus. Any or all of the byte sections of the data bus (D24–D31, D16–D23, D8–D15, and D0–D7) are selected by SIZ0–SIZ1 and A0–A1. During S2, the processor drives $\overline{\text{DBEN}}$ active to enable external data buffers. In systems that use two-clock synchronous bus cycles, the timing of $\overline{\text{DBEN}}$ may prevent its use. At the beginning of S2, the processor samples the level of $\overline{\text{STERM}}$. If $\overline{\text{STERM}}$ is recognized, the processor latches the incoming data at the end of S2. If the selected data is not to be cached for the current cycle or if the device cannot supply 32 bits, $\overline{\text{CIIN}}$ must be asserted at the same time as $\overline{\text{STERM}}$. In addition, the state of $\overline{\text{CBACK}}$ is latched when $\overline{\text{STERM}}$ is recognized.

Since $\overline{\text{CIIN}}$, $\overline{\text{CBACK}}$, and $\overline{\text{STERM}}$ are synchronous signals, they must meet the synchronous input setup and hold times for all rising edges of the clock while $\overline{\text{AS}}$ is asserted. If $\overline{\text{STERM}}$ is negated at the beginning of S2, wait states are inserted after S2, and $\overline{\text{STERM}}$ is sampled on every rising edge thereafter until it is recognized. Once $\overline{\text{STERM}}$ is recognized, data is latched on the next falling edge of the clock (corresponding to the beginning of S3).

State 3

The processor negates $\overline{\text{AS}}$, $\overline{\text{DS}}$, and $\overline{\text{DBEN}}$ during S3. It holds the address valid during S3 to simplify memory interfaces. R/$\overline{\text{W}}$, SIZ0–SIZ1, and FC0–FC2 also remain valid throughout S3.

The external device must keep its data asserted throughout the synchronous hold time for data from the beginning of S3. The device must remove its data within one clock after asserting $\overline{\text{STERM}}$ and negate $\overline{\text{STERM}}$ within two clocks after asserting $\overline{\text{STERM}}$; otherwise, the processor may inadvertently use $\overline{\text{STERM}}$ for the next bus cycle.

7.3.5 Synchronous Write Cycle

A synchronous write cycle is terminated differently from an asynchronous write cycle and the data strobe may not be useful. Otherwise, the cycles assert and respond to the same signal, in the same sequence. $\overline{\text{STERM}}$ is asserted by the external device to terminate a synchronous write cycle. The discussion of $\overline{\text{STERM}}$ in the preceding section applies to write cycles as well as to read cycles.

$\overline{\text{DS}}$ is not asserted for two-clock synchronous write cycles; therefore, the clock (CLK) may be used as the timing signal for latching the data. In addition, there is no time from the latest assertion of $\overline{\text{AS}}$ and the required assertion of $\overline{\text{STERM}}$ for any two-clock synchronous bus cycle. The system must qualify a memory write with the assertion of $\overline{\text{AS}}$ to ensure that the write is not aborted by internal conditions within the MC68030.

Figure 7-33 is a flowchart of a synchronous write cycle. Figure 7-34 is a functional timing diagram of this operation with wait states.

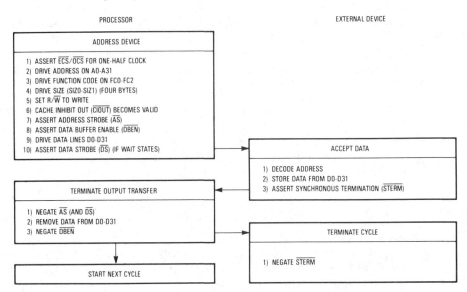

Figure 7-33. Synchronous Write Cycle Flowchart

State 0

The write cycle starts with S0. The processor drives $\overline{\text{ECS}}$ low, indicating the beginning of an external cycle. When the cycle is the first cycle of a write operation, $\overline{\text{OCS}}$ is driven low at the same time. During S0, the processor places a valid address on A0–A31 and valid function codes on FC0–FC2. The function codes select the address space for the cycle. The processor drives R/$\overline{\text{W}}$ low for a write cycle. SIZ0–SIZ1 become valid, indicating the number of bytes to be transferred. $\overline{\text{CIOUT}}$ also becomes valid, indicating the state of the MMU CI bit in the address translation descriptor or in the appropriate TTx register.

State 1

One-half clock later in S1, the processor asserts $\overline{\text{AS}}$, indicating that the address on the address bus is valid. The processor also asserts $\overline{\text{DBEN}}$ during S1, which may be used to enable the external data buffers. In addition, the $\overline{\text{ECS}}$ (and $\overline{\text{OCS}}$, if asserted) signal is negated during S1.

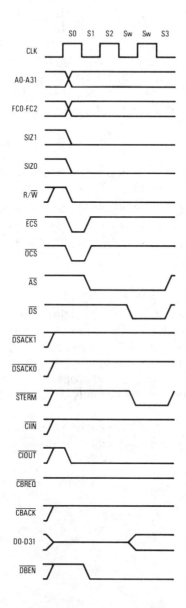

Figure 7-34. Synchronous Write Cycle with Wait States — CIOUT Asserted

State 2

During S2, the processor places the data to be written onto D0–D31. The selected device uses R/W, CLK, SIZ0–SIZ1, and A0–A1 to latch data from the appropriate section(s) of the data bus (D24–D31, D16–D23, D8–D15, and D0–D7). SIZ0–SIZ1 and A0–A1 select the data bus sections. The device asserts $\overline{\text{STERM}}$ when it has successfully stored the data. If the device does not assert $\overline{\text{STERM}}$ by the rising edge of S2, the processor inserts wait states until it is recognized. The processor asserts $\overline{\text{DS}}$ at the end of S2 if wait states are inserted. For zero-wait-state synchronous write cycles, $\overline{\text{DS}}$ is not asserted.

State 3

The processor negates $\overline{\text{AS}}$ (and $\overline{\text{DS}}$, if necessary) during S3. It holds the address and data valid during S3 to simplify memory interfaces. R/W, SIZ0–SIZ1, FC0–FC2, and $\overline{\text{DBEN}}$ also remain valid throughout S3.

The addressed device must negate $\overline{\text{STERM}}$ within two clock periods after asserting it, or the processor may use $\overline{\text{STERM}}$ for the next bus cycle.

7.3.6 Synchronous Read-Modify-Write Cycle

A synchronous read-modify-write operation differs from an asynchronous read-modify-write operation only in the terminating signal of the read and write cycles and in the use of CLK instead of $\overline{\text{DS}}$ latching data in the write cycle. Like the asynchronous operation, the synchronous read-modify-write operation is indivisible. Although the operation is synchronous, the burst mode is never used during read-modify-write cycles.

Figure 7-35 is a flowchart of the synchronous read-modify-write operation. Timing for the cycle is shown in Figure 7-36.

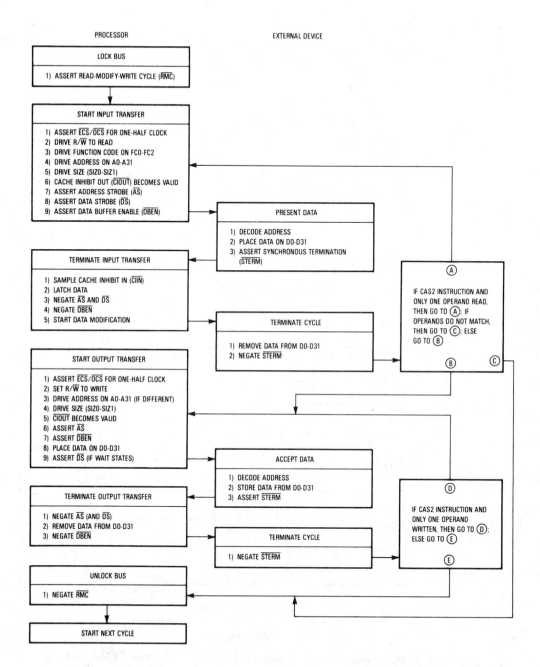

Figure 7-35. Synchronous Read-Modify-Write Cycle Flowchart

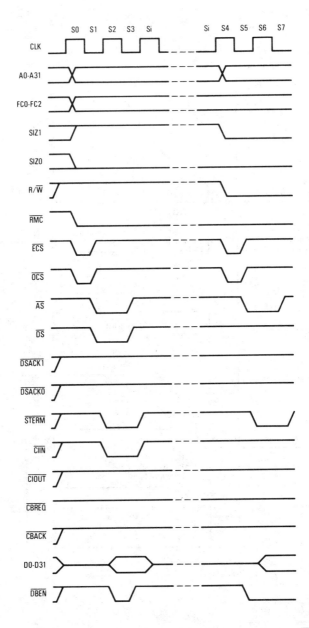

Figure 7-36. Synchronous Read-Modify-Write Cycle Timing — CIIN Asserted

State 0

The processor asserts $\overline{\text{ECS}}$ and $\overline{\text{OCS}}$ in S0 to indicate the beginning of an external operand cycle. The processor also asserts $\overline{\text{RMC}}$ in S0 to identify a read-modify-write cycle. The processor places a valid address on A0–A31 and valid function codes on FC0–FC2. The function codes select the address space for the operation. SIZ0–SIZ1 become valid in S0 to indicate the operand size. The processor drives R/$\overline{\text{W}}$ high for a read cycle and sets $\overline{\text{CIOUT}}$ to the value of the MMU CI bit in the address translation descriptor or in the appropriate TTx register. The processor drives $\overline{\text{DBEN}}$ inactive to disable the data buffers.

State 1

One-half clock later in S1, the processor asserts $\overline{\text{AS}}$, indicating that the address on the address bus is valid. The processor also asserts $\overline{\text{DS}}$ during S1. In addition, the $\overline{\text{ECS}}$ (and $\overline{\text{OCS}}$, if asserted) signal is negated during S1.

State 2

The selected device uses R/$\overline{\text{W}}$, SIZ0–SIZ1, A0–A1, and $\overline{\text{CIOUT}}$ to place its information on the data bus. Any or all of the byte sections (D24–D31, D16–D23, D8–D15, and D0–D7) are selected by SIZ0–SIZ1 and A0–A1. During S2, the processor drives $\overline{\text{DBEN}}$ active to enable external data buffers. In systems that use two-clock synchronous bus cycles, the timing of $\overline{\text{DBEN}}$ may prevent its use. At the beginning of S2, the processor samples the level of $\overline{\text{STERM}}$. If $\overline{\text{STERM}}$ is recognized, the processor latches the incoming data. If the selected data is not to be cached for the current cycle or if the device cannot supply 32 bits, $\overline{\text{CIIN}}$ must be asserted at the same time as $\overline{\text{STERM}}$.

Since $\overline{\text{CIIN}}$ and $\overline{\text{STERM}}$ are synchronous signals, they must meet the synchronous input setup and hold times for all rising edges of the clock while $\overline{\text{AS}}$ is asserted. If $\overline{\text{STERM}}$ is negated at the beginning of S2, wait states are inserted after S2, and $\overline{\text{STERM}}$ is sampled on every rising edge thereafter until it is recognized. Once $\overline{\text{STERM}}$ is recognized, data is latched on the next falling edge of the clock (corresponding to the beginning of S3).

7

State 3

The processor negates $\overline{AS}$, $\overline{DS}$, and $\overline{DBEN}$ during S3. If more than one read cycle is required to read in the operand(s), S0–S3 are repeated accordingly. When finished with the read cycle, the processor holds the address, R/$\overline{W}$, and FC0–FC2 valid in preparation for the write portion of the cycle.

The external device must keep its data asserted throughout the synchronous hold time for data from the beginning of S3. The device must remove the data within one-clock cycle after asserting $\overline{STERM}$ to avoid bus contention. It must also negate $\overline{STERM}$ within two clocks after asserting $\overline{STERM}$; otherwise, the processor may inadvertently use $\overline{STERM}$ for the next bus cycle.

Idle States

The processor does not assert any new control signals during the idle states, but it may begin the modify portion of the cycle at this time. The R/$\overline{W}$ signal remains in the read mode until S4 to prevent bus conflicts with the preceding read portion of the cycle; the data bus is not driven until S6.

State 4

The processor asserts $\overline{ECS}$ and $\overline{OCS}$ in S4 to indicate that an external cycle is beginning. The processor drives R/$\overline{W}$ low for a write cycle. CIOUT also becomes valid, indicating the state of the MMU CI bit in the address translation descriptor or in the appropriate TTx register. Depending on the write operation to be performed, the address lines may change during S4.

State 5

In state 5 (S5), the processor asserts $\overline{AS}$ to indicate that the address on the address bus is valid. The processor also asserts $\overline{DBEN}$ during S5, which can be used to enable external data buffers.

State 6

During S6, the processor places the data to be written onto the D0–D31.

The selected device uses R/$\overline{W}$, CLK, SIZ0–SIZ1, and A0–A1 to latch data from the appropriate byte(s) of the data bus (D24–D31, D16–D23, D8–D15, and D0–D7). SIZ0–SIZ1 and A0–A1 select the data bus sections. The device asserts $\overline{STERM}$ when it has successfully stored the data. If the device does not assert $\overline{STERM}$ by the rising edge of S6, the processor inserts wait states until it is recognized. The processor asserts $\overline{DS}$ at the end of S6 if wait states are inserted. Note that for zero-wait-state synchronous write cycles, $\overline{DS}$ is not asserted.

State 7

The processor negates $\overline{AS}$ (and $\overline{DS}$, if necessary) during S7. It holds the address and data valid during S7 to simplify memory interfaces. $R/\overline{W}$ and FC0–FC2 also remain valid throughout S7.

If more than one write cycle is required, S8–S11 are repeated for each write cycle.

The external device must negate $\overline{STERM}$ within two clock periods after asserting it, or the processor may inadvertently use $\overline{STERM}$ for the next bus cycle.

7.3.7 Burst Operation Cycles

The MC68030 supports a burst mode for filling the on-chip instruction and data caches.

The MC68030 provides a set of handshake control signals for the burst mode. When a miss occurs in one of the caches, the MC68030 initiates a bus cycle to obtain the required data or instruction stream fetch. If the data or instruction can be cached, the MC68030 attempts to fill a cache entry. Depending on the alignment for a data access, the MC68030 may attempt to fill two cache entries. The processor may also assert $\overline{CBREQ}$ to request a burst fill operation. That is, the processor can fill additional entries in the line. The MC68030 allows a burst of as many as four long words.

The mechanism that asserts the $\overline{CBREQ}$ signal for burstable cache entries is enabled by the data burst enable (DBE) and instruction burst enable (IBE) bits of the cache control register (CACR) for the data and instruction caches, respectively. Either of the following conditions cause the MC68030 to initiate a cache burst request (and assert $\overline{CBREQ}$) for a cachable read cycle:

- The logical address and function code signals of the current instruction or data fetch do not match the indexed tag field in the respective instruction or data cache.

- All four long words corresponding to the indexed tag in the appropriate cache are marked invalid.

However, the MC68030 does not assert $\overline{CBREQ}$ during the first portion of a misaligned access if the remainder of the access does not correspond to the same cache line. Refer to **6.1.3.1 SINGLE ENTRY MODE** for details.

If the appropriate cache is not enabled or if the cache freeze bit for the cache is set, the processor does not assert $\overline{\text{CBREQ}}$. $\overline{\text{CBREQ}}$ is not asserted during the read or write cycles of any read-modify-write operation.

The MC68030 allows burst filling only from 32-bit ports that terminate bus cycles with $\overline{\text{STERM}}$ and respond to $\overline{\text{CBREQ}}$ by asserting $\overline{\text{CBACK}}$. When the MC68030 recognizes $\overline{\text{STERM}}$ and $\overline{\text{CBACK}}$ and it has asserted $\overline{\text{CBREQ}}$, it maintains $\overline{\text{AS}}$, $\overline{\text{DS}}$, R/$\overline{\text{W}}$, A0–A31, FC0–FC2, SIZ0–SIZ1 in their current state throughout the burst operation. The processor continues to accept data on every clock during which $\overline{\text{STERM}}$ is asserted until the burst is complete or an abnormal termination occurs.

$\overline{\text{CBACK}}$ indicates that the addressed device can respond to a cache burst request by supplying one more long word of data in the burst mode. It can be asserted independently of the $\overline{\text{CBREQ}}$ signal, and burst mode is only initiated if both of these signals are asserted for a synchronous cycle. If the MC68030 executes a full burst operation and fetches four long words, $\overline{\text{CBREQ}}$ is negated after $\overline{\text{STERM}}$ is asserted for the third cycle, indicating that the MC68030 only requests one more long word (the fourth cycle). $\overline{\text{CBACK}}$ can then be negated, and the MC68030 latches the data for the fourth cycle and completes the cache line fill.

The following conditions can abort a burst fill:

- $\overline{\text{CIIN}}$ asserted,

- $\overline{\text{BERR}}$ asserted, or

- $\overline{\text{CBACK}}$ negated prematurely.

The processing of a bus error during a burst fill operation is described in **7.5.1 Bus Errors**.

For the purposes of halting the processor or arbitrating the bus away from the processor with $\overline{\text{BR}}$, a burst operation is a single cycle since $\overline{\text{AS}}$ remains asserted during the entire operation. If the $\overline{\text{HALT}}$ signal is asserted during a burst operation, the processor halts at the end of the operation. Refer to **7.5.3 Halt Operation** for more information about the halt operation. An alternate bus master requesting the bus with $\overline{\text{BR}}$ may become bus master at the end of the operation provided $\overline{\text{BR}}$ is asserted early enough to be internally synchronized before another processor cycle begins. Refer to **7.7 BUS ARBITRATION** for more information about bus arbitration.

The simultaneous assertion of $\overline{\text{BERR}}$ and $\overline{\text{HALT}}$ during a bus cycle normally indicates that the cycle should be retried. However, during the second, third, or fourth cycle of a burst operation, this signal combination indicates a bus error condition, which aborts the burst operation. In addition, the processor remains in the halted state until $\overline{\text{HALT}}$ is negated. For information about bus error processing, refer to **7.5.1. Bus Errors**.

Figure 7-37 is a flowchart of the burst operation. The following timing diagrams show various burst operations. Figure 7-38 shows burst operations for long-word requests with two wait states inserted in the first access and one wait cycle inserted in the subsequent accesses. Figure 7-39 shows a burst operation that fails to complete normally due to $\overline{\text{CBACK}}$ negating prematurely. Figure 7-40 shows a burst operation that is deferred because the entire operand does not correspond to the same cache line. Figure 7-41 shows a burst operation aborted by $\overline{\text{CIIN}}$. Because $\overline{\text{CBACK}}$ corresponds to the *next* cycle, three long words are transferred even though $\overline{\text{CBACK}}$ is only asserted for two clock periods.

The burst operation sequence begins with states S0–S3, which are very similar to those states for a synchronous read cycle except that $\overline{\text{CBREQ}}$ is asserted. S4–S9 perform the final three reads for a complete burst operation.

State 0

The burst operation starts with S0. The processor drives $\overline{\text{ECS}}$ low, indicating the beginning of an external cycle. When the cycle is the first cycle of a read operation, $\overline{\text{OCS}}$ is driven low at the same time. During S0, the processor places a valid address on A0–A31 and valid function codes on FC0–FC2. The function codes select the address space for the cycle. The processor drives R/$\overline{\text{W}}$ high, indicating a read cycle, and drives $\overline{\text{DBEN}}$ inactive to disable the data buffers. SIZ0–SIZ1 become valid, indicating the number of operand bytes to be transferred. $\overline{\text{CIOUT}}$ also becomes valid, indicating the state of the MMU CI bit in the address translation descriptor or in the appropriate TTx register.

State 1

One-half clock later in S1, the processor asserts $\overline{\text{AS}}$ to indicate that the address on the address bus is valid. The processor also asserts $\overline{\text{DS}}$ during S1. $\overline{\text{CBREQ}}$ is also asserted, indicating that the MC68030 can perform a burst operation into one of its caches and can read in four long words. In addition, $\overline{\text{ECS}}$ (and $\overline{\text{OCS}}$, if asserted) is negated during S1.

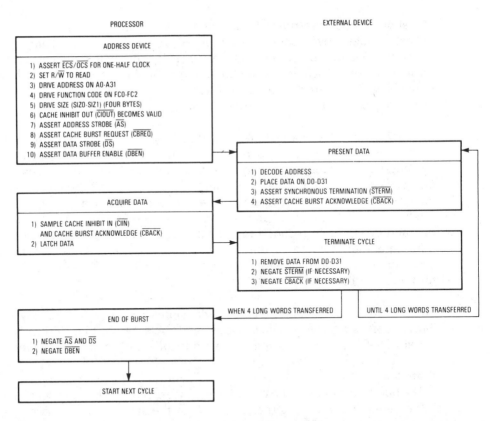

Figure 7-37. Burst Operation Flowchart — Four Long Words Transferred

State 2

The selected device uses R/$\overline{W}$, SIZ0–SIZ1, A0–A1, and $\overline{CIOUT}$ to place the data on the data bus. (The first cycle must supply the long word at the corresponding long-word boundary.) All of the byte sections (D24–D31, D16–D23, D8–D15, and D0–D7) of the data bus must be driven since the burst operation latches 32 bits on every cycle. During S2, the processor drives $\overline{DBEN}$ active to enable external data buffers. In systems that use two-clock synchronous bus cycles, the timing of $\overline{DBEN}$ may prevent its use. At the beginning of S2, the processor tests the level of $\overline{STERM}$. If $\overline{STERM}$ is recognized, the processor latches the incoming data at the end of S2. For the burst operation to proceed, $\overline{CBACK}$ must be asserted when $\overline{STERM}$ is recognized. If the data for the current cycle is not to be cached, $\overline{CIIN}$ must be asserted at the same time as $\overline{STERM}$. The assertion of $\overline{CIIN}$ also has the effect of aborting the burst operation.

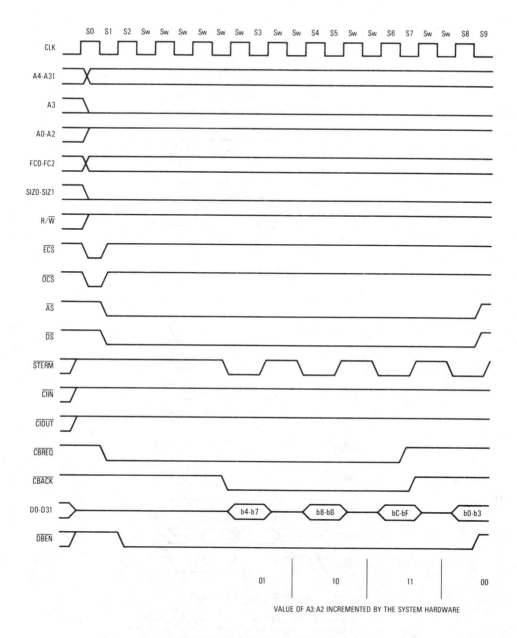

**Figure 7-38. Long-Word Operand Request from $07 with
Burst Request and Wait Cycle**

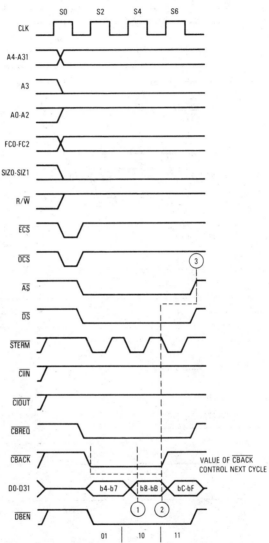

VALUE OF A3:A2 INCREMENTED BY THE SYSTEM HARDWARE

NOTES:
1. Assertion of $\overline{CBACK}$ causes data to be placed on D0-D31.
2. Continued assertion of $\overline{CBACK}$ causes data to be placed on D0-D31.
3. Negation of $\overline{CBACK}$ cause $\overline{AS}$ to be negated.

**Figure 7-39. Long-Word Operand Request from $07 with
Burst Request — CBACK Negated Early**

MC68030 USER'S MANUAL

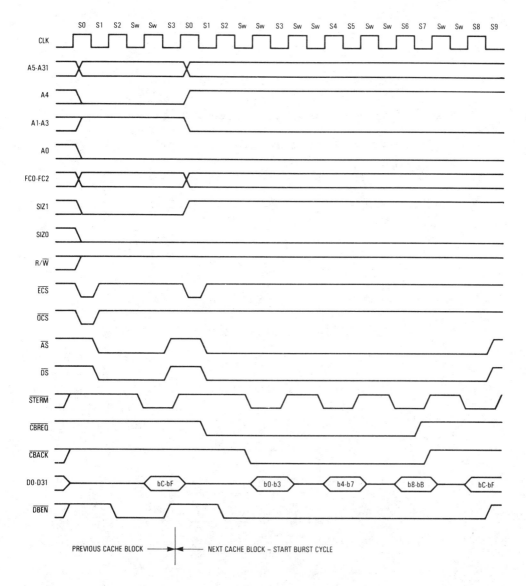

Figure 7-40. Long-Word Operand Request from $0E — Burst Fill Deferred

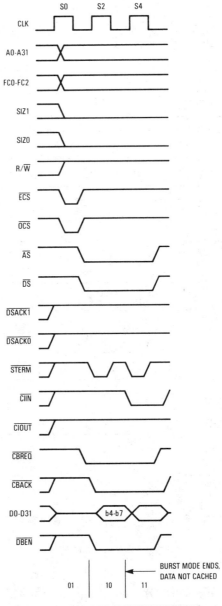

Figure 7-41. Long-Word Operand Request from $07 with
Burst Request — CBACK and CIIN Asserted

MC68030 USER'S MANUAL

MOTOROLA

Since $\overline{\text{CIIN}}$, $\overline{\text{CBACK}}$, and $\overline{\text{STERM}}$ are synchronous signals, they must meet the synchronous input setup and hold times for all rising edges of the clock while $\overline{\text{AS}}$ is asserted. If $\overline{\text{STERM}}$ is negated at the beginning of S2, wait states are inserted after S2, and $\overline{\text{STERM}}$ is sampled on every rising edge of the clock thereafter until it is recognized. Once $\overline{\text{STERM}}$ is recognized, data is latched on the next falling edge of the clock (corresponding to the beginning of S3).

State 3

The processor maintains $\overline{\text{AS}}$, $\overline{\text{DS}}$, and $\overline{\text{DBEN}}$ asserted during S3. It also holds the address valid during S3 for continuation of the burst. R/$\overline{\text{W}}$, SIZ0–SIZ1, and FC0–FC2 also remain valid throughout S3.

The external device must keep the data driven throughout the synchronous hold time for data from the beginning of S3. The device must negate $\overline{\text{STERM}}$ within one clock after asserting $\overline{\text{STERM}}$; otherwise, the processor may inadvertently use $\overline{\text{STERM}}$ prematurely for the next burst access. $\overline{\text{STERM}}$ need not be negated if subsequent accesses do not require wait cycles.

State 4

At the beginning of S4, the processor tests the level of $\overline{\text{STERM}}$. This state signifies the beginning of burst mode, and the remaining states correspond to burst fill cycles. If $\overline{\text{STERM}}$ is recognized, the processor latches the incoming data at the end of S4. This data corresponds to the second long word of the burst. If $\overline{\text{STERM}}$ is negated at the beginning of S4, wait states are inserted instead of S4 and S5, and $\overline{\text{STERM}}$ is sampled on every rising edge of the clock thereafter until it is recognized. As for synchronous cycles, the states of $\overline{\text{CBACK}}$ and $\overline{\text{CIIN}}$ are latched at the time $\overline{\text{STERM}}$ is recognized. The assertion of $\overline{\text{CBACK}}$ at this time indicates that the burst operation should continue, and the assertion of $\overline{\text{CIIN}}$ indicates that the data latched at the end of S4 should not be cached and that the burst should abort.

State 5

The processor maintains all the signals on the bus driven throughout S5 for continuation of the burst. The same hold times for $\overline{\text{STERM}}$ and data described for S3 apply here.

State 6

This state is identical to S4 except that once $\overline{\text{STERM}}$ is recognized, the third long word of data for the burst is latched at the end of S6.

State 7

During this state, the processor negates $\overline{\text{CBREQ}}$, and the memory device may negate $\overline{\text{CBACK}}$. Aside from this, all other bus signals driven by the processor remain driven. The same hold times for $\overline{\text{STERM}}$ and data described for S3 apply here.

State 8

This state is identical to S4 except that $\overline{\text{CBREQ}}$ is negated, indicating that the processor cannot continue to accept more data after this. The data latched at the end of S8 corresponds to the fourth long word of the burst.

State 9

The processor negates $\overline{\text{AS}}$, $\overline{\text{DS}}$, and $\overline{\text{DBEN}}$ during S9. It holds the address, R/$\overline{\text{W}}$, SIZ0–SIZ1, and FC0–FC2 valid throughout S9. The same hold times for data described for S3 apply here.

Note that the address bus of the MC68030 remains driven to a constant value for the duration of a burst transfer operation (including the first transfer before burst mode is entered). If an external memory system requires incrementing of the long-word base address to supply successive long words of information, this function must be performed by external hardware. Additionally, in the case of burst transfers that cross a 16-byte boundary (i.e., the first long word transferred is not located at A3/A2 = 00), the external hardware must correctly control the continuation or termination of the burst transfer as desired. The burst may be terminated by negating $\overline{\text{CBACK}}$ during the transfer of the most significant long word of the 16-byte image (A3/A2 = 11) or may be continued (with $\overline{\text{CBACK}}$ asserted) by providing the long word located at A3/A2 = 00 (i.e., the count sequence wraps back to zero and continues as necessary). The MC68030 caches assume the higher order address lines (A4–A31) remain unchanged as the long-word accesses wrap back around to A3/A2 = 00.

7.4 CPU SPACE CYCLES

FC0–FC2 select user and supervisor program and data areas as listed in Table 4-1. The area selected by FC0–FC2 = $7 is classified as the CPU space. The interrupt acknowledge, breakpoint acknowledge, and coprocessor communication cycles described in the following sections utilize CPU space.

The CPU space type is encoded on A16–A19 during a CPU space operation and indicates the function that the processor is performing. On the MC68030, three of the encodings are implemented as shown in Figure 7-42. All unused values are reserved by Motorola for future additional CPU space types.

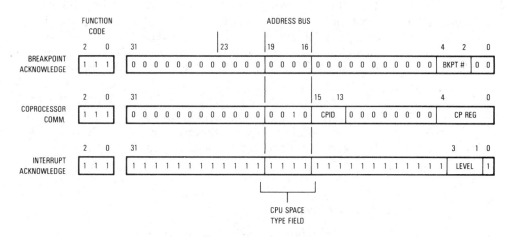

Figure 7-42. MC68030 CPU Space Address Encoding

7.4.1 Interrupt Acknowledge Bus Cycles

When a peripheral device signals the processor (with the $\overline{IPL0}$–$\overline{IPL2}$ signals) that the device requires service, and the internally synchronized value on these signals indicates a higher priority than the interrupt mask in the status register (or that a transition has occurred in the case of a level 7 interrupt), the processor makes the interrupt a pending interrupt. Refer to **8.1.9 Interrupt Exceptions** for details on the recognition of interrupts.

The MC68030 takes an interrupt exception for a pending interrupt within one instruction boundary (after processing any other pending exception with a higher priority). The following paragraphs describe the various kinds of interrupt acknowledge bus cycles that can be executed as part of interrupt exception processing.

7.4.1.1 INTERRUPT ACKNOWLEDGE CYCLE — TERMINATED NORMALLY. When the MC68030 processes an interrupt exception, it performs an interrupt acknowledge cycle to obtain the number of the vector that contains the starting location of the interrupt service routine.

Some interrupting devices have programmable vector registers that contain the interrupt vectors for the routines they use. The following paragraphs describe the interrupt acknowledge cycle for these devices. Other interrupting conditions or devices cannot supply a vector number and use the autovector cycle described in **7.4.1.2 AUTOVECTOR INTERRUPT ACKNOWLEDGE CYCLE.**

The interrupt acknowledge cycle is a read cycle. It differs from the asynchronous read cycle described in **7.3.1 Asynchronous Read Cycle** or the synchronous read cycle described in **7.3.4 Synchronous Read Cycle** in that it accesses the CPU address space. Specifically, the differences are:

1. FC0–FC2 are set to seven (FC0/FC1/FC2 = 111) for CPU address space.

2. A1, A2, and A3 are set to the interrupt request level (the inverted values of $\overline{\text{IPL0}}$, $\overline{\text{IPL1}}$, and $\overline{\text{IPL2}}$, respectively).

3. The CPU space type field (A16–A19) is set to $F, the interrupt acknowledge code.

4. A20–A31, A4–A15, and A0 are set to one.

The responding device places the vector number on the data bus during the interrupt acknowledge cycle. Beyond this, the cycle is terminated normally with either $\overline{\text{STERM}}$ or $\overline{\text{DSACKx}}$. Figure 7-43 is the flowchart of the interrupt acknowledge cycle.

MC68030 USER'S MANUAL

MOTOROLA

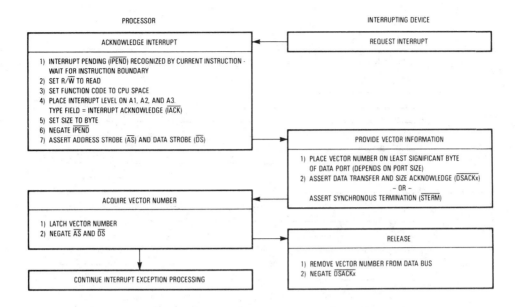

Figure 7-43. Interrupt Acknowledge Cycle Flowchart

Figure 7-44 shows the timing for an interrupt acknowledge cycle terminated with $\overline{\text{DSACKx}}$.

7.4.1.2 AUTOVECTOR INTERRUPT ACKNOWLEDGE CYCLE. When the interrupting device cannot supply a vector number, it requests an automatically generated vector or autovector. Instead of placing a vector number on the data bus and asserting $\overline{\text{DSACKx}}$ or $\overline{\text{STERM}}$, the device asserts the autovector signal ($\overline{\text{AVEC}}$) to terminate the cycle. Neither $\overline{\text{STERM}}$ nor $\overline{\text{DSACKx}}$ may be asserted during an interrupt acknowledge cycle terminated by $\overline{\text{AVEC}}$.

The vector number supplied in an autovector operation is derived from the interrupt level of the current interrupt. When $\overline{\text{AVEC}}$ is asserted instead of $\overline{\text{DSACK}}$ or $\overline{\text{STERM}}$ during an interrupt acknowledge cycle, the MC68030 ignores the state of the data bus and internally generates the vector number, the sum of the interrupt level plus 24 ($18). There are seven distinct autovectors that can be used, corresponding to the seven levels of interrupt available with signals $\overline{\text{IPL0}}$–$\overline{\text{IPL2}}$. Figure 7-45 shows the timing for an autovector operation.

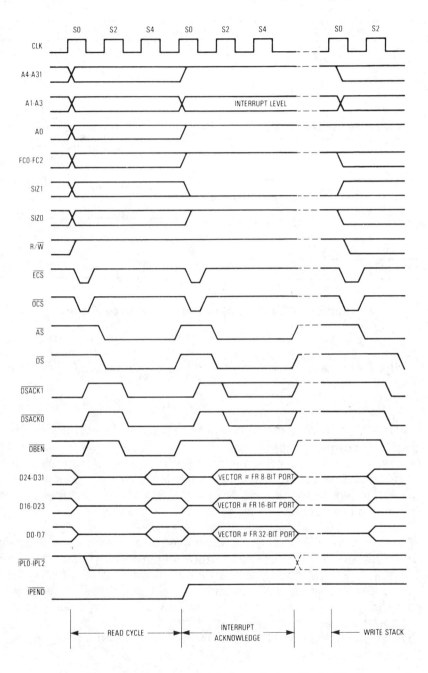

Figure 7-44. Interrupt Acknowledge Cycle Timing

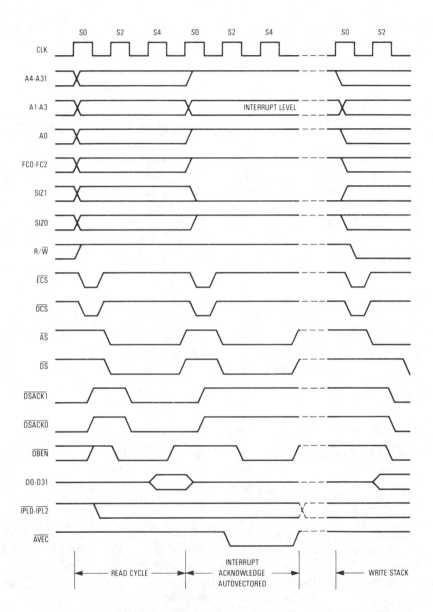

Figure 7-45. Autovector Operation Timing

7.4.1.3 SPURIOUS INTERRUPT CYCLE. When a device does not respond to an interrupt acknowledge cycle with $\overline{\text{AVEC}}$, $\overline{\text{STERM}}$, or $\overline{\text{DSACKx}}$, the external logic typically returns $\overline{\text{BERR}}$. The MC68030 automatically generates the spurious interrupt vector number, 24, instead of the interrupt vector number in this case. If $\overline{\text{HALT}}$ is also asserted, the processor retries the cycle.

7.4.2 Breakpoint Acknowledge Cycle

The breakpoint acknowledge cycle is generated by the execution of a breakpoint instruction (BKPT). The breakpoint acknowledge cycle allows the external hardware to provide an instruction word directly into the instruction pipeline as the program executes. This cycle accesses the CPU space with a type field of zero and provides the breakpoint number specified by the instruction on address lines A2–A4. If the external hardware terminates the cycle with $\overline{\text{DSACKx}}$ or $\overline{\text{STERM}}$, the data on the bus (an instruction word) is inserted into the instruction pipe, replacing the breakpoint opcode, and is executed after the breakpoint acknowledge cycle completes. The breakpoint instruction requires a word to be transferred so that if the first bus cycle accesses an 8-bit port, a second cycle is required. If the external logic terminates the breakpoint acknowledge cycle with $\overline{\text{BERR}}$ (i.e., no instruction word available), the processor takes an illegal instruction exception. Figure 7-46 is a flowchart of the breakpoint acknowledge cycle. Figure 7-47 shows the timing for a breakpoint acknowledge cycle that returns an instruction word. Figure 7-48 shows the timing for a breakpoint acknowledge cycle that signals an exception.

7.4.3 Coprocessor Communication Cycles

The MC68030 coprocessor interface provides instruction-oriented communication between the processor and as many as seven coprocessors. The bus communication required to support coprocessor operations uses the MC68030 CPU space with a type field of $2.

Coprocessor accesses use the MC68030 bus protocol except that the address bus supplies access information rather than a 32-bit address. The CPU space type field (A16–A19) for a coprocessor operation is $2. A13–A15 contain the coprocessor identification number (CpID), and A0–A4 specify the coprocessor interface register to be accessed. Coprocessor accesses to a CpID of zero correspond to MMU instructions and are not generated by the MC68030 as a result of the coprocessor interface. These cycles can only be generated by the MOVES instruction. Refer to **SECTION 10 COPROCESSOR INTERFACE DESCRIPTION** for further information.

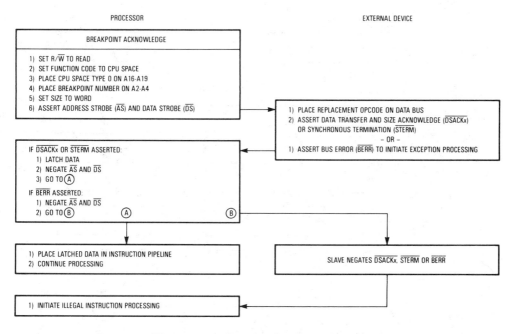

Figure 7-46. Breakpoint Operation Flow

7.5 BUS EXCEPTION CONTROL CYCLES

The MC68030 bus architecture requires assertion of either $\overline{\text{DSACKx}}$ or $\overline{\text{STERM}}$ from an external device to signal that a bus cycle is complete. $\overline{\text{DSACKx}}$, $\overline{\text{STERM}}$, or $\overline{\text{AVEC}}$ is not asserted if:

- The external device does not respond.

- No interrupt vector is provided.

- Various other application-dependent errors occur.

External circuitry can provide $\overline{\text{BERR}}$ when no device responds by asserting $\overline{\text{DSACKx}}$, $\overline{\text{STERM}}$, or $\overline{\text{AVEC}}$ within an appropriate period of time after the processor asserts $\overline{\text{AS}}$. This allows the cycle to terminate and the processor to enter exception processing for the error condition.

The MMU can also detect an internal bus error. This occurs when the processor attempts to access an address in a protected area of memory (a user program attempts to access supervisor data, for example) or after the MMU receives a bus error while searching the address table for an address translation description.

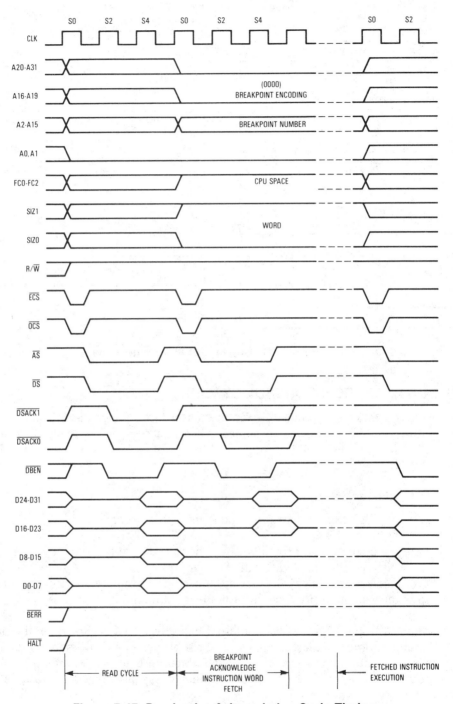

Figure 7-47. Breakpoint Acknowledge Cycle Timing

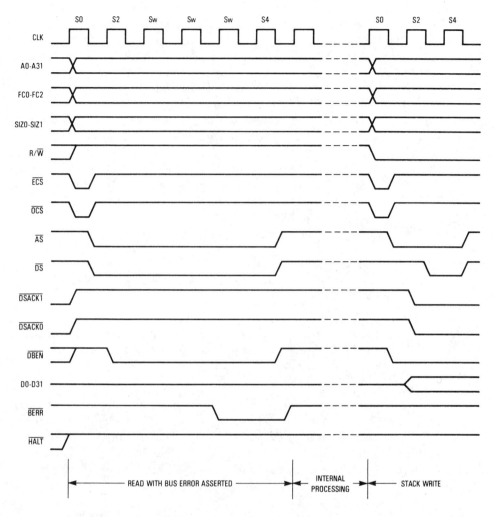

Figure 7-48. Breakpoint Acknowledge Cycle Timing (Exception Signaled)

Another signal that is used for bus exception control is $\overline{\text{HALT}}$. This signal can be asserted by an external device for debugging purposes to cause single bus cycle operation or (in combination with $\overline{\text{BERR}}$) a retry of a bus cycle in error.

To properly control termination of a bus cycle for a retry or a bus error condition, $\overline{\text{DSACKx}}$, $\overline{\text{BERR}}$, and $\overline{\text{HALT}}$ can be asserted and negated with the rising edge of the MC68030 clock. This assures that when two signals are asserted simultaneously, the required setup time (#47A) and hold time (#47B) for both of them is met for the same falling edge of the processor clock. (Refer to MC68030EC/D, *MC68030 Electrical Specifications* for timing requirements.) This or some equivalent precaution should be designed into the external circuitry that provides these signals.

The acceptable bus cycle terminations for asynchronous cycles are summarized in relation to $\overline{\text{DSACKx}}$ assertion as follows (case numbers refer to Table 7-8):

Normal Termination:
    $\overline{\text{DSACKx}}$ is asserted; $\overline{\text{BERR}}$ and $\overline{\text{HALT}}$ remain negated (case 1).

Halt Termination:
    $\overline{\text{HALT}}$ is asserted at same time or before $\overline{\text{DSACKx}}$, and $\overline{\text{BERR}}$ remains negated (case 2).

Bus Error Termination:
    $\overline{\text{BERR}}$ is asserted in lieu of, at the same time, or before $\overline{\text{DSACKx}}$ (case 3) or after $\overline{\text{DSACKx}}$ (case 4), and $\overline{\text{HALT}}$ remains negated; $\overline{\text{BERR}}$ is negated at the same time or after $\overline{\text{DSACKx}}$.

Retry Termination:
    $\overline{\text{HALT}}$ and $\overline{\text{BERR}}$ are asserted in lieu of, at the same time, or before $\overline{\text{DSACKx}}$ (case 5) or after $\overline{\text{DSACKx}}$ (case 6); $\overline{\text{BERR}}$ is negated at the same time or after $\overline{\text{DSACKx}}$; $\overline{\text{HALT}}$ may be negated at the same time or after $\overline{\text{BERR}}$.

7

Table 7-8. DSACK, BERR, and HALT Assertion Results

Case No.	Control Signal	Asserted on Rising Edge of State		Result
		N	N+2	
1	DSACKx	A	S	Normal cycle terminate and continue.
	BERR	NA	NA	
	HALT	NA	X	
2	DSACKx	A	S	Normal cycle terminate and halt. Continue when HALT negated.
	BERR	NA	NA	
	HALT	A/S	S	
3	DSACKx	NA/A	X	Terminate and take bus error exception, possibly deferred.
	BERR	A	S	
	HALT	NA	NA	
4	DSACKx	A	X	Terminate and take bus error exception, possibly deferred.
	BERR	NA	A	
	HALT	NA	NA	
5	DSACKx	NA/A	X	Terminate and retry when HALT negated.
	BERR	A	S	
	HALT	A/S	S	
6	DSACKx	A	X	Terminate and retry when HALT negated.
	BERR	NA	A	
	HALT	NA	A	

LEGEND:
- N — The number of current even bus state (e.g., S2, S4, etc.)
- A — Signal is asserted in this bus state
- NA — Signal is not asserted in this state
- X — Don't care
- S — Signal was asserted in previous state and remains asserted in this state

Table 7-8 shows various combinations of control signal sequences and the resulting bus cycle terminations. To ensure predictable operation, BERR and HALT should be negated according to the specifications in MC68030EC/D, *MC68030 Electrical Specifications*. DSACKx, BERR, and HALT may be negated after AS. If DSACKx or BERR remain asserted into S2 of the next bus cycle, that cycle may be terminated prematurely.

The termination signal for a synchronous cycle is STERM. An analogous set of bus cycle termination cases exists in relationship to STERM assertion. Note that STERM and DSACKx must never both be asserted in the same cycle. STERM has setup time (#60) and hold time (#61) requirements relative to each rising edge of the processor clock while AS is asserted. Bus error and retry terminations during burst cycles operate as described in **6.1.3.2 BURST MODE FILLING, 7.5.1 Bus Error**, and **7.5.2 Retry Operation**.

For $\overline{\text{STERM}}$, the bus cycle terminations are summarized as follows (case numbers refer to Table 7-9):

Normal Termination:
$\overline{\text{STERM}}$ is asserted; $\overline{\text{BERR}}$ and $\overline{\text{HALT}}$ remain negated (case 1).

Halt Termination:
$\overline{\text{HALT}}$ is asserted before $\overline{\text{STERM}}$, and $\overline{\text{BERR}}$ remains negated (case 2).

Bus Error Termination:
$\overline{\text{BERR}}$ is asserted in lieu of, at the same time, or before $\overline{\text{STERM}}$ (case 3) or after $\overline{\text{STERM}}$ (case 4), and $\overline{\text{HALT}}$ remains negated; $\overline{\text{BERR}}$ is negated at the same time or after $\overline{\text{STERM}}$.

Retry Termination:
$\overline{\text{HALT}}$ and $\overline{\text{BERR}}$ are asserted in lieu of, at the same time, or before $\overline{\text{STERM}}$ (case 5) or after $\overline{\text{STERM}}$ (case 6); $\overline{\text{BERR}}$ is negated at the same time or after $\overline{\text{STERM}}$; $\overline{\text{HALT}}$ may be negated at the same time or after $\overline{\text{BERR}}$.

7

Table 7-9. STERM, BERR, and HALT Assertion Results

Case No.	Control Signal	Asserted on Rising Edge of State		Result
		N	N+2	
1	STERM	A	—	Normal cycle terminate and continue.
	BERR	NA	—	
	HALT	NA	—	
2	STERM	NA	A	Normal cycle terminate and halt. Continue when HALT negated.
	BERR	NA	NA	
	HALT	A/S	S	
3	STERM	NA	A	Terminate and take bus error exception, possibly deferred.
	BERR	A/S	S	
	HALT	NA	NA	
4	STERM	A	—	Terminate and take bus error exception, possibly deferred.
	BERR	A	—	
	HALT	NA	—	
5	STERM	NA	A	Terminate and retry when HALT negated.
	BERR	A	S	
	HALT	A/S	S	
6	STERM	A	—	Terminate and retry when HALT negated.
	BERR	A	—	
	HALT	A	—	

LEGEND:
- N — The number of current even bus state (e.g., S2, S4, etc.)
- A — Signal is asserted in this bus state
- NA — Signal is not asserted in this state
- X — Don't care
- S — Signal was asserted in previous state and remains asserted in this state
- — — State N+2 not part of bus cycle

EXAMPLE A:

A system uses a watchdog timer to terminate accesses to an unpopulated address space. The timer asserts BERR after timeout (case 3).

7

EXAMPLE B:

A system uses error detection and correction on RAM contents. The designer may:

1. Delay $\overline{DSACKx}$ until data is verified; assert $\overline{BERR}$ and $\overline{HALT}$ simultaneously to indicate to the processor to automatically retry the error cycle (case 5) or, if data is valid, assert $\overline{DSACKx}$ (case 1).

2. Delay $\overline{DSACKx}$ until data is verified and assert $\overline{BERR}$ with or without $\overline{DSACKx}$ if data is in error (case 3). This initiates exception processing for software handling of the condition.

3. Return $\overline{DSACKx}$ prior to data verification. If data is invalid, $\overline{BERR}$ is asserted on the next clock cycle (case 4). This initiates exception processing for software handling of the condition.

4. Return $\overline{DSACKx}$ prior to data verification; if data is invalid, assert $\overline{BERR}$ and $\overline{HALT}$ on the next clock cycle (case 6). The memory controller can then correct the RAM prior to or during the automatic retry.

7.5.1 Bus Errors

The bus error signal can be used to abort the bus cycle and the instruction being executed. $\overline{BERR}$ takes precedence over $\overline{DSACKx}$ or $\overline{STERM}$ provided it meets the timing constraints described in MC68030EC/D, *MC68030 Electrical Specifications*. If $\overline{BERR}$ does not meet these constraints, it may cause unpredictable operation of the MC68030. If $\overline{BERR}$ remains asserted into the next bus cycle, it may cause incorrect operation of that cycle.

When the bus error signal is issued to terminate a bus cycle, the MC68030 may enter exception processing immediately following the bus cycle, or it may defer processing the exception. The instruction prefetch mechanism requests instruction words from the bus controller and the instruction cache before it is ready to execute them. If a bus error occurs on an instruction fetch, the processor does not take the exception until it attempts to use that instruction word. Should an intervening instruction cause a branch or should a task switch occur, the bus error exception does not occur.

The bus error signal is recognized during a bus cycle in any of the following cases:

- $\overline{\text{DSACKx}}$ (or $\overline{\text{STERM}}$) and $\overline{\text{HALT}}$ are negated and $\overline{\text{BERR}}$ is asserted.
- $\overline{\text{HALT}}$ and $\overline{\text{BERR}}$ are negated and $\overline{\text{DSACKx}}$ is asserted. $\overline{\text{BERR}}$ is then asserted within one clock cycle ($\overline{\text{HALT}}$ remains negated).
- $\overline{\text{BERR}}$ is asserted and recognized on the next falling clock edge following the rising clock edge on which $\overline{\text{STERM}}$ is asserted and recognized ($\overline{\text{HALT}}$ remains negated).

When the processor recognizes a bus error condition, it terminates the current bus cycle in the normal way. Figure 7-49 shows the timing of a bus error for the case in which neither $\overline{\text{DSACKx}}$ nor $\overline{\text{STERM}}$ is asserted. Figure 7-50 shows the timing for a bus error that is asserted after $\overline{\text{DSACKx}}$. Exceptions are taken in both cases. (Refer to **8.1.2 Bus Error Exception** for details of bus error exception processing.) When $\overline{\text{BERR}}$ is asserted during a read cycle that supplies data to either on-chip cache, the data in the cache is marked invalid. However, when a write cycle that writes data into the data cache results in an externally generated bus error, the data in the cache is not marked invalid.

In the second case, where $\overline{\text{BERR}}$ is asserted after $\overline{\text{DSACKx}}$ is asserted, $\overline{\text{BERR}}$ must be asserted within specification #48 (refer to MC68030EC/D, *MC68030 Electrical Specifications*) for purely asynchronous operation, or it must be asserted and remain stable during the sample window, defined by specifications #27A and #47B, around the next falling edge of the clock after $\overline{\text{DSACKx}}$ is recognized. If $\overline{\text{BERR}}$ is not stable at this time, the processor may exhibit erratic behavior. $\overline{\text{BERR}}$ has priority over $\overline{\text{DSACKx}}$. In this case, data may be present on the bus, but may not be valid. This sequence may be used by systems that have memory error detection and correction logic and by external cache memories.

The assertion of $\overline{\text{BERR}}$ described in the third case (recognized after $\overline{\text{STERM}}$) has requirements similar to those described in the preceding paragraph. $\overline{\text{BERR}}$ must be stable throughout the sample window for the next falling edge of the clock, as defined by specifications #27A and #28A. Figure 7-51 shows the timing for this case.

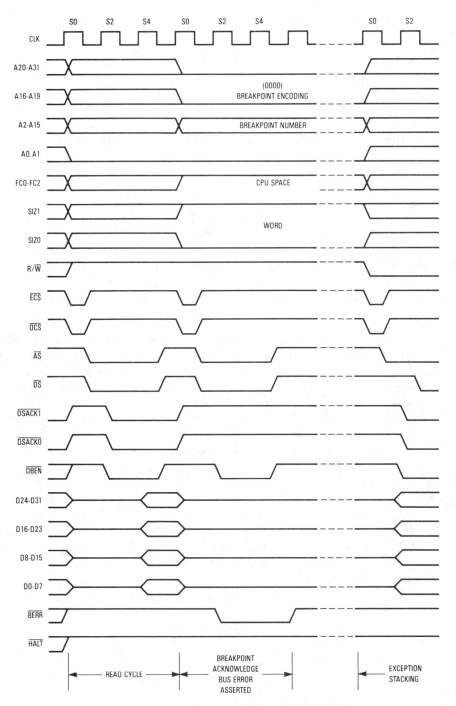

Figure 7-49. Bus Error without $\overline{\text{DSACK}}$x

MC68030 USER'S MANUAL

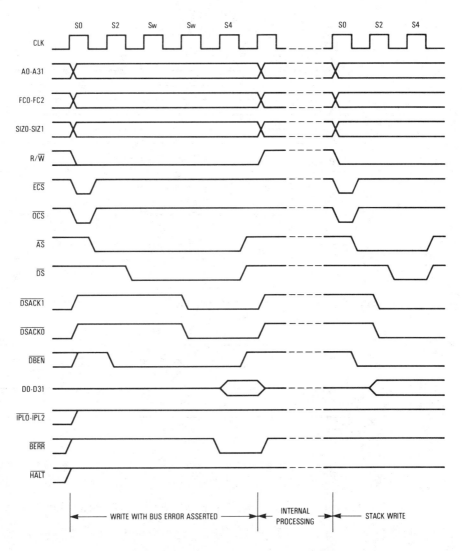

Figure 7-50. Late Bus Error with $\overline{\text{DSACKx}}$

A bus error occurring during a burst fill operation is a special case. If a bus error occurs during the first cycle of a burst, the data is ignored, the entire cache line is marked invalid, and the burst operation is aborted. If the cycle is for an instruction fetch, a bus error exception is made pending. This bus error is processed only if the execution unit attempts to use either of the two

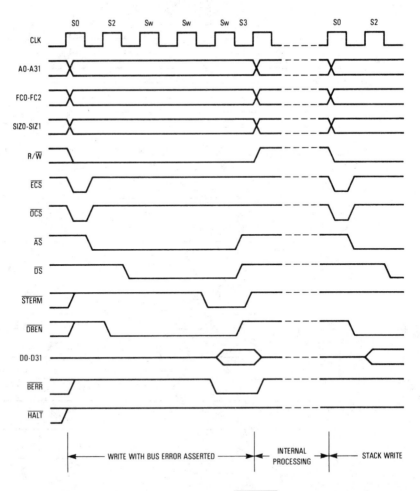

Figure 7-51. Late Bus Error with $\overline{\text{STERM}}$ — Exception Taken

words latched during the bus cycle. If the cycle is for a data fetch, the bus error exception is taken immediately. Refer to **SECTION 11 INSTRUCTION EXECUTION TIMING** for more information about pipeline operation.

When a bus error occurs after the burst mode has been entered (that is, on the second access or later), the processor terminates the burst operation, and the cache entry corresponding to that cycle is marked invalid, but the processor does not take an exception (see Figure 7-52). If the second cycle is for a portion of a misaligned operand fetch, the processor runs another

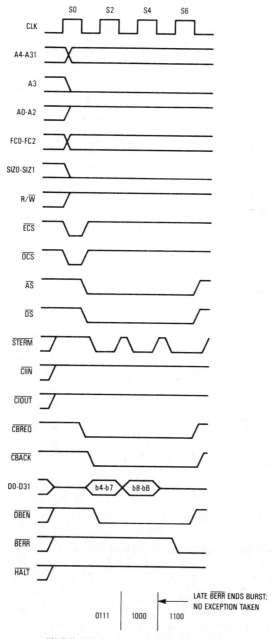

Figure 7-52. Long-Word Operand Request — Late $\overline{\text{BERR}}$ on Third Access

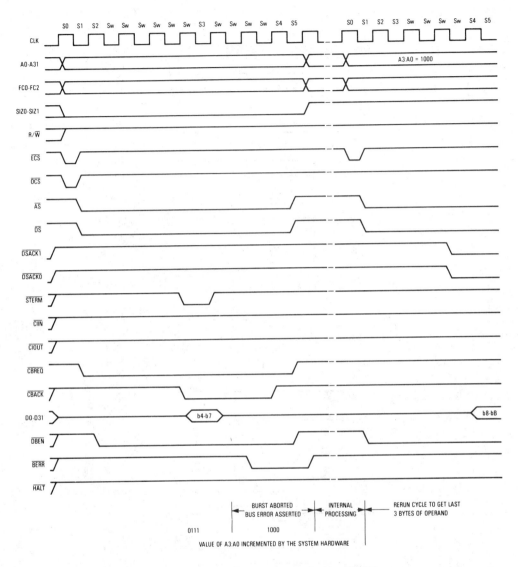

Figure 7-53. Long-Word Operand Request — $\overline{\text{BERR}}$ on Second Access

read cycle for the second portion with $\overline{\text{CBREQ}}$ negated, as shown in Figure 7-53. If $\overline{\text{BERR}}$ is asserted again, the MC68030 then takes an exception. The MC68030 supports late bus errors during a burst fill operation; the timing is the same relative to $\overline{\text{STERM}}$ and the clock as for a late bus error in a normal synchronous cycle.

MC68030 USER'S MANUAL

7.5.2 Retry Operation

When the $\overline{\text{BERR}}$ and $\overline{\text{HALT}}$ signals are both asserted by an external device during a bus cycle, the processor enters the retry sequence. A delayed retry, similar to the delayed bus error signal described previously, can also occur, both for synchronous and asynchronous cycles.

The processor terminates the bus cycle, places the control signals in their inactive state, and does not begin another bus cycle until the $\overline{\text{HALT}}$ signal is negated by external logic. After a synchronization delay, the processor retries the previous cycle using the same access information (address, function code, size, etc.) The $\overline{\text{BERR}}$ signal should be negated before S2 of the read cycle to ensure correct operation of the retried cycle. Figure 7-54 shows a retry operation of an asynchronous cycle, and Figure 7-55 shows a retry operation of a synchronous cycle.

The processor retries any read or write cycle of a read-modify-write operation separately; $\overline{\text{RMC}}$ remains asserted during the entire retry sequence.

On the initial access of a burst operation, a retry (indicated by the assertion of $\overline{\text{BERR}}$ and $\overline{\text{HALT}}$) causes the processor to retry the bus cycle and assert $\overline{\text{CBREQ}}$ again. Figure 7-56 shows a late retry operation that causes an initial burst operation to be repeated. However, signaling a retry with simultaneous $\overline{\text{BERR}}$ and $\overline{\text{HALT}}$ during the second, third, or fourth cycle of a burst operation does not cause a retry operation, even if the requested operand is misaligned. Assertion of $\overline{\text{BERR}}$ and $\overline{\text{HALT}}$ during a subsequent cycle of a burst operation causes independent $\overline{\text{BERR}}$ and $\overline{\text{HALT}}$ operations. The external bus activity remains halted until $\overline{\text{HALT}}$ is negated and the processor acts as previously described for the bus error during a burst operation.

Asserting $\overline{\text{BR}}$ along with $\overline{\text{BERR}}$ and $\overline{\text{HALT}}$ provides a relinquish and retry operation. The MC68030 does not relinquish the bus during a read-modify-write operation, except during the first read cycle. Any device that requires the processor to give up the bus and retry a bus cycle during a read-modify-write cycle must either assert $\overline{\text{BERR}}$ and $\overline{\text{BR}}$ only ($\overline{\text{HALT}}$ must not be included) or use the single wire arbitration method discussed in **7.7.4 Bus Arbitration Control**. The bus error handler software should examine the read-modify-write bit in the special status word (refer to **8.2.1 Special Status Word**) and take the appropriate action to resolve this type of fault when it occurs.

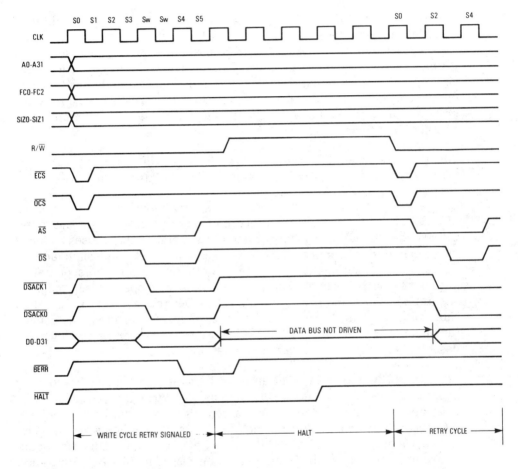

Figure 7-54. Asynchronous Late Retry

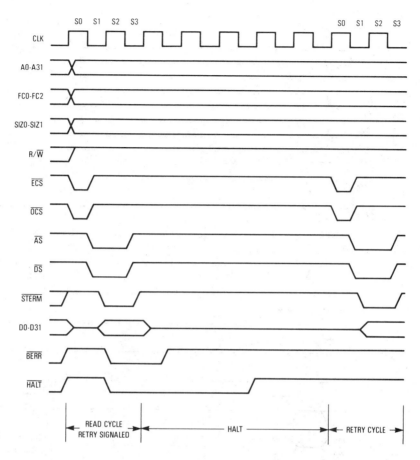

Figure 7-55. Synchronous Late Retry

7.5.3 Halt Operation

When $\overline{\text{HALT}}$ is asserted and $\overline{\text{BERR}}$ is not asserted, the MC68030 halts external bus activity at the next bus cycle boundary. $\overline{\text{HALT}}$ by itself does not terminate a bus cycle. Negating and reasserting $\overline{\text{HALT}}$ in accordance with the correct timing requirements provides a single-step (bus cycle to bus cycle) operation. The $\overline{\text{HALT}}$ signal affects external bus cycles only; thus, a program that resides in the instruction cache and performs no data writes (or reads that miss in the data cache) may continue executing, unaffected by the $\overline{\text{HALT}}$ signal.

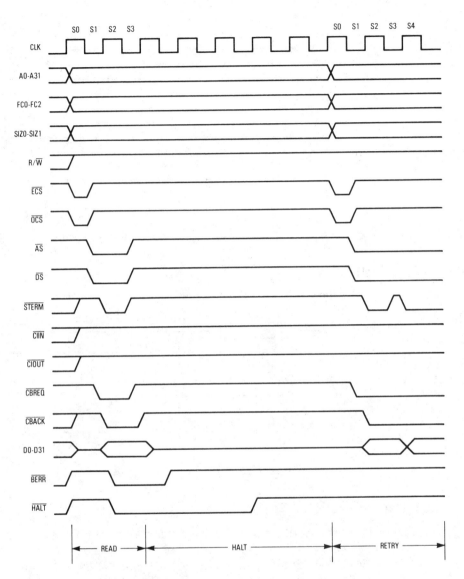

Figure 7-56. Late Retry Operation for a Burst

The single-cycle mode allows the user to proceed through (and debug) external processor operations, one bus cycle at a time. Figure 7-57 shows the timing requirements for a single-cycle operation. Since the occurrence of a bus error while $\overline{\text{HALT}}$ is asserted causes a retry operation, the user must anticipate retry cycles while debugging in the single-cycle mode. The single-

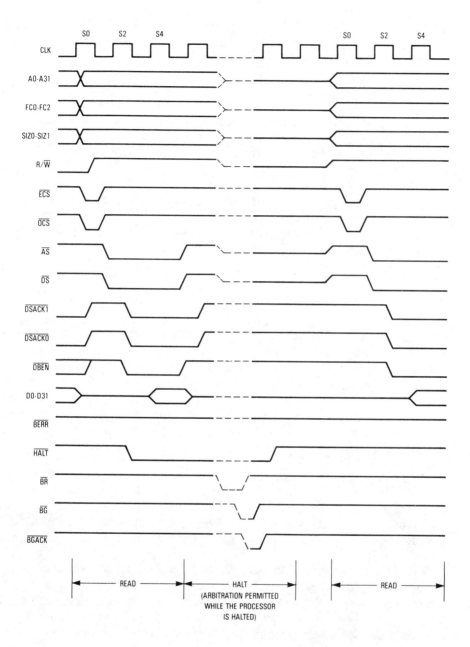

Figure 7-57. Halt Operation Timing

step operation and the software trace capability allow the system debugger to trace single bus cycles, single instructions, or changes in program flow. These processor capabilities, along with a software debugging package, give complete debugging flexibility.

When the processor completes a bus cycle with the $\overline{\text{HALT}}$ signal asserted, the data bus is placed in the high-impedance state, and bus control signals are driven inactive (not high-impedance state); the address, function code, size, and read/write signals remain in the same state. The halt operation has no effect on bus arbitration (refer to **7.7 BUS ARBITRATION**). When bus arbitration occurs while the MC68030 is halted, the address and control signals are also placed in the high-impedance state. Once bus mastership is returned to the MC68030, if $\overline{\text{HALT}}$ is still asserted, the address, function code, size, and read/write signals are again driven to their previous states. The processor does not service interrupt requests while it is halted, but it may assert the $\overline{\text{IPEND}}$ signal as appropriate.

7.5.4 Double Bus Fault

When a bus error or an address error occurs during the exception processing sequence for a previous bus error, a previous address error, or a reset exception, the bus or address error causes a double bus fault. For example, the processor attempts to stack several words containing information about the state of the machine while processing a bus error exception. If a bus error exception occurs during the stacking operation, the second error is considered a double bus fault. Only an external reset operation can restart a halted processor. However, bus arbitration can still occur (refer to **7.7 BUS ARBITRATION**).

The MC68030 indicates that a double bus fault condition has occurred by continuously asserting the $\overline{\text{STATUS}}$ signal until the processor is reset. The processor asserts $\overline{\text{STATUS}}$ for one, two, or three clock periods to signal other microsequencer status indications. Refer to **SECTION 12 APPLICATIONS IN-FORMATION** for a description of the interpretation of the $\overline{\text{STATUS}}$ signal.

A second bus error or address error that occurs after exception processing has completed (during the execution of the exception handler routine or later) does not cause a double bus fault. A bus cycle that is retried does not constitute a bus error or contribute to a double bus fault. The processor continues to retry the same bus cycle as long as the external hardware requests it.

7.6 BUS SYNCHRONIZATION

The MC68030 overlaps instruction execution; that is, during bus activity for one instruction, instructions that do not use the external bus can be executed. Due to the independent operation of the on-chip caches relative to the operation of the bus controller, many subsequent instructions can be executed, resulting in seemingly nonsequential instruction execution. When this is not desired and the system depends on sequential execution following bus activity, the NOP instruction can be used. The NOP instruction forces instruction and bus synchronization in that it freezes instruction execution until all pending bus cycles have completed.

An example of the use of the NOP instruction for this purpose is the case of a write operation of control information to an external register, where the external hardware attempts to control program execution based on the data that is written with the conditional assertion of $\overline{BERR}$. If the data cache is enabled and the write cycle results in a hit in the data cache, the cache is updated. That data, in turn, may be used in a subsequent instruction before the external write cycle completes. Since the MC68030 cannot process the bus error until the end of the bus cycle, the external hardware has not successfully interrupted program execution. To prevent a subsequent instruction from executing until the external cycle completes, a NOP instruction can be inserted after the instruction causing the write. In this case, bus error exception processing proceeds immediately after the write before subsequent instructions are executed. This is an irregular situation, and the use of the NOP instruction for this purpose is not required by most systems.

Note that even in a system with error detection/correction circuitry, the NOP is not required for this synchronization. Since the MMU always checks the validity of write cycles before they proceed to the data cache and are executed externally, the MC68030 is guaranteed to write correct data to the cache. Thus, there is no danger in subsequent instructions using erroneous data from the cache before an external bus error signals an error.

A bus synchronization example is given in Figure 7-58.

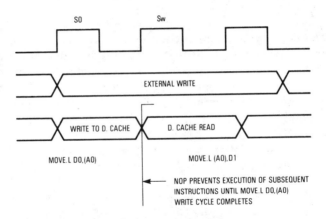

Figure 7-58. Bus Synchronization Example

7.7 BUS ARBITRATION

The bus design of the MC68030 provides for a single bus master at any one time: either the processor or an external device. One or more of the external devices on the bus can have the capability of becoming bus master. Bus arbitration is the protocol by which an external device becomes bus master; the bus controller in the MC68030 manages the bus arbitration signals so that the processor has the lowest priority. External devices that need to obtain the bus must assert the bus arbitration signals in the sequences described in the following paragraphs. Systems having several devices that can become bus master require external circuitry to assign priorities to the device so that, when two or more external devices attempt to become bus master at the same time, the one having the highest priority becomes bus master first. The sequence of the protocol is:

1. An external device asserts the bus request signal.

2. The processor asserts the bus grant signal to indicate that the bus will become available at the end of the current bus cycle.

3. The external device asserts the bus grant acknowledge signal to indicate that it has assumed bus mastership.

$\overline{BR}$ may be issued any time during a bus cycle or between cycles. $\overline{BG}$ is asserted in response to $\overline{BR}$; it is usually asserted as soon as $\overline{BR}$ has been synchronized and recognized, except when the MC68030 has made an internal decision to execute a bus cycle. Then, the assertion of $\overline{BG}$ is deferred until the bus cycle has begun. Additionally, $\overline{BG}$ is not asserted until the end of a read-modify-write operation (when $\overline{RMC}$ is negated) in response to a $\overline{BR}$

signal. When the requesting device receives $\overline{BG}$ and more than one external device can be bus master, the requesting device should begin whatever arbitration is required. The external device asserts $\overline{BGACK}$ when it assumes bus mastership and maintains $\overline{BGACK}$ during the entire bus cycle (or cycles) for which it is bus master. The following conditions must be met for an external device to assume mastership of the bus through the normal bus arbitration procedure:

- It must have received $\overline{BG}$ through the arbitration process.

- $\overline{AS}$ must be negated, indicating that no bus cycle is in progress, and the external device must ensure that all appropriate processor signals have been placed in the high-impedance state (by observing specification #7 in MC68030EC/D, *MC68030 Electrical Specifications*).

- The termination signal ($\overline{DSACKx}$ or $\overline{STERM}$) for the most recent cycle must have become inactive, indicating that external devices are off the bus (optional, refer to **7.7.3 Bus Grant Acknowledge**).

- $\overline{BGACK}$ must be inactive, indicating that no other bus master has claimed ownership of the bus.

Figure 7-59 is a flowchart showing the detail involved in bus arbitration for a single device. Figure 7-60 is a timing diagram for the same operation. This technique allows processing of bus requests during data transfer cycles.

The timing diagram shows that $\overline{BR}$ is negated at the time that $\overline{BGACK}$ is asserted. This type of operation applies to a system consisting of the processor and one device capable of bus mastership. In a system having a number of devices capable of bus mastership, the bus request line from each device can be wire-ORed to the processor. In such a system, more than one bus request can be asserted simultaneously.

The timing diagram in Figure 7-60 shows that $\overline{BG}$ is negated a few clock cycles after the transition of the $\overline{BGACK}$ signal. However, if bus requests are still pending after the negation of $\overline{BG}$, the processor asserts another $\overline{BG}$ within a few clock cycles after it was negated. This additional assertion of $\overline{BG}$ allows external arbitration circuitry to select the next bus master before the current bus master has finished with the bus. The following paragraphs provide additional information about the three steps in the arbitration process.

Bus arbitration requests are recognized during normal processing, $\overline{RESET}$ assertion, $\overline{HALT}$ assertion, and even when the processor has halted due to a double bus fault.

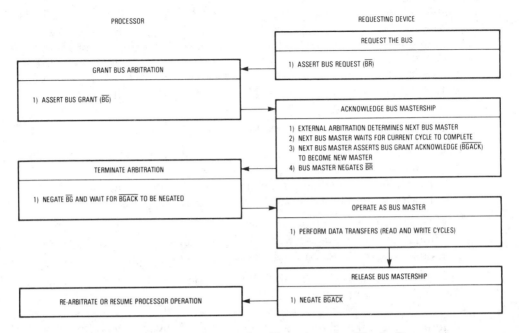

Figure 7-59. Bus Arbitration Flowchart for Single Request

7.7.1 Bus Request

External devices capable of becoming bus masters request the bus by asserting $\overline{BR}$. This can be a wire-ORed signal (although it need not be constructed from open-collector devices) that indicates to the processor that some external device requires control of the bus. The processor is effectively at a lower bus priority level than the external device and relinquishes the bus after it has completed the current bus cycle (if one has started).

If no acknowledge is received while the $\overline{BR}$ is active, the processor remains bus master once $\overline{BR}$ is negated. This prevents unnecessary interference with ordinary processing if the arbitration circuitry inadvertently responds to noise or if an external device determines that it no longer requires use of the bus before it has been granted mastership.

MC68030 USER'S MANUAL   MOTOROLA

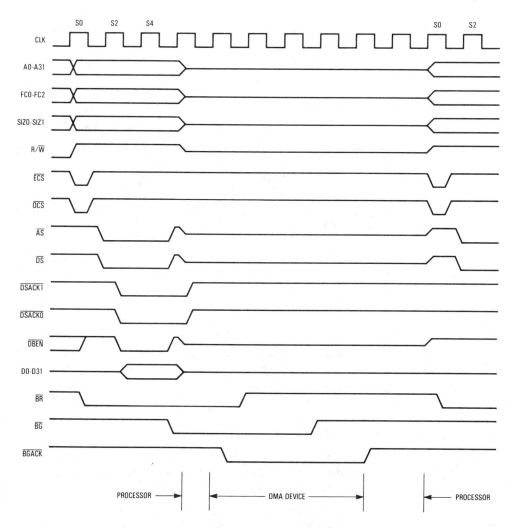

Figure 7-60. Bus Arbitration Operation Timing

7.7.2 Bus Grant

The processor asserts $\overline{BG}$ as soon as possible after receipt of $\overline{BR}$. This is immediately following internal synchronization except during a read-modify-write cycle or following an internal decision to execute a bus cycle. During a read-modify-write cycle, the processor does not assert $\overline{BG}$ until the entire operation has completed. $\overline{RMC}$ is asserted to indicate that the bus is locked. In the case an internal decision to execute another bus cycle, $\overline{BG}$ is deferred until the bus cycle has begun.

$\overline{\text{BG}}$ may be routed through a daisy-chained network or through a specific priority-encoded network. The processor allows any type of external arbitration that follows the protocol.

7.7.3 Bus Grant Acknowledge

Upon receiving $\overline{\text{BG}}$, the requesting device waits until $\overline{\text{AS}}$, $\overline{\text{DSACKx}}$ (or synchronous termination, $\overline{\text{STERM}}$), and $\overline{\text{BGACK}}$ are negated before asserting its own $\overline{\text{BGACK}}$. The negation of the $\overline{\text{AS}}$ indicates that the previous master releases the bus after specification #7 (refer to MC68030EC/D, *MC68030 Electrical Specifications*). The negation of $\overline{\text{DSACKx}}$ or $\overline{\text{STERM}}$ indicates that the previous slave has completed its cycle with the previous master. Note that in some applications, $\overline{\text{DSACKx}}$ might not be used in this way.

General-purpose devices are then connected to be dependent only on $\overline{\text{AS}}$. When $\overline{\text{BGACK}}$ is asserted, the device is the bus master until it negates $\overline{\text{BGACK}}$. $\overline{\text{BGACK}}$ should not be negated until all bus cycles required by the alternate bus master are completed. Bus mastership terminates at the negation of $\overline{\text{BGACK}}$. The $\overline{\text{BR}}$ from the granted device should be negated after $\overline{\text{BGACK}}$ is asserted. If a $\overline{\text{BR}}$ is still pending after the assertion of $\overline{\text{BGACK}}$, another $\overline{\text{BG}}$ is asserted within a few clocks of the negation of $\overline{\text{BG}}$, as described in the **7.7.4 Bus Arbitration Control**. Note that the processor does not perform any external bus cycles before it reasserts $\overline{\text{BG}}$ in this case.

7.7.4 Bus Arbitration Control

The bus arbitration control unit in the MC68030 is implemented with a finite state machine. As discussed previously, all asynchronous inputs to the MC68030 are internally synchronized in a maximum of two cycles of the processor clock.

As shown in Figure 7-61, input signals labeled R and A are internally synchronized versions of the $\overline{\text{BR}}$ and $\overline{\text{BGACK}}$ signals, respectively. The $\overline{\text{BG}}$ output is labeled G, and the internal high-impedance control signal is labeled T. If T is true, the address, data, and control buses are placed in the high-impedance state after the next rising edge following the negation of $\overline{\text{AS}}$ and $\overline{\text{RMC}}$. All signals are shown in positive logic (active high), regardless of their true active voltage level.

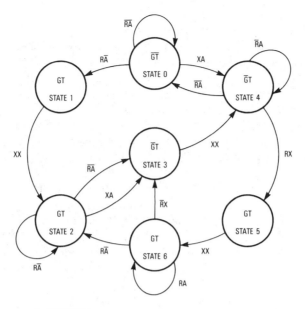

R - BUS REQUEST
A - BUS GRANT ACKNOWLEDGE
G - BUS GRANT
T - THREE-STATE CONTROL TO BUS CONTROL LOGIC
X - DON'T CARE

NOTE: The $\overline{BG}$ output will not be asserted while $\overline{RMC}$ is asserted.

Figure 7-61. Bus Arbitration State Diagram

State changes occur on the next rising edge of the clock after the internal signal is valid. The $\overline{BG}$ signal transitions on the falling edge of the clock after a state is reached during which G changes. The bus control signals (controlled by T) are driven by the processor, immediately following a state change, when bus mastership is returned to the MC68030.

State 0, at the top center of the diagram, in which G and T are both negated, is the state of the bus arbiter while the processor is bus master. Request R and acknowledge A keep the arbiter in state 0 as long as they are both negated. When a request R is received, both grant G and signal T are asserted (in state 1 at the top left). The next clock causes a change to state 2, at the lower left, in which G and T are held. The bus arbiter remains in that state until acknowledge A is asserted or request R is negated. Once either occurs, the arbiter changes to the center state, state 3, and negates grant G. The next clock takes the arbiter to state 4, at the upper right, in which grant G remains negated and signal T remains asserted. With acknowledge A asserted, the arbiter remains in state 4 until A is negated or request R is again asserted. When A is negated, the arbiter returns to the original state, state 0, and negates signal T. This sequence of states follows the normal sequence of signals for relinquishing the bus to an external bus master. Other states apply to other possible sequences of combinations of R and A. As shown by the path from state 0 to state 4, $\overline{BGACK}$ alone can be used to place the processor's external bus buffers in the high-impedance state, providing single-wire arbitration capability.

The read-modify-write sequence is normally indivisible to support semaphore operations and multiprocessor synchronization. During this indivisible sequence, the MC68030 asserts the $\overline{RMC}$ signal and causes the bus arbitration state machine to ignore bus requests (assertions of $\overline{BR}$) that occur after the first read cycle of the read-modify-write sequence by not issuing bus grants (asserting $\overline{BG}$).

In some cases, however, it may be necessary to force the MC68030 to release the bus during an read-modify-write sequence. One way for an alternate bus master to force the MC68030 to release the bus applies only to the first read cycle of an read-modify-write sequence. The MC68030 allows normal bus arbitration during this read cycle; a normal relinquish and retry operation (asserting $\overline{BERR}$, $\overline{HALT}$, and $\overline{BR}$ at the same time) is used. Note that this method applies only to the first read cycle of the read-modify-write sequence, but this method preserves the integrity of the read-modify-write sequence without imposing any constraint on the alternate bus master.

A second method is single-wire arbitration, the timing of which is shown in Figure 7-62. An alternate master forces the MC68030 to release the bus by asserting $\overline{BGACK}$ and waits for $\overline{AS}$ to negate before taking the bus. It applies to all bus cycles of a read-modify-write sequence, but can cause system integrity problems if used improperly. The alternate bus master must guarantee the integrity of the read-modify-write sequence by not altering the contents of memory locations accessed by the read-modify-write sequence. Note that for the method to operate properly, $\overline{AS}$ must be observed to be negated (high) on two consecutive clock edges before the alternate bus master takes the bus. Waiting for this condition ensures that any current or pending bus activity has completed or has been pre-empted.

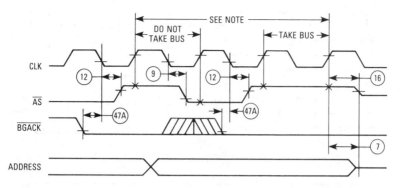

NOTE: The alternate bus master must sample AS high on two consecutive rising edges of the clock (after BGACK is recognized low) before taking the bus.

Figure 7-62. Single-Wire Bus Arbitration Timing Diagram

A timing diagram of the bus arbitration sequence during a processor bus cycle is shown in Figure 7-60. The bus arbitration sequence while the bus is inactive (i.e., executing internal operations such as a multiply instruction) is shown in Figure 7-63.

7.8 RESET OPERATION

RESET is a bidirectional signal with which an external device resets the system or the processor resets external devices. When power is applied to the system, external circuitry should assert RESET for a minimum of 520 clocks after V$_{CC}$ is within tolerance. Figure 7-64 is a timing diagram of the powerup reset operation, showing the relationships between RESET, V$_{CC}$, and bus signals. The clock signal is required to be stable by the time V$_{CC}$ reaches the minimum operating specification. During the reset period, the entire bus three-states (except for non-three-statable signals, which are driven to their inactive state). Once RESET negates, all control signals are driven to their inactive state, the data bus is in read mode, and the address bus is driven. After this, the first bus cycle for reset exception processing begins.

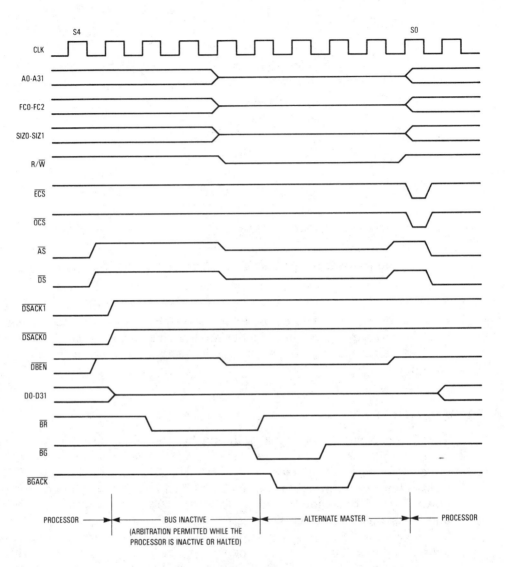

Figure 7-63. Bus Arbitration Operation (Bus Inactive)

The external RESET signal resets the processor and the entire system. Except for the initial reset, RESET should be asserted for at least 520 clock periods to ensure that the processor resets. Asserting RESET for 10 clock periods is sufficient for resetting the processor logic; the additional clock periods prevent a reset instruction from overlapping the external RESET signal.

MC68030 USER'S MANUAL   MOTOROLA

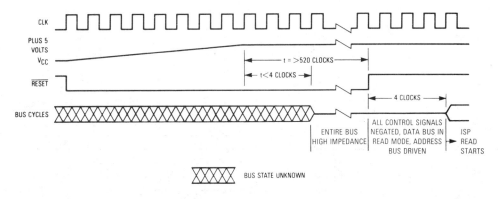

Figure 7-64. Initial Reset Operation Timing

Resetting the processor causes any bus cycle in progress to terminate as if DSACKx, BERR, or STERM had been asserted. In addition, the processor initializes registers appropriately for a reset exception. Exception processing for a reset operation is described in **8.1.1 Reset Exception**.

When a reset instruction is executed, the processor drives the RESET signal for 512 clock cycles. In this case, the processor resets the external devices of the system, and the internal registers of the processor are unaffected. The external devices connected to the RESET signal are reset at the completion of the reset instruction. An external RESET signal that is asserted to the processor during execution of a reset instruction must extend beyond the reset period of the instruction by at least eight clock cycles to reset the processor. Figure 7-65 shows the timing information for the reset instruction.

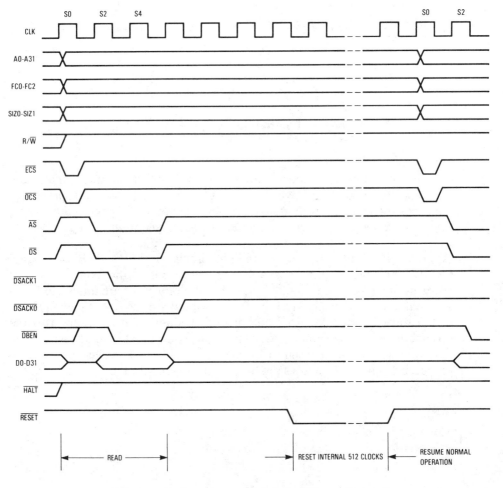

Figure 7-65. Processor-Generated Reset Operation

SECTION 8
EXCEPTION PROCESSING

Exception processing is defined as the activities performed by the processor in preparing to execute a handler routine for any condition that causes an exception. In particular, exception processing does not include execution of the handler routine itself. An introduction to exception processing, as one of the processing states of the MC68030 processor, was given in **SECTION 4 PROCESSING LEVELS**. This section describes exception processing in detail, describing the processing for each type of exception. It describes the return from an exception and bus fault recovery. This section also describes the formats of the exception stack frames. For details of MMU-related exceptions, refer to **SECTION 9 MEMORY MANAGEMENT UNIT**. For more detail on protocol violation and coprocessor-related exceptions, refer to **SECTION 10 COPROCESSOR INTERFACE DESCRIPTION**. Also, for more detail on exceptions defined for floating-point coprocessors, refer to the user's manual for the MC68881/MC68882.

8

8.1 EXCEPTION PROCESSING SEQUENCE

Exception processing occurs in four functional steps. However, all individual bus cycles associated with exception processing (vector acquisition, stacking, etc.) are not guaranteed to occur in the order in which they are described in this section. Nonetheless, all addresses and offsets from the stack pointer are guaranteed to be as described.

The first step of exception processing involves the status register. The processor makes an internal copy of the status register. Then the processor sets the S bit, changing to the supervisor privilege level. Next, the processor inhibits tracing of the exception handler by clearing the T1 and T0 bits. For the reset and interrupt exceptions, the processor also updates the interrupt priority mask.

In the second step, the processor determines the vector number of the exception. For interrupts, the processor performs an interrupt acknowledge cycle (a read from the CPU address space type $F; see Figures 7-45 and 7-46) to obtain the vector number. For coprocessor-detected exceptions, the vector number is included in the coprocessor exception primitive response.

(Refer to **SECTION 10 COPROCESSOR INTERFACE DESCRIPTION** for a complete discussion of coprocessor exceptions.) For all other exceptions, internal logic provides the vector number. This vector number is used in the last step to calculate the address of the exception vector. Throughout this section, 9vector numbers are given in decimal notation.

For all exceptions other than reset, the third step is to save the current processor context. The processor creates an exception stack frame on the active supervisor stack and fills it with context information appropriate for the type of exception. Other information may also be stacked, depending on which exception is being processed and the state of the processor prior to the exception. If the exception is an interrupt and the M bit of the status register is set, the processor clears the M bit in the status register and builds a second stack frame on the interrupt stack.

The last step initiates execution of the exception handler. The processor multiplies the vector number by four to determine the exception vector offset. It adds the offset to the value stored in the vector base register to obtain the memory address of the exception vector. Next, the processor loads the program counter (and the interrupt stack pointer (ISP) for the reset exception) from the exception vector table in memory. After prefetching the first three words to fill the instruction pipe, the processor resumes normal processing at the address in the program counter. Table 8-1 contains a description of all the exception vector offsets defined for the MC68030.

Table 8-1. Exception Vector Assignments (Sheet 1 of 2)

Vector Number(s)	Vector Offset		Assignment	STATUS Asserted
	Hex	Space		
0	000	SP	Reset Initial Interrupt Stack Pointer	—
1	004	SP	Reset Initial Program Counter	—
2	008	SD	Bus Error	Yes
3	00C	SD	Address Error	Yes
4	010	SD	Illegal Instruction	No
5	014	SD	Zero Divide	No
6	018	SD	CHK, CHK2 Instruction	No
7	01C	SD	cpTRAPcc, TRAPcc, TRAPV Instructions	No
8	020	SD	Privilege Violation	No
9	024	SD	Trace	Yes
10	028	SD	Line 1010 Emulator	No
11	02C	SD	Line 1111 Emulator	Yes
12	030	SD	(Unassigned, Reserved)	—
13	034	SD	Coprocessor Protocol Violation	No
14	038	SD	Format Error	No
15	03C	SD	Uninitialized Interrupt	Yes

Table 8-1. Exception Vector Assignments (Sheet 2 of 2)

Vector Number(s)	Vector Offset		Assignment	STATUS Asserted
	Hex	Space		
16 Through 23	040 05C	SD SD	Unassigned, Reserved	—
24	060	SD	Spurious Interrupt	Yes
25	064	SD	Level 1 Interrupt Autovector	Yes
26	068	SD	Level 2 Interrupt Autovector	Yes
27	06C	SD	Level 3 Interrupt Autovector	Yes
28	070	SD	Level 4 Interrupt Autovector	Yes
29	074	SD	Level 5 Interrupt Autovector	Yes
30	078	SD	Level 6 Interrupt Autovector	Yes
31	07C	SD	Level 7 Interrupt Autovector	Yes
32 Through 47	080 0BC	SD SD	TRAP #0–15 Instruction Vectors	No
48	0C0	SD	FPCP Branch or Set on Unordered Condition	No
49	0C4	SD	FPCP Inexact Result	No
50	0C8	SD	FPCP Divide by Zero	No
51	0CC	SD	FPCP Underflow	No
52	0D0	SD	FPCP Operand Error	No
53	0D4	SD	FPCP Overflow	No
54	0D8	SD	FPCP Signaling NAN	No
55	0DC	SD	Unassigned, Reserved	No
56	0E0	SD	MMU Configuration Error	No
57	0E4	SD	Defined for MC68851 not used by MC68030	—
58	0E8	SD	Defined for MC68851 not used by MC68030	—
59 Through 63	0EC 0FC	SD SD	Unassigned, Reserved	—
64 Through 255	100 3FC	SD SD	User Defined Vectors (192)	Yes

SP = Supervisor Program Space
SD = Supervisor Data Space

As shown in Table 8-1, the first 64 vectors are defined by Motorola and 192 vectors are reserved for interrupt vectors defined by the user. However, external devices may use vectors reserved for internal purposes at the discretion of the system designer.

8

The MC68030 provides the $\overline{\text{STATUS}}$ signal to identify instruction boundaries and some exceptions. As shown in Table 8-2, $\overline{\text{STATUS}}$ indicates an instruction boundary and exceptions to be processed, depending on the state of the internal microsequencer. In addition, $\overline{\text{STATUS}}$ indicates when an MMU address translation cache miss has occurred and the processor is about to begin a table search access for the logical address that caused the miss. Instruction-related exceptions do not cause the assertion of $\overline{\text{STATUS}}$ as shown in Table 8-1. For $\overline{\text{STATUS}}$ signal timing information, refer to **SECTION 12 APPLICATIONS INFORMATION**.

Table 8-2. Microsequencer $\overline{\text{STATUS}}$ Indications

Asserted for	Indicates
1 Clock	Sequencer at instruction boundary will begin execution of next instruction.
2 Clocks	Sequencer at instruction boundary but will not begin the next instruction immediately due to: • pending trace exception OR • pending interrupt exception
3 Clocks	MMU address translation cache miss — processor to begin table serach OR Exception processing to begin for: • reset OR • bus error OR • address error OR • spurious interrupt OR • autovectored interrupt OR • F-line instruction (no coprocessor responded)
Continuously	Processor halted due to double bus fault.

8

       MC68030 USER'S MANUAL   MOTOROLA

8.1.1 Reset Exception

Assertion by external hardware of the $\overline{\text{RESET}}$ signal causes a reset exception. For details on the requirements for the assertion of $\overline{\text{RESET}}$, refer to **7.8 RESET OPERATION**.

The reset exception has the highest priority of any exception; it provides for system initialization and recovery from catastrophic failure. When reset is recognized, it aborts any processing in progress, and that processing cannot be recovered. Figure 8-1 is a flowchart of the reset exception, which performs the following operations:

1. Clears both trace bits in the status register to disable tracing.

2. Places the processor in the interrupt mode of the supervisor privilege level by setting the supervisor bit and clearing the master bit in the status register.

3. Sets the processor interrupt priority mask to the highest priority level (level 7).

4. Initializes the vector base register to zero ($00000000).

5. Clears the enable, freeze, and burst enable bits for both on-chip caches and the write-allocate bit for the data cache in the cache control register.

6. Invalidates all entries in the instruction and data caches.

7. Clears the enable bit in the translation control register and the enable bits in both transparent translation registers of the MMU.

8. Generates a vector number to reference the reset exception vector (two long words) at offset zero in the supervisor program address space.

9. Loads the first long word of the reset exception vector into the interrupt stack pointer.

10. Loads the second long word of the reset exception vector into the program counter.

After the initial instruction prefetches, program execution begins at the address in the program counter. The reset exception does not flush the address translation cache (ATC), nor does it save the value of either the program counter or the status register.

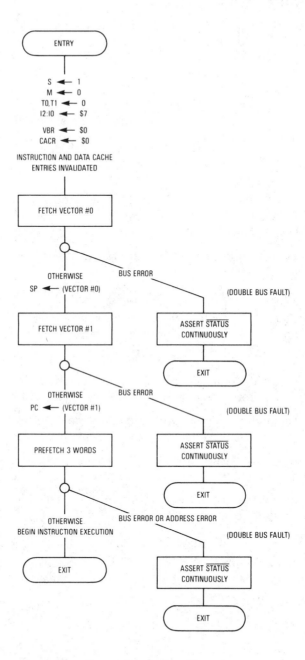

Figure 8-1. Reset Operation Flowchart

As described in **7.5.4 Double Bus Fault**, if bus error or address error occur during the exception processing sequence for a reset, a double bus fault occurs. The processor halts, and the $\overline{\text{STATUS}}$ signal is asserted continuously to indicate the halted condition.

Execution of the reset instruction does not cause a reset exception, nor does it affect any internal registers, but it does cause the MC68030 to assert the $\overline{\text{RESET}}$ signal, resetting all external devices.

8.1.2 Bus Error Exception

A bus error exception occurs when external logic aborts a bus cycle by asserting the $\overline{\text{BERR}}$ input signal. If the aborted bus cycle is a data access, the processor immediately begins exception processing. If the aborted bus cycle is an instruction prefetch, the processor may delay taking the exception until it attempts to use the prefetched information. The assertion of the $\overline{\text{BERR}}$ signal during the second, third, or fourth access of a burst operation does not cause a bus error exception, but the burst is aborted. Refer to **6.1.3.2 BURST MODE FILLING** and **7.5.1 Bus Errors** for details on the effects of bus errors during burst operation.

A bus error exception also occurs when the MMU detects that a successful address translation is not possible. Furthermore, when an ATC miss occurs and an external bus cycle is required, the MMU must abort the bus cycle, search the translation tables in memory for the mapping, and then retry the bus cycle. If a valid translation for the logical address is not available due to a problem encountered during the table search (the attempt to access the appropriate page descriptor in the translation tables for that page), a bus error exception occurs when the aborted bus cycle is retried.

The problem encountered could be a limit violation, an invalid descriptor, or the assertion of the $\overline{\text{BERR}}$ signal during a bus cycle used to access the translation tables. A miss in the ATC causes the processor to automatically initiate a table search but does not cause a bus error exception unless one of the specific conditions mentioned above is encountered.

8

The processor begins exception processing for a bus error by making an internal copy of the current status register. The processor then enters the supervisor privilege level (by setting the S bit in the status register) and clears the trace bits. The processor generates exception vector number 2 for the bus error vector. It saves the vector offset, program counter, and the internal copy of the status register on the stack. The saved program counter value is the logical address of the instruction that was executing at the time the fault was detected. This is not necessarily the instruction that initiated the bus cycle, since the processor overlaps execution of instructions. The processor also saves the contents of some of its internal registers. The information saved on the stack is sufficient to identify the cause of the bus fault and recover from the error.

For efficiency, the MC68030 uses two different bus error stack frame formats. When the bus error exception is taken at an instruction boundary, less information is required to recover from the error, and the processor builds the short bus fault stack frame as shown in Table 8-7. When the exception is taken during the execution of an instruction, the processor must save its entire state for recovery and uses the long bus fault stack frame shown in Table 8-7. The format code in the stack frame distinguishes the two stack frame formats. Stack frame formats are described in detail in **8.4 EXCEPTION STACK FRAME FORMATS**.

If a bus error occurs during the exception processing for a bus error, address error, or reset or while the processor is loading internal state information from the stack during the execution of an RTE instruction, a double bus fault occurs, and the processor enters the halted state as indicated by the continuous assertion of the $\overline{\text{STATUS}}$ signal. In this case, the processor does not attempt to alter the current state of memory. Only an external $\overline{\text{RESET}}$ can restart a processor halted by a double bus fault.

8.1.3 Address Error Exception

An address error exception occurs when the processor attempts to prefetch an instruction from an odd address. This exception is similar to a bus error exception, but is internally initiated. A bus cycle is not executed, and the processor begins exception processing immediately. After exception processing commences, the sequence is the same as that for bus error exceptions described in the preceding paragraphs, except that the vector number is 3 and the vector offset in the stack frame refers to the address error vector. Either a short or long bus fault stack frame may be generated. If an address error occurs during the exception processing for a bus error, address error, or reset, a double bus fault occurs.

8.1.4 Instruction Trap Exception

Certain instructions are used to explicitly cause trap exceptions. The TRAP #n instruction always forces an exception and is useful for implementing system calls in user programs. The TRAPcc, TRAPV, cpTRAPcc, CHK, and CHK2 instructions force exceptions if the user program detects an error, which may be an arithmetic overflow or a subscript value that is out of bounds.

The DIVS and DIVU instructions force exceptions if a division operation is attempted with a divisor of zero.

When a trap exception occurs, the processor copies the status register internally, enters the supervisor privilege level, and clears the trace bits. If tracing is enabled for the instruction that caused the trap, a trace exception is taken after the RTE instruction from the trap handler is executed, and the trace corresponds to the trap instruction; the trap handler routine is not traced. The processor generates a vector number according to the instruction being executed; for the TRAP #n instruction, the vector number is 32 plus n. The stack frame saves the trap vector offset, the program counter, and the internal copy of the status register on the supervisor stack. The saved value of the program counter is the logical address of the instruction following the instruction that caused the trap. For all instruction traps other than TRAP #n, a pointer to the instruction that caused the trap is also saved. Instruction execution resumes at the address in the exception vector after the required instruction prefetches.

8.1.5 Illegal Instruction and Unimplemented Instruction Exceptions

An illegal instruction is an instruction that contains any bit pattern in its first word that does not correspond to the bit pattern of the first word of a valid MC68030 instruction or is a MOVEC instruction with an undefined register specification field in the first extension word. An illegal instruction exception corresponds to vector number 4 and occurs when the processor attempts to execute an illegal instruction.

An illegal instruction exception is also taken if a breakpoint acknowledge bus cycle (see **7.4.2 Breakpoint Acknowledge Cycle**) is terminated with the assertion of the bus error signal. This implies that the external circuitry did not supply an instruction word to replace the BKPT instruction word in the instruction pipe.

Instruction word patterns with bits [15:12] equal to $A are referred to as unimplemented instructions with A-line opcodes. When the processor attempts to execute an unimplemented instruction with an A-line opcode, an exception is generated with vector number 10, permitting efficient emulation of unimplemented instructions.

Instructions that have word patterns with bits [15:12] equal to $F, bits [11:9] equal to $0, and defined word patterns for subsequent words are legal MMU instructions. Instructions that have bits [15:12] of the first words equal to $F, bits [11:9] equal to $0, and undefined patterns in subsequent words are treated as unimplemented instructions with F-line opcodes when execution is attempted in supervisor mode. When execution of the same instruction is attempted in user mode, a privilege violation exception is taken. The exception vector number for an unimplemented instruction with an F-line opcode is number 11.

The word patterns with bits [15:12] equal to $F and bits [11:9] not equal to zero are used for coprocessor instructions. When the processor identifies a coprocessor instruction, it runs a bus cycle referencing CPU space type $2 (refer to **4.2 ADDRESS SPACE TYPES**) and addressing one of seven coprocessors (1–7, according to bits [11:9]). If the addressed coprocessor is not included in the system and the cycle terminates with the assertion of the bus error signal, the instruction takes an unimplemented instruction (F-line opcode) exception. The system can emulate the functions of the coprocessor with an F-line exception handler. Refer to **SECTION 10 COPROCESSOR INTERFACE DESCRIPTION** for more details.

Exception processing for illegal and unimplemented instructions is similar to that for instruction traps. When the processor has identified an illegal or unimplemented instruction, it initiates exception processing instead of attempting to execute the instruction. The processor copies the status register, enters the supervisor privilege level, and clears the trace bits, disabling further tracing. The processor generates the vector number, either 4, 10, or 11, according to the exception type. The illegal or unimplemented instruction vector offset, current program counter, and copy of the status register are saved on the supervisor stack, with the saved value of the program counter being the address of the illegal or unimplemented instruction. Instruction execution resumes at the address contained in the exception vector. It is the responsibility of the handling routine to adjust the stacked program counter if the instruction is emulated in software or is to be skipped on return from the handler.

8.1.6 Privilege Violation Exception

To provide system security, the following instructions are privileged:
ANDI TO SR
EOR to SR
cpRESTORE
cpSAVE
MOVE from SR
MOVE to SR
MOVE USP
MOVEC
MOVES
ORI to SR
PFLUSH
PLOAD
PMOVE
PTEST
RESET
RTE
STOP

An attempt to execute one of the privileged instructions while at the user privilege level causes a privilege violation exception. Also, a privilege violation exception occurs if a coprocessor requests a privilege check and the processor is at the user level.

Exception processing for privilege violations is similar to that for illegal instructions. When the processor identifies a privilege violation, it begins exception processing before executing the instruction. The processor copies the status register, enters the supervisor privilege level, and clears the trace bits. The processor generates vector number 8, the privilege violation exception vector, and saves the privilege violation vector offset, the current program counter value, and the internal copy of the status register on the supervisor stack. The saved value of the program counter is the logical address of the first word of the instruction that caused the privilege violation. Instruction execution resumes after the required prefetches from the address in the privilege violation exception vector.

8.1.7 Trace Exception

To aid in program development, the M68000 processors include instruction-by-instruction tracing capability. The MC68030 can be programmed to trace all instructions or only instructions that change program flow. In the trace mode, an instruction generates a trace exception after it completes execution, allowing a debugger program to monitor execution of a program.

The T1 and T0 bits in the supervisor portion of the status register control tracing. The state of these bits when an instruction begins execution determines whether the instruction generates a trace exception after the instruction completes. Clearing both T bits disables tracing, and instruction execution proceeds normally. Clearing the T1 bit and setting the T0 bit causes an instruction that forces a change of flow to take a trace exception. Instructions that increment the program counter normally do not take the trace exception. Instructions that are traced in this mode include all branches, jumps, instruction traps, returns, and coprocessor instructions that modify the program counter flow. This mode also includes status register manipulations, because the processor must re-prefetch instruction words to fill the pipe again any time an instruction that can modify the status register is executed. The execution of the BKPT instruction causes a change of flow if the opcode replacing the BKPT is an instruction that causes a change of flow (i.e., a jump, branch, etc.). Setting the T1 bit and clearing the T0 bit causes the execution of all instructions to force trace exceptions. Table 8-3 shows the trace mode selected by each combination of T1 and T0.

Table 8-3. Tracing Control

T1	T0	Tracing Function
0	0	No Tracing
0	1	Trace on Change of Flow (BRA, JMP, etc.)
1	0	Trace on Instruction Execution (Any Instruction)
1	1	Undefined, Reserved

In general terms, a trace exception is an extension to the function of any traced instruction — that is, the execution of a traced instruction is not complete until the trace exception processing is completed. If an instruction does not complete due to a bus error or address error exception, trace exception processing is deferred until after the execution of the suspended instruction is resumed and the instruction execution completes normally. If an interrupt is pending at the completion of an instruction, the trace exception processing occurs before the interrupt exception processing starts. If an instruction forces an exception as part of its normal execution, the forced exception processing occurs before the trace exception is processed. See **8.1.12 Multiple Exceptions** for a more complete discussion of exception priorities.

When the processor is in the trace mode and attempts to execute an illegal or unimplemented instruction, that instruction does not cause a trace exception since it is not executed. This is of particular importance to an instruction emulation routine that performs the instruction function, adjusts the stacked program counter to skip the unimplemented instruction, and returns. Before returning, the trace bits of the status register on the stack should be checked. If tracing is enabled, the trace exception processing should also be emulated for the trace exception handler to account for the emulated instruction.

The exception processing for a trace starts at the end of normal processing for the traced instruction and before the start of the next instruction. The processor makes an internal copy of the status register and enters the supervisor privilege level. It also clears the T0 and T1 bits of the status register, disabling further tracing. The processor supplies vector number 9 for the trace exception and saves the trace exception vector offset, program counter value, and the copy of the status register on the supervisor stack. The saved value of the program counter is the logical address of the next instruction to be executed. Instruction execution resumes after the required prefetches from the address in the trace exception vector.

The STOP instruction does not perform its function when it is traced. A STOP instruction that begins execution with T1 = 1 and T0 = 0 forces a trace exception after it loads the status register. Upon return from the trace handler routine, execution continues with the instruction following the STOP, and the processor never enters the stopped condition.

8.1.8 Format Error Exception

Just as the processor checks that prefetched instructions are valid, the processor (with the aid of a coprocessor, if needed) also performs some checks of data values for control operations, including the coprocessor state frame format word for a cpRESTORE instruction and the stack frame format for an RTE instruction.

The RTE instruction checks the validity of the stack format code. For long bus cycle fault format frames, the RTE instruction also compares the internal version number of the processor to that contained in the frame at memory location SP + 54 (SP + $36). This check ensures that the processor can correctly interpret internal state information from the stack frame.

The cpRESTORE instruction passes the format word of the coprocessor state frame to the coprocessor for validation. If the coprocessor does not recognize the format value, it signals the MC68030 to take a format error exception. Refer to **SECTION 10 COPROCESSOR INTERFACE DESCRIPTION** for details of coprocessor-related exceptions.

If any of the checks previously described determine that the format of the stacked data is improper, the instruction generates a format error exception. This exception saves a short format stack frame, generates exception vector number 14, and continues execution at the address in the format exception vector. The stacked program counter value is the logical address of the instruction that detected the format error.

8.1.9 Interrupt Exceptions

When a peripheral device requires the services of the MC68030 or is ready to send information that the processor requires, it may signal the processor to take an interrupt exception. The interrupt exception transfers control to a routine that responds appropriately.

The peripheral device uses the active-low interrupt priority level signals (IPL0–IPL2) to signal an interrupt condition to the processor and to specify the priority of that condition. The three signals encode a value of zero through seven (IPL0 is the least significant bit). High levels on all three signals correspond to no interrupt requested (level 0) and low levels on IPL0–IPL2 correspond to interrupt request level 7. Values 1–7 specify one of seven levels of prioritized interrupts; level seven has the highest priority. External circuitry can chain or otherwise merge signals from devices at each level, allowing an unlimited number of devices to interrupt the processor.

The IPL0–IPL2 interrupt signals must maintain the interrupt request level until the MC68030 acknowledges the interrupt to guarantee that the interrupt is recognized. The MC68030 continuously samples the IPL0–IPL2 signals on consecutive falling edges of the processor clock to synchronize and debounce these signals. An interrupt request that is the same for two consecutive falling clock edges is considered a valid input. Although the protocol requires that the request remain until the processor runs an interrupt acknowledge cycle for that interrupt value, an interrupt request that is held for as short a period as two clock cycles could be recognized.

The status register of the MC68030 contains an interrupt priority mask (I2, I1, I0, bits 10–8). The value in the interrupt mask is the highest priority level that the processor ignores. When an interrupt request has a priority higher than the value in the mask, the processor makes the request a pending interrupt. Figure 8-2 is a flowchart of the procedure for making an interrupt pending.

8

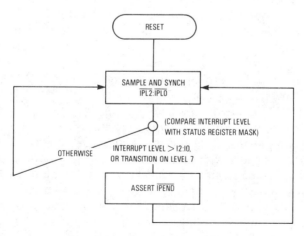

Figure 8-2. Interrupt Pending Procedure

When several devices are connected to the same interrupt level, each device should hold its interrupt priority level constant until its corresponding interrupt acknowledge cycle to ensure that all requests are processed.

Table 8-4 lists the interrupt levels, the states of $\overline{IPL2}-\overline{IPL0}$ that define each level, and the mask value that allows an interrupt at each level.

Table 8-4. Interrupt Levels and Mask Values

Requested Interrupt Level	Control Line Status			Interrupt Mask Level Required for Recognition
	$\overline{IP2}$	$\overline{IP1}$	$\overline{IP0}$	
0*	High	High	High	N/A*
1	High	High	Low	0
2	High	Low	High	0-1
3	High	Low	Low	0-2
4	Low	High	High	0-3
5	Low	High	Low	0-4
6	Low	Low	High	0-5
7	Low	Low	Low	0-7

*Indicates that no interrupt is requested.

Priority level 7, the nonmaskable interrupt (NMI), is a special case. Level 7 interrupts cannot be masked by the interrupt priority mask, and they are transition sensitive. The processor recognizes an interrupt request each time the external interrupt request level changes from some lower level to level 7, regardless of the value in the mask. Figure 8-3 shows two examples of interrupt recognitions, one for level 6 and one for level 7. When the MC68030 processes a level 6 interrupt, the status register mask is automatically updated with a value of 6 before entering the handler routine so that subsequent level 6 interrupts are masked. Provided no instruction that lowers the mask value is executed, the external request can be lowered to level 3 and then raised back to level 6 and a second level 6 interrupt is not processed. However, if the MC68030 is handling a level 7 interrupt (status register mask set to 7) and the external request is lowered to level 3 and than raised back to level 7, a second level 7 interrupt is processed. The second level 7 interrupt is processed because the level 7 interrupt is transition sensitive. A level 7 interrupt is also generated by a level comparison if the request level and mask level are at seven and the priority mask is then set to a lower level (with the MOVE to SR or RTE instruction, for example). As shown in Figure 8-3 for level 6 interrupt request level and mask level, this is the case for all interrupt levels.

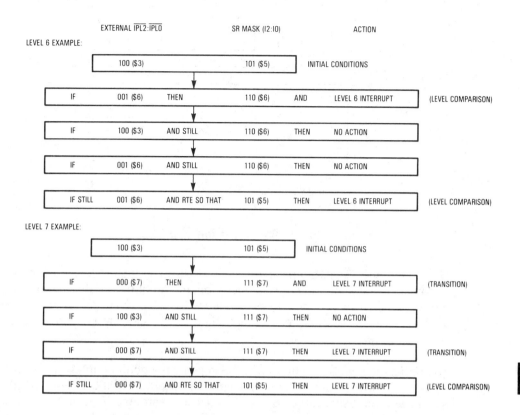

Figure 8-3. Interrupt Recognition Examples

Note that a mask value of 6 and a mask value of 7 both inhibit request levels 1–6 from being recognized. In addition, neither masks a transition to an interrupt request level of 7. The only difference between mask values of 6 and 7 occurs when the interrupt request level is 7 and the mask value is 7. If the mask value is lowered to 6, a second level 7 interrupt is recognized.

The MC68030 asserts the interrupt pending signal (IPEND) when it makes an interrupt request pending. Figure 8-4 shows the assertion of IPEND relative to the assertion of an interrupt level on the IPL lines. IPEND signals to external devices that an interrupt exception will be taken at an upcoming instruction boundary (following any higher priority exception).

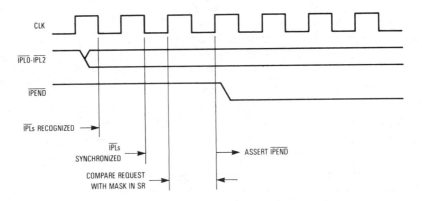

Figure 8-4. Assertion of IPEND

The state of the IPEND signal is internally checked by the processor once per instruction, independently of bus operation. In addition, it is checked during the second instruction prefetch associated with exception processing. Figure 8-5 is a flowchart of the interrupt recognition and associated exception processing sequence.

To predict the instruction boundary during which a pending interrupt is processed, the timing relationship between the assertion of IPEND for that interrupt and the assertion of STATUS must be examined. Figure 8-6 shows two examples of interrupt recognition. The first assertion of STATUS after IPEND is denoted as STAT0. The next assertion of STATUS is denoted as STAT1. If STAT0 begins on the falling edge of the clock immediately following the clock edge that caused IPEND to assert (as shown in example 1), STAT1 is at least two clocks long, and, when there are no other pending exceptions, the interrupt is acknowledged at the boundary defined by STAT1. If IPEND is asserted with more setup time to STAT0, the interrupt may be acknowledged at the boundary defined by STAT0 (as shown in example 2). In that case, STAT0 is asserted for two clocks, signaling this condition.

If no higher priority interrupt has been synchronized, the IPEND signal is negated during state 0 (S0) of an interrupt acknowledge cycle (refer to **7.4.1.1 INTERRUPT ACKNOWLEDGE CYCLE — TERMINATED NORMALLY**), and the IPLx signals for the interrupt being acknowledged can be negated at this time.

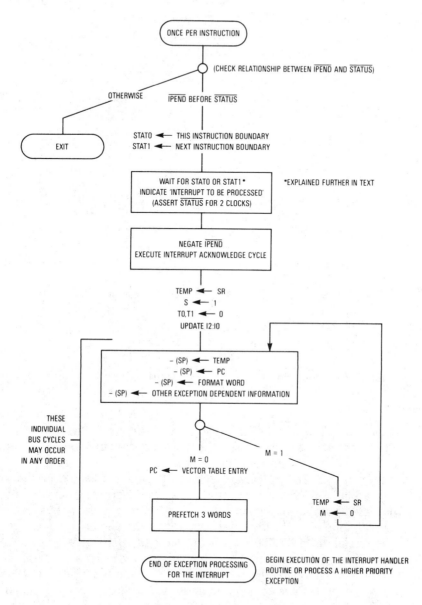

Figure 8-5. Interrupt Exception Processing Flowchart

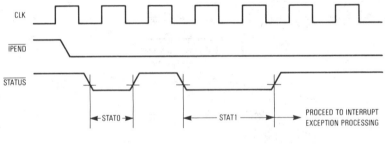

EXAMPLE 1: INTERRUPT EXCEPTION SIGNALED DURING STAT1

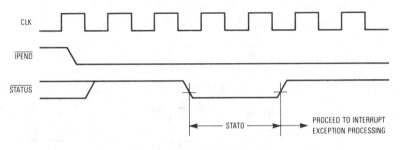

EXAMPLE 2: INTERRUPT EXCEPTION SIGNALED DURING STAT0

Figure 8-6. Examples of Interrupt Recognition and Instruction Boundaries

When processing an interrupt exception, the processor first makes an internal copy of the status register, sets the privilege level to supervisor, suppresses tracing, and sets the processor interrupt mask level to the level of the interrupt being serviced. The processor attempts to obtain a vector number from the interrupting device using an interrupt acknowledge bus cycle with the interrupt level number output on pins A1–A3 of the address bus. For a device that cannot supply an interrupt vector, the autovector signal ($\overline{\text{AVEC}}$) can be asserted, and the MC68030 uses an internally generated autovector, which is one of vector numbers 25–31, that corresponds to the interrupt level number. If external logic indicates a bus error during the interrupt acknowledge cycle, the interrupt is considered spurious, and the processor generates the spurious interrupt vector number, 24. Refer to **7.4.1 Interrupt Acknowledge Bus Cycles** for complete interrupt bus cycle information.

Once the vector number is obtained, the processor saves the exception vector offset, program counter value, and the internal copy of the status register on the active supervisor stack. The saved value of the program counter is the logical address of the instruction that would have been executed had the interrupt not occurred. If the interrupt was acknowledged during the execution of a coprocessor instruction, further internal information is saved on the stack so that the MC68030 can continue executing the coprocessor instruction when the interrupt handler completes execution.

If the M bit of the status register is set, the processor clears the M bit and creates a throwaway exception stack frame on top of the interrupt stack as part of interrupt exception processing. This second frame contains the same program counter value and vector offset as the frame created on top of the master stack, but has a format number of 1 instead of 0 or 9. The copy of the status register saved on the throwaway frame is exactly the same as that placed on the master stack except that the S bit is set in the version placed on the interrupt stack. (It may or may not be set in the copy saved on the master stack.) The resulting status register (after exception processing) has the S bit set and the M bit cleared.

The processor loads the address in the exception vector into the program counter, and normal instruction execution resumes after the required prefetches for the interrupt handler routine.

Most M68000 Family peripherals use programmable interrupt vector numbers as part of the interrupt request/acknowledge mechanism of the system. If this vector number is not initialized after reset and the peripheral must acknowledge an interrupt request, the peripheral usually returns the vector number for the uninitialized interrupt vector, 15.

8.1.10 MMU Configuration Exception

When the MC68030 executes a PMOVE instruction that attempts to move invalid data into the TC, CRP, or SRP register of the MMU, the PMOVE instruction causes an MMU configuration exception. The exception is a post-instruction exception; it is processed after the instruction completes. The processor generates exception vector number 56 when an MMU configuration exception occurs. Refer to **SECTION 9 MEMORY MANAGEMENT UNIT** for a description of the valid configurations for the MMU registers.

The processor copies the status register, enters the supervisor privilege level, and clears the trace bits. The processor saves the vector offset, the scanPC value (which points to the next instruction), and the copy of the status register on the supervisor stack. It also saves the logical address of the PMOVE instruction on the stack. Then the processor resumes normal instruction execution after the required prefetches from the address in the exception vector.

8.1.11 Breakpoint Instruction Exception

To use the MC68030 in a hardware emulator, it must provide a means of inserting breakpoints in the emulator code and of performing appropriate operations at each breakpoint. For the MC68000 and MC68008, this can be done by inserting an illegal instruction at the breakpoint and detecting the illegal instruction exception from its vector location. However, since the vector base register on the MC68010, MC68020, and MC68030 allows arbitrary relocation of exception vectors, the exception address cannot reliably identify a breakpoint. The MC68020 and MC68030 processors provide a breakpoint capability with a set of breakpoint instructions, $4848–$484F, for eight unique breakpoints. The breakpoint facility also allows external hardware to monitor the execution of a program residing in the on-chip instruction cache without severe performance degradation.

When the MC68030 executes a breakpoint instruction, it performs a break-point acknowledge cycle (read cycle) from CPU space type $0 with address lines A2–A4 corresponding to the breakpoint number. Refer to Figure 7-44 for the CPU space type $0 addresses and to **7.4.2 Breakpoint Acknowledge Cycle** for a description of the breakpoint acknowledge cycle. The external hardware can return either $\overline{BERR}$, $\overline{DSACKx}$, or $\overline{STERM}$ with an instruction word on the data bus. If the bus cycle terminates with $\overline{BERR}$, the processor performs illegal instruction exception processing. If the bus cycle terminates with $\overline{DSACKx}$ or $\overline{STERM}$, the processor uses the data returned to replace the breakpoint instruction in the internal instruction pipe and begins execution of that instruction. The remainder of the pipe remains unaltered. In addition, no stacking or vector fetching is involved with the execution of the instruction. Figure 8-7 is a flowchart of the breakpoint instruction execution.

MC68030 USER'S MANUAL   MOTOROLA

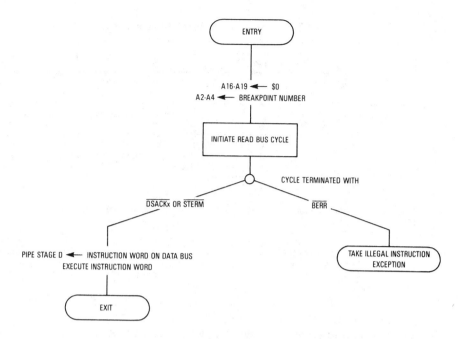

Figure 8-7. Breakpoint Instruction Flowchart

8.1.12 Multiple Exceptions

When several exceptions occur simultaneously, they are processed according to a fixed priority. Table 8-5 lists the exceptions, grouped by characteristics. Each group has a priority from 0–4. Priority 0 has the highest priority.

As soon as the MC68030 has completed exception processing for a condition when another exception is pending, it begins exception processing for the pending exception instead of executing the exception handler for the original exception condition. Also, whenever a bus error or address error occurs, its exception processing takes precedence over lower priority exceptions and occurs immediately. For example, if a bus error occurs during the exception processing for a trace condition, the system processes the bus error and executes its handler before completing the trace exception processing. However, most exceptions cannot occur during exception processing, and very few combinations of the exceptions shown in Table 8-5 can be pending simultaneously.

Table 8-5. Exception Priority Groups

Group/Priority	Exception and Relative Priority	Characteristics
0	0.0 — Reset	Aborts all processing (instruction or exception) and does not save old context.
1	1.0 — Address Error 1.1 — Bus Error	Suspends processing (instruction or exception) and saves internal context.
2	2.0 — BKPT #n, CHK, CHK2, cp Mid-Instruction, cp Protocol Violation, cp-TRAPcc, Divide by Zero, RTE, TRAP #n, TRAPV, MMU Configuration	Exception processing is part of instruction execution.
3	3.0 — Illegal Instruction, Line A, Unimplemented Line F, Privilege Violation, cp Pre-Instruction	Exception processing begins before instruction is executed.
4	4.0 — cp Post-Instruction 4.1 — Trace 4.2 — Interrupt	Exception processing begins when current instruction or previous exception processing is completed.

0.0 is the highest priority, 4.2 is the lowest.

The priority scheme is very important in determining the order in which exception handlers execute when several exceptions occur at the same time. As a general rule, the lower the priority of an exception, the sooner the handler routine for that exception executes. For example, if simultaneous trap, trace, and interrupt exceptions are pending, the exception processing for the trap occurs first, followed immediately by exception processing for the trace and then for the interrupt. When the processor resumes normal instruction execution, it is in the interrupt handler, which returns to the trace handler, which returns to the trap exception handler. This rule does not apply to the reset exception; its handler is executed first even though it has the highest priority because the reset operation clears all other exceptions.

8.1.13 Return from Exception

After the processor has completed exception processing for all pending exceptions, the processor resumes normal instruction execution at the address in the vector for the last exception processed. Once the exception handler has completed execution, the processor must return to the system context prior to the exception (if possible). The RTE instruction returns from the handler to the previous system context for any exception.

When the processor executes an RTE instruction, it examines the stack frame on top of the active supervisor stack to determine if it is a valid frame and what type of context restoration it requires. This section describes the processing for each of the stack frame types; refer to **8.3 COPROCESSOR CONSIDERATIONS** for a description of the stack frame type formats.

For a normal four-word frame, the processor updates the status register and program counter with the data read from the stack, increments the stack pointer by eight, and resumes normal instruction execution.

For the throwaway four-word stack, the processor reads the status register value from the frame, increments the active stack pointer by eight, updates the status register with the value read from the stack, and then begins RTE processing again, as shown in Figure 8-8. The processor reads a new format word from the stack frame on top of the active stack (which may or may not be the same stack used for the previous operation) and performs the proper operations corresponding to that format. In most cases, the throwaway frame is on the interrupt stack and when the status register value is read from the stack, the S and M bits are set. In that case, there is a normal four-word frame or a ten-word coprocessor mid-instruction frame on the master stack. However, the second frame may be any format (even another throwaway frame) and may reside on any of the three system stacks.

For the six-word stack frame, the processor restores the status register and program counter values from the stack, increments the active supervisor stack pointer by 12, and resumes normal instruction execution.

For the coprocessor mid-instruction stack frame, the processor reads the status register, program counter, instruction address, internal register values, and the evaluated effective address from the stack, restores these values to the corresponding internal registers, and increments the stack pointer by 20. The processor then reads from the response register of the coprocessor that initiated the exception to determine the next operation to be performed. Refer to **SECTION 10 COPROCESSOR INTERFACE DESCRIPTION** for details of coprocessor-related exceptions.

For both the short and long bus fault stack frames, the processor first checks the format value on the stack for validity. In addition, for the long stack frame, the processor compares the version number in the stack with its own version number. The version number is located in the most significant nibble (bits 15–12) of the word at location SP + $36 in the long stack frame. This validity check is required in a multiprocessor system to ensure that the data is properly interpreted by the RTE instruction. The RTE instruction also reads from

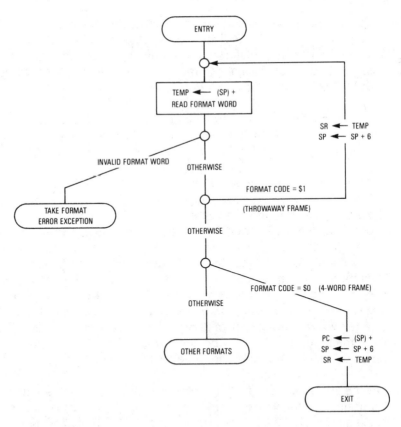

Figure 8-8. RTE Instruction for Throwaway Four-Word Frame

both ends of the stack frame to make sure it is accessible. If the frame is invalid or inaccessible, the processor takes a format error or a bus error exception, respectively. Otherwise, the processor reads the entire frame into the proper internal registers, deallocates the stack, and resumes normal processing. Once the processor begins to load the frame to restore its internal state, the assertion of the $\overline{\text{BERR}}$ signal causes the processor to enter the halted state with the continuous assertion of the $\overline{\text{STATUS}}$ signal. Refer to **8.2 BUS FAULT RECOVERY** for a description of the processing that occurs after the frame is read into the internal registers.

If a format error or bus error exception occurs during the frame validation sequence of the RTE instruction, either due to any of the errors previously described or due to an illegal format code, the processor creates a normal four-word or a bus fault stack frame below the frame that it was attempting to use. In this way, the faulty stack frame remains intact. The exception handler can examine or repair the faulty frame. In a multiprocessor system, the faulty frame can be left to be used by another processor of a different type (e.g., an MC68010, MC68020, or a future M68000 processor) when appropriate.

8.2 BUS FAULT RECOVERY

An address error exception or a bus error exception indicates a bus fault. The saving of the processor state for a bus error or address error is described in **8.1.2 Bus Error Exception**, and the restoring of the processor state by an RTE instruction is described in **8.1.13 Return from Exception**.

Processor accesses of either data items or the instruction stream can result in bus errors. When a bus error exception occurs while accessing a data item, the exception is taken immediately after the bus cycle terminates. Bus errors reported by the on-chip MMU are also processed immediately. A bus error occurring during an instruction stream access is not processed until the processor attempts to use the information (if ever) that the access should have provided. For instruction faults, when the short format frame applies, the address of the pipe stage B word is the value in the program counter plus four, and the address of the stage C word is the value in the program counter plus two. For the long format, the long word at SP+$24 contains the address of the stage B word; the address of the stage C word is the address of the stage B word minus two. Address error faults occur only for instruction stream accesses, and the exceptions are taken before the bus cycles are attempted.

8

8.2.1 Special Status Word (SSW)

The internal SSW (see Figure 8-9) is one of several registers saved as part of the bus fault exception stack frame. Both the short bus cycle fault format and the long bus cycle fault format include this word at offset $A. The bus cycle fault stack frame formats are described in detail at the end of this section.

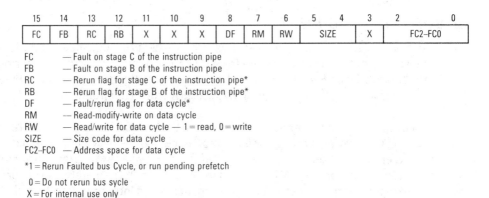

15	14	13	12	11	10	9	8	7	6	5	4	3	2		0
FC	FB	RC	RB	X	X	X	DF	RM	RW	SIZE		X	FC2–FC0		

FC — Fault on stage C of the instruction pipe
FB — Fault on stage B of the instruction pipe
RC — Rerun flag for stage C of the instruction pipe*
RB — Rerun flag for stage B of the instruction pipe*
DF — Fault/rerun flag for data cycle*
RM — Read-modify-write on data cycle
RW — Read/write for data cycle — 1 = read, 0 = write
SIZE — Size code for data cycle
FC2–FC0 — Address space for data cycle

*1 = Rerun Faulted bus Cycle, or run pending prefetch

 0 = Do not rerun bus sycle
 X = For internal use only

Figure 8-9. Special Status Word (SSW)

The SSW information indicates whether the fault was caused by an access to the instruction stream, data stream, or both. The high-order half of the SSW contains two status bits each for the B and C stages of the instruction pipe. The fault bits (FB and FC) indicate that the processor attempted to use a stage (B or C) and found it to be marked invalid due to a bus error on the prefetch for that stage. The fault bits can be used by a bus error handler to determine the cause(s) of a bus error exception. The rerun flag bits (RB and RC) are set to indicate that a fault occurred during a prefetch for the corresponding stage. A rerun bit is always set when the corresponding fault bit is set. The rerun bits indicate that the word in a stage of the instruction pipe is invalid, and the state of the bits can be used by a handler to repair the values in the pipe after an address error or a bus error, if necessary. If a rerun bit is set when the processor executes an RTE instruction, the processor may execute a bus cycle to prefetch the instruction word for the corresponding stage of the pipe (if it is required). If the rerun and fault bits are set for a stage of the pipe, the RTE instruction automatically reruns the prefetch cycle for that stage. The address space for the bus cycle is the program space for the privilege level indicated in the copy of the status register on the stack. If a rerun bit is cleared, the words on the stack for the corresponding stages

8

of the pipe are accepted as valid; the processor assumes that there is no prefetch pending for the corresponding stage and that software has repaired or filled the image of the stage, if necessary.

If an address error exception occurs, the fault bits written to the stack frame are not set (they are only set due to a bus error, as previously described), and the rerun bits alone show the cause of the exception. Depending on the state of the pipeline, either RB and RC are both set, or RC alone is set. To correct the pipeline contents and continue execution of the suspended instruction, software must place the correct instruction stream data in the stage C and/or stage B images requested by the rerun bits and clear the rerun bits. The least significant half of the SSW applies to data cycles only. If the DF bit of the SSW is set, a data fault has occurred and caused the exception. If the DF bit is set when the processor reads the stack frame, it reruns the faulted data access; otherwise, it assumes that the data input buffer value on the stack is valid for a read or that the data has been correctly written to memory for a write (or that no data fault occurred). The RM bit of the SSW identifies a read-modify-write operation and the RW bit indicates whether the cycle was a read or write operation. The SIZE field indicates the size of the operand access, and the FC field specifies the address space for the data cycle. Data and instruction stream faults may be pending simultaneously; the fault handler should be able to recognize any combination of the FC, FB, RC, RB, and DF bits.

8.2.2 Using Software To Complete the Bus Cycles

One method of completing a faulted bus cycle is to use a software handler to emulate the cycle. This is the only method for correcting address errors. The handler should emulate the faulted bus cycle in a manner that is transparent to the instruction that caused the fault. For instruction stream faults, the handler may need to run bus cycles for both the B and C stages of the instruction pipe. The RB and RC bits identify the stages that may require a bus cycle; the FB and FC bits indicate that a stage was invalid when an attempt was made to use its contents. Those stages must be repaired. For each faulted stage, the software handler should copy the instruction word from the proper address space as indicated by the S bit of the copy of the status register saved on the stack to the image of the appropriate stage in the stack frame. In addition, the handler must clear the rerun bit associated with the stage that it has corrected. The handler should not change the fault bits FB and FC.

8

To repair data faults (indicated by DF = 1), the software should first examine the RM bit in the SSW to determine if the fault was generated during a read-modify-write operation. If RM = 0, the handler should then check the R/W bit of the SSW to determine if the fault was caused by a read or a write cycle. For data write faults, the handler must transfer the properly sized data from the data output buffer (DOB) on the stack frame to the location indicated by the data fault address in the address space defined by the SSW. (Both the DOB and the data fault address are part of the stack frame at SP + $18 and SP + $10, respectively.) Data read faults only generate the long bus fault frame and the handler must transfer properly sized data from the location indicated by the fault address and address space to the image of the data input buffer (DIB) at location SP + $2C of the long format stack frame. Byte, word, and 3-byte operands are right-justified in the 4-byte data buffers. In addition, the software handler must clear the DF bit of the SSW to indicate that the faulted bus cycle has been corrected.

To emulate a read-modify-write cycle, the exception handler must first read the operation word at the program counter address (SP + 2 of the stack frame). This word identifies the CAS, CAS2, or TAS instruction that caused the fault. Then the handler must emulate this entire instruction (which may consist of up to four long word transfers) and update the condition code portion of the status register appropriately, because the RTE instruction expects the entire operation to have been completed if the RM bit is set and the DF bit is cleared. This is true even if the fault occurred on the first read cycle.

To emulate the entire instruction, the handler must save the data and address registers for the instruction (with a MOVEM instruction, for example). Next, the handler reads and modifies (if necessary) the memory location. It clears the DF bit in the SSW of the stack frame and modifies the condition codes in the status register copy and the copies of any data or address registers required for the CAS and CAS2 instructions. Last, the handler restores the registers that it saved at the beginning of the emulation. Except for the data input buffer (DIB), the copy of the status register, and the SSW, the handler should not modify a bus fault stack frame. The only bits in the SSW that may be modified are DF, RB, and RC; all other bits, including those defined for internal use, must remain unchanged.

Address error faults must be repaired in software. Address error faults can be distinguished from bus error faults by the value in the vector offset field of the format word.

8.2.3 Completing the Bus Cycles with RTE

Another method of completing a faulted bus cycle is to allow the processor to rerun the bus cycles during execution of the RTE instruction that terminates the exception handler. This method cannot be used to recover from address errors. The RTE instruction is always executed. Unless the handler routine has corrected the error and cleared the fault (and cleared the rerun and DF bits of the SSW), the RTE instruction can complete the bus cycle(s). If the DF bit is still set at the time of the RTE execution, the faulted data cycle is rerun by the RTE instruction. If the fault bit for a stage of the pipe is set and the corresponding rerun bit was not cleared by the software, the RTE reruns the associated instruction prefetch. The fault occurs again unless the cause of the fault, such as a non-resident page in a virtual memory system, has been corrected. If the rerun bit is set for a stage of the pipe and the fault bit is cleared, the associated prefetch cycle may or may not be run by the RTE instruction (depending on whether the stage is required).

If a fault occurs when the RTE instruction attempts to rerun the bus cycle(s), the processor creates a new stack frame on the supervisor stack after de-allocating the previous frame, and address error or bus error exception processing starts in the normal manner.

The read-modify-write operations of the MC68030 can also be completed by the RTE instruction that terminates the handler routine. The rerun operation, executed by the RTE instruction with the DF bit of the SSW set, reruns the entire instruction. If the cause of the error has been corrected, the handler does not need to emulate the instruction but can leave the DF bit set and execute the RTE instruction.

Systems programmers and designers should be aware that the MMU of the MC68030 treats any bus cycle with $\overline{RMC}$ asserted as a write operation for protection checking, regardless of the state of R/$\overline{W}$ signal. Otherwise, the potential for partially destroying system pointers with CAS and CAS2 instructions exists since one portion of the write operation could take place and the remainder be aborted by a bus error.

8

8.3 COPROCESSOR CONSIDERATIONS

Exception handler programmers should consider carefully whether to save and restore the context of a coprocessor at the beginning and end of handler routines for exceptions that can occur during the execution of a coprocessor instruction (i.e., bus errors, interrupts, and coprocessor-related exceptions). The nature of the coprocessor and the exception handler routine determines whether or not saving the state of one or more coprocessors with the cpSAVE and cpRESTORE instructions is required. If the coprocessor allows multiple coprocessor instructions to be executed concurrently, it may require its state to be saved and restored for all coprocessor-generated exceptions, regardless of whether or not the coprocessor is accessed during the handler routine. The MC68882 floating-point coprocessor is an example of this type of co-processor. On the other hand, the MC68881 floating-point coprocessor requires FSAVE and FRESTORE instructions within an exception handler routine only if the exception handler itself uses the coprocessor.

8.4 EXCEPTION STACK FRAME FORMATS

The MC68030 provides six different stack frames for exception processing. The set of frames includes the normal four- and six-word stack frames, the four-word throwaway stack frame, the coprocessor mid-instruction stack frame, and the short and long bus fault stack frames.

When the MC68030 writes or reads a stack frame, it uses long-word operand transfers wherever possible. Using a long-word-aligned stack pointer with memory that is on a 32-bit port greatly enhances exception processing performance. The processor does not necessarily read or write the stack frame data in sequential order.

The system software should not depend on a particular exception generating a particular stack frame. For compatibility with future devices, the software should be able to handle any type of stack frame for any type of exception.

Table 8-6 summarizes the stack frames defined for the M68000 Family.

8

Table 8-6. Exception Stack Frames (Sheet 1 of 2)

Stack Frames	Exception Types (Stacked PC Points to)
15 0 SP → STATUS REGISTER +$02 PROGRAM COUNTER +$06 0 0 0 0 VECTOR OFFSET FOUR WORD STACK FRAME - FORMAT $0	• Interrupt [Next instruction] • Format Error [RTE or cpRESTORE instruction] • TRAP #N [Next instruction] • Illegal Instruction [Illegal instruction] • A-Line Instruction [A-line instruction] • F-Line Instruction [F-line instruction] • Privilege Violation [First word of instruction causing Privilege Violation] • Coprocessor Pre-Instruction [Op-Word of instruction that returned the Take Pre-Instruction primitive]
15 0 SP → STATUS REGISTER +$02 PROGRAM COUNTER +$06 0 0 0 1 VECTOR OFFSET THROWAWAY FOUR WORD STACK FRAME - FORMAT $1	• Created on Interrupt Stack [Next instruction — same during interrupt exception as on master stack] processing when transition from master state to interrupt state occurs
15 0 SP → STATUS REGISTER +$02 PROGRAM COUNTER +$06 0 0 1 0 VECTOR OFFSET +$08 INSTRUCTION ADDRESS SIX WORD STACK FRAME - FORMAT $2	• CHK [Next instruction for all these exceptions] • CHK2 • cpTRAPcc • TRAPcc INSTRUCTION ADDRESS • TRAPV is the address of the • Trace instruction that caused • Zero Divide the exception • MMU Configuration • Coprocessor Post-Instruction
15 0 SP → STATUS REGISTER +$02 PROGRAM COUNTER +$06 1 0 0 1 VECTOR OFFSET +$08 INSTRUCTION ADDRESS +$0C INTERNAL REGISTERS, 4 WORDS +$12 COPROCESSOR MID-INSTRUCTION STACK FRAME (10 WORDS) - FORMAT $9	• Coprocessor Mid-Instruction [Next word to be fetched from instruction stream for all these exceptions] • Main-Detected Protocol Violation • Interrupt Detected INSTRUCTION ADDRESS During Coprocessor is the address of the Instruction (supported instruction that caused the with 'null come again exception with interrupts allowed' primitive)

8

Table 8-6. Exception Stack Frames (Sheet 2 of 2)

Stack Frames	Exception Types (Stacked PC Points to)

Stack Frame (top):

```
       15                          0
SP →   |        STATUS REGISTER         |
+$02   |        PROGRAM COUNTER         |
+$06   | 1 0 1 0 |   VECTOR OFFSET      |
+$08   |        INTERNAL REGISTER       |
+$0A   |        SPECIAL STATUS WORD     |
+$0C   |      INSTRUCTION PIPE STAGE C  |
+$0E   |      INSTRUCTION PIPE STAGE B  |
+$10   |                                |
+$12   |      DATA CYCLE FAULT ADDRESS  |
+$14   |        INTERNAL REGISTER       |
+$16   |        INTERNAL REGISTER       |
+$18   |                                |
+$1A   |        DATA OUTPUT BUFFER      |
+$1C   |        INTERNAL REGISTER       |
+$1E   |        INTERNAL REGISTER       |
```

SHORT BUS CYCLE FAULT STACK FRAME (16 WORDS) - FORMAT $A

- Address Error or Bus Error — Execution Unit at Instruction Boundary   [Next instruction]

Stack Frame (bottom):

```
       15                          0
SP →   |        STATUS REGISTER         |
+$02   |        PROGRAM COUNTER         |
+$06   | 1 0 1 1 |   VECTOR OFFSET      |
+$08   |        INTERNAL REGISTER       |
+$0A   |        SPECIAL STATUS WORD     |
+$0C   |      INSTRUCTION PIPE STAGE C  |
+$0E   |      INSTRUCTION PIPE STAGE B  |
+$10   |                                |
+$12   |      DATA CYCLE FAULT ADDRESS  |
+$14   |        INTERNAL REGISTER       |
+$16   |        INTERNAL REGISTER       |
+$18   |                                |
+$1A   |        DATA OUTPUT BUFFER      |
+$1C   |                                |
       |      INTERNAL REGISTERS, 4 WORDS |
+$22   |                                |
+$24   |        STAGE B ADDRESS         |
+$28   |      INTERNAL REGISTERS, 2 WORDS |
+$2A   |                                |
+$2C   |        DATA INPUT BUFFER       |
+$30   |      INTERNAL REGISTERS, 3 WORDS |
+$34   |                                |
+$36   | VERSION # |  INTERNAL INFORMATION |
+$38   |      INTERNAL REGISTERS,        |
       |      18 WORDS                   |
+$5A   |                                |
```

LONG BUS CYCLE FAULT STACK FRAME (46 WORDS) - FORMAT $B

- Address Error or Bus Error — Instruction Execution in Progress   [Address of instruction in execution when fault occurred — may not be the instruction that generated the faulted bus cycle]

8

SECTION 9
MEMORY MANAGEMENT UNIT

The MC68030 includes a memory management unit (MMU) that supports a demand-paged virtual memory environment. The memory management is "demand" in that programs do not specify required memory areas in advance, but request them by accessing logical addresses. The physical memory is paged, meaning that it is divided into blocks of equal size called page frames. The logical address space is divided into pages of the same size. The operating system assigns pages to page frames as they are required to meet the needs of programs.

The principal function of the MMU is the translation of logical addresses to physical addresses using translation tables stored in memory. The MMU contains an address translation cache (ATC) in which recently used logical-to-physical address translations are stored. As the MMU receives each logical address from the CPU core, it searches the ATC for the corresponding physical address. When the translation is not in the ATC, the processor searches the translation tables in memory for the translation information. The address calculations and bus cycles required for this search are performed by microcode and dedicated logic in the MC68030. In addition, the MMU contains two transparent translation registers (TT0 and TT1) that identify blocks of memory that can be accessed without translation. The features of the MMU are:

- 32-Bit Logical Address Translated to 32-Bit Physical Address with 3-Bit Function Code

- Supports Two-Clock Cycle Processor Accesses to Physical Address Spaces

- Addresses Translated in Parallel with Accesses to Data and Instruction Caches

- On-Chip Fully Associative 22-Entry ATC

- Translation Table Search Controlled by Microcode

- Eight Page Sizes: 256, 512, 1K, 2K, 4K, 8K, 16K and 32K Bytes

- Separate User and Supervisor Translation Table Trees Are Supported

- Two Independent Blocks Can Be Defined as Transparent (Untranslated)

- Multiple Levels of Translation Tables

- 0–15 Upper Logical Address Bits Can Be Ignored (Using Initial Shift)
- Portions of Tables Can Be Undefined (Using Limits)
- Write Protection and Supervisor Protection
- History Bits Automatically Maintained in Page Descriptors
- Cache Inhibit Output ($\overline{\text{CIOUT}}$) Signal Asserted on Page Basis
- External Translation Disable Input Signal ($\overline{\text{MMUDIS}}$)
- Subset of Instruction Set Defined by MC68851

The MMU completely overlaps address translation time with other processing activity when the translation is resident in the ATC. ATC accesses operate in parallel with the on-chip instruction and data caches.

Figure 9-1 is a block diagram of the MC68030 showing the relationship of the MMU to the execution unit and the bus controller. For an instruction or operand access, the MC68030 simultaneously searches the caches and searches for a physical address in the ATC. If the translation is available, the MMU provides the physical address to the bus controller and allows the bus cycle to continue. When the instruction or operand is in either of the on-chip caches on a read cycle, the bus controller aborts the bus cycle before address strobe is asserted. Similarly, the MMU causes a bus cycle to abort before the assertion of address strobe when a valid translation is not available in the ATC or when an invalid access is attempted.

An MMU disable input signal ($\overline{\text{MMUDIS}}$) is provided that dynamically disables address translation for emulation, diagnostic, or other purposes.

The programming model of the MMU (see Figure 9-2) consists of two root pointer registers, a control register, two transparent translation registers, and a status register. These registers can only be accessed by supervisor programs. The CPU root pointer register points to an address translation tree structure in memory that describes the logical-to-physical mapping for user accesses or for both user and supervisor accesses. The supervisor root pointer register optionally points to an address translation tree structure for supervisor mappings. The translation control register is comprised of fields that control the translation operation. Each transparent translation register can define a block of logical addresses that are used as physical addresses (without translation). The MMU status register contains accumulated status information from a translation performed as a part of a PTEST instruction.

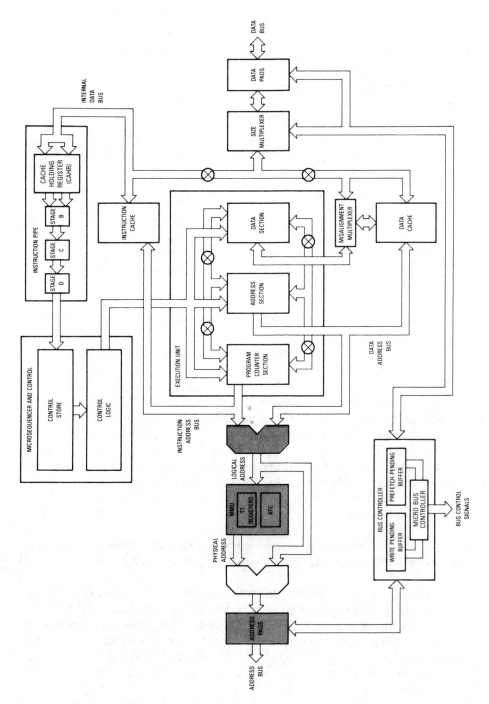

Figure 9-1. MMU Block Diagram

9

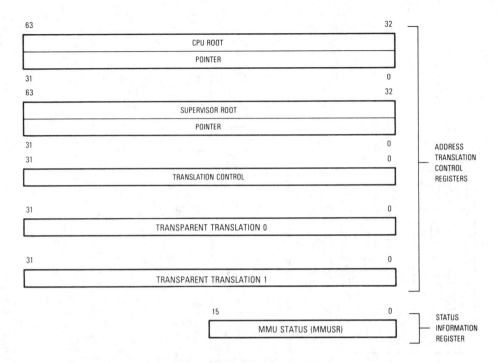

Figure 9-2. MMU Programming Model

The ATC in the MMU is a fully associative cache that stores 22 logical-to-physical address translations and associated page information. It compares the logical address and function code internally supplied by the processor with all tag entries in the ATC. When the access address and function code matches a tag in the ATC (a hit occurs) and no access violation is detected, the ATC outputs the corresponding physical address to the bus controller, which continues the external bus cycle. Function codes are routed to the bus controller unmodified.

Each ATC entry contains a logical address, a physical address, and status bits. Among the status bits are the write protect and cache inhibit bits.

When the ATC does not contain the translation for a logical address (a miss occurs) and an external bus cycle is required, the MMU aborts the access and causes the processor to initiate bus cycles that search the translation tables in memory for the correct translation. If the table search completes without any errors, the MMU stores the translation in the ATC and provides the physical address for the access, allowing the bus controller to retry the original bus cycle.

An MMU translation table has a tree structure with the base of the first table defined by a root pointer descriptor. The root pointer descriptor of the current translation table is resident in one of two root pointer registers. The general tree structure is shown in Figure 9-3. Table entries at the upper levels of a tree point to other tables. The table leaf entries are page frame addresses. All addresses stored in the translation tables are physical addresses; the translation tables reside in the physical address space.

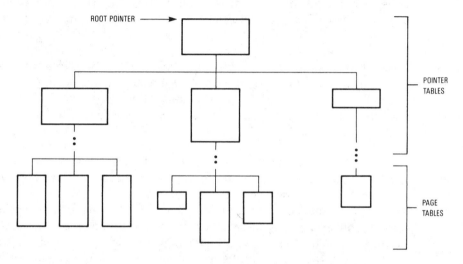

Figure 9-3. Translation Table Tree

System software selects the parameters for the translation tables by configuring the translation control register (TC) appropriately. The function codes or a portion of the logical address can be defined as the index into the first level of lookup in the table. The TC register specifies how many bits of the logical address are used as the index for each level of the lookup (as many as 15 bits can be used at a given level).

9.1 TRANSLATION TABLE STRUCTURE

The M68030 uses the ATC and translation tables stored in memory to perform the translation from a logical to a physical address. Translation tables for a program are loaded into memory by the operating system.

The general translation table structure supported by the MC68030 is a tree structure of tables. The pointer tables form the branches of the tree. These tables contain the base addresses of other tables. Page descriptors can reside in pointer tables and, in that case, are called early termination descriptors. The tables at the leaves of the tree are called page tables. Only a portion of the translation table for the entire logical address space is required to be resident in memory at any time: specifically, only the portion of the table that translates the logical addresses that the currently executing process(es) use(s) must be resident. Portions of translation tables can be dynamically allocated as the process requires additional memory.

As shown in Figure 9-4, the root pointer for a table is a descriptor that contains the base address of the top level table for the tree. The pointer tables and page tables also consist of descriptors. A descriptor in a pointer table typically contains the base address of a table at the next level of the tree. A table descriptor can also contain limits for the index into the next table, protection information, and history information pertaining to the descriptor. Each table is indexed by a field extracted from the logical address. In the example shown in Figure 9-4, the A field of the logical address, $00A, is added to the root pointer value to select a descriptor at the A level of the translation tree. The selected descriptor points to the base of the appropriate page table, and the B field of the logical address ($006) is added to this base address to select a descriptor within the page table. A descriptor in a page table contains the physical base address of the page, protection information, and history information for the page. A page descriptor can also reside in a pointer table or even in a root pointer to define a contiguous block of pages. A two-level page task is shown. The 32-bit logical address space is divided into 4096 segments of 1024 bytes each.

Figure 9-5 shows a possible layout of this example translation tree in memory.

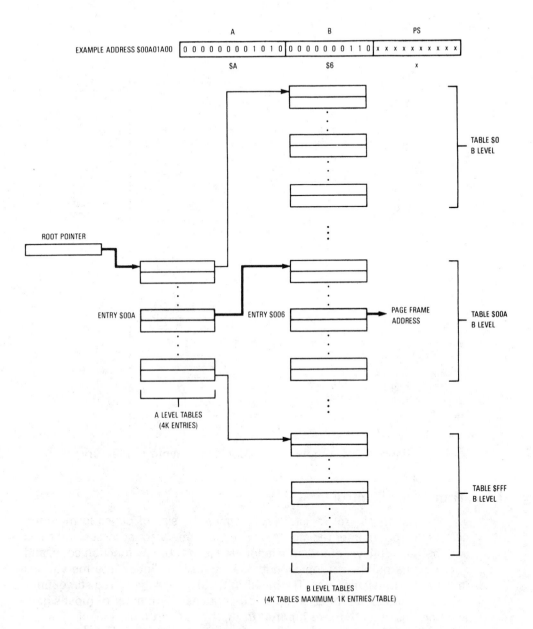

Figure 9-4. Example Translation Table Tree

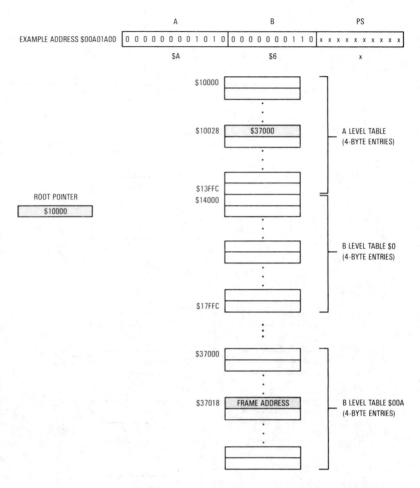

Figure 9-5. Example Translation Tree Layout in Memory

9.1.1 Translation Control

The translation control register (TC) defines the size of pages in memory, selects the root pointer register to be used for supervisor accesses, indicates whether the top level of the translation tree is indexed by function code, and specifies the number of logical address bits used to index into the various levels of the translation tree. The initial shift (IS) field of the TC register defines the size of the logical address space; it contains the number of most significant address bits that are ignored in the translation table lookup. For example, if the IS field is set to zero, the logical address space is 2^{32} bytes. On the other hand, if the IS field is set to 15, the logical address space contains only $2^{32} - 2^{15}$ bytes.

The page size (PS) field of the TC register specifies the page size for the system. The number of pages in the system is equal to the logical address space divided by the page size. The maximum number of pages that can be defined by a translation tree is greater than 16 million ($2^{32}/2^8$). The minimum number is 4 ($2^{17}/2^{15}$). The function code can also be used in the table lookup, defining as many as seven regions of the above size (FC = 0–6). The entire range of the logical address space(s) can be defined by translation tables of many sizes. The MC68030 provides flexibility that simplifies the implementation of large translation tables.

The use of a tree structure with as many as five levels of tables provides granularity in translation table design. The LIMIT field of the root pointer can limit the value of the first index and limits the actual number of descriptors required. Optionally, the top level of the structure can be indexed by function code bits. In this case, the pointer table at this level contains eight descriptors. The next level of the structure (or the top level when the FCL bit of the TC register is set to zero) is indexed by the most significant bits of the logical address (disregarding the number of bits specified by the IS field). The number of logical address bits used for this index is specified by the TIA field of the TC register. If, for example, the TIA field contains the value 5, the index for this level contains five bits, and the pointer table at this level contains at most 32 descriptors.

Similarly, the TIB, TIC, and TID fields of the TC register define the indexes for lower levels of the translation table tree. When one of these fields contains zero, the remaining TIx fields are ignored; the last nonzero TIx field defines the index into the lowest level of the tree structure. The tables selected by the index at this level are page tables; every descriptor in these tables is (or represents) a page descriptor. Figure 9-6 shows how the TIx fields of the TC register apply to a function code and logical address.

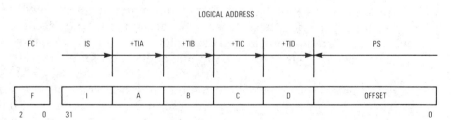

Figure 9-6. Derivation of Table Index Fields

For example, a TC register in which the FCL bit is set to one, the TIA field contains five, the TIB field contains nine, and the TIC and TID fields contain zero defines a three-level translation tree. The top level is indexed by the function code, the next level by five logical address bits, and the bottom level by nine logical address bits. If the TIC field contained nine instead of zero, the translation tree would have four levels, and the two bottom levels would each be indexed by 9-bit portions of the logical address.

The following equation for fields in the TC register must be satisfied:
$$IS + PS + TIA + TIB^1 + TIC^1 + TID^1 = 32$$
That is, every bit of the logical address either addresses a byte within the page, is part of the index at some level of the address table, or is explicitly ignored by initial shift.

Table 9-1 lists the valid sizes of the table indexes at each of the levels indexed by the TIx fields and the position of each table index within the logical address. When the function code is also used to select a descriptor, a total of five levels can be defined by the logical address. The function code lookup level and levels B, C, and D can be suppressed.

Table 9-1. Size Restrictions

Field	Starting Bit Position	Size Restrictions
A	31-IS	1–15 (TIA must be greater than zero; minimum of two if TIB = 0)
B	31-IS-TIA	0–15
C	31-IS-TIA-TIB	0–15 (ignored if TIB is zero)
D	31-IS-TIA-TIB-TIC	0–15 (ignored if TIB or TIC is zero)

9.1.2 Translation Table Descriptors

The address translation trees consist of tables of descriptors. These descriptors can be one of four basic types: table descriptors, page descriptors (normal or early termination), invalid descriptors, or indirect descriptors. Each of these descriptors has both a long-format and a short-format representation.

A root pointer descriptor defines the root of a tree and can be a table descriptor or an early termination page descriptor. A table descriptor points to a descriptor table in memory that defines the next lower level in the translation tree. An early termination page descriptor causes immediate termi-

---

NOTE 1: If any of these fields are zero, the remaining fields are ignored.

nation of the table search and contains the physical address of an area in memory that contains page frames corresponding to contiguous logical addresses (Refer to **9.5.3.1 EARLY TERMINATION AND CONTIGUOUS MEMORY**).

Tables at intermediate levels of a translation tree contain descriptors that are similar to the root pointer descriptors. They can contain table descriptors or early termination page descriptors and can also contain invalid descriptors.

The descriptor tables at the lowest level of a translation tree can only contain page descriptors, indirect descriptors, and invalid descriptors. A page descriptor in the lowest level of a translation tree defines the physical address of a page frame in memory that corresponds to the logical address of a page. An indirect descriptor contains a pointer to the actual page descriptor and can be used when a single page descriptor is accessed by two or more logical addresses.

To enhance the flexibility of translation table design, descriptors (except for root pointer descriptors) can be either short or long format. The short-format descriptors consist of one long word and have no index-limiting capabilities or supervisor-only protection. The long-format descriptors consist of two long words and contain all defined descriptor fields for the MC68030. The pointer and page tables can each contain either short- or long-format descriptors, but no single table can contain both sizes. Tables at different levels of the translation tree can contain different formats of descriptors. Tables at the same level can also contain descriptors of different formats, but all descriptors in a particular pointer table or page table must be of the same format. Figure 9-7 shows a translation tree that uses several different format descriptors.

All descriptors contain a descriptor type (DT) field, which identifies the descriptor or specifies the size of the descriptors in the table to which the descriptor points. It is always the two least significant bits of the most significant (or only) long word of a descriptor.

Invalid descriptors can be used at any level of the translation tree except the root. When a table search for a normal translation encounters an invalid descriptor, the processor takes a bus error exception. The invalid descriptor can be used to identify either a page or branch of the tree that has been stored on an external device and is not resident in memory or a portion of the translation table that has not yet been defined. In these two cases, the exception routine can either restore the page from disk or add to the translation table.

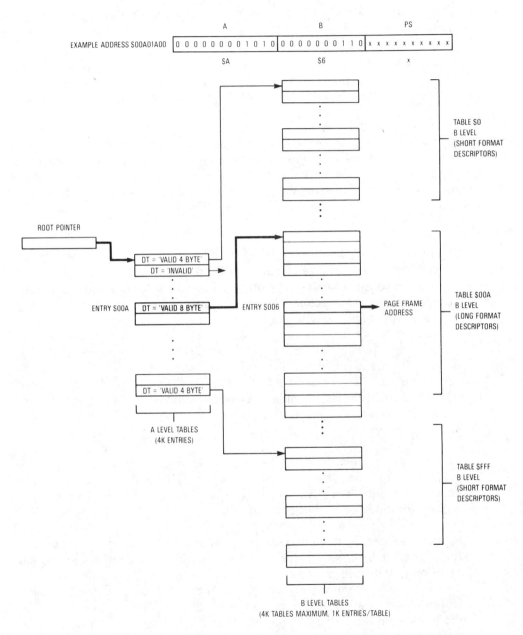

Figure 9-7. Example Translation Tree Using Different Format Descriptors

MC68030 USER'S MANUAL

MOTOROLA

All long-format descriptors and short-format invalid descriptors include one or two unused fields. The operating system can use these fields for its own purposes. For example, the operating system can encode these fields to specify the type of invalid descriptor. Alternately, the external device address of a page that is not resident in main memory can be stored in the unused field.

9.2 ADDRESS TRANSLATION

The function of the MMU is to translate logical addresses to physical addresses according to control information stored by the system in the MMU registers and in translation table trees resident in memory.

9.2.1 General Flow for Address Translation

A CPU space address (FC0–FC2 = $7) is a special case that is immediately used as a physical address without translation. For other accesses, the translation process proceeds as follows:

1. Search the on-chip data and instruction caches for the required instruction word or operand on read accesses.

2. Compare the logical address and function code to the transparent translation parameters in the transparent translation registers, and use the logical address as a physical address for the memory access when one or both of the registers match.

3. Compare the logical address and function code to the tag portions of the entries in the ATC and use the corresponding physical address for the memory access when a match occurs.

4. When no on-chip cache hit occurs (on a read) and no TTx register matches or valid ATC entry matches, initiate a table search operation to obtain the corresponding physical address from the corresponding translation tree, create a valid ATC entry for the logical address, and repeat step 3.

Figure 9-8 is a general flowchart for address translation. The top branch of the flowchart applies to CPU space accesses (FC0–FC2 = $7). The next branch applies to read accesses only. When either of the on-chip caches hits (contains the required data or instruction), no memory access is necessary. The third branch applies to transparent translation. The bottom three branches apply to ATC translation as follows. If the requested access misses in the ATC, the memory cycle is aborted, and a table search operation proceeds. An ATC entry is created after the table search, and the access is retried. If an access

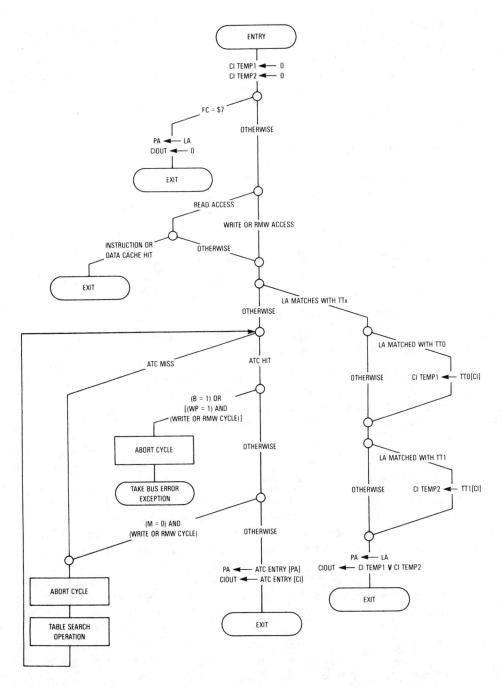

Figure 9-8. Address Translation General Flowchart

hits in the ATC but a bus error was detected during the table search that created the ATC entry, the memory access is aborted, and a bus error exception is taken.

If an access results in an ATC hit but the access is either a write or read-modify-write access and the page is write protected, the memory cycle is also aborted, and a bus error exception is taken. For a write or read-modify-write access, when the modified bit of the ATC entry is not set, the memory cycle is aborted, a table search proceeds to set the modified bit in both the page descriptor in memory and in the ATC, and the access is retried. If the modified bit of the ATC entry is set and the bus error bit is not, assuming that neither TTx register matches and the access is not to CPU space, the ATC provides the address translation to the bus controller under two conditions: 1) if a read access does not hit in either on-chip cache and 2) if a write or read-modify-write access is not write protected.

The preceding description of the general flowchart specifies several conditions that cause the memory cycle to be aborted. In these cases, the bus cycle is aborted before the assertion of $\overline{AS}$.

9.2.2 Effect of $\overline{RESET}$ on MMU

When the MC68030 is reset by the assertion of the $\overline{RESET}$ signal, the E bits of the TC and TTx registers are cleared, disabling address translation. This causes logical addresses to be passed through as physical addresses to the bus controller, allowing an operating system to set up the translation tables and MMU registers, as required. After it has initialized the translation tables and registers, the E bit of the TC register can be set, enabling address translation. A reset of the processor does not invalidate any entries in the ATC. An MMU instruction (such as PMOVE) that flushes the ATC must be executed to flush all existing valid entries from the ATC after a reset operation and before translation is enabled.

9.2.3 Effect of $\overline{MMUDIS}$ on Address Translation

The assertion of $\overline{MMUDIS}$ prevents the MMU from performing searches of the ATC and the execution unit from performing table searches. With address translation disabled, logical addresses are used as physical addresses. When an initial access to a long-word-aligned data operand that is larger than the addressed port size is performed, the successive bus cycles for additional portions of the operand always use the same higher order address bits that were used for the initial bus cycle (changing A0 and A1 appropriately). Thus, if $\overline{\text{MMUDIS}}$ is asserted during this type of operation, the disabling of address translation does not become effective until the entire transfer is complete. Note that the assertion of $\overline{\text{MMUDIS}}$ does not affect the operation of the transparent translation registers.

9.3 TRANSPARENT TRANSLATION

Two independent transparent translation registers (TT0 and TT1) in the MMU optionally define two blocks of the logical address space that are directly translated to the physical address spaces. The MMU does not explicitly check write protection for the addresses in these blocks, but a block can be specified as transparent only for read cycles. The blocks of addresses defined by the TTx registers include at least 16M bytes of logical address space; the two blocks can overlap, or they can be separate.

The following description of the address comparison assumes that both TT0 and TT1 are enabled; however, each TTx register can be independently disabled. A disabled TTx register is completely ignored.

When the MMU receives an address to be translated, the function code and the eight high-order bits of the address are compared to the block of addresses defined by TT0 and TT1. The address space block for each TTx register is defined by the base function code, the function code mask, the logical base address, and the logical address mask. When a bit in a mask field is set, the corresponding bit of the base function code or logical base address is ignored in the function code and address comparison. Setting successively higher order bits in the address mask increases the size of the transparently translated block.

The address for the current bus cycle and a TTx register address match when the function code bits and address bits (not including masked bits) are equal. Each TTx register can specify read accesses or write accesses as transparent. In that case, the internal read/write signal must match the R/$\overline{\text{W}}$ bit in the TTx register for the match to occur. The selection of the type of access (read or write) can also be masked. The read/write mask bit (RWM) must be set for transparent translation of addresses used by instructions that execute read-modify-write operations. Otherwise, neither the read nor write portions of read-modify-write operations are mapped transparently with the TTx registers, regardless of the function code and address bits for the individual cycles within a read-modify-write operation.

MC68030 USER'S MANUAL MOTOROLA

By appropriately configuring a transparent translation register, flexible transparent mapping can be specified. For instance, to transparently translate user program space with a TTx register, the RWM bit of the register is set to 1, the FC BASE is set to $2, and the FC MASK is set to $0. To transparently translate supervisor data read accesses of addresses $00000000–$0FFFFFFF, the LOGICAL BASE ADDRESS field is set to $0X, the LOGICAL ADDRESS MASK is set to $0F, the R/W bit is set to 1, the RWM bit is set to 0, the FC BASE is set to $5, and the FC MASK field is set to $0. Since only read cycles are specified by the TTx register for this example, write accesses for this address range can be translated with the translation tables and write protection can be implemented as required.

Each TTx register can specify that the contents of logical addresses in its block should not be stored in either an internal or external cache. The cache inhibit out signal (CIOUT) is asserted when an address matches the address specified by a TTx register and the cache inhibit bit in that TTx register is set. CIOUT is used by the on-chip instruction and data caches to inhibit caching of data associated with this address. The signal is available to external caches for the same purpose.

For an access, if either of these registers match, the access is transparently translated. If both registers match, the CI bits are ORed together to generate the CIOUT signal.

Transparent translation can also be implemented by the translation tables of the translation trees if the physical addresses of pages are set equal to the logical addresses.

9.4 ADDRESS TRANSLATION CACHE

The ATC is a 22-entry fully associative (content addressable) cache that contains address translations in a form similar to the corresponding page descriptors in memory to provide fast address translation of a recently used logical address.

The MC68030 is organized such that the translation time of the ATC is always completely overlapped by other operations; thus, no performance penalty is associated with ATC searches. The address translation occurs in parallel with on-chip instruction and data cache accesses before an external bus cycle begins.

If possible, when the ATC stores a new address translation, it replaces an entry that is no longer valid. When all entries in the ATC are valid, the ATC selects a valid entry to be replaced, using a pseudo least recently used algorithm. The ATC uses a validity bit and an internal history bit to implement this replacement algorithm. ATC hit rates are application dependent, but hit rates ranging from 98% to greater than 99% can be expected.

Each ATC entry consists of a logical address and information from a corresponding page descriptor that contains the physical address. The 28-bit logical (or tag) portion of each entry consists of three fields:

27	26 24	23 0
V	FC	LOGICAL ADDRESS

V — VALID

This bit indicates the validity of the entry. If V is set, this entry is valid. This bit is set when the MC68030 loads an entry. A flush operation clears the bit. Specifically, any of these operations clear the V bit of an entry:

- A PMOVE instruction with the FD bit equal to zero that loads a value into the CRP, SRP, TC, TT0, or TT1 register.

- A PFLUSHA instruction.

- A PFLUSH instruction that selects this entry.

- A PLOAD instruction for a logical address and FC that matches the tag for this entry. The instruction writes a new entry (with the V bit set) for the specified logical address.

- The selection of this entry for replacement by the replacement algorithm of the ATC.

FC — FUNCTION CODE

This 3-bit field contains the function code bits (FC0–FC2) corresponding to the logical address in this entry.

LOGICAL ADDRESS

This 24-bit field contains the most significant logical address bits for this entry. All 24 bits of this field are used in the comparison of this entry to an incoming logical address when the page size is 256 bytes. For larger page sizes, the appropriate number of least significant bits of this field are ignored.

Each logical portion of an entry has a corresponding 28-bit physical (or data) portion. The physical portion contains these fields:

27	26	25	24	23	0
B	CI	WP	M	PHYSICAL ADDRESS	

B — BUS ERROR

This bit is set for an entry if a bus error, an invalid descriptor, a supervisor violation, or a limit violation is encountered during the table search corresponding to this entry. When B is set, a subsequent access to the logical address causes the MC68030 to take a bus error exception. Since an ATC miss causes an immediate retry of the access after the table search operation, the bus error exception is taken on the retry. The B bit remains set until a PFLUSH instruction or a PLOAD instruction for this entry invalidates the entry or until the replacement algorithm for the ATC replaces it.

CI — CACHE INHIBIT

This bit is set when the cache inhibit bit of the page descriptor corresponding to this entry is set. When the MC68030 accesses the logical address of an entry with the CI bit set, it asserts the cache inhibit out signal ($\overline{CIOUT}$) during the corresponding bus cycle. This signal inhibits caching in the on-chip caches and can also be used for external caches.

WP — WRITE PROTECT

This bit is set when a WP bit is set in any of the descriptors encountered during the table search for this entry. Setting a WP bit in a table descriptor write protects all pages accessed with that descriptor. When the WP bit is set, a write access or a read-modify-write access to the logical address corresponding to this entry causes a bus error exception to be taken immediately.

M — MODIFIED

This bit is set when a valid write access to the logical address corresponding to the entry occurs. If the M bit is clear and a write access to this logical address is attempted, the MC68030 aborts the access and initiates a table search, setting the M bit in the page descriptor, invalidating the old ATC entry, and creating a new entry with the M bit set. The MMU then allows the original write access to be performed. This assures that the first write operation to a page sets the M bit in both the ATC and the page descriptor in the translation tables even when a previous read operation to the page had created an entry for that page in the ATC with the M bit clear.

9

PHYSICAL ADDRESS
This 24-bit field contains the physical address bits (A31–A8) from the page descriptor corresponding to the logical address. When the page size is larger than 256 bytes, not all bits in the physical address field are used. All page index bits of the logical address are transferred to the bus controller without translation.

9.5 TRANSLATION TABLE DETAILS

The details of translation tables and their use include detailed descriptions of the descriptors, table searching, translation table structure variations, and the protection techniques available with the MC68030 MMU.

9.5.1 Descriptor Details

The descriptor details include detailed descriptions of the short- and long-format descriptors used in the translation trees. The fields that apply to all descriptors are described in the first paragraph.

9.5.1.1 DESCRIPTOR FIELD DEFINITIONS. All descriptor fields are used in more than one type of descriptor. This section lists these fields and describes the use of each field.

DT
This 2-bit field contains the descriptor type; the first two types apply to the descriptor itself. The other two types apply to the descriptors in the table at the next level of the tree. The values are defined as follows:

$0   INVALID
This code identifies the current descriptor as an invalid descriptor. A table search ends when an invalid descriptor is encountered.

$1   PAGE DESCRIPTOR
This code identifies the current descriptor as a page descriptor. The page descriptor is a normal page descriptor when it resides in a page table (in the bottom level of the translation tree). A page descriptor at a higher level is an early termination page descriptor. A table search ends when a page descriptor of either type is encountered.

$2   VALID 4 BYTE

This code specifies that the next table to be accessed contains short-format descriptors. The MC68030 multiplies the index for the next table by four to access the next descriptor. (Short-format descriptors must be long-word aligned.) When used in a page table (bottom level of an translation tree), this code identifies an indirect descriptor that points to a short-format page descriptor.

$3   VALID 8 BYTE

This code specifies that the next table to be accessed contains long-format descriptors. The MC68030 multiplies the index for the next table by eight to access the next descriptor. (Long-format descriptors must be quad-word aligned.) When used in a page table (bottom level of an address translation tree), this code identifies an indirect descriptor that points to a long-format page descriptor.

U

This bit is automatically set by the processor when a descriptor is accessed in which the U bit is clear except after a supervisor violation is detected. In a page descriptor table, this bit is set to indicate that the page corresponding to the descriptor has been accessed. In a pointer table, this bit is set to indicate that the pointer has been accessed by the MC68030 as part of a table search. Note that a pointer may be fetched, and its U bit set, for an address to which access is denied at another level of the tree. Updates of the U bit are performed before the MC68030 allows a page to be accessed. The processor never clears this bit.

WP

This bit provides write protection. The states of all WP bits encountered during a table search are logically ORed, and the result is copied to the ATC entry at the end of a table search for a logical address. During a table search for a PTEST instruction, the processor copies this result into the MMU status register (MMUSR). When WP is set, the MC68030 does not allow the logical address space mapped by that descriptor to be written by any program (i.e., this protection is absolute). If the WP bit is clear, the MC68030 allows write accesses using this descriptor (unless access is restricted at some other level of the translation tree).

CI

This bit is set to inhibit caching of items within this page by the on-chip instruction and data caches and, also, to cause the assertion of the $\overline{\text{CIOUT}}$ signal by the MC68030 for bus cycles accessing items within this page.

L/U

This bit specifies the type of limit in the LIMIT field. When the L/U bit is set, the LIMIT field contains the unsigned lower limit; the index value for the next level of the tree must be greater than or equal to the value in the LIMIT field. When the bit is cleared, the limit is an unsigned upper limit, and the index value must be less than or equal to the LIMIT. An out-of-bounds access causes the B bit in the ATC entry for the address to be set and causes the table search to abort.

LIMIT

This 15-bit field contains a limit to which the index portion of an address is compared to detect an out-of-bounds index. The limit check applies to the index into the table at the next lower level of the translation tree. If the descriptor is an early termination page descriptor, the limit field is still used as a check on the next index field of the logical address.

M

This bit identifies a modified page. The MC68030 sets the M bit in the corresponding page descriptor before a write operation to a page for which the M bit is zero, except after a descriptor with the WP bit set is encountered, or after a supervisor violation is encountered. An access is considered to be a write for updating purposes if either the R/$\overline{\text{W}}$ or $\overline{\text{RMC}}$ signal is low. The MC68030 never clears this bit.

PAGE ADDRESS

This 24-bit field contains the physical base address of a page in memory. The low-order bits of the address are supplied by the logical address. When the page size is larger than 256 bytes, one or more of the least significant bits of this field are not used. The number of unused bits is equal to the PS field value in the TC register minus eight.

S

This bit identifies a pointer table or a page as a supervisor only table or page. When the S bit is set, only programs operating at the supervisor privilege level are allowed to access the portion of the logical address mapped by this descriptor. If this bit is clear, accesses using this descriptor are not restricted to supervisor-only unless the access is restricted by some other level of the translation tree.

TABLE ADDRESS

This 28-bit field contains the physical base address of a table of descriptors. The low-order bits of the address are supplied by the logical address.

DESCRIPTOR ADDRESS

This 30-bit field, which contains the physical address of a page descriptor, is only used in short- and long-format indirect descriptors.

UNUSED

The bits in this field are not used by the MC68030 and may be used by the system software.

RESERVED

Descriptor fields designated by a one or a zero are reserved by Motorola for future definition. These bits should be consistently written as either a one or a zero as appropriate. In the root pointers, these bits are not alterable. In memory-resident descriptors, the values in these fields are neither checked nor altered by the MC68030. Use of these bits by system software for any purpose may not be supported in future products.

9.5.1.2 ROOT POINTER DESCRIPTOR. A root pointer descriptor contains the address of the top-level pointer table of a translation tree. This type of descriptor is loaded into the CRP and SRP registers with the PMOVE instruction. The field descriptions in the preceding section apply to corresponding fields of the CRP and SRP with two minor exceptions. A descriptor-type code of $00 (invalid) is not allowed; an attempt to load zero into the DT field of the CRP or SRP register results in an MMU configuration exception. Also, when the FCL field of the TC register is set, the L/U and LIMIT fields of the root pointer registers are unused. Figure 9-9 shows the root pointer descriptor format.

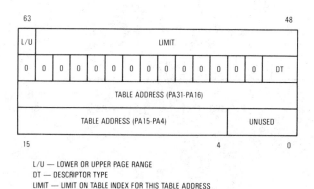

L/U — LOWER OR UPPER PAGE RANGE
DT — DESCRIPTOR TYPE
LIMIT — LIMIT ON TABLE INDEX FOR THIS TABLE ADDRESS
TABLE ADDRESS — ADDRESS OF TABLE AT NEXT LEVEL OR PAGE OFFSET IF DT = 1

Figure 9-9. Root Pointer Descriptor Format

9.5.1.3 SHORT-FORMAT TABLE DESCRIPTOR.   The field descriptions in **9.5.1.1 DE-SCRIPTOR FIELD DEFINITIONS** apply to corresponding fields of this descriptor. Figure 9-10 shows the format of the short-format table descriptor.

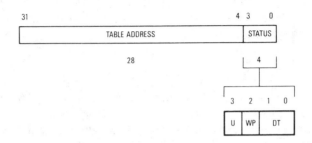

Figure 9-10. Short-Format Table Descriptor

9.5.1.4 LONG-FORMAT TABLE DESCRIPTOR.   The field descriptions in **9.5.1.1 DE-SCRIPTOR FIELD DEFINITIONS** apply to corresponding fields of this descriptor. During address computations, the MC68030 internally replaces the UNUSED field with zeros. Figure 9-11 shows the format of the long-format table descriptor.

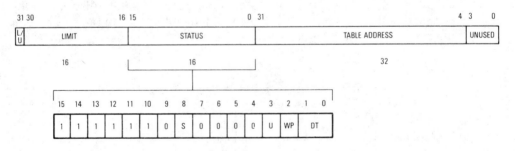

Figure 9-11. Long-Format Table Descriptor

9.5.1.5 SHORT-FORMAT EARLY TERMINATION PAGE DESCRIPTOR. The short-format early termination page descriptor contains the page descriptor code in the DT field but resides in a pointer table. That is, the table in which an early termination page descriptor is located is not at the bottom level of the address translation tree. The field descriptions in **9.5.1.1 DESCRIPTOR FIELD DEFINITIONS** apply to corresponding fields of this descriptor. Figure 9-12 shows the format of the short-format early termination page descriptor.

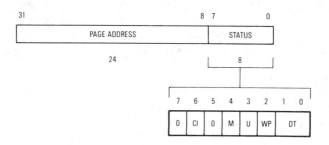

Figure 9-12. Short-Format Page Descriptor and Short-Format Early Termination Page Descriptor

9.5.1.6 LONG-FORMAT EARLY TERMINATION PAGE DESCRIPTOR. The long-format early termination page descriptor contains the page descriptor code in the DT field but resides in a pointer table like the short-format early termination page descriptor. The field descriptions in **9.5.1.1 DESCRIPTOR FIELD DEFINITIONS** apply to corresponding fields of this descriptor. Figure 9-13 shows the format of the long-format early termination page descriptor. The LIMIT field of the long-format descriptor provides a means of limiting the number of pages to which the descriptor applies.

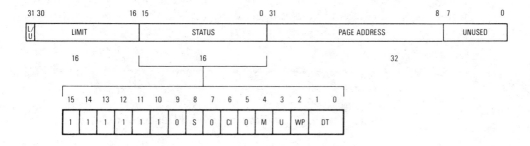

Figure 9-13. Long-Format Early Termination Page Descriptor

9.5.1.7 SHORT-FORMAT PAGE DESCRIPTOR. The short-format page descriptor is used in the page tables (the bottom level of the address table). The field descriptions in **9.5.1.1 DESCRIPTOR FIELD DEFINITIONS** apply to the corresponding fields of this descriptor. The short-format page descriptor is identical to of the short-format early termination page descriptor shown in Figure 9-12.

9.5.1.8 LONG-FORMAT PAGE DESCRIPTOR. The long-format page descriptor is also used in the page tables. The field descriptions in **9.5.1.1 DESCRIPTOR FIELD DEFINITIONS** apply to the corresponding fields of this descriptor. Figure 9-14 shows the format of the long-format page descriptor.

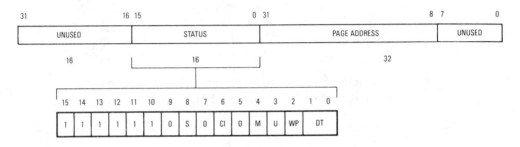

Figure 9-14. Long-Format Page Descriptor

9.5.1.9 SHORT-FORMAT INVALID DESCRIPTOR. The short-format invalid descriptor consists of a DT field that contains zeros, identifying it as an invalid descriptor. It can be used at any level of the address translation tree except at the root pointer level. The 30-bit unused field is available to the operating system to identify unallocated portions of the table or portions of the table that reside on an external device. For example, the disk address of disk-resident tables or pages can be stored in this field. Figure 9-15 shows the format of a short-format invalid descriptor.

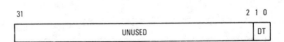

Figure 9-15. Short-Format Invalid Descriptor

9.5.1.10 LONG-FORMAT INVALID DESCRIPTOR. The long-format invalid descriptor is used in pointer and page tables that contain long-format descriptors. It is used in the same way as the short-format invalid descriptor in the preceding section. The first long word contains the DT field in the lowest order bits. The second long word is an unused field, also available to the operating system. Figure 9-16 shows the format of the long-format invalid descriptor.

Figure 9-16. Long-Format Invalid Descriptor

9.5.1.11 SHORT-FORMAT INDIRECT DESCRIPTOR. The short-format indirect descriptor does not have a unique descriptor-type code. Rather, it resides in a page table (the bottom level of the address translation tree) that contains short-format descriptors and is neither a page descriptor nor an invalid descriptor. The descriptor-type field contains either the code for a valid 4-byte descriptor or for a valid 8-byte descriptor, depending upon the size of the referenced page descriptor. The field descriptions in **9.5.1.1 DESCRIPTOR FIELD DEFINITIONS** apply to the corresponding fields of this descriptor. Figure 9-17 shows the format of a short-format indirect descriptor.

Figure 9-17. Short-Format Indirect Descriptor

9.5.1.12 LONG-FORMAT INDIRECT DESCRIPTOR. The long-format indirect descriptor has all the attributes of the short-format indirect descriptor described in the preceding section. The only differences are that it is used in a page table that contains long-format descriptors and that it has two unused fields. The field descriptions in **9.5.1.1 DESCRIPTOR FIELD DEFINITIONS** apply to corresponding fields of this descriptor. Figure 9-18 shows the format of a long-format indirect descriptor.

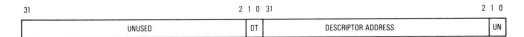

31		2 1 0	31		2 1 0
	UNUSED	DT		DESCRIPTOR ADDRESS	UN

Figure 9-18. Long-Format Indirect Descriptor

9.5.2 General Table Search

When the ATC does not contain a descriptor for the logical address of a processor access and a translation is required, the MC68030 searches the translation tables in memory and obtains the physical address and status information for the page corresponding to the logical address. When a table search is required, the CPU suspends instruction execution activity and, at the end of a successful table search, stores the address mapping in the ATC and retries the access. The access then results in a match (it hits) and the translated address is transferred to the bus controller (provided no exceptions were encountered).

The table search begins by selecting the translation tree, using function code bit FC2 and the SRE bit of the TC register, as shown in Table 9-2. SRE is set to enable the supervisor root pointer, and FC2 is set for supervisor-level accesses. The translation tree with its root defined by the SRP register is selected only when SRE and FC2 are both set. Otherwise, the translation table with its root defined by the CRP register is selected. A simplified flowchart of the table search procedure is shown in Figure 9-19.

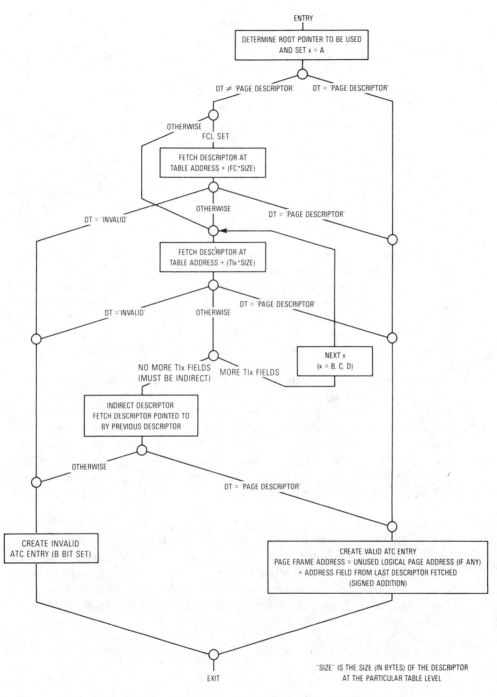

Figure 9-19. Simplified Table Search Flowchart

Table 9-2. Translation Tree Selection

FC2	SRE	Translation Table Root Pointer
0	0	CRP
0	1	CRP
1	0	CRP
1	1	SRP

The table search procedure uses physical addresses to access the translation tables. The read-modify-write ($\overline{\text{RMC}}$) signal is asserted on the first bus cycle of the search and remains asserted throughout, ensuring that the entire table search completes without interruption.

The first bus cycle of the search uses the table address field of the appropriate root pointer as the base address of the first table. The low-order bits of the address are supplied by the logical address. The table is indexed by either the function code or the set of logical address bits defined by the TIA field of the TC register. The FCL field of the TC register determines whether or not the function code is used. In either case, the descriptor-type field of the root pointer selects the scale factor (or multiplier) for the index.

The first access obtains a descriptor. If the descriptor is a table descriptor, the MC68030 again accesses memory. The next access uses the table address in the descriptor as the base address for the next table. The low-order bits of the address are supplied by the logical address. The table is indexed by a set of bits from the logical address using a scale factor determined by the descriptor type code in the descriptor. If the first table access used the function code, the second access uses the bits selected by the TIA field of the TC register. Otherwise, the second access uses the bits selected by the TIB field.

Additional accesses are performed, using the logical address bits specified in TIB, TIC, or TID in order, until an access obtains a page descriptor or an invalid descriptor or until a limit violation occurs. At this point, whether or not all levels of the address table have been accessed, the table search is over. The page descriptor contains the physical address and other information needed for the ATC entry; the MC68030 creates the ATC entry and retries the original bus access.

Figure 9-20 shows a table search using the function code and all four TIx fields.

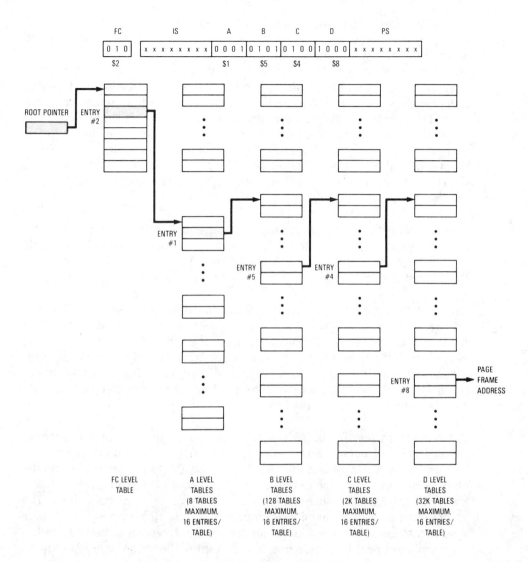

Figure 9-20. Five-Level Table Search

The MC68030 enforces a limit on the index value for the next level of a table search when long-format descriptors are used.

The root pointer includes a limit field that applies when the function code lookup is not used (the FCL bit of the TC register is zero). The index used to access the next level table is compared to the contents of the limit field. The limit field effectively reduces the portion of the address space to which a descriptor applies and also reduces the size of the translation table. The index must reside within the range defined by the limit field. The limit can be a lower limit or an upper limit, according to the L/U bit value. When the L/U bit is set, the limit is a lower limit, and an index less than the limit is out of bounds. When the L/U bit is zero, the limit is an upper limit, and an index greater than the limit is out of bounds. The limit field is effectively disabled if L/U is set and the limit field contains zero or if L/U is clear and the limit field contains $7FFF.

During a table search for an normal translation or a PLOAD instruction, if a limit violation is detected, the ATC is loaded with an entry having the bus error (B) bit set. If a limit violation is detected during a table search for a PTEST instruction, the invalid (I) and limit (L) bits are set in the MMUSR.

During a table search, the U bit in each descriptor that is encountered is checked and set if it is not already set. Similarly, when the table search is for a write access and the M bit of the page descriptor is clear, the processor sets the bit if the table search does not encounter a set WP bit or a supervisor violation. Since the read-modify-write ($\overline{RMC}$) signal is asserted throughout the entire table search operation, the read and write operations to update the history bits are guaranteed to be uninterrupted.

A table search terminates successfully when a page descriptor is encountered. The occurrence of an invalid descriptor, a limit violation, or a bus error also terminates a table search, and the MC68030 takes an exception on the retry of the cycle because of these conditions. The exception routine should distinguish between anticipated conditions and true error conditions. The routine can correct an invalid descriptor that indicates a nonresident page or one that identifies a portion of the translation table yet to be allocated. A limit violation or a bus error due to a system malfunction may result in an error message and termination of the task.

9.5.3 Variations in Translation Table Structure

Many aspects of the MMU translation tree structure are software configurable, allowing the system designer flexibility to optimize the performance of the MMU for a particular system. The following paragraphs discuss the variations of the tree structure from the general structure discussed previously.

9.5.3.1 EARLY TERMINATION AND CONTIGUOUS MEMORY. The MMU provides the ability to map a contiguous range of the logical address space (an integral number of logical pages) to an equivalent contiguous physical address range with a single descriptor. This is done by placing the code for page descriptor ($1) in the descriptor type (DT) field of a descriptor at a level of the tree that would normally contain a table pointer, thereby deleting a subtree of the table.

The table search ends when the search encounters a page descriptor, whether or not the page descriptor is in a page descriptor table at the lowest level of the translation tree.

Termination of the table search by a page descriptor in a pointer descriptor table (i.e., the MC68030 has not encountered a TIx field of zero) is called an early termination. The terminating page descriptor is called an early termination page descriptor.

An early termination page descriptor takes the place of many page descriptors in a translation table. It applies to all pages that would exist on the branch on which the descriptor has been placed, and on any branches from that branch. An early termination page descriptor can be used where contiguous pages in physical memory correspond to contiguous logical pages. If an early termination page descriptor is a long format, the limit field is applied to the next index field of the logical address. This allows the number of pages mapped contiguously to be restricted. Refer to **9.1.2 Translation Table Descriptors** for additional information.

If n low-order bits of the logical page address are unused when a page descriptor encoding is encountered, the single descriptor creates a mapping of a contiguous region of the logical address space starting at the logical page address (with n unused bits set to zero) to a contiguous region in the physical address space starting at the page frame base address with a size of 2^{PS+n} bytes.

When a search is made for a logical address to which an early termination page descriptor applies, the MC68030 creates an entry in the ATC for the logical address; the physical address in the ATC entry is the sum of the page address field in the descriptor plus an offset. The offset is the logical address with the bits used in the search set to zero.

Although the early termination page descriptor creates a contiguous logical-to-physical mapping without having to maintain individual descriptors in the translation tree for each page that is a member of the contiguous region, the ATC contains one entry for each page mapped. These entries are created internally each time a page boundary (as determined by the page size) is crossed in the contiguous region. Figure 9-21 shows an example translation table with a portion of the logical address space translated as a contiguous block.

Note that the DT field can be set to page descriptor at any level of the translation tree including the root pointer level. Setting the DT field of a root pointer to page descriptor creates a direct mapping from the logical to the physical address space with a constant offset as determined by the value in the table address field of the root pointer.

9.5.3.2 INDIRECTION. The MC68030 provides the ability to replace an entry in a page table with a pointer to an alternate entry. The indirection capability allows multiple tasks to share a physical page while maintaining only a single set of history information for the page (i.e., the "modified" indication is maintained only in the single descriptor). The indirection capability also allows the page frame to appear at arbitrarily different addresses in the logical address spaces of each task.

Using the indirection capability, single entries or entire tables can be shared between multiple tasks. Figure 9-22 shows two tasks sharing a page using indirect descriptors.

When the MC68030 has completed a normal table search (has exhausted all index fields of the logical page address), it examines the descriptor-type field of the last entry fetched from the translation tables. If the DT field contains a "valid long" ($2) or "valid short" ($3) encoding, this indicates that the address contained in the highest order 30 bits of the table address field of the descriptor is a pointer to the page descriptor that is to be used to map the logical address. The processor then fetches the page descriptor of the indicated format from this address and uses the page address field of the page descriptor as the physical mapping for the logical address.

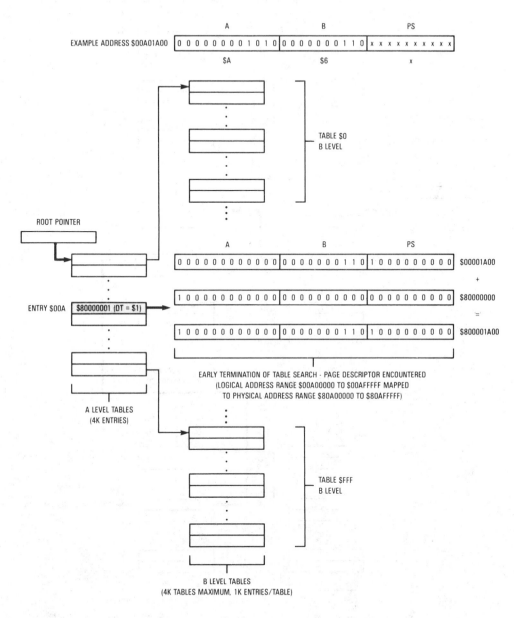

Figure 9-21. Example Translation Tree Using Contiguous Memory

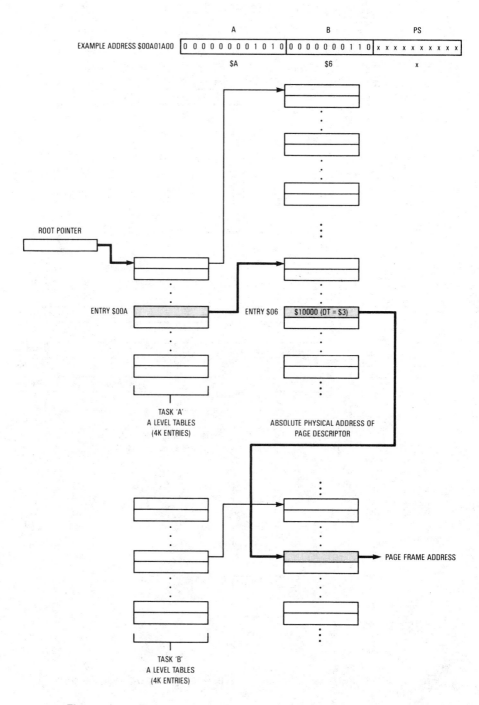

Figure 9-22. Example Translation Tree Using Indirect Descriptors

The page descriptor located at the address given by the indirect descriptor must not have a DT field with a long or short encoding (it must either be a page descriptor or invalid). Otherwise, the descriptor is treated as invalid, and the MC68030 creates an ATC entry with an error condition signaled (bit set).

9.5.3.3 TABLE SHARING BETWEEN TASKS. A page or pointer table can be shared between tasks by placing a pointer to the shared table in the address translation tables of more than one task. The upper (nonshared) tables can contain different settings of protection bits allowing different tasks to use the area with different permissions. In Figure 9-23 two tasks share the memory translated by the table at the B level. Note that task "A" cannot write to the shaded area. Task "B", however, has the WP bit clear in its pointer to the shared table; thus, it can read and write the shared area. Also note that the shared area appears at different logical addresses for each task.

9.5.3.4 PAGING OF TABLES. It is not required that the entire address translation tree for an active task be resident in main memory at once. In the same way that only the working set of pages must reside in main memory, only the tables that describe the resident set of pages need be available in main memory. This paging of tables is implemented by placing the "invalid" code ($0) in the DT field of the table descriptor that points to the absent table(s). When a task attempts to use an address that would be translated by an absent table, the MC68030 is unable to locate a translation and takes a bus error exception when the execution unit retries the bus cycle that caused the table search to be initiated.

It is the responsibility of the system software to determine that the invalid code in the descriptor corresponds to nonresident tables. This determination can be facilitated by using the unused bits in the descriptor to store status information concerning the invalid encoding. When the MC68030 encounters an invalid descriptor, it makes no interpretation (or modification) of any fields of this descriptor other than the DT field, allowing the operating system to store system-defined information in the remaining bits. Typical information that is stored includes the reason for the invalid encoding (tables paged-out, region not allocated, . . ., etc.) and possibly the disk address for nonresident tables.

Figure 9-24 shows an address translation table in which only a single page table (table n) is resident and all other page tables are not resident.

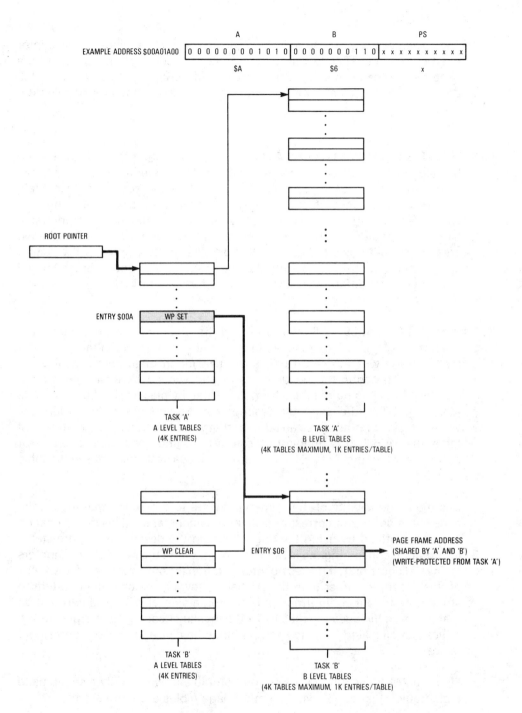

Figure 9-23. Example Translation Tree Using Shared Tables

MC68030 USER'S MANUAL

MOTOROLA

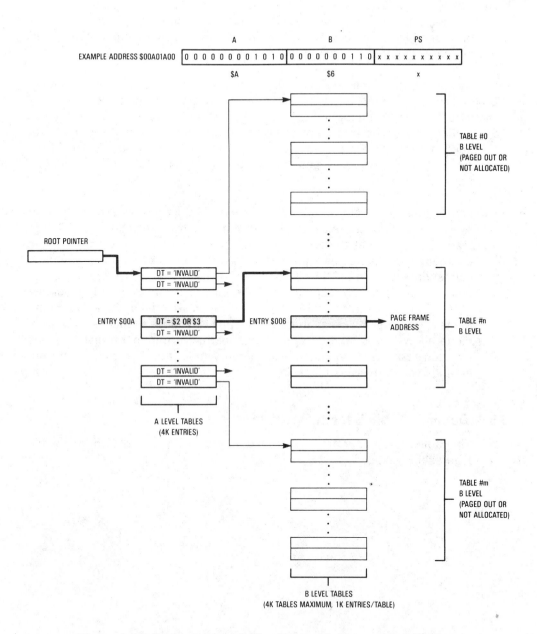

Figure 9-24. Example Translation Tree with Nonresident Tables

9.5.3.5 DYNAMIC ALLOCATION OF TABLES.

Similar to the case of paged tables, it is not required that a complete translation tree exist for an active task. The translation tree can be dynamically allocated by the operating system based on requests for access to particular areas.

As in the case of demand paging, it is difficult, if not impossible, to predict the areas of memory that are used by a task over any extended period of time. Instead of attempting to predict the requirements of the task, the operating system performs no action for a task until a demand is made requesting access to a previously unused area or an area that is no longer resident in memory. This same technique can be used to efficiently create a translation tree for a task.

For example, consider an operating system that is preparing the system to execute a previously unexecuted task that has no translation tree. Rather than guessing what the memory usage requirements of the task are, the operating system creates a translation tree for the task that maps one page corresponding to the initial value of the program counter for that task, and possibly, one page corresponding to the initial stack pointer of the task. All other branches of the translation tree for this task remain unallocated until the task requests access to the areas mapped by these branches. This technique allows the operating system to construct a minimal translation tree for each task, conserving physical memory utilization and minimizing operating system overhead.

9.5.4 Detail of Table Search Operations

The table search operations described in this section are shown in detail in Figures 9-25–9-29.

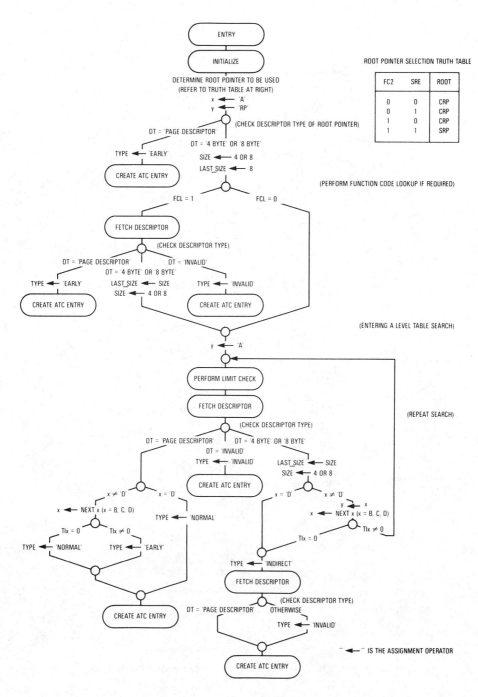

ROOT POINTER SELECTION TRUTH TABLE

FC2	SRE	ROOT
0	0	CRP
0	1	CRP
1	0	CRP
1	1	SRP

Figure 9-25. Detailed Flowchart of MMU Table Search Operation

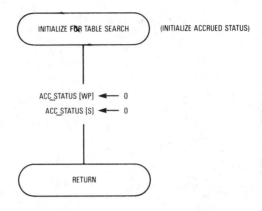

Figure 9-26. Table Search Initialization Flowchart

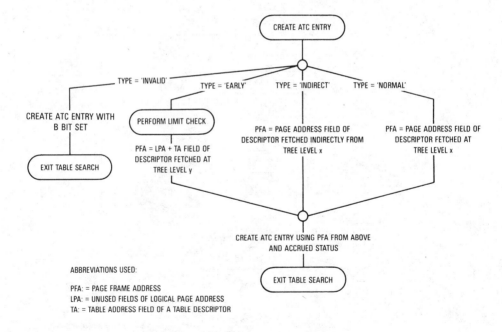

ABBREVIATIONS USED:

PFA: = PAGE FRAME ADDRESS
LPA: = UNUSED FIELDS OF LOGICAL PAGE ADDRESS
TA: = TABLE ADDRESS FIELD OF A TABLE DESCRIPTOR

Figure 9-27. ATC Entry Creation Flowchart

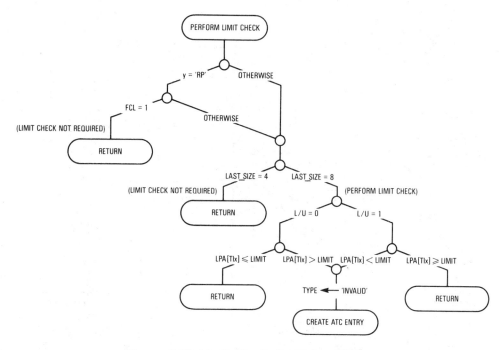

Figure 9-28. Limit Check Procedure Flowchart

9.5.5 Protection

M68000 Family processors provide an indication of the context in which they are operating on a cycle-by-cycle basis by means of the function code signals. These signals identify accesses to the user program space, the user data space, the supervisor program space, and the supervisor data space. The function code signals can be used for protection mechanisms by setting the function code lookup (FCL) bit in the translation control (TC) register.

The MC68030 MMU provides the capability for separate translation trees for supervisor and user spaces to be used. When the supervisor root pointer enable bit (SRE) in the TC register is set, the root pointer register for the supervisor space translation tree is selected for supervisor program or data accesses.

The translation table trees contain both mapping and protection information. Each table and page descriptor includes a write-protect (WP) bit, which can be set to provide write protection at any level. Each long-format table and page descriptor also contains a supervisor-only (S) bit, which can limit access to programs operating at the supervisor privilege level.

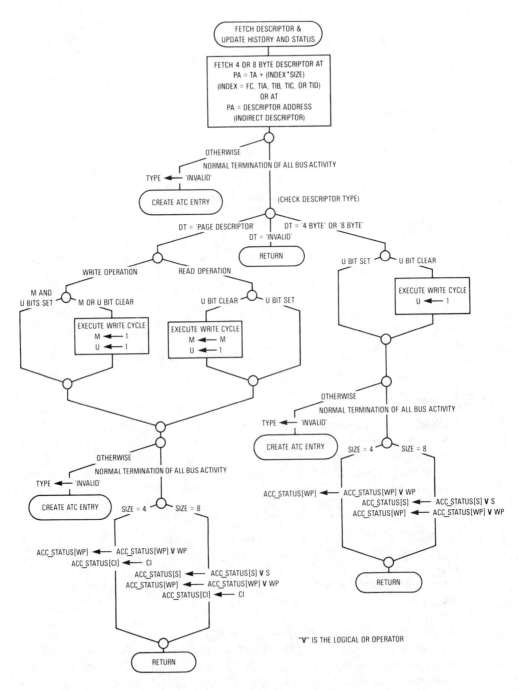

Figure 9-29. Detailed Flowchart of Descriptor Fetch Operation

The protection mechanisms can be used individually or in any combination to protect:

- Supervisor program and data spaces from access by user programs.

- User program and data spaces from access by other user programs or supervisor programs (except with the MOVES instruction).

- Supervisor and user program spaces from write accesses (except by the supervisor using the MOVES instruction).

- One or more pages of memory from write accesses.

9.5.5.1 FUNCTION CODE LOOKUP. One way of protecting supervisor and user spaces from unauthorized access is to set the FCL bit in the TC register. This effectively segments the logical address space into a supervisor program space, a supervisor data space, a user program space, and a user data space, as shown in Figure 9-30. Each task has an address translation tree with unique mappings for the logical addresses in its user spaces. The translation tables for mapping the supervisor spaces can be copied into each task's translation tree. Figure 9-31 shows a translation tree using function code lookup, and Figure 9-32 shows translation trees for two tasks that share common supervisor spaces.

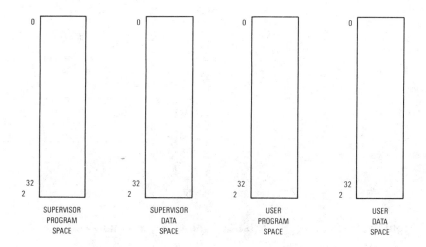

Figure 9-30. Logical Address Map Using Function Code Lookup

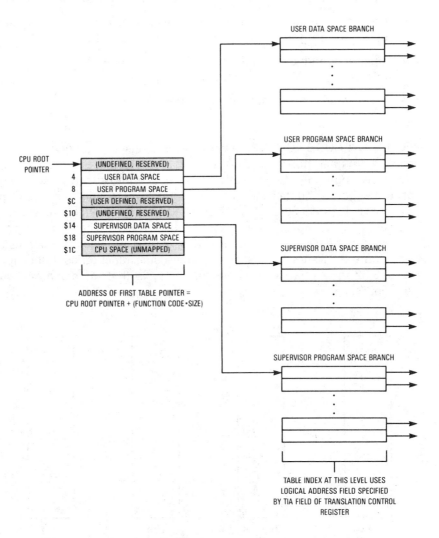

CPU ROOT POINTER →

	(UNDEFINED, RESERVED)
4	USER DATA SPACE
8	USER PROGRAM SPACE
$C	(USER DEFINED, RESERVED)
$10	(UNDEFINED, RESERVED)
$14	SUPERVISOR DATA SPACE
$18	SUPERVISOR PROGRAM SPACE
$1C	CPU SPACE (UNMAPPED)

ADDRESS OF FIRST TABLE POINTER =
CPU ROOT POINTER + (FUNCTION CODE•SIZE)

USER DATA SPACE BRANCH

USER PROGRAM SPACE BRANCH

SUPERVISOR DATA SPACE BRANCH

SUPERVISOR PROGRAM SPACE BRANCH

TABLE INDEX AT THIS LEVEL USES
LOGICAL ADDRESS FIELD SPECIFIED
BY TIA FIELD OF TRANSLATION CONTROL
REGISTER

Figure 9-31. Example Translation Tree Using Function Code Lookup

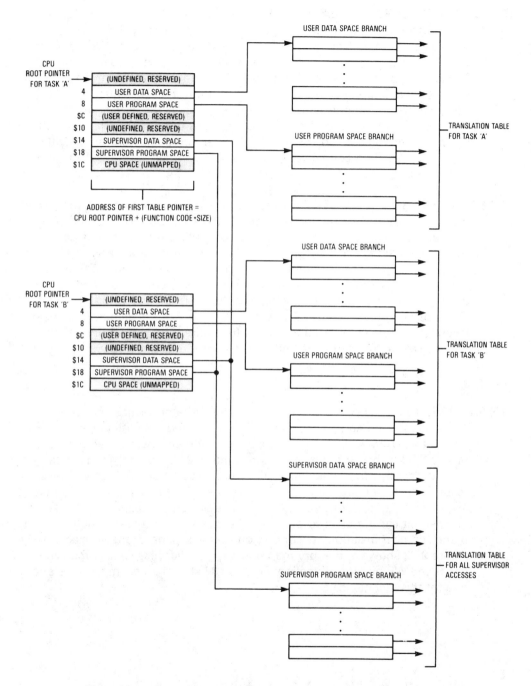

Figure 9-32. Example Translation Tree Structure for Two Tasks

9.5.5.2 SUPERVISOR TRANSLATION TREE. A second protection mechanism uses a supervisor translation tree. A supervisor translation tree protects supervisor programs and data from access by user programs and user programs and data from access by supervisor programs. Access is granted to the supervisor programs which can access any area of memory with the move address space (MOVES) instruction. When the SRE bit in the TC register is set, the translation tree pointed to by the SRP is selected for all supervisor level accesses. This translation tree can be common to all tasks. This technique segments the logical address space into user and supervisor areas without adding the function code level to the translation trees.

9.5.5.3 SUPERVISOR ONLY. A third mechanism protects supervisor programs and data without segmenting the logical address space into supervisor and user address spaces. The long formats of table descriptors and page descriptors contain S bits to protect areas of memory from access by user programs. When a table search for a user access encounters an S bit set in any table or page descriptor, the table search is completed and an ATC descriptor corresponding to the logical address is created with the B bit set. The subsequent retry of the user access results in a bus error exception being taken. The S bit can be used to protect the entire area of memory defined in a branch of the translation tree or only one or more pages from user program access.

9.5.5.4 WRITE PROTECT. The MC68030 provides write protection independently of the segmented address spaces for programs and data. All table and page descriptors contain WP bits to protect areas of memory from write accesses of any kind. When a table search encounters a WP bit set in any table or page descriptor, the table search is completed and an ATC descriptor corresponding to the logical address is created with the WP bit set. The subsequent retry of the write access results in a bus error exception being taken. The WP bit can be used to protect the entire area of memory defined in a branch of the translation tree, or only one or more pages from write accesses. Figure 9-33 shows a memory map of the logical address space organized to use S and WP bits for protection. Figure 9-34 shows an example translation tree for this technique.

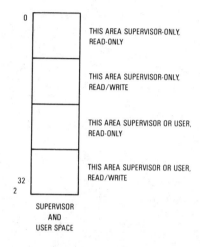

Figure 9-33. Example Logical Address Map with Shared Supervisor and User Address Spaces

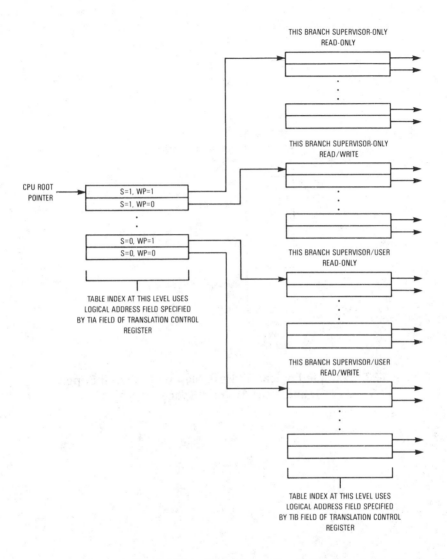

Figure 9-34. Example Translation Tree Using S and WP Bits to Set Protection

MC68030 USER'S MANUAL

MOTOROLA

9.6 MC68030 AND MC68851 MMU DIFFERENCES

The MC68851 paged memory management unit provides memory management for the MC68020 as a coprocessor. The on-chip MMU of the MC68030 provides many of the features of the MC68020/MC68851 combination. The following functions of the MC68851 are not available in the MC68030 MMU:

- Access Levels

- Breakpoint Registers

- Root Pointer Table

- Aliases for Tasks

- Lockable Entries in the ATC

- ATC Entries Defined as Shared Globally

In addition, the following features of the MC68030 MMU differ from the MC68020/MC68851 pair:

- 22-Entry ATC

- Reduced Instruction Set

- Only Control-Alterable Addressing Modes Supported for MMU Instructions

In general, the MC68030 is program compatible with the MC68020/MC68851 combination. However, in a program for the MC68030, the following instructions must be avoided or emulated in the exception routine for F-line unimplemented instructions: PVALID, PFLUSHR, PFLUSHS, PBcc, PDBcc, PScc, PTRAPcc, PSAVE, PRESTORE, and PMOVE for unsupported registers (CAL, VAL, SCC, BAD, BACx, DRP, and AC). Additionally, the effective addressing modes supported on the MC68851 that are not emulated by the MC68030 must be simulated or avoided.

9

9.7 REGISTERS

The registers of the MMU described here are part of the supervisor programming model for the MC68030.

The six registers that control and provide status information for address translation in the MC68030 are the CPU root pointer register (CRP), the supervisor root pointer register (SRP), the translation control register (TC), two independent transparent translation control registers (TT0 and TT1), and the MMU status register (MMUSR). These registers can be accessed directly by programs that execute only at the supervisor level.

9.7.1 Root Pointer Registers

The supervisor root pointer (SRP), used for supervisor accesses only, is enabled or disabled in software. The CPU root pointer (CRP) corresponds to the current translation table for user space (when the SRP is enabled) or for both user and supervisor space (when the SRP is disabled). The CRP is a 64-bit register that contains the address and related status information of the root of the translation table tree for the current task. When a new task begins execution, the operating system typically writes a new root pointer descriptor to the CRP. A new translation table address implies that the contents of the address translation cache (ATC) may no longer be valid. Therefore, the instruction that loads the CRP can optionally flush the ATC.

The SRP is a 64-bit register that optionally contains the address and related status information of the root of the translation table for supervisor area accesses. The SRP is used when operating at the supervisor privilege level only when the supervisor root pointer enable bit (SRE) of the translation control register (TC) is set. The instruction that loads the SRP can optionally flush the ATC. The format of the CRP and SRP is shown in Figure 9-35 and defines the following fields:

Lower/Upper (L/U)
Specifies that the value contained in the limit field is to be used as the unsigned lower limit of indexes into the translation tables when this bit is set. When this bit is cleared, the limit field is the unsigned upper limit of the translation table indexes.

Limit

Specifies a maximum or minimum value for the index to be used at the next level of table search (the function code level cannot be limited). To suppress the limit function, the L/U bit is cleared and the limit field is set to ones ($7FFF in the word containing both fields), or the L/U bit is set and the limit field is cleared ($8000 in that word).

Descriptor Type (DT)

Specifies the type of descriptor contained in either the root pointer or in the first level of the translation table identified by the root pointer. The values are:

$0 INVALID

This value is not allowed at the root pointer level. When a root pointer register is loaded with an invalid root pointer descriptor, an MMU configuration exception is taken.

$1 PAGE DESCRIPTOR

A translation table for this root pointer does not exist. The MC68030 internally calculates an ATC entry (page descriptor) for accesses using this root pointer within the current page by adding (unsigned) the value in the table address field to the incoming logical address. This results in direct mapping with a constant offset (the table address). For this case, the processor performs a limit check, regardless of the state of the FCL bit in the TC register.

$2 VALID 4 BYTE

The translation table at the root of the translation tree contains short-format descriptors. The MC68030 must scale the table index for this level of the table search by 4 bytes to access the next descriptor.

$3 VALID 8 BYTE

The translation table at the root of the translation tree contains long-format descriptors. The MC68030 must scale the table index for this level of the table search by 8 bytes to access the next descriptor.

Table Address

Contains the physical base address (in bits 31–4) of the translation table at the root pointer level. When the DT field contains $1, the value in the table address field is the offset used to calculate the physical address for the page descriptor. The table address field can contain zero (for zero offset).

Unused

Bits 3–0 of the root pointer are not used and are ignored when written. All other unused bits must always be zeros.

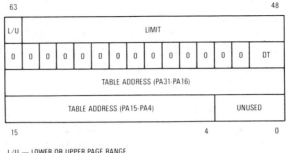

L/U — LOWER OR UPPER PAGE RANGE
DT — DESCRIPTOR TYPE
LIMIT — LIMIT ON TABLE INDEX FOR THIS TABLE ADDRESS
TABLE ADDRESS — ADDRESS OF TABLE AT NEXT LEVEL OR PAGE OFFSET IF DT = 1

Figure 9-35. Root Pointer Register (CRP, SRP) Format

9.7.2 Translation Control Register

The translation control register (TC) is a 32-bit register that contains the control fields for address translation. All unimplemented fields of this register are read as zeros and must always be written as zeros.

Writing to this register optionally causes a flush of the entire ATC. When written with the E bit (bit 31) set (translation enabled), a consistency check is performed on the values of PS, IS, and Tlx as follows. The Tlx fields are added together until a zero field is reached, and this sum is added to PS and IS. The total must be 32, or an MMU configuration exception (refer to **9.7.5.3 MMU CONFIGURATON EXCEPTION**) is taken. If an MMU configuration exception occurs, the TC register is updated with the data, and the E bit is cleared. The translation control register is shown in Figure 9-36.

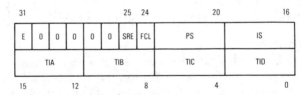

E — ENABLE
SRE — SUPERVISOR ROOT POINTER ENABLE
FCL — FUNCTION CODE LOOKUP ENABLE
PS — PAGE SIZE
IS — INITIAL SHIFT
TIA, TIB, TIC, TID — TABLE INDICES

Figure 9-36. Translation Control Register (TC) Format

The fields of the TC register are:

Enable (E)

This bit enables and disables address translation:

0 — Translation disabled

1 — Translation enabled

A reset operation clears this bit. When translation is disabled, logical addresses are used as physical addresses. The MMU instructions (PTEST, PLOAD, PMOVE, PFLUSH) can be executed successfully, regardless of the state of the E bit. Additionally, even if the E bit is set, the TC register can be updated with a value whose E bit is set. The state of the E bit does not affect the use of the transparent translation registers.

Supervisor Root Pointer Enable (SRE)

This bit controls the use of the supervisor root pointer register (SRP):

0 — SRP disabled

1 — SRP enabled

When the SRP is disabled, both user and supervisor accesses use the translation table defined by the CRP. When the SRP is enabled, user accesses use the CRP, and supervisor accesses use the SRP.

Function Code Lookup (FCL)

This bit enables the use of function code lookup for searching the address translation tables:

0 — Function code lookup disabled

1 — Function code lookup enabled

When function code lookup is disabled, the first level of pointer tables within the translation table structure is indexed by the logical address field defined by TIA. When function code lookup is enabled, the first table of the translation table structure is indexed by function code. In this case, the limit field of CRP or SRP is ignored.

9

Page Size (PS)

This 4-bit field specifies the system page size:

1000 — 256 bytes
1001 — 512 bytes
1010 — 1K bytes
1011 — 2K bytes
1100 — 4K bytes
1101 — 8K bytes
1110 — 16K bytes
1111 — 32K bytes

All other bit combinations are reserved by Motorola for future use; an attempt to load other values into this field of the TC register causes an MMU configuration exception.

Initial Shift (IS)

This 4-bit field contains the number of high-order bits of the logical address that are ignored during table search operations. The field contains an integer, 0–15, which sets the effective size of the logical address to 32–17 bits, respectively. Since all 32 bits of the address are compared during address translation, bits ignored due to initial shift cannot have random values. They must be specified and be consistent with the translation table values in order to ensure that subsequent address translations match the corresponding entries in the ATC.

Table Index (TIA, TIB, TIC, and TID)

These 4-bit fields specify the numbers of logical address bits used as the indexes for the four possible levels of the translation tables (not including the optional level indexed by the function codes). The index into the highest level table (following the function code, when used) is specified by TIA, and the lowest level, by TID. The fields contain integers, 0–15. When a zero value in a TIx field is encountered during a table search operation, the search is over unless the indexed descriptor is a table (indirect) descriptor.

9

9.7.3 Transparent Translation Registers

The transparent translation registers (TT0 and TT1) are 32-bit registers that define blocks of logical address space that are transparently translated. Logical addresses in a transparently translated block are used as physical addresses, without modification and without protection checking. The minimum size block that can be defined by either TTx register is 16 Mbytes of logical address space. The two TTx registers can specify blocks that overlap. The TTx registers operate independently of the E bit in the TC register and the state of the $\overline{\text{MMUDIS}}$ signal. A transparent translation register is shown in Figure 9-37.

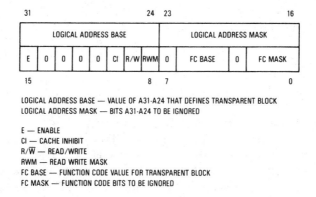

LOGICAL ADDRESS BASE — VALUE OF A31-A24 THAT DEFINES TRANSPARENT BLOCK
LOGICAL ADDRESS MASK — BITS A31-A24 TO BE IGNORED

E — ENABLE
CI — CACHE INHIBIT
R/$\overline{\text{W}}$ — READ/WRITE
RWM — READ WRITE MASK
FC BASE — FUNCTION CODE VALUE FOR TRANSPARENT BLOCK
FC MASK — FUNCTION CODE BITS TO BE IGNORED

Figure 9-37. Transparent Translation Register (TT0 and TT1) Format

The fields of the transparent translation register are:

Enable (E)
   This bit enables transparent translation of the block defined by this register:
   0 — Transparent translation disabled
   1 — Transparent translation enabled
   A reset operation clears this bit.

Cache Inhibit (CI)

This bit inhibits caching for the transparent block:

0 — Caching allowed

1 — Caching inhibited

When this bit is set, the contents of a matching address are not stored in the internal instruction or data cache. Additionally, the cache inhibit out signal ($\overline{\text{CIOUT}}$) is asserted when this bit is set, and a matching address is accessed, signaling external caches to inhibit caching for those accesses.

Read/Write (R/W)

This bit defines the type of access that is transparently translated (for a matching address):

0 — Write accesses transparent

1 — Read accesses transparent

Read/Write Mask (RWM)

This bit masks the R/W field:

0 — R/W field used

1 — R/W field ignored

When RWM is set to one, both read and write accesses of a matching address are transparently translated. For transparent translation of read-modify-write cycles with matching addresses, RWM must be set to one. If the RWM bit equals zero, neither the read nor the write of any read-modify-write cycle is transparently translated with the TTx register.

Function Code Base (FC BASE)

This 3-bit field defines the base function code for accesses to be transparently translated with this register. Addresses with function codes that match the FC BASE field (and are otherwise eligible) are transparently translated.

Function Code Mask (FC MASK)

This 3-bit field contains a mask for the FC BASE field. Setting a bit in this field causes the corresponding bit of the FC BASE field to be ignored.

LOGICAL ADDRESS BASE

This 8-bit field is compared with address bits A31–A24. Addresses that match in this comparison (and are otherwise eligible) are transparently translated.

LOGICAL ADDRESS MASK

This 8-bit field contains a mask for the LOGICAL ADDRESS BASE field. Setting a bit in this field causes the corresponding bit of the LOGICAL ADDRESS BASE field to be ignored. Blocks of memory larger than 16 Mbytes can be transparently translated by setting some of the logical address mask bits to ones. Normally, the low-order bits of this field are set to define contiguous blocks larger than 16 Mbytes, although this is not required.

9.7.4 MMU Status Register

The MMU status register (MMUSR) is a 16-bit register that contains the status information returned by execution of the PTEST instruction. The PTEST instruction searches either the ATC (PTEST with level 0) or the translation tables (PTEST with levels of 1–7) to determine status information about the translation of a specified logical address. The MMUSR is shown in Figure 9-38.

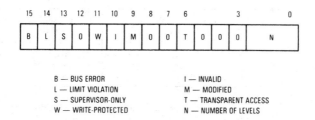

Figure 9-38. MMU Status Register (MMUSR) Format

The bits in the MMUSR have different meanings for the two kinds of PTEST instructions, as shown in Table 9-3.

Table 9-3. MMUSR Bit Definitions

MMUSR Bit	PTEST, Level 0	PTEST, Level 1–7
Bus Error (B)	This bit is set if the bus error bit is set in the ATC entry for the specified logical address.	This bit is set if a bus error is encountered during the table search for the PTEST instruction.
Limit (L)	This bit is cleared.	This bit is set if an index exceeds a limit during the table search.
Supervisor Violation (S)	This bit is cleared.	This bit is set if the S bit of a long (S) format table descriptor or long format page descriptor encountered during the search is set, and the FC2 bit of the function code specified by the PTEST instruction is not equal to one. The S bit is undefined if the I bit is set.
Write Protected (W)	This bit is set if the WP bit of the ATC entry is set. It is undefined if the I bit is set.	This bit is set if a descriptor or page descriptor is encountered with the WP bit set during the table search. The W bit is undefined if the I bit is set.
Invalid (I)	This bit indicates an invalid translation. The I bit is set if the translation for the specified logical address is not resident in the ATC or if the B bit of the corresponding ATC entry is set.	This bit indicates an invalid translation. The I bit is set if the DT field of a table or a page descriptor encountered during the serach is set to invalid or if either the B or L bits of the MMUSR are set during the table search.
Modified (M)	This bit is set if the ATC entry corresponding to the specified address has the modified bit set. It is undefined if the I bit is set.	This bit is set if the page descriptor for the specified address has the modified bit set. It is undefined if I is set.
Transparent (T)	This bit is set if a match occurred in either (or both) of the transparent translation registers (TT0 or TT1). If the T bit is set, all remaining MMUSR bits are undefined.	This bit is set to zero.
Number of Levels (N)	This 3-bit field is cleared to zero.	This 3-bit field contains the actual number of tables accessed during the search.

9

9.7.5 Register Programming Considerations

If the entries in the address translation cache (ATC) are no longer valid when a reset operation occurs, an explicit flush operation must be specified by the software. The assertion of $\overline{\text{RESET}}$ disables translations by clearing the E bits of the TC and TTx registers, but it does not flush the ATC. Flushing of the ATC is optional under control of the FD bit of the PMOVE instruction that loads a new value into the SRP, CRP, TT0, TT1, or TC register.

The programmer of the MMU must be aware of effects resulting from loading certain registers. A subsequent section describes these effects. The MMUSR values lend themselves to the use of a case structure for branching to appropriate routines in a bus error handler. An example of a flowchart that implements this technique is shown in another section. A third section describes the conditions that result in MMU exceptions.

9.7.5.1 REGISTER SIDE EFFECTS. The PMOVE instruction is used to load or read any of the MMU registers (CRP, SRP, TC, MMUSR, TT0, and TT1). Since loading the root pointers, the translation control register, or the transparent translation registers with new values can cause some or all of the address translations to change, it may be desired to flush the ATC of its contents any time these registers are written. The opcodes of the PMOVE instructions that write to CRP, SRP, TC, TT0, and TT1 contain a flush disable (FD) bit that optionally flushes the ATC when these instructions are executed. If the FD bit equals one, the ATC is not flushed when the instruction is executed. If the FD bit equals zero, the ATC is flushed during the execution of the PMOVE instruction.

9.7.5.2 MMU STATUS REGISTER DECODING. The seven status bits in the MMU status register (MMUSR) indicate conditions to which the operating system should respond. In a typical bus error handler routine, the flows shown in Figures 9-39 and 9-40 can be used to determine the cause of an MMU fault. The PTEST instructions set the bits in the MMUSR appropriately, and the program can branch to the appropriate code segment for the condition. Figure 9-39 shows the flow for a PTEST instruction for the ATC (level 0), and Figure 9-40 shows the flow for a PTEST instruction that accesses an address translation tree (levels 1–7).

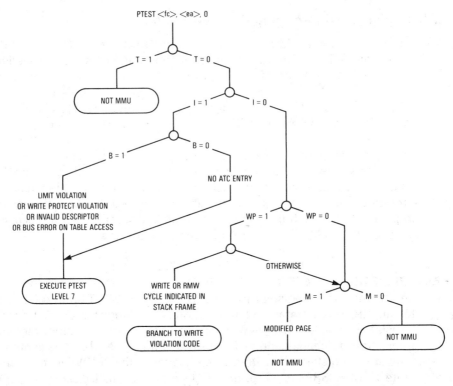

Figure 9-39. MMU Status Interpretation PTEST Level 0

9.7.5.3 MMU CONFIGURATION EXCEPTION.

The exception vector table in the MC68030 assigns a vector for an MMU configuration error exception. The configuration exception occurs as the result of loading invalid data into the TC, SRP, or CRP register.

When the TC register is loaded with the E bit set, the MMU performs a consistency check of the values in all the four bit fields. The values in the TIx fields are added until the first zero is encountered. The values in the PS and IS fields are added to the sum of the TIx fields. If the sum is not equal to 32, the PMOVE instruction causes an MMU configuration exception. The instruction also causes a configuration exception when a reserved value ($0–$7) is placed in the PS field of the TC register.

A PMOVE instruction that loads either the CRP or the SRP causes an MMU configuration exception if the new value of the DT field is zero (invalid). In this case, the register is loaded with the new value before the exception is taken.

MC68030 USER'S MANUAL

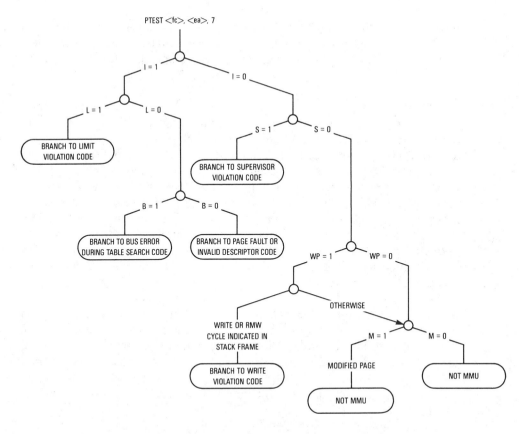

Figure 9-40. MMU Status Interpretation PTEST Level 7

9.8 MMU INSTRUCTIONS

The MC68030 instruction set includes four privileged instructions that perform MMU operations. A brief description of each of these instructions follows.

The PMOVE instruction transfers data between a CPU register or memory location and any one of the six MMU registers. The operating system uses the PMOVE instruction to control and monitor MMU operation by manipulating and reading these registers. Optionally, a PMOVE instruction flushes the ATC when it loads a value into the TC, SRP, CRP, TT0, or TT1 register.

The PFLUSH instruction flushes (invalidates) address translation descriptors in the ATC. PFLUSHA, a version of the PFLUSH instruction, flushes all entries. The PFLUSH instruction flushes all entries with a specified function code or the entry with a specified function code and logical address.

The PLOAD instruction performs a table search operation for a specified function code and logical address and then loads the translation for the address into the ATC. The operating system can use this instruction to initialize the ATC to minimize table searching during program execution. Any existing entry in the ATC that translates the specified address is flushed. The preload can be executed for either read or write attributes. If the write attribute is selected (PLOADW), the MC68030 performs the table search and updates all history information in the translation tables (used and modified bits) as if a write operation to that address had occurred. Similarly, if the read attribute is selected (PLOADR), the history information in the translation table (used bit) is updated as if a read operation had occurred. The PLOAD instruction does not alter the MMUSR.

The PTEST instruction either searches the ATC or performs a table search operation for a specified function code and logical address, and sets the appropriate bits in the MMUSR to indicate conditions encountered during the search. The physical address of the last descriptor fetched can be returned in an address register. The exception routines of the operating system can use this instruction to identify MMU faults. The PTEST instruction does not alter the ATC.

This instruction is primarily used in bus error handling routines. For example, if a bus error has occurred, the handler can execute an instruction such as:

        PTESTW   #1,([A7, offset]),#7,A0

This instruction requests that the MC68030 search the translation tables for an address in user data space (#1) and examine protection information. This particular logical address is obtained from the exception stack frame ([A7, offset]). The MC68030 is instructed to search to the bottom of the table (#7 — there cannot be more than six levels) and return the physical address of the last table entry used in register A0. After executing this instruction, the handler can examine the MMUSR for the source of the fault and use A0 to access the last descriptor. Note that the PTESTR and PTESTW instructions have identical results except for PTEST0 when either TTx register matches the logical address and the R/W bit of that register is not masked.

The MMU instructions use the same opcodes and coprocessor identification (CpID) as the corresponding instructions of the MC68851. All F-line instructions with CpID = 0 (including MC68851 instructions) that the MC68030 does not support automatically cause F-line unimplemented instruction exceptions when their execution is attempted in the supervise mode. If execution of a unimplemented F-line instruction with CpID = 0 is attempted in the user mode, the MC68030 takes a privilege violation exception. F-line instructions with a CpID other than zero are executed as coprocessor instructions by the MC68030.

9.9 DEFINING AND USING PAGE TABLES IN AN OPERATING SYSTEM

Many factors must be considered when determining how to use the MMU in an operating system. The MC68030 provides the flexibility required to optimize an operating system for many system implementations. The example operating system described in the next section presents one approach to operating system design, with many of the tradeoffs discussed.

9.9.1 Root Pointer Registers

An operating system can use the CPU root pointer (CRP) register alone or both the CRP and the supervisor root pointer (SRP) registers to point to the top level address translation table(s). The choice depends on the complexity of the memory layout for the system. When only the CRP is used, it must point to a translation table that maps all supervisor and user references. However, the supervisor and user translation tables can be separate even when only the CRP register is used. When the index to the top level translation table is the function code value (FCL in TC register is set), supervisor and user tables are separate at all lower levels. With proper structuring of the address tables, both methods can provide the same functionality, but each has its advantages.

When the translation tables use the CRP and function code lookup, supervisor and user accesses are separate, and each task can have different supervisor and user mappings. Alternatively, the entries in the function code tables that correspond to the supervisor spaces for each task can all point to the same tables to provide a common mapping for all supervisor references.

When the mapping of the supervisor address space is identical for all tasks, the SRP can be used in conjunction with the CRP to provide a more simple and efficient way to define the mapping. This technique suppresses the use of the function code (unless the program and data spaces require distinct mappings) and separates supervisor and user accesses at the root pointer level of the translation tables. A single translation table maps all supervisor accesses without maintaining a large number of supervisor pointers in the translation tables for each task, resulting in reduced bus activity for table searches.

9.9.2 Task Memory Map Definition

The MC68030 provides several different means by which the supervisor can access the user address spaces. The supervisor can access any user address, regardless of how the virtual space is partitioned, with the MOVES (move space) instruction. Some systems provide a complete 4-Gbyte virtual memory map for each task. Indeed, an operating system that runs other operating systems in a virtual machine environment must provide a complete map to accurately emulate the full addressing range for the subordinate operating system.

With the large address space of the MC68030, each individual user task or all user tasks can share the address space with the operating system. One method of performing this function is implemented in the example operating system in the next section. Sharing the address space provides direct access to user data items by the operating system. Another advantage of this mapping method is that tasks can easily share code. Common routines such as file I/O handlers and arithmetic conversion packages can be written re-entrantly and be restricted to read-only access from all user tasks in the system.

The simplest example of a shared virtual address space system is one in which each user and supervisor process is given a unique virtual address range within the single 4-Gbyte virtual address space. In other words, the system has only one linear virtual address space; all processes run somewhere in that space. Only one translation table tree is required for the entire system, but each task can have individual tables if desired. With the common tree approach, the operating system can access any item of any task without modifying the root pointer. Otherwise, only the currently active task is immediately accessible, which often is adequate. To switch tasks, the operating system only has to update the user program and user data pointers in the highest level translation table indexed by the function code. This gives each task access to its own data only. This scheme has the advantages of simple table management and easy sharing of common items by giving them the same virtual address for all tasks in the system. This scheme might be ideal for real-time systems that do not require more complexity in memory management facilities.

The next logical step toward increased operating system complexity, with shared user and supervisor virtual memory maps, is to keep the supervisor addresses separate but to give each user task its own use of the remainder of the virtual space. For example, each user task could have the virtual memory space from zero to 512 Mbytes; the operating system programs and data would occupy the remainder of the space, from 512 Mbytes up to 4 Gbytes. Each user task has its own set of translation tables. The supervisor root pointer may or may not be used, depending on whether the user tables also map the supervisor space. As in the preceding method, the user cannot access the operating system portion of the address space unless the operating system allows it or wishes to share common routines. The advantages of this scheme are that it provides a much larger virtual address space for each user task and it avoids virtual memory fragmentation problems. Disadvantages of this scheme include the requirement for slightly more complex table management and the restriction of operating system access to only the current user task.

There are few absolute rules in the use of the MC68030 MMU. In general, the statement regarding restricting operating system access to only one user task using the scheme described in the preceding paragraph holds true. However, by using the entire 4-Gbyte virtual address space and cross mapping the address space, the supervisor can access each user task space as a distinct portion of its own supervisor map. If each user task is limited to a 16-Mbyte virtual address space and the supervisor only requires a 16-Mbyte address space, 256 such address spaces can be mapped simultaneously. The supervisor translation tables can include each of these spaces, and the supervisor can access each task using indexed addressing with a register that contains the proper constant for a particular task. This constant provides a supervisor-to-user virtual address conversion. A systems programmer can implement some very sophisticated functions that exploit the flexibility of the MMU.

The most complex systems and those that implement virtual machine capability completely separate the virtual address spaces of the supervisor and all user tasks, or possibly even those of individual supervisor tasks. Each user or supervisor task has its own virtual memory space starting at zero and extending to 4 Gbytes. Using the function code, a 4-Gbyte address space for the program and another for its data can be provided for each task. Both the SRP and the CRP are probably used, since nothing is common among the various spaces. The operating system uses the MOVES instruction to interact with the user space. The advantages of this implementation are the maximum availability of the virtual space and a complete logical separation of addresses. Virtual machine implementations require maximum availability of virtual space. The disadvantages are the more complex table management and the more restrictive accesses to other address spaces.

9.9.3 Impact of MMU Features on Table Definition

The features of the MMU that impact table definition are usually considered after deciding how to map memory for the tasks. For some systems, these features can affect the mapping decision and should be considered when making that decision.

9.9.3.1 NUMBER OF TABLE LEVELS. The MMU supports from zero to five levels (six levels with the use of indirection) in the address translation tables. The zero-level case is early termination at the root pointer. This provides a limit check on the range of physical addresses for the system. It is used primarily in systems that require the limit check on physical addresses.

Systems that support large page sizes or that require only limited amounts of virtual memory space can use single-level tables. A single-level translation tree with 32K-byte pages may be the best choice for systems that are primarily numerically intensive (i.e., the system is involved in arithmetic manipulations rather than data movement) where the overhead of virtual page faults and paging I/O must be minimized. This type of system can map a 16-Mbyte address space with only 2K bytes of page table space. With this much mapped address space, table search time becomes insignificant.

At another extreme is a single-user business system that only needs a 2-Mbyte virtual address space. A 512-byte page size might be best for this system, because the block size formats of many Winchester hard disk file systems is 512 bytes. A page table that completely maps the 2-Mbyte space requires only 16K bytes of memory, and the ATC entries directly map 11K bytes of virtual space at any one time. The page tables for this system and the one described in the preceding paragraph are small enough to be permanently allocated in the operating system data area. They incur virtually no management or swapping overhead.

A two-level address translation table provides a lower page level similar to the page tables in the two preceding paragraphs and additional direction at a higher level. For example, in a system using 32K-byte pages and 512-entry page tables, the upper level translation table contains 256 entries of short-format descriptors, requiring 1K bytes for the table. Each of the upper table

9

entries maps a 16-Mbyte region of the virtual address space. The primary advantage of a two-level table for large "number-crunching" system is the operating system designer's ability to make a tradeoff between page size and table size. The system designer may choose a smaller page size to fit the block sizes on available I/O devices, yet keep the tables manageable. However, the designer must also consider the performance penalty associated with smaller page sizes. Systems with smaller page sizes have a higher frequency of page faults requiring more table search time and paging I/O. With the flexibility of the MC68030 MMU, the designer has enough choices to optimize table structure design and page size.

Three-level translation tables are useful when the operating system makes heavy use of shared memory spaces and/or shared page tables. Sophisticated systems often share translation tables or program and data areas defined at the page table level. When a table entry can point to a translation table also used by a different task, sharing memory areas becomes efficient. The direct access to user address space by the supervisor is an example of sharing memory.

Some artificial intelligence systems require very large virtual address spaces with only small fragments of memory allocated among these widely differing addresses. This fragmentation is due to the complex and recursive actions the system performs on lists of data. These actions require the system to constantly allocate and free sophisticated pointers and linked lists in the memory map. The fragmentation suggests a small page size to utilize memory most efficiently. However, small pages in a large virtual memory map require relatively large translation tables. For example, to map 4 Gbytes of virtual address space with 256-byte pages, the page tables alone require 64 Mbytes. With a three- or four-level table structure, the number of actual translation table entries can be drastically reduced. The designer can use invalid descriptors to represent blocks of unused addresses and the limit fields in valid descriptors to minimize the sizes of pointer and page tables. In addition, paging of the address tables themselves reduces memory requirements.

9.9.3.2 INITIAL SHIFT COUNT. The initial shift field (IS) of the translation control register (TC) can decrease the size of translation tables. When the required virtual address space can be addressed with fewer than 32 bits, the IS field reduces the size of the virtual address space by discarding the appropriate number of the most significant logical address bits. This technique inhibits the system's ability to detect very large illegal (i.e., out-of-bounds) addresses. Using the full 32-bit address and reducing the table size with invalid descriptors and limited pointer and page table sizes prevents this problem.

9.9.3.3 LIMIT FIELDS Except for a table indexed by function code, every pointer and page table can have a defined limit on its size. Defining limits provides flexibility in the operating system and saves memory in the translation tables. The limit field of a table descriptor limits the size of the table to which it points. The limit can be either an upper or a lower limit, using either the lower or higher addresses within the range of the table. Since a task seldom requires the maximum number of possible virtual pages, this reduction in table size is practical.

For example, when an operating system uses 4K-byte pages and runs numerous small tasks that average 80K bytes each in size, each task requires a 20-entry page table. The system can limit the size of each table to 80 bytes, or 800 bytes for ten tasks. Without the limit, an operating system running ten of these tasks would require 40K bytes of space for the page tables alone (one table per page).

Memory savings required for translation tables is especially significant for artificial intelligence systems these systems tend to require very large memory maps. By using limit fields, each table is only as large as the number of active entries within it. This limit can change as the table grows. For higher level tables, each table only grows as the additional entries require. The use of three or four levels of tables facilitates the management of these tables.

9.9.3.4 EARLY TERMINATION PAGE DESCRIPTORS. A page descriptor residing in a pointer table is an early termination page descriptor mapping an entire block of pages. That is, it maps a contiguous range of virtual addresses to a contiguous range of physical addresses. For example, an operating system could reserve a 32K-byte area for special supervisor I/O peripheral devices. This area can be mapped with a single early termination descriptor to save translation table size and table search overhead. The descriptor can use the limit field to reduce the size of the contiguous block when the block size is smaller than the virtual address space that the particular descriptor represents. The MC68030 creates multiple ATC entries (one for each page) for the range of virtual addresses represented by the early termination descriptor as the pages are accessed.

An operating system can use an early termination page descriptor to map a contiguous block of memory for each task (both program and data). The tasks can be relocated by changing the physical address portion of the descriptor. This scheme is useful when the tasks in a system consist of one or a few sequential blocks of memory that can be swapped as a group. The operating system memory map can treat the entire address space within these blocks as a uniform virtual space available for all tasks. The system only requires one translation table; by the use of limit fields and early termination page descriptors, it maps complete segments of memory.

9.9.3.5 INDIRECT DESCRIPTORS. An indirect descriptor is a table descriptor residing in a page table. It points to another page descriptor in the translation tree. Using an indirect descriptor for a page makes the page common to several tasks. History information for a common page is maintained in only one descriptor. Access to the page sets the used (U) bit, and a write operation to the page sets the M (modified) bit for that page. When the operating system is searching for an available page, it simply checks the page table containing the descriptor for the common page to determine its status. With other methods of page sharing, the system would have to check page tables for all sharing tasks to determine the status of the common page.

9.9.3.6 USING UNUSED DESCRIPTOR BITS. In general, the bits in the unused fields of many types of descriptors are available to the operating system for its own purposes. The invalid descriptor, in particular, uses only two bits of the 32 (short) or 64 (long) bits available with that format. An operating system typically uses these fields for the software flags, indicating whether the virtual address space is allocated and whether an image resides on the paging device. Also, these fields often contain the physical address of the image.

The operating system often maintains information in an unused field about a page resident in memory. This information may be an aging counter or some other indication of the page's frequency of use. This information helps the operating system to identify the pages that are least likely to impact system performance if they are reallocated. The system should first use physical page frames that are not allocated to a virtual page. Next it should use pages with the longest time since the most recent access. Pages that do not have the M (modified) bit set should be taken first, since they do not need to be copied to the paging device (the existing image remains valid).

9

An aging counter can be set up in an unused field of a page descriptor. The system can periodically check the U (used) bit for the page and increment the count when the page has not been used since the previous check. The system can identify the least recently used page from the counts in the aging counter. When the counter for a page overflows, the system can list the page in a queue of least recently used pages from which it chooses the next page to be reallocated.

Many schemes afford the operating system designer a variety in selecting a page to be taken. One operating system scans page tables, starting at the lowest priority task, looking for aged pages to steal. Another system maintains a system-wide list of all page frames as they are used and scans the list, starting at the oldest, to find a page to steal. A sophisticated system keeps a working set model of active pages for each individual task. From this information, it can swap a complete block of pages in and out with a single I/O operation. The method chosen can have a dramatic impact on limiting page fault overhead in a heavily used system.

9.10 AN EXAMPLE OF PAGING IMPLEMENTATION IN AN OPERATING SYSTEM

This section describes an example operating system design that illustrates some of the MMU features. The description suggests alternatives to provide variations of the design. Memory management algorithms that can be implemented to derive the actual code are shown. A bus error handler routine is shown also. Implementing the algorithms develops the basic code for the memory management services of an operating system.

9.10.1 System Description

The example system has the ability to map a large virtual memory task space, which is required for execution of predominantly numerically intensive processing tasks. Most of these tasks do not need more than 16 Mbytes of memory, but the system can supply a larger virtual memory space (as large as 496 Mbytes) to the occasional task that requires more. The system uses the relatively large page size of 8K bytes to minimize thrashing and translation table searches. With a larger page size, fewer descriptors can map a large area of virtual memory. Also, in a given period of time, the MC68030 experiences fewer ATC misses and performs fewer table searches. The larger page size requires the paging I/O operations to transfer larger blocks of data, and sometimes only a small part of the page is actually used. However, preliminary software model simulations show that 8K-byte pages provide optimum performance for this type of processing.

The average task for this system is a compiler or text editor that requires only 192K bytes of memory, or 24 8K-byte pages. Using short page descriptors, the page table occupies 96 bytes.

Page tables can reside at any 16-byte boundary; the limit fields of the MMU can provide the area needed without requiring excess space. This results in an address table area small enough to be completely resident in physical memory. The operating system does not need to page the table areas.

The paging hardware of many computer systems requires lower level tables to reside at page boundaries, effectively using one or more entire pages. This requires 80K bytes for the page tables for 10 tasks (10 tables, one 8K-byte page per table). Then, when the memory required for an upper level of tables is added, at a minimum of 8K bytes per task, the total comes to over 160K bytes. Table base addresses in the MC68030 are zero modulo 16 addresses. This results in a dramatic savings of memory for address table space; instead of using 80K bytes for the page tables for 10 tasks, (10 tables, one 8K-byte page per table), the MC68030 needs 960 bytes. Instead of 8K bytes per task for the upper level of tables, the tables require 2560 bytes in the MC68030. The fragmentation that may occur in allocating smaller tables could increase the memory requirement but would still remain less than 160K bytes.

The translation table tree for the example system consists of two levels. The upper level is a fixed table that contains 32 entries, each of which is a long-format table descriptor that points to a lower level page table. Each page table maps as many as 16 Mbytes of virtual address space. Since the upper level table is small (256 bytes), it can easily fit in the main control block of the task. When the system dispatches a new task, it loads a pointer to the upper level table for the task into the CRP register. Each lower level table consists of 0–2048 short-format page descriptors. The limit entry in the table descriptor for a page table determines the size of the table. For the average 192K-byte task, the upper level table usually has one valid entry, and this entry points to a lower level table with an average size of 96 bytes. A task that requires more than 16 Mbytes uses more than one valid entry in the higher level table.

9

In a typical computer system, with 64K bytes of boot and diagnostics ROM, a 64K I/O area, and 1 Mbyte of RAM, the physical mapping appears as follows:

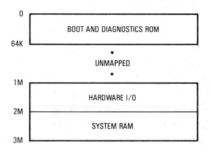

The operating system must control memory allocation for physical memory (page frames) to hold the pages of virtual memory. All available physical memory is divided into page frames, each of which can hold a page of virtual memory. A system with 4 Mbytes of actual memory is divided into 512 8K-byte frames that can theoretically hold 512 pages of active virtual memory at any one time. Usually, operating system components (exception handlers, the kernel, private memory pool) permanently reside in some of the memory. Only the remaining page frames are available for virtual memory pages.

The operating system maintains a linked list of all unallocated page frames. One simple way to do this is for each unallocated frame to contain a pointer to the next frame. The operating system takes the first page frame on the list when a frame is required. An operating system primitive called GetFrame performs this function and returns the physical address of an available frame. When all frames are allocated, GetFrame steals a frame from another task. GetFrame first looks for an unmodified frame to steal. An unmodified frame could be stolen without waiting for the page to be copied back to the external storage device that stores virtual page images. (This device is called the paging device or the backing store.) If no unmodified page frame is available, GetFrame must wait while the system copies a modified page to the paging device, then steals the page frame and returns to the caller with the physical address.

Next, the operating system needs physical memory management routines to allocate and free supervisor work memory. The routine must allocate pieces of memory on boundaries of at least modulo 16, the requirement for address translation tables. Typically, this type of routine allocates pieces of certain sizes. GetReal is the allocation routine; ReturnReal is the return routine. They use physical addresses.

With physical memory allocation provided for, the operating system must be able to manage virtual memory for all tasks. To do this, the system must be aware of the virtual memory map. It must know the total amount of virtual memory space, how much is allocated, and which areas are available to be assigned to tasks. The virtual memory map looks like this:

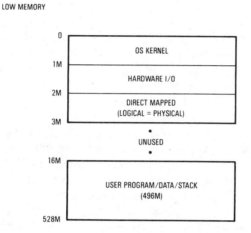

Virtual addresses for this virtual memory are subdivided:

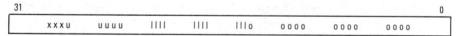

x — Ignored (3 bits)
u — Upper level index (5 bits), maps 32 long-table entries
l — Lower level index (11 bits), maps 2048 short-page entries

The translation table structure consists of:
CRP♦ upper level table in the task control block, which contains 32 long
pointers:
  [0] ♦ lower level table common to all tasks; maps all operating system
areas (first 4 Mbytes of virtual space). This common table contains
512 short-page entries (2K bytes).
  [1] ♦ lower level table for first 16 Mbytes of user program/data/stack area.
     •
     •
     •
  [31]♦ lower level table for last 16 Mbytes (of 496 total) of user program/
data/stack area.

The user program can only access virtual addresses starting at 16 Mbytes
and extending upward to the limit of 512 Mbytes. The code, the data, and
the stacks for user tasks are allocated in this area of virtual memory. Supervisor programs can access the entire virtual map; they can access addresses
that directly access the I/O ports as well as the entire physical memory at
untranslated addresses. The address tables are set up so that virtual addresses are equal to the physical addresses for the supervisor between 1 and
3 Mbytes. Folding the physical address space into the virtual space greatly
simplifies operations that use physical addresses. The folding does not necessarily mean that the virtual addresses are the same as the physical addresses. For example, the boot/diagnostic ROM at physical address zero could
be assigned a virtual address of 3 Mbytes. However, any external bus masters
or circuitry (such as breakpoint registers) resident on the physical side of the
bus must have physical addresses. This requires the overhead of operating
system code to perform address translation.

This virtual memory map provides supervisor addresses that are unique with
respect to user addresses; all supervisor routines can directly access any
user area without being restricted to certain instructions or addressing modes.
The separate user and supervisor maps suggest that two root pointers should
be used, one for the supervisor map and one for the user map. However,
the supervisor must be able to access user translation tables for proper access
to user data items. With separate root pointers, the supervisor table structure
must be linked to that of the user. To do this requires an additional level of
table lookup (function code level) for the supervisor address table.

This example uses a simpler scheme instead. Only the CPU root pointer is
used, and, for each task, the first entry of the upper level table (for the
supervisor portion, the first 16 Mbytes of virtual address space) points to the
same lower level table. This common lower level table has supervisor pro-

tection and maps the entire virtual operating system, physical I/O, and physical memory areas. This scheme avoids the requirement for extra lookup levels or pointer manipulations during a task switch to furnish correct access across the user/supervisor boundary. All the operating system has to do when creating the address table for a new task is to set the first upper level table entry to point to the common page table of the supervisor.

To solve the problem of accounting for virtual memory areas assigned to a user task, the operating system uses the existing translation tables to identify these areas. When a valid descriptor points to a given virtual address page, this 8K-byte page of memory has been allocated. This scheme provides areas of memory that are multiples of the 8K-byte page size. Due to the 8K granularity, this scheme would be inadequate for tasks that continually request and return virtual memory space. As a result, some other technique would be used (perhaps auxiliary tables to show virtual space availability). The tasks in this system seldom request additional memory space; any request made is for a large area. This scheme suffices. The application programs and utilities that run in the UNIX (r) environment have similar requirements for memory.

The operating system primitive GetVirtual allocates virtual memory space for tasks. The input parameter is a block size, in bytes; GetVirtual returns the virtual address for the new block. GetVirtual first checks that the requested size is not too large. Then it scans the translation tables looking for an unallocated virtual memory area large enough to hold the requested block. If it does not find enough space, GetVirtual attempts to increase the page table size to its maximum. If this does not provide the space, GetVirtual returns an error indication. When the routine finds enough virtual space for the block, it sets the page descriptors for the block to virgin status (invalid, but allocated). When these pages are first used, a page fault is generated. The operating system allocates a page frame for the page and replaces the descriptor with a valid page descriptor. The status (indicated by a software flag in the invalid descriptor) tells the operating system that the paging device does not have a page image for this page; no read operation from the paging device is required.

When the status of an invalid descriptor indicates that a page image must be read in, primitive SwapInPage, reads in the image. The input parameter for this routine is the invalid descriptor, which contains the disk address of the page image. Before returning, SwapInPage replaces the invalid descriptor with a valid page descriptor that contains the page address. The page is now ready for use.

These routines provide many of the functions required for the memory management services of an operating system, but a complete memory management system requires a complementary function for each routine. The complementary function usually performs the same steps in the reverse order. The complement of GetVirtual could be ReturnVirtual; for SwapInPage, the complement might be SwapOutPage. These counterparts can be derived to perform similar steps in the reverse order.

9.10.2 Allocation Routines

This section describes the central routine Vallocate, which user programs call to obtain memory. In this section (and the next), a loose high-level language syntax is used for the code. The code takes many liberties to enhance readability. For example, the code assigns descriptive strings for return status values. These strings typically represent binary values. Also, the code uses empty brackets to represent obvious subscripts in loops that scan tables. In such a loop, the subscript on the second line is obvious:

```
for Upper_Table_Index = 1 to 31 do
    if Upper_Table [Upper_Table_Index].Status = invalid then ...
```
In the code shown here, the second line is:
```
    if Upper_Table [].Status = invalid then ...
```
The code uses flag operations that are assumed to be defined elsewhere in the system. They may imply more complex operations than bit manipulations. For example, page table status of invalid virgin can be implemented with an invalid descriptor instead of the page descriptor, and a software flag bit in the descriptor that indicates the page is allocated but has never been used (the paging device has no page image).

Vallocate has a single input parameter, the required memory size in bytes. It returns status information and the virtual address of the start of the area (if the memory is allocated). To simplify the routine, it always returns a multiple of the system page size and never allocates a block that crosses a 16-Mbyte boundary. It could allocate a portion of a page by implementing a control structure to subdivide a page, but, if the control structure were within the allocated page, the user could corrupt it. The block could cross a 16-Mbyte boundary if the routine included code to keep track of consecutive free blocks when scanning the lower level tables, each of which represents 16 Mbytes of address space. Once the total area is located, Vallocate allocates the consecutive blocks and returns the address of the lowest block.

The 32 upper level table entries are long pointer types; each represents 16 Mbytes of virtual address space. Each entry is either invalid (has no lower page tables) or allocated (has lower page tables and a limit field that defines the table size). By convention, the first entry maps the supervisor address space and has supervisor protection. The routine never modifies this first entry. The 31 entries after the first are available to be allocated as user address space.

A routine similar to this that linearly extends (grows) a previously allocated memory block could be written. A stack is a good example. The operating system can allocate the top of the memory (the thirty-second upper level table entry) as a stack that grows downward from the highest address. If a task needs several large stacks, a 16-Mbyte block can be used for each stack, with a software flag set to indicate growth in a downward direction.

The logic of Vallocate is:

1. Validate the request and calculate number of pages required.

2. Scan each upper table entry's lower page tables (where they exist) looking for an adequate group of unallocated pages.

3. If no space is found, see if the lower table is less than its maximum size and if the block can be allocated by expanding it at the end.

4. If still no space is found, use the next free upper table entry and initialize its new lower level page table to allocate the block here.

5. Set allocated page entries to indicate virgin status (allocated, invalid, and not swapped out).

6. Return status. If status is OK, also return virtual address.

The code for Vallocate is:

```
Vallocate (SizeInBytes, VirtualAddressReturned, Status);

/* The following are global to all routines                                    */

/* Symbolicly define the upper level pointer table                             */

Declare Upper_Table[32] Record of
            Status=(unallocated, allocated),     /* lower table here or not     */
            Limit_Field=(0 to 4k),               /* limit for lower page table  */
            Pointer;                             /*address of lower page table if allocated */

/* Symbolicly define the lower level page table                                */

Declare Lower_Table[0 to Limit_Field] Based Record of
            Status=(invalid_unallocated,         /*not allocated to User        */
                    invalid_paged_out,           /*allocated but paged out      */
                    invalid_virgin,              /*allocated but not yet used    */
                    valid_in_memory),            /*allocated and in memory      */
                Pointer;                         /*physical address or disk address of page */
```

```
Declare Upper_Table_Index, Lower_Level_Index;        /*table indexes                                    */

Declare NumPages;                                     /* number of pages required to hold request        */

Status = "Out of virtual Memory";                     /* default result status to this error             */

if SizeInBytes > 16 megabytes then exit Vallocate;

NumPages = (SizeInBytes+PageSize-1)/PageSize;          /* Pages needed                                    */

/* Scan User eligible page tables                                                                         */

for Upper_Table_Index = 1 to 31 do
        If Upper_Table[].Status = allocated  then call SearchPageTable;
        If Status = "OK" then Exit Vallocate;
        end;

/* Block not found so find upper level entry unallocated and call SearchPageTable that will 'expand' */
/* the null table to hold the block.                                                                      */

for Upper_Table_Index = 1 to 31
        If Upper_Table[].Status = unallocated then call SearchPageTable;

/* No more virtual space, exit leaving Status =  "out of virtual memory"                                   */

exit Vallocate;

Procedure SearchPageTable;

/* Scan table pointed to by upper level index to see if it can hold the block.  If not, see if  it can be  */
/* be expanded.   If successful then set flags in the page entries, set status to "OK" and User's          */
/* virtual address                                                                                        */

        Declare Maxfound;                             /* Count of consecutive free blocks found            */

        Maxfound = 0;
        For Lower_Level_Index = 0 to Upper_Table[].Limit_Field

                /* count consecutive free pages until Maxfound met or not                                  */
                If Lower_Table[].Status = invalid_unallocated then do
                        Maxfound = Maxfound+1;
                        if Maxfound >= NumPages then do
```

```
                            /* Found!  Now flag the page entries, update the  MC68030 and    */
                            /* return the User's virtual address                             */
                            while (Maxfound > 0) do
                                    Lower_Table[].Status = invalid_virgin;
                                    Lower_Level_Index = Lower_Level_Index-1;
                            end;

                            Status = "OK";
                            VirtualAddressReturned =
                                    Upper_Level_Index*16Meg +
                                    Lower_Level_Index*8k;
                            PLOAD (VirtualAddressReturned);
                            exit SearchPageTables;
                            end;
                    end;

    /* allocated page hit so start counting from zero again                                  */
    else Maxfound = 0;


    /* If we get here there was not room.  See if we can expand the page table to hold the new block */
    /* If so grow it and set the new page entries as virgin                                  */

    If Upper_Table[].Limit + NumPages < 4k then do
            NewLimit = Upper_Table[].Limit + NumPages;

            /* We can grow the page table! First get area for new table                      */
            Call GetReal(4*NewLimit, NewPageTable);

            /* Now copy the first part of the old table into the new                         */
            for Lower_Table_Index = 0 to Upper_Table[].Limit
                    NewPageTable->Lower_Table[] = Lower_Table[]

            /* Return the old table and install the new table pointer                        */
            Call ReturnReal(4*Upper_Table[].Limit, Upper_Table[].Pointer);

    Upper_Table[].Pointer = NewPageTable;

            /* Set returned virtual address and load it replacing the old                    */
            VirtualAddressReturned = Upper_Level_Index*16Meg + Lower_Level_Index*8k;
            PLOAD (VirtualAddressReturned)                    /* refresh MC68030            */

            /* Set all the new entries at the end to virgin status                           */
            While (Lower_Table_Index < NewLimit) do
                    Lower_Table_Index = Lower_Table_Index + 1;
                    Lower_Table[].Status = invalid_virgin;
                    end;

            /* Set OK status and return with it                                              */
            Status = "OK";
            exit SearchPageTables;
            end;

    /* cannot expand the table.  return with status unchanged (failed)                       */
    end SearchPageTables;
```

9

9.10.3 Bus Error Handler Routine

The routine that processes bus error exceptions is the most critical part of the memory management services provided by the example operating system. This routine must determine the validity of page faults and perform the necessary processing. It must identify the conditions that aborted the executing task. The PTEST instruction can investigate the cause of a bus error by performing a table search using the address and type of access that produced the error, accumulating status information during the search.

When the PTEST instruction does not find any error, the bus error was most likely a malfunction (for example, a transient memory failure). The operating system must respond appropriately.

The table search performed by the PTEST instruction may end in a bus error termination. Either the address translation tables are not correctly built or main memory has failed (either a transient or permanent failure).

A supervisor protection violation or a write protection violation usually indicates that the task generating the exception attempted to access an area of the virtual address space that is not part of the task's address space. The operating system usually recovers from such an error by terminating (aborting) the task.

When the PTEST instruction returns the invalid status, the bus error is a page fault, and the operating system must identify the specific type of page fault. When the limit violation bit returned by the PTEST instruction is set, the task that took the exception was trying to access a page that has not been allocated. The example system aborts the task in this case. In other systems, this is an implicit request for more virtual memory, particularly if the reference is in a stack area.

When no limit violation occurred, a descriptor is invalid. Typically, the descriptor contains software flags that provide relevant information. The example operating system checks to see if the invalid descriptor is in an upper level or a lower level table. When the descriptor is in the upper level table, the task was attempting to access unallocated virtual memory, and the system aborts the task. When the descriptor is in a lower level table, the system checks software flags to identify the invalid descriptor.

When the software flags indicate that the descriptor corresponds to an unallocated page, the system aborts the task. When the descriptor refers to a virgin page (allocated, but not yet accessed) and the request for the page

9

was a read request, the page is actually invalid because the read operation reads unknown data. However, the example operating system does not consider the type of request, but assigns a physical page frame to the page and writes the page descriptor to the page table. Some systems clear virgin pages to zero.

When the software flags indicate that the page is allocated and the image has been copied to the paging device, the operating system assigns a page frame, reads the page image into the frame, and writes the page descriptor to the page table. Another possible type of invalid descriptor is one that requires special processing, such as one that refers to a virtual I/O device area in a virtual machine.

Obtaining a page frame for a virtual page may be an obvious operation. However, when no idle page frame is available, the system must steal one. If the page in the stolen frame has been modified in memory, the system must save the page image on the paging device. The system must alter the translation table of the task that loses the frame to show that the page is allocated and swapped out. Typically, the translation table entry shows the address of the page image on the paging device.

The method a system uses to select a page frame to steal varies a great deal from system to system. A simple system may just steal a page from the lowest priority task. More advanced systems select the page frame that has not been accessed for the longest time. This process, called aging, is done in several ways. One method uses bits of the page descriptor as an aging counter. Periodically, the operating system examines the U (used) bits and increments the count for pages that have not been used. The system maintains a list of pages with aging counters that have overflowed. The pages on this list are available for stealing.

Some systems keep a separate list of pages that have not been modified since the page image was read from memory. The page frames that contain these pages can be stolen without swapping out because the existing page image on the paging device remains valid.

Page stealing software can involve many dynamics of the system. It can consider task priority, I/O activity, working-set determinations, the number of executing tasks, a thrashing level, and other factors.

9

The example bus error exception routine is called BusErrorHandler. It is more general than Vallocate because it relies on several operating-system-dependent items. The variable pointer VictimTask is assumed to point to a table from a task that is losing a page frame. This assumption is necessary because control block layout and the method of searching for and finding other tasks in the example operating system are not defined. The code is further simplified by omitting the function code value and the read/write status, which do not affect the basic logic of the program.

```
/* Paging Bus Error Handler for example O.S.                                                    */

Procedure BusErrorHandler (BusErrAddress);

/* Global Variables to all code                                                                 */

Declare TableEntry;                              /*Pointer returned by PTEST instruction        */
                                                 /* pointing to the lowest level entry in the   */
                                                 /* translation tables.                         */

/* Use MC68030 PTEST instruction to get fault status and table entry                            */
case PTEST (BusErrAddress,TableEntry) of

        /* Bus Error - translation table is invalid or  memory hardware problems.  Terminate the task.  */
        B: AbortTask("Invalid table or memory hardware error");

        /* Supervisor Violation - task tried accessing restricted memory                        */
        S: AbortTask("Attempted access of Supervisor-only memory");

        /* Write Protected - tried writing into read-only memory                                */
        W: AbortTask("Attempted write into read-only memory");

        /* Limit Violation - tried accessing unmapped virtual space.  This happens in our example  */
        /* O.S. when accessing within a 16 megabyte segment in User memory past what is          */
        /* currently allocated for the lower page table as determined   by the upper level limit field.  */
        L: AbortTask("Invalid address");

        /* Invalid - pointer indicates invalid.  Must determine status.                         */
        I: begin

                /* If upper level entry then that 16 Meg chunk of the virtual space is unallocated  */
                /* and has no page tables.                                                       */
                If TableEntry is upper level then AbortTask("Invalid address");

                /* We are at a page table entry.  Look at software flags.                        */

                /* If this page unallocated to the User then abort task                          */
                If EntryStatus=invalid_unallocated then
                                AbortTask("Invalid Address");

                /* If this page is virgin then assign to it a physical frame                     */
                if EntryStatus = invalid_virgin then do
                        GetFrame(TableEntry);          /* address returned in entry              */
                        PLOAD (BusErrAddress);         /* update MC68030 entry                   */
                        exit BusErrorHandler;          /* done so continue task                  */
                        end do;
```

```
                    /* If this page is swapped out then read it back in */
                    if EntryStatus = invalid_swapped_out then do
                            /* first get a frame to hold the new page */
                            DiskAddress = TableEntry.Pointer;        /* disk location              */

                            GetFrame(TableEntry);                    /* address returned in entry  */

                            /* Now read in the virtual page image */
                            call SwapPageIn(TableEntry,DiskAddress);
                            PLOAD (BusErrAddress);                   /* update MC68851 entry       */
                            exit BusErrorHandler;                    /* done so continue task      */
                            end do;


            end begin;


    /* No MC68030 status bits on.  Must be memory malfunction or RMW cycle with no     */
    /* ATC entry                                                                       */
    Otherwise:          If Stack_Frame shows RMW instruction (SSW) then
                                /* ATC did not have descriptor loaded and MC68030 cannot   */
                                /* search tables to load it.  Explicitly load it and allow the task to */
                                /* continue normally                                       */

                        Begin
                                PLOAD (BusErrAddress); /* update ATC                       */
                                exit BueErrorHandler;   /* done so re-execute instruction */
                                end Begin

                        Else: AbortTask("Memory Malfunction");

    end case;
```

Procedure GetFrame(FrameTableEntry);

```
    /* This module returns the address of a physical frame in the passed table entry.  It obtains one */
    /* from the free frame list.  If none there it scans a queue pointing to pages that have been      */
    /* recorded as having aged by not being accessed frequently.  It first tries to find a read-only   */
    /* page in the queue but if none it returns the first (oldest) entry after swapping the page out   */
    /* to disk and altering the translation tables of the owning task.  If nothing in the queue it waits */
    /* for some other task to free a  frame by terminating or deallocating memory                      */

Restart:
    if Free_Frame_Queue NOT null then
            Dequeue first entry and return its value.

    if Aged_Frame_Queue NOT null then begin

            /* First try to find a read-only page                                  */
            If scanning finds read-only page then use and dequeue it
                else dequeue the first entry (which is the oldest);

            Find owning task and the frames current page entry;

            /* Invalidate owning task's page                                       */
            PFLUSH (User_Space,VictimTask.VirtualAddress);
```

```
                    /* If modified page swap it out.  SwapPageOut either gives control to other tasks    */
                    /* during the I/O or copies the page returning immediately.                          */
                    If modified then call SwapPageOut(VictimTask.TableEntry);
                    /* Disk address now in Victim's page entry                                           */

                    /* Now set the old task's page status and return the frame                           */
                    VictimTask.TableEntry.Status = invalid_swapped_out;
                    return physical frame value;
                    end do;

              /* At this point we can use some other stealing method but we just wait until another task frees */
              /* a frame by terminating or freeing memory.                                             */
              call wait (Free_Frame);
              go to Restart;


          end GetFrame;


    Procedure SwapPageIn (SwapInTableEntry,DiskAddress);
              /* This procedure takes the disk address and reads the page from the paging external media  */
              /* into the physical address residing in the table entry pointer.                          */
              end SwapPageIn;


    Procedure SwapPageOut(SwapoutTableEntry);
              /* This procedure performs output on the external paging device and then replaces the       */
              /* physical page frame address in the page entry pointer field with the disk address of the */
              /* block holding the image of the page.                                                    */
              end SwapPageOut;

    Procedure AbortTask(TerminationMsg);
              /* This procedure terminates the current task and issues a diagnostic message.              */
              end AbortTask;

    end BusErrorHandler;
```

SECTION 10
COPROCESSOR INTERFACE DESCRIPTION

The M68000 Family of general-purpose microprocessors provides a level of performance that satisfies a wide range of computer applications. Special-purpose hardware, however, can often provide a higher level of performance for a specific application. The coprocessor concept allows the capabilities and performance of a general-purpose processor to be enhanced for a particular application without encumbering the main processor architecture. A coprocessor can efficiently meet specific capability requirements that must typically be implemented in software by a general-purpose processor. With a general-purpose main processor and the appropriate coprocessor(s), the processing capabilities of a system can be tailored to a specific application.

The MC68030 supports the M68000 coprocessor interface described in this section. The section is intended for designers who are implementing coprocessors to interface with the MC68030.

The designer of a system that uses one or more Motorola coprocessors (the MC68881 or MC68882 floating-point coprocessor, for example) does not require a detailed knowledge of the M68000 coprocessor interface. Motorola coprocessors conform to the interface described in this section. Typically, they implement a subset of the interface, and that subset is described in the coprocessor user's manual. These coprocessors execute Motorola defined instructions that are described in the user's manual for each coprocessor.

10.1 INTRODUCTION

The distinction between standard peripheral hardware and a M68000 coprocessor is important from a perspective of the programming model. The programming model of the main processor consists of the instruction set, register set, and memory map available to the programmer. An M68000 coprocessor is a device or set of devices that communicates with the main processor through the protocol defined as the M68000 coprocessor interface. The programming model for a coprocessor is different than that for a peripheral device. A coprocessor adds additional instructions and generally additional registers and data types to the programming model that are not directly supported by the main processor architecture. The additional instructions are dedicated coprocessor instructions that utilize the coprocessor capabilities. The necessary interactions between the main processor and the coprocessor that provide a given service are transparent to the programmer. That is, the programmer does not need to know the specific communication protocol between the main processor and the coprocessor because this protocol is implemented in hardware. Thus, the coprocessor can provide capabilities to the user without appearing separate from the main processor.

In contrast, standard peripheral hardware is generally accessed through interface registers mapped into the memory space of the main processor. To use the services provided by the peripheral, the programmer accesses the peripheral registers with standard processor instructions. While a peripheral could conceivably provide capabilities equivalent to a coprocessor for many applications, the programmer must implement the communication protocol between the main processor and the peripheral necessary to use the peripheral hardware.

The communication protocol defined for the M68000 coprocessor interface is described in **10.2 COPROCESSOR INSTRUCTION TYPES**. The algorithms that implement the M68000 coprocessor interface are provided in the microcode of the MC68030 and are completely transparent to the MC68030 programmer's model. For example, floating-point operations are not implemented in the MC68030 hardware. In a system utilizing both the MC68030 and the MC68881 or MC68882 floating-point coprocessor, a programmer can use any of the instructions defined for the coprocessor without knowing that the actual computation is performed by the MC68881 or MC68882 hardware.

10.1.1 Interface Features

The M68000 coprocessor interface design incorporates a number of flexible capabilities. The physical coprocessor interface uses the main processor external bus, which simplifies the interface since no special-purpose signals are involved. With the MC68030, a coprocessor can use either the asynchronous or synchronous bus transfer protocol. Since standard bus cycles transfer information between the main processor and the coprocessor, the coprocessor can be implemented in whatever technology is available to the coprocessor designer. A coprocessor can be implemented as a VLSI device, as a separate system board, or even as a separate computer system.

Since the main processor and a M68000 coprocessor can communicate using the asynchronous bus, they can operate at different clock frequencies. The system designer can choose the speeds of a main processor and coprocessor that provide the optimum performance for a given system. If the coprocessor uses the synchronous bus interface all coprocessor signals and data must be synchronized with the main processor clock. Both the MC68881 and MC68882 floating-point coprocessors use the asynchronous bus handshake protocol.

The M68000 coprocessor interface also facilitates the design of coprocessors. The coprocessor designer must only conform to the coprocessor interface and does not need an extensive knowledge of the architecture of the main processor. Also, the main processor can operate with a coprocessor without having explicit provisions made in the main processor for the capabilities of that coprocessor. This provides a great deal of freedom in the implementation of a given coprocessor.

10.1.2 Concurrent Operation Support

The programmer's model for the M68000 Family of microprocessors is based on sequential, nonconcurrent instruction execution. This implies that the instructions in a given sequence must appear to be executed in the order in which they occur. To maintain a uniform programmer's model, any coprocessor extensions should also maintain the model of sequential, nonconcurrent instruction execution at the user level. Consequently, the programmer can assume that the images of registers and memory affected by a given instruction have been updated when the next instruction in the sequence accessing these registers or memory locations is executed.

The M68000 coprocessor interface provides full support of all operations necessary for nonconcurrent operation of the main processor and its associated coprocessors. Although the M68000 coprocessor interface allows concurrency in coprocessor execution, the coprocessor designer is responsible for implementing this concurrency while maintaining a programming model based on sequential nonconcurrent instruction execution.

For example, if the coprocessor determines that instruction "B" does not use or alter resources to be altered or used by instruction "A", instruction "B" can be executed concurrently (if the execution hardware is also available). Thus, the required instruction interdependencies and sequences of the program are always respected. The MC68882 coprocessor offers concurrent instruction execution while the MC68881 coprocessor does not. However, the MC68030 can execute instructions concurrently with coprocessor instruction execution in the MC68881.

10

10.1.3 Coprocessor Instruction Format

The instruction set for a given coprocessor is defined by the design of that coprocessor. When a coprocessor instruction is encountered in the main processor instruction stream, the MC68030 hardware initiates communication with the coprocessor and coordinates any interaction necessary to execute the instruction with the coprocessor. A programmer needs to know only the instruction set and register set defined by the coprocessor in order to use the functions provided by the coprocessor hardware.

The instruction set of an M68000 coprocessor uses a subset of the F-line operation words in the M68000 instruction set. The operation word is the first word of any M68000 Family instruction. The F-line operation word contains ones in bits 15–12 ([15:12] = 1111; refer to Figure 10-1); the remaining bits are coprocessor and instruction dependent. The F-line operation word may be followed by as many extension words as are required to provide additional information necessary for the execution of the coprocessor instruction.

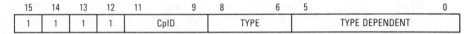

Figure 10-1. F-Line Coprocessor Instruction Operation Word

As shown in Figure 10-1, bits 9–11 of the F-line operation word encode the coprocessor identification code (CpID). The MC68030 uses the coprocessor identification field to indicate the coprocessor to which the instruction applies. F-line operation words, in which the CpID is zero, are not coprocessor instructions for the MC68030. If the CpID (bits 9–11) and the type field (bits 6–8) contain zeros, the instruction accesses the on-chip memory management unit of the MC68030. Instructions with a CpID of zero and a nonzero type field are unimplemented instructions that cause the MC68030 to begin exception processing. The MC68030 never generates coprocessor interface bus cycles with the CpID equal to zero (except via the MOVES instruction).

CpID codes of 001–101 are reserved for current and future Motorola coprocessors and CpID codes of 110–111 are reserved for user-defined coprocessors. The Motorola CpID code that is currently defined is 001 for the MC68881 or MC68882 floating-point coprocessor. By default, Motorola assemblers will use CpID code 001 when generating the instruction operation codes for the MC68881 or MC68882 coprocessor instructions.

10

The encoding of bits 0–8 of the coprocessor instruction operation word is dependent on the particular instruction being implemented (see **10.2 CO-PROCESSOR INSTRUCTION TYPES**).

10.1.4 Coprocessor System Interface

The communication protocol between the main processor and coprocessor necessary to execute a coprocessor instruction uses a group of interface registers, called coprocessor interface registers, resident within the coprocessor. By accessing one of these interface registers, the MC68030 hardware initiates coprocessor instructions. The coprocessor uses a set of response primitive codes and format codes defined for the M68000 coprocessor interface to communicate status and service requests to the main processor through these registers. The coprocessor interface registers (CIRs) are also used to pass operands between the main processor and the coprocessor. The CIR set, response primitives, and format codes are discussed in **10.3 COPROCESSOR INTERFACE REGISTER SET** and **10.4 COPROCESSOR RESPONSE PRIMITIVES**.

10.1.4.1 COPROCESSOR CLASSIFICATION. M68000 coprocessors can be classified into two categories depending on their bus interface capabilities. The first category, non-DMA coprocessors, consists of coprocessors that always operate as bus slaves. The second category, DMA coprocessors, consists of coprocessors that operate as bus slaves while communicating with the main processor across the coprocessor interface, but also have the ability to operate as bus masters, directly controlling the system bus.

If the operation of a coprocessor does not require a large portion of the available bus bandwidth or has special requirements not directly satisfied by the main processor, that coprocessor can be efficiently implemented as a non-DMA coprocessor. Since non-DMA coprocessors always operate as bus slaves, all external bus-related functions that the coprocessor requires are performed by the main processor. The main processor transfers operands from the coprocessor by reading the operand from the appropriate CIR and then writing the operand to a specified effective address with the appropriate address space specified on the function code lines. Likewise, the main processor transfers operands to the coprocessor by reading the operand from a specified effective address (and address space) and then writing that operand to the appropriate CIR using the coprocessor interface. The bus interface circuitry of a coprocessor operating as a bus slave is not as complex as that of a device operating as a bus master.

To improve the efficiency of operand transfers between memory and the coprocessor, a coprocessor that requires a relatively high amount of bus bandwidth or has special bus requirements can be implemented as a DMA coprocessor. DMA coprocessors can operate as bus masters. The coprocessor provides all control, address, and data signals necessary to request and obtain the bus and then performs DMA transfers using the bus. DMA coprocessors, however, must still act as bus slaves when they require information or services of the main processor using the M68000 coprocessor interface protocol.

10.1.4.2 PROCESSOR-COPROCESSOR INTERFACE. Figure 10-2 is a block diagram of the signals involved in an asynchronous non-DMA M68000 coprocessor interface. The synchronous interface is similar. Since the CpID on signals A13–A15 of the address bus is used with other address signals to select the coprocessor, the system designer can use several coprocessors of the same type and assign a unique CpID to each one.

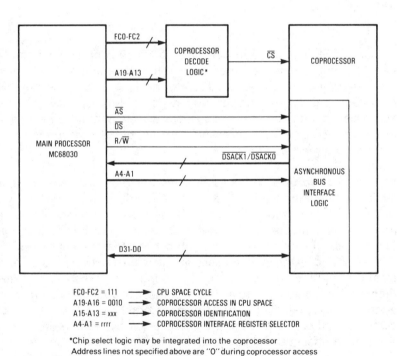

FC0-FC2 = 111	→	CPU SPACE CYCLE
A19-A16 = 0010	→	COPROCESSOR ACCESS IN CPU SPACE
A15-A13 = xxx	→	COPROCESSOR IDENTIFICATION
A4-A1 = rrrr	→	COPROCESSOR INTERFACE REGISTER SELECTOR

*Chip select logic may be integrated into the coprocessor
Address lines not specified above are "0" during coprocessor access

**Figure 10-2. Asynchronous Non-DMA M68000 Coprocessor
Interface Signal Usage**

The MC68030 accesses the registers in the CIR set using standard asynchronous or synchronous bus cycles. Thus, the bus interface implemented by a coprocessor for its interface register set must satisfy the MC68030 address, data, and control signal timing. The MC68030 timing information for read and write cycles is illustrated in Figures 13-5–13-8 on foldout pages in the back of this manual. The MC68030 never requests a burst operation during a coprocessor (CPU space) bus cycle, nor does it internally cache data read or written during coprocessor (CPU space) bus cycles. The MC68030 bus operation is described in detail in **SECTION 7 BUS OPERATION**.

During coprocessor instruction execution, the MC68030 executes CPU space bus cycles to access the CIR set. The MC68030 drives the three function code outputs high (FC2:FC0 = 111) identifying a CPU space bus cycle. The CIR set is mapped into CPU space in the same manner that a peripheral interface register set is generally mapped into data space. The information encoded on the function code lines and address bus of the MC68030 during a coprocessor access is used to generate the chip select signal for the coprocessor being accessed. Other address lines select a register within the interface set. The information encoded on the function code and address lines of the MC68030 during a coprocessor access is illustrated in Figure 10-3.

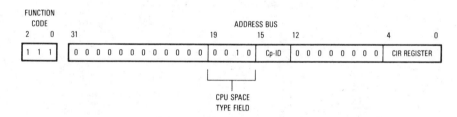

Figure 10-3. MC68030 CPU Space Address Encodings

Address signals A16–A19 specify the CPU space cycle type for a CPU space bus cycle. The types of CPU space cycles currently defined for the MC68030 are interrupt acknowledge, breakpoint acknowledge, and coprocessor access cycles. CPU space type $2 (A19:A16 = 0010) specifies a coprocessor access cycle.

Signals A13–A15 of the MC68030 address bus specify the coprocessor identification code CpID for the coprocessor being accessed. This code is transferred from bits 9–11 of the coprocessor instruction operation word (refer to Figure 10-1) to the address bus during each coprocessor access. Thus, decoding the MC68030 function code signals and bits A13–A19 of the address bus provides a unique chip select signal for a given coprocessor. The function code signals and A16–A19 indicate a coprocessor access; A13–A15 indicate which of the possible seven coprocessors (001–111) is being accessed. Bits A20–A31 and A5–A12 of the MC68030 address bus are always zero during a coprocessor access.

The MC68010 can emulate coprocessor access cycles in CPU space using the MOVES instruction.

10.1.4.3 COPROCESSOR INTERFACE REGISTER SELECTION. Figure 10-4 shows that the value on the MC68030 address bus during a coprocessor access addresses a unique region of the main processor's CPU address space. Signals A0–A4 of the MC68030 address bus select the CIR being accessed. The register map for the M68000 coprocessor interface is shown in Figure 10-5. The individual registers are described in detail in **10.3 COPROCESSOR IN-TERFACE REGISTER SET**.

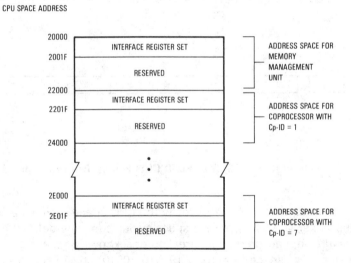

Figure 10-4. Coprocessor Address Map in MC68030 CPU Space

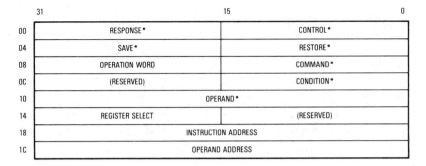

	31		15		0

00	RESPONSE* / CONTROL*
04	SAVE* / RESTORE*
08	OPERATION WORD / COMMAND*
0C	(RESERVED) / CONDITION*
10	OPERAND*
14	REGISTER SELECT / (RESERVED)
18	INSTRUCTION ADDRESS
1C	OPERAND ADDRESS

Figure 10-5. Coprocessor Interface Register Set Map

10.2 COPROCESSOR INSTRUCTION TYPES

The M68000 coprocessor interface supports four categories of coprocessor instructions: general, conditional, context save, and context restore. The category name indicates the type of operations provided by the coprocessor instructions in the category. The instruction category also determines the CIR accessed by the MC68030 to initiate instruction and communication protocols between the main processor and the coprocessor necessary for instruction execution.

During the execution of instructions in the general or conditional categories, the coprocessor uses the set of coprocessor response primitive codes defined for the MC68000 coprocessor interface to request services from and indicate status to the main processor. During the execution of the instructions in the context save and context restore categories, the coprocessor uses the set of coprocessor format codes defined for the M68000 coprocessor interface to indicate its status to the main processor.

10.2.1 Coprocessor General Instructions

The general coprocessor instruction category contains data processing instructions and other general-purpose instructions for a given coprocessor.

10

10.2.1.1 FORMAT. Figure 10-6 shows the format of a general type instruction.

15	14	13	12	11		9	8	7	6	5		0
1	1	1	1		CpID		0	0	0		EFFECTIVE ADDRESS	
COPROCESSOR COMMAND												
OPTIONAL EFFECTIVE ADDRESS OR COPROCESSOR-DEFINED EXTENSION WORDS												

Figure 10-6. Coprocessor General Instruction Format (cpGEN)

The mnemonic cpGEN is a generic mnemonic used in this discussion for all general instructions. The mnemonic of a specific general instruction usually suggests the type of operation it performs and the coprocessor to which it applies. The actual mnemonic and syntax used to represent a coprocessor instruction is determined by the syntax of the assembler or compiler that generates the object code.

A coprocessor general type instruction consists of at least two words. The first word of the instruction is an F-line operation code (bits [15:12] = 1111). The CpID field of the F-line operation code is used during the coprocessor access to indicate which of the coprocessors in the system executes the instruction. During accesses to the coprocessor interface registers (refer to **10.1.4.2 PROCESSOR-COPROCESSOR INTERFACE**), the processor places the CpID on address lines A13–A15.

Bits [8:6] = 000 indicate that the instruction is in the general instruction category. Bits 0–5 of the F-line operation code sometimes encodes a standard M68000 effective address specifier (refer to **2.5 EFFECTIVE ADDRESS ENCODING SUMMARY**). During the execution of a cpGEN instruction, the coprocessor can use a coprocessor response primitive to request that the MC68030 perform an effective address calculation necessary for that instruction. Using the effective address specifier field of the F-line operation code, the processor then determines the effective addressing mode. If a coprocessor never requests effective address calculation, bits 0–5 can have any value (don't cares).

The second word of the general-type instruction is the coprocessor command word. The main processor writes this command word to the command CIR to initiate execution of the instruction by the coprocessor.

An instruction in the coprocessor general instruction category optionally includes a number of extension words following the coprocessor command word. These words can provide additional information required for the coprocessor instruction. For example, if the coprocessor requests that the MC68030 calculate an effective address during coprocessor instruction execution, information required for the calculation must be included in the instruction format as effective address extension words.

10.2.1.2 PROTOCOL. The execution of a cpGEN instruction follows the protocol shown in Figure 10-7. The main processor initiates communication with the coprocessor by writing the instruction command word to the command CIR. The coprocessor decodes the command word to begin processing the cpGEN instruction. Coprocessor design determines the interpretation of the coprocessor command word; the MC68030 does not attempt to decode it.

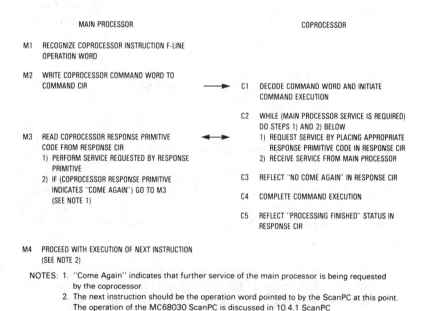

MAIN PROCESSOR

M1 RECOGNIZE COPROCESSOR INSTRUCTION F-LINE OPERATION WORD

M2 WRITE COPROCESSOR COMMAND WORD TO COMMAND CIR

M3 READ COPROCESSOR RESPONSE PRIMITIVE CODE FROM RESPONSE CIR
   1) PERFORM SERVICE REQUESTED BY RESPONSE PRIMITIVE
   2) IF (COPROCESSOR RESPONSE PRIMITIVE INDICATES "COME AGAIN") GO TO M3 (SEE NOTE 1)

M4 PROCEED WITH EXECUTION OF NEXT INSTRUCTION (SEE NOTE 2)

COPROCESSOR

C1 DECODE COMMAND WORD AND INITIATE COMMAND EXECUTION

C2 WHILE (MAIN PROCESSOR SERVICE IS REQUIRED) DO STEPS 1) AND 2) BELOW
   1) REQUEST SERVICE BY PLACING APPROPRIATE RESPONSE PRIMITIVE CODE IN RESPONSE CIR
   2) RECEIVE SERVICE FROM MAIN PROCESSOR

C3 REFLECT "NO COME AGAIN" IN RESPONSE CIR

C4 COMPLETE COMMAND EXECUTION

C5 REFLECT "PROCESSING FINISHED" STATUS IN RESPONSE CIR

NOTES: 1. "Come Again" indicates that further service of the main processor is being requested by the coprocessor
2. The next instruction should be the operation word pointed to by the ScanPC at this point. The operation of the MC68030 ScanPC is discussed in 10.4.1 ScanPC

Figure 10-7. Coprocessor Interface Protocol for General Category Instructions

10

While the coprocessor is executing an instruction, it requests any required services from and communicates status to the main processor by placing coprocessor response primitive codes in the response CIR. After writing to the command CIR, the main processor reads the response CIR and responds appropriately. When the coprocessor has completed the execution of an instruction or no longer needs the services of the main processor to execute the instruction, it provides a response to release the processor. The main processor can then execute the next instruction in the instruction stream. However, if a trace exception is pending, the MC68030 does not terminate communication with the coprocessor until the coprocessor indicates that it has completed all processing associated with the cpGEN instruction (refer to **10.5.2.5 TRACE EXCEPTIONS**).

The coprocessor interface protocol shown in Figure 10-7 allows the coprocessor to define the operation of each general category instruction. That is, the main processor initiates the instruction execution by writing the instruction command word to the command CIR and by reading the response CIR to determine its next action. The execution of the coprocessor instruction is then defined by the internal operation of the coprocessor and by its use of response primitives to request services from the main processor. This instruction protocol allows a wide range of operations to be implemented in the general instruction category.

10.2.2 Coprocessor Conditional Instructions

The conditional instruction category provides program control based on the operations of the coprocessor. The coprocessor evaluates a condition and returns a true/false indicator to the main processor. The main processor completes the execution of the instruction based on this true/false condition indicator.

The implementation of instructions in the conditional category promotes efficient use of both the main processor's and the coprocessor's hardware. The condition specified for the instruction is related to the coprocessor operation and is, therefore, evaluated by the coprocessor. The instruction completion following the condition evaluation is, however, directly related to the operation of the main processor. The main processor performs the change of flow, the setting of a byte, or the TRAP operation, since its architecture explicitly implements these operations for its instruction set.

10

Figure 10-8 shows the protocol for a conditional category coprocessor instruction. The main processor initiates execution of an instruction in this category by writing a condition selector to the condition CIR. The coprocessor decodes the condition selector to determine the condition to evaluate. The coprocessor can use response primitives to request that the main processor provide services required for the condition evaluation. After evaluating the condition, the coprocessor returns a true/false indicator to the main processor by placing a null primitive (refer to **10.4.4 Null Primitive**) in the response CIR. The main processor completes the coprocessor instruction execution when it receives the condition indicator from the coprocessor.

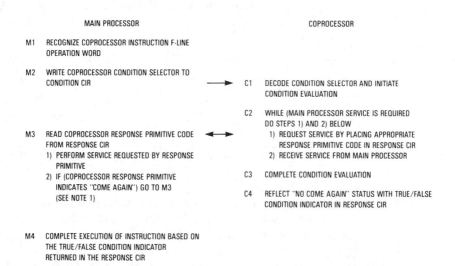

MAIN PROCESSOR   COPROCESSOR

M1   RECOGNIZE COPROCESSOR INSTRUCTION F-LINE
      OPERATION WORD

M2   WRITE COPROCESSOR CONDITION SELECTOR TO
      CONDITION CIR   ⟶   C1   DECODE CONDITION SELECTOR AND INITIATE
                                                        CONDITION EVALUATION

                                                  C2   WHILE (MAIN PROCESSOR SERVICE IS REQUIRED
                                                        DO STEPS 1) AND 2) BELOW
M3   READ COPROCESSOR RESPONSE PRIMITIVE CODE ⟷   1) REQUEST SERVICE BY PLACING APPROPRIATE
      FROM RESPONSE CIR   RESPONSE PRIMITIVE CODE IN RESPONSE CIR
      1) PERFORM SERVICE REQUESTED BY RESPONSE   2) RECEIVE SERVICE FROM MAIN PROCESSOR
         PRIMITIVE
      2) IF (COPROCESSOR RESPONSE PRIMITIVE   C3   COMPLETE CONDITION EVALUATION
         INDICATES "COME AGAIN") GO TO M3
         (SEE NOTE 1)   C4   REFLECT "NO COME AGAIN" STATUS WITH TRUE/FALSE
                                                        CONDITION INDICATOR IN RESPONSE CIR

M4   COMPLETE EXECUTION OF INSTRUCTION BASED ON
      THE TRUE/FALSE CONDITION INDICATOR
      RETURNED IN THE RESPONSE CIR

NOTES: 1. All coprocessor response primitives, except the Null primitive, that allow the "Come Again"
          primitive attribute must indicate "Come Again" when used during the execution of a
          conditional category instruction. If a "Come Again" attribute is not indicated in one of these
          primitives, the main processor will initiate protocol violation exception processing (see 10.6.2.1
          PROTOCOL VIOLATIONS)

**Figure 10-8. Coprocessor Interface Protocol for Conditional
Category Instructions**

10.2.2.1 BRANCH ON COPROCESSOR CONDITION INSTRUCTION.

The conditional instruction category includes two formats of the M68000 Family branch instruction. These instructions branch on conditions related to the coprocessor operation. They execute similarly to the conditional branch instructions provided in the M68000 Family instruction set.

10.2.2.1.1 Format. Figure 10-9 shows the format of the branch on coprocessor condition instruction that provides a word-length displacement. Figure 10-10 shows the format of the instruction that includes a long-word displacement.

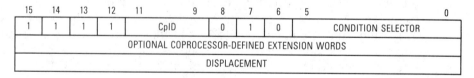

Figure 10-9. Branch on Coprocessor Condition Instruction (cpBcc.W)

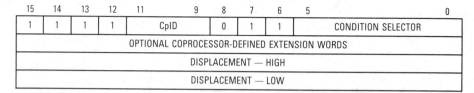

Figure 10-10. Branch On Coprocessor Condition Instruction (cpBcc.L)

The first word of the branch on coprocessor condition instruction is the F-line operation word. Bits [15:12] = 1111 and bits [11:9] contain the identification code of the coprocessor that is to evaluate the condition. The value in bits [8:6] identifies either the word or the long-word displacement format of the branch instruction, which is specified by the cpBcc.W or cpBcc.L mnemonic, respectively.

Bits [0–5] of the F-line operation word contain the coprocessor condition selector field. The MC68030 writes the entire operation word to the condition CIR to initiate execution of the branch instruction by the coprocessor. The coprocessor uses bits [0–5] to determine which condition to evaluate.

If the coprocessor requires additional information to evaluate the condition, the branch instruction format can include this information in extension words. Following the F-line operation word, the number of extension words is determined by the coprocessor design. The final word(s) of the cpBcc instruction format contains the displacement used by the main processor to calculate the destination address when the branch is taken.

10.2.2.1.2 Protocol. Figure 10-8 shows the protocol for the cpBcc.L and cpBcc.W instructions. The main processor initiates the instruction by writing the F-line operation word to the condition CIR to transfer the condition selector to the coprocessor. The main processor then reads the response CIR to determine its next action. The coprocessor can return a response primitive to request services necessary to evaluate the condition. If the coprocessor returns the false condition indicator, the main processor executes the next instruction in the instruction stream. If the coprocessor returns the true condition indicator, the processor adds the displacement to the MC68030 scanPC (refer to **10.4.1 ScanPC**) to determine the address of the next instruction for the main processor to execute. The scanPC must be pointing to the location of the first word of the displacement in the instruction stream when the address is calculated. The displacement is a twos-complement integer that can be either a 16-bit word or a 32-bit long word. The processor sign-extends the 16-bit displacement to a long-word value for the destination address calculation.

10.2.2.2 SET ON COPROCESSOR CONDITION INSTRUCTION. The set on coprocessor condition instructions set or reset a flag (a data alterable byte) according to a condition evaluated by the coprocessor. The operation of this instruction is similar to the operation of the Scc instruction in the M68000 Family instruction set. Although the Scc instruction and the cpScc instruction do not explicitly cause a change of program flow, they are often used to set flags that control program flow.

10.2.2.2.1 Format. Figure 10-11 shows the format of the set on coprocessor condition instruction, denoted by the cpScc mnemonic.

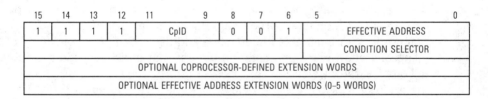

Figure 10-11. Set On Coprocessor Condition (cpScc)

The first word of the cpScc instruction is the F-line operation word. This word contains the CpID field in bits [9–11] and 001 in bits [8:6] to identify the cpScc instruction. The lower six bits of the F-line operation word are used to encode an M68000 Family effective addressing mode (refer to **2.5 EFFECTIVE ADDRESS ENCODING SUMMARY**).

The second word of the cpScc instruction format contains the coprocessor condition selector in bits [0–5]. Bits [6–15] of this word are reserved by Motorola and should be zero to ensure compatibility with future M68000 products. This word is written to the condition CIR to initiate the cpScc instruction.

If the coprocessor requires additional information to evaluate the condition, the instruction can include extension words to provide this information. The number of these extension words, which follow the word containing the coprocessor condition selector field, is determined by the coprocessor design.

The final portion of the cpScc instruction format contains zero to five effective address extension words. These words contain any additional information required to calculate the effective address specified by bits [0–5] of the F-line operation word.

10.2.2.2.2 Protocol.   Figure 10-8 shows the protocol for the cpScc instruction. The MC68030 transfers the condition selector to the coprocessor by writing the word following the F-line operation word to the condition CIR. The main processor then reads the response CIR to determine its next action. The coprocessor can return a response primitive to request services necessary to evaluate the condition. The operation of the cpScc instruction depends on the condition evaluation indicator returned to the main processor by the coprocessor. When the coprocessor returns the false condition indicator, the main processor evaluates the effective address specified by bits [0–5] of the F-line operation word and sets the byte at that effective address to FALSE (all bits cleared). When the coprocessor returns the true condition indicator, the main processor sets the byte at the effective address to TRUE (all bits set to one).

10.2.2.3 TEST COPROCESSOR CONDITION, DECREMENT AND BRANCH INSTRUC-
TION. The operation of the test coprocessor condition, decrement and branch instruction is similar to that of the DBcc instruction provided in the M68000 Family instruction set. This operation uses a coprocessor evaluated condition and a loop counter in the main processor. It is useful for implementing DO-UNTIL constructs used in many high-level languages.

10.2.2.3.1 Format. Figure 10-12 shows the format of the test coprocessor condition, decrement and branch instruction, denoted by the cpDBcc mnemonic.

15	14	13	12	11		9	8	7	6	5	4	3	2		0
1	1	1	1	\multicolumn{2}{c	}{CpID}	0	0	1	0	0	1	\multicolumn{3}{c	}{EFFECTIVE ADDRESS}

(RESERVED)	CONDITION SELECTOR

OPTIONAL COPROCESSOR-DEFINED EXTENSION WORDS

DISPLACEMENT

Figure 10-12. Test Coprocessor Condition, Decrement and Branch Instruction Format (cpDBcc)

The first word of the cpDBcc instruction is the F-line operation word. This word contains the CpID field in bits [9–11] and 001001 in bits [8:3] to identify the cpDBcc instruction. Bits [0:2] of this operation word specify the main processor data register used as the loop counter during the execution of the instruction.

The second word of the cpDBcc instruction format contains the coprocessor condition selector in bits [0–5] and should contain zeros in bits [6–15] to maintain compatibility with future M68000 products. This word is written to the condition CIR to initiate execution of the cpDBcc instruction by the coprocessor.

If the coprocessor requires additional information to evaluate the condition, the cpDBcc instruction can include this information in extension words. These extension words follow the word containing the coprocessor condition selector field in the cpDBcc instruction format.

The last word of the instruction contains the displacement for the cpDBcc instruction. This displacement is a twos-complement 16-bit value that is sign-extended to long-word size when it is used in a destination address calculation.

10.2.2.3.2 Protocol. Figure 10-8 shows the protocol for the cpDBcc instructions. The MC68030 transfers the condition selector to the coprocessor by writing the word following the operation word to the condition CIR. The main processor then reads the response CIR to determine its next action. The coprocessor can use a response primitive to request any services necessary to evaluate the condition. If the coprocessor returns the true condition indicator, the main processor executes the next instruction in the instruction stream. If the coprocessor returns the false condition indicator, the main processor decrements the low-order word of the register specified by bits [0–2] of the F-line operation word. If this register contains minus one (− 1) after being decremented, the main processor executes the next instruction in the instruction stream. If the register does not contain minus one (− 1) after being decremented, the main processor branches to the destination address to continue instruction execution.

The MC68030 adds the displacement to the scanPC (refer to **10.4.1 ScanPC**) to determine the address of the next instruction. The scanPC must point to the 16-bit displacement in the instruction stream when the destination address is calculated.

10.2.2.4 TRAP ON COPROCESSOR CONDITION. The trap on coprocessor condition instruction allows the programmer to initiate exception processing based on conditions related to the coprocessor operation.

10.2.2.4.1 Format. Figure 10-13 shows the format of the trap on coprocessor condition instruction, denoted by the cpTRAPcc mnemonic.

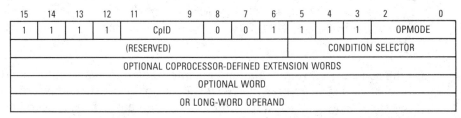

Figure 10-13. Trap On Coprocessor Condition (cpTRAPcc)

The F-line operation word contains the CpID field in bits [9–11] and 001111 in bits [8:3] to identify the cpTRAPcc instruction. Bits [0–2] of the cpTRAPcc F-line operation word specify the number of optional operand words in the instruction format. The instruction format can include zero, one, or two operand words.

The second word of the cpTRAPcc instruction format contains the coprocessor condition selector in bits [0–5] and should contain zeros in bits [6–15] to maintain compatibility with future M68000 products. This word is written to the condition CIR of the coprocessor to initiate execution of the cpTRAPcc instruction by the coprocessor.

If the coprocessor requires additional information to evaluate a condition, the instruction can include this information in extension words. These extension words follow the word containing the coprocessor condition selector field in the cpTRAPcc instruction format.

The operand words of the cpTRAPcc F-line operation word follow the coprocessor-defined extension words. These operand words are not explicitly used by the MC68030, but can be used to contain information referenced by the cpTRAPcc exception handling routines. The valid encodings for bits [0–2] of the F-line operation word and the corresponding numbers of operand words are listed in Table 10-1. Other encodings of these bits are invalid for the cpTRAPcc instruction.

Table 10-1. cpTRAPcc Opmode Encodings

Opmode	Optional Words in Instruction Format
010	One
011	Two
100	Zero

10.2.2.4.2 Protocol. Figure 10-8 shows the protocol for the cpTRAPcc instructions. The MC68030 transfers the condition selector to the coprocessor by writing the word following the operation word to the condition CIR. The main processor then reads the response CIR to determine its next action. The coprocessor can, using a response primitive, request any services necessary to evaluate the condition. If the coprocessor returns the true condition indicator, the main processor initiates exception processing for the cpTRAPcc exception (refer to **10.5.2.4 cpTRAPcc INSTRUCTION TRAPS**). If the coprocessor returns the false condition indicator, the main processor executes the next instruction in the instruction stream.

10.2.3 Coprocessor Save and Restore Instructions

The coprocessor context save and context restore instruction categories in the M68000 coprocessor interface support multitasking programming environments. In a multitasking environment, the context of a coprocessor may need to be changed asynchronously with respect to the operation of that coprocessor. That is, the coprocessor may be interrupted at any point in the execution of an instruction in the general or conditional category to begin context change operations.

In contrast to the general and conditional instruction categories, the context save and context restore instruction categories do not use the coprocessor response primitives. A set of format codes defined by the M68000 coprocessor interface communicates status information to the main processor during the execution of these instructions. These coprocessor format codes are discussed in detail in **10.2.3.2 COPROCESSOR FORMAT WORDS**.

10.2.3.1 COPROCESSOR INTERNAL STATE FRAMES. The context save (cpSAVE) and context restore (cpRESTORE) instructions transfer an internal coprocessor state frame between memory and a coprocessor. This internal coprocessor state frame represents the state of coprocessor operations. Using the cpSAVE and cpRESTORE instructions, it is possible to interrupt coprocessor operation, save the context associated with the current operation, and initiate coprocessor operations with a new context.

A cpSAVE instruction stores a coprocessor's internal state frame as a sequence of long-word entries in memory. Figure 10-14 shows the format of a coprocessor state frame. During execution of the cpSAVE instruction, the MC68030 calculates the state frame effective address from information in the operation word of the instruction and stores a format word at this effective address. The processor writes the long words that form the coprocessor state frame to descending memory addresses, beginning with the address specified by the sum of the effective address and the format word-length field multiplied by four. During execution of the cpRESTORE instruction, the MC68030 reads the format word and long words in the state frame from ascending addresses, beginning with the effective address specified in the instruction operation word.

SAVE ORDER	RESTORE ORDER	31	23	15	0
0	0	FORMAT	LENGTH	(UNUSED, RESERVED)	
n	1	COPROCESSOR-DEPENDENT INFORMATION			
n-1	2				
n-2	3				
•	•			•	
•	•			•	
•	•			•	
1	n				

Figure 10-14. Coprocessor State Frame Format in Memory

The processor stores the coprocessor format word at the lowest address of the state frame in memory, and this word is the first word transferred for both the cpSAVE and the cpRESTORE instructions. The word following the format word does not contain information relevant to the coprocessor state frame, but serves to keep the information in the state frame a multiple of four bytes in size. The number of entries following the format word (at higher addresses) is determined.

The information in a coprocessor state frame describes a context of operation for that coprocessor. This description of a coprocessor context includes the program invisible state information and, optionally, the program visible state information. The program invisible state information consists of any internal registers or status information that cannot be accessed by the program but is necessary for the coprocessor to continue its operation at the point of suspension. Program visible state information includes the contents of all registers that appear in the coprocessor programming model and that can be directly accessed using the coprocessor instruction set. The information saved by the cpSAVE instruction must include the program invisible state information. If cpGEN instructions are provided to save the program visible state of the coprocessor, the cpSAVE and cpRESTORE instructions should only transfer the program invisible state information to minimize interrupt latency during a save or restore operation.

10.2.3.2 COPROCESSOR FORMAT WORDS. The coprocessor communicates status information to the main processor during the execution of cpSAVE and cpRESTORE instructions using coprocessor format words. The format words defined for the M68000 coprocessor interface are listed in Table 10-2.

Table 10-2. Coprocessor Format Word Encodings

Format Code	Length	Meaning
00	xx	Empty/Reset
01	xx	Not Ready, Come Again
02	xx	Invalid Format
03–0F	xx	Undefined, Reserved
10–FF	Length	Valid Format, Coprocessor Defined

The upper byte of the coprocessor format word contains the code used to communicate coprocessor status information to the main processor. The MC68030 recognizes four types of format words: empty/reset, not ready, invalid format, and valid format. The MC68030 interprets the reserved format codes ($03–$0F) as invalid format words. The lower byte of the coprocessor format word specifies the size in bytes (which must be a multiple of four) of the coprocessor state frame. This value is only relevant when the code byte contains the valid format code (refer to **10.2.3.2.4 Valid Format Word**).

10.2.3.2.1 Empty/Reset Format Word. The coprocessor returns the empty/reset format code during a cpSAVE instruction to indicate that the coprocessor contains no user-specific information. That is, no coprocessor instructions have been executed since either a previous cpRESTORE of an empty/reset format code or the previous hardware reset. If the main processor reads the empty/reset format word from the save CIR during the initiation of a cpSAVE instruction, it stores the format word at the effective address specified in the cpSAVE instruction and executes the next instruction.

When the main processor reads the empty/reset format word from memory during the execution of the cpRESTORE instruction, it writes the format word to the restore CIR. The main processor then reads the restore CIR and, if the coprocessor returns the empty/reset format word, executes the next instruction. The main processor can initialize the coprocessor by writing the empty/reset format code to the restore CIR. When the coprocessor receives the empty/reset format code, it terminates any current operations and waits for the main processor to initiate the next coprocessor instruction. In particular, after the cpRESTORE of the empty/reset format word, the execution of a cpSAVE should cause the empty/reset format word to be returned when a cpSAVE instruction is executed before any other coprocessor instructions. Thus, an empty/reset state frame consists only of the format word and the following reserved word in memory (refer to Figure 10-14).

10.2.3.2.2 Not Ready Format Word. When the main processor initiates a cpSAVE instruction by reading the save CIR the coprocessor can delay the save operation by returning a not ready format word. The main processor then services any pending interrupts and reads the save CIR again. The not ready format word delays the save operation until the coprocessor is ready to save its internal state. The cpSAVE instruction can suspend execution of a general or conditional coprocessor instruction; the coprocessor can resume execution of the suspended instruction when the appropriate state is restored with a cpRESTORE. If no further main processor services are required to complete coprocessor instruction execution, it may be more efficient to complete the instruction and thus reduce the size of the saved state. The coprocessor designer should consider the efficiency of completing the instruction or of suspending and later resuming the instruction when the main processor executes a cpSAVE instruction.

When the main processor initiates a cpRESTORE instruction by writing a format word to the restore CIR, the coprocessor should usually terminate any current operations and restore the state frame supplied by the main processor. Thus, the not ready format word should usually not be returned by the coprocessor during the execution of a cpRESTORE instruction. If the coprocessor must delay the cpRESTORE operation for any reason, it can return the not ready format word when the main processor reads the restore CIR. If the main processor reads the not ready format word from the restore CIR during the cpRESTORE instruction, it reads the restore CIR again without servicing any pending interrupts.

10.2.3.2.3 Invalid Format Word. When the format word placed in the restore CIR to initiate a cpRESTORE instruction does not describe a valid coprocessor state frame, the coprocessor returns the invalid format word in the restore CIR. When the main processor reads this format word during the cpRESTORE instruction, it writes the abort mask to the control CIR and initiates format error exception processing. The two least significant bits of the abort mask are 01; the fourteen most significant bits are undefined.

A coprocessor should usually not place an invalid format word in the save CIR when the main processor initiates a cpSAVE instruction. A coprocessor, however, may not be able to support the initiation of a cpSAVE instruction while it is executing a previously initiated cpSAVE or cpRESTORE instruction. In this situation, the coprocessor can return the invalid format word when the main processor reads the save CIR to initiate the cpSAVE instruction while either another cpSAVE or cpRESTORE instruction is executing. If the main processor reads an invalid format word from the save CIR, it writes the abort mask to the control CIR and initiates format error exception processing (refer to **10.5.1.5 FORMAT ERRORS**).

10.2.3.2.4 Valid Format Word. When the main processor reads a valid format word from the save CIR during the cpSAVE instruction, it uses the length field to determine the size of the coprocessor state frame to save. The length field in the lower eight bits of a format word is relevant only in a valid format word. During the cpRESTORE instruction, the main processor uses the length field in the format word read from the effective address in the instruction to determine the size of the coprocessor state frame to restore.

The length field of a valid format word, representing the size of the coprocessor state frame, must contain a multiple of four. If the main processor detects a value that is not a multiple of four in a length field during the execution of a cpSAVE or cpRESTORE instruction, the main processor writes the abort mask (refer to **10.2.3.2.3 Invalid Format Word**) to the control CIR and initiates format error exception processing.

10.2.3.3 COPROCESSOR CONTEXT SAVE INSTRUCTION. The M68000 coprocessor context save instruction category consists of one instruction. The coprocessor context save instruction, denoted by the cpSAVE mnemonic, saves the context of a coprocessor dynamically without relation to the execution of coprocessor instructions in the general or conditional instruction categories. During the execution of a cpSAVE instruction, the coprocessor communicates status information to the main processor by using the coprocessor format codes.

10.2.3.3.1 Format. Figure 10-15 shows the format of the cpSAVE instruction. The first word of the instruction is the F-line operation word, which contains the coprocessor identification code in bits [9–11] and an M68000 effective address code in bits [0–5]. The effective address encoded in the cpSAVE instruction is the address at which the state frame associated with the current context of the coprocessor is saved in memory.

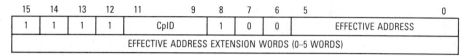

15	14	13	12	11		9	8	7	6	5		0
1	1	1	1	CpID			1	0	0	EFFECTIVE ADDRESS		
EFFECTIVE ADDRESS EXTENSION WORDS (0–5 WORDS)												

Figure 10-15. Coprocessor Context Save Instruction Format (cpSAVE)

The control alterable and predecrement addressing modes are valid for the cpSAVE instruction. Other addressing modes cause the MC68030 to initiate F-line emulator exception processing as described in **10.5.2.2 F-LINE EMULATOR EXCEPTIONS**.

The instruction can include as many as five effective address extension words following the cpSAVE instruction operation word. These words contain any additional information required to calculate the effective address specified by bits [0–5] of the operation word.

10.2.3.3.2 Protocol. Figure 10-16 shows the protocol for the coprocessor context save instruction. The main processor initiates execution of the cpSAVE instruction by reading the save CIR. Thus, the cpSAVE instruction is the only coprocessor instruction that begins by reading from a CIR. (All other coprocessor instructions write to a CIR to initiate execution of the instruction by the coprocessor.) The coprocessor communicates status information associated with the context save operation to the main processor by placing coprocessor format codes in the save CIR.

If the coprocessor is not ready to suspend its current operation when the main processor reads the save CIR, it returns a "not ready" format code. The main processor services any pending interrupts and then reads the save CIR again. After placing the not ready format code in the save CIR, the coprocessor should either suspend or complete the instruction it is currently executing.

Once the coprocessor has suspended or completed the instruction it is executing, it places a format code representing the internal coprocessor state in the save CIR. When the main processor reads the save CIR, it transfers the format word to the effective address specified in the cpSAVE instruction. The lower byte of the coprocessor format word specifies the number of bytes of state information, not including the format word and associated null word,

```
        MAIN PROCESSOR                                           COPROCESSOR

M1  RECOGNIZE COPROCESSOR INSTRUCTION F-LINE
    OPERATION WORD

M2  READ SAVE CIR TO INITIATE THE cpSAVE INSTRUCTION      C1  IF (NOT READY TO BEGIN CONTEXT SAVE OPERATION)
                                                              DO STEPS 1) AND 2) BELOW
M3  IF (FORMAT = NOT READY) DO STEPS 1) AND 2) BELOW  ◄───      1)  PLACE NOT READY FORMAT CODE IN SAVE CIR
      1)  SERVICE PENDING INTERRUPTS                           2)  SUSPEND OR COMPLETE CURRENT OPERATIONS
      2)  GO TO M2

                                                          C2  PLACE APPROPRIATE FORMAT WORD IN SAVE CIR

M3  EVALUATE EFFECTIVE ADDRESS SPECIFIED IN F-LINE        C3  TRANSFER NUMBER OF BYTES INDICATED IN
    OPWORD AND STORE FORMAT WORD AT                           FORMAT WORD THROUGH OPERAND CIR
    EFFECTIVE ADDRESS

M4  IF (FORMAT = EMPTY) GO TO M5
    ELSE, TRANSFER NUMBER OF BYTES INDICATED
    IN FORMAT WORD FROM OPERAND CIR TO
    EFFECTIVE ADDRESS

M5  PROCEED WITH EXECUTION OF NEXT INSTRUCTION
```

Figure 10-16. Coprocessor Context Save Instruction Protocol

to be transferred from the coprocessor to the effective address specified. If the state information is not a multiple of four bytes in size, the MC68030 initiates format error exception processing (refer to **10.5.1.5 FORMAT ERRORS**). The coprocessor and main processor coordinate the transfer of the internal state of the coprocessor using the operand CIR. The MC68030 completes the coprocessor context save by repeatedly reading the operand CIR and writing the information obtained into memory until all the bytes specified in the coprocessor format word have been transferred. Following a cpSAVE instruction, the coprocessor should be in an idle state — that is, not executing any coprocessor instructions.

The cpSAVE instruction is a privileged instruction. When the main processor identifies a cpSAVE instruction, it checks the supervisor bit in the status register to determine whether it is operating at the supervisor privilege level. If the MC68030 attempts to execute a cpSAVE instruction while at the user privilege level (status register bit [13] = 0), it initiates privilege violation exception processing without accessing any of the coprocessor interface registers (refer to **10.5.2.3 PRIVILEGE VIOLATIONS**).

The MC68030 initiates format error exception processing if it reads an invalid format word (or a valid format word whose length field is not a multiple of four bytes) from the save CIR during the execution of a cpSAVE instruction (refer to **10.2.3.2.3 Invalid Format Word**). The MC68030 writes an abort mask (refer to **10.2.3.2.3 Invalid Format Word**) to the control CIR to abort the coprocessor instruction prior to beginning exception processing. Figure 10-16 does not include this case since a coprocessor usually returns either a not ready or a valid format code in the context of the cpSAVE instruction. The coprocessor can return the invalid format word, however, if a cpSAVE is initiated while the coprocessor is executing a cpSAVE or cpRESTORE instruction and the coprocessor is unable to support the suspension of these two instructions.

10.2.3.4 COPROCESSOR CONTEXT RESTORE INSTRUCTION. The M68000 coprocessor context restore instruction category includes one instruction. The coprocessor context restore instruction, denoted by the cpRESTORE mnemonic, forces a coprocessor to terminate any current operations and to restore a former state. During the execution of a cpRESTORE instruction, the coprocessor can communicate status information to the main processor by placing format codes in the restore CIR.

10.2.3.4.1 Format. Figure 10-17 shows the format of the cpRESTORE instruction.

15	14	13	12	11	9	8	7	6	5	0
1	1	1	1	CpID		1	0	1	EFFECTIVE ADDRESS	
EFFECTIVE ADDRESS EXTENSION WORDS (0–5 WORDS)										

Figure 10-17. Coprocessor Context Restore Instruction Format (cpRESTORE)

The first word of the instruction is the F-line operation word, which contains the coprocessor identification code in bits [9–11] and an M68000 effective addressing code in bits [0–5]. The effective address encoded in the cpRESTORE instruction is the starting address in memory where the coprocessor context is stored. The effective address is that of the coprocessor format word that applies to the context to be restored to the coprocessor.

The instruction can include as many as five effective address extension words following the first word in the cpRESTORE instruction format. These words contain any additional information required to calculate the effective address specified by bits [0–5] of the operation word.

All memory addressing modes except the predecrement addressing mode are valid. Invalid effective address encodings cause the MC68030 to initiate F-line emulator exception processing (refer to **10.5.2.2 F-LINE EMULATOR EXCEPTIONS**).

10

10.2.3.4.2 Protocol. Figure 10-18 shows the protocol for the coprocessor context restore instruction. When the main processor executes a cpRESTORE instruction, it first reads the coprocessor format word from the effective address in the instruction. This format word contains a format code and a length field. During cpRESTORE operation, the main processor retains a copy of the length field to determine the number of bytes to be transferred to the coprocessor during the cpRESTORE operation and writes the format word to the restore CIR to initiate the coprocessor context restore.

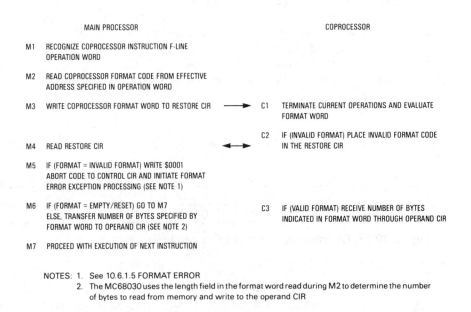

MAIN PROCESSOR   COPROCESSOR

M1   RECOGNIZE COPROCESSOR INSTRUCTION F-LINE
      OPERATION WORD

M2   READ COPROCESSOR FORMAT CODE FROM EFFECTIVE
      ADDRESS SPECIFIED IN OPERATION WORD

M3   WRITE COPROCESSOR FORMAT WORD TO RESTORE CIR ⟶ C1   TERMINATE CURRENT OPERATIONS AND EVALUATE
                                              FORMAT WORD

                                                  C2   IF (INVALID FORMAT) PLACE INVALID FORMAT CODE
M4   READ RESTORE CIR ⟷ IN THE RESTORE CIR

M5   IF (FORMAT = INVALID FORMAT) WRITE $0001
      ABORT CODE TO CONTROL CIR AND INITIATE FORMAT
      ERROR EXCEPTION PROCESSING (SEE NOTE 1)

M6   IF (FORMAT = EMPTY/RESET) GO TO M7   C3   IF (VALID FORMAT) RECEIVE NUMBER OF BYTES
      ELSE, TRANSFER NUMBER OF BYTES SPECIFIED BY   INDICATED IN FORMAT WORD THROUGH OPERAND CIR
      FORMAT WORD TO OPERAND CIR (SEE NOTE 2)

M7   PROCEED WITH EXECUTION OF NEXT INSTRUCTION

NOTES: 1. See 10.6.1.5 FORMAT ERROR
         2. The MC68030 uses the length field in the format word read during M2 to determine the number
            of bytes to read from memory and write to the operand CIR

Figure 10-18. Coprocessor Context Restore Instruction Protocol

When the coprocessor receives the format word in the restore CIR, it must terminate any current operations and evaluate the format word. If the format word represents a valid coprocessor context as determined by the coprocessor design, the coprocessor returns the format word to the main processor through the restore CIR and prepares to receive the number of bytes specified in the format word through its operand CIR.

After writing the format word to the restore CIR the main processor continues the cpRESTORE dialog by reading that same register. If the coprocessor returns a valid format word, the main processor transfers the number of bytes specified by the format word at the effective address to the operand CIR.

If the format word written to the restore CIR does not represent a valid coprocessor state frame, the coprocessor places an invalid format word in the restore CIR and terminates any current operations. The main processor receives the invalid format code, writes an abort mask (refer to **10.2.3.2.3 Invalid Format Word**) to the control CIR, and initiates format error exception processing (refer to **10.5.1.5 FORMAT ERRORS**).

The cpRESTORE instruction is a privileged instruction. When the main processor accesses a cpRESTORE instruction, it checks the supervisor bit in the status register. If the MC68030 attempts to execute a cpRESTORE instruction while at the user privilege level (status register bit [13] = 0), it initiates privilege violation exception processing without accessing any of the coprocessor interface registers (refer to **10.5.2.3 PRIVILEGE VIOLATIONS**).

10.3 COPROCESSOR INTERFACE REGISTER SET

The instructions of the M68000 coprocessor interface use registers of the CIR set to communicate with the coprocessor. These CIRs are not directly related to the coprocessor's programming model.

Figure 10-4 is a memory map of the CIR set. The registers denoted by asterisks (*) must be included in a coprocessor interface that implements coprocessor instructions in all four categories. The complete register model must be implemented if the system uses all of the coprocessor response primitives defined for the M68000 coprocessor interface.

The following paragraphs contain detailed descriptions of the registers.

10.3.1 Response CIR

The coprocessor uses the 16-bit response CIR to communicate all service requests (coprocessor response primitives) to the main processor. The main processor reads the response CIR to receive the coprocessor response primitives during the execution of instructions in the general and conditional instruction categories. The offset from the base address of the CIR set for the response CIR is $00. Refer to **10.4 COPROCESSOR RESPONSE PRIMITIVES**.

10

10.3.2 Control CIR

The main processor writes to the 2-bit control CIR to acknowledge coprocessor-requested exception processing or to abort the execution of a coprocessor instruction. The offset from the base address of the CIR set for the control CIR is $02. The control CIR occupies the two least significant bits of the word at that offset. The 14 most significant bits of the word are undefined. Figure 10-19 shows the format of this register.

Figure 10-19. Control CIR Format

When the MC68030 receives one of the three take exception coprocessor response primitives, it acknowledges the primitive by writing the exception acknowledge mask (10_2) to the control CIR, which sets the exception acknowledge (XA) bit. The MC68030 writes the abort mask (01_2), which sets the abort (AB) bit, to the control CIR to abort any coprocessor instruction in progress. (The most significant 14 bits of both masks are undefined.) The MC68030 aborts a coprocessor instruction when it detects one of the following exception conditions:

- An F-line emulator exception condition after reading a response primitive

- A privilege violation exception as it performs a supervisor check in response to a supervisor check primitive

- A format error exception when it receives an invalid format word or a valid format word that contains an invalid length

10.3.3 Save CIR

The coprocessor uses the 16-bit save CIR to communicate status and state frame format information to the main processor while executing a cpSAVE instruction. The main processor reads the save CIR to initiate execution of the cpSAVE instruction by the coprocessor. The offset from the base address of the CIR set for the save CIR is $04. Refer to **10.2.3.2 COPROCESSOR FORMAT WORDS**.

10.3.4 Restore CIR

The main processor initiates the cpRESTORE instruction by writing a coprocessor format word to the 16-bit restore register. During the execution of the cpRESTORE instruction, the coprocessor communicates status and state frame format information to the main processor through the restore CIR. The offset from the base address of the CIR set for the restore CIR is $06. Refer to **10.2.3.2 COPROCESSOR FORMAT WORDS**.

10.3.5 Operation Word CIR

The main processor writes the F-line operation word of the instruction in progress to the 16-bit operation word CIR in response to a transfer operation word coprocessor response primitive (refer to **10.4.6 Transfer Operation Word Primitive**). The offset from the base address of the CIR set for the operation word CIR is $08.

10.3.6 Command CIR

The main processor initiates a general category instruction by writing the instruction command word, which follows the instruction F-line operation word in the instruction stream, to the 16-bit command CIR. The offset from the base address of the CIR set for the command CIR is $0A.

10.3.7 Condition CIR

The main processor initiates a conditional category instruction by writing the condition selector to the 16-bit condition CIR. The offset from the base address of the CIR set for the condition CIR is $0E. Figure 10-20 shows the format of the condition CIR.

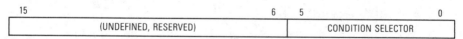

Figure 10-20. Condition CIR Format

10.3.8 Operand CIR

When the coprocessor requests the transfer of an operand, the main processor performs the transfer by reading from or writing to the 32-bit operand CIR. The offset from the base address of the CIR set for the operand CIR is $10.

The MC68030 aligns all operands transferred to and from the operand CIR to the most significant byte of this CIR. The processor performs a sequence of long-word transfers to read or write any operand larger than four bytes. If the operand size is not a multiple of four bytes, the portion remaining after the initial long-word transfers is aligned to the most significant byte of the operand CIR. Figure 10-21 shows the operand alignment used by the MC68030 when accessing the operand CIR.

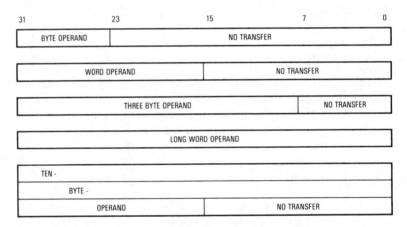

Figure 10-21. Operand Alignment for Operand CIR Accesses

10.3.9 Register Select CIR

When the coprocessor requests the transfer of one or more main processor registers or a group of coprocessor registers, the main processor reads the 16-bit register select CIR to identify the number or type of registers to be transferred. The offset from the base address of the CIR set for the register select CIR is $14. The format of this register depends on the primitive that is currently using it. Refer to **10.4 COPROCESSOR RESPONSE PRIMITIVES**.

10.3.10 Instruction Address CIR

When the coprocessor requests the address of the instruction it is currently executing, the main processor transfers this address to the 32-bit instruction address CIR. Any transfer of the scanPC is also performed through the instruction address CIR (refer to **10.4.17 Transfer Status Register and ScanPC Primitive**). The offset from the base address of the CIR set for the instruction address CIR is $18.

10.3.11 Operand Address CIR

When a coprocessor requests an operand address transfer between the main processor and the coprocessor, the address is transferred through the 32-bit operand address CIR. The offset from the base address of the CIR set for the operand address CIR is $1C.

10.4 COPROCESSOR RESPONSE PRIMITIVES

The response primitives are primitive instructions that the coprocessor issues to the main processor during the execution of a coprocessor instruction. The coprocessor uses response primitives to communicate status information and service requests to the main processor. In response to an instruction command word written to the command CIR or a condition selector in the condition CIR, the coprocessor returns a response primitive in the response CIR. Within the general and conditional instruction categories, individual instructions are distinguished by the operation of the coprocessor hardware and also by services specified by coprocessor response primitives provided by the main processor.

Subsequent paragraphs, beginning with **10.4.2 Coprocessor Response Primitive General Format**, consist of detailed descriptions of the M68000 coprocessor response primitives supported by the MC68030. Any response primitive that the MC68030 does not recognize causes it to initiate protocol violation exception processing (refer to **10.5.2.1 PROTOCOL VIOLATIONS**). This processing of undefined primitives supports emulation of extensions to the M68000 coprocessor response primitive set by the protocol violation exception handler. Exception processing related to the coprocessor interface is discussed in **10.5 EXCEPTIONS**.

10.4.1 ScanPC

Several of the response primitives involve the scanPC, and many of them require the main processor to use it while performing services requested. These paragraphs describe the scanPC and tell how it operates.

During the execution of a coprocessor instruction, the program counter in the MC68030 contains the address of the F-line operation word of that instruction. A second register, called the scanPC, sequentially addresses the remaining words of the instruction.

If the main processor requires extension words to calculate an effective address or destination address of a branch operation, it uses the scanPC to address these extension words in the instruction stream. Also, if a coprocessor requests the transfer of extension words, the scanPC addresses the extension words during the transfer. As the processor references each word, it increments the scanPC to point to the next word in the instruction stream. When an instruction is completed, the processor transfers the value in the scanPC to the program counter to address the operation word of the next instruction.

The value in the scanPC when the main processor reads the first response primitive after beginning to execute an instruction depends on the instruction being executed. For a cpGEN instruction, the scanPC points to the word following the coprocessor command word. For the cpBcc instructions, the scanPC points to the word following the instruction F-line operation word. For the cpScc, cpTRAPcc, and cpDBcc instructions, the scanPC points to the word following the coprocessor condition specifier word.

If a coprocessor implementation uses optional instruction extension words with a general or conditional instruction, the coprocessor must use these words consistently so that the scanPC is updated accordingly during the instruction execution. Specifically, during the execution of general category instructions, when the coprocessor terminates the instruction protocol, the MC68030 assumes that the scanPC is pointing to the operation word of the next instruction to be executed. During the execution of conditional category instructions, when the coprocessor terminates the instruction protocol, the MC68030 assumes that the scanPC is pointing to the word following the last of any coprocessor-defined extension words in the instruction format.

10

10.4.2 Coprocessor Response Primitive General Format

The M68000 coprocessor response primitives are encoded in a 16-bit word that is transferred to the main processor through the response CIR. Figure 10-22 shows the format of the coprocessor response primitives.

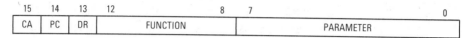

Figure 10-22. Coprocessor Response Primitive Format

The encoding of bits [0–12] of a coprocessor response primitive depends on the individual primitive. Bits [13–15], however, specify optional additional operations that apply to most of the primitives defined for the M68000 co-processor interface.

Bit [15], the CA bit, specifies the "come again" operation of the main processor. When the main processor reads a response primitive from the response CIR with the come again bit set to one, it performs the service indicated by the primitive and then reads the response CIR again. Using the CA bit, a coprocessor can transfer several response primitives to the main processor during the execution of a single coprocessor instruction.

Bit [4], the PC bit, specifies the pass program counter operation. When the main processor reads a primitive with the PC bit set from the response CIR, the main processor immediately passes the current value in its program counter to the instruction address CIR as the first operation in servicing the primitive request. The value in the program counter is the address of the F-line operation word of the coprocessor instruction currently executing. The PC bit is implemented in all of the coprocessor response primitives currently defined for the M68000 coprocessor interface.

When an undefined primitive or a primitive that requests an illegal operation is passed to the main processor, the main processor initiates exception processing for either an F-line emulator or a protocol violation exception (refer to **10.5.2 Main-Processor-Detected Exceptions**). If the PC bit is set in one of these response primitives, however, the main processor passes the program counter to the instruction address CIR before it initiates exception processing.

When the main processor initiates a cpGEN instruction that can be executed concurrently with main processor instructions, the PC bit is usually set in the first primitive returned by the coprocessor. Since the main processor proceeds with instruction stream execution once the coprocessor releases it, the coprocessor must record the instruction address to support any possible exception processing related to the instruction. Exception processing related to concurrent coprocessor instruction execution is discussed in **10.5.1 Co-processsor-Detected Exceptions**.

Bit [13], the DR bit, is the direction bit. It applies to operand transfers between the main processor and the coprocessor. If DR = 0, the direction of transfer is from the main processor to the coprocessor (main processor write). If DR = 1, the direction of transfer is from the coprocessor to the main processor (main processor read). If the operation indicated by a given response primitive does not involve an explicit operand transfer, the value of this bit depends on the particular primitive encoding.

10.4.3 Busy Primitive

The busy response primitive causes the main processor to reinitiate a coprocessor instruction. This primitive applies to instructions in the general and conditional categories. Figure 10-23 shows the format of the busy primitive.

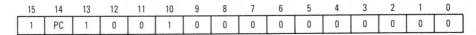

15	14	13	12	11	10	9	8	7	6	5	4	3	2	1	0
1	PC	1	0	0	1	0	0	0	0	0	0	0	0	0	0

Figure 10-23. Busy Primitive Format

This primitive uses the PC bit as previously described.

Coprocessors that can operate concurrently with the main processor but cannot buffer write operations to their command or condition CIR use the busy primitive. A coprocessor may execute a cpGEN instruction concurrently with an instruction in the main processor. If the main processor attempts to initiate an instruction in the general or conditional instruction category while the coprocessor is concurrently executing a cpGEN instruction, the coprocessor can place the busy primitive in the response CIR. When the main processor reads this primitive, it services pending interrupts (using a pre-instruction exception stack frame, refer to Figure 10-41). The processor then restarts the general or conditional coprocessor instruction that it had attempted to initiate earlier.

MC68030 USER'S MANUAL

MOTOROLA

The busy primitive should only be used in response to a write to the command or condition CIR. It should be the first primitive returned after the main processor attempts to initiate a general or conditional category instruction. In particular, the busy primitive should not be issued after program-visible resources have been altered by the instruction. (Program-visible resources include coprocessor and main processor program-visible registers and operands in memory, but not the scanPC.) The restart of an instruction after it has altered program-visible resources causes those resources to have inconsistent values when the processor reinitiates the instruction.

The MC68030 responds to the busy primitive differently in a special case that can occur during a breakpoint operation (refer to **8.1.12 Multiple Exceptions**). This special case occurs when a breakpoint acknowledge cycle initiates a coprocessor F-line instruction, the coprocessor returns the busy primitive in response to the instruction initiation, and an interrupt is pending. When these three conditions are met, the processor re-executes the breakpoint acknowledge cycle after the interrupt exception processing has been completed. A design that uses a breakpoint to monitor the number of passes through a loop by incrementing or decrementing a counter may not work correctly under these conditions. This special case may cause several breakpoint acknowledge cycles to be executed during a single pass through a loop.

10.4.4 Null Primitive

The null coprocessor response primitive communicates coprocessor status information to the main processor. This primitive applies to instructions in the general and conditional categories. Figure 10-24 shows the format of the null primitive.

15	14	13	12	11	10	9	8	7	6	5	4	3	2	1	0
CA	PC	0	0	1	0	0	IA	0	0	0	0	0	0	PF	TF

Figure 10-24. Null Primitive Format

This primitive uses the CA and PC bits as previously described.

Bit [8], the IA bit, specifies the interrupts allowed optional operation. This bit determines whether the MC68030 services pending interrupts prior to re-reading the response CIR after receiving a null primitive. Interrupts are allowed when the IA bit is set.

Bit [1], the PF bit, shows the "processing finished" status of the coprocessor. That is, PF = 1 indicates that the coprocessor has completed all processing associated with an instruction.

Bit [0], the TF bit, indicates the true/false condition during the execution of a conditional category instruction. TF = 1 is the true condition specifier, and TF = 0 is the false condition specifier. The TF bit is only relevant for null primitives with CA = 0 that are used by the coprocessor during the execution of a conditional instruction.

The MC68030 processes a null primitive with CA = 1 in the same manner whether executing a general or conditional category coprocessor instruction. If the coprocessor sets CA and IA to one in the null primitive, the main processor services pending interrupts (using a mid-instruction stack frame, refer to Figure 10-43) and reads the response CIR again. If the coprocessor sets CA to one and IA to zero in the null primitive, the main processor reads the response CIR again without servicing any pending interrupts.

A null, CA = 0 primitive provides a condition evaluation indicator to the main processor during the execution of a conditional instruction and ends the dialogue between the main processor and coprocessor for that instruction. The main processor completes the execution of a conditional category coprocessor instruction when it receives the primitive. The PF bit is not relevant during conditional instruction execution since the primitive itself implies completion of processing.

Usually, when the main processor reads any primitive that does not have CA = 1 while executing a general category instruction, it terminates the dialogue between the main processor and coprocessor. If a trace exception is pending, however, the main processor does not terminate the instruction dialogue until it reads a null, CA = 0, PF = 1 primitive from the response CIR (refer to **10.5.2.5 TRACE EXCEPTIONS**). Thus, the main processor continues to read the response CIR until it receives a null, CA = 0, PF = 1 primitive, and then performs trace exception processing. When IA = 1, the main processor services pending interrupts before reading the response CIR again.

A coprocessor can be designed to execute a cpGEN instruction concurrently with the execution of main processor instructions and, also, buffer one write operation to either its command or condition CIR. This type of coprocessor issues a null primitive with CA = 1 when it is concurrently executing a cpGEN instruction, and the main processor initiates another general or conditional coprocessor instruction. This primitive indicates that the coprocessor is busy and the main processor should read the response CIR again without reinitiating the instruction. The IA bit of this null primitive usually should be set to minimize interrupt latency while the main processor is waiting for the coprocessor to complete the general category instruction.

Table 10-3 summarizes the encodings of the null primitive.

Table 10-3. Null Coprocessor Response Primitive Encodings

CA	PC	IA	PF	TF	General Instructions	Conditional Instructions
x	1	x	x	x	Pass Program Counter to Instruction Address CIR, Clear PC Bit, and Proceed with Operation Specified by CA, IA, PF, and TF Bits	Same as General Category
1	0	0	x	x	Reread Response CIR, Do Not Service Pending Interrupts	Same as General Category
1	0	1	x	x	Service Pending Interrupts and Reread the Response CIR	Same as General Category
0	0	0	0	c	If (Trace Pending) Reread Response CIR; Else, Execute Next Instruction	Main Processor Completes Instruction Execution Based on TF = c
0	0	1	0	c	If (Trace Pending) Service Pending Interrupts and Reread Response CIR; Else, Execute Next Instruction	Main Processor Completes Instruction Execution Based on TF = c
0	0	x	1	c	Coprocessor Instruction Completed; Service Pending Exceptions or Execute Next Instruction	Main Processor Completes Instruction Execution Based on TF = c.

x = Don't Care
c = 1 or 0 Depending on Coprocessor Condition Evaluation

10

10.4.5 Supervisor Check Primitive

The supervisor check primitive verifies that the main processor is operating in the supervisor state while executing a coprocessor instruction. This primitive applies to instructions in the general and conditional coprocessor instruction categories. Figure 10-25 shows the format of the supervisor check primitive.

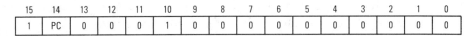

15	14	13	12	11	10	9	8	7	6	5	4	3	2	1	0
1	PC	0	0	0	1	0	0	0	0	0	0	0	0	0	0

Figure 10-25. Supervisor Check Primitive Format

This primitive uses the PC bit as previously described. Bit [15] is shown as one, but during execution of a general category instruction, this primitive performs the same operations regardless of the value of bit [15]. If this primitive is issued with bit [15]=0 during a conditional category instruction, however, the main processor initiates protocol violation exception processing.

When the main processor reads the supervisor check primitive from the response CIR, it checks the value of the S bit in the status register. If S=0 (main processor operating at user privilege level), the main processor aborts the coprocessor instruction by writing an abort mask (refer to **10.3.2 Control CIR**) to the control CIR. The main processor then initiates privilege violation exception processing (refer to **10.5.2.3 PRIVILEGE VIOLATIONS**). If the main processor is at the supervisor privilege level when it receives this primitive, it reads the response CIR again.

The supervisor check primitive allows privileged instructions to be defined in the coprocessor general and conditional instruction categories. This primitive should be the first one issued by the coprocessor during the dialog for an instruction that is implemented as privileged.

10.4.6 Transfer Operation Word Primitive

The transfer operation word primitive requests a copy of the coprocessor instruction operation word for the coprocessor. This primitive applies to general and conditional category instructions. Figure 10-26 shows the format of the transfer operation word primitive.

15	14	13	12	11	10	9	8	7	6	5	4	3	2	1	0
CA	PC	0	0	0	1	1	1	0	0	0	0	0	0	0	0

Figure 10-26. Transfer Operation Word Primitive Format

This primitive uses the CA and PC bits as previously described. If this primitive is issued with CA = 0 during a conditional category instruction, the main processor initiates protocol violation exception processing.

When the main processor reads this primitive from the response CIR, it transfers the F-line operation word of the currently executing coprocessor instruction to the operation word CIR. The value of the scanPC is not affected by this primitive.

10.4.7 Transfer from Instruction Stream Primitive

The transfer from instruction stream primitive initiates transfers of operands from the instruction stream to the coprocessor. This primitive applies to general and conditional category instructions. Figure 10-27 shows the format of the transfer from instruction stream primitive.

15	14	13	12	11	10	9	8	7				0
CA	PC	0	0	1	1	1	1			LENGTH		

Figure 10-27. Transfer from Instruction Stream Primitive Format

This primitive uses the CA and PC bits as previously described. If this primitive is issued with CA = 0 during a conditional category instruction, the main processor initiates protocol violation exception processing.

Bits [0–7] of the primitive format specify the length, in bytes, of the operand to be transferred from the instruction stream to the coprocessor. The length must be an even number of bytes. If an odd length is specified, the main processor initiates protocol violation exception processing (refer to **10.5.2.1 PROTOCOL VIOLATIONS**).

This primitive transfers coprocessor-defined extension words to the coprocessor. When the main processor reads this primitive from the response CIR, it copies the number of bytes indicated by the length field from the instruction stream to the operand CIR. The first word or long word transferred is at the location pointed to by the scanPC when the primitive is read by the main processor, and the scanPC is incremented after each word or long word is transferred. When execution of the primitive has completed, the scanPC has been incremented by the total number of bytes transferred and points to the word following the last word transferred. The main processor transfers the operands from the instruction stream using a sequence of long-word writes to the operand CIR. If the length field is not an even multiple of four bytes, the last two bytes from the instruction stream are transferred using a word write to the operand CIR.

10.4.8 Evaluate and Transfer Effective Address Primitive

The evaluate and transfer effective address primitive evaluates the effective address specified in the coprocessor instruction operation word and transfers the result to the coprocessor. This primitive applies to general category instructions. If this primitive is issued by the coprocessor during the execution of a conditional category instruction, the main processor initiates protocol violation exception processing. Figure 10-28 shows the format of the evaluate and transfer effective address primitive.

15	14	13	12	11	10	9	8	7	6	5	4	3	2	1	0
CA	PC	0	0	1	0	1	0	0	0	0	0	0	0	0	0

Figure 10-28. Evaluate and Transfer Effective Address Primitive Format

This primitive uses the CA and PC bits as previously described.

When the main processor reads this primitive while executing a general category instruction, it evaluates the effective address specified in the instruction. At this point, the scanPC contains the address of the first of any required effective address extension words. The main processor increments the scanPC by two after it references each of these extension words. After the effective address is calculated, the resulting 32-bit value is written to the operand address CIR.

The MC68030 only calculates effective addresses for control alterable addressing modes in response to this primitive. If the addressing mode in the operation word is not a control alterable mode, the main processor aborts the instruction by writing a $0001 to the control CIR and initiates F-line emulation exception processing (refer to **10.5.2.2 F-LINE EMULATOR EXCEPTIONS**).

10

10.4.9 Evaluate Effective Address and Transfer Data Primitive

The evaluate effective address and transfer data primitive transfers an operand between the coprocessor and the effective address specified in the coprocessor instruction operation word. This primitive applies to general category instructions. If the coprocessor issues this primitive during the execution of a conditional category instruction, the main processor initiates protocol violation exception processing. Figure 10-29 shows the format of the evaluate effective address and transfer data primitive.

15	14	13	12	11	10	8	7	0
CA	PC	DR	1	0	VALID EA		LENGTH	

Figure 10-29. Evaluate Effective Address and Transfer Data Primitive Format

This primitive uses the CA, PC, and DR bits as previously described.

The valid effective address field (bits [8–10]) of the primitive format specifies the valid effective address categories for this primitive. If the effective address specified in the instruction operation word is not a member of the class specified by bits [8–10], the main processor aborts the coprocessor instruction by writing an abort mask (refer to **10.3.2 Control CIR**) to the control CIR and by initiating F-line emulation exception processing. Table 10-4 lists the valid effective address field encodings.

Table 10-4. Valid Effective Address Codes

Field	Category
000	Control Alterable
001	Data Alterable
010	Memory Alterable
011	Alterable
100	Control
101	Data
110	Memory
111	Any Effective Address (No Restriction)

Even when the valid effective address fields specified in the primitive and in the instruction operation word match, the MC68030 initiates protocol violation exception processing if the primitive requests a write to a nonalterable effective address.

The length in bytes of the operand to be transferred is specified by bits [0–7] of the primitive format. Several restrictions apply to operand lengths for certain effective addressing modes. If the effective address is a main processor register (register direct mode), only operand lengths of one, two, or four bytes are valid; all other lengths (zero, for example) cause the main processor to initiate protocol violation exception processing. Operand lengths of 0–255 bytes are valid for the memory addressing modes.

The length of 0–255 bytes does not apply to an immediate operand. The length of an immediate operand must be one byte or an even number of bytes (less than 256), and the direction of transfer must be to the coprocessor; otherwise, the main processor initiates protocol violation exception processing.

When the main processor receives this primitive during the execution of a general category instruction, it verifies that the effective address encoded in the instruction operation word is in the category specified by the primitive. If so, the processor calculates the effective address using the appropriate effective address extension words at the current scanPC address and increments the scanPC by two for each word referenced. The main processor then transfers the number of bytes specified in the primitive between the operand CIR and the effective address using long-word transfers whenever possible. Refer to **10.3.8 Operand CIR** for information concerning operand alignment for transfers involving the operand CIR.

The DR bit specifies the direction of the operand transfer. DR = 0 requests a transfer from the effective address to the operand CIR, and DR = 1 specifies a transfer from the operand CIR to the effective address.

10

If the effective addressing mode specifies the predecrement mode, the address register used is decremented by the size of the operand before the transfer. The bytes within the operand are then transferred to or from ascending addresses beginning with the location specified by the decremented address register. In this mode, if A7 is used as the address register and the operand length is one byte, A7 is decremented by two to maintain a word-aligned stack.

For the postincrement effective addressing mode, the address register used is incremented by the size of the operand after the transfer. The bytes within the operand are transferred to or from ascending addresses beginning with the location specified by the address register. In this mode, if A7 is used as the address register and the operand length is one byte, A7 is incremented by two after the transfer to maintain a word aligned stack. Transferring odd length operands longer than one byte using the −(A7) or (A7)+ addressing modes can result in a stack pointer that is not word aligned.

The processor repeats the effective address calculation each time this primitive is issued during the execution of a given instruction. The calculation uses the current contents of any required address and data registers. The instruction must include a set of effective address extension words for each repetition of a calculation that requires them. The processor locates these words at the current scanPC location and increments the scanPC by two for each word referenced in the instruction stream.

The MC68030 sign-extends a byte or word-sized operand to a long-word value when it is transferred to an address register (A0–A7) using this primitive with the register direct effective addressing mode. A byte or word-sized operand transferred to a data register (D0–D7) only overwrites the lower byte or word of the data register.

10

10.4.10 Write to Previously Evaluated Effective Address Primitive

The write to previously evaluated effective address primitive transfers an operand from the coprocessor to a previously evaluated effective address. This primitive applies to general category instructions. If the coprocessor uses this primitive during the execution of a conditional category instruction, the main processor initiates protocol violation exception processing. Figure 10-30 shows the format of the write to previously evaluated effective address primitive.

Figure 10-30. Write to Previously Evaluated Effective Address Primitive Format

This primitive uses the CA and PC bits as previously described.

Bits [0–7] of the primitive format specify the length of the operand in bytes. The MC68030 transfers operands between zero and 255 bytes in length.

When the main processor receives this primitive during the execution of a general category instruction, it transfers an operand from the operand CIR to an effective address specified by a temporary register within the MC68030. When a previous primitive for the current instruction has evaluated the effective address, this temporary register contains the evaluated effective address. Primitives that store an evaluated effective address in a temporary register of the main processor are the evaluate and transfer effective address, evaluate effective address and transfer data, and transfer multiple coprocessor registers primitive. If this primitive is used during an instruction in which the effective address specified in the instruction operation word has not been calculated, the effective address used for the write is undefined. Also, if the previously evaluated effective address was register direct, the address written to in response to this primitive is undefined.

The function code value during the write operation indicates either supervisor or user data space, depending on the value of the S bit in the MC68030 status register when the processor reads this primitive. While a coprocessor should request writes to only alterable effective addressing modes, the MC68030 does not check the type of effective address used with this primitive. For example, if the previously evaluated effective address was program counter relative and the MC68030 is at the user privilege level (S = 0 in status register), the MC68030 writes to user data space at the previously calculated program relative address (the 32-bit value in the temporary internal register of the processor).

Operands longer than four bytes are transferred in increments of four bytes (operand parts) when possible. The main processor reads a long-word operand part from the operand CIR and transfers this part to the current effective address. The transfers continue in this manner using ascending memory locations until all of the long-word operand parts are transferred, and any remaining operand part is then transferred using a one-, two-, or three-byte transfer as required. The operand parts are stored in memory using ascending addresses beginning with the address in the MC68030 temporary register.

The execution of this primitive does not modify any of the registers in the MC68030 programmer's model, even if the previously evaluated effective address mode is the predecrement or postincrement mode. If the previously evaluated effective addressing mode used any of the MC68030 internal address or data registers, the effective address value used is the final value from the preceding primitive. That is, this primitive uses the value from an evaluate and transfer effective address, evaluate effective address and transfer data, or transfer multiple coprocessor registers primitive without modification.

The take address and transfer data primitive described in the next section does not replace the effective address value that has been calculated by the MC68030. The address that the main processor obtains in response to the take address and transfer data primitive is not available to the write to previously evaluated effective address primitive.

A coprocessor can issue an evaluate effective address and transfer data primitive followed by this primitive to perform a read-modify-write operation that is not indivisible. The bus cycles for this operation are normal bus cycles that can be interrupted, and the bus can be arbitrated between the cycles.

10

10.4.11 Take Address and Transfer Data Primitive

The take address and transfer data primitive transfers an operand between the coprocessor and an address supplied by the coprocessor. This primitive applies to general and conditional category instructions. Figure 10-31 shows the format of the take address and transfer data primitive.

15	14	13	12	11	10	9	8	7	0
CA	PC	DR	0	0	1	0	1	LENGTH	

Figure 10-31. Take Address and Transfer Data Primitive Format

This primitive uses the CA, PC, and DR bits as previously described. If the coprocessor issues this primitive with CA = 0 during a conditional category instruction, the main processor initiates protocol violation exception processing.

Bits [0–7] of the primitive format specify the operand length, which can be from 0–255 bytes.

The main processor reads a 32-bit address from the operand address CIR. Using a series of long-word transfers, the processor transfers the operand between this address and the operand CIR. The DR bit determines the direction of the transfer. The processor reads or writes the operand parts to ascending addresses, starting at the address from the operand address CIR. If the operand length is not a multiple of four bytes, the final operand part is transferred using a one-, two-, or three-byte transfer as required.

The function code used with the address read from the operand address CIR indicates either supervisor or user data space according to the value of the S bit in the MC68030 status register.

10.4.12 Transfer to/from Top of Stack Primitive

The transfer to/from top of stack primitive transfers an operand between the coprocessor and the top of the currently active main processor stack (refer to **2.8.1 System Stack**). This primitive applies to general and conditional category instructions. Figure 10-32 shows the format of the transfer to/from top of stack primitive.

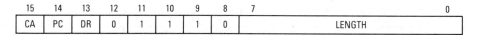

15	14	13	12	11	10	9	8	7		0
CA	PC	DR	0	1	1	1	0		LENGTH	

Figure 10-32. Transfer To/From Top of Stack Primitive Format

This primitive uses the CA, PC, and DR bits as previously described. If the coprocessor issues this primitive with CA = 0 during a conditional category instruction, the main processor initiates protocol violation exception processing.

Bits [0–7] of the primitive format specify the length in bytes of the operand to be transferred. The operand may be one, two, or four bytes in length; other length values cause the main processor to initiate protocol violation exception processing.

If DR = 0, the main processor transfers the operand from the currently active system stack to the operand CIR. The implied effective address mode used for the transfer is the (A7) + addressing mode. A one-byte operand causes the stack pointer to be incremented by two after the transfer to maintain word alignment of the stack.

If DR = 1, the main processor transfers the operand from the operand CIR to the currently active stack. The implied effective address mode used for the transfer is the – (A7) addressing mode. A one-byte operand causes the stack pointer to be decremented by two before the transfer to maintain word alignment of the stack.

10

10.4.13 Transfer Single Main Processor Register Primitive

The transfer single main processor register primitive transfers an operand between one of the main processor's data or address registers and the co-processor. This primitive applies to general and conditional category instructions. Figure 10-33 shows the format of the transfer single main processor register primitive.

15	14	13	12	11	10	9	8	7	6	5	4	3	2		0
CA	PC	DR	0	1	1	0	0	0	0	0	0	D/A	REGISTER		

Figure 10-33. Transfer Single Main Processor Register Primitive Format

This primitive uses the CA, PC, and DR bits as previously described. If the coprocessor issues this primitive with CA = 0 during a conditional category instruction, the main processor initiates protocol violation exception processing.

Bit [3], the D/A bit, specifies whether the primitive transfers an address or data register. D/A = 0 indicates a data register, and D/A = 1 indicates an address register. Bits [2–0] contain the register number.

If DR = 0, the main processor writes the long-word operand in the specified register to the operand CIR. If DR = 1, the main processor reads a long-word operand from the operand CIR and transfers it to the specified data or address register.

10.4.14 Transfer Main Processor Control Register Primitive

The transfer main processor control register primitive transfers a long-word operand between one of its control registers and the coprocessor. This primitive applies to general and conditional category instructions. Figure 10-34 shows the format of the transfer main processor control register primitive. This primitive uses the CA, PC, and DR bits as previously described. If the coprocessor issues this primitive with CA = 0 during a conditional category instruction, the main processor initiates protocol violation exception processing.

15	14	13	12	11	10	9	8	7	6	5	4	3	2	1	0
CA	PC	DR	0	1	1	0	1	0	0	0	0	0	0	0	0

Figure 10-34. Transfer Main Processor Control Register Primitive Format

When the main processor receives this primitive, it reads a control register select code from the register select CIR. This code determines which main processor control register is transferred. Table 10-5 lists the valid control register select codes. If the control register select code is not valid, the MC68030 initiates protocol violation exception processing (refer to **10.5.2.1 PROTOCOL VIOLATIONS**).

**Table 10-5. Main Processor Control
Register Selector Codes**

Hex	Control Register
x000	Source Function Code (SFC) Register
x001	Destination Function Code (DFC) Register
x002	Cache Control Register (CACR)
x800	User Stack Pointer (USP)
x801	Vector Base Register (VBR)
x802	Cache Address Register (CAAR)
x803	Master Stack Pointer (MSP)
x804	Interrupt Stack Pointer (ISP)
All other codes cause a protocol violation exception	

After reading a valid code from the register select CIR, if DR = 0, the main processor writes the long-word operand from the specified control register to the operand CIR. If DR = 1, the main processor reads a long-word operand from the operand CIR and places it in the specified control register.

10

10.4.15 Transfer Multiple Main Processor Registers Primitive

The transfer multiple main processor registers primitive transfers long-word operands between one or more of its data or address registers and the coprocessor. This primitive applies to general and conditional category instructions. Figure 10-35 shows the format of the transfer multiple main processor registers primitive.

15	14	13	12	11	10	9	8	7	6	5	4	3	2	1	0
CA	PC	DR	0	0	1	1	0	0	0	0	0	0	0	0	0

Figure 10-35. Transfer Multiple Main Processor Registers Primitive Format

This primitive uses the CA, PC, and DR bits as previously described. If the coprocessor issues this primitive with CA = 0 during a conditional category instruction, the main processor initiates protocol violation exception processing.

When the main processor receives this primitive, it reads a 16-bit register select mask from the register select CIR. The format of the register select mask is shown in Figure 10-36. A register is transferred if the bit corresponding to the register in the register select mask is set to one. The selected registers are transferred in the order D0–D7 and then A0–A7.

15	14	13	12	11	10	9	8	7	6	5	4	3	2	1	0
A7	A6	A5	A4	A3	A2	A1	A0	D7	D6	D5	D4	D3	D2	D1	D0

Figure 10-36. Register Select Mask Format

If DR = 0, the main processor writes the contents of each register indicated in the register select mask to the operand CIR using a sequence of long-word transfers. If DR = 1, the main processor reads a long-word operand from the operand CIR into each register indicated in the register select mask. The registers are transferred in the same order, regardless of the direction of transfer indicated by the DR bit.

10.4.16 Transfer Multiple Coprocessor Registers Primitive

The transfer multiple coprocessor registers primitive transfers from 0–16 operands between the effective address specified in the coprocessor instruction and the coprocessor. This primitive applies to general category instruc-

10

tions. If the coprocessor issues this primitive during the execution of a conditional category instruction, the main processor initiates protocol violation exception processing. Figure 10-37 shows the format of the transfer multiple coprocessor registers primitive.

15	14	13	12	11	10	9	8	7		0
CA	PC	DR	0	0	0	0	1		LENGTH	

Figure 10-37. Transfer Multiple Coprocessor Registers Primitive Format

This primitive uses the CA, PC, and DR bits as previously described.

Bits [7–0] of the primitive format indicate the length in bytes of each operand transferred. The operand length must be an even number of bytes; odd length operands cause the MC68030 to initiate protocol violation exception processing (refer to **10.5.2.1 PROTOCOL VIOLATIONS**).

When the main processor reads this primitive, it calculates the effective address specified in the coprocessor instruction. The scanPC should be pointing to the first of any necessary effective address extension words when this primitive is read from the response CIR; the scanPC is incremented by two for each extension word referenced during the effective address calculation. For transfers from the effective address to the coprocessor (DR = 0), the control addressing modes and the postincrement addressing mode are valid. For transfers from the coprocessor to the effective address (DR = 1), the control alterable and predecrement addressing modes are valid. Invalid addressing modes cause the MC68030 to abort the instruction by writing an abort mask (refer to **10.3.2 Control CIR**) to the control CIR and to initiate F-line emulator exception processing (refer to **10.5.2.2 F-LINE EMULATOR EXCEPTIONS**).

After performing the effective address calculation, the MC68030 reads a 16-bit register select mask from the register select CIR. The coprocessor uses the register select mask to specify the number of operands to transfer; the MC68030 counts the number of ones in the register select mask to determine the number of operands. The order of the ones in the register select mask is not relevant to the operation of the main processor. As many as 16 operands can be transferred by the main processor in response to this primitive. The total number of bytes transferred is the product of the number of operands transferred and the length of each operand specified in bits [0–7] of the primitive format.

10

If DR=1, the main processor reads the number of operands specified in the register select mask from the operand CIR and writes these operands to the effective address specified in the instruction using long-word transfers whenever possible. If DR=0, the main processor reads the number of operands specified in the register select mask from the effective address and writes them to the operand CIR.

For the control addressing modes, the operands are transferred to or from memory using ascending addresses. For the postincrement addressing mode, the operands are read from memory with ascending addresses also, and the address register used is incremented by the size of an operand after each operand is transferred. The address register used with the (An)+ addressing mode is incremented by the total number of bytes transferred during the primitive execution.

For the predecrement addressing mode, the operands are written to memory with descending addresses, but the bytes within each operand are written to memory with ascending addresses. As an example, Figure 10-38 shows the format in long-word-oriented memory for two 12-byte operands transferred from the coprocessor to the effective address using the −(An) addressing mode. The processor decrements the address register by the size of an operand before the operand is transferred. It writes the bytes of the operand to ascending memory addresses. When the transfer is complete, the address register has been decremented by the total number of bytes transferred. The MC68030 transfers the data using long-word transfers whenever possible.

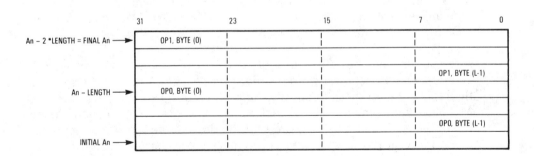

NOTE: OP0, Byte (0) is the first byte written to memory
OP0, Byte (L-1) is the last byte of the first operand written to memory
OP1, Byte (0) is the first byte of the second operand written to memory
OP1, Byte (L-1) is the last byte written to memory

Figure 10-38. Operand Format in Memory for Transfer to −(An)

10.4.17 Transfer Status Register and ScanPC Primitive

Both the transfer status register and the scanPC primitive transfers values between the coprocessor and the main processor status register. On an optional basis, the scanPC also makes transfers. This primitive applies to general category instructions. If the coprocessor issues this primitive during the execution of a conditional category instruction, the main processor initiates protocol violation exception processing. Figure 10-39 shows the format of the transfer status register and scanPC primitive.

15	14	13	12	11	10	9	8	7	6	5	4	3	2	1	0
CA	PC	DR	0	0	0	1	SP	0	0	0	0	0	0	0	0

Figure 10-39. Transfer Status Register and ScanPC Primitive Format

This primitive uses the CA, PC, and DR bits as previously described.

Bit [8], the SP bit, selects the scanPC option. If SP = 1, the primitive transfers both the scanPC and status register. If SP = 0, only the status register is transferred.

If SP = 0 and DR = 0, the main processor writes the 16-bit status register value to the operand CIR. If SP = 0 and DR = 1, the main processor reads a 16-bit value from the operand CIR into the main processor status register.

If SP = 1 and DR = 0, the main processor writes the long-word value in the scanPC to the instruction address CIR and then writes the status register value to the operand CIR. If SP = 1 and DR = 1, the main processor reads a 16-bit value from the operand CIR into the status register and then reads a long-word value from the instruction address CIR into the scanPC.

With this primitive, a general category instruction can change the main processor program flow by placing a new value in the status register, in the scanPC, or new values in both the status register and the scanPC. By accessing the status register, the coprocessor can determine and manipulate the main processor condition codes, supervisor status, trace modes, selection of the active stack, and interrupt mask level.

10

The MC68030 discards any instruction words that have been prefetched beyond the current scanPC location when this primitive is issued with DR = 1 (transfer to main processor). The MC68030 then refills the instruction pipe from the scanPC address in the address space indicated by the status register S bit.

If the MC68030 is operating in the trace on change of flow mode (T1:T0 in the status register contains 01) when the coprocessor instruction begins to execute and if this primitive is issued with DR = 1 (from coprocessor to main processor), the MC68030 prepares to take a trace exception. The trace exception occurs when the coprocessor signals that it has completed all processing associated with the instruction. Changes in the trace modes due to the transfer of the status register to main processor take effect on execution of the next instruction.

10.4.18 Take Pre-Instruction Exception Primitive

The take pre-instruction exception primitive initiates exception processing using a coprocessor-supplied exception vector number and the pre-instruction exception stack frame format. This primitive applies to general and conditional category instructions. Figure 10-40 shows the format of the take pre-instruction exception primitive.

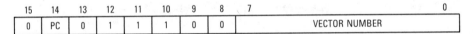

15	14	13	12	11	10	9	8	7	0
0	PC	0	1	1	1	0	0	VECTOR NUMBER	

Figure 10-40. Take Pre-Instruction Exception Primitive Format

The primitive uses the PC bit as previously described. Bits [0–7] contain the exception vector number used by the main processor to initiate exception processing.

When the main processor receives this primitive, it acknowledges the coprocessor exception request by writing an exception acknowledge mask (refer to **10.3.2 Control CIR**) to the control CIR. The MC68030 then proceeds with exception processing as described in **8.1 EXCEPTION PROCESSING SEQUENCE**. The vector number for the exception is taken from bits [0–7] of the primitive, and the MC68030 uses the four-word stack frame format shown in Figure 10-41.

10

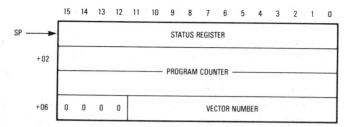

Figure 10-41. MC68030 Pre-Instruction Stack Frame

The value of the program counter saved in this stack frame is the F-line operation word address of the coprocessor instruction during which the primitive was received. Thus, if the exception handler routine does not modify the stack frame, an RTE instruction causes the MC68030 to return and reinitiate execution of the coprocessor instruction.

The take pre-instruction exception primitive can be used when the coprocessor does not recognize a value written to either its command CIR or condition CIR to initiate a coprocessor instruction. This primitive can also be used if an exception occurs in the coprocessor instruction before any program-visible resources are modified by the instruction operation. This primitive should not be used during a coprocessor instruction if program-visible resources have been modified by that instruction. Otherwise, since the MC68030 reinitiates the instruction when it returns from exception processing, the restarted instruction receives the previously modified resources in an inconsistent state.

One of the most important uses of the take pre-instruction exception primitive is to signal an exception condition in a cpGEN instruction that was executing concurrently with the main processor's instruction execution. If the coprocessor no longer requires the services of the main processor to complete a cpGEN instruction and the concurrent instruction completion is transparent to the programmer's model, the coprocessor can release the main processor by issuing a primitive with CA=0. The main processor usually executes the next instruction in the instruction stream, and the coprocessor completes its operations concurrently with the main processor operation. If an exception occurs while the coprocessor is executing an instruction concurrently, the exception is not processed until the main processor attempts to initiate the next general or conditional instruction. After the main processor writes to the command or condition CIR to initiate a general or conditional instruction, it then reads the response CIR. At this time, the coprocessor can return the take pre-instruction exception primitive. This protocol allows the main processor to proceed with exception processing related to the previous concurrently executing coprocessor instruction and then return and reinitiate the coprocessor instruction during which the exception was signaled. The coprocessor should record the addresses of all general category instructions that can be executed concurrently with the main processor and that support exception recovery. Since the exception is not reported until the next coprocessor instruction is initiated, the processor usually requires the instruction address to determine which instruction the coprocessor was executing when the exception occurred. A coprocessor can record the instruction address by setting PC = 1 in one of the primitives it uses before releasing the main processor.

10.4.19 Take Mid-Instruction Exception Primitive

The take mid-instruction exception primitive initiates exception processing using a coprocessor-supplied exception vector number and the mid-instruction exception stack frame format. This primitive applies to general and conditional category instructions. Figure 10-42 shows the format of the take mid-instruction exception primitive.

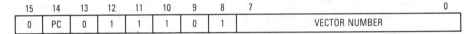

15	14	13	12	11	10	9	8	7							0
0	PC	0	1	1	1	0	1				VECTOR NUMBER				

Figure 10-42. Take Mid-Instruction Exception Primitive Format

This primitive uses the PC bit as previously described. Bits [7–0] contain the exception vector number used by the main processor to initiate exception processing.

When the main processor receives this primitive, it acknowledges the coprocessor exception request by writing an exception acknowledge mask (refer to **10.3.2 Control CIR**) to the control CIR. The MC68030 then performs exception processing as described in **8.1 EXCEPTION PROCESSING SEQUENCE**. The vector number for the exception is taken from bits [0–7] of the primitive and the MC68030 uses the 10-word stack frame format shown in Figure 10-43.

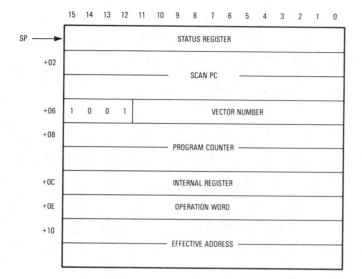

Figure 10-43. MC68030 Mid-Instruction Stack Frame

The program counter value saved in this stack frame is the operation word address of the coprocessor instruction during which the primitive is received. The scanPC field contains the value of the MC68030 scanPC when the primitive is received. If the current instruction does not evaluate an effective address prior to the exception request primitive, the value of the effective address field in the stack frame is undefined.

The coprocessor uses this primitive to request exception processing for an exception during the instruction dialog with the main processor. If the exception handler does not modify the stack frame, the MC68030 returns from the exception handler and reads the response CIR. Thus, the main processor attempts to continue executing the suspended instruction by reading the response CIR and processing the primitive it receives.

10

10.4.20 Take Post-Instruction Exception Primitive

The take post-instruction exception primitive initiates exception processing using a coprocessor-supplied exception vector number and the post-instruction exception stack frame format. This primitive applies to general and conditional category instructions. Figure 10-44 shows the format of the take post-instruction exception primitive.

Figure 10-44. Take Post-Instruction Exception Primitive Format

This primitive uses the PC bit as previously described. Bits [0–7] contain the exception vector number used by the main processor to initiate exception processing.

When the main processor receives this primitive, it acknowledges the coprocessor exception request by writing an exception acknowledge mask (refer to **10.3.2 Control CIR**) to the control CIR. The MC68030 then performs exception processing as described in **8.1 EXCEPTION PROCESSING SEQUENCE**. The vector number for the exception is taken from bits [0-7] of the primitive, and the MC68030 uses the six-word stack frame format shown in Figure 10-45.

The value in the main processor scanPC at the time this primitive is received is saved in the scanPC field of the post-instruction exception stack frame. The value of the program counter saved is the F-line operation word address of the coprocessor instruction during which the primitive is received.

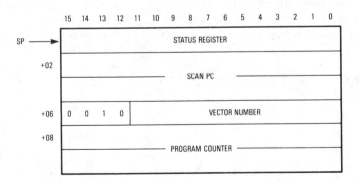

Figure 10-45. MC68030 Post-Instruction Stack Frame

When the MC68030 receives the take post-instruction exception primitive, it assumes that the coprocessor either completed or aborted the instruction with an exception. If the exception handler does not modify the stack frame, the MC68030 returns from the exception handler to begin execution at the location specified by the scanPC field of the stack frame. This location should be the address of the next instruction to be executed.

The coprocessor uses this primitive to request exception processing when it completes or aborts an instruction while the main processor is awaiting a normal response. For a general category instruction, the response is a release; for a conditional category instruction, it is an evaluated true/false condition indicator. Thus, the operation of the MC68030 in response to this primitive is compatible with standard M68000 Family instruction related exception processing (for example, the divide-by-zero exception).

10.5 EXCEPTIONS

Various exception conditions related to the execution of coprocessor instructions may occur. Whether an exception is detected by the main processor or by the coprocessor, the main processor coordinates and performs exception processing. Servicing these coprocessor-related exceptions is an extension of the protocol used to service standard M68000 Family exceptions. That is, when either the main processor detects an exception or is signaled by the coprocessor that an exception condition has occurred, the main processor proceeds with exception processing as described in **8.1 EXCEPTION PROCESSING SEQUENCE.**

10.5.1 Coprocessor-Detected Exceptions

Exceptions that the coprocessor detects, also those that the main processor detects, are usually classified as coprocessor-detected exceptions. These exceptions can occur during M68000 coprocessor interface operations, internal operations, or other system-related operations of the coprocessor.

Most coprocessor-detected exceptions are signaled to the main processor through the use of one of the three take exception primitives defined for the M68000 coprocessor interface. The main processor responds to these primitives as previously described. However, not all coprocessor-detected exceptions are signaled by response primitives. Coprocessor-detected format errors during the cpSAVE or cpRESTORE instruction are signaled to the main processor using the invalid format word described in **10.2.3.4.3 Invalid Format Words.**

10

10.5.1.1 COPROCESSOR-DETECTED PROTOCOL VIOLATIONS. Protocol violation exceptions are communication failures between the main processor and coprocessor across the M68000 coprocessor interface. Coprocessor-detected protocol violations occur when the main processor accesses entries in the coprocessor interface register set in an unexpected sequence. The sequence of operations that the main processor performs for a given coprocessor instruction or coprocessor response primitive has been described previously in this section.

A coprocessor can detect protocol violations in various ways. According to the M68000 coprocessor interface protocol, the main processor always accesses the operation word, operand, register select, instruction address, or operand address CIRs synchronously with respect to the operation of the coprocessor. That is, the main processor accesses these five registers in a certain sequence, and the coprocessor expects them to be accessed in that sequence. As a minimum, all M68000 coprocessors should detect a protocol violation if the main processor accesses any of these five registers when the coprocessor is expecting an access to either the command or condition CIR. Likewise, if the coprocessor is expecting an access to the command or condition CIR and the main processor accesses one of these five registers, the coprocessor should detect and signal a protocol violation.

According to the M68000 coprocessor interface protocol, the main processor can perform a read of either the save or response CIRs or a write of either the restore or control CIRs asynchronously with respect to the operation of the coprocessor. That is, an access to one of these registers without the coprocessor explicitly expecting that access at that point can be a valid access. Although the coprocessor can anticipate certain accesses to the restore, response, and control coprocessor interface registers, these registers can be accessed at other times also.

The coprocessor cannot signal a protocol violation to the main processor during the execution of cpSAVE or cpRESTORE instructions. If a coprocessor detects a protocol violation during the cpSAVE or cpRESTORE instruction, it should signal the exception to the main processor when the next coprocessor instruction is initiated.

The main philosophy of the coprocessor-detected protocol violation is that the coprocessor should always acknowledge an access to one of its interface registers. If the coprocessor determines that the access is not valid, it should assert $\overline{DSACKx}$, to the main processor and signal a protocol violation when the main processor next reads the response CIR. If the coprocessor fails to assert $\overline{\text{DSACKx}}$, the main processor waits for the assertion of that signal (or some other bus termination signal) indefinitely. The protocol previously described ensures that the coprocessor cannot halt the main processor.

The coprocessor can signal a protocol violation to the main processor with the take mid-instruction exception primitive. To maintain consistency, the vector number should be 13, as it is for a protocol violation detected by the main processor. When the main processor reads this primitive, it proceeds as described in **10.4.19 Take Mid-Instruction Exception Primitive**. If the exception handler does not modify the stack frame, the MC68030 returns from the exception handler and reads the response CIR.

10.5.1.2 COPROCESSOR-DETECTED ILLEGAL COMMAND OR CONDITION WORDS.
Illegal coprocessor command or condition words are values written to the command CIR or condition CIR that the coprocessor does not recognize. If a value written to either of these registers is not valid, the coprocessor should return the take pre-instruction exception primitive in the response CIR. When it receives this primitive, the main processor takes a pre-instruction exception as described in **10.4.18 Take Pre-Instruction Exception Primitive**. If the exception handler does not modify the main processor stack frame, an RTE instruction causes the MC68030 to reinitiate the instruction that took the exception. The coprocessor designer should ensure that the state of the coprocessor is not irrecoverably altered by an illegal command or condition exception if the system supports emulation of the unrecognized command or condition word.

All Motorola M68000 coprocessors signal illegal command and condition words by returning the take pre-instruction exception primitive with the F-line emulator exception vector number 11.

10.5.1.3 COPROCESSOR DATA-PROCESSING EXCEPTIONS.
Exceptions related to the internal operation of a coprocessor are classified as data-processing-related exceptions. These exceptions are analogous to the divide-by-zero exception defined by M68000 microprocessors and should be signaled to the main processor using one of the three take exception primitives containing an appropriate exception vector number. Which of these three primitives is used to signal the exception is usually determined by the point in the instruction operation where the main processor should continue the program flow after exception processing. Refer to **10.4.18 Take Pre-Instruction Exception Primitives**, **10.4.19 Take Mid-Instruction Exception Primitive**, and **10.4.20 Take Post-Instruction Exception Primitive**.

10

10.5.1.4 COPROCESSOR SYSTEM-RELATED EXCEPTIONS. System-related exceptions detected by a DMA coprocessor include those associated with bus activity and any other exceptions (interrupts, for example) occurring external to the coprocessor. The actions taken by the coprocessor and the main processor depend on the type of exception that occurs.

When an address or bus error is detected by a DMA coprocessor, the coprocessor should store any information necessary for the main processor exception handling routines in system-accessible registers. The coprocessor should place one of the three take exception primitives encoded with an appropriate exception vector number in the response CIR. Which of the three primitives is used depends upon the point in the coprocessor instruction at which the exception was detected and the point in the instruction execution at which the main processor should continue after exception processing.

10.5.1.5 FORMAT ERRORS. Format errors are the only coprocessor-detected exceptions that are not signaled to the main processor with a response primitive. When the main processor writes a format word to the restore CIR during the execution of a cpRESTORE instruction, the coprocessor decodes this word to determine if it is valid (refer to **10.2.3.3 COPROCESSOR CONTEXT SAVE INSTRUCTION**). If the format word is not valid, the coprocessor places the invalid format code in the restore CIR. When the main processor reads the invalid format code, it aborts the coprocessor instruction by writing an abort mask (refer to **10.3.2 Control CIR**) to the control CIR. The main processor then performs exception processing using a four-word pre-instruction stack frame and the format error exception vector number 14. Thus, if the exception handler does not modify the stack frame, the MC68030 restarts the cpRESTORE instruction when the RTE instruction in the handler is executed. If the coprocessor returns the invalid format code when the main processor reads the save CIR to initiate a cpSAVE instruction, the main processor performs format error exception processing as outlined for the cpRESTORE instruction.

10

10.5.2 Main-Processor-Detected Exceptions

A number of exceptions related to coprocessor instruction execution are detected by the main processor instead of the coprocessor (they are still serviced by the main processor). These exceptions can be related to the execution of coprocessor response primitives, communication across the M68000 coprocessor interface, or the completion of conditional coprocessor instructions by the main processor.

10.5.2.1 PROTOCOL VIOLATIONS. The main processor detects a protocol violation when it reads a primitive from the response CIR that is not a valid primitive. The protocol violations that can occur in response to the primitives defined for the M68000 coprocessor interface are summarized in Table 10-6.

10

Table 10-6. Exceptions Related to Primitive Processing (Sheet 1 of 2)

Primitive	Protocol	F-Line	Other
Busy			
NULL			
Supervisory Check* Other: Privilege Violation if "S" Bit=0			X
Transfer Operation Word*			
Transfer from Instruction Stream* Protocol: If Length Field is Odd (Zero Length Legal)	X		

Evaluate and Transfer Effective Address
   Protocol: If Used with Conditional Instruction
   F-Line: If EA in Op-Word is NOT Control Alterable
	X	X	

Evaluate Effective Address and Transfer Data
   Protocol:
     1. If Used with Conditional Instructions
     2. Length is Not 1, 2, or 4 and EA=Register Direct
     3. If EA=Immediate and Length Odd and Greater Than 1
     4. Attempt to Write to Nonalterable Address Even if Address Declared Legal in Primitive
   F-Line: Valid EA Field Does Not Match EA in Op-Word
	X	X	

Write to Previously Evaluated Effective Address Protocol: If Used with Conditional Instruction	X		
Busy			
Take Address and Transfer Data*			
Transfer To/From Top of Stack* Protocol: Length Field Other Than 1, 2, or 4	X		
Transfer To/From Main Processor Register*			
Transfer To/From Main Processor Control Register Protocol: Invalid Control Register Select Code	X		
Transfer Multiple Main Processor Registers*			

Transfer Multiple Coprocessor Registers
   Protocol:
     1. If Used with Conditional Instructions
     2. Odd Length Value
   F-Line:
     1. EA Not Control Alterable or (An)+ for CP to Memory Transfer
     2. EA Not Control Alterable or −(An) for Memory to CP Transfer
	X
	X		

10

Table 10-6. Exceptions Related to Primitive Processing (Sheet 2 of 2)

Primitive	Protocol	F-Line	Other

Transfer Status and/or ScanPC
  Protocol: If Used with Conditional Instruction
  Other:
    1. Trace — Trace Made Pending if MC68020 in "Trace on Change
       of Flow" Mode and DR = 1
    2. Address Error — If Odd value Written to ScanPC
	X		X

Take Pre-Instruction, Mid-Instruction, or Post-Instruction Exception Exception Depends on Vector Supplies in Primitive	X	X	X

*Use of this primitive with CA = 0 will cause protocol violation on conditional instructions.

Abbreviations:
    EA = Effective Address
    CP = Coprocessor

When the MC68030 detects a protocol violation, it does not automatically notify the coprocessor of the resulting exception by writing to the control CIR. The exception handling routine may, however, use the MOVES instruction to read the response CIR and thus determine the primitive that caused the MC68030 to initiate protocol violation exception processing. The main processor initiates exception processing using the mid-instruction stack frame (refer to Figure 10-43) and the coprocessor protocol violation exception vector number 13. If the exception handler does not modify the stack frame, the main processor reads the response CIR again following the execution of an RTE instruction to return from the exception handler. This protocol allows extensions to the M68000 coprocessor interface to be emulated in software by a main processor that does not provide hardware support for these extensions. Thus, the protocol violation is transparent to the coprocessor if the primitive execution can be emulated in software by the main processor.

10

10.5.2.2 F-LINE EMULATOR EXCEPTIONS. The F-line emulator exceptions detected by the MC68030 are either explicitly or implicitly related to the encodings of F-line operation words in the instruction stream. If the main processor determines that an F-line operation word is not valid, it initiates F-line emulator exception processing. Any F-line operation word with bits [8:6] = 110 or 111 causes the MC68030 to initiate exception processing without initiating any communication with the coprocessor for that instruction. Also, an operation word with bits [8:6] = 000–101 that does not map to one of the valid coprocessor instructions in the instruction set causes the MC68030 to initiate F-line emulator exception processing. If the F-line emulator exception is either of these two situations, the main processor does not write to the control CIR prior to initiating exception processing.

F-line exceptions can also occur if the operations requested by a coprocessor response primitive are not compatible with the effective address type in bits [0–5] of the coprocessor instruction operation word. The F-line emulator exceptions that can result from the use of the M68000 coprocessor response primitives are summarized in Table 10-6. If the exception is caused by receiving an invalid primitive, the main processor aborts the coprocessor instruction in progress by writing an abort mask (refer to **10.3.2 Control CIR**) to the control CIR prior to F-line emulator exception processing.

Another type of F-line emulator exception occurs when a bus error occurs during the coprocessor interface register access that initiates a coprocessor instruction. The main processor assumes that the coprocessor is not present and takes the exception.

When the main processor initiates F-line emulator exception processing, it uses the four-word pre-instruction exception stack frame (refer to Figure 10-41) and the F-line emulator exception vector number 11. Thus, if the exception handler does not modify the stack frame, the main processor attempts to restart the instruction that caused the exception after it executes an RTE instruction to return from the exception handler.

If the cause of the F-line exception can be emulated in software, the handler stores the results of the emulation in the appropriate registers of the programmer's model and in the status register field of the saved stack frame. The exception handler adjusts the program counter field of the saved stack frame to point to the next instruction operation word and executes the RTE instruction. The MC68030 then executes the instruction following the instruction that was emulated.

10

The exception handler should also check the copy of the status register on the stack to determine whether tracing is on. If tracing is on, the trace exception processing should also be emulated. Refer to **8.1.7 Trace Exception** for additional information.

10.5.2.3 PRIVILEGE VIOLATIONS. Privilege violations can result from the cpSAVE and cpRESTORE instructions and, also, from the supervisor check coprocessor response primitive. The main processor initiates privilege violation exception processing if it attempts to execute either the cpSAVE or cpRESTORE instruction when it is in the user state (S = 0 in status register). The main processor initiates this exception processing prior to any communication with the coprocessor associated with the cpSAVE or cpRESTORE instructions.

If the main processor is executing a coprocessor instruction in the user state when it reads the supervisor check primitive, it aborts the coprocessor instruction in progress by writing an abort mask (refer to **10.3.2 Control CIR**) to the control CIR. The main processor then performs privilege violation exception processing.

If a privilege violation occurs, the main processor initiates exception processing using the four-word pre-instruction stack frame (refer to Figure 10-41) and the privilege violation exception vector number 8. Thus, if the exception handler does not modify the stack frame, the main processor attempts to restart the instruction during which the exception occurred after it executes an RTE to return from the handler.

10.5.2.4 cpTRAPcc INSTRUCTION TRAPS. If, during the execution of a cpTRAPcc instruction, the coprocessor returns the TRUE condition indicator to the main processor with a null primitive, the main processor initiates trap exception processing. The main processor uses the six-word post-instruction exception stack frame (refer to Figure 10-45) and the trap exception vector number 7. The scanPC field of this stack frame contains the address of the instruction following the cpTRAPcc instruction. The processing associated with the cpTRAPcc instruction can then proceed, and the exception handler can locate any immediate operand words encoded in the cpTRAPcc instruction using the information contained in the six-word stack frame. If the exception handler does not modify the stack frame, the main processor executes the instruction following the cpTRAPcc instruction after it executes an RTE instruction to exit from the handler.

10

10.5.2.5 TRACE EXCEPTIONS. The MC68030 supports two modes of instruction tracing, discussed in **8.1.7 Trace Exception**. In the trace on instruction execution mode, the MC68030 takes a trace exception after completing each instruction. In the trace on change of flow mode, the MC68030 takes a trace exception after each instruction that alters the status register or places an address other than the address of the next instruction in program counter.

The protocol used to execute coprocessor cpSAVE, cpRESTORE, or conditional category instructions does not change when a trace exception is pending in the main processor. The main processor performs a pending trace on instruction execution exception after completing the execution of that instruction. If the main processor is in the trace on change of flow mode and an instruction places an address other than that of the next instruction in the program counter, the processor takes a trace exception after it executes the instruction.

If a trace exception is not pending during a general category instruction, the main processor terminates communication with the coprocessor after reading any primitive with CA = 0. Thus, the coprocessor can complete a cpGEN instruction concurrently with the execution of instructions by the main processor. When a trace exception is pending, however, the main processor must ensure that all processing associated with a cpGEN instruction has been completed before it takes the trace exception. In this case, the main processor continues to read the response CIR and to service the primitives until it receives either a null, CA = 0, PF = 1 primitive, or until exception processing caused by a take post-instruction exception primitive has completed. The coprocessor should return the null, CA = 0 primitive with PF = 0, while it is completing the execution of the cpGEN instruction. The main processor may service pending interrupts between reads of the response CIR if IA = 1 in these primitives (refer to Table 10-3). This protocol ensures that a trace exception is not taken until all processing associated with a cpGEN instruction has completed.

If T1:T0 = 01 in the MC68030 status register (trace on change of flow) when a general category instruction is initiated, a trace exception is taken for the instruction only when the coprocessor issues a transfer status register and scanPC primitive with DR = 1 during the execution of that instruction. In this case, it is possible that the coprocessor is still executing the cpGEN instruction concurrently when the main processor begins execution of the trace exception handler. A cpSAVE instruction executed during the trace on change of flow exception handler could thus suspend the execution of a concurrently operating cpGEN instruction.

10

10.5.2.6 INTERRUPTS. Interrupt processing, discussed in **8.1.9 Interrupt Exceptions**, can occur at any instruction boundary. Interrupts are also serviced during the execution of a general or conditional category instruction under either of two conditions. If the main processor reads a null primitive with CA = 1 and IA = 1, it services any pending interrupts prior to reading the response CIR. Similarly, if a trace exception is pending during cpGEN instruction execution and the main processor reads a null primitive with CA = 0, IA = 1, and PF = 0 (refer to **10.5.2.5 TRACE EXCEPTIONS**), the main processor services pending interrupts prior to reading the response CIR again.

The MC68030 uses the ten-word mid-instruction stack frame when it services interrupts during the execution of a general or conditional category coprocessor instruction. Since it uses this stack frame, the main processor can perform all necessary processing and then return to read the response CIR. Thus, it can continue the coprocessor instruction during which the interrupt exception was taken.

The MC68030 also services interrupts if it reads the not ready format word from the save CIR during a cpSAVE instruction. The MC68030 uses the normal four word pre-instruction stack frame when it services interrupts after reading the not ready format word. Thus, the processor can service any pending interrupts and execute an RTE to return and re-initiate the cpSAVE instruction by reading the save CIR.

10.5.2.7 FORMAT ERRORS. The MC68030 can detect a format error while executing a cpSAVE or cpRESTORE instruction if the length field of a valid format word is not a multiple of four bytes in length. If the MC68030 reads a format word with an invalid length field from the save CIR during the cpSAVE instruction, it aborts the coprocessor instruction by writing an abort mask (refer to **10.3.2 Control CIR**) to the control CIR and initiates format error exception processing. If the MC68030 reads a format word with an invalid length field from the effective address specified in the cpRESTORE instruction, the MC68030 writes that format word to the restore CIR and then reads the coprocessor response from the restore CIR. The MC68030 then aborts the cpRESTORE instruction by writing an abort mask (refer to **10.3.2 Control CIR**) to the control CIR and initiates format error exception processing.

The MC68030 uses the four-word pre-instruction stack frame and the format error vector number 14 when it initiates format error exception processing. Thus, if the exception handler does not modify the stack frame, the main processor attempts to restart the instruction during which the exception occurred after it executes an RTE to return from the handler.

10

10.5.2.8 ADDRESS AND BUS ERRORS. Coprocessor-instruction-related bus faults can occur during main processor bus cycles to CPU space to communicate with a coprocessor or during memory cycles run as part of the coprocessor instruction execution. If a bus error occurs during the coprocessor interface register access that is used to initiate a coprocessor instruction, the main processor assumes that the coprocessor is not present and takes an F-line emulator exception as described in **10.5.2.2 F-LINE EMULATOR EXCEPTIONS**. That is, the processor takes an F-line emulator exception when a bus error occurs during the initial access to a CIR by a coprocessor instruction. If a bus error occurs on any other coprocessor access or on a memory access made during the execution of a coprocessor instruction, the main processor performs bus error exception processing as described in **8.1.2 Bus Error Exceptions**. After the exception handler has corrected the cause of the bus error, the main processor can return to the point in the coprocessor instruction at which the fault occurred.

An address error occurs if the MC68030 attempts to prefetch an instruction from an odd address. This can occur if the calculated destination address of a cpBcc or cpDBcc instruction is odd or if an odd value is transferred to the scanPC with the transfer status register and the scanPC response primitive. If an address error occurs, the MC68030 performs exception processing for a bus fault as described in **8.1.3 Address Error Exception**.

10.5.3 Coprocessor Reset

Either an external reset signal or a RESET instruction can reset the external devices of a system. The system designer can design a coprocessor to be reset and initialized by both reset types or by external reset signals only. To be consistent with the MC68030 design, the coprocessor should be affected by external reset signals only and not by RESET instructions, because the coprocessor is an extension to the main processor programming model and to the internal state of the MC68030.

10.6 COPROCESSOR SUMMARY

Coprocessor instruction formats are presented for reference. Refer to the M68000PM/AD, *M68000 Programmer's Reference Manual*, for detailed information on coprocessor instructions.

The M68000 coprocessor response primitive formats are shown in this section. Any response primitive with bits [13:8] = $00 or $3F causes a protocol violation exception. Response primitives with bits [13:8] = $0B, $18–$1B, $1F, $28–$2B, and $38–3B currently cause protocol violation exceptions; they are undefined and reserved for future use by Motorola.

BUSY

15	14	13	12	11	10	9	8	7	6	5	4	3	2	1	0
1	PC	1	0	0	1	0	0	0	0	0	0	0	0	0	0

TRANSFER MULTIPLE COPROCESSOR REGISTERS

15	14	13	12	11	10	9	8	7							0
CA	PC	DR	0	0	0	0	1	LENGTH							

TRANSFER STATUS REGISTER AND SCANPC

15	14	13	12	11	10	9	8	7	6	5	4	3	2	1	0
CA	PC	DR	0	0	0	1	SP	0	0	0	0	0	0	0	0

SUPERVISOR CHECK

15	14	13	12	11	10	9	8	7	6	5	4	3	2	1	0
1	PC	0	0	0	1	0	0	0	0	0	0	0	0	0	0

TAKE ADDRESS AND TRANSFER DATA

15	14	13	12	11	10	9	8	7							0
CA	PC	DR	0	0	1	0	1	LENGTH							

TRANSFER MULTIPLE MAIN PROCESSOR REGISTERS

15	14	13	12	11	10	9	8	7	6	5	4	3	2	1	0
CA	PC	DR	0	0	1	1	0	0	0	0	0	0	0	0	0

TRANSFER OPERATION WORD

15	14	13	12	11	10	9	8	7	6	5	4	3	2	1	0
CA	PC	0	0	0	1	1	1	0	0	0	0	0	0	0	0

10

NULL

15	14	13	12	11	10	9	8	7	6	5	4	3	2	1	0
CA	PC	0	0	1	0	0	IA	0	0	0	0	0	0	PF	TF

EVALUATE AND TRANSFER EFFECTIVE ADDRESS

15	14	13	12	11	10	9	8	7	6	5	4	3	2	1	0
CA	PC	0	0	1	0	1	0	0	0	0	0	0	0	0	0

TRANSFER SINGLE MAIN PROCESSOR REGISTER

15	14	13	12	11	10	9	8	7	6	5	4	3	2		0
CA	PC	DR	0	1	1	0	0	0	0	0	0	D/A	REGISTER		

TRANSFER MAIN PROCESSOR CONTROL REGISTER

15	14	13	12	11	10	9	8	7	6	5	4	3	2	1	0
CA	PC	DR	0	1	1	0	1	0	0	0	0	0	0	0	0

TRANSFER TO/FROM TOP OF STACK

15	14	13	12	11	10	9	8	7		0
CA	PC	DR	0	1	1	1	0	LENGTH		

TRANSFER FROM INSTRUCTION STREAM

15	14	13	12	11	10	9	8	7		0
CA	PC	0	0	1	1	1	1	LENGTH		

EVALUATE EFFECTIVE ADDRESS AND TRANSFER DATA

15	14	13	12	11	10	9	8	7		0
CA	PC	DR	1	0	VALID EA			LENGTH		

TAKE PRE-INSTRUCTION EXCEPTION

15	14	13	12	11	10	9	8	7		0
0	PC	0	1	1	1	0	0	VECTOR NUMBER		

TAKE MID-INSTRUCTION EXCEPTION

15	14	13	12	11	10	9	8	7		0
0	PC	0	1	1	1	0	1	VECTOR NUMBER		

TAKE POST-INSTRUCTION EXCEPTION

15	14	13	12	11	10	9	8	7		0
0	PC	0	1	1	1	1	0	VECTOR NUMBER		

WRITE TO PREVIOUSLY EVALUATED EFFECTIVE ADDRESS

15	14	13	12	11	10	9	8	7		0
CA	PC	1	0	0	0	0	0	LENGTH		

10

SECTION 11
INSTRUCTION EXECUTION TIMING

This section describes the instruction execution and operations (table searches, etc.) of the MC68030 in terms of external clock cycles. It provides accurate execution and operation timing guidelines but not exact timings for every possible circumstance. This approach is used since exact execution time for an instruction or operation is highly dependent on memory speeds and other variables. The timing numbers presented in this section allow the assembly language programmer or compiler writer to predict actual cache-case and average no-cache-case timings needed to evaluate the performance of the MC68030. Additionally, the timings for exception processing, context switching, and interrupt processing are included so that designers of multi-tasking or real-time systems can predict task switch overhead, maximum interrupt latency, and similar timing parameters.

In this section, instruction and operation times are shown in clock cycles to eliminate clock frequency dependencies.

11.1 PERFORMANCE TRADEOFFS

The MC68030 maximizes average performance at the expense of worst case performance. The time spent executing one instruction can vary from zero to over 100 clocks. Factors affecting the execution time are the preceding and following instructions, the instruction stream alignment, residency of operands and instruction words in the caches, residency of address translations in the address translation cache, and operand alignment.

To increase the average performance of the MC68030, certain tradeoffs were made to increase best case performance and to decrease the occurrence of worst case behavior. For example, burst filling increases performance by prefetching data for later accesses, but it commits the external bus controller and a cache for a longer period.

The MC68030 can overlap data writes with instruction cache reads, data cache reads, and/or microsequencer execution. Instruction cache reads can be overlapped with data cache fills and/or microsequencer activity. Similarly, data cache reads can be overlapped with instruction cache fills and/or microsequencer activity. The execution of an instruction that only accesses on-chip registers can be overlapped entirely with a concurrent data write generated by a previous instruction, if prefetches generated by that instruction are resident in the instruction cache.

11.2 RESOURCE SCHEDULING

Some of the variability in instruction execution timings results from the overlap of resource utilization. The processor can be viewed as consisting of eight independently scheduled resources. Since very little of the scheduling is directly related to instruction boundaries, it is impossible to make accurate estimates of the time required to execute a particular instruction without knowing the complete context within which the instruction is executing. The position of these resources within the MC68030 is shown in Figure 11-1.

11.2.1 Microsequencer

The microsequencer is either executing microinstructions or awaiting completion of accesses that are necessary to continue executing microcode. The bus controller is responsible for all bus activity. The microsequencer controls the bus controller, instruction execution, and internal processor operations such as calculation of effective addresses and setting of condition codes. The microsequencer initiates instruction word prefetches and controls the validation of instruction words in the instruction pipe.

11.2.2 Instruction Pipe

The MC68030 contains a three-word instruction pipe where instruction op-codes are decoded. As shown in Figure 11-1, instruction words (instruction operation words and all extension words) enter the pipe at stage B and proceed to stages C and D. An instruction word is completely decoded when it reaches stage D of the pipe. Each of the pipe stages has a status bit that reflects whether the word in the stage was loaded with data from a bus cycle that was terminated abnormally. Stages of the pipe are only filled in response to specific prefetch requests issued by the microsequencer.

Words are loaded into the instruction pipe from the cache holding register. While the individual stages of the pipe are only 16 bits wide, the cache holding register is 32 bits wide and contains the entire long word. This long word is obtained from the instruction cache or the external bus in response to a prefetch request from the microsequencer. When the microsequencer re-

11

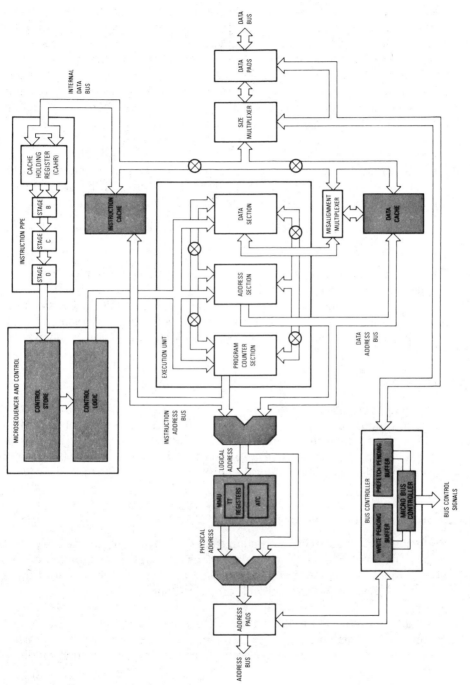

Figure 11-1. Block Diagram — Eight Independent Resources

11

quests an even-word (long-word aligned) prefetch, the entire long word is accessed from the instruction cache or the external bus and loaded into the cache holding register, and the high-order word is also loaded into stage B of the pipe. The instruction word for the next sequential prefetch can then be accessed directly from the cache holding register, and no external bus cycle or instruction cache access is required. The cache holding register provides instruction words to the pipe, regardless of whether the instruction cache is enabled or disabled.

Prefetch requests are simultaneously submitted to the cache holding register, the instruction cache, and the bus controller. Thus, even if the instruction cache is disabled, an instruction prefetch may hit in the cache holding register and cause an external bus cycle to be aborted.

11.2.3 Instruction Cache

The instruction cache services the instruction prefetch portion of the microsequencer. The prefetch of an instruction that hits in the on-chip instruction cache causes no delay in instruction execution since no external bus activity is required for the prefetch. The instruction cache also interacts with the external bus during instruction cache fills following instruction cache misses.

11.2.4 Data Cache

The data cache services data reads and is updated on data writes. Data operands required by the execution unit that are accessed from the data cache cause no delay in instruction execution due to external bus activity for the data fetch. The data cache also interacts with the external bus during data cache fills following data cache misses.

11.2.5 Bus Controller Resources

Prefetches that miss in the instruction cache cause an external memory cycle to be performed. Similarly, when data reads miss in the on-chip data cache, an external memory cycle is required. The time required for either of these bus cycles may be overlapped with other internal activity.

The bus controller and microsequencer can operate on an instruction concurrently. The bus controller can perform a read or write while the microsequencer controls an effective address calculation or sets the condition codes. The microsequencer may also request a bus cycle that the bus controller cannot perform immediately. In this case, the bus cycle is queued and the bus controller runs the cycle when the current cycle is complete.

The bus controller consists of the micro bus controller, the instruction fetch pending buffer, and the write pending buffer. These three resources carry out all writes and reads that miss in the on-chip caches.

11.2.5.1 INSTRUCTION FETCH PENDING BUFFER. The instruction prefetch mechanism includes a single long-word instruction fetch pending buffer. Interlocks are provided to prevent this buffer from being overwritten by an instruction prefetch request before a previously requested prefetch is completed.

11.2.5.2 WRITE PENDING BUFFER. The MC68030 incorporates a single write pending buffer, allowing the microsequencer to continue execution after the request for a write cycle proceeds to the bus controller. Interlocks prevent the microsequencer from overwriting this buffer.

11.2.5.3 MICRO BUS CONTROLLER. The micro bus controller performs the bus cycles issued to the bus controller by the rest of the processor. It implements any dynamic bus sizing required and also controls burst operations.

When prefetching instructions from external memory, the micro bus controller utilizes long-word read cycles. The processor reads two words, which may load two instructions at once or two words of a multi-word instruction into the cache holding register (and the instruction cache if it is enabled and not frozen). A special case occurs when prefetch, that corresponds to an instruction word at an odd-word boundary, is not found in the cache holding register (e.g., due to a branch to an odd-word location) with an instruction cache miss. From a 32-bit memory, the MC68030 reads both the even and odd words associated with the long-word base address in one bus cycle. From an 8- or 16-bit memory, the processor reads the even word before the odd word. Both the even and odd word are loaded into the cache holding register (and the instruction cache if it is enabled and not frozen).

11

11.2.6 Memory Management Unit

The MC68030 includes a memory management unit (MMU) that translates logical addresses to physical addresses for external accesses when required. The MMU uses an address translation cache (ATC) to store recently used translations. When the physical address corresponding to a logical address resides in the ATC, the address translation time is completely overlapped with on-chip cache accesses and has no effect on instruction timing.

When the ATC does not contain the translation for a logical address, the processor performs a table search operation to external memory. The amount of time required for a table search depends on the structure of the address translation tree and whether a nonresident portion of the translation tree is required.

The MMU supports demand-paged virtual memory. When a table search terminates with an exception, indicating that the requested instruction or data is not resident, additional time to bring the appropriate page into memory is required. The time required is dependent on the handling routine for the exception.

11.3 INSTRUCTION EXECUTION TIMING CALCULATIONS

The instruction-cache-case timing, overlap, average no-cache-case timing, and actual instruction-cache-case execution time calculations are discussed in the following paragraphs.

11.3.1 Instruction-Cache Case

The instruction-cache-case (CC) time for an instruction is the total number of clock periods required to execute the instruction, provided all the corresponding instruction prefetches are resident in the on-chip instruction cache. All bus cycles are assumed to take two clock periods. The instruction-cache-case time does not assume any overlap with other instructions nor does it take into account hits in the on-chip data cache. The overall instruction-cache-case time for some instructions is divided into the instruction-cache-case time for the required effective address calculation (CCea) and the instruction-cache-case time for the remainder of the operation (CCop). The instruction-cache-case times for all instructions and addressing modes are listed in the tables of **11.6 INSTRUCTION TIMING TABLES**.

11

11.3.2 Overlap and Best Case

Overlap is the time, measured in clock periods, that an instruction executes concurrently with the previous instruction. In Figure 11-2, a portion of instructions A and B execute simultaneously. The overlap time decreases the overall execution time for the two instructions. Similarly, an overlap period between instructions B and C reduces the overall execution time of these two instructions.

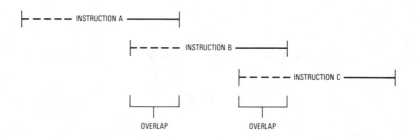

Figure 11-2. Simultaneous Instruction Execution

Each instruction contributes to the total overlap time. As shown in Figure 11-2, a portion of time at the beginning of the execution of instruction B can overlap the end of the execution time of instruction A. This time period is called the head of instruction B. The portion of time at the end of instruction A that can overlap the beginning of instruction B is called the tail of instruction A. The total overlap time between instructions A and B consists of the lesser of the tail of instruction A or the head of instruction B. Refer to the instruction timing tables in **11.6 INSTRUCTION TIMING TABLES** for head and tail times.

Figure 11-3 shows the timing relationship of the factors that comprise the instruction-cache case time for either an effective address calculation (CCea) or for an operation (CCop). In Figure 11-12, the best case execution time for instruction B occurs when the instruction-cache-case times for instruction B and instruction A overlap so that the head of instruction B is completely overlapped with the tail of instruction A.

11

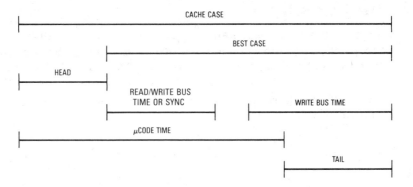

Figure 11-3. Derivation of Instruction Overlap Time

The nature of the instruction overlap and the fact that the heads of some instructions equal the total instruction-cache-case time for those instructions makes a zero net execution time possible. The execution time of an instruction is completely absorbed by overlap with the previous instruction.

11.3.3 Average No-Cache Case

The average no-cache-case (NCC) time for an instruction takes into account the time required for the microcode to execute plus the time required for all external bus activity. This time is calculated assuming both caches miss and the associated instruction prefetches require one external bus cycle per two instruction prefetches. Refer to **11.2.2 Instruction Pipe**. The average no-cache-case time also assumes no overlap. *All bus cycles are assumed to take two clock periods.* Average no-cache-case times for instructions and effective address calculations are listed in **11.6 INSTRUCTION TIMING TABLES**. *Because the no-cache-case times assume no overlap, the head and tail values listed in these tables do not apply to the no-cache-case values.*

Since the actual no-cache-case time depends on the alignment of prefetches associated with an instruction, both alignment cases were considered, and the value shown in the table is the average of the odd-word-aligned case and the even-word-aligned case (rounded up to an integral number of clocks). Similarly, the number of prefetch bus cycles is the average of these two cases rounded up to an integral number of bus cycles.

The effect of instruction alignment on timing is illustrated by the following example. The assumptions referred to in **11.6 INSTRUCTION TIMING TABLES** apply. Both the data cache and instruction cache miss on all accesses.

Instruction

1. MOVE.L $(d_{16},An,Dn),Dn$
2. CMPI.W $\#\langle data\rangle.W,(d_{16},An)$

The instruction stream is positioned with even alignment in 32-bit memory as:

Address			
n	MOVE	EA Ext	
n + 4	d_{16}	CMPI	
n + 8	$\#\langle data.W\rangle$	d_{16}	
n + 12	. . .	. . .	

Figure 11-4 shows processor activity for even alignment of the given instruction stream. It shows the activity of the external bus, the bus controller, and the sequencer.

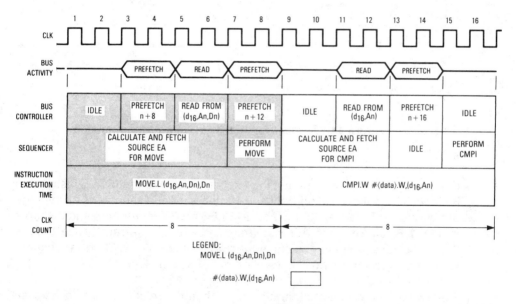

Figure 11-4. Processor Activity — Even Alignment

Figure 11-5 shows processor activity for odd alignment. The instruction stream is positioned in 32-bit memory as:

Address	n	. . .	MOVE
	n + 4	EA Ext	d_{16}
	n + 8	CMPI	#⟨data.W⟩
	n + 12	d_{16}	. . .

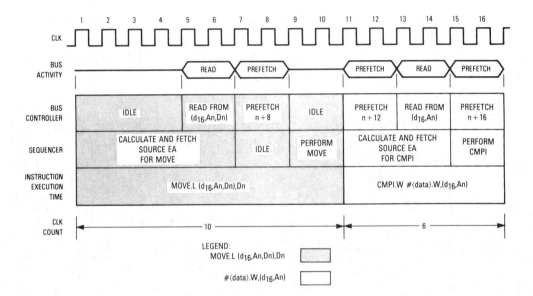

Figure 11-5. Processor Activity — Odd Alignment

Comparing the two alignments, the execution time of the MOVE instruction is eight clocks for even alignment and 10 clocks for odd alignment, an average of nine clocks. Referring to the table in **11.6.6 MOVE Instruction** and the table in **11.6.1 Fetch Effective Address (fea)**, the average no-cache-case time is $2 + 7 = 9$ clocks. A similar calculation can be made of the CMPI instruction, which has an average no-cache-case time of seven clocks.

The average no-cache-case timing rather than the maximum no-cache-case timing gives a closer approximation of the actual timing of an instruction stream in many cases. The total execution time of the two instructions in the previous example is 16 clocks for both even and odd alignment. Adding the average no-cache-case timing of the given instructions also gives 16 clocks ($9 + 7 = 16$ clocks). It should be noted again that the no-cache-case time assumes no overlap. Therefore, the actual execution time of an instruction stream may be less than that given by adding the no-cache-case times. To factor in the effect of wait states for the no-cache case, refer to **11.5 EFFECT OF WAIT STATES**.

11.3.4 Actual Instruction-Cache-Case Execution Time Calculations

The overall execution time for an instruction may depend on the overlap with the previous and following instructions. Therefore, to calculate instruction execution time estimations, the entire code sequence to be evaluated must be analyzed as a whole. To derive the actual instruction-cache-case execution times for an instruction sequence (under the assumptions listed in **11.6 INSTRUCTION TIMING TABLES**), the instruction-cache-case times listed in the tables must be used, and the proper overlap must be subtracted for the entire sequence. The formula for this calculation is:

$$CC_1 + [CC_2 - \min(H_2, T_1)] + [(CC_3 - \min(H_3, T_2)] + \ldots \qquad (11\text{-}1)$$

where:
    CC_n is the instruction-cache-case time for an instruction,
    T_n is the tail time for an instruction,
    H_n is the head time for an instruction, and
    $\min(a,b)$ is the minimum of parameters a and b.

The instruction-cache-case time for most instructions is composed of the instruction-cache-case time for the effective address calculation (CCea) overlapped with the instruction-cache-case time for the operation (CCop). The more specific formula is:

$$CCea_1 + [CCop_1 - \min(Hop_1, Tea_1)] + [CCea_2 - \min(Hea_2, Top_1)] +$$
$$[CCop_2 - \min(Hop_2, Tea_2)] + [CCea_3 - \min(Hea_3, Top_2)] + \ldots \qquad (11\text{-}2)$$

where:
    $CCea_n$ is the effective address time for the instruction-cache case,
    $CCop_n$ is the instruction-cache-case time for the operation portion of an instruction,
    Tea_n is the tail time for the effective address of an instruction,
    Hop_n is the head time for the operation portion of an instruction,
    Top_n is the tail time for the operation portion of an instruction,
    Hea_n is the head time for the effective address of an instruction, and
    $\min(a,b)$ is the minimum of parameters a and b.

11

The instructions that require the instruction-cache case, head, and tail of an effective address (CCea, Hea, and Tea) to be overlapped with CCop, Hop, and Top are footnoted in **11.6 INSTRUCTION TIMING TABLES**.

The actual instruction-cache-case execution time for a stream of instructions can be computed using Equation (11-1) or the general Equation (11-2). Equation (11-1) is used unless the instruction-cache case, head, and tail of an effective address are required.

An example using a series of instructions that require Equation (11-1) to calculate the instruction-cache-case execution time follows. The assumptions referred to in **11.6 INSTRUCTION TIMING TABLES** apply.

Instruction

1. ADD.L   A1,D1
2. SUBA.L   D1,A2

Referring to the timing table in **11.6.8 Arithmetic/Logical Instructions**, the head, tail, and instruction-cache-case (CC) times for ADD.L A1,D1 and SUBA.L D1,A2 are found. There is no footnote directing the user to add an effective address time for either instruction. Since both of the instructions use register operands only, there is no need to add effective address calculation times. Therefore, the general Equation (11-1) can be used for both.

		Head	Tail	CC
1.	ADD.L A1,D1	2	0̲	2
2.	SUBA.L D1,A2	4̲	0	4

NOTE

The underlined numbers show the typical pattern for the comparison of head and tail in the following equation.

The following computations use Equation (11-1):

$$
\begin{aligned}
\text{Execution Time} &= CC_1 + [CC_2 - \min(H_2, T_1)] \\
&= 2 + [4 - \min(4, 0)] \\
&= 2 + [4 - 0] \\
&= 6 \text{ clocks}
\end{aligned}
$$

Instructions that require the addition of an effective address calculation time from an appropriate table use the general Equation (11-2) to calculate the actual CC time. The CCea, Hea, and Tea values must be extracted from the appropriate effective address table (either fetch effective address, fetch immediate effective address, calculate effective address, calculate immediate effective address, or jump effective address) as indicated and included in Equation (11-2). All of the following instructions (except the last) require general Equation (11-2). The last instruction uses Equation (11-1).

Instruction

1.	ADD.L	$-(A1),D1$
2.	AND.L	$D1,([A2])$
3.	MOVE.L	$(A6),(8,A1)$
4.	TAS	$(A3)+$
5.	NEG	$D3$

Using the appropriate operation and effective address tables from **11.6 IN-STRUCTION TIMING TABLES**:

		Head	Tail	CC
1.	ADD.L $-(A1),D1$			
	Fetch Effective Address (fea) $-(An)$	2	2	4
	ADD EA,Dn	0	0	2
2.	AND.L $D1,([A2])$			
	fea ([B])	4	0	10
	AND Dn,EA	0	1	3
3.	MOVE.L $(A6),(8,A1)$			
	fea (An)	1	1	3
	MOVE Source,(d_{16},An)	2	0	4
4.	TAS $(A3)+$			
	Calculate Effective Address (cea) $(An)+$	0	0	2
	TAS Mem	3	0	12
5.	NEG D3	2	0	2

The following calculations use Equations (11-1) and (11-2):

$$\text{Execution Time} = CCea_1 + [CCop_1 - \min(Hop_1, Tea_1)] + [CCea_2 - \min(Hea_2, Top_1)] +$$
$$[CCop_2 - \min(Hop_2, Tea_2)] + [CCea_3 - \min(Hea_3, Top_2)] +$$
$$[CCop_3 - \min(Hop_3, Tea_3)] + [CCea_4 - \min(Hop_4, Top_3)] +$$
$$[CCop_4 - \min(Hop_4, Top_3)] + [CCop_5 - \min(Hop_5, Top_4)]$$

$$= 4 + [2 - \min(0,2)] + [10 - \min(4,0)] + [3 - \min(0,0)] + [3 - \min(1,1)] +$$
$$[4 - \min(2,1)] + [2 - \min(0,0)] + [12 - \min(3,0)] + [2 - \min(2,0)]$$

$$= 4 + 2 + 10 + 3 + 2 + 3 + 2 + 12 + 2$$

$$= 40 \text{ clock periods}$$

Notice that the last instruction did not require the general Equation (11-2) since there were no effective address (ea) additions. Therefore, Equation (11-1) is used:

$$CCop_5 - \min(Hop_5, Top_4)$$

When using the fetch immediate effective address (fiea) or the calculate immediate effective address (ciea) tables, the size of the data is significant in the timing calculations. For each effective address, a line is listed for word data, #<data>.W, and for long data, #<data>.L.

The total head of some effective address types extends through the effective address calculation and includes the head of the operation. These effective address calculations are marked in the head column as follows:

$$X + op\ head$$

where:
    X is the head of the effective address alone.

An example using the fiea table and the $X + op$ head notation is:

	Instruction	
1.	EORI.W	#$400, −(A1)
2.	ADDI.L	#$6000FF,D1

		Head	Tail	CC
1.	EORI.W #$400, −(A1)			
	fiea #<data>.W, −(An)	2	2	4
	EORI #<data>,Mem	0	1	3
2.	ADDI.L #$6000FF,D1			
	fiea #<data>.L,D1	4 + op head	0	4
		6	0	4
	ADDI #<data>,Dn	2(op head)	0	2

The following calculations use the general Equation (11-2):

$$\text{Execution Time} = CCea_1 + [CCop_1 - \min(Hop_1, Tea_1)] + [CCea_2 - \min(Hea_2, Top_1)] + [CCop_2 - \min(Hop_2, Tea_2)]$$

$$= 4 + [3 - \min(0,2)] + [4 - \min(6,1)] + [2 - \min(2,0)]$$

$$= 4 + 3 + 3 + 2$$

$$= 12 \text{ clock periods}$$

Note that for the head of fiea #<data>.L,D1, 4+op head, the resulting head of 6 is larger than the instruction-cache-case time of the fetch. A negative number for the execution time of that portion could result (e.g., 4−min(6,6)=−2). This result would produce the correct execution time since the fetch was completely overlapped and the operation was partially overlapped by the same tail. No changes in the calculation for the operation execution time are required.

Many two-word instructions (e.g., MULU.L, DIV.L, BFSET, etc.) include the fetch immediate effective address (fiea) time or the calculate immediate effective address (ciea) time in the execution time calculation. The timing for immediate data of word length (#<data>.W) is used for these calculations. If the instruction has a source and a destination, the source EA is used for the table lookup. If the instruction is single operand, the effective address of that operand is used.

The following example includes multi-word instructions that refer to the fetch immediate effective address and calculate immediate effective address tables in **11.6 INSTRUCTION TIMING TABLES**.

	Instruction	
1.	MULU.L	(D7),D1:D2
2.	BFCLR	$6000{0:8}
3.	DIVS.L	#$10000,D3:D4

		Head	**Tail**	**CC**
1.	MULU.L (D7),D1:D2			
	fiea #<data>.W,Dn	2+op head	0	2
		4	0	2
	MUL.L EA, Dn	2(op head)	0	44
2.	BFCLR $6000{0:8}			
	fiea #<data>.W,$XXX.W	4	2	6
	BFCLR Mem(<5 bytes)	6	0	14
3.	DIVS.L #$10000,D3:D4			
	fiea #<data>.W,#<data>.L	6+op head	0	6
		6	0	6
	DIVS.L EA,Dn	0(op head)	0	90

11

Use the general Equation (11-2) to compute:

$$
\begin{aligned}
\text{Execution Time} \quad &= CCea_1 + [CCop_1 - \min(Hop_1, Tea_1)] + [CCea_2 - \min(Hea_2, Top_1)] + \\
&\quad [CCop_2 - \min(Hop_2, Tea_2)] + [CCea_3 - \min(Hea_3, Top_2)] + \\
&\quad [CCop_3 - \min(Hop_3, Tea_3)] \\
&= 2 + [44 - \min(2,0)] + [6 - \min(4,0)] + [14 - \min(6,2)] + [6 - \min(6,0)] + \\
&\quad [90 - \min(0,0)] \\
&= 2 + 44 + 6 + 12 + 6 + 90 \\
&= 160 \text{ clock periods}
\end{aligned}
$$

NOTE

This CC time is a maximum since the times given for the MULU.L and DIVS.L are maximums.

11.4 EFFECT OF DATA CACHE

When the data accesses required by an instruction are in the data cache, reading these operands requires no bus cycles, and the execution time for the instruction may be minimized. Write accesses, however, always require bus cycles because the data cache is a writethrough cache.

The effect of the data cache on operand read accesses can be factored into the actual instruction execution time as follows.

When a data cache hit occurs for the data fetch corresponding to either the fetch effective address table or the fetch immediate effective address table in **11.6 INSTRUCTION TIMING TABLES**, the following rules apply:

1a. if $Tail_t = 0$: No change in timing.

1b. if $Tail_t = 1$: $Tail = Tail_t - 1$
$CC = CC_t - 1$

1c. if $Tail_t > 1$: $Tail = Tail_t - (Tail_t - 1) = 1$
$CC = CC_t - (Tail_t - 1)$

where:
$Tail_t$ and CC_t are the values listed in the tables.

2. If the EA mode is memory indirect (two data reads), the tail and CC time are calculated as for one data read.

11

NOTE

Data cache hits cannot easily be accounted for in instruction and operation timings that include an operand fetch in the CCop (e.g., BFFFO and CHK2). The effect of a data cache hit on such CCop's has been ignored for computational purposes.

RMC cycles (e.g., TAS and CAS) are forced to miss on data cache reads. Therefore, a data cache hit has no effect on these instructions.

The following example assumes data cache hits. The lines that are corrected for data cache hits are printed in **boldface** type. These lines are used to calculate the instruction-cache-case execution time. References are to the preceding rules.

	Instruction	
1.	ADD.L	$-$(A1),D1
2.	AND.L	D1,([A2])
3.	MOVE.L	(A6),(8,A1)
4.	TAS	(A3)

	Head	Tail	CC
1. ADD.L $-$(A1),D1			
Fetch Effective Address			
fea $-$(An)	2	2$-$1	4$-$1(1/0/0)
*1c	**2**	**1**	**3(1/0/0)**
*ADD EA,Dn	**0**	**0**	**2(0/0/1)**
2. AND.L D1,([A2])			
*1a & 2 fea ([B])	**4**	**0**	**10(2/0/0)**
*AND Dn,EA	**0**	**1**	**3(0/0/1)**
3. MOVE.L (A6),(8,A1)			
fea (An)	1	1$-$1	3$-$1(1/0/0)
*1b	**1**	**0**	**2(1/0/0)**
*MOVE Source, (d_{16},An)	**2**	**0**	**4(0/0/1)**
4. TAS (A3)$+$			
*Cea (An)$+$	**0**	**0**	**2(0/0/0)**
*TAS Mem	**0**	**0**	**12(1/0/1)**

*Corrected for data cache hits.

NOTE

It is helpful to include the number of operand reads and writes along with the number of instruction accesses in the CC column for computing the effect of data cache hits on execution time.

The following computations use the general Equation (11-2):

$$\text{Execution Time} = CCea_1 + [CCop_1 - \min(Hop_1, Tea_1)] + [CCea_2 - \min(Hea_2, Top_1)] +$$
$$[CCop_2 - \min(Hop_2, Tea_2)] + [CCea_3 - \min(Hea_3, Top_2)] +$$
$$[CCop_3 - \min(Hop_3, Tea_3)] + [CCea_4 - \min(Hea_4, Top_3)] +$$
$$[CCop_4 - \min(Hop_4, Tea_4)]$$

$$= 3 + [2 - \min(0,1)] + [10 - \min(4,0)] + [3 - \min(0,0)] + [2 - \min(1,1)] +$$
$$[4 - \min(2,0)] + [2 - \min(0,0)] + [12 - \min(0,0)]$$

$$= 3 + 2 + 10 + 3 + 1 + 4 + 2 + 12$$

$$= 37 \text{ clock periods}$$

11.5 EFFECT OF WAIT STATES

The constraints of a system design may require the insertion of wait states in memory cycles. When the bus or the memory device requires many wait states, instruction execution time is increased. However, one or two wait states may have little effect on instruction timing. Often the only effect of one or more wait states is to reduce bus idle time.

The effect of wait states on data accesses may be accounted for in the instruction-cache-case timings.

To add the effect of wait states on data accesses:

1a. For nonmemory indirect effective address timings that include an operand read, add the number of wait states (in clocks) to the tail and instruction-cache-case (CC) times. The head is not affected.

1b. For memory indirect effective address timings that use the calculate <ea> tables and have only one data read (for the address fetch), add the number of wait states to the CC time only. The head and tail are not affected.

1c. For memory indirect effective address timings (fetch <ea>) that have two data reads (for the address fetch), add the number of wait states for two reads to the CC time. Add the number of wait states for one data read to the tail. The head is not affected.

11

2a. For operation timings that include a data read (e.g., BFFF0 and TAS), add the number of wait states to the CC time only. Neither the head nor the tail are affected.

NOTE

The CC timing and tail of the MOVEM instruction are special cases for both data reads and writes. Equations for both the CC timing and the tail as a function of wait states are footnoted in the table in **11.6.7 Special-Purpose MOVE Instruction**.

2b. If the operation has more than one data read, add the total amount of wait states for all reads to the CC time. Neither the head nor the tail are affected. Refer to preceding note.

3a. For operation timings that include a data write, the number of wait states is added to the tail and the CC time. The head is not affected. Refer to preceding note.

3b. If there is more than one write in the operation, the tail is only increased by the wait states for one write. The CC timing is increased by the total amount of wait states for all writes. Refer to preceding note.

The following example calculates the instruction-cache-case execution time for the specified instruction stream with two wait states (four-clock reads and writes). The lines that are corrected for wait states are printed in boldface type and are used to calculate the instruction execution time. References are to the preceding rules.

	Instruction	
1.	MOVE.L	($800,A2,D3),(A5,D2)
2.	ADD.L	D1,([$30,A4])
3.	BFCLR	($20,A5){1:5} — (<5 bytes)
4.	BFTST	($10,A3,D3){31:31} — (5 bytes)
5.	MOVEM	([A1,D1]),A1-A4 — 4 registers

Wait States = 2

		Head	Tail	CC
1.	MOVE.L ($800,A2,D3),(A5,D2)			
	fea (d$_{16}$,An,Xn)	4	0 + 2	6 + 2(1/0/0)
	*1a	**4**	**2**	**8(1/0/0)**
	MOVE Source,(B)	4	0 + 2	8 + 2(0/0/1)
	*3a	**4**	**2**	**10(0/0/1)**
2.	ADD.L D1,([$30,A4])			
	fea ([d$_{16}$,B])	4	0 + 2	12 + 4(2/0/0)
	*1c	**4**	**2**	**16(2/0/0)**
	ADD Dn,EA	0	1 + 2	3 + 2(0/0/1)
	*3a	**0**	**3**	**5(0/0/1)**
3.	BFCLR ($20,A5){1:5}			
	*ciea #<data>.W,(d$_{16}$,An)	**10**	**0**	**4(0/0/0)**
	Single EA Format			
	BFCLR Mem (< 5 bytes)	6	0 + 2	14 + 4(1/0/1)
	*2a & 3a	**6**	**2**	**18(1/0/1)**
4.	BFTST ($10,A3,D3){31:31}			
	*ciea (d$_{16}$,An,Xn)	**14**	**0**	**8(0/0/0)**
	BFTST Mem (5 bytes)	6	0	14 + 4(2/0/0)
	*2b	**6**	**0**	**18(2/0/0)**
5.	MOVEM ([A1,D1]),A1-A4			
	ciea ([B])	6	0	12 + 2(1/0/0)
	*1b	**6**	**0**	**14(1/0/0)**
	MOVEM EA,RL	2	0	24 + 0(4/0/0)
	*2a & 2b	**2**	**0**	**24(4/0/0)**

*Corrected for wait states.

11

NOTE

It is helpful to include the number of operand read and writes along with the number of instruction accesses in the CC column for computing the effect of wait states on execution time.

Using the general Equation (11-2), calculate as follows:

Execution Time $= CCea_1 + [CCop_1 - min(Hop_1, Tea_1)] + [CCea_2 - min(Hea_2, Top_1)] +$
$[CCop_2 - min(Hop_2, Tea_2)] + [CCea_3 - min(Hea_3, Top_2)] +$
$[CCop_3 - min(Hop_3, Tea_3)] + [CCea_4 - min(Hea_4, Top_3)] +$
$[CCop_4 - min(Hop_4, Tea_4)] + [CCea_5 - min(Hea_5, Top_4)] +$
$[CCop_5 - min(Hop_5, Tea_5)]$

$= 8 + [10 - min(4,2)] + [16 - min(4,2)] +$
$[5 - min(0,2)] + [4 - min(10,3)] + [18 - min(6,0)] + [8 - min(14,2)] +$
$[18 - min(6,0)] + [14 - min(6,0)] +$
$[24 - min(2,0)]$

$= 8 + 8 + 14 + 5 + 1 + 18 + 6 + 18 + 14 + 24$

$= 116$ clock periods

The next example is the data cache hit example from **11.4 EFFECT OF DATA CACHE** with two wait states per cycle (four-clock read/write). Hits in the data cache and instruction cache are assumed. Three lines are shown for each timing. The first is the timing from the appropriate table. The second is the timing adjusted for a data cache hit. The third *adds wait states only to write operations*, since the read operations hit in the cache and cause no delay. The third line for each timing is used to calculate the instruction cache execution time; it is shown in boldface type.

	Instruction	
1.	ADD.L	$-(A1),D1$
2.	AND.L	D1,([A2])
3.	MOVE.L	(A6),(8,A1)
4.	TAS	(A3)+

		Head	Tail	CC
1.	ADD.L −(A1),D1			
	fea −(An)	2	2	4(1/0/0)
	*	2	1	3(1/0/0)
	**	**2**	**1**	**3(1/0/0)**
	ADD.L EA,Dn	0	0	2(0/1/0)
	*	0	0	2(0/1/0)
	**	**0**	**0**	**2(0/1/0)**
2.	AND.L D1,([A1])			
	fea ([B])	4	0	10(1/0/0)
	*	4	0	10(1/0/0)
	***	**4**	**0**	**12(1/0/0)**
	AND Dn,EA	0	1	3(0/0/1)
	*	0	1	3(0/0/1)
	**	**0**	**3**	**5(0/0/1)**
3.	MOVE.L (A6),(8,A1)			
	fea (An)	1	1	3(1/0/0)
	*	1	0	2(1/0/0)
	**	**1**	**0**	**2(1/0/0)**
	MOVE Source,(d_{16},An)	2	0	4(0/0/1)
	*	2	0	4(0/0/1)
	**	**2**	**2**	**6(0/0/1)**
4.	TAS (A3)+			
	Cea (An)	0	0	2(0/0/0)
	*	0	0	2(0/0/0)
	**	**0**	**0**	**2(0/0/0)**
	TAS Mem	3	0	12(1/0/1)
	*	3	0	12(1/0/1)
	**	**3**	**0**	**14(1/0/1)**

NOTES:
   *Corrected for data cache hits.
  **Corrected for wait states also (only on data writes).
 ***No data cache hit assumed for address fetch.

Using the general Equation (11-2), calculate as follows:

Execution Time $= CCea_1 + [CCop_1 - \min(Hea_1, Top_1)] + [CCea_2 - \min(Hea_2, Top_1)] +$
$[CCop_2 - \min(Hop_2, Tea_2)] + [CCea_3 - \min(Hea_3, Top_2)] +$
$[CCop_3 - \min(Hop_3, Tea_3)] + [CCea_4 - \min(Hea_4, Top_3)] +$
$[CCop_4 - \min(Hop_4, Tea_4)]$

$= 3 + [2 - \min(0,1)]m + [12 - \min(4,0)] +$
$[5 - \min(0,0)] + [2 - \min(1,3)] +$
$[6 - \min(2,0)] + [2 - \min(0,2)] +$
$[14 - \min(3,0)$

$= 3 + 2 + 12 + 5 + 1 + 6 + 2 + 14$

$= 45$ clock periods

A similar analysis can be constructed for the average no-cache case. Since the average no-cache-case time assumes two clock periods per bus cycle (i.e., no wait states), the timing given in the tables does not apply directly to systems with wait states. To approximate the average no-cache-case time for an instruction or effective address with W wait states, use the following formula:

$$NCC = NCC_t + (\# \text{ of data reads and writes}) \cdot W + (\text{max.} \# \text{ of instruction accesses}) \cdot W$$

where:

NCC_t is the no-cache-case timing value from the appropriate table.

The number of data reads, data writes, and maximum instruction accesses are found in the appropriate table.

The average no-cache-case timing obtained from this formula is equal to or greater than the actual no-cache-case timing since the number of instruction accesses used is a maximum (the values in the tables are always rounded up) and no overlap is assumed.

11.6 INSTRUCTION TIMING TABLES

All the following assumptions apply to the times shown in the tables in this section:

- All memory accesses occur with two-clock bus cycles and no wait states.

- All operands in memory, including the system stack, are long-word aligned.

- A 32-bit bus is used for communications between the MC68030 and system memory.

- The data cache is not enabled.

- No exceptions occur (except as specified).

- Required address translations for all external bus cycles are resident in the address translation cache.

Four values are listed for each instruction and effective address:

1. Head,

2. Tail,

3. Instruction-cache case (CC) when the instruction is in the cache but has no overlap, and

4. Average no-cache case (NCC) when the instruction is not in the cache or the cache is disabled and there is no instruction overlap.

The only instances for which the size of the operand has any effect are the instructions with immediate operands and the ADDA and SUBA instructions. Unless specified otherwise, immediate byte and word operands have identical execution times.

The instruction-cache-case and average no-cache-case columns of the instruction timing tables contain four sets of numbers, three of which are enclosed in parentheses. The outer number is the total number of clocks for the given cache case and instruction. The first number inside the parentheses is the number of operand read cycles performed by the instruction. The second value inside the parentheses is the maximum number of instruction bus cycles performed by the instruction, including all prefetches to keep the instruction pipe filled. Because the second value is the average of the odd-word-aligned case and the even-word-aligned case (rounded up to an integral number of bus cycles), it is always greater than or equal to the actual number of bus cycles (one bus cycle per two instruction prefetches). The third value within the parentheses is the number of write cycles performed by the instruction. One example from the instruction timing table is:

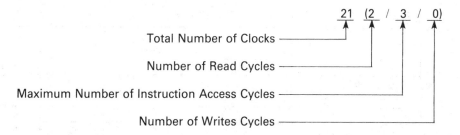

The total numbers of bus-activity clocks and internal clocks (not overlapped by bus activity) of the instruction in this example are derived as follows:

(2 Reads•2 Clocks/Read) + (3 Instruction Accesses•2 Clocks/Access) +
(0 Writes•2 Clocks/Write) = 10 Clocks of Bus Activity
21 Total Clocks − 10 Bus Activity Clocks = 11 Internal Clocks

The example used here is taken from a no-cache-case 'fetch effective address' time. The addressing mode is ([d$_{32}$,B],I,d$_{32}$). The same addressing mode under the instruction-cache-case execution time entry is 18(2/0/0). For the instruction-cache-case execution time, no instruction accesses are required because the cache is enabled and the sequencer does not have to access external memory for the instruction words.

The first five timing tables deal exclusively with fetching and calculating effective addresses and immediate operands. The remaining tables are instruction and operation timings. Some instructions use addressing modes that are not included in the corresponding instruction timings. These cases refer to footnotes that indicate the additional table needed for the timing calculation. All read and write accesses are assumed to take two clock periods.

11.6.1 Fetch Effective Address (fea)

The fetch effective address table indicates the number of clock periods needed for the processor to calculate and fetch the specified effective address. The effective addresses are divided by their formats (refer to **2.5 Effective Address Encoding Summary**). For instruction-cache case and for no-cache case, the total number of clock cycles is outside the parentheses. The number of read, prefetch, and write cycles is given inside the parentheses as (r/p/w). The read, prefetch, and write cycles are included in the total clock cycle number.

All timing data assumes two-clock reads and writes.

Address Mode	Head	Tail	I-Cache Case	No-Cache Case
SINGLE EFFECTIVE ADDRESS INSTRUCTION FORMAT				
% Dn	—	—	0(0/0/0)	0(0/0/0)
% An	—	—	0(0/0/0)	0(0/0/0)
(An)	1	1	3(1/0/0)	3(1/0/0)
(An)+	0	1	3(1/0/0)	3(1/0/0)
−(An)	2	2	4(1/0/0)	4(1/0/0)
(d_{16},An) or (d_{16},PC)	2	2	4(1/0/0)	4(1/1/0)
(xxx).W	2	2	4(1/0/0)	4(1/1/0)
(xxx).L	1	0	4(1/0/0)	5(1/1/0)
#(data).B	2	0	2(0/0/0)	2(0/1/0)
#(data).W	2	0	2(0/0/0)	2(0/1/0)
#(data).L	4	0	4(0/0/0)	4(0/1/0)
BRIEF FORMAT EXTENSION WORD				
(d_8,An,Xn) or (d_8,PC,Xn)	4	2	6(1/0/0)	6(1/1/0)

11.6.1 Fetch Effective Address (fea) (Continued)

Address Mode	Head	Tail	I-Cache Case	No-Cache Case
FULL FORMAT EXTENSION WORD(S)				
(d_{16},An) or (d_{16},PC)	2	0	**6**(1/0/0)	**7**(1/1/0)
(d_{16},An,Xn) or (d_{16},PC,Xn)	4	0	**6**(1/0/0)	**7**(1/1/0)
$([d_{16},An])$ or $([d_{16},PC])$	2	0	**10**(2/0/0)	**10**(2/1/0)
$([d_{16},An],Xn)$ or $([d_{16},PC],Xn)$	2	0	**10**(2/0/0)	**10**(2/1/0)
$([d_{16},An],d_{16})$ or $([d_{16},PC],d_{16})$	2	0	**12**(2/0/0)	**13**(2/2/0)
$([d_{16},An],Xn,d_{16})$ or $([d_{16},PC],Xn,d_{16})$	2	0	**12**(2/0/0)	**13**(2/2/0)
$([d_{16},An],d_{32})$ or $([d_{16},PC],d_{32})$	2	0	**12**(2/0/0)	**14**(2/2/0)
$([d_{16},An],Xn,d_{32})$ or $([d_{16},PC],Xn,d_{32})$	2	0	**12**(2/0/0)	**14**(2/2/0)
(B)	4	0	**6**(1/0/0)	**7**(1/1/0)
(d_{16},B)	4	0	**8**(1/0/0)	**10**(1/1/0)
(d_{32},B)	4	0	**12**(1/0/0)	**13**(1/2/0)
([B])	4	0	**10**(2/0/0)	**10**(2/1/0)
([B],I)	4	0	**10**(2/0/0)	**10**(2/1/0)
$([B],d_{16})$	4	0	**12**(2/0/0)	**13**(2/1/0)
$([B],I,d_{16})$	4	0	**12**(2/0/0)	**13**(2/1/0)
$([B],d_{32})$	4	0	**12**(2/0/0)	**14**(2/2/0)
$([B],I,d_{32})$	4	0	**12**(2/0/0)	**14**(2/2/0)
$([d_{16},B])$	4	0	**12**(2/0/0)	**13**(2/1/0)
$([d_{16},B],I)$	4	0	**12**(2/0/0)	**13**(2/1/0)
$([d_{16},B],d_{16})$	4	0	**14**(2/0/0)	**16**(2/2/0)
$([d_{16},B],I,d_{16})$	4	0	**14**(2/0/0)	**16**(2/2/0)
$([d_{16},B],d_{32})$	4	0	**14**(2/0/0)	**17**(2/2/0)
$([d_{16},B],I,d_{32})$	4	0	**14**(2/0/0)	**17**(2/2/0)
$([d_{32},B])$	4	0	**16**(2/0/0)	**17**(2/2/0)
$([d_{32},B],I)$	4	0	**16**(2/0/0)	**17**(2/2/0)
$([d_{32},B],d_{16})$	4	0	**18**(2/0/0)	**20**(2/2/0)
$([d_{32},B],I,d_{16})$	4	0	**18**(2/0/0)	**20**(2/2/0)
$([d_{32},B],d_{32})$	4	0	**18**(2/0/0)	**21**(2/3/0)
$([d_{32},B],I,d_{32})$	4	0	**18**(2/0/0)	**21**(2/3/0)

B = Base Address; 0, An, PC, Xn, An + Xn, PC + Xn. Form does not affect timing.
I = Index; 0, Xn
% = No clock cycles incurred by effective address fetch.

NOTE: Xn cannot be in B and I at the same time. Scaling and size of Xn do not affect timing.

11.6.2 Fetch Immediate Effective Address (fiea)

The fetch immediate effective address table indicates the number of clock periods needed for the processor to fetch the immediate source operand and to calculate and fetch the specified destination operand. In the case of two-word instructions, this table indicates the number of clock periods needed for the processor to fetch the second word of the instruction and to calculate and fetch the specified source operand or single operand. The effective addresses are divided by their formats (refer to **2.5 Effective Address Encoding Summary**). For instruction-cache case and for no-cache case, the total number of clock cycles is outside the parentheses. The number of read, prefetch, and write cycles is given inside the parentheses as (r/p/w). The read, prefetch, and write cycles are included in the total clock cycle number.

All timing data assumes two-clock reads and writes.

Address Mode	Head	Tail	I-Cache Case	No-Cache Case
SINGLE EFFECTIVE ADDRESS INSTRUCTION FORMAT				
% #⟨data⟩.W,Dn	2 + op head	0	**2**(0/0/0)	**2**(0/1/0)
% #⟨data⟩.L,Dn	4 + op head	0	**4**(0/0/0)	**4**(0/1/0)
#⟨data⟩.W,(An)	1	1	**3**(1/0/0)	**4**(1/1/0)
#⟨data⟩.L,(An)	1	0	**4**(1/0/0)	**5**(1/1/0)
#⟨data⟩.W,(An) +	2	1	**5**(1/0/0)	**5**(1/1/0)
#⟨data⟩.L,(An) +	4	1	**7**(1/0/0)	**7**(1/1/0)
#⟨data⟩.W, − (An)	2	2	**4**(1/0/0)	**4**(1/1/0)
#⟨data⟩.L, − (An)	2	0	**4**(1/0/0)	**5**(1/1/0)
#⟨data⟩.W,(d$_{16}$,An)	2	0	**4**(1/0/0)	**5**(1/1/0)
#⟨data⟩.L,(d$_{16}$,An)	4	0	**6**(1/0/0)	**8**(1/2/0)
#⟨data⟩.W,$XXX.W	4	2	**6**(1/0/0)	**6**(1/1/0)
#⟨data⟩.L,$XXX.W	6	2	**8**(1/0/0)	**8**(1/2/0)
#⟨data⟩.W,$XXX.L	3	0	**6**(1/0/0)	**7**(1/2/0)
#⟨data⟩.L,$XXX.L	5	0	**8**(1/0/0)	**9**(1/2/0)
#⟨data⟩.W,#⟨data⟩.L	6 + op head	0	**6**(0/0/0)	**6**(0/2/0)
BRIEF FORMAT EXTENSION WORD				
#⟨data⟩.W,(d$_8$,An,Xn) or (d$_8$,PC,Xn)	6	2	**8**(1/0/0)	**8**(1/2/0)
#⟨data⟩.L,(d$_8$,An,Xn) or (d$_8$,PC,Xn)	8	2	**10**(1/0/0)	**10**(1/2/0)

11.6.2 Fetch Immediate Effective Address (fiea) (Continued)

Address Mode	Head	Tail	I-Cache Case	No-Cache Case
FULL FORMAT EXTENSION WORD(S)				
#⟨data⟩.W,(d$_{16}$,An) or (d$_{16}$,PC)	4	0	8(1/0/0)	9(1/2/0)
#⟨data⟩.L,(d$_{16}$,An) or (d$_{16}$,PC)	6	0	10(1/0/0)	11(1/2/0)
#⟨data⟩.W,(d$_{16}$,An,Xn) or (d$_{16}$,PC,Xn)	6	0	8(1/0/0)	9(1/2/0)
#⟨data⟩.L,(d$_{16}$,An,Xn) or (d$_{16}$,PC,Xn)	8	0	10(1/0/0)	11(1/2/0)
#⟨data⟩.W,([d$_{16}$,An]) or ([d$_{16}$,PC])	4	0	12(2/0/0)	12(2/2/0)
#⟨data⟩.L,([d$_{16}$,An]) or ([d$_{16}$,PC])	6	0	14(2/0/0)	14(2/2/0)
#⟨data⟩.W,([d$_{16}$,An],Xn) or ([d$_{16}$,PC],Xn)	4	0	12(2/0/0)	12(2/2/0)
#⟨data⟩.L,([d$_{16}$,An],Xn) or ([d$_{16}$,PC],Xn)	6	0	14(2/0/0)	14(2/2/0)
#⟨data⟩.W,([d$_{16}$,An],d$_{16}$) or ([d$_{16}$,PC],d$_{16}$)	4	0	14(2/0/0)	15(2/2/0)
#⟨data⟩.L,([d$_{16}$,An],d$_{16}$) or ([d$_{16}$,PC],d$_{16}$)	6	0	16(2/0/0)	17(2/3/0)
#⟨data⟩.W,([d$_{16}$,An],Xn,d$_{16}$) or ([d$_{16}$,PC],Xn,d$_{16}$)	4	0	14(2/0/0)	15(2/2/0)
#⟨data⟩.L,([d$_{16}$,An],Xn,d$_{16}$) or ([d$_{16}$,PC],Xn,d$_{16}$)	6	0	16(2/0/0)	17(2/3/0)
#⟨data⟩.W,([d$_{16}$,An],d$_{32}$) or ([d$_{16}$,PC],d$_{32}$)	4	0	14(2/0/0)	16(2/3/0)
#⟨data⟩.L,([d$_{16}$,An],d$_{32}$) or ([d$_{16}$,PC],d$_{32}$)	6	0	16(2/0/0)	18(2/3/0)
#⟨data⟩.W,([d$_{16}$,An],Xn,d$_{32}$) or ([d$_{16}$,PC],Xn,d$_{32}$)	4	0	14(2/0/0)	16(2/3/0)
#⟨data⟩.L,([d$_{16}$,An],Xn,d$_{32}$) or ([d$_{16}$,PC],Xn,d$_{32}$)	6	0	16(2/0/0)	18(2/3/0)
#⟨data⟩.W,(B)	6	0	8(1/0/0)	9(1/1/0)
#⟨data⟩.L,(B)	8	0	10(1/0/0)	11(1/2/0)
#⟨data⟩.W,(d$_{16}$,B)	6	0	10(1/0/0)	12(1/2/0)
#⟨data⟩.L,(d$_{16}$,B)	8	0	12(1/0/0)	14(1/2/0)
#⟨data⟩.W,(d$_{32}$,B)	10	0	14(1/0/0)	16(1/2/0)
#⟨data⟩.L,(d$_{32}$,B)	12	0	16(1/0/0)	18(1/3/0)
#⟨data⟩.W,([B])	6	0	12(2/0/0)	12(2/1/0)
#⟨data⟩.L,([B])	8	0	14(2/0/0)	14(2/2/0)
#⟨data⟩.W,([B],I)	6	0	12(2/0/0)	12(2/1/0)
#⟨data⟩.L,([B],I)	8	0	14(2/0/0)	14(2/2/0)
#⟨data⟩.W,([B],d$_{16}$)	6	0	14(2/0/0)	15(2/2/0)
#⟨data⟩.L,([B],d$_{16}$)	8	0	16(2/0/0)	17(2/2/0)
#⟨data⟩.W,([B],I,d$_{16}$)	6	0	14(2/0/0)	15(2/2/0)
#⟨data⟩.L,([B],I,d$_{16}$)	8	0	16(2/0/0)	17(2/2/0)
#⟨data⟩.W,([B],d$_{32}$)	6	0	14(2/0/0)	16(2/2/0)
#⟨data⟩.L,([B],d$_{32}$)	8	0	16(2/0/0)	18(2/3/0)
#⟨data⟩.W,([B],I,d$_{32}$)	6	0	14(2/0/0)	16(2/2/0)
#⟨data⟩.L,([B],I,d$_{32}$)	8	0	16(2/0/0)	18(2/3/0)
#⟨data⟩.W,([d$_{16}$,B])	6	0	14(2/0/0)	15(2/2/0)
#⟨data⟩.L,([d$_{16}$,B])	8	0	16(2/0/0)	17(2/2/0)
#⟨data⟩.W,([d$_{16}$,B],I)	6	0	14(2/0/0)	15(2/2/0)
#⟨data⟩.L,([d$_{16}$,B],I)	8	0	16(2/0/0)	17(2/2/0)

11

11.6.2 Fetch Immediate Effective Address (fiea) (Continued)

Address Mode	Head	Tail	I-Cache Case	No-Cache Case
FULL FORMAT EXTENSION WORD(S) (CONTINUED)				
#⟨data⟩.W,([d_{16},B],d_{16})	6	0	**16**(2/0/0)	**18**(2/2/0)
#⟨data⟩.L,([d_{16},B],d_{16})	8	0	**18**(2/0/0)	**20**(2/3/0)
#⟨data⟩.W,([d_{16},B],I,d_{16})	6	0	**16**(2/0/0)	**18**(2/2/0)
#⟨data⟩.L,([d_{16},B],I,d_{16})	8	0	**18**(2/0/0)	**20**(2/3/0)
#⟨data⟩.W,([d_{16},B],d_{32})	6	0	**16**(2/0/0)	**19**(2/3/0)
#⟨data⟩.L,([d_{16},B],d_{32})	8	0	**18**(2/0/0)	**21**(2/3/0)
#⟨data⟩.W,([d_{16},B],I,d_{32})	6	0	**16**(2/0/0)	**19**(2/3/0)
#⟨data⟩.L,([d_{16},B],I,d_{32})	8	0	**18**(2/0/0)	**21**(2/3/0)
#⟨data⟩.W,([d_{32},B])	6	0	**18**(2/0/0)	**19**(2/2/0)
#⟨data⟩.L,([d_{32},B])	8	0	**20**(2/0/0)	**21**(2/3/0)
#⟨data⟩.W,([d_{32},B],I)	6	0	**18**(2/0/0)	**19**(2/2/0)
#⟨data⟩.L,([d_{32},B],I)	8	0	**20**(2/0/0)	**21**(2/3/0)
#⟨data⟩.W,([d_{32},B],d_{16})	6	0	**20**(2/0/0)	**22**(2/3/0)
#⟨data⟩.L,([d_{32},B],d_{16})	8	0	**22**(2/0/0)	**24**(2/3/0)
#⟨data⟩.W,([d_{32},B],I,d_{16})	6	0	**20**(2/0/0)	**22**(2/3/0)
#⟨data⟩.L,([d_{32},B],I,d_{16})	8	0	**22**(2/0/0)	**24**(2/3/0)
#⟨data⟩.W,([d_{32},B],d_{32})	6	0	**20**(2/0/0)	**23**(2/3/0)
#⟨data⟩.L,([d_{32},B],d_{32})	8	0	**22**(2/0/0)	**25**(2/4/0)
#⟨data⟩.W,([d_{32},B],I,d_{32})	6	0	**20**(2/0/0)	**23**(2/3/0)
#⟨data⟩.L,([d_{32},B],I,d_{32})	8	0	**22**(2/0/0)	**25**(2/4/0)

B = Base Address: 0, An, PC, Xn, An + Xn, PC + Xn. Form does not affect timing.
I = Index: 0, Xn
% = Total head for fetch immediate effective address timing includes the head time for the operation.

NOTE: Xn cannot be in B and I at the same time. Scaling and size of Xn do not affect timing.

11.6.3 Calculate Effective Address (cea)

The calculate effective address table indicates the number of clock periods needed for the processor to calculate the specified effective address. Fetch time is only included for the first level of indirection on memory indirect addressing modes. The effective addresses are divided by their formats (refer to **2.5 Effective Address Encoding Summary**). For instruction-cache case and for no-cache case, the total number of clock cycles is outside the parentheses. The number of read, prefetch, and write cycles is given inside the parentheses as (r/p/w). The read, prefetch, and write cycles are included in the total clock cycle number.

All timing data assumes two-clock reads and writes.

11.6.3 Calculate Effective Address (cea) (Continued)

Address Mode	Head	Tail	I-Cache Case	No-Cache Case
SINGLE EFFECTIVE ADDRESS INSTRUCTION FORMAT				
% Dn	—	—	**0**(0/0/0)	**0**(0/0/0)
% An	—	—	**0**(0/0/0)	**0**(0/0/0)
(An)	2 + op head	0	**2**(0/0/0)	**2**(0/0/0)
(An) +	0	0	**2**(0/0/0)	**2**(0/0/0)
– (An)	2 + op head	0	**2**(0/0/0)	**2**(0/0/0)
(d_{16},An) or (d_{16},PC)	2 + op head	0	**2**(0/0/0)	**2**(0/1/0)
(xxx).W	2 + op head	0	**2**(0/0/0)	**2**(0/1/0)
(xxx).L	4 + op head	0	**4**(0/0/0)	**4**(0/1/0)
BRIEF FORMAT EXTENSION WORD				
(d_8,An,Xn) or (d_8,PC,Xn)	4 + op head	0	**4**(0/0/0)	**4**(0/1/0)
FULL FORMAT EXTENSION WORD(S)				
(d_{16},An) or (d_{16},PC)	2	0	**6**(0/0/0)	**6**(0/1/0)
(d_{16},An,Xn) or (d_{16},PC,Xn)	6 + op head	0	**6**(0/0/0)	**6**(0/1/0)
$([d_{16},An])$ or $([d_{16},PC])$	2	0	**10**(1/0/0)	**10**(1/1/0)
$([d_{16},An],Xn)$ or $([d_{16},PC],Xn)$	2	0	**10**(1/0/0)	**10**(1/1/0)
$([d_{16},An],d_{16})$ or $([d_{16},PC],d_{16})$	2	0	**12**(1/0/0)	**13**(1/2/0)
$([d_{16},An],Xn,d_{16})$ or $([d_{16},PC],Xn,d_{16})$	2	0	**12**(1/0/0)	**13**(1/2/0)
$([d_{16},An],d_{32})$ or $([d_{16},PC],d_{32})$	2	0	**12**(1/0/0)	**13**(1/2/0)
$([d_{16},An],Xn,d_{32})$ or $([d_{16},PC],Xn,d_{32})$	2	0	**12**(1/0/0)	**13**(1/2/0)
(B)	6 + op head	0	**6**(0/0/0)	**6**(0/1/0)
(d_{16},B)	4	0	**8**(0/0/0)	**9**(0/1/0)
(d_{32},B)	4	0	**12**(0/0/0)	**12**(0/2/0)
([B])	4	0	**10**(1/0/0)	**10**(1/1/0)
([B],I)	4	0	**10**(1/0/0)	**10**(1/1/0)
$([B],d_{16})$	4	0	**12**(1/0/0)	**13**(1/1/0)
$([B],I,d_{16})$	4	0	**12**(1/0/0)	**13**(1/1/0)
$([B],d_{32})$	4	0	**12**(1/0/0)	**13**(1/2/0)
$([B],I,d_{32})$	4	0	**12**(2/0/0)	**13**(1/2/0)
$([d_{16},B])$	4	0	**12**(1/0/0)	**13**(1/1/0)
$([d_{16},B],I)$	4	0	**12**(1/0/0)	**13**(1/1/0)
$([d_{16},B],d_{16})$	4	0	**14**(1/0/0)	**16**(1/2/0)
$([d_{16},B],I,d_{16})$	4	0	**14**(1/0/0)	**16**(1/2/0)

11

11.6.3 Calculate Effective Address (cea) (Continued)

Address Mode	Head	Tail	I-Cache Case	No-Cache Case

FULL FORMAT EXENSION WORD(S) (CONTINUED)

Address Mode	Head	Tail	I-Cache Case	No-Cache Case
([d$_{16}$,B],d$_{32}$)	4	0	**14**(1/0/0)	**16**(1/2/0)
([d$_{16}$,B],I,d$_{32}$)	4	0	**14**(1/0/0)	**16**(1/2/0)
([d$_{32}$,B])	4	0	**16**(1/0/0)	**17**(1/2/0)
([d$_{32}$,B],I)	4	0	**16**(1/0/0)	**17**(1/2/0)
([d$_{32}$,B],d$_{16}$)	4	0	**18**(1/0/0)	**20**(1/2/0)
([d$_{32}$,B],I,d$_{16}$)	4	0	**18**(1/0/0)	**20**(1/2/0)
([d$_{32}$,B],d$_{32}$)	4	0	**18**(1/0/0)	**20**(1/3/0)
([d$_{32}$,B],I,d$_{32}$)	4	0	**18**(1/0/0)	**20**(1/3/0)

B = Base address; 0, An, PC, Xn, An + Xn, PC + Xn. Form does not affect timing.
I = Index; 0, Xn
% = No clock cycles incurred by effective address calculation.

NOTE: Xn cannot be in B and I at the same time. Scaling and size of Xn do not affect timing.

11.6.4 Calculate Immediate Effective Address (ciea)

The calculate immediate effective address table indicates the number of clock periods needed for the processor to fetch the immediate source operand and calculate the specified destination effective address. In the case of two-word instructions, this table indicates the number of clock periods needed for the processor to fetch the second word of the instruction and calculate the specified source operand or single operand. Fetch time is only included for the first level of indirection on memory indirect addressing modes. The effective addresses are divided by their formats (refer to **2.5 Effective Address Encoding Summary**). For instruction-cache case and for no-cache case, the total number of clock cycles is outside the parentheses. The number of read, prefetch, and write cycles is given inside the parentheses as (r/p/w). The read, prefetch, and write cycles are included in the total clock cycle number.

All timing data assumes two-clock reads and writes.

Address Mode	Head	Tail	I-Cache Case	No-Cache Case

SINGLE EFFECTIVE ADDRESS INSTRUCTION FORMAT

Address Mode	Head	Tail	I-Cache Case	No-Cache Case
% #⟨data⟩.W,Dn	2 + op head	0	**2**(0/0/0)	**2**(0/1/0)
% #⟨data⟩.L,Dn	4 + op head	0	**4**(0/0/0)	**4**(0/1/0)
% #⟨data⟩.W,(An)	2 + op head	0	**2**(0/0/0)	**2**(0/1/0)
% #⟨data⟩.L,(An)	4 + op head	0	**4**(0/0/0)	**4**(0/1/0)
#⟨data⟩.W,(An) +	2	0	**4**(0/0/0)	**4**(0/1/0)
#⟨data⟩.L,(An) +	4	0	**6**(0/0/0)	**6**(0/1/0)
% #⟨data⟩.W, − (An)	2 + op head	0	**2**(0/0/0)	**2**(0/1/0)
% #⟨data⟩.L, − (An)	4 + op head	0	**4**(0/0/0)	**4**(0/1/0)
% #⟨data⟩.W,(d_{16},An)	4 + op head	0	**4**(0/0/0)	**4**(0/1/0)
% #⟨data⟩.L,(d_{16},An)	6 + op head	0	**6**(0/0/0)	**7**(0/2/0)
% #⟨data⟩.W,$XXX.W	4 + op head	0	**4**(0/0/0)	**4**(0/1/0)
% #⟨data⟩.L,$XXX.W	6 + op head	0	**6**(0/0/0)	**6**(0/2/0)
% #⟨data⟩.W,$XXX.L	6 + op head	0	**6**(0/0/0)	**6**(0/2/0)
% #⟨data⟩.L,$XXX.L	8 + op head	0	**8**(0/0/0)	**8**(0/2/0)

BRIEF FORMAT EXTENSION WORD

Address Mode	Head	Tail	I-Cache Case	No-Cache Case
% #⟨data⟩.W,(d_8,An,Xn) or (d_8,PC,Xn)	6 + op head	0	**6**(0/0/0)	**6**(0/2/0)
% #⟨data⟩.L,(d_8,An,Xn) or (d_8,PC,Xn)	8 + op head	0	**8**(0/0/0)	**8**(0/2/0)

FULL FORMAT EXTENSION WORD(S)

Address Mode	Head	Tail	I-Cache Case	No-Cache Case
#⟨data⟩.W,(d_{16},An) or (d_{16},PC)	4	0	**8**(0/0/0)	**8**(0/2/0)
#⟨data⟩.L,(d_{16},An) or (d_{16},PC)	6	0	**10**(0/0/0)	**10**(0/2/0)
% #⟨data⟩.W,(d_{16},An,Xn) or (d_{16},PC,Xn)	8 + op head	0	**8**(0/0/0)	**8**(0/2/0)
% #⟨data⟩.L,(d_{16},An,Xn) or (d_{16},PC,Xn)	10 + op head	0	**10**(0/0/0)	**10**(0/2/0)
#⟨data⟩.W,([d_{16},An]) or ([d_{16},PC])	4	0	**12**(1/0/0)	**12**(1/2/0)
#⟨data⟩.L,([d_{16},An]) or ([d_{16},PC])	6	0	**14**(1/0/0)	**14**(1/1/0)
#⟨data⟩.W,([d_{16},An],Xn) or ([d_{16},PC],Xn)	4	0	**12**(1/0/0)	**12**(1/2/0)
#⟨data⟩.L,([d_{16},An],Xn) or ([d_{16},PC],Xn)	6	0	**14**(1/0/0)	**14**(1/1/0)
#⟨data⟩.W,([d_{16},An],d_{16}) or ([d_{16},PC],d_{16})	4	0	**14**(1/0/0)	**15**(1/2/0)
#⟨data⟩.L,([d_{16},An],d_{16}) or ([d_{16},PC],d_{16})	6	0	**16**(1/0/0)	**17**(1/3/0)
#⟨data⟩.W,([d_{16},An],Xn,d_{16}) or ([d_{16},PC],Xn,d_{16})	4	0	**14**(1/0/0)	**15**(1/2/0)
#⟨data⟩.L,([d_{16},An],Xn,d_{16}) or ([d_{16},PC],Xn,d_{16})	6	0	**16**(1/0/0)	**17**(1/3/0)
#⟨data⟩.W,([d_{16},An],d_{32}) or ([d_{16},PC],d_{32})	4	0	**14**(1/0/0)	**16**(1/3/0)
#⟨data⟩.L,([d_{16},An],d_{32}) or ([d_{16},PC],d_{32})	6	0	**16**(1/0/0)	**17**(1/3/0)
#⟨data⟩.W,([d_{16},An],Xn,d_{32}) or ([d_{16},PC],Xn,d_{32})	4	0	**14**(1/0/0)	**15**(1/3/0)
#⟨data⟩.L,([d_{16},An],Xn,d_{32}) or ([d_{16},PC],Xn,d_{32})	6	0	**16**(1/0/0)	**17**(1/3/0)
% #⟨data⟩.W,(B)	8 + op head	0	**8**(0/0/0)	**8**(0/1/0)
% #⟨data⟩.L,(B)	10 + op head	0	**10**(0/0/0)	**10**(0/2/0)

11

11.6.4 Calculate Immediate Effective Address (ciea) (Continued)

Address Mode	Head	Tail	I-Cache Case	No-Cache Case
FULL FORMAT EXTENSION WORD(S) (CONTINUED)				
#⟨data⟩.W,(d$_{16}$,B)	6	0	**10**(0/0/0)	**11**(0/2/0)
#⟨data⟩.L,(d$_{16}$,B)	8	0	**12**(0/0/0)	**13**(0/2/0)
#⟨data⟩.W,(d$_{32}$,B)	6	0	**14**(0/0/0)	**15**(0/2/0)
#⟨data⟩.L,(d$_{32}$,B)	8	0	**16**(0/0/0)	**17**(0/3/0)
#⟨data⟩.W,([B])	6	0	**12**(1/0/0)	**12**(1/1/0)
#⟨data⟩.L,([B])	8	0	**14**(1/0/0)	**14**(1/2/0)
#⟨data⟩.W,([B],I)	6	0	**12**(1/0/0)	**12**(1/1/0)
#⟨data⟩.L,([B],I)	8	0	**14**(1/0/0)	**14**(1/2/0)
#⟨data⟩.W,([B],d$_{16}$)	6	0	**14**(1/0/0)	**15**(1/2/0)
#⟨data⟩.L,([B],d$_{16}$)	8	0	**16**(1/0/0)	**17**(1/2/0)
#⟨data⟩.W,([B],I,d$_{16}$)	6	0	**14**(1/0/0)	**15**(1/2/0)
#⟨data⟩.L,([B],I,d$_{16}$)	8	0	**16**(2/0/0)	**17**(1/2/0)
#⟨data⟩.W,([B],d$_{32}$)	6	0	**14**(1/0/0)	**15**(1/2/0)
#⟨data⟩.L,([B],d$_{32}$)	8	0	**16**(1/0/0)	**17**(1/3/0)
#⟨data⟩.W,([B],I,d$_{32}$)	6	0	**14**(1/0/0)	**15**(1/2/0)
#⟨data⟩.L,([B],I,d$_{32}$)	8	0	**16**(1/0/0)	**17**(1/3/0)
#⟨data⟩.W,([d$_{16}$,B])	6	0	**14**(1/0/0)	**15**(1/2/0)
#⟨data⟩.L,([d$_{16}$,B])	8	0	**16**(1/0/0)	**17**(1/2/0)
#⟨data⟩.W,([d$_{16}$,B],I)	6	0	**14**(1/0/0)	**15**(1/2/0)
#⟨data⟩.L,([d$_{16}$,B],I)	8	0	**16**(1/0/0)	**17**(1/2/0)
#⟨data⟩.W,([d$_{16}$,B],d$_{16}$)	6	0	**16**(1/0/0)	**18**(1/2/0)
#⟨data⟩.L,([d$_{16}$,B],d$_{16}$)	8	0	**18**(1/0/0)	**20**(1/3/0)
#⟨data⟩.W,([d$_{16}$,B],I,d$_{16}$)	6	0	**16**(1/0/0)	**18**(1/2/0)
#⟨data⟩.L,([d$_{16}$,B],I,d$_{16}$)	8	0	**18**(1/0/0)	**20**(1/3/0)
#⟨data⟩.W,([d$_{16}$,B],d$_{32}$)	6	0	**16**(1/0/0)	**18**(1/3/0)
#⟨data⟩.L,([d$_{16}$,B],d$_{32}$)	8	0	**18**(1/0/0)	**20**(1/3/0)
#⟨data⟩.W,([d$_{16}$,B],I,d$_{32}$)	6	0	**16**(1/0/0)	**18**(1/3/0)
#⟨data⟩.L,([d$_{16}$,B],I,d$_{32}$)	8	0	**18**(1/0/0)	**20**(1/3/0)
#⟨data⟩.W,([d$_{32}$,B])	6	0	**18**(1/0/0)	**19**(1/2/0)
#⟨data⟩.L,([d$_{32}$,B])	8	0	**20**(1/0/0)	**21**(1/3/0)
#⟨data⟩.W,([d$_{32}$,B],I)	6	0	**18**(1/0/0)	**19**(1/2/0)
#⟨data⟩.L,([d$_{32}$,B],I)	8	0	**20**(1/0/0)	**21**(1/3/0)
#⟨data⟩.W,([d$_{32}$,B],d$_{16}$)	6	0	**20**(1/0/0)	**22**(1/3/0)
#⟨data⟩.L,([d$_{32}$,B],d$_{16}$)	8	0	**22**(1/0/0)	**24**(1/3/0)
#⟨data⟩.W,([d$_{32}$,B],I,d$_{16}$)	6	0	**20**(1/0/0)	**22**(1/3/0)
#⟨data⟩.L,([d$_{32}$,B],I,d$_{16}$)	8	0	**22**(1/0/0)	**24**(1/3/0)

11.6.4 Calculate Immediate Effective Address (ciea) (Continued)

Address Mode	Head	Tail	I-Cache Case	No-Cache Case

FULL FORMAT EXTENSION WORD(S) (CONTINUED)

Address Mode	Head	Tail	I-Cache Case	No-Cache Case
#⟨data⟩.W,([d$_{32}$,B],d$_{32}$)	6	0	**20**(1/0/0)	**22**(1/3/0)
#⟨data⟩.L,([d$_{32}$,B],d$_{32}$)	8	0	**22**(1/0/0)	**24**(1/4/0)
#⟨data⟩.W,([d$_{32}$,B],I,d$_{32}$)	6	0	**20**(1/0/0)	**22**(1/3/0)
#⟨data⟩.L,([d$_{32}$,B],I,d$_{32}$)	8	0	**22**(1/0/0)	**24**(1/4/0)

B = Base address; 0, An, PC, Xn, An + Xn, PC + Xn. Form does not affect timing.
I = Index; 0, Xn
% = Total head for address timing includes the head time for the operation.

NOTE: Xn cannot be in B and I at the same time. Scaling and size of Xn do not affect timing.

11.6.5 Jump Effective Address

The jump effective address table indicates the number of clock periods needed for the processor to calculate the specified effective address for the JMP or JSR instructions. Fetch time is only included for the first level of indirection on memory indirect addressing modes. The effective addresses are divided by their formats (refer to **2.5 Effective Address Encoding Summary**). For instruction-cache case and for no-cache case, the total number of clock cycles is outside the parentheses. The number of read, prefetch, and write cycles is given inside the parentheses as (r/p/w). The read, prefetch, and write cycles are included in the total clock cycle number.

All timing data assumes two-clock reads and writes.

Address Mode	Head	Tail	I-Cache Case	No-Cache Case

SINGLE EFFECTIVE ADDRESS INSTRUCTION FORMAT

Address Mode	Head	Tail	I-Cache Case	No-Cache Case
% (An)	2 + op head	0	**2**(0/0/0)	**2**(0/0/0)
% (d$_{16}$,An)	4 + op head	0	**4**(0/0/0)	**4**(0/0/0)
% (xxx).W	2 + op head	0	**2**(0/0/0)	**2**(0/0/0)
% (xxx).L	2 + op head	0	**2**(0/0/0)	**2**(0/0/0)

BRIEF FORMAT EXTENSION WORD

Address Mode	Head	Tail	I-Cache Case	No-Cache Case
% (d$_8$,An,Xn) or (d$_8$,PC,Xn)	6 + op head	0	**6**(0/0/0)	**6**(0/0/0)

11

Address Mode	Head	Tail	I-Cache Case	No-Cache Case

FULL FORMAT EXTENSION WORD(S) (CONTINUED)

Address Mode	Head	Tail	I-Cache Case	No-Cache Case
(d_{16},An) or (d_{16},PC)	2	0	**6**(0/0/0)	**6**(0/0/0)
% (d_{16},An,Xn) or (d_{16},PC,Xn)	6 + op head	0	**6**(0/0/0)	**6**(0/0/0)
$([d_{16},An])$ or $([d_{16},PC])$	2	0	**10**(1/0/0)	**10**(1/1/0)
$([d_{16},An],Xn)$ or $([d_{16},PC],Xn)$	2	0	**10**(1/0/0)	**10**(1/1/0)
$([d_{16},An],d_{16})$ or $([d_{16},PC],d_{16})$	2	0	**12**(1/0/0)	**12**(1/1/0)
$([d_{16},An],Xn,d_{16})$ or $([d_{16},PC],Xn,d_{16})$	2	0	**12**(1/0/0)	**12**(1/1/0)
$([d_{16},An],d_{32})$ or $([d_{16},PC],d_{32})$	2	0	**12**(1/0/0)	**12**(1/1/0)
$([d_{16},An],Xn,d_{32})$ or $([d_{16},PC],Xn,d_{32})$	2	0	**12**(1/0/0)	**12**(1/1/0)
% (B)	6 + op head	0	**6**(0/0/0)	**6**(0/0/0)
(d_{16},B)	4	0	**8**(0/0/0)	**9**(0/1/0)
(d_{32},B)	4	0	**12**(0/0/0)	**13**(0/1/0)
([B])	4	0	**10**(1/0/0)	**10**(1/1/0)
([B],I)	4	0	**10**(1/0/0)	**10**(1/1/0)
$([B],d_{16})$	4	0	**12**(1/0/0)	**12**(1/1/0)
$([B],I,d_{16})$	4	0	**12**(1/0/0)	**12**(1/1/0)
$([B],d_{32})$	4	0	**12**(1/0/0)	**12**(1/1/0)
$([B],d_{32})$	4	0	**12**(1/0/0)	**12**(1/1/0)
$([B],I,d_{32})$	4	0	**12**(1/0/0)	**12**(1/1/0)
$([d_{16},B])$	4	0	**12**(1/0/0)	**13**(1/1/0)
$([d_{16},B],I)$	4	0	**12**(1/0/0)	**13**(1/1/0)
$([d_{16},B],d_{16})$	4	0	**14**(1/0/0)	**15**(1/1/0)
$([d_{16},B],I,d_{16})$	4	0	**14**(1/0/0)	**15**(1/1/0)
$([d_{16},B],d_{32})$	4	0	**14**(1/0/0)	**15**(1/1/0)
$([d_{16},B],I,d_{32})$	4	0	**14**(1/0/0)	**15**(1/1/0)
$([d_{32},B])$	4	0	**16**(1/0/0)	**17**(1/2/0)
$([d_{32},B],I)$	4	0	**16**(1/0/0)	**17**(1/2/0)
$([d_{32},B],d_{16})$	4	0	**18**(1/0/0)	**19**(1/2/0)
$([d_{32},B],I,d_{16})$	4	0	**18**(1/0/0)	**19**(1/2/0)
$([d_{32},B],d_{32})$	4	0	**18**(1/0/0)	**19**(1/2/0)
$([d_{32},B],I,d_{32})$	4	0	**18**(1/0/0)	**19**(1/2/0)

B = Base address; 0, An, PC, Xn, An + Xn, PC + Xn. Form does not affect timing.
I = Index; 0, Xn
% = Total head for effective address timing includes the head time for the operation.

NOTE: Xn cannot be in B and I at the same time. Scaling and size of Xn do not affect timing.

11

11.6.6 MOVE Instruction

The MOVE instruction timing table indicates the number of clock periods needed for the processor to calculate the destination effective address and perform the MOVE or MOVEA instruction, including the first level of indirection on memory indirect addressing modes. The fetch effective address table is needed on most MOVE operations (source, destination dependent). The destination effective addresses are divided by their formats (refer to **2.5 Effective Address Encoding Summary**). For instruction-cache case and for no-cache case, the total number of clock cycles is outside the parentheses. The number of read, prefetch, and write cycles is given inside the parentheses as (r/p/w). The read, prefetch, and write cycles are included in the total clock cycle number.

All timing data assumes two-clock reads and writes.

MOVE Source,Destination	Head	Tail	I-Cache Case	No-Cache Case
SINGLE EFFECTIVE ADDRESS INSTRUCTION FORMAT				
MOVE Rn, Dn	2	0	2(0/0/0)	2(0/1/0)
MOVE Rn, An	2	0	2(0/0/0)	2(0/1/0)
* MOVE EA,An	0	0	2(0/0/0)	2(0/1/0)
* MOVE EA,Dn	0	0	2(0/0/0)	2(0/1/0)
MOVE Rn,(An)	0	1	3(0/0/1)	4(0/1/1)
* MOVE SOURCE, (An)	2	0	4(0/0/1)	5(0/1/1)
MOVE Rn,(An)+	0	1	3(0/0/1)	4(0/1/1)
* MOVE SOURCE, (An)+	2	0	4(0/0/1)	5(0/1/1)
MOVE Rn,−(An)	0	2	4(0/0/1)	4(0/1/1)
* MOVE SOURCE, −(An)	2	0	4(0/0/1)	5(0/1/1)
* MOVE EA, (d_{16},An)	2	0	4(0/0/1)	5(0/1/1)
* MOVE EA,XXX.W	2	0	4(0/0/1)	5(0/1/1)
* MOVE EA,XXX.L	0	0	6(0/0/1)	7(0/2/1)
BRIEF FORMAT EXTENSION WORD				
* MOVE EA, (d_8,An,Xn)	4	0	6(0/0/1)	7(0/1/1)

11

11.6.6 MOVE Instruction (Continued)

MOVE Source,Destination	Head	Tail	I-Cache Case	No-Cache Case

FULL FORMAT EXTENSION WORD(S)

MOVE Source,Destination	Head	Tail	I-Cache Case	No-Cache Case
* MOVE EA, (d_{16},An) or (d_{16},PC)	2	0	8(0/0/1)	9(0/2/1)
* MOVE EA, (d_{16},An,Xn) or (d_{16},PC,Xn)	2	0	8(0/0/1)	9(0/2/1)
* MOVE EA, $([d_{16},An],Xn)$ or $([d_{16},PC],Xn)$	2	0	10(1/0/1)	11(1/2/1)
* MOVE EA,$([d_{16},An],d_{16})$ or $([d_{16},PC],d_{16})$	2	0	12(1/0/1)	14(1/2/1)
* MOVE EA,$([d_{16},An],Xn,d_{16})$ or $([d_{16},PC],Xn,d_{16})$	2	0	12(1/0/1)	14(1/2/1)
* MOVE EA,$([d_{16},An],d_{32})$ or $([d_{16},PC],d_{32})$	2	0	14(1/0/1)	16(1/3/1)
* MOVE EA,$([d_{16},An],Xn,d_{32})$ or $([d_{16},PC],Xn,d_{32})$	2	0	14(1/0/1)	16(1/3/1)
* MOVE EA,(B)	4	0	8(0/0/1)	9(0/1/1)
* MOVE EA,(d_{16},B)	4	0	10(0/0/1)	12(0/2/1)
* MOVE EA,(d_{32},B)	4	0	14(0/0/1)	16(0/2/1)
* MOVE EA,([B])	4	0	10(1/0/1)	11(1/1/1)
* MOVE EA,([B],I)	4	0	10(1/0/1)	11(1/1/1)
* MOVE EA,$([B],d_{16})$	4	0	12(1/0/1)	14(1/2/1)
* MOVE EA,$([B],I,d_{16})$	4	0	12(1/0/1)	14(1/2/1)
* MOVE EA,$([B],d_{32})$	4	0	14(1/0/1)	16(1/2/1)
* MOVE EA,$([B],I,d_{32})$	4	0	14(1/0/1)	16(1/2/1)
* MOVE EA,$([d_{16},B])$	4	0	12(1/0/1)	14(1/2/1)
* MOVE EA,$([d_{16},B],I)$	4	0	12(1/0/1)	14(1/2/1)
* MOVE EA,$([d_{16},B],d_{16})$	4	0	14(1/0/1)	17(1/2/1)
* MOVE EA,$([d_{16},B],I,d_{16})$	4	0	14(1/0/1)	17(1/2/1)
* MOVE EA,$([d_{16},B],d_{32})$	4	0	16(1/0/1)	19(1/3/1)
* MOVE EA,$([d_{16},B],I,d_{32})$	4	0	16(1/0/1)	19(1/3/1)
* MOVE EA,$([d_{32},B])$	4	0	16(1/0/1)	18(1/2/1)
* MOVE EA,$([d_{32},B],I)$	4	0	16(1/0/1)	18(1/2/1)
* MOVE EA,$([d_{32},B],d_{16})$	4	0	18(1/0/1)	21(1/3/1)
* MOVE EA,$([d_{32},B],I,d_{16})$	4	0	18(1/0/1)	21(1/3/1)
* MOVE EA,$([d_{32},B],d_{32})$	4	0	20(1/0/1)	23(1/3/1)
* MOVE EA,$([d_{32},B],I,d_{32})$	4	0	20(1/0/1)	23(1/3/1)

*   Add Fetch Effective Address Time   SOURCE Is Memory or Immediate Data Address Mode
Rn Is a Data or Address Register   EA   Is any Effective Address

11.6.7 Special-Purpose MOVE Instruction

The special-purpose MOVE timing table indicates the number of clock periods needed for the processor to fetch, calculate, and perform the special-purpose MOVE operation on the control registers or specified effective address. Footnotes indicate when to account for the appropriate effective address times. The total number of clock cycles is outside the parentheses. The number of read, prefetch, and write cycles is given inside the parentheses as (r/p/w). The read, prefetch, and write cycles are included in the total clock cycle number.

All timing data assumes two-clock reads and writes.

	Instruction		Head	Tail	I-Cache Case	No-Cache Case
	EXG	Ry,Rx	4	0	**4**(0/0/0)	**4**(0/1/0)
	MOVEC	Cr,Rn	6	0	**6**(0/0/0)	**6**(0/1/0)
	MOVEC	Rn,Cr − A	6	0	**6**(0/0/0)	**6**(0/1/0)
	MOVEC	Rn,Cr − B	4	0	**12**(0/0/0)	**12**(0/1/0)
	MOVE	CCR,Dn	2	0	**4**(0/0/0)	**4**(0/1/0)
*	MOVE	CCR,Mem	2	0	**4**(0/0/1)	**5**(0/1/1)
	MOVE	Dn,CCR	4	0	**4**(0/0/0)	**4**(0/1/0)
*	MOVE	EA,CCR	0	0	**4**(0/0/0)	**4**(0/1/0)
	MOVE	SR,Dn	2	0	**4**(0/0/0)	**4**(0/1/0)
*	MOVE	SR,Mem	2	0	**4**(0/0/1)	**5**(0/1/1)
#	MOVE	EA,SR	0	0	**8**(0/0/0)	**10**(0/2/0)
% +	MOVEM	EA,RL	2	0	$\mathbf{8+4n}$(n/0/0)	$\mathbf{8+4n}$(n/1/0)
% +	MOVEM	RL,EA	2	0	$\mathbf{4+2n}$(0/0/n)	$\mathbf{4+2n}$(0/1/n)
	MOVEP.W	Dn,(d_{16},An)	4	0	**10**(0/0/2)	**10**(0/1/2)
	MOVEP.W	(d_{16},An),Dn	2	0	**10**(2/0/0)	**10**(2/1/0)
	MOVEP.L	Dn,(d_{16},An)	4	0	**14**(0/0/4)	**14**(0/1/4)
	MOVEP.L	(d_{16},An),Dn	2	0	**14**(4/0/0)	**14**(4/1/0)
%	MOVES	EA,Rn	3	0	**7**(1/0/0)	**7**(1/1/0)
%	MOVES	Rn,EA	2	1	**5**(0/0/1)	**6**(0/1/1)
	MOVE	USP,An	4	0	**4**(0/0/0)	**4**(0/1/0)
	MOVE	An,USP	4	0	**4**(0/0/0)	**4**(0/1/0)
	SWAP	Dn	4	0	**4**(0/0/0)	**4**(0/1/0)

CR − A Control Registers USP, VBR, CAAR, MSP, and ISP
CR − B Control Registers SFC, DFC, and CACR
n   Number of Register to Transfer (n>0)
RL   Register List
*   Add Calculate Effective Address Time
\#   Add Fetch Effective Address Time
%   Add Calculate Immediate Address Time

\+   MOVEM EA,RL — For n Registers (n > 0) and w Wait States
      I-Cache Case Timing = $w \leqslant 2$: $(8+4n)$
                          $w > 2$: $(8+4n)+(w-2)n$
    Tail = 0 for all Wait States
    MOVEM RL,EA — For n Registers (n > 0) and w Wait States
      I-Cache Case Timing = $w \leqslant 2$: $(4+2n)+(n-1)w$
                          $w > 2$: $(4+2n)+(n-1)w+(w-2)$
        Tail = $w \leqslant 2$: $(n-1)w$
                 $w > 2$: $(n)w+(n)(w-2)$

11

11.6.8 Arithmetical/Logical Instructions

The arithmetical/logical operation timing table indicates the number of clock periods needed for the processor to perform the specified arithmetical/logical instruction using the specified addressing mode. Footnotes indicate when to account for the appropriate fetch effective address or fetch immediate effective address times. For instruction-cache case and for no-cache case, the total number of clock cycles is outside the parentheses. The number of read, prefetch, and write cycles is given inside the parentheses as (r/p/w). The read, prefetch, and write cycles are included in the total clock cycle number.

All timing data assumes two-clock reads and writes.

Instruction		Head	Tail	I-Cache Case	No-Cache Case
ADD	Rn,Dn	2	0	2(0/0/0)	2(0/1/0)
ADDA.W	Rn,An	4	0	4(0/0/0)	4(0/1/0)
ADDA.L	Rn,An	2	0	2(0/0/0)	2(0/1/0)
* ADD	EA,Dn	0	0	2(0/0/0)	2(0/1/0)
* ADD.W	EA,An	0	0	4(0/0/0)	4(0/1/0)
* ADDA.L	EA,An	0	0	2(0/0/0)	2(0/1/0)
* ADD	Dn,EA	0	1	3(0/0/1)	4(0/1/1)
AND	Dn,Dn	2	0	2(0/0/0)	2(0/1/0)
* AND	EA,Dn	0	0	2(0/0/0)	2(0/1/0)
* AND	Dn,EA	0	1	3(0/0/1)	4(0/1/1)
EOR	Dn,Dn	2	0	2(0/0/0)	2(0/1/0)
* EOR	Dn,EA	0	1	3(0/0/1)	4(0/1/1)
OR	Dn,Dn	2	0	2(0/0/0)	2(0/1/0)
* OR	EA,Dn	0	0	2(0/0/0)	2(0/1/0)
* OR	Dn,EA	0	1	3(0/0/1)	4(0/1/1)
SUB	Rn,Dn	2	0	2(0/0/0)	2(0/1/0)
* SUB	EA,Dn	0	0	2(0/0/0)	2(0/1/0)

11

11.6.8 Arithmetical/Logical Instructions (Continued)

	Instruction		Head	Tail	I-Cache Case	No-Cache Case
*	SUB	Dn,EA	0	1	3(0/0/1)	4(0/1/1)
	SUBA.W	Rn,An	4	0	4(0/0/0)	4(0/1/0)
	SUBA.L	Rn,An	2	0	2(0/0/0)	2(0/1/0)
*	SUBA.W	EA,An	0	0	4(0/0/0)	4(0/1/0)
*	SUBA.L	EA,An	0	0	2(0/0/0)	2(0/1/0)
	CMP	Rn,Dn	2	0	2(0/0/0)	2(0/1/0)
*	CMP	EA,Dn	0	0	2(0/0/0)	2(0/1/0)
	CMPA	Rn,An	4	0	4(0/0/0)	4(0/1/0)
*	CMPA	EA,An	0	0	4(0/0/0)	4(0/1/0)
** +	CMP2	EA,Rn	2	0	20(1/0/0)	20(1/1/0)
* +	MULS.W	EA,Dn	2	0	28(0/0/0)	28(0/1/0)
** +	MULS.L	EA,Dn	2	0	44(0/0/0)	44(0/1/0)
* +	MULU.W	EA,Dn	2	0	28(0/0/0)	28(0/1/0)
** +	MULU.L	EA,Dn	2	0	44(0/0/0)	44(0/1/0)
+	DIVS.W	Dn,Dn	2	0	56(0/0/0)	56(0/1/0)
* +	DIVS.W	EA,Dn	0	0	56(0/0/0)	56(0/1/0)
** +	DIVS.L	Dn,Dn	6	0	90(0/0/0)	90(0/1/0)
** +	DIVS.L	EA,Dn	0	0	90(0/0/0)	90(0/1/0)
+	DIVU.W	Dn,Dn	2	0	44(0/0/0)	44(0/1/0)
* +	DIVU.W	EA,Dn	0	0	44(0/0/0)	44(0/1/0)
** +	DIVU.L	Dn,Dn	6	0	78(0/0/0)	78(0/1/0)
** +	DIVU.L	EA,Dn	0	0	78(0/0/0)	78(0/1/0)

*Add Fetch Effective Address Time
**Add Fetch Immediate Effective Address Time
+Indicates Maximum Time (Acutal time is data dependent)

11

11.6.9 Immediate Arithmetical/Logical Instructions

The immediate arithmetical/logical operation timing table indicates the number of clock periods needed for the processor to fetch the source immediate data value and to perform the specified arithmetic/logical operation using the specified destination addressing mode. Footnotes indicate when to account for the appropriate fetch effective or fetch immediate effective address times. For instruction-cache case and for no-cache case, the total number of clock cycles is outside the parentheses. The number of read, prefetch, and write cycles is given inside the parentheses as (r/p/w). The read, prefetch, and write cycles are included in the total clock cycle number.

All timing data assumes two-clock reads and writes.

Instruction		Head	Tail	I-Cache Case	No-Cache Case
MOVEQ	#⟨data⟩,Dn	2	0	2(0/0/0)	2(0/1/0)
ADDQ	#⟨data⟩,Rn	2	0	2(0/0/0)	2(0/1/0)
* ADDQ	#⟨data⟩,Mem	0	1	3(0/0/1)	4(0/1/1)
SUBQ	#⟨data⟩,Rn	2	0	2(0/0/0)	2(0/1/0)
* SUBQ	#⟨data⟩,Mem	0	1	3(0/0/1)	4(0/1/1)
** ADDI	#⟨data⟩,Dn	2	0	2(0/0/0)	2(0/1/0)
** ADDI	#⟨data⟩,Mem	0	1	3(0/0/1)	4(0/1/1)
** ANDI	#⟨data⟩,Dn	2	0	2(0/0/0)	2(0/1/0)
** ANDI	#⟨data⟩,Mem	0	1	3(0/0/1)	4(0/1/1)
** EORI	#⟨data⟩,Dn	2	0	2(0/0/0)	2(0/1/0)
** EORI	#⟨data⟩,Mem	0	1	3(0/0/1)	4(0/1/1)
** ORI	#⟨data⟩,Dn	2	0	2(0/0/0)	2(0/1/0)
** ORI	#⟨data⟩,Mem	0	1	3(0/0/1)	4(0/1/1)
** SUBI	#⟨data⟩,Dn	2	0	2(0/0/0)	2(0/1/0)
** SUBI	#⟨data⟩,Mem	0	1	3(0/0/1)	4(0/1/1)
** CMPI	#⟨data⟩,Dn	2	0	2(0/0/0)	2(0/1/0)
** CMPI	#⟨data⟩,Mem	0	0	2(0/0/0)	2(0/1/0)

*Add Fetch Effective Address Time
**Add Fetch Immediate Effective Address Time

11

11.6.10 Binary-Coded Decimal and Extended Instructions

The binary-coded decimal and extended instruction table indicates the number of clock periods needed for the processor to perform the specified operation using the given addressing modes. No additional tables are needed to calculate total effective execution time for these instructions. For instruction-cache case and for no-cache case, the total number of clock cycles is outside the parentheses. The number of read, prefetch, and write cycles is given inside the parentheses as (r/p/w). The read, prefetch, and write cycles are included in the total clock cycle number.

All timing data assumes two-clock reads and writes.

Instruction		Head	Tail	I-Cache Case	No-Cache Case
ABCD	Dn,Dn	0	0	**4**(0/0/0)	**4**(0/1/0)
ABCD	−(An),−(An)	2	1	**13**(2/0/1)	**14**(2/1/1)
SBCD	Dn,Dn	0	0	**4**(0/0/0)	**4**(0/1/0)
SBCD	−(An),−(An)	2	1	**13**(2/0/1)	**14**(2/1/1)
ADDX	Dn,Dn	2	0	**2**(0/0/0)	**2**(0/1/0)
ADDX	−(An),−(An)	2	1	**9**(2/0/1)	**10**(2/1/1)
SUBX	Dn,Dn	2	0	**2**(0/0/0)	**2**(0/1/0)
SUBX	−(An),−(An)	2	1	**9**(2/0/1)	**10**(2/1/1)
CMPM	(An)+,(An)+	0	0	**8**(2/0/0)	**8**(2/1/0)
PACK	Dn,Dn,#⟨data⟩	6	0	**6**(0/0/0)	**6**(0/1/0)
PACK	−(An),−(An),#⟨data⟩	2	1	**11**(1/0/1)	**11**(1/1/1)
UNPK	Dn,Dn,#⟨data⟩	8	0	**8**(0/0/0)	**8**(0/1/0)
UNPK	−(An),−(An),#⟨data⟩	2	1	**11**(1/0/1)	**11**(1/1/1)

11

11.6.11 Single Operand Instructions

The single operand instruction table indicates the number of clock periods needed for the processor to perform the specified operation on the given addressing mode. Footnotes indicate when it is necessary to account for the appropriate effective address time. For instruction-cache case and for no-cache case, the total number of clock cycles is outside the parentheses. The number of read, prefetch, and write cycles is given inside the parentheses as (r/p/w). The read, prefetch, and write cycles are included in the total clock cycle number.

All timing data assumes two-clock reads and writes.

	Instruction		Head	Tail	I-Cache Case	No-Cache Case
	CLR	Dn	2	0	2(0/0/0)	2(0/1/0)
**	CLR	Mem	0	1	3(0/0/1)	4(0/1/1)
	NEG	Dn	2	0	2(0/0/0)	2(0/1/0)
*	NEG	Mem	0	1	3(0/0/1)	4(0/1/1)
	NEGX	Dn	2	0	2(0/0/0)	2(0/1/0)
*	NEGX	Mem	0	1	3(0/0/1)	4(0/1/1)
	NOT	Dn	2	0	2(0/0/0)	2(0/1/0)
*	NOT	Mem	0	1	3(0/0/1)	4(0/1/1)
	EXT	Dn	4	0	4(0/0/0)	4(0/1/0)
	NBCD	Dn	0	0	6(0/0/0)	6(0/1/0)
	Scc	Dn	4	0	4(0/0/0)	4(0/1/0)
**	Scc	Mem	0	1	5(0/0/1)	5(0/1/1)
	TAS	Dn	4	0	4(0/0/0)	4(0/1/0)
**	TAS	Mem	3	0	12(1/0/1)	12(1/1/1)
	TST	Dn	0	0	2(0/0/0)	2(0/1/0)
*	TST	Mem	0	0	2(0/0/0)	2(0/1/0)

*Add Fetch Effective Address Time
**Add Calculate Effective Address Time

11

MC68030 USER'S MANUAL   MOTOROLA

11.6.12 Shift/Rotate Instructions

The shift/rotate instruction table indicates the number of clock periods needed for the processor to perform the specified operation on the given addressing mode. Footnotes indicate when it is necessary to account for the appropriate effective address time. The number of bits shifted does not affect the execution time, unless noted. For instruction-cache case and for no-cache case, the total number of clock cycles is outside the parentheses. The number of read, prefetch, and write cycles is given inside the parentheses as (r/p/w). The read, prefetch, and write cycles are included in the total clock cycle number.

All timing data assumes two-clock reads and writes.

	Instruction		Head	Tail	I-Cache Case	No-Cache Case
	LSd	#⟨data⟩,Dy	4	0	4(0/0/0)	4(0/1/0)
%	LSd	Dx,Dy	6	0	6(0/0/0)	6(0/1/0)
+	LSd	Dx,Dy	8	0	8(0/0/0)	8(0/1/0)
*	LSd	Mem by 1	0	0	4(0/0/1)	4(0/1/1)
	ASL	#⟨data⟩,Dy	2	0	6(0/0/0)	6(0/1/0)
	ASL	Dx,Dy	4	0	8(0/0/0)	8(0/1/0)
*	ASL	Mem by 1	0	0	6(0/0/1)	6(0/1/1)
	ASR	#⟨data⟩,Dy	4	0	4(0/0/0)	4(0/1/0)
%	ASR	Dx,Dy	6	0	6(0/0/0)	6(0/1/0)
+	ASR	Dx,Dy	10	0	10(0/0/0)	10(0/1/0)
*	ASR	Mem by 1	0	0	4(0/0/1)	4(0/1/1)
	ROd	#⟨data⟩,Dy	4	0	6(0/0/0)	6(0/1/0)
	ROd	Dx,Dy	6	0	8(0/0/0)	8(0/1/0)
*	ROd	Mem by 1	0	0	6(0/0/1)	6(0/1/1)
	ROXd	Dn	10	0	12(0/0/0)	12(0/1/0)
*	ROXd	Mem by 1	0	0	4(0/0/0)	4(0/1/0)

d   Direction of shift/rotate: L or R
*   Add Fetch Effective Address Time
%   Indicates shift count is less than or equal to the size of data
+   Indicates shift count is greater than size of data

11

11.6.13 Bit Manipulation Instructions

The bit manipulation instruction table indicates the number of clock periods needed for the processor to perform the specified bit operation on the given addressing mode. Footnotes indicate when it is necessary to account for the appropriate effective address time. For instruction-cache case and for no-cache case, the total number of clock cycles is outside the parentheses. The number of read, prefetch, and write cycles is given inside the parentheses as (r/p/w). The read, prefetch, and write cycles are included in the total clock cycle number.

All timing data assumes two-clock reads and writes.

	Instruction		Head	Tail	I-Cache Case	No-Cache Case
	BTST	#⟨data⟩,Dn	4	0	4(0/0/0)	4(0/1/0)
	BTST	Dn,Dn	4	0	4(0/0/0)	4(0/1/0)
#	BTST	#⟨data⟩,Mem	0	0	4(0/0/0)	4(0/1/0)
*	BTST	Dn,Mem	0	0	4(0/0/0)	4(0/1/0)
	BCHG	#⟨data⟩,Dn	6	0	6(0/0/0)	6(0/1/0)
	BCHG	Dn,Dn	6	0	6(0/0/0)	6(0/1/0)
#	BCHG	#⟨data⟩,Mem	0	0	6(0/0/1)	6(0/1/1)
*	BCHG	Dn,Mem	0	0	6(0/0/1)	6(0/1/1)
	BCLR	#⟨data⟩,Dn	6	0	6(0/0/0)	6(0/1/0)
	BCLR	Dn,Dn	6	0	6(0/0/0)	6(0/1/0)
#	BCLR	#⟨data⟩,Mem	0	0	6(0/0/1)	6(0/1/1)
*	BCLR	Dn,Mem	0	0	6(0/0/1)	6(0/1/1)
	BSET	#⟨data⟩,Dn	6	0	6(0/0/0)	6(0/1/0)
	BSET	Dn,Dn	6	0	6(0/0/0)	6(0/1/0)
#	BSET	#⟨data⟩,Mem	0	0	6(0/0/1)	6(0/1/1)
*	BSET	Dn,Mem	0	0	6(0/0/1)	6(0/1/1)

*Add Fetch Effective Address Time
#Add Fetch Immediate Effective Address Time

11

11.6.14 Bit Field Manipulation Instructions

The bit field manipulation instruction table indicates the number of clock periods needed for the processor to perform the specified bit field operation using the given addressing mode. Footnotes indicate when it is necessary to account for the appropriate effective address time. For instruction-cache case and for no-cache case, the total number of clock cycles is outside the parentheses. The number of read, prefetch, and write cycles is given inside the parentheses as (r/p/w). The read, prefetch, and write cycles are included in the total clock cycle number.

All timing data assumes two-clock reads and writes.

Instruction		Head	Tail	I-Cache Case	No-Cache Case
BFTST	Dn	8	0	8(0/0/0)	8(0/1/0)
* BFTST	Mem (<5 Bytes)	6	0	10(1/0/0)	10(1/1/0)
* BFTST	Mem (5 Bytes)	6	0	14(2/0/0)	14(2/1/0)
BFCHG	Dn	14	0	14(0/0/0)	14(0/1/0)
* BFCHG	Mem (<5 Bytes)	6	0	14(1/0/1)	14(1/1/1)
* BFCHG	Mem (5 Bytes)	6	0	22(2/0/2)	22(2/1/2)
BFCLR	Dn	14	0	14(0/0/0)	14(0/1/0)
* BFCLR	Mem (<5 Bytes)	6	0	14(1/0/1)	14(1/1/1)
* BFCLR	Mem (5 Bytes)	6	0	22(2/0/2)	22(2/1/2)
BFSET	Dn	14	0	14(0/0/0)	14(0/1/0)
* BFSET	Mem (<5 Bytes)	6	0	14(1/0/1)	14(1/1/1)
* BFSET	Mem (5 Bytes)	6	0	22(2/0/2)	22(2/1/2)
BFEXTS	Dn	10	0	10(0/0/0)	10(0/1/0)
* BFEXTS	Mem (<5 Bytes)	6	0	12(1/0/0)	12(1/1/0)
* BFEXTS	Mem (5 Bytes)	6	0	18(2/0/0)	18(2/1/0)
BFEXTU	Dn	10	0	10(0/0/0)	10(0/1/0)
* BFEXTU	Mem (<5 Bytes)	6	0	12(1/0/0)	12(1/1/0)
* BFEXTU	Mem (5 Bytes)	6	0	18(2/0/0)	18(2/1/0)
BFINS	Dn	12	0	12(0/0/0)	12(0/1/0)
* BFINS	Mem (<5 Bytes)	6	0	12(1/0/1)	12(1/1/1)
* BFINS	Mem (5 Bytes)	6	0	18(2/0/2)	18(2/1/2)
BFFFO	Dn	20	0	20(0/0/0)	20(0/1/0)
* BFFFO	Mem (<5 Bytes)	6	0	22(1/0/0)	22(1/1/0)
* BFFFO	Mem (5 Bytes)	6	0	28(2/0/0)	28(2/1/0)

*Add Calculate Immediate Effective Address Time

NOTE: A bit field of 32 bits may span 5 bytes that require two operand cycles to access or may span 4 bytes that require only one operand cycle to access.

11

11.6.15 Conditional Branch Instructions

The conditional branch instruction table indicates the number of clock periods needed for the processor to perform the specified branch on the given branch size, with complete execution times given. No additional tables are needed to calculate total effective execution time for these instructions. For instruction-cache case and for no-cache case, the total number of clock cycles is outside the parenthees. The number of read, prefetch, and write cycles is given inside the parentheses as (r/p/w). The read, prefetch, and write cycles are included in the total clock cycle number.

All timing data assumes two-clock reads and writes.

Instruction		Head	Tail	I-Cache Case	No-Cache Case
Bcc	(Taken)	6	0	6(0/0/0)	8(0/2/0)
Bcc.B	(Not Taken)	4	0	4(0/0/0)	4(0/1/0)
Bcc.W	(Not Taken)	6	0	6(0/0/0)	6(0/1/0)
Bcc.L	(Not Taken)	6	0	6(0/0/0)	8(0/2/0)
DBcc	(cc = False, Count Not Expired)	6	0	6(0/0/0)	8(0/2/0)
DBcc	(cc = False, Count Expired)	10	0	10(0/0/0)	13(0/3/0)
DBcc	(cc = True)	6	0	6(0/0/0)	8(0/1/0)

MC68030 USER'S MANUAL

11.6.16 Control Instructions

The control instruction table indicates the number of clock periods needed for the processor to perform the specified operation. Footnotes indicate when it is necessary to account for the appropriate effective address time. For instruction-cache case and for no-cache case, the total number of clock cyclces is outside the parentheses. The number of read, prefetch, and write cycles is given inside the parentheses as (r/p/w). The read, prefetch, and write cycles are included in the total clock cycle number.

All timing data assumes two-clock reads and writes.

Instruction			Head	Tail	I-Cache Case	No-Cache Case
ANDI to SR			4	0	**12**(0/0/0)	**14**(0/2/0)
EORI to SR			4	0	**12**(0/0/0)	**14**(0/2/0)
ORI to SR			4	0	**12**(0/0/0)	**14**(0/2/0)
ANDI to CCR			4	0	**12**(0/0/0)	**14**(0/2/0)
EORI to CCR			4	0	**12**(0/0/0)	**14**(0/2/0)
ORI to CCR			4	0	**12**(0/0/0)	**14**(0/2/0)
BSR			2	0	**6**(0/0/1)	**9**(0/2/1)
## CAS		(Successful Compare)	1	0	**13**(1/0/1)	**13**(1/1/1)
## CAS		(Unsuccessful Compare)	1	0	**11**(1/0/0)	**11**(1/1/0)
+ CAS2		(Successful Compare)	2	0	**24**(2/0/2)	**26**(2/2/2)
+ CAS2		(Unsuccessful Compare)	2	0	**24**(2/0/0)	**24**(2/2/0)
CHK	Dn,Dn	(No Exception)	8	0	**8**(0/0/0)	**8**(0/1/0)
+ CHK	Dn,Dn	(Exception Taken)	4	0	**28**(1/0/4)	**30**(1/3/4)
* CHK	EA,Dn	(No Exception)	0	0	**8**(0/0/0)	**8**(0/1/0)
* + CHK	EA,Dn	(Exception Taken)	0	0	**28**(1/0/4)	**30**(1/3/4)
# + CHK2	Mem,Rn	(No Exception)	2	0	**18**(1/0/0)	**18**(1/1/0)
# + CHK2	Mem,Rn	(Exception Taken)	2	0	**40**(2/0/4)	**42**(2/3/4)
% JMP			4	0	**4**(0/0/0)	**6**(0/2/0)
% JSR			0	0	**4**(0/0/1)	**7**(0/2/1)
** LEA			2	0	**2**(0/0/0)	**2**(0/1/0)
LINK.W			0	0	**4**(0/0/1)	**5**(0/1/1)
LINK.L			2	0	**6**(0/0/1)	**7**(0/2/1)
NOP			0	0	**2**(0/0/0)	**2**(0/1/0)
** PEA			0	2	**4**(0/0/1)	**4**(0/1/1)
RTD			2	0	**10**(1/0/0)	**12**(1/2/0)
RTR			1	0	**12**(2/0/0)	**14**(2/2/0)
RTS			1	0	**9**(1/0/0)	**11**(1/2/0)
UNLK			0	0	**5**(1/0/0)	**5**(1/1/0)

+ Indicates Maximum Time
* Add Fetch Effective Address Time
** Add Calculate Effective Address Time
# Add Fetch Immediate Address Time
Add Calculate Immediate Address Time
% Add Jump Effective Address Time

11

11.6.17 Exception-Related Instructions and Operations

The exception-related instruction and operation table indicates the number of clock periods needed for the processor to perform the specified exception-related action. No additional tables are needed to calculate total effective execution time for these operations. For instruction-cache case and for no-cache case, the total number of clock cycles is outside the parentheses. The number of read, prefetch, and write cycles is given inside the parentheses as (r/p/w). The read, prefetch, and write cycles are included in the total clock cycle number.

All timing data assumes two-clock reads and writes.

Instruction/Operation	Head	Tail	I-Cache Case	No-Cache Case
BKPT	1	0	**9**(1/0/0)	**9**(1/0/0)
Interrupt (I-Stack)	0	0	**23**(2/0/4)	**24**(2/2/4)
Interrupt (M-Stack)	0	0	**33**(2/0/8)	**34**(2/2/8)
RESET Instruction	0	0	**518**(0/0/0)	**518**(0/1/0)
STOP	0	0	**8**(0/0/0)	**8**(0/2/0)
TRACE	0	0	**22**(1/0/5)	**24**(1/2/5)
TRAP #n	0	0	**18**(1/0/4)	**20**(1/2/4)
Illegal Instruction	0	0	**18**(1/0/4)	**20**(1/2/4)
A-Line Trap	0	0	**18**(1/0/4)	**20**(1/2/4)
F-Line Trap	0	0	**18**(1/0/4)	**20**(1/2/4)
Privilege Violation	0	0	**18**(1/0/4)	**20**(1/2/4)
TRAPcc (Trap)	2	0	**22**(1/0/5)	**24**(1/2/5)
TRAPcc (No Trap)	4	0	**4**(0/0/0)	**4**(0/1/0)
TRAPcc.W (Trap)	5	0	**24**(1/0/5)	**26**(1/3/5)
TRAPcc.W (No Trap)	6	0	**6**(0/0/0)	**6**(0/1/0)
TRAPcc.L (Trap)	6	0	**26**(1/0/5)	**28**(1/3/5)
TRAPcc.L (No Trap)	8	0	**8**(0/0/0)	**8**(0/2/0)
TRAPV (Trap)	2	0	**22**(1/0/5)	**24**(1/2/5)
TRAPV (No Trap)	4	0	**4**(0/0/0)	**4**(0/1/0)

11.6.18 Save and Restore Operations

The save and restore operation table indicates the number of clock periods needed for the processor to perform the specified state save or to return from exception, with complete execution times and stack length given. No additional tables are needed to calculate total effective execution time for these operations. For instruction-cache case and for no-cache case, the total number of clock cycles is outside the parentheses. The number of read, prefetch, and write cycles is given inside the parentheses as (r/p/w). The read, prefetch, and write cycles are included in the total clock cycle number.

All timing data ssumes two-clock reads and writes.

Operation	Head	Tail	I-Cache Case	No-Cache Case
Bus Cycle Fault (Short)	0	0	**36**(1/0/10)	**38**(1/2/10)
Bus Cycle Fault (Long)	0	0	**62**(1/0/24)	**64**(1/2/24)
RTE (Normal Four Word)	1	0	**18**(4/0/0)	**20**(4/2/0)
RTE (Six Word)	1	0	**18**(4/0/0)	**20**(4/2/0)
RTE (Throwaway)	1	0	**12**(4/0/0)	**12**(4/0/0)
RTE (Coprocessor)	1	0	**26**(7/0/0)	**26**(7/2/0)
RTE (Short Fault)	1	0	**36**(10/0/0)	**26**(10/2/0)
RTE (Long Fault)	1	0	**76**(25/0/0)	**76**(25/2/0)

11.7 Address Translation Tree Search Timing

The time required for a search of the address translation tree depends on the configuration of the tree structure and the descriptors in the tree, the states of the used (U) and modified (M) bits in the descriptors, bus cycle time, and other factors. The large number of variables involved implies that search time can best be calculated by a program. To determine the time required for the MC68030 to perform the table search for a specific configuration, the following interactive program can be used. It is a shell script suitable for use with **sh(1)** on either UNIX® System V or BSD 4.2. To use the program, run the script and answer the questions about the system configuration and current state. The values shown in square brackets at the ends of the question lines are the default values that the program uses when carriage returns are entered.

The shell script assumes that the data bus between the MC68030 and memory is 32 bits wide. To calculate the search time for a narrower bus, enter the appropriate multiple of the bus cycle time in response to the bus cycle time

---

UNIX is a registered trademark of AT&T Bell Laboratories.

prompt. Use the time required for two bus cycles in the case of a 16-bit data bus. Use the time required for four bus cycles in the case of an 8-bit data bus.

The times provided by this program include all phases of the translation tree search. With various mask versions of the MC68030, times may differ slightly from those calculated by the program.

```
##################################################################################
#
#       This Shell script is suitable for use with sh(1) on either System V or
#       BSD 4.2.  When run, it will prompt for several parameters, print a
#       configuration message, and then print the number of clocks and bus
#       cycles required for the table search.  Questions may be answered with
#       a carriage return, and the default in square brackets will be selected.
#
#       The following things should be noted by the user:
#
#       1. This script gives an approximation for the time taken for a table
#          search and associated overhead for a miss in the ATC.  The exact time
#          will vary with the instruction sequence being executed at the time of the
#          miss, and may vary plus or minus 2 clocks (see pre-walk overhead, below).
#
#       2. It will give accurate times for normal table walks (due to misses
#          in the ATC) and for PLOAD table walks but not for PTEST table walks.
#          Table walks due to the PTEST instruction will be somewhat longer.
#
#       3. It does little error checking.  It is possible to describe
#          inconsistent and impossible configurations in the script.
#
#
echo -n "Enter bus cycle time (in clocks) [2]: "
read bus
if test ! "$bus"; then
        bus=2
fi

echo -n "Enter 1 if there is a function code lookup, 0 otherwise [0]: "
read fcl
if test ! "$fcl"; then
        fcl=0
fi

echo -n "Enter number of long descriptors (page and pointer), including FCL ones [1]: "
read long
if test ! "$long"; then
        long=1
fi

echo -n "Enter number of short descriptors (page or pointer), including FCL ones [1]: "
read short
if test ! "$short"; then
        short=1
fi
```

```
echo -n "Enter 1 if there is a long indirect descriptor, 0 otherwise [0]: "
read l_ind
if test ! "$l_ind"; then
        l_ind=0
fi

echo -n "Enter 1 if there is a short indirect descriptor, 0 otherwise [0]: "
read s_ind
if test ! "$s_ind"; then
        s_ind=0
fi

echo -n "Enter number of cleared ubits encountered in pointer descriptors [0]: "
read pointer_ubits
if test ! "$pointer_ubits"; then
        pointer_ubits=0
fi

echo -n "Enter 1 if the page descriptor ubit and/or mbit is clear, 0 otherwise [0]: "
read page_m_ubit
if test ! "$page_m_ubit"; then
        page_m_ubit=0
fi

echo -n "Enter 1 if the page descriptor is encountered unexpectedly, 0 otherwise [0]: "
read et
if test ! "$et"; then
        et=0
fi

echo -n "Enter 1 if the page descriptor is long (and no rp et) [0]: "
read long_page
if test ! "$long_page"; then
        long_page=0
fi

################################################################################
#
# Print Configuration message.
#

levels=`expr $short + $long + $l_ind + $s_ind`

if test $fcl -eq 1; then
    tmp1=" (one for FCL)"
else
    tmp1=""
fi

out1="Configuration:  $levels levels $tmp1  - "

if test $long -ne 0 ;  then
out1="$out1 $long long descriptor(s) "
fi

if test $short -ne 0 ;  then
out1="$out1 $short short descriptor(s)"
fi

if test $l_ind -eq 1 ; then
    out1="$out1 long indirection"
elif test $s_ind -eq 1 ; then
    out1="$out1 short indirection"
fi
```

11

```
    if test $pointer_ubits -ne 0 ;  then
        out2="$out2 $pointer_ubits  pointer ubits clear, "
    fi

    if test $page_m_ubit -eq 1 ; then
        out2="$out2 page ubit and/or mbit  clear, "
    fi

    if test $et -eq 1 ; then
        out2="$out2 early termination, "
    fi

    if test $long_page -eq 1 ; then
        out2="$out2 page is long;"
    else
        out2="$out2 page is short;"
    fi


    out3="$bus clock bus cycle time."

    echo
    echo $out1
    echo "            " $out2
    echo "            " $out3

#################################################################################
#
# Calculate result.
#
# Variables:
#
#   cough  --- the number of clocks from the start of the bus cycle that will miss to
#              the first clock of the first micro-instruction.
#
#   startup -- microcode startup overhead common to all flows
#
#   termination -- microcode termination overhead common to all flows
#
#   bus_max_4 bus_max_3  the maximum value of the bus cycle time (in clocks) and
#                        4 or 3, respectively.
#
#

bus_reads=0
bus_writes=0
ind_clocks=0

# time from BEGINNING of bus cycle which misses to first box
# this is 6 to 9 clocks depending on i- and d-state at miss-- use 7 as average
cough=7

# 4 boxes of startup, when no FCL.
startup=8

# 4 boxes of termination.
termination=8

# Bus accesses begin sooner if FCL - no limit check.
if test $fcl -eq 1 ; then
    startup=`expr $startup - 2`
fi

# calculate max((bus-4),0) for overlap
bus_max_4=`expr $bus - 4`

if test $bus_max_4 -lt 0; then
        bus_max_4=0
fi
```

```
# calculate max((bus-3),0) for overlap
bus_max_3='expr $bus - 3'

if test $bus_max_3 -lt 0; then
        bus_max_3=0
fi

overhead='expr $cough + $startup + $termination'

# number of clock due to long descriptors
l_clocks='expr $long \* \( 6 + $bus + $bus_max_4 \)'

#long page is one box less than long pointer
if test $long_page -eq 1; then
        l_clocks='expr $l_clocks - 2'
fi

bus_reads='expr $bus_reads + \( $long \* 2 \)'

# number of clock due to short descriptors
s_clocks='expr $short \* \( 3 + $bus \)'
bus_reads='expr $bus_reads + $short'

# total clocks due to descriptor fetches
t_clocks='expr $l_clocks + $s_clocks'

if test $t_clocks -eq 0 ; then
    if test $et -ne 1 ; then
        echo Error: 0 bus accesses must imply unexpected page encountered.
    fi
    et=0
fi

# now caculate clocks due to setting u bits in pointer descriptor

u_clocks='expr $pointer_ubits \* \( 4 + $bus_max_3 \)'
bus_writes='expr $bus_writes + $pointer_ubits + $page_m_ubit'

# clocks due to setting u/m bits in page descriptor
page_clocks='expr $page_m_ubit \* \( 2 + $bus_max_3 \)'
bus_writes='expr $bus_writes + $page_m_ubit'

# clocks due to indirect level (long)
if test $l_ind -ne 0; then
        ind_clocks='expr 2 + \( $bus \* 2 \)'
        bus_reads='expr $bus_reads + 2'
fi

# clocks due to indirect level (short)
if test $s_ind -ne 0; then
        ind_clocks='expr 3 + $bus'
        bus_reads='expr $bus_reads + 1'
fi

# early termination penalty
if test $et -eq 1; then
        et_delay=3
else
        et_delay=0
fi
```

11

```
################################################################################
#
# Perform the calculation.
#

clocks=`expr $overhead   \
        + $1_clocks      \
        + $s_clocks      \
        + $u_clocks      \
        + $page_clocks   \
        + $ind_clocks    \
        + $et_delay`

out="    Clocks required (from beginning of missed bus cycle): $clocks"
echo
echo $out

write_accesses=`expr $pointer_ubits + $page_m_ubit`

out="    Bus Reads:                                    $bus_reads"
echo $out

print_total=0
if test $write_accesses -ne 0 ; then
    out="    Bus Writes:                               $write_accesses"
    echo $out
    print_total=1
fi

bus_accesses=`expr $bus_reads + $write_accesses`

if test $print_total -eq 1 ; then
    out="    Total Bus Cycles:                         $bus_accesses"
    echo $out
fi
```

The following table gives some sample times obtained using the shell script. Each row of the table indicates a translation table configuration. The identifier on each row consists of five positions. Each position may have either an "x", meaning that there is no table at the level; an "S", meaning that the table at the level is composed of short-format descriptors; or an "L", meaning that the table at the level is composed of long-format descriptors. The format of the entries is:

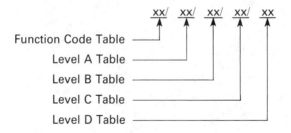

Each entry in the table consists of three numbers that give the number of clock cycles, the number of bus reads, and the number of bus writes required for a table search. An RMC cycle to set the U bit is counted as one read and one write. The format of the entires is:

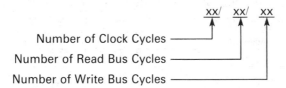

Number of Clock Cycles
Number of Read Bus Cycles
Number of Write Bus Cycles

The table is calculated based on the following assumptions:

1. Bus cycle time is two clock cycles,
2. There are no indirect descriptors,
3. There are no page descriptors encountered unexpectedly (no early termination), and
4. The memory port is 32 bits wide.

Table Format	All U and M Bits Must be Set	Page U and M Bits Only Must be Set	No U and M Bits Must be Set
LLxxx	41/4/2	37/4/1	35/4/0
LLLxx	53/6/3	45/6/1	43/6/0
LLLLx	65/8/4	53/8/1	51/8/0
LLLLL	77/10/5	61/10/1	59/10/0
SSxxx	37/2/2	33/2/1	31/2/0
SSSxx	46/3/3	38/3/1	36/3/0
SSSSx	55/4/4	43/4/1	41/4/0
SSSSS	64/5/5	48/5/1	46/5/0
xSSxx	39/2/2	35/2/1	33/2/0
xSLxx	40/3/2	36/3/1	34/3/0
xLSxx	42/3/2	38/3/1	36/3/0
xLLxx	43/4/2	39/4/1	37/4/0
xSSSx	48/3/3	40/3/1	38/3/0
xSSLx	49/4/3	41/4/1	39/4/0
xSLSx	51/4/3	43/4/1	41/4/0
xSLLx	52/5/3	44/5/1	44/5/0
xLSSx	51/4/3	43/4/1	41/4/0
xLSLx	52/5/3	44/5/1	42/5/0
xLLSx	54/5/3	46/5/1	44/5/0
xLLLx	55/6/3	47/6/1	45/6/0

11

11.7.1 MMU Effective Address Calculation

The calculate effective address table for MMU instructions lists the number of clock periods needed for the processor to calculate various effective addresses. Fetch time is only included for the first level of indirection on memory indirect addressing modes. The total number of clock cycles is outside the parentheses. This total includes the number of read, prefetch, and write cycles, which are shown inside the parentheses as (r/pr/w).

Address Mode	Head	Tail	I-Cache Case	No-Cache Case
(An)	4 + op head	0	**4**(0/0/0)	**4**(0/1/0)
(d_{16},An)	4 + op head	0	**4**(0/0/0)	**4**(0/1/0)
(xxx).W	4 + op head	0	**4**(0/0/0)	**4**(0/1/0)
(xxx).L	6 + op head	0	**6**(0/0/0)	**6**(0/2/0)
(d_8,An,Xn)	4 + op head	0	**4**(0/0/0)	**4**(0/1/0)

FULL FORMAT EXTENSION WORD(S)

Address Mode	Head	Tail	I-Cache Case	No-Cache Case
(d_{16},An)	4	0	**8**(0/0/0)	**8**(0/2/0)
(d_{16},An,Xn)	4	0	**8**(0/0/0)	**8**(0/2/0)
$([d_{16},An])$	4	0	**12**(1/0/0)	**12**(1/2/0)
$([d_{16},An],Xn)$	4	0	**12**(1/0/0)	**12**(1/2/0)
$([d_{16},An],d_{16})$	2	0	**12**(1/0/0)	**12**(1/2/0)
$([d_{16},An],Xn,d_{16})$	4	0	**12**(1/0/0)	**12**(1/2/0)
$([d_{16},An],d_{32})$	4	0	**14**(1/0/0)	**14**(1/3/0)
$([d_{16},An],Xn,d_{32})$	4	0	**14**(1/0/0)	**14**(1/3/0)
(B)	8 + op head	0	**8**(0/0/0)	**8**(0/1/0)
(d_{16},B)	6	0	**10**(0/0/0)	**10**(0/2/0)
(d_{32},B)	6	0	**16**(0/0/0)	**16**(0/2/0)
$([B])$	6	0	**12**(1/0/0)	**12**(1/1/0)
$([B],I)$	6	0	**12**(1/0/0)	**12**(1/1/0)
$([B],d_{16})$	6	0	**12**(1/0/0)	**12**(1/2/0)
$([B],I,d_{16})$	6	0	**12**(1/0/0)	**12**(1/2/0)
$([B],d_{32})$	6	0	**14**(1/0/0)	**14**(1/2/0)
$([B],I,d_{32})$	6	0	**14**(1/0/0)	**14**(1/2/0)
$([d_{16},B])$	6	0	**14**(1/0/0)	**14**(1/2/0)
$([d_{16},B],I)$	6	0	**14**(1/0/0)	**14**(1/2/0)
$([d_{16},B],d_{16})$	6	0	**14**(1/0/0)	**14**(1/2/0)
$([d_{16},B],I,d_{16})$	6	0	**14**(1/0/0)	**14**(1/2/0)
$([d_{16},B],d_{32})$	6	0	**16**(1/0/0)	**16**(1/3/0)

11.7.1 MMU Effective Address Calculation (Continued)

Address Mode	Head	Tail	I-Cache Case	No-Cache Case

FULL FORMATION EXTENSION WORD(S) (CONTINUED)

Address Mode	Head	Tail	I-Cache Case	No-Cache Case
$([d_{32},B])$	6	0	**20**(1/0/0)	**20**(1/2/0)
$([d_{32},B],I)$	6	0	**20**(1/0/0)	**20**(1/2/0)
$([d_{32},B],d_{16})$	6	0	**20**(1/0/0)	**20**(1/3/0)
$([d_{32},B],I,d_{16})$	6	0	**20**(1/0/0)	**20**(1/3/0)
$([d_{32},B],d_{32})$	6	0	**22**(1/0/0)	**22**(1/3/0)
$([d_{32},B],I,d_{32})$	6	0	**22**(1/0/0)	**22**(1/3/0)

B = Base address; O, An, Xn, An + Xn. Form does not affect timing.
I = Index; O, Xn

*No separation on effective address and operation in timing. Head and tail are the operation's.

NOTE: Xn cannot be in B and I at the same time. Scaling and size of Xn do not affect timing.

11.7.2 MMU Instruction Timing

The MMU instruction timing table lists the numbers of clock periods needed for the MMU to perform the MMU instructions. The total number of clock cycles is outside the parentheses. It includes the numbers of read, prefetch, and write cycles, which are shown inside the parentheses as (r/pr/w).

Instruction	Head	Tail	I-Cache Case	No-Cache Case
PMOVE (from CRP, SRP)*	0	0	**4**(0/0/2)	**5**(0/1/2)
PMOVE (to CRP, SRP, valid)*	0	0	**12**(2/0/0)	**14**(2/2/0)
PMOVE (to CRP, SRP, invalid)[1]*	0	0	**28**(3/0/4)	**30**(3/2/4)
PMOVE (from TT0, TT1)*	0	0	**8**(0/0/1)	**8**(0/1/1)
PMOVE (to TT0, TT1)*	0	0	**12**(1/0/0)	**14**(1/2/0)
PMOVE (from MMUSR)*	2	0	**4**(0/0/1)	**5**(0/1/1)
PMOVE (to MMUSR)*	0	0	**6**(1/0/0)	**6**(1/1/0)
PMOVE (from TC)*	2	0	**4**(0/0/1)	**5**(0/1/1)
PMOVE (to TC, valid)[2]*	0	0	**38**(1/0/0)	**40**(1/2/0)
PMOVE (to TC, invalid)[3]*	0	0	**56**(2/0/4)	**58**(2/2/4)
PMOVE (to TC)[4]*	0	0	**14**(1/0/0)	**16**(1/2/0)
PFLUSHA	0	0	**12**(0/0/0)	**14**(0/2/0)
PFLUSH ⟨fc⟩,#⟨mask⟩ (fc is immediate or data register)	0	0	**16**(0/0/0)	**18**(0/2/0)
PFLUSH ⟨fc⟩,#⟨mask⟩ (fc is in SFC or DFC register)	0	0	**20**(0/0/0)	**22**(0/2/0)
PFLUSH ⟨fc⟩,#⟨mask⟩,⟨ea⟩ (fc is immediate or data register)*	0	0	**16**(0/0/0)	**18**(0/2/0)
PFLUSH ⟨fc⟩,#⟨mask⟩,⟨ea⟩ (fc is in SFC or DFC register)*	0	0	**20**(0/0/0)	**22**(0/2/0)
PLOAD[R:W] ⟨fc⟩,⟨ea⟩ (fc is immediate or data register)**	0	0	**8**(0/0/0)	**10**(0/2/0)
PLOAD[R:W] ⟨fc⟩,⟨ea⟩ (fc is in SFC or DFC register)**	0	0	**12**(0/0/0)	**14**(0/2/0)
PTEST[R:W] ⟨fc⟩,⟨ea⟩,#6 * ***	0	0	**88**(12/0/0)	**88**(12/1/0)
PTEST[R:W] ⟨fc⟩,⟨ea⟩,#0*	0	0	**22**(0/0/0)	**22**(0/1/0)

NOTES:
1. Attempt to load invalid root pointer.
2. Translation enabled.
3. Number is maximum, assuming valid page size but Tlx fields do not add up to 32. Translation enabled.
4. Translation disabled.

  *Add the appropriate effective address calculation time.
 **Add the appropriate effective address calculation time and the table search time.
***Number given is the maximum for a six-level table (FC lookup, a, b, c, and d levels with indirect level, all long descriptors).

11.8 Interrupt Latency

In real-time systems, the response time required for a processor to service an interrupt is a very important factor pertaining to overall system performance. Processors in the M68000 Family support asynchronous assertion of interrupts and begin processing them on subsequent instruction boundaries. The average interrupt latency is quite short, but the maximum latency is often critical because real-time interrupts cannot require servicing in less than the maximum interrupt latency. The maximum interrupt latency for the MC68030 alone is approximately 200 clock cycles (for the MOVEM.L ($[d_{32},An],Xn,d_{32}$), D0-D7/A0-A7 instruction where the last data fetch is aborted with a bus error), but when the MMU is enabled, some operations can take several times longer to execute.

Interrupt latency in systems using the MMU is affected by the length of the main processor instructions, the address translation tree configuration, the number of translation tree searches required by the instructions, the access time of main memory, and the width of the data bus connecting the MC68030 to main memory. It is important to note that the address translation tree configuration is under software control and can strongly affect the system interrupt latency. The maximum interrupt latency for a given system configuration can be computed by adding the length of the longest main processor instruction to the time required for the maximum number of translation tree searches that the instruction could require. For the MC68030 microprocessor, one instruction of particular interest is a memory-to-memory move with memory indirect addressing for both the source and destination, with all of the code and data items crossing page boundaries. The assembler syntax for this instruction is:

MOVE.L (od,[bd,An,Rm]),(od,[bd,An,Rm])

This instruction can cause ten address translation tree searches: two for the instruction stream, two for the source indirect address, two for the destination indirect address, two for the operand fetch, and two for the destination write. System software can reduce the maximum number of translation searches by placing additional restrictions on generated code. For example, if the language translators in the system only generate long words aligned on long-word boundaries, the indirect address and operands can cause only one translation search each. This reduces the number of searches for the instruction to a maximum of six.

11

11.9 Bus Arbitration Latency

In a system that uses the MMU, the bus arbitration latency is affected by several factors. The MC68030 does not relinquish the physical bus while it is performing a read-modify-write operation. Since the address translation search is an extended read-modify-write operation, the no-cache-case latency is incurred by the longest address translation search required by the system.

Another bus arbitration delay occurs when a coprocessor or other device delays or fails to assert $\overline{DSACKx}$ or $\overline{STERM}$ signals to terminate a bus cycle. The maximum delay in this case is undefined; it depends on the length of the delay in asserting the signals.

SECTION 12
APPLICATIONS INFORMATION

This section provides guidelines for using the MC68030. First, it discusses the requirements for adapting the MC68030 to MC68020 designs. Then, it describes the use of the MC68881 and MC68882 coprocessors with the MC68030. The byte select logic is described next, followed by memory interface information. A description of external caches, the use of the $\overline{\text{STATUS}}$ and $\overline{\text{REFILL}}$ signals, and power and ground considerations complete the section.

12.1 ADAPTING THE MC68030 TO MC68020 DESIGNS

Perhaps the easiest way to first utilize the MC68030 is in a system designed for the MC68020. This is possible due to the complete compatibility of the asynchronous buses of the MC68020 and MC68030. This section describes how to configure an adapter for the MC68030 to allow insertion into an existing MC68020-based system. Software and architectural differences between the two processors are also discussed. The need for an adapter is absolute because the MC68020 and MC68030 are NOT pin compatible. Use of the adapter board provides the immediate capability for evaluating the programmer's model and instruction set of the MC68030 and for developing software to utilize the MC68030's additional enhanced features. This adapter board also provides a relatively simple method for increasing the performance of an existing MC68020 or MC68020/MC68851 system by insertion of a more advanced 32-bit MPU with an on-chip data cache and an on-chip MMU. Since the adapter board does not support of the synchronous bus interface of the MC68030, performance measurements for the MC68030 used in this manner may be misleading when compared to a system designed specifically for the MC68030.

The adapter board plugs into the CPU socket of an MC68020 target system, drawing power, ground, and clock signals through the socket and running bus cycles in a fashion compatible with the MC68030. The only support hardware necessary is a single 1K-ohm pullup resistor and two capacitors for decoupling power and ground on the adapter board.

12

12.1.1 Signal Routing

Figure 12-1 shows the complete schematic for routing the signals of the MC68030 to the MC68020 header. All signals common to both processors are directly routed to the corresponding signal of the other processor. The signals on the MC68030 that do not have a compatible signal on the MC68020 are either pulled up or left unconnected:

Pulled Up	No Connect
$\overline{\text{STERM}}$	STATUS
$\overline{\text{CBACK}}$	REFILL
$\overline{\text{CIIN}}$	$\overline{\text{CBREQ}}$
$\overline{\text{MMUDIS}}$	CIOUT

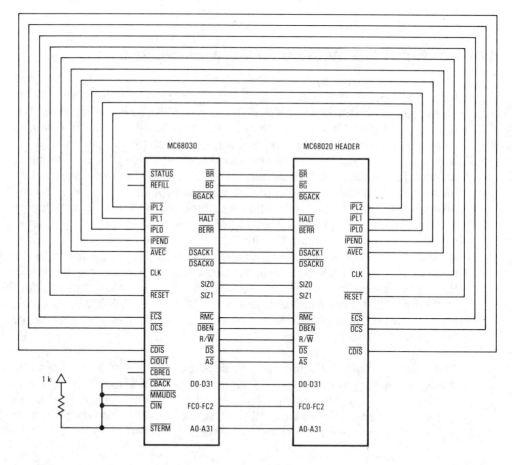

Figure 12-1. Signal Routing for Adapting the MC68030 to MC68020 Designs

12.1.2 Hardware Differences

Before enabling the on-chip caches of the MC68030, an important system feature must be checked. Because of the MC68030 cache organization and implementation, cachable read bus cycles are expected to transfer the entire port width of data (as indicated by the $\overline{\text{DSACKx}}$ encoding), regardless of how many bytes are actually requested by the SIZx pins. The MC68020 did not have this requirement, and system memory banks or peripherals may or may not supply the amount of data required by the MC68030. If the target system does not supply the full port width with valid data for any cachable instruction or data access the user should either designate that area of memory as noncachable (with the MMU) or not enable the corresponding on-chip cache(s). In some systems, modifying the target system hardware may also be an option; frequently, the byte select logic is generated by a single PAL, which might easily be replaced or reprogrammed to select all bytes during read cycles from multibyte ports.

The $\overline{\text{HALT}}$ input-only signal of the MC68030 is slightly different than the bidirectional $\overline{\text{HALT}}$ signal of the MC68020. However, this should not cause any problems beyond eliminating an indication to the external system (e.g., lighting an LED) that the processor has halted due to a double bus fault.

When used in a system originally designed for both an MC68020 and an MC68851, the MC68851 may be left in the system or removed (and replaced with a jumpered header). However, if left in the system, the MC68851 is not accessible to the programmer with the M68000 coprocessor interface. All MMU instructions access the MC68030's on-chip MMU. This is true even if the MC68030's $\overline{\text{MMUDIS}}$ signal is asserted. The benefit in removing the MC68851 is that the minimum asynchronous bus cycle time to the physical bus is reduced from four clock cycles to three.

If the MC68851 is removed and replaced with a jumpered header, the following MC68851 signals may need special system-specific consideration: $\overline{\text{CLI}}$, $\overline{\text{RMC}}$, $\overline{\text{LBRO}}$, $\overline{\text{LBG}}$, LBGACK, and $\overline{\text{LBGI}}$. During translation table searches, the MC68851 asserts the cache load inhibit ($\overline{\text{CLI}}$) signal but not $\overline{\text{RMC}}$; whereas,

12

the MC68030 asserts $\overline{\text{RMC}}$ but not $\overline{\text{CIOUT}}$. In simple MC68020/MC68851 systems without logical bus arbitration or logical caches, the MC68851's jumper can have the following signals connected together:

$\overline{\text{LAS}}$ ◀▶ $\overline{\text{PAS}}$
$\overline{\text{LBRO}}$ ◀▶ $\overline{\text{PBR}}$
$\overline{\text{LBGI}}$ ◀▶ $\overline{\text{PBG}}$
$\overline{\text{LBGACK}}$ ◀▶ $\overline{\text{PBGACK}}$
LA(8-31) ◀▶ PA(8-31)
$\overline{\text{CLI}}$ ◀▶ no connect or $\overline{\text{LAS}}$

$\overline{\text{CLI}}$ has two connection options because some systems may use $\overline{\text{CLI}}$ to qualify the occurrence of CPU space cycles since the MC68851's $\overline{\text{PAS}}$ does not assert.

12.1.3 Software Differences

The instruction cache control bits in the cache control register (CACR) of the MC68030 are in the identical bit positions as the corresponding bits as the MC68020's CACR. However, the MC68030 has additional control bits for burst enable and data cache control. Because this adapter board does not support synchronous bus cycles (and thus burst mode), enabling burst mode through the CACR does not affect system operation in any way. Refer to **SECTION 6 ON-CHIP CACHE MEMORIES** for more information on the bit positions and functions of the CACR bits.

When used in a system originally designed for an MC68020, a difference a programmer must be aware of is that the MC68030 does not support the CALLM and RTM instructions of the MC68020. If code is executed on the MC68030 using either the CALLM or RTM instructions, an unimplemented instruction exception is taken. If no MMU software development capability is desired and the cache behavior described under hardware differences is understood, the user may ignore the MC68030 MMU.

When the adapter is used in a system originally designed for the MC68020/ MC68851 pair, the software differences described below also apply. The MC68030's MMU offers a subset of the MC68851 features. The features not supported by the MC68030 MMU are listed below:

- On-chip breakpoint registers

- Task aliasing

- Instructions: PBcc, PDBcc, PRESTORE, PSAVE, PScc, PTRAPcc, PVALID

12

Only control-alterable addressing modes are allowed for MMU instructions on the MC68030.

A feature new to the MC68030 MMU (and not on the MC68851) is the transparent translation of two logical address blocks with the transparent translation registers. See **SECTION 9 MEMORY MANAGEMENT UNIT**.

12.2 FLOATING-POINT UNITS

Floating-point support for the MC68030 is provided by the MC68881 floating-point coprocessor and the MC68882 enhanced floating-point coprocessor. Both devices offer a full implementation of the *IEEE Standard for Binary Floating-Point Arithmetic* (754). The MC68882 is a pin and software-compatible upgrade of the MC68881, with an optimized MPU interface that provides over 1.5 times the performance of the MC68881 at the same clock frequency.

Both coprocessors provide a logical extension to the integer data processing capabilities of the main processor. They contain a very high performance floating-point arithmetic unit and a set of floating-point data registers that are utilized in a manner that is analogous to the use of the integer data registers of the processor. The MC68881/MC68882 instruction set is a natural extension of all earlier members of the M68000 Family and supports all of the addressing modes and data types of the host MC68030. The programmer perceives the MC68030/coprocessor execution model as if both devices are implemented on one chip. In addition to supporting the full IEEE standard, the MC68881 and MC68882 provide a full set of trigonometric and transcendental functions, on-chip constants, and a full 80-bit extended-precision-real data format.

The interface of the MC68030 to the MC68881 or the MC68882 is easily tailored to system cost/performance needs. The MC68030 and the MC68881/MC68882 communicate via standard asynchronous M68000 bus cycles. All data transfers are performed by the main processor at the request of the MC68881/MC68882; thus memory management, bus errors, address errors, and bus arbitration function as if the MC68881/MC68882 instructions are executed by the main processor. The floating-point unit and the processor may operate at different clock speeds, and up to seven floating-point coprocessors may reside in an MC68030 system simultaneously.

Figure 12-2 illustrates the coprocessor interface connection of an MC68881/MC68882 to an MC68030 (uses entire 32-bit data bus). The MC68881/MC68882 is configured to operate with a 32-bit data bus when both the A0 and $\overline{\text{SIZE}}$

12

pins are connected to V_{CC}. Refer to the MC68881UM/AD *MC68881/MC68882 Floating-Point Coprocessor User's Manual* for configuring the MC68881/ MC68882 for smaller data bus widths. Note that the MC68030 cache inhibit input ($\overline{\text{CIIN}}$) signal is not used for the coprocessor interface because the MC68030 does not cache data obtained during CPU space accesses.

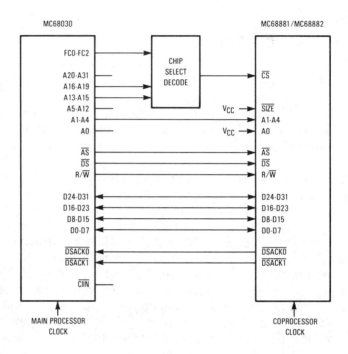

Figure 12-2. 32-Bit Data Bus Coprocessor Connection

The chip select ($\overline{\text{CS}}$) decode circuitry is asynchronous logic that detects when a particular floating-point coprocessor is addressed. The MC68030 signals used by the logic include the function code signals (FC0–FC2), and the address lines (A13–A19). Refer to **SECTION 10 COPROCESSOR INTERFACE DESCRIPTION** for more information concerning the encoding of these signals. All or just a subset of these lines may be decoded depending on the number of coprocessors in the system and the degree of redundant mapping allowed in the system.

12

The major concern of a system designer is to design a $\overline{CS}$ interface that meets the AC electrical specifications for both the MC68030 (MPU) and the MC68881/MC68882 (FPCP) without adding unnecessary wait states to FPCP accesses. The following maximum specifications (relative to CLK low) meet these objectives:

$$t_{CLK} \text{ low to } \overline{AS} \text{ low} \leq (\text{MPU Spec 1} - \text{MPU Spec 47A} - \text{FPCP Spec 19}) \quad (1)$$

$$t_{CLK} \text{ low to } \overline{CS} \text{ low} \leq (\text{MPU Spec 1} - \text{MPU Spec 47A} - \text{FPCP Spec 19}) \quad (2)$$

Even though requirement (1) is not met under worst case conditions, if the MPU $\overline{AS}$ is loaded within specifications and the $\overline{AS}$ input to the FPCP is unbuffered, the requirement is met under typical conditions. Designing the $\overline{CS}$ generation circuit to meet requirement (2) provides the highest probability that accesses to the FPCP occur without unnecessary wait states. A PAL 16L8 (see Figure 12-3) with a maximum propagation delay of 10 ns, programmed according to the equations in Figure 12-4, can be used to generate $\overline{CS}$. For a 25-MHz system, t_{CLK} low to $\overline{CS}$ low is less than or equal to 10 ns when this design is used. Should worst case conditions cause t_{CLK} low to $\overline{AS}$ low to exceed requirement (1), one wait state is inserted in the access to the FPCP; no other adverse effect occurs. Figure 12-5 shows the bus cycle timing for this interface. Refer to MC68881UM/AD, *MC68881/MC68882 Floating-Point Coprocessor User's Manual*, for FPCP specifications.

The circuit that generates $\overline{CS}$ must meet another requirement. When a non-floating-point access immediately follows a floating-point access, $\overline{CS}$ (for the floating-point access) must be negated before $\overline{AS}$ and $\overline{DS}$ (for the subsequent access) are asserted. The PAL circuit previously described also meets this requirement.

For example, if a system has only one coprocessor, the full decoding of the ten signals (FC0–FC2 and A13–A19) provided by the PAL equations in Figure 12-4 is not absolutely necessary. It may be sufficient to use only FC0–FC1 and A16–A17. FC0–FC1 indicate when a bus cycle is operating in either CPU space ($7) or user-defined space ($3), and A16–A17 encode CPU space type as coprocessor space ($2). A13–A15 can be ignored in this case because they encode the coprocessor identification code (CpID) used to differentiate between multiple coprocessors in a system. Motorola assemblers always default to a CpID of $1 for floating-point instructions; this can be controlled with assembler directives if a different CpID is desired or if multiple coprocessors exist in the system.

12

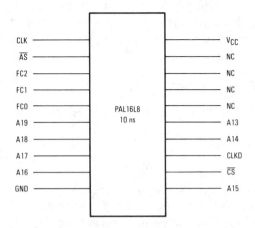

Figure 12-3. Chip-Select Generation PAL

PAL16l8
FPCP CS GENERATION CIRCUITRY FOR 25 MHz OPERATION
MOTOROLA INC., AUSTIN, TEXAS

CLK	AS	FC2	FC1	FC0	A19	A18	A17	A16	GND
A15	/CS	/CLKD	A14	A13	NC	NC	NC	NC	V$_{CC}$

```
CS  = FC2   * FC1   * FC0               ;cpu space = $7
      * /A19  * /A18  * A17   * /A16     ;coprocessor access = $2
      * /A15  * /A14  * A13             ;coprocessor id = $1
      * /CLK                            ;qualified by MPU clock low

      + FC2   * FC1   * FC0             ;cpu space = $7
      * /A19  * /A18  * A17   * /A16     ;coprocessor access = $2
      * /A15  * /A14  * A13             ;coprocessor id = $1
      * /AS                            ;qualified by address strobe low

      + FC2   * FC1   * FC0
      * /A19  * /A18  * A17   * /A16     ;coprocessor access = $2
      * /A15  * /A14  * A13             ;coprocessor id = $1
      * /CLKD                          ;qualified by CLKD (delayed CLK)

CLKD = CLK
```

Description: There are three terms to the CS generation. The first term denotes the earliest time CS can be asserted. The second term is used to assert CS until the end of the FPCP access. The third term is to ensure that no race condition occurs in case of a late AS.

Figure 12-4. PAL Equations

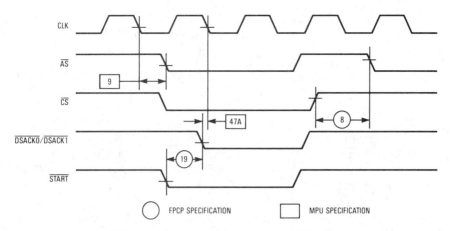

Figure 12-5. Bus Cycle Timing Diagram

12.3 BYTE SELECT LOGIC FOR THE MC68030

The architecture of the MC68030 allows it to support byte, word, and long-word operand transfers to any 8-, 16-, or 32-bit data port regardless of alignment. This feature allows the programmer to write code that is not bus-width specific. When accessed, the peripheral or memory subsystem reports its actual port size to the processor, and the MC68030 then dynamically sizes the data transfer accordingly, using multiple bus cycles when necessary. Hardware designers also have the flexibility to choose implementations independent of software prejudices. The following paragraphs describe the generation of byte select control signals that enable the dynamic bus sizing mechanism, the transfer of differently sized operands, and the transfer of misaligned operands to operate correctly.

The following signals control the MC68030 operand transfer mechanism:

- A1, A0 = Address lines. The most significant byte of the operand to be transferred is addressed directly.

- SIZ1, SIZ0 = Transfer size. Output of the MC68030. These indicate the number of bytes of an operand remaining to be transferred during a given bus cycle.

- R/$\overline{W}$ = Read/Write. Output of the MC68030. For byte select generation in MC68030 systems, R/$\overline{W}$ must be included in the logic if the data from the device is cachable.

- $\overline{\text{DSACK1}}$, $\overline{\text{DSACK0}}$ = Data transfer and size acknowledge. Driven by an asynchronous port to indicate the actual bus width of the port.

- $\overline{\text{STERM}}$ = Synchronous termination. Driven by a 32-bit synchronous port only.

The MC68030 assumes that 16-bit ports are situated on data lines D16–D31, and that 8-bit ports are situated on data lines D24–D31. This ensures that the following logic works correctly with the MC68030's on-chip internal-to-external data bus multiplexer. Refer to **SECTION 7 BUS OPERATION** for more details on the dynamic bus sizing mechanism.

The need for byte select signals is best illustrated by an example. Consider a long-word write cycle to an odd address in word-organized memory. The transfer requires three bus cycles to complete. The first bus cycle transfers the most significant byte of the long word on D16–D23. The second bus cycle transfers a word on D16–D31, and the last bus cycle transfers the least significant byte of the original long word on D24–D31. In order not to overwrite those bytes which are not used these transfers, a unique byte data strobe must be generated for each byte when using devices with 16- and 32-bit port widths.

For noncachable read cycles and all write cycles, the required active bytes of the data bus for any given bus transfer are a function of the size (SIZ0/SIZ1) and lower address (A0/A1) outputs and are shown in Table 12-1. Individual strobes or select signals can be generated by decoding these four signals for every bus cycle. Devices residing on 8-bit ports can utilize data strobe ($\overline{\text{DS}}$) alone since there is only one valid byte for any transfer.

During cachable read cycles, the addressed device must provide valid data over its full bus width (as indicated by $\overline{\text{DSACKx}}$ or $\overline{\text{STERM}}$). While instructions are always prefetched as long-word-aligned accesses, data fetches can occur with any alignment and size. Because the MC68030 assumes that the entire data bus port size contains valid data, cachable data read bus cycles must provide as much data as signaled by the port size during a bus cycle. To satisfy this requirement, the R/$\overline{\text{W}}$ signal must be included in the byte select logic for the MC68030.

Figure 12-6 shows a block diagram of an MC68030 system with two memory banks. The PAL provides memory-mapped byte select signals for an asynchronous 32-bit port and unmapped byte select signals for other memory banks or ports. Figure 12-7 provides sample equations for the PAL.

12

Table 12-1. Data Bus Activity for Byte, Word, and Long-Word Ports

Transfer Size	SIZ1	SIZ0	A1	A0	Data Bus Active Sections Byte (B) – Word (W) – Long-Word (L) Ports			
					D31-D24	D23-D16	D15-D8	D7-D0
Byte	0	1	0	0	B W L	—	—	—
	0	1	0	1	B	W L	—	—
	0	1	1	0	B W	—	L	—
	0	1	1	1	B	W	—	L
Word	1	0	0	0	B W L	W L	—	—
	1	0	0	1	B	W L	L	—
	1	0	1	0	B W	W	L	L
	1	0	1	1	B	W	—	L
Three Byte	1	1	0	0	B W L	W L	L	—
	1	1	0	1	B	W L	L	L
	1	1	1	0	B W	W	L	L
	1	1	1	1	B	W	—	L
Long Word	0	0	0	0	B W L	W L	L	L
	0	0	0	1	B	W L	L	L
	0	0	1	0	B W	W	L	L
	0	0	1	1	B	W	—	L

The PAL equations and circuits presented here are not intended to be the optimal implementation for every system. Depending on the CPU's clock frequency, memory access times, and system architecture, different circuits may be required.

12.4 MEMORY INTERFACE

The MC68030 is capable of running three types of external bus cycles as determined by the cycle termination and handshake signals (refer to **SECTION 7 BUS OPERATION**). These three types of bus cycles are:

1. Asynchronous cycles, terminated by the $\overline{\text{DSACKx}}$ signals, have a minimum duration of three processor clock periods in which up to four bytes are transferred.

2. Synchronous cycles, terminated by the $\overline{\text{STERM}}$ signal, have a minimum duration of two processor clock periods in which up to four bytes are transferred.

3. Burst operation cycles, terminated by the $\overline{\text{STERM}}$ and $\overline{\text{CBACK}}$ signals, have a duration of as little as five processor clock periods in which up to four long words (16 bytes) are transferred.

12

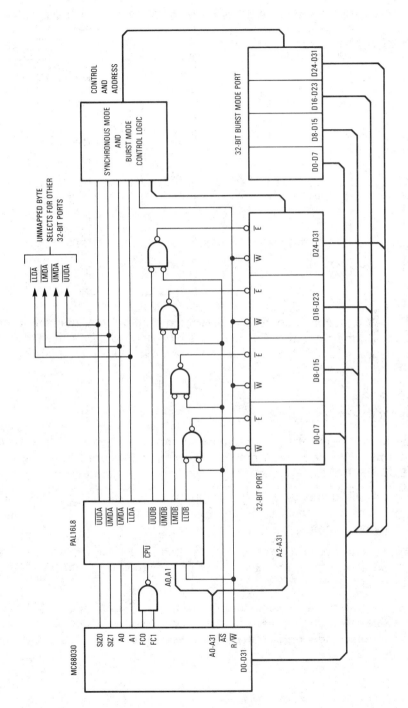

Figure 12-6. Example MC68030 Byte Select PAL System Configuration

PAL16L8
U1
MC68030 BYTE DATA SELECT GENERATION FOR 32-BIT PORTS, MAPPED AND UNMAPPED.
MOTOROLA INC., AUSTIN, TEXAS

A0	A1	SIZ0	SIZ1	RW	A18	A19	A20	A21	GND
/CPU	/UUDA	/UMDA	/LMDA	/LLDA	/UUDA	/UMDB	/LMDB	/LLDB	VCC

UUDA = RW	;enable upper byte on read of 32-bit port
+ /A0 * /A1	;directly addressed, any size
UMDA = RW	;enable upper middle byte on read of 32-bit port
+ A0 * /A1	;directly addressed, any size
+ /A1 * /SIZ0	;word aligned, size byte or three byte
+ /A1 * SIZ1	;word aligned, size is word or long word
LMDA = RW	;enable lower middle byte on read of 32-bit port
+ /A0 * A1	;directly addressed, any size
+ /A1 * /SIZ0 * /SIZ1	;word aligned, size is long word
+ /A1 * SIZ0 * SIZ1	;word aligned, size is three byte
+ /A1 * A0 * /SIZ0	;word aligned, size is word or long word
LLDA = RW	;enable lower byte on read of 32-bit port
+ A0 * A1	;directly addressed, any size
+ A0 * SIZ0 * SIZ1	;odd alignment, three byte size
+ /SIZ0 * /SIZ1	;size is long word, any address
+ A1 * SIZ1	;word aligned, word or three byte size

UUDB = RW * /CPU * (addressb)	;enable upper byte on read of 32-bit port
+ /A0 * /A1 * /CPU * (addressb)	;directly addressed, any size
UMDB = RW * /CPU * (addressb)	;enable upper middle byte on read of 32-bit port
+ A0 * /A1 * /CPU * (addressb)	;directly addressed, any size
+ /A1 * /SIZ0 * /CPU * (addressb)	;word aligned, size byte or three byte
+ /A1 * SIZ1 * /CPU * (addressb)	;word aligned, size is word or long word
LMDB = RW * /CPU * (addressb)	;enable lower middle byte on read of 32-bit port
+ /A0 * A1 * /CPU * (addressb)	;directly addressed, any size
+ /A1 * /SIZ0 * /SIZ1 * /CPU * (addressb)	;word aligned, size is long word
+ /A1 * SIZ0 * SIZ1 * /CPU * (addressb)	;word aligned, size is three byte
+ /A1 * A0 * /SIZ0 * /CPU * (addressb)	;word aligned, size is word or long word
LLDB = RW * /CPU * (addressb)	;enable lower byte on read of 32-bit port
+ A0 * A1 * /CPU * (addressb)	;directly addressed, any size
+ A0 * SIZ0 * SIZ1 * /CPU * (addressb)	;odd alignment, three byte size
+ /SIZ0 * /SIZ1 * /CPU * (addressb)	;size is long word, any address
+ A1 * SIZ1 * /CPU * (addressb)	;word aligned, word or three byte size

DESCRIPTION: Byte select signals for writing. On reads, all bytes selects are asserted if the respective memory block is addressed. The input signal /CPU prevents byte select assertion during CPU space cycles and is derived from NANDing FC0-FC1 or FC0-FC2. The label, (addressb), is a designer-selectable combination of address lines used to generate the proper address decode for the system's memory bank. With the address lines given here the decode block size is 256K bytes. A similar address might be included in the equations for UUDA, UMDA, etc. if the designer wishes them to be memory mapped also.

Figure 12-7. MC68030 Byte Select PAL Equations

During read operations, M68000 processors latch data on the last falling clock edge of the bus cycle, one-half clock before the bus cycle ends (burst mode is a special case). Latching data here, instead of the next rising clock edge, helps to avoid data bus contention with the next bus cycle and allows the MC68030 to receive the data into its execution unit sooner for a net performance increase.

Write operations also use this data bus timing to allow data hold times from the negating strobes and to avoid any bus contention with the following bus cycle. This usually allows the system to be designed with a minimum of bus buffers and latches.

One of the benefits of the MC68030's on-chip caches is that the effect of external wait states on performance is lessened because the caches are always accessed in fewer than "no wait states", regardless of the external memory configuration. This feature makes the MC68030 (and MC68020) unique among other general-purpose microprocessors.

12.4.1 Access Time Calculations

The timing paths that are typically critical in any memory interface are illustrated and defined in Figure 12-8. For burst transfers, the first long word transferred also uses these parameters, but the subsequent transfers are different and are discussed in **12.4.2 Burst Mode Cycles**.

The type of device that is interfaced to the MC68030 determines exactly which of the paths is most critical. The address-to-data paths are typically the critical paths for static devices since there is no penalty for initiating a cycle to these devices and later validating that access with the appropriate bus control signal. Conversely, the address-strobe-to-data-valid path is often most critical for dynamic devices since the cycle must be validated before an access can be initiated. For devices that signal termination of a bus cycle before data is validated (e.g., error detection and correction hardware and some external caches) to improve performance, the critical path may be from the address or strobes to the assertion of $\overline{BERR}$ (or $\overline{BERR}$ and $\overline{HALT}$). Finally, the address-valid-to-$\overline{DSACKx}$-or-$\overline{STERM}$-asserted path is most critical for very fast devices and external caches, since the time available between when the address is valid and when $\overline{DSACKx}$ or $\overline{STERM}$ must be asserted to terminate the bus cycle is minimal. Table 12-2 provides the equations required to calculate the various memory access times assuming a 50-percent duty cycle clock.

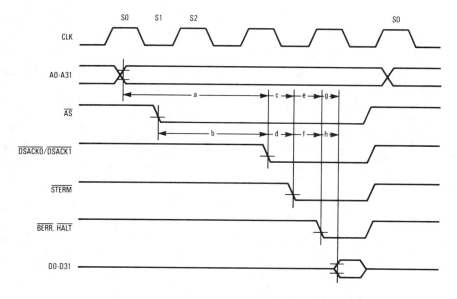

NOTE: This diagram illustrates access time calculations only. $\overline{DSACK0}/\overline{DSACK1}$ and $\overline{STERM}$ should never be asserted together during the same bus cycle.

Parameter	Description	System	Equation
a	Address Valid to $\overline{DSACKx}$ Asserted	t_{AVDL}	12-1
b	Address Strobe Asserted to $\overline{DSACKx}$ Asserted	t_{SADL}	12-2
c	Address Valid to $\overline{STERM}$ Asserted	t_{AVSL}	12-3
d	Address Strobe Asserted to $\overline{STERM}$ Asserted	t_{SASL}	12-4
e	Address Valid to $\overline{BERR}/\overline{HALT}$ Asserted	t_{AVBHL}	12-5
f	Address Strobe Asserted to $\overline{BERR}/\overline{HALT}$ Asserted	t_{SABHL}	12-6
g	Address Valid to Data Valid	t_{AVDV}	12-7
h	Address Strobe Asserted to Data Valid	t_{SADV}	12-8

Figure 12-8. Access Time Computation Diagram

During asynchronous bus cycles, $\overline{DSACK1}$ and $\overline{DSACK0}$ are used to terminate the current bus cycle. In true asynchronous operations, such as accesses to peripherals operating at a different clock frequency, either or both signals may be asserted without regard to the clock, and then data must be valid a certain amount of time later as defined by specification #31. With a 16.67-MHz processor, this time is 50 ns after $\overline{DSACKx}$ asserts; with a 20.0-MHz processor, this time is 43 ns after $\overline{DSACK}$ asserts (both numbers vary with the actual clock frequency).

Table 12-2. Memory Access Time Equations at 20 MHz

	N = 2	N = 3	N = 4	N = 5	N = 6
(12-1) $t_{AVDL} = (N-1) \cdot t1 - t2 - t6 - t47A$	—	46 ns	96 ns	146 ns	196 ns
(12-2) $t_{SADL} = (N-2) \cdot t1 - t9 - t47A$	—	26 ns	76 ns	126 ns	176 ns
(12-3) $t_{AVSL} = (N-1) \cdot t1 - t6 - t60$	21 ns	71 ns	121 ns	171 ns	221 ns
(12-4) $t_{SASL} = (N-1) \cdot t1 - t3 - t9 - t60$	1 ns	51 ns	101 ns	151 ns	201 ns
(12-5) $t_{AVBHL} = N \cdot t1 - t2 - t6 - t27A$	40 ns	90 ns	140 ns	190 ns	240 ns
(12-6) $t_{SABHL} = (N-1) \cdot t1 - t9 - t27A$	20 ns	70 ns	120 ns	170 ns	220 ns
(12-7) $t_{AVDV} = N \cdot t1 - t2 - t6 - t27$	46 ns	96 ns	146 ns	196 ns	246 ns
(12-8) $t_{SADV} = (N-1) \cdot t1 - t9 - t27$	26 ns	76 ns	126 ns	176 ns	226 ns

where:

tX	=	Refers to AC Electrical Specification #X
$t1$	=	The Clock Period
$t2$	=	The Clock Low Time
$t3$	=	The Clock High Time
$t6$	=	The Clock High to Address Valid Time
$t9$	=	The Clock Low to $\overline{AS}$ Low Delay
$t27$	=	The Data-In to Clock Low Setup Time
$t27A$	=	The $\overline{BERR}/\overline{HALT}$ to Clock Low Setup Time
$t47A$	=	The Asynchronous Input Setup Time
$t60$	=	The Synchronous Input to CLK High Setup Time
N	=	The Total Number of Clock Periods in the Bus Cycle (Nonburst)
		($N \geq 2$ for Synchronous Cycles; $N \geq 3$ for Asynchronous Cycles)

However, many local memory systems do not operate in a truly asynchronous manner because the memory control logic can either be related to the MC68030's clock or worst case propagation delays are known; thus, asynchronous setup times for the $\overline{DSACKx}$ signals can be guaranteed. The timing requirements for this pseudo-synchronous $\overline{DSACKx}$ generation is governed by the equation for t_{AVDL}.

Synchronous cycles use the $\overline{STERM}$ signal to terminate the current bus cycle. In bus cycles of equal length, $\overline{STERM}$ has more relaxed timing requirements than $\overline{DSACKx}$ since an additional 30 ns is available when comparing t_{AVSL} (or t_{SASL}) to t_{AVDL} (or t_{SADL}). The only additional restriction is that $\overline{STERM}$ must meet the setup and hold times as defined by specifications #60 and #61, respectively, for all rising edges of the clock during a bus cycle. The value for t_{SASL} when the total number of clock periods (N) equals two in Table 12-2 requires further explanation. Because the calculated value of this access time (see Equation 12-4 of Table 12-2) is zero under certain conditions, hardware cannot always qualify $\overline{STERM}$ with $\overline{AS}$ at all frequencies. However, such qualification is not a requirement for the MC68030. $\overline{STERM}$ can be generated by the assertion of $\overline{ECS}$, the falling edge of S0, or most simply by the output(s) of an address decode or comparator logic. Note that other

12

devices in the system may require qualification of the access with $\overline{AS}$ since the MC68030 has the capability to initiate bus cycles and then abort them before the assertion of $\overline{AS}$.

Another way to optimize the CPU to memory access times in a system is to use a clock frequency less than the rated maximum of the specific MC68030 device. Table 12-3 provides calculated t_{AVDV} (see Equation 12-7 of Table 12-2) results for an MC68030RC16 and MC68030RC20 operating at various clock frequencies. If the system uses other clock frequencies, the above equations can be used to calculate the exact access times.

Table 12-3. Calculated t_{AVDV} Values for Operation at Frequencies Less Than or Equal to the CPU Maximum Frequency Rating

Equation 12-7 t_{AVDV}		MC68030RC20		MC68030RC25		
Clocks Per Bus Cycle (N) and Type	Wait States	Clock at 16.67 MHz	Clock at 20 MHz	Clock at 16.67 MHz	Clock at 20 MHz	Clock at 25 MHz
2 Clock Synchronous	0	61	46	68	53	38 —
3 Clock Synchronous	1	121	96	128	103	78
3 Clock Asynchronous	0	121	96	128	103	78
4 Clock Synchronous	2	181	146	188	153	118
4 Clock Asynchronous	1	181	146	188	153	118
5 Clock Synchronous	3	241	196	248	203	158
5 Clock Asynchronous	2	241	196	248	203	158
6 Clock Synchronous	4	301	246	308	253	198
6 Clock Asynchronous	3	301	246	308	253	198

12.4.2 Burst Mode Cycles

The memory access times for burst mode bus cycles follow the above equations for the first access only. For the subsequent (second, third, and fourth) accesses, the memory access time calculations depend on the architecture of the burst mode memory system.

Architectural tradeoffs include the width of the burst memory and the type of memory used. If the memory is 128 bits wide, the subsequent operand accesses do not affect the critical timing paths. For example, if a 3-1-1-1 burst accesses 128-bit-wide memory, the first access is governed by the equations in Table 12-2 for N equal to three. The subsequent accesses also use these values as a base but have additional clock periods added in. The second access has one additional clock period, the third access has two additional clock periods, and the fourth has three additional clock periods. Thus, the access time for the first cycle determines the critical timing paths.

Memory that is 64 bits wide presents a compromise between the two configurations listed above.

12.5 STATIC RAM MEMORY BANKS

When the MC68030 is operating at a high clock frequency, a no-wait-state external memory system will most likely be composed of static RAMs. The following paragraphs discuss three static memory banks, which may be used as shown or as a starting point for an external cache design. The designs offer different levels of performance, bus utilization, and cost.

12.5.1 A Two-Clock Synchronous Memory Bank Using SRAMs

The MC68030 normally attains its highest performance when the external memory system can support a two-clock synchronous bus protocol. This section describes a complete memory bank containing 64K bytes that can operate with a 20-MHz MC68030 using two-clock accesses. Also discussed are several options and minor alterations to reduce cost or power consumption.

Figure 12-9 shows the complete memory bank and its connection to the MC68030. As drawn, the required parts include:
- (8) 16K × 4 SRAMs, 35-ns access time with separate I/O pins
- (4) 74F244 buffers
- (2) 74F32 OR gates
- (1) PAL16L8D (or equivalent)

The system must also provide any $\overline{STERM}$ consolidation circuitry as required (e.g., by the presence of multiple synchronous memory banks or ports). In Figure 12-9, this consolidation circuitry is shown as an AND gate.

The memory bank can be divided into three sections:

1. The byte select and address decode section (provided by the PAL),

2. The actual memory section (SRAMs), and

3. The buffer section.

12

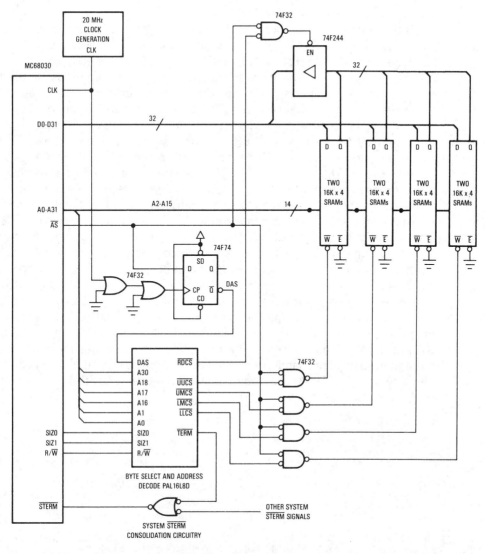

Figure 12-9. Example Two-Clock Read, Three-Clock Write Memory Bank

The first section consists of two 74F32 OR gates, a 74F74 D-type flip-flop, and a PAL16L8D. Example PAL equations are provided in Figure 12-10. The PAL generates six memory-mapped signals; four byte select signals for write operations, a buffer control signal, and the cycle termination signal. The byte select signals are only asserted during write operations when the processor is addressing the 64K bytes contained in the memory bank, and then only when the appropriate byte (or bytes) is being written to as indicated by the SIZ0, SIZ1, A0, and A1 signals. The four signals, $\overline{\text{UUCS}}$, $\overline{\text{UMCS}}$, $\overline{\text{LMCS}}$, and $\overline{\text{LLCS}}$, control data bits D24–D31, D16–D23, D8–D15, and D0–D7, respectively. $\overline{\text{AS}}$ is used to qualify the byte select signals to avoid spurious writes to memory before the address is valid. During read operations, the read chip select ($\overline{\text{RDCS}}$) signal, qualified with $\overline{\text{AS}}$, controls the data buffers only (since the memory is already enabled with its $\overline{\text{E}}$ input grounded). The last signal generated by the PAL is the $\overline{\text{TERM}}$ signal. As its equation shows, $\overline{\text{TERM}}$ consists of two events: one for read cycles and the other for write cycles. For read cycles, $\overline{\text{TERM}}$ is an address decode signal that is asserted whenever the address corresponds to the encoded memory-mapped bank of SRAM. For write operations, a delayed form of $\overline{\text{AS}}$ (DAS) is used to qualify the same address decode, which lengthens write operations to three clock cycles. The DAS signal generation is delayed from the clock edge by running the clock signal through two 74F32 OR gates before connecting to the 74F74 D-type flip-flop. This guarantees that the maximum propagation delay to generate the $\overline{\text{TERM}}$ signal does not violate the synchronous input hold time of the MC68030. By increasing write operation to three clock cycles, the MC68030 can easily meet the specified data setup time to the SRAMs before the negation of the write strobes ($\overline{\text{W}}$). $\overline{\text{TERM}}$ is then connected to the system's $\overline{\text{STERM}}$ consolidation circuity. The consolidation circuitry should have no more than 15 ns of propagation delay. If the system has no other synchronous memory or ports, $\overline{\text{TERM}}$ may be connected directly to $\overline{\text{STERM}}$.

UUCS = /A0 * /A1 8 /RW */A16*/A17*/A18*A30*   ;directly addressed, any size

UMCS = A0 * /A1 * /RW * /A16*/A17*/A18*A30*   ;directly addressed, any size
   + /A1 * /SIZ0 * /RW * /A16*/A17*/A18*A30*   ;word aligned, size byte or three byte
   + /A1 *SIZ1 * /RW * /A16*/A17*/A18*A30*   ;word aligned, size is word or long word

LMCS = /A0 *A1 * /RW * /A16*/A17*/A18*A30*   ;directly addressed, any size
   + /A1 * /SIZ0 * /SIZ1 * /RW * /A16*/A17*/A18*A30*   ;word aligned, size is long word
 + /A1 * SIZ0 * SIZ1 * /RW * /A16*/A17*/A18*A30*   ;word aligned, size is three byte
 + /A1 * A0 * /SIZ0 * /RW * /A16*/A17*/A18*A30*   ;word aligned, size is word or long word

LLCS = A0 * A1 /RW * /A16*/A17*/A18*A30*   ;directly addressed, any size
   + A0 * SIZ0 *SIZ1 * /RW * /A16*/A17*/A18*A30*   ;odd alignment, three byte size
   + /SIZ0 * /SIZ1 * /RW * /A16*/A17*/A18*A30*   ;size is long word, any address
   + A1 * SIZ1 * /RW * /A16*/A17*/A18*A30*   ;word aligned, word or three byte size

RDCS = /A16*/A17*/A18*A30*RW   ;immediate $\overline{\text{STERM}}$ with proper address
   + /A15 * /A17 * /A18*A30* /RW*DAS   ;write cycles take three clocks

DESCRIPTION: Byte select signals. The byte select signals are asserted only during write operations when the particular byte is being written. The synchronous bank of memory is always enabled, and writes are controlled by $\overline{\text{W}}$ on the memory. $\overline{\text{RDCS}}$ is for buffer control and only asserts for read operations. $\overline{\text{TERM}}$ is the cycle termination signals to the MC68030.

Figure 12-10. Example PAL Equations for Two-Clock Memory Bank

12

The second section contains the memory devices. Eight devices are used, but some designs may wish to increase this to support EDAC or to increase density. The most important feature of the memory devices used in this design is the separate data-in and data-out pins, which allow the SRAMs to be enabled before address decode is complete without causing data bus contention. The enable pins on the SRAMs have been grounded for both simplicity and improved memory access timing. If the designer wishes to include some type of enable circuitry to take advantage of low bus utilization for lower power consumption, the timing in this design will be preserved if the memory's $\overline{E}$ signal is asserted before the falling edge of state S0 (at the same time as or before the address becomes valid). Two possible enable circuits are shown in Figure 12-11.

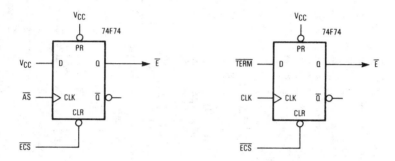

Figure 12-11. Additional Memory Enable Circuits

The third section of the memory bank is the data buffers. The data buffers are shown as 74F244, but 74AS244s may also be used. The $\overline{RDCS}$ signal, qualified with $\overline{AS}$, controls the data buffers during read operations as described above.

To maximize performance, both read and write operations should be capable of completing in two clock cycles. Figure 12-12 shows a two-clock read and write memory bank. The required parts include:

- (8)   16K×4 SRAMs, 25-ns access time with separate I/O pins
- (4)   74F244 buffers
- (2)   74F32 OR gates
- (1)   PAL16L8D (or equivalent)
- (1)   74F74 D-type flip-flop
- (2)   74F373 transparent latches
- (1)   74AS21 AND gate
- (1)   74F04 inverter

12

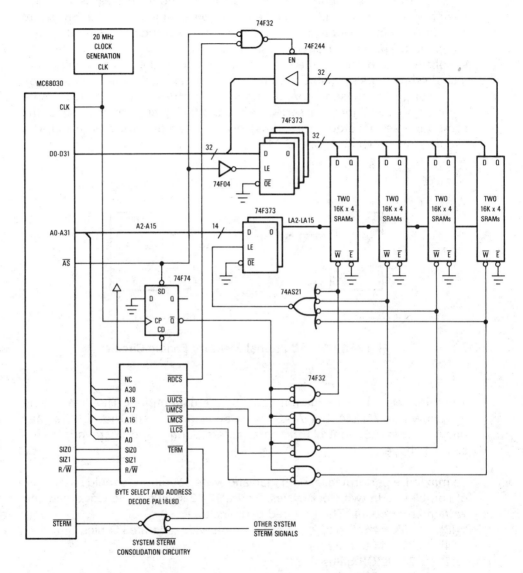

Figure 12-12. Example Two-Clock Read and Write Memory Bank

The structure of this design is very similiar to the previous design and can similarly be divided into three main sections:

1. The byte select and address decode section (provided by the PAL).

2. The actual memory section (SRAMs).

3. The buffer/latch section (address and data).

The same PAL equations listed in Figure 12-10 are used with the exception of the $\overline{\text{TERM}}$ signal. Figure 12-13 shows the equation for $\overline{\text{TERM}}$, which is used by the two clock read and write design.

TERM = /A16 * /A17 * /A16 * A30   ;immediate $\overline{\text{STERM}}$ for both reads and writes

Figure 12-13. Example PAL Equation for Two-Clock Read and Write Memory Bank

$\overline{\text{TERM}}$ is simply an address decode signal in this design because both read and write operations complete in two clock periods. The other signals generated by the PAL have already been discussed in the previous design and are not repeated here. A latched version of $\overline{\text{AS}}$ is generated by a 74F74 D-type flip-flop and used to qualify the individual byte select signals from the PAL. The required SRAM data setup time on write cycles is ensured by keeping the write strobes ($\overline{\text{W}}$) active to the SRAMs until the rising edge of the clock that completes the MC68030 write operation.

The memory section in this design uses 25-ns SRAMs rather than the 35-ns SRAMs used in the previous design. The faster SRAMs compensate for the 74F373 transparent latches used on the address lines. Since the memory write operations complete after the MC68030 write bus cycle, both address and data are latched and held valid to the SRAMs until the write strobes ($\overline{\text{W}}$) negate. During read operations, the transparent latches on the address lines remain in the transparent mode, allowing the SRAMs to provide data through the 74F244 buffers in time to meet the specified data setup time to the MC68030.

Not all systems require the performance of 20-MHz two-clock bus cycles, nor will all systems be able to afford the fast devices. Fortunately, several small changes to this design could assist designers with different cost/performance ratios. The simplest and most direct method is to reduce the clock frequency of the MC68030. For instance, if the clock frequency is below approximately 18.1 MHz, the same control logic supports two-clock bus cycles with 45-ns memory (55 ns if < 15.8 MHz). If 20 MHz is still the frequency of choice, the designer may choose to run three-clock bus cycles. This can be accomplished with the addition of a flip-flop to delay the $\overline{\text{TERM}}$ signal by one clock. The resulting memory access time is over 85 ns with a 20-MHz processor running with three-clock bus cycles.

12.5.2 A 2-1-1-1 Burst Mode Memory Bank Using SRAMs

The MC68030 normally attains its lowest bus utilization when the external memory system can support a 2-1-1-1 burst protocol. However, exceptions to this can occur. For instance, when a large amount of memory accesses are not governed by the locality of reference principles, burst accesses may not decrease bus utilization. This section describes a complete 2-1-1-1 memory bank with 256K bytes that can operate with a 20-MHz MC68030. Nonburst reads and all write cycles execute in two clocks.

Figure 12-14 shows the complete memory bank and its connection to the MC68030. The required parts include:

- (32) 64K × 1 SRAMs 25 ns access time (Motorola's MCM6287-25 or equivalent)
- (2) 74ALS244 buffers
- (4) 74AS373 latches
- (2) 74F32 OR gates
- (4) 74F191 counters
- (1) PAL16L8D (or equivalent)
- (1) 74F04 inverter

The system must also provide any $\overline{\text{STERM}}$ or $\overline{\text{CBACK}}$ consolidation circuitry as required (e.g., due to the presence of multiple synchronous memory banks or ports). In Figure 12-14, this consolidation circuitry is shown as an AND gate.

The memory bank can be divided into four sections:

1. The byte select and address decode section (provided by the PAL).

2. The burst address generator (provided by the counters).

3. The actual memory section (SRAMs).

4. The buffer section (address and data).

The first section is completely contained within the PAL16L8D. The PAL equations are the same as those provided in Figure 12-8 for the two-clock read, three-clock write memory bank, although slightly modified to support the

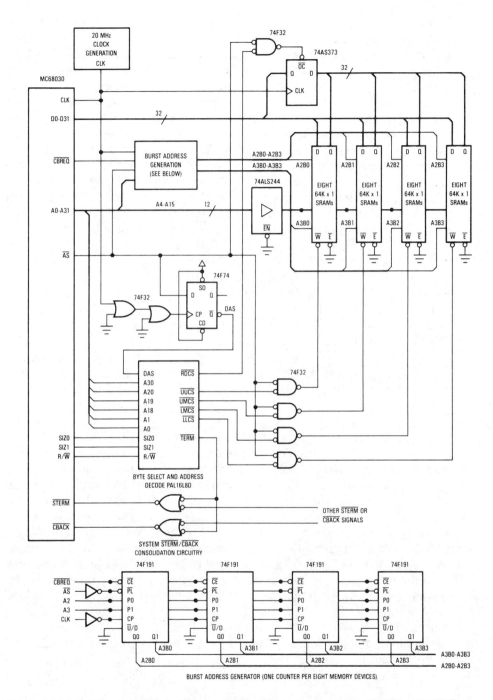

Figure 12-14. Example 2-1-1-1 Burst Mode Memory Bank at 20 MHz, 256K Bytes

larger block of memory (use A18–A20 instead of A16–A18). The PAL generates six memory-mapped signals: four byte select signals for write operations, a buffer control signal, and the cycle termination signal. The byte select signals are only asserted during write operations when the processor is addressing the 256K bytes contained in the memory bank, and then only when the appropriate byte or bytes is being written to as indicated by the SIZ0, SIZ1, A0, and A1 signals. The four signals, $\overline{\text{UUCS}}$, $\overline{\text{UMCS}}$, $\overline{\text{LMCS}}$, and $\overline{\text{LLCS}}$, control data bits D24–D31, D16–D23, D8–15, and D0–D7 respectively. $\overline{\text{AS}}$ is used to qualify the byte select signals to avoid spurious writes to memory before the address is valid. During read operations, the read chip select ($\overline{\text{RDCS}}$) signal, qualified with $\overline{\text{AS}}$, controls the data latches only (since the memory is already enabled with its $\overline{\text{E}}$ input grounded). The last signal generated by the PAL is the $\overline{\text{TERM}}$ signal. As the equation shows, $\overline{\text{TERM}}$ consists of two events: one for read cycles and the other for write cycles. For read cycles, $\overline{\text{TERM}}$ is an address decode signal that is asserted whenever the address corresponds to the encoded memory-mapped bank of SRAM. Write operations use the DAS signal to qualify the address decode, which lengthens write cycles to three clock periods. If a two-clock write cycle is required, this design can be modified to incorporate the address and data latches used in Figure 12-12. $\overline{\text{TERM}}$ is connected to the system's $\overline{\text{STERM}}$ and $\overline{\text{CBACK}}$ consolidation circuitry such that both are asserted when $\overline{\text{TERM}}$ is asserted. The consolidation circuitry should have a maximum propagation delay of 15 ns or less. If the system has no other synchronous memory or ports, $\overline{\text{TERM}}$ can be connected directly to $\overline{\text{STERM}}$, and $\overline{\text{CBACK}}$ may be grounded.

The second section is the burst address generator which contains the four counters and the inverter. The counters serve to both buffer the MC68030's address lines (A2 and A3) and to provide the next long-word address during a burst operation. The 74F191s are asynchronously preset at the beginning of every bus cycle when $\overline{\text{AS}}$ is negated. When $\overline{\text{AS}}$ asserts, the counting is dependent on the $\overline{\text{CBREQ}}$ signal and the CLK signal. During writes, $\overline{\text{CBREQ}}$ is always negated, and the counters serve only as address buffers. During reads, if $\overline{\text{CBREQ}}$ asserts, the current value of counter bits Q1:Q0 are incremented on every falling clock edge of the MC68030's clock after $\overline{\text{AS}}$ asserts. Four counters are used to provide enough drive capability to avoid an additional buffer propagation delay. Each counter drives eight memory devices.

The third section contains the memory devices. The most important feature of the memory devices used in this design is the separate data-in and data-out pins, which allow the SRAMs to be constantly enabled before address decode is complete without causing data bus contention. If the designer

12

wishes to include some type of enable circuitry to take advantage of low bus utilization, the timing in this design will be preserved if the memory's $\overline{E}$ signal is asserted within 13 ns after the falling edge of state S0.

The fourth and last section of the memory bank is the address and data buffers. The address buffers are shown as 74ALS244s, but 74AS244s and 74F244s are also acceptable. Two inputs to the address buffers remain unused allowing the possibility for expansion up to 1 Mbyte without any additional devices when SRAMs of suitable density become available. The $\overline{RDCS}$ signal, qualified with $\overline{AS}$, controls the data buffers during read operations. The address buffers are always enabled.

Some modifications to this design can improve performance. Specifically, circuitry to control $\overline{CBACK}$ and thus prevent or discontinue a burst cycle is a simple addition. The circuitry should have two functions: to prevent wraparound and to prevent bursting when a data operand crosses a long-word boundary.

Not all systems require the performance of 20-MHz 2-1-1-1 burst cycles, nor will all systems be able to afford the fast devices of this design. If the clock frequency is below approximately 17.5 MHz, the same support logic supports 2-1-1-1 burst cycles with 35-ns memory. If 20 MHz is still the frequency of choice, the designer may choose to run 3-1-1-1 burst cycles.

12.5.3 A 3-1-1-1 Burst Mode Memory Bank Using SRAMs

Figure 12-15 shows the complete 3-1-1-1 memory bank with 256K bytes that can operate with a 20-MHz MC68030. The required parts include:

- (32) 64K × 1 SRAMs 35-ns access time (Motorola's MCM6287-35 or equivalent)
- (4) 74ALS244 buffers
- (4) 74F374 latches
- (2) 74F32 OR gates
- (4) 74F191 counters
- (1) PAL16L8D (or equivalent)
- (2) inverters
- (1) flip-flop

12

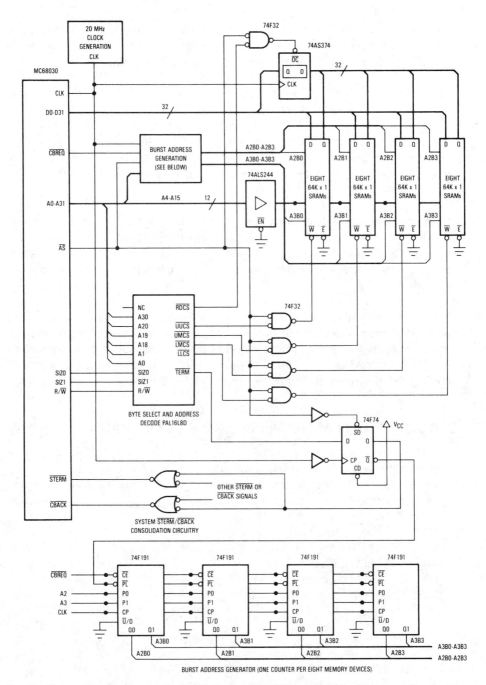

Figure 12-15. Example 3-1-1-1 Pipelined Burst Mode Memory Bank at 20 MHz, 256K Bytes

The structure of this memory bank is very similiar to the 2-1-1-1 memory bank described in **12.5.2 A 2-1-1-1 Burst Mode Memory Bank Using SRAMs**. In fact, the PAL and address buffers are exactly the same. The PAL equations are provided in Figure 12-10. The most important differences occur in the data latches, which are now flip-flops. Also, the D-type flip-flop has been moved from the input side of the PAL to the $\overline{\text{TERM}}$ output.

The data flip-flops allow the long words out of the memory to be pipelined such that setup and hold times are easier to satisfy. The memory devices are generating the next long word of data even before the MC68030 has latched the "current" long word. This alteration eases access timing requirements such that 35-ns memory can be used with a clock frequency of 20 MHz. If the clock frequency is less than 17 MHz, 45-ns memory can be used. Another benefit of the slower cycle is a relaxed timing requirement for the enable inputs of the SRAMs. Although Figure 12-15 has all the SRAM chip enables grounded, the timing in this design will be preserved if the memory's $\overline{\text{E}}$ signal is asserted within 10 ns after the rising edge of state S2. Figure 12-16 shows four possible enable circuits.

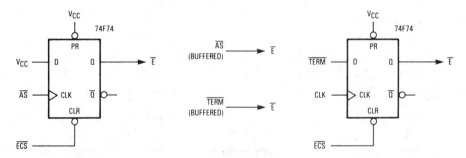

Figure 12-16. Additional Memory Enable Circuits

The flip-flop connected to the $\overline{\text{TERM}}$ signal serves two purposes: first, the $\overline{\text{TERM}}$ signal is delayed at the beginning of the cycle to insert the wait state for the first long word, and second, the burst address generator is also prevented from incrementing the long word base address until the first long-word has been latched by the 74F374s.

The performance enhancing modifications described for the 2-1-1-1 design also apply to this design. Specifically, circuitry can be added to control $\overline{\text{CBACK}}$ and thus prevent or discontinue a burst cycle. The circuitry should have two functions: first, to prevent wraparound and second, to prevent bursting when

12

a data operand crosses a long-word boundary. Another enhancement might be to alter the $\overline{\text{TERM}}$ control circuitry with the addition of a write latch mechanism to run two-clock writes.

The critical path for the 3-1-1-1 memory bank is not the first long-word access as in the 2-1-1-1 memory bank, but rather the subsequent long words during burst cycles. No alternative architecture can correct the critical path for the 2-1-1-1 burst cycle. However, for 3-1-1-1 burst cycles, the designer might consider memory banks which are 64 or 128 bits wide. In this manner, the access time for the subsequent long words can be hidden underneath the access of the previous long word(s).

12.6 EXTERNAL CACHES

To provide lower average access times to memory, some systems implement caches local to the main processor that store recently used instructions and/or data. For the MC68030, several architectural options are available to the cache designer. The primary decisions are whether to configure the cache as an asynchronous or synchronous device and whether the cache accesses are terminated early (before the cache lookup is complete) or only after validation.

The MC68030 late $\overline{\text{BERR}}/\overline{\text{HALT}}$ facility allows an external device to signal completion of a bus cycle by asserting $\overline{\text{DSACKx}}$ or $\overline{\text{STERM}}$ and later (approximately one clock period or one-half clock, respectively) aborting or retrying that cycle if an error condition is detected. Since one critical access path in many memory structures is the assertion of $\overline{\text{DSACKx}}/\overline{\text{STERM}}$ to avoid additional wait states, the late abort capability allows the memory controller to terminate a bus cycle before data is valid on the processor data bus. If the data validation fails, the memory controller can then abort ($\overline{\text{BERR}}$) or retry ($\overline{\text{BERR}}/\overline{\text{HALT}}$) the cycle. This technique is useful in memory error detection schemes where the cycle can be terminated as soon as data becomes available and the error checking can occur during the period between the signaling of termination of the cycle and the latching of data by the processor with a late retry or abort signaled upon error indication. Likewise, this technique can be used in cache implementations in which the cache tag validation cannot be completed before termination of the cycle must be signaled but the validation is completed before late abort or retry must be indicated.

The major consideration in choosing whether or not to utilize late retry for an external cache miss is the overhead involved in retrying a bus cycle after a miss in the cache. The minimum penalty is the four clock periods required

12

to retry the cycle (two clocks during which the miss is detected and two clocks idle bus time), assuming that the bus control strobes ($\overline{\text{BERR}}$ and $\overline{\text{HALT}}$) are negated soon enough after the completion of the aborted cycle that the next cycle can begin immediately. In evaluating this overhead, the projected cache miss rate determines the percentage of cycles that must be retried. Additionally, the degree of parallelism in the system should be considered. If, after a cache miss, it is possible to continue the bus cycle to main memory while the processor is retrying the cycle, it is possible to avoid some, or all, of the performance penalty associated with late retry (although the control circuitry required may be more complex).

For a two-clock bus or burst capability, use of the synchronous bus is mandated, but for a three or more clock, nonburst cache, the choice of synchronous versus asynchronous operation must be made. If the bus cycle is terminated only after validation, use of the synchronous bus is recommended since the address-valid-to-$\overline{\text{STERM}}$-asserted timing requirement is longer than the address-valid-to-$\overline{\text{DSACK}}$-asserted timing for bus cycles of the same length. If the cache implements late retry, the choice of which bus control mode to use is less important and depends on system-specific features and control structures. Some external caches might use both synchronous and asynchronous transfers: synchronous for hits and asynchronous for misses or vice versa. The following discussion assumes that the external cache uses the synchronous two-clock protocol, but most statements also apply to the asynchronous protocol.

If the MC68030 MMU is disabled, all bus cycles use logical addresses. If the MMU is enabled, the external address bus uses physical addresses (including directly mapped logical-to-physical addresses from the transparent translation (TTx) registers). These two modes of operation, logical and physical, affect the maintenance of external caches. For example, when the external cache uses physical addresses, the cache need not be flushed on each context switch. Since each task in a system may have its own unique mapping of the logical address space, a logical cache must be flushed of all entries any time the logical-to-physical mapping of the system changes (as occurs during a context switch). Since there is only a single physical address space, this problem does not occur with a physical cache because all references to a particular operand must utilize the same physical address.

The intended cache size should be evaluated when considering the utility of allowing multiple tasks to maintain cache entries. If the cache is relatively small and the time between context switches is large, each task will tend to fill the cache and remove all entries created during the execution of previous

12

tasks. Conversely, if the cache size is relatively large and the period between context switches is relatively small, the cache may provide an efficient sharing of entries.

12.6.1 Cache Implementation

An example organization of an external cache is shown in Figure 12-15. With this organization, the cache timing controller does not terminate a bus cycle until the cache has had sufficient time to validate the access as a "hit" or a "miss". When a hit decision is made, the cache controller asserts the $\overline{STERM}$ signal and also blocks propagation of $\overline{AS}$ (A) to the external system. If the cache decision cannot be completed before $\overline{AS}$ would normally be asserted by the MC68030, some provision must be made to delay the propagation of $\overline{AS}$ until the decision is valid. Otherwise, spurious assertions of the $\overline{AS}$ signal are likely to occur.

The cache control circuit (B) contains all logic required to clear or create cache entries. Also contained in (B) is the decision logic required to determine whether a hit or miss has occurred and the timing logic that is required to prevent propagation of the "hit" signal until the lookup and compare circuitry has had sufficient time to generate a valid decision. The critical path in the design of this cache is from the output of valid address by the MC68030 to the assertion of $\overline{STERM}$ by the cache controller (see Equation 12-3 of Table 12-2). After a cache hit decision has been made, the hit signal directly drives the $\overline{STERM}$ signal. Qualifying $\overline{STERM}$ with $\overline{AS}$ is not necessary assuming the appropriate setup and hold times are respected when $\overline{AS}$ is asserted. Operating at 20 MHz with no wait states, 21 ns are available from the presentation of valid address by the MC68030 to the assertion of $\overline{STERM}$ by the cache controller while 46 ns are available from valid address to data valid at the processor.

If the access times cannot be met due to the particular cache architecture, size, cost, or other consideration, the system designer may choose to utilize an early termination approach, as discussed above, that increases the decision time available to the cache controller by meeting the critical path from address valid to $\overline{BERR}/\overline{HALT}$ asserted (see Equation 12-5 of Table 12-2). The only required changes to the cache structure shown in Figure 12-17 is the generation of $\overline{STERM}$. Figure 12-18 shows an example circuit that could be positioned between the MC68030 and the external cache to provide the early termination or late retry function.

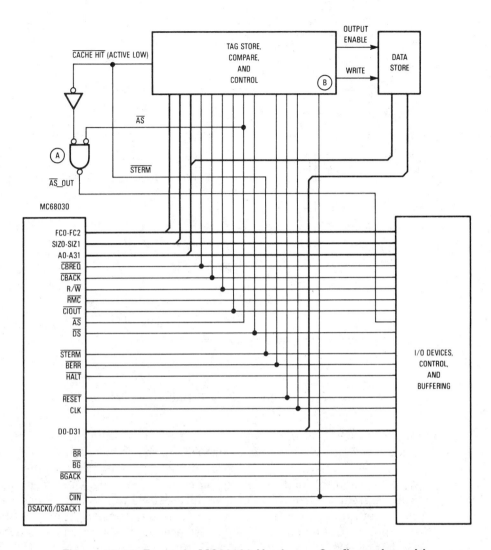

Figure 12-17. Example MC68030 Hardware Configuration with External Physical Cache

Normally, as soon as $\overline{AS}$ is asserted, circuit (C) immediately asserts the $\overline{STERM}$ signal to terminate the bus cycle, assuming that the cache will produce a valid hit later in the cycle. Circuit (C) also prevents the early termination from occurring from those cycles that access operands that are noncachable or had missed in the cache on the previous cycle (and have not already been retried). In this example, (C) prevents early termination of all CPU space accesses, all write cycles (assuming a writethrough cache is implemented),

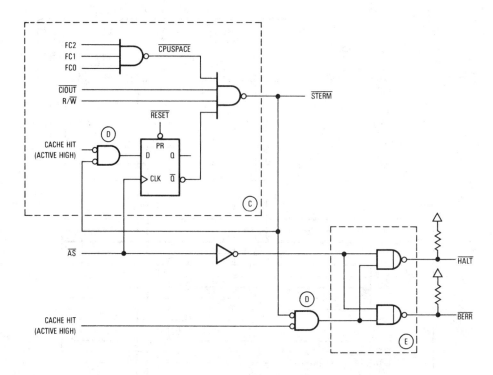

Figure 12-18. Example Early Termination Control Circuit

cycles with $\overline{\text{CIOUT}}$ asserted, and all cycles that missed in the cache on the previous cycle and were not accesses to noncachable locations. The flip-flop in (C) latches the termination condition of the current bus cycle at the rising edge of $\overline{\text{AS}}$, and this status is used during the next cycle. Other conditions to suppress early termination may be included as required by a particular system, but propagation delays must be carefully considered in order that the output of (C) be valid before the rising edge of state S1 (see Equation 12-3 of Table 12-2).

The late termination circuit is formed by the gates (D) and (E). If the current cycle is accessing a cachable location, as determined by the output of (C), and a cache hit has not occurred (D), then the $\overline{\text{BERR}}$ and $\overline{\text{HALT}}$ signals are driven low (E).

Note that the logic depicted in Figure 12-18 is designed to support a cache operating with no wait states. A provision for generating wait states may be included by placing additional timing stages between (C) and the MC68030 to delay propagation of this output by the required number of clock periods.

To minimize the potential for delays in retrying a bus cycle, the negation path of the bus error and halt signals should be carefully controlled. Light capacitive loading of these signals lines as well as the use of a properly sized pullup resistor for any open collector drivers, or some equivalent method, is recommended.

The available cache tag lookup, compare, and logic delay (D) and (E) time for this implementation is given by Equation 12-5 of Table 12-2 (40 ns at 20.0 MHz with no wait states).

A further design consideration is the response of the main memory controller to accesses that miss in the cache and are retried. During a retry operation and in the absence of arbitration for the logical bus, the MC68030 continuously drives the address bus with the address that caused the retry to be signaled. This presents the designer with the opportunity to utilize this information to continue (or initiate) the access in the main memory (by latching the state of the $\overline{AS}$ signal during the initial bus cycle and holding it asserted for the duration of the retry), thus decreasing the overhead associated with retrying the cycle.

12.6.2 Instruction-Only External Cache Implementations

In some cases, particularly in multiprocessing systems where cache coherence is a concern, it is desirable to store only instruction operands since they are not considered to be alterable and, hence, cannot generate stale data. In general, this is feasible with the MC68000 architecture as long as PC relative addressing modes are not used. This restriction allows program and data accesses to be distinguished externally by decoding the function code signals.

12.7 DEBUGGING AIDS

The MC68030 supports the monitoring of internal microsequencer activity with the $\overline{STATUS}$ and $\overline{REFILL}$ signals. The use of these signals is described in the following paragraph. A useful device to aid programming debugging is described in **12.7.2 Real-Time Instruction Trace**.

12

12.7.1 STATUS and REFILL

The MC68030 provides the STATUS and REFILL signals to identify internal microsequencer activity associated with the processing of data in the pipeline. Since bus cycles are independently controlled and scheduled by the bus controller, information concerning the processing state of the microsequencer is not available by monitoring bus signals by themselves. The internal activity identified by the STATUS and REFILL signals include instruction boundaries, some exception conditions, when the microsequencer has halted, and instruction pipeline refills. STATUS and REFILL track only the internal microsequencer activity and are not directly related to bus activity.

As shown in Table 12-4, the number of consecutive clocks during which STATUS is asserted indicates an instruction boundary, an exception to be processed, or that the processor has halted. Note that the processor halted condition is an internal error state in which the microsequencer has shut itself down due to a double bus fault and is not related to the external assertion of the HALT input signal. The HALT signal only affects bus operation, not the microsequencer.

Table 12-4. Microsequencer STATUS Indications

Asserted for	Indicates
1 Clock	Sequencer at instruction boundary will begin execution of next instruction
2 Clocks	Sequencer at instruction boundary but will not begin next instruction immediately due to: • pending trace exception OR • pending interrupt exception
3 Clocks	MMU address translation cache miss — processor to begin table search OR Exception processing to begin for: • reset OR • bus error OR • address error OR • spurious interrupt OR • autovectored interrupt OR • F-line instruction (no coprocessor responded)
Continuously	Processor halted due to double bus fault

The REFILL signal identifies when the microsequencer requests an instruction pipeline refill. Refill requests are a result of having to break sequential instruction execution to handle nonsequential events. Both exceptions and instructions can cause the assertion of REFILL. Instructions that cause refills include branches, jumps, instruction traps, returns, coprocessor general instructions that modify the program counter flow, and status register manipulations. Logical and arithmetic operations affecting the condition codes of the status register do not result in a refill request. However, operations like the MOVE <ea>,SR instruction, which updates the status register, cause a refill request since this can change the program space as defined by the function codes. When the program space changes, the processor must fetch data from the new space to replace data already prefetched from the old program space. Similarly, operations which affect the address translation mechanism of the memory management unit (MMU) cause a refill request. An instruction like the PMOVE <ea>,TC, which changes the translation control register, requires the processor to fetch data from the new address translation base. The Test Condition, Decrement, and Branch (DBcc) instruction causes two refill requests when the condition being tested is false. To optimize branching performance, the DBcc instruction requests a refill before the condition is tested. If the condition is false, another refill is requested to continue with the next sequential instruction.

Figure 12-19 illustrates the relation between the CLK signal and normal instruction boundaries as identified by the STATUS signal. STATUS asserting for one clock cycle identifies normal instruction boundaries. Note that the assertion of REFILL does not necessarily correspond to the assertion of STATUS. Both STATUS and REFILL assert and negate from the falling edge of the CLK signal.

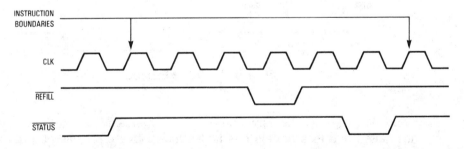

Figure 12-19. Normal Instruction Boundaries

Figure 12-20 shows a normal instruction boundary followed by a trace or interrupt exception boundary. STATUS asserting for two clock cycles identifies a trace or interrupt exception. Instruction boundary information is still present since both trace and interrupt exceptions are processed only at instruction boundaries. Before the exception handler instructions are prefetched, the REFILL signal asserts (not shown) to identify a change in program flow.

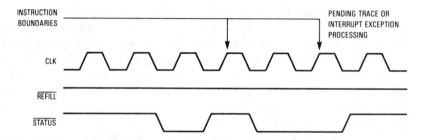

Figure 12-20. Trace or Interrupt Exception

Figure 12-21 illustrates the assertion of the $\overline{\text{STATUS}}$ signal for other exception conditions, which include MMU address translation cache miss, reset, bus error, address error, spurious interrupt, autovectored interrupt, and F-line instruction when no coprocessor responds. Exception processing causes $\overline{\text{STATUS}}$ to assert for three clock cycles to indicate that normal instruction processing has stopped. Instruction boundaries cannot be determined in this case since these exceptions are processed immediately, not just at instruction boundaries.

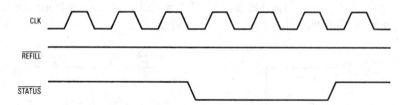

Figure 12-21. Other Exceptions

Figure 12-22 shows the assertion of $\overline{\text{STATUS}}$, indicating that the processor has halted due to a double bus fault. Once a bus error has occurred, any additional bus error exception occurring before the execution of the first instruction of the bus error handler routine constitutes a double bus fault. The processor also halts if it receives a bus error or address error during the vector table read operations or the prefetch for the first instruction after an external reset. $\overline{\text{STATUS}}$ remains asserted until the processor is reset.

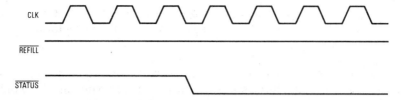

Figure 12-22. Processor Halted

12.7.2 Real-Time Instruction Trace

Microprocessor-based systems used for real-time applications typically lack development aids for program debug. The real-time environment does not allow program instruction execution to arbitrarily stop to handle debugging events. These systems include control applications where mechanical events cannot halt, such as robotics, automotive, and industrial control and emulator systems which may need to keep the target system executing in real time.

To solve the problems inherent with real-time systems, the MC68030 incorporates extra hardware-based features to enhance program debug. Real-time systems cannot take advantage of the trace exception mechanism built into all M68000 Family processors since this takes processing time away from real-time events. Additional output pins have been incorporated into the MC68030 to gain real-time visibility into the processor. Tracing capability can be added by decoding MC68030 control signals to detect which cycles are important for tracking. Post analysis of collected data allows for program debug.

Several problems exist with an external trace mechanism. These problems include determining which cycles are important for tracking program flow, detecting if instructions obtained in prefetch operations are discarded by the execution unit, and the inability of external trace circuitry to capture accesses to on-chip cache memories.

External trace hardware used for program debug must be synchronized to the MC68030 bus activity. Since all clock cycles are not traced in a program debug environment, the trace hardware requires a sampling signal. For external read and write operations, trace sampling occurs when the data bus contains valid data. Two modes of external bus operation are possible: the synchronous mode in which the system returns the $\overline{\text{STERM}}$ signal and the asynchronous mode in which the system responds with the $\overline{\text{DSACK1}}$ and/or the $\overline{\text{DSACK0}}$ signals. Both modes of bus operation need to generate a sampling signal when valid data is present on the bus. This allows for tracing data flow in and out of the processor, which is the basis for tracking program execution.

The pipelined architecture of the MC68030 prefetches instructions and operands to keep the three stages of the instruction pipe full. The pipeline allows concurrent operations to occur for up to three words of a single instruction or for up to three consecutive instructions. While sequential instruction execution is the norm, it is possible that prefetched data is not used by the execution unit due to a nonsequential event. The $\overline{\text{STATUS}}$ signal allows trace hardware to mark the progress of the execution unit as it processes program memory operands and allows marking of some exceptions. Nonsequential events, where the entire pipeline needs to reload before continuing execution, are marked by the $\overline{\text{REFILL}}$ signal.

External hardware typically has no visibility into on-chip cache memory operations. However, the MC68030 provides a local address reference to increase visibility. Write operations are totally visible since the MC68030 implements a writethrough policy allowing external hardware to capture data. For read operations from on-chip cache memories, the least significant byte of the address bus provides a local address reference.

The MC68030 begins an external cycle by driving the address bus and asserting the external cycle start ($\overline{\text{ECS}}$) signal. Address strobe ($\overline{\text{AS}}$) asserts later in the cycle to validate the address. If a hit occurs in the cache or the cache holding register, then the external cycle is aborted and $\overline{\text{AS}}$ is not asserted. In addition, the low-order address bits (A0–A7) are not involved in the address translation process performed by the on-chip MMU, creating a local address reference which can be used by trace functions. All read cycles from the on-chip cache memories cannot be captured externally since the cache access does not depend on the availability of the external bus.

Figure 12-23 shows a trace interface circuit which can be used with a logic analyzer for program debug. The nine input signals ($\overline{\text{DSACK1}}$, $\overline{\text{DSACK0}}$, CLK, $\overline{\text{AS}}$, $\overline{\text{RESET}}$, $\overline{\text{STATUS}}$, $\overline{\text{REFILL}}$, $\overline{\text{STERM}}$, and $\overline{\text{ECS}}$) are connected to the MC68030 processor in the system under development. Six output signals are generated to aid in capturing and analyzing data. In addition to connecting the logic analyzer to the address bus, the data bus, and the bus control signals, the trace interface signals (SAMPLE, PHALT, FILL, EP, IE, and $\overline{\text{ECSC}}$) should also be connected. The external clock probe of the logic analyzer connects to the system CLK signal for synchronization. Setting up the logic analyzer for data capture requires that samples be taken on the falling edge of the CLK signal when the SAMPLE signal is high. Table 12-5 lists the parts required to implement this circuit.

12

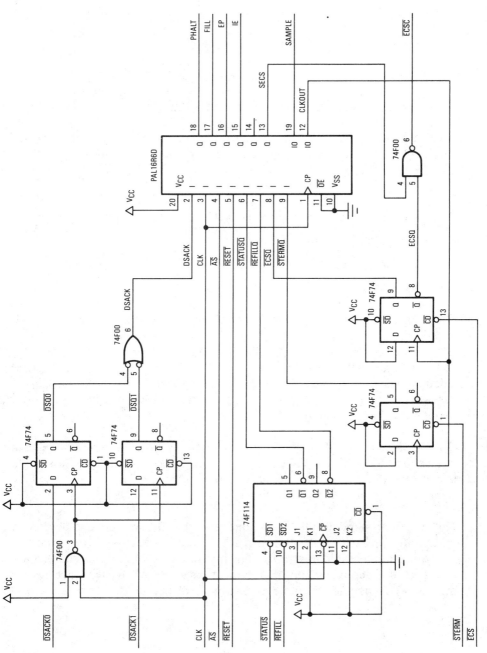

Figure 12-23. Trace Interface Circuit

Table 12-5. List of Parts

Quantity	Part	Part Description
1	74F00	Quad 2 Input NAND Gate
1	74F114	Dual JK Negative Edge-Triggered Flip-Flop
2	74F74	Dual D-Type Positive Edge-Triggered Flip-Flop
1	PAL16R6D	Programmable Logic Array, Ultra High Speed

The sample signal (SAMPLE) is an active-high signal which qualifies the next falling edge of the CLK signal as the sampling point. Five types of conditions cause SAMPLE to assert:

1. An external bus cycle

2. An internal cache hit, including a hit in the cache holding register

3. An instruction boundary

4. Exception processing as marked by the EP signal discussed below

5. The processor halting

The remaining five output signals are used to qualify the information collected.

The processor halt (PHALT) signal indicates that the MC68030 has received a double bus fault and needs a reset operation to continue processing. PHALT asserts after the assertion of STATUS for greater than three clock cycles and generates a SAMPLE signal.

The FILL signal indicates a break in sequential instruction execution. FILL is a latched version of the REFILL signal and remains asserted until a sample is collected as indicated by the assertion of SAMPLE. The assertion of FILL does not generate a SAMPLE signal.

The exception pending (EP) signal indicates that the MC68030 is beginning exception processing for either a reset, bus error, address error, spurious interrupt, autovectored interrupt, F-line instruction, MMU address translation cache miss, trace exception, or interrupt exception. The EP signal asserts after STATUS negates from a two- or three-clock cycle assertion. The assertion of EP does generate a SAMPLE signal.

The instruction executed (IE) signal indicates the execution unit has just finished processing an instruction. The IE signal asserts after $\overline{STATUS}$ negates from a one-clock cycle assertion. The assertion of IE also generates a SAMPLE signal.

The external cycle start condition ($\overline{ECSC}$) signal is used in conjunction with the $\overline{AS}$ signal to determine if the address bus and data bus are valid in the current trace sample. Table 12-6 lists the possible combinations of $\overline{AS}$ and $\overline{ECSC}$ and shows what parts of the traced address and data bus are valid. The assertion of $\overline{ECSC}$ does not generate a SAMPLE signal.

Table 12-6. $\overline{AS}$ and $\overline{ECSC}$ Indications

$\overline{AS}$	$\overline{ECSC}$	Indicates
0	0	Both Address and Data Bus Are Valid
0	1	Both Address and Data Bus Are Valid
1	0	Address Bits (A0–A7) are Valid Address Bits (A8–A31) Are Invalid Data Bus Is Invalid
1	1	Both Address and Data Bus Are Invalid

Figure 12-24 shows the pin definitions for the PAL16R6 package used in the trace circuit. These definitions are used by the PAL equations listed in Figure 12-25.

12.8 POWER AND GROUND CONSIDERATIONS

The MC68030 is fabricated in Motorola's advanced HCMOS process, contains approximately 275,000 total transistor sites, and is capable of operating at clock frequencies of up to 33.33 MHz. While the use of CMOS for a device containing such a large number of transistors allows significantly reduced power consumption in comparison to an equivalent NMOS circuit, the high clock speed makes the characteristics of power supplied to the device very important. The power supply must be able to supply large amounts of instantaneous current when the MC68030 performs certain operations, and it must remain within the rated specification at all times. To meet these requirements, more detailed attention must be given to the power supply connection to the MC68030 than is required for NMOS devices that operate at slower clock rates.

12

```
/********************************************************/
/*  This device generates a sampling signal for tracing processor activity on    *
/*  an instruction level basis for the MC68030. In the pin definitions and        *
/*  equations listed below the following symbols are used:                        *
/*                      Symbol    Definition                                      *
/*                        !       Logical NOT                                      *
/*                        #       Logical OR                                       *
/*                        &       Logical AND                                      *
/*  In addition, the '.d' extension on signal names refers to the 'D' input of     *
/*  the internal PAL flip flop.                                                    *
/********************************************************/
/*  Allowable Target Device Types : PAL16R6D High Speed PAL                        *
/********************************************************/
/**     Inputs    **/
PIN 1       =   clk         ;       /* same as pin 3 CLK            */
PIN 2       =   DSACK       ;       /* Data Strobe Acknowledge      */
PIN 3       =   CLK         ;       /* MPU Clock Signal             */
PIN 4       =   !AS         ;       /* Address Strobe               */
PIN 5       =   !RESET      ;       /* System Reset Signal          */
PIN 6       =   !STATUSQ    ;       /* Latched STATUS Signal        */
PIN 7       =   !REFILLQ    ;       /* Latched REFILL Signal        */
PIN 8       =   !ECSQ       ;       /* Latched ECS Signal           */
PIN 9       =   !STERMQ     ;       /* Latched STERM Signal         */

/**     Outputs   **/
PIN 19      =   SAMPLE      ;       /* Sample Signal                */
PIN 18      =   PHALT       ;       /* Processor Halted             */
PIN 17      =   FILL        ;       /* REFILL received              */
PIN 16      =   EP          ;       /* Exception Pending            */
PIN 15      =   IE          ;       /* Instruction Executed         */
PIN 14      =   sc          ;       /* status complete              */
PIN 13      =   secs        ;       /* sampled ECS signal           */
PIN 12      =   CLKOUT      ;       /* Delayed CLK Signal           */
```

Figure 12-24. PAL Pin Definitions

To supply a solid power supply interface, 10 V_{CC} pins and 14 GND pins are provided. This allows two V_{CC} and four GND pins to supply power for the address bus and two V_{CC} and four GND pins to supply the data bus; the remaining V_{CC} and GND pins are used by the internal logic and clock generation circuitry. Table 12-7 lists the V_{CC} and GND pin assignments.

To reduce the amount of noise in the power supplied to the MC68030 and to provide for instantaneous current requirements, common capacitive decoupling techniques should be observed. While there is no recommended layout for this capacitive decoupling, it is essential that the inductance between these devices and the MC68030 be minimized to provide sufficiently fast response time to satisfy momentary current demands and to maintain

12

```
/**   Intermediate Equations     **/              /*    State   =  PHALT   SC   EP   IE  */
    S0  =  !PHALT  &  !SC  &  !EP  &  !IE;     /*     0     =     0      0    0    0  */
    S1  =  !PHALT  &  !SC  &  !EP  &   IE;     /*     1     =     0      0    0    1  */
    S2  =  !PHALT  &  !SC  &   EP  &   IE;     /*     2     =     0      0    1    1  */
    S3  =  !PHALT  &  !SC  &   EP  &  !IE;     /*     3     =     0      0    1    0  */
    S4  =   PHALT  &   SC  &   EP  &   IE;     /*     4     =     1      1    1    1  */
    S5  =  !PHALT  &   SC  &  !EP  &   IE;     /*     5     =     0      1    0    1  */
    S6  =  !PHALT  &   SC  &   EP  &   IE;     /*     6     =     0      1    1    1  */
    S7  =  !PHALT  &   SC  &   EP  &  !IE;     /*     7     =     0      1    1    0  */


/**   Logic Equations    **/
!SAMPLE      = !SC  &   !AS  &  !SECS  #
               !SC  &  !DSACK  &  !STERMQ  &  !SECS  #
               !SC  &   AS  &  !DSACK  &  !STERMQ  &  SECS;

!PHALT.d    = !STATUSQ  #  !EP  #  IE  #  RESET;

!SC.d       = RESET  #
              S0  #
              S1  &   STATUSQ  #
              S2  &   STATUSQ  #
              S4  &  !STATUSQ  #
              SC  &  !PHALT;

!EP.d       = RESET  #
              S0  #
              S1  &  !STATUSQ  #
              S4  &  !STATUSQ  #
              SC  &  !PHALT;

!IE.d       = RESET  #
              S0  &  !STATUSQ  #
              S2  &   STATUSQ  #
              S3  &  !STATUSQ  #
              SC  &  !STATUSQ;

!SECS.d     = !ECSQ;

!CLKOUT     = !CLK;

!FILL.d     = !REFILLQ  &  SAMPLE  #
              !FILL  &  !REFILLQ  #
              RESET;
```

Figure 12-25. Logic Equations

Table 12-7. V$_{CC}$ and GND Pin Assignments

Pin Group	V$_{CC}$	GND
Address Bus	C6, D10	C5, C7, C9, E11
Data Bus	L6, K10	J11, L9, L7, L5
ECS, SIZx, $\overline{DS}$, $\overline{AS}$, $\overline{DBEN}$, $\overline{CBREQ}$, R/$\overline{W}$	K4	J3
FC0–FC2, $\overline{RMC}$, $\overline{OCS}$, $\overline{CIOUT}$, $\overline{BG}$	D4	E3
Internal Logic, $\overline{RESET}$, STATUS, REFILL, Misc.	H3, F2, F11, H11	L8, G3, F3, G11

a constant supply voltage. It is suggested that a combination of low, middle, and high frequency, high-quality capacitors be placed as close to the MC68030 as possible (e.g., a set of 10 μF, 0.1 μF, and 330 pF capacitors in parallel provides filtering for most frequencies prevalent in a digital system). Similar decoupling techniques should also be observed for other VLSI devices in the system.

In addition to the capacitive decoupling of the power supply, care must be taken to ensure a low-impedance connection between all MC68030 V$_{CC}$ and GND pins and the system power supply planes. Failure to provide connections of sufficient quality between the MC68030 power supply pins and the system supplies will result in increased assertion delays for external signals, decreased voltage noise margins, and potential errors in internal logic.

SECTION 13
ELECTRICAL CHARACTERISTICS

The following paragraphs provide information on the maximum rating and thermal characteristics for the MC68030. Detailed information on timing specifications for power considerations, DC electrical characteristics, and AC timing specifications can be found in the MC68030EC/D, *MC68030 Electrical Specifications*.

13.1 MAXIMUM RATINGS

Rating	Symbol	Value	Unit
Supply Voltage*	V_{CC}	−0.3 to +7.0	V
Input Voltage	V_{in}	−0.5 to +7.0	V
Operating Temperature Range	T_A	0 to 70	°C
Storage Temperature Range	T_{stg}	−55 to 150	°C

*A continuous clock must be supplied to the MC68030 when it is powered up.

13.2 THERMAL CHARACTERISTICS — PGA PACKAGE

Characteristic	Symbol	Value	Rating
Thermal Resistance — Ceramic			°C/W
Junction to Ambient	θ_{JA}	30*	
Junction to Case	θ_{JC}	15*	

*Estimated

13

SECTION 14
ORDERING INFORMATION AND MECHANICAL DATA

This section contains the pin assignments and package dimensions of the MC68030. In addition, detailed information is provided to be used as a guide when ordering.

14.1 STANDARD MC68030 ORDERING INFORMATION

Package Type	Frequency (MHz)	Temperature	Order Number
Pin Grid Array	20.0	0°C to 70°C	MC68030RC20
RC Suffix	25.0	0°C to 70°C	MC68030RC25
	33.33	0°C to 70°C	MC68030RC33
Ceramic Surface Mount	20.0	0°C to 70°C	MC68030FE20
FE Suffix	25.0	0°C to 70°C	MC68030FE25
	33.33	0°C to 70°C	MC68030FE33

14

14.2 PIN ASSIGNMENTS — PIN GRID ARRAY (RC SUFFIX)

The V_{CC} and GND pins are separated into three groups to provide individual power supply connections for the address bus buffers, data bus buffers, and all other output buffers and internal logic.

Pin Group	V_{CC}	GND
Address Bus	C6, D10	C5, C7, C9, E11
Data Bus	L6, K10	J11, L9, L7, L5
$\overline{ECS}$, SIZx, $\overline{DS}$, $\overline{AS}$, $\overline{DBEN}$, $\overline{CBREQ}$, R/$\overline{W}$	K4	J3
FC0–FC2, $\overline{RMC}$, $\overline{OCS}$, $\overline{CIOUT}$, $\overline{BG}$	D4	E3
Internal Logic, $\overline{RESET}$, STATUS, REFILL, Misc.	H3, F2, F11, H11	L8, G3, F3, G11

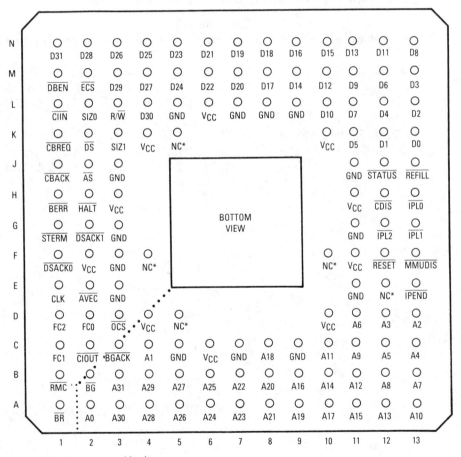

*NC — Do not connect to this pin.

14

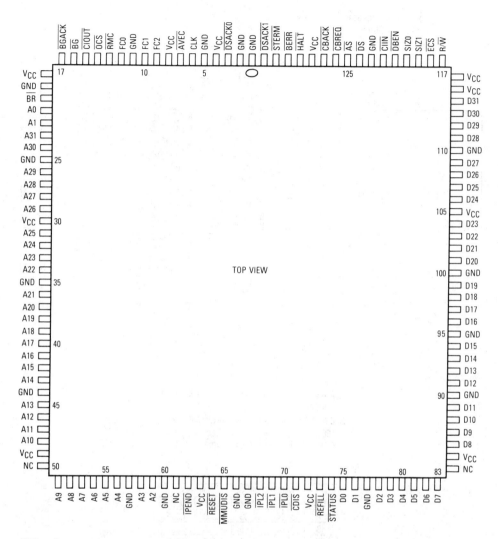

*NC — Do not connect to this pin.

14.4 PACKAGE DIMENSIONS

MC68030
RC Suffix Package
Case 789C-01

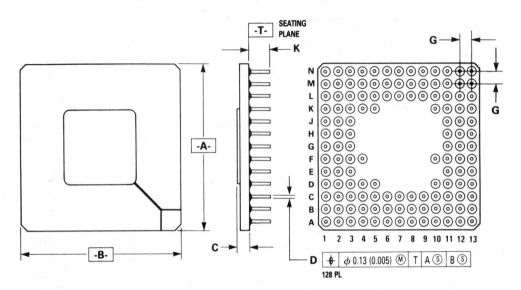

NOTES:
1. A AND B ARE DATUMS AND T IS A DATUM SURFACE.
2. DIMENSIONING AND TOLERANCING PER Y14.5M, 1982.
3. CONTROLLING DIMENSION: INCH.

DIM	MILLIMETERS		INCHES	
	MIN	MAX	MIN	MAX
A	34.04	35.05	1.340	1.380
B	34.04	35.05	1.340	1.380
C	2.54	3.81	0.100	0.150
D	0.44	0.55	0.017	0.022
G	2.54 BSC		0.100 BSC	
K	4.32	4.95	0.170	0.195

14

MC68030
FE Suffix Package
Case 831-01

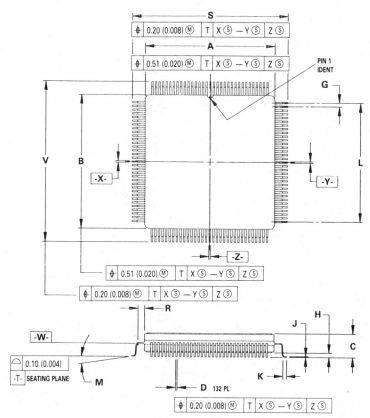

DIM	MILLIMETERS		INCHES	
	MIN	MAX	MIN	MAX
A	21.85	22.86	0.860	0.900
B	21.85	22.86	0.860	0.900
C	3.94	4.31	0.155	0.170
D	0.204	0.292	0.0080	0.0115
G	0.64 BSC		0.025 BSC	
H	0.64	0.88	0.025	0.035
J	0.13	0.20	0.005	0.008
K	0.51	0.76	0.020	0.030
L	20.32 REF		0.800 REF	
M	0°	8°	0°	8°
R	0.64	—	0.025	—
S	27.31	27.55	1.075	1.085
V	27.31	27.55	1.075	1.085

NOTES:
1. DIMENSIONING AND TOLERANCING
   PER ANSI Y14.5M, 1982.
2. CONTROLLING DIMENSION: INCH.
3. DIM A AND B DEFINE MAXIMUM CERAMIC BODY
   DIMENSIONS INCLUDING GLASS PROTRUSION
   AND MISMATCH OF CERAMIC BODY TOP AND
   BOTTOM.
4. DATUM PLANE -W- IS LOCATED AT THE
   UNDERSIDE OF LEADS WHERE LEADS EXIT
   PACKAGE BODY.
5. DATUMS X–Y AND Z TO BE DETERMINED
   WHERE CENTER LEADS EXIT PACKAGE BODY AT
   DATUM -W-.
6. DIM S AND V TO BE DETERMINED AT SEATING
   PLANE, DATUM -T-.
7. DIM A AND B TO BE DETERMINED AT DATUM
   PLANE -W-.

14

APPENDIX A
M68000 FAMILY SUMMARY

This Appendix summarizes the characteristics of the microprocessors in the M68000 Family. Refer to M68000 PM/AD, *M68000 Programmer's Reference Manual*, for more detailed information about MC68000 and MC68010 differences.

	MC68000	MC68008	MC68010	MC68020	MC68030
Data Bus Size (Bits)	16	8	16	8,16,32	8,16,32
Address Bus Size (Bits)	24	20	24	32	32
Instruction Cache (in words)	—	—	3[1]	128	128
Data Cache (in words)	—	—	—	—	128

Note 1. The MC68010 supports a three-word cache for the loop mode.

Virtual Memory/Machine

MC68010, MC68020, and MC68030	Provide Bus Error Detection, Fault Recovery
MC68030	On-Chip MMU

Coprocessor Interface

MC68000, MC68008, and MC68010	Emulated in Software
MC68020 and MC68030	In Microcode

A

Word/Long-Word Data Alignment
MC68000,
MC68008, and   Word/Long Data, Instructions, and Stack Must be
MC68010   Word Aligned

MC68020 and   Only Instructions Must be Word Aligned
MC68030   (Data Alignment Improves Performance)

Control Registers
MC68000 and
MC68008   None

MC68010   SFC, DFC, VBR

MC68020   SFC, DFC, VBR, CACR, CAAR

MC68030   SFC, DFC, VBR, CACR, CAAR, CRP, SRP, TC, TT0,
                       TT1, PSR

Stack Pointers
MC68000,
MC68008, and   USP, SSP
MC68010

MC68020 and
MC68030   USP, SSP (MSP, ISP)

Status Register Bits
MC68000,
MC68008, and   T, S, I0/I1/I2, X/N/Z/V/C
MC68010

MC68020 and
MC68030   T0/T1, S, M, I0/I1/I2, X/N/Z/V/C

A

Function Code/Address Space
MC68000 and
MC68008   FC0-FC2 = 7 is Interrupt Acknowledge Only

MC68010,
MC68020, and   FC0-FC2 = 7 is CPU Space
MC68030

Indivisible Bus Cycles
MC68000,
MC68008, and   Use $\overline{\text{AS}}$ Signal
MC68010

MC68020 and
MC68030   Use $\overline{\text{RMC}}$ Signal

Stack Frames
MC68000 and
MC68008   Support Original Set

MC68010   Supports Formats $0, $8

MC68020 and
MC68030   Support Formats $0, $1, $2, $9, $A, $B

Addressing Modes
MC68020 and   Memory indirect addressing modes, scaled index,
MC68030 extensions: and larger displacements. Refer to specific data
                        sheets for details.

A

MC68020 and MC68030 Instruction Set Extensions

Bcc	Supports 32-Bit Displacements
BFxxxx	Bit Field Instructions (BFCHG, BFCLR, BFEXTS, BFEXTU, BFFFO, BFINS, BFSET, BFTST)
BKPT	New Instruction Functionality
BRA	Supports 32-Bit Displacements
BSR	Supports 32-Bit Displacements
CALLM	New Instruction (MC68020 only)
CAS, CAS2	New Instructions
CHK	Supports 32-Bit Operands
CHK2	New Instruction
CMPI	Supports Program Counter Relative Addressing Modes
CMP2	New Instruction
cp	Coprocessor Instructions
DIVS/DIVU	Supports 32-Bit and 64-Bit Operands
EXTB	Supports 8-Bit Extend to 32 Bits
LINK	Supports 32-Bit Displacement
MOVEC	Supports New Control Registers
MULS/MULU	Supports 32-Bit Operands
PACK	New Instruction
PFLUSH	MMU Instruction (MC68030 only)
PLOAD	MMU Instruction (MC68030 only)
PMOVE	MMU Instruction (MC68030 only)
PTEST	MMU Instruction (MC68030 only)
RTM	New Instruction (MC68020 only)
TST	Supports Program Counter Relative Addressing Modes
TRAPcc	New Instruction
UNPK	New Instruction

MC68030 USER'S MANUAL

MOTOROLA

INDEX

— C —

I

— F —

— G —

— H —

I

Protocol
 Processor General Instruction, 10-7
 Violations,
  Coprocessor Detected, 10-62
  Main Processor Detected, 10-65

— Q —

Queue, 2-39

— R —

R/W̄ Signal, 5-5, 7-4, 7-36ff
RAM, Static, 12-18–12-24
Ratings, Maximum, 13-1
Read Cycle,
 Asynchronous, 32-Bit Port, Timing, 7-33
 Data Bus Requirements, 7-10
 Synchronous, 7-48
  CIIN Asserted, CBACK Negated, Timing, 7-50
Read-Modify-Write
 Accesses, 6-10
 Cycle,
  Asynchronous, 7-45
  Asynchronous, Byte, 32-Bit Port, Timing, 7-45
  Asynchronous, Flowchart, 7-44
  Synchronous, 7-52
  Synchronous, CIIN Asserted, Flowchart, 7-56
  Synchronous, Flowchart, 7-55
 Signal, 5-5, 7-4, 7-36ff, 12-3
Read/Write Signal, 5-5, 7-4, 7-36ff
Real Time Instruction Trace, 12-39–12-43
Recovery,
 Bus Fault, 8-27
 RTE, 8-25
REFILL Signal, 5-10, 6-5
Register,
 Cache Address, 1-9, 2-5, 6-23
 Cache Control, 1-9, 2-5, 6-1, 6-3, 6-20, 6-21
 Condition Code, 2-4, 3-14
 Coprocessor Interface, 10-8, 10-29
 MMU Status, 1-9, 2-5, 9-60–9-63
 Status, 1-8, 2-4, 6-5
 Translation Control, 1-9, 2-5, 9-8, 9-54
 Vector Base, 1-8, 2-5
 Data Organization, 2-2
Register Select CIR, 10-32
Registers,
 Address, 1-6, 2-4
 Data, 1-6, 2-2
 Function Code, 1-8, 2-5
 Transparent Translation, 1-9, 2-5, 9-16, 9-55
Representation, Internal Operand, 7-8
Request, Bus, 7-98
Requirements, Data Bus, Read Cycle, 7-10
Reset,
 Cache, 6-20

Reset (Continued)
 Coprocessor, 10-72
 Exception, 8-5, 8-6
 Operation, 7-103
 Signal, 5-9, 7-97ff, 9-15, 9-61
RESET Signal, 5-9, 7-97ff, 9-15, 9-61
Resource Scheduling, 11-1
Response CIR, 10-29
Restore CIR, 10-31
Restore Operation Timing Table, 11-51
Retry Operation, 7-89
 Late,
  Asynchronous, Timing, 7-90
  Burst, Timing, 7-92
  Synchronous, Timing, 7-91
Return from Exception, 8-24
RMC Signal, 5-5, 7-4, 7-36
Root Pointer Descriptor, 9-23
Rotate Instructions, 3-7
Routine,
 AbortTask, 9-86
 Bus Error, 9-84
 GetFrame, 9-85
 SwapPageIn, 9-86
 Vallocate, 9-79
RTE
 Bus Fault Recovery, 8-26
 Instruction, 8-24

— S —

Save CIR, 10-30
Save Operation Timing Table, 11-51
ScanPC, 10-15, 10-18, 10-34
Scheduling, Resource, 11-1
Script, Table Search Timing, 11-51
Search, Table, 9-28, 9-30
Sequence, Exception Processing, 8-1
Set, Instruction, 1-10, 1-13
Set on Coprocessor Condition Instruction, 10-15
SFC, 1-8, 2-5
Shared Supervisor/User Address Space Logical
 Address Map, 9-49
Sharing, Table, 9-37, 9-39
Shift Instructions, 3-7
Shift/Rotate Instruction Timing Table, 11-45
Short Format
 Early Termination Page Descriptor, 9-24
 Indirect Descriptor, 9-26
 Invalid Descriptor, 9-25
 Page Descriptor, 9-25
 Table Descriptor, 9-24
Side Effects, MMU Register, 9-61
Signal,
 Address Strobe, 5-5, 7-3, 7-4, 7-26ff
 AS, 5-5, 7-3, 7-4, 7-26ff
 Autovector, 5-8, 7-6, 7-29, 7-71ff

I

ISBN 0-13-566423-3 PRINTED IN USA EVANS PRESS EPHP 1507 1,500